# Creating And
# Implementing
# Virtual Private Networks

Casey Wilson

Peter Doak

**President, CEO**
*Keith Weiskamp*

**Publisher**
*Steve Sayre*

**Acquisitions Editor**
*Stephanie Wall*

**Marketing Specialist**
*Tracy Scofield*

**Project Editor**
*Greg Balas*

**Technical Reviewer**
*Michael Norian*

**Production Coordinator**
*Wendy Littley*

**Cover Design**
*Jody Winkler*

**Layout Design**
*April Nielsen*

Creating And Implementing Virtual Private Networks
© 2000 The Coriolis Group. All Rights Reserved.

The Coriolis Group, LLC
14455 North Hayden Road
Suite 220
Scottsdale, Arizona 85260

480/483-0192
FAX 480/483-0193
http://www.coriolis.com

Library of Congress Cataloging-in-Publication Data
Wilson, Casey
    Virtual private networks gold book / by Casey Wilson and Peter Doak.
        p.    cm.
    Includes index.
    ISBN 1-57610-430-3
    1. Extranets (Computer networks)   2. Business enterprises-
-Computer networks.   3. Internet (Computer network)   4. Computer
networks--Security measures.   I. Doak, Peter.   II. Title.
TK5105.875.E87W55    2000
658'.05468—dc21                                                    99-43077
                                                                          CIP

Printed in the United States of America
10 9 8 7 6 5 4 3 2 1

14455 North Hayden Road • Suite 220 • Scottsdale, Arizona 85260

Dear Reader:

Coriolis Technology Press was founded to create a very elite group of books: the ones you keep closest to your machine. Sure, everyone would like to have the Library of Congress at arm's reach, but in the real world, you have to choose the books you rely on every day *very* carefully.

To win a place for our books on that coveted shelf beside your PC, we guarantee several important qualities in every book we publish. These qualities are:

- *Technical accuracy*—It's no good if it doesn't work. Every Coriolis Technology Press book is reviewed by technical experts in the topic field, and is sent through several editing and proofreading passes in order to create the piece of work you now hold in your hands.

- *Innovative editorial design*—We've put years of research and refinement into the ways we present information in our books. Our books' editorial approach is uniquely designed to reflect the way people learn new technologies and search for solutions to technology problems.

- *Practical focus*—We put only pertinent information into our books and avoid any fluff. Every fact included between these two covers must serve the mission of the book as a whole.

- *Accessibility*—The information in a book is worthless unless you can find it quickly when you need it. We put a lot of effort into our indexes, and heavily cross-reference our chapters, to make it easy for you to move right to the information you need.

Here at The Coriolis Group we have been publishing and packaging books, technical journals, and training materials since 1989. We're programmers and authors ourselves, and we take an ongoing active role in defining what we publish and how we publish it. We have put a lot of thought into our books; please write to us at **ctp@coriolis.com** and let us know what you think. We hope that you're happy with the book in your hands, and that in the future, when you reach for software development and networking information, you'll turn to one of our books first.

Keith Weiskamp
President and CEO

Jeff Duntemann
VP and Editorial Director

# Look For These Other Books From The Coriolis Group:

*Cisco Routers for IP Routing Little Black Book*

*Windows 2000 Active Directory Black Book*

*Windows 2000 Systems Programming Black Book*

*Windows 2000 Server Architecture and Planning*

*Active Server Pages Black Book*

*XML Black Book*

*For Florence, who believed in me enough to let me do it—MTYLTT*

*—Casey Wilson*

*For Henrietta, who put our life on hold while I worked on writing this book.*

*—Peter Doak*

&

# About The Authors

**Casey Wilson** turned full-time freelance writer after 37 years and hundreds of thousands of written words working for the federal government. His first personal computer was a VIC-20, and during his career with the government, Casey took delivery of one of the first seven IBM-XT computers purchased by the U.S. Navy. Part of his work in infrared technology was designing and installing data interfaces between computers and infrared radiometers. Since becoming a freelance writer, Casey's articles have appeared in national and regional magazines. Two of his scripts have been produced for television, and he has edited an anthology. In 1998, he received the coveted Jack London meritorious service award from the prestigious 90-year-old California Writers' Club and serves as president on its corporate board of directors.

**Peter Doak** has more than 20 years experience in the computer field. He has been a tenured associate professor in electronics and computer systems technology for more than 11 years. Within the management structure of College of the Mainland in Texas, Peter is administrator for the courses in Electronics Technology, Microcomputer Systems Specialist, and Industrial Instrumentation. In 1988, with his proven experience installing and supporting Novell NetWare, he was instrumental in establishing the first PC-based network system at COM. In 1991, he implemented a new program at COM for electronics technology and computer sciences. When computer networking surged in 1993, Peter established the college as a Novell Education Academic partner, the first community college in the area to offer NetWare certification courses. Microsoft Windows NT certification courses were added to the curriculum soon after. The original LAN has grown from 25 users with one server to nearly 1,000 computers on 12 servers with its own T1 line. The network comprises all 11 buildings of the campus including administrative and support staff. At this writing, Peter is guiding COM in the incorporation of a Virtual Private Network subnet.

# *Acknowledgments*

It takes more than one or two authors to make this sort of book possible. It takes a platoon of people—concealed and camouflaged—working quietly in the wings to bring it off. We would like to thank them. Some, because of the way we made them suffer, deserve that we call them out by name and march them front and center for special commendation. This particular book started with a series of emails with Stephanie Wall, an acquisitions editor for The Coriolis Group. "I know its going to be tough," Stephanie said, "but I know you can do it." Well, here it is. Then came Greg Balas, our project editor, freshly displaced from the northeast, and plunked down in the Arizona desert. Greg was faced with not only learning the system himself, but teaching it to us. Should this book be deemed a success, it will be because Ellen Strader strived to make it that. Ellen was, you see, the copy editor for this adventure. She snatched out commas from where they did not belong and inserted them where they were missing. Her suggestions for rewrites were superb. Next on our list is Michael Norian, the technical editor, who was faced with the challenges of keeping us on track by testing our procedures, step by step, and checking out all the URLs we stuffed in. Great job, Michael. The graphics and production staff at Coriolis deserves more than casual kudos for the way they made our sketches and drafts into professional presentations. Among them are production coordinator, Wendy Littley; compositor, Carol Bowers; proofreader, Rachel Anderson; and indexer, Alexandra Nickerson.

Thank you—all.

Now its time to shove the keyboard under the desk and go to the beach!

—*Casey Wilson*

I would like to thank the Board of Trustees and the Administration at College of the Mainland, Texas City, Texas, for their continuing commitment to advanced technical applications, and for allowing me practically unlimited access to facilities and equipment during the book's development. Without their encouragement and support, this book would not have been possible.

Many individuals and groups helped with this book, and I will probably forget to mention someone. I offer my apologies in advance for the oversight. Among those I can recall are Gordon Evans, Umesh Muniyappa, and Simon Kandah with the Novell BorderManger™ development team in San Jose, California; Jeff Sommers with AMP Incorporated; Brendon Howe with Indus River Networks; Barry Shilmover for the tip about screen captures; and finally, Penny, Barbara, Angela, Mark, and all the rest at my favorite ISP, **www.phoenix.net**. I must also thank the Technical Education Team at College of the Mainland, especially my network guru Frank Williams for his help and advice along with Mona Beth and Bonnie for putting up with me while this book was being developed.

—*Peter Doak*

# Contents At A Glance

Chapter 1    VPN, What's It All About?    1

Chapter 2    A Review Of Local Area Networks    15

Chapter 3    Wide Area Networks    65

Chapter 4    Development Of VPN Standards    115

Chapter 5    How Manufacturers Are Implementing
VPN Standards    147

Chapter 6    Incorporating VPN Into An Existing Network    173

Chapter 7    Basic NetWare VPN Model    199

Chapter 8    Basic VPN Using Microsoft Solutions    273

Chapter 9    Expanding The VPN    319

Chapter 10    VPN Security    379

Chapter 11    VPN Management And Maintenance    423

Chapter 12    Connecting Your Network To The World    463

Appendix A    Acronyms    471

Appendix B    Selected Requests For Comments    481

Appendix C    VPN Vendors    491

Appendix D    Installation And Administration Checklists    497

Appendix E    Recommended Reading    541

# Table Of Contents

Introduction ........................................................ xv

Chapter 1  VPN, What's It All About? .................................. 1
History   1
Advantages And Disadvantages Of VPN   7
A Peek Into The Millenium   10
Summary   14

Chapter 2   A Review Of Local Area Networks ................. 15
What Is A LAN   15
Architecture   16
Network Models   18
Each Device Is Different—Physical Addressing   32
Which Media Are We Using?   32
Hardware   41
Network Operating Systems—The Software   54
Security Issues   64

Chapter 3   Wide Area Networks ........................................ 65
What Makes The Difference?   65
WAN Service Providers, AKA POTS, AKA Plain Old
  Telephone Service   68
WAN Protocols   78
Physical Components   85
The Routing Process, Part One   89
The Routing Process, Part Two   93
The Routing Process, Part Three   94
Gateways   95
The Routing Process, Part Four   98
Remote Access For Users   107
Implementations Of WAN Protocols By Selected
  Software Vendors   109
Network Security, It's Everyone's Concern   113

**Chapter 4   Development Of VPN Standards** .................. 115

The Venerable TCP/IP Protocol Suite (Yet Again)   115
How Internet Standards Are Developed   116
Virtual Private Networks—A Definition   118
Standards Relating To VPN   119
Tunneling, Part Deux   122
A Look At The Development Of Two VPN Protocols—PPTP
  And L2F/L2TP   128
Making IP Secure, IPsec   134
Key Management Protocol (KMP) With Oakley Key Exchange   141
Final Notes About VPN Protocols   143
Wrap Up   145

**Chapter 5   How Manufacturers Are Implementing
VPN Standards** ............................................. 147

Seeking A Common Ground—Caveats And Disclaimers   147
Who Is Using What?   148
Firewalls   148
(Some) People That Make It Work   151
Microsoft *Et Al.*, The PPTP Forum   152
Novell   158
Cisco Systems   164
Indus River Software   168

**Chapter 6   Incorporating VPN Into An
Existing Network** ......................................... 173

The Human Factor   174
Design Consideration   185
Hidden Costs And Other Considerations   192
Words Of Wit And Wisdom   197
Summary   197

**Chapter 7   Basic NetWare VPN Model** .......................... 199

Simplified System With Limited Capability   199
Architecture   200
Traffic Patterns   202
Vintage Air On The Internet   203
Network Access And Use Policy   203
Future Plans   203

Installation And Configuration Items Related To The
  New VPN Model    207
Implementing Novell NetWare VPN    210
M & M (But Not The Candy Kind)    266
Wrap Up    272

Chapter 8    Basic VPN Using Microsoft Solutions ...........273
VPN Using NT 4 With PPTP Protocol    273
Wrap Up    317

Chapter 9    Expanding The VPN .......................................319
Why's And Where's—Some Basic Theory    319
Product Comparisons    326
VPN Client Installation Procedure    328
The Novell BorderManager VPN    333
The Windows NT PPTP Connection    353
Remote User Administration    367
Troubleshooting The Remote User    372

Chapter 10    VPN Security .................................................379
Security Defined    380
Threats    381
The Inside Intruder    382
System Defenses    393
System Backup    397
Hardware    404
Software    410
Encryption    418

Chapter 11    VPN Management And Maintenance ...........423
Moving From Implementation To Operations    423
Administrative Checklists    436
VPN Maintenance Tasks    438
Troubleshooting Your VPN    440
Problem Isolation    447
Stick With A System    458
Summary    461

Chapter 12    Connecting Your Network To The World .......463
What The Future Looks Like    463
Prediction #1    464

Prediction #2  465
Prediction #3  465
Some Closing Words  466
Our Recommendations About Your VPN  466
Things We Missed And Mistakes We Made  468
Recommended Reading  469
Coming Events  469
Conclusion  469

Appendix A  Acronyms ..................................................... 471

Appendix B  Selected Requests For Comments ................ 481

Appendix C  VPN Vendors ............................................... 491

Appendix D  Installation And Administration Checklists ... 497

Appendix E  Recommended Reading ............................. 541

Index ......................................................... 545

# Introduction

I remember reading somewhere that "...what is our technology today was once the magic of mages..." I can't help but wonder what Blaise Pascal (1623–1662) would have thought about a 400MHz Pentium laptop sitting next to his mechanical calculator. I would like to peek over the shoulder of Sam Morse, with a pair of wires stuck into the back of his 56K modem, reading an email from Alex Bell.

Writing a book like this is a continuing series of daunting challenges. From the start, we said that we would write this book primarily for network administrators and anyone else that has an interest in Virtual Private Networks. We wanted to make this book technically complete, without making it technically complex (which may be a contradiction in terms). We were faced with writing about a technology that evolved further with every page; that changed as theory became fact while we tapped away on the keyboard. What we did between these covers was brush as broad a stroke as possible over the subject of Virtual Private Networking—emerging magic.

VPN is far from mature—four years ago, we would have been writing science fiction—but it has coalesced into describable form. Using technology that is available right now, large and small businesses with VPNs use the Internet to connect to any outlying facility or any user they can reach by telephone. From Bangor, Maine, to Cape Town, South Africa—with just the click of a mouse an enterprise can privately conduct business and share data confidentially.

In this book, my co-author and I sorted through piles of information to give you what you need to put VPN technology to work in your business. By necessity, we built the text around Novell® and Microsoft, touching other VPN vendors as often as we could. We tried to show the technology without making any sales pitches while we were at it. Pete is the brain behind the book—as an associate professor at the College of the Mainland in Texas, this is his forte.

We chose as a target audience the network administrators, MIS managers, Information Technologists, and technicians with experience in networking. We intend that this book will be a resource for planning, implementing, and maintaining a Virtual Private Network. We invented a couple paradigm companies (Specialty Training and Vintage Air) and used them as examples.

In Chapter 1 we take a ride back through time to visit some of the earlier mages and discover how this all came about, this thing they call Internet. This chapter will give you the pros and cons of a VPN and tell you what it can, or cannot, do for your enterprise.

We use Chapters 2 and 3 to revisit Local- and Wide-Area-Networks. We presume you already have one or more networks and use this to make sure we are using the same language. Obviously, two chapters could not possibly offer a tutorial. We could not do that with two books.

In Chapters 4 and 5, we will explore the somewhat esoteric subject of developing standards. You will learn who is behind the rules imposed on the networking community in general, and the Internet in particular—along with how and why the rules exist. If you think it is chaotic, believe us, without standards the Internet would not exist. We will show some examples of how various vendors have incorporated standards for their benefit and sometimes benefited by collaborations with seeming competitors.

Chapter 6 is where we will discuss evolving your existing network system(s) into incorporating VPN technology. We will lay the groundwork for incorporating the Internet into your company's *Network Acceptable Use* policy. If your company does not already have policies in place we will convince you why it needs policies and give you a foundation for building them. We will use this chapter to begin discussing security—what it really means to you. Next, will come some thoughts about training: how to make life a lot easier on yourself by getting correct information into the minds of your users. Finally, we will use Chapter 6 to help you determine the most cost-efficient way of implementing this exciting technology.

Novell and Microsoft will take up Chapters 7 and 8. In each chapter, we will take you through a step-by-step process of installing and configuring a VPN. Screen shots will show you where you should be as we explain in detail why you make certain entries. We think it is important for you to know why you will do things in certain ways. At this stage, we will set up simple site-to-site VPNs showing how you can connect two networks via local telephone connections. One site could be in Texas and another in New Zealand and users could share data between the sites for the cost of a local call.

Then we step up in Chapter 9 and expand the VPNs to incorporate client-to-site users. The goal here will be to expand the system for the telecommuters and/or road warriors. The goal is to reduce that monthly telephone bill while still letting your remote users have access to the system wherever they are, including Cut 'N Shoot, Texas.

We cannot ignore security. In this book, all of Chapter 10 is concerned about security although we know any competent pair of authors could fill an entire book and have materials left over. One goal will be to show you how you can broach the Internet with a private tunnel between networks using VPN technology. Nevertheless, we shall also show that security is not merely encrypting a bunch of bits and bytes. Security is maintaining the integrity of your data and that includes protecting it from a wide range of threats. Some of them may be lurking in a cubicle down the hall or in a power station miles away.

M&M (not the candy kind) is the subject of Chapter 11. In this case, we mean Management and Maintenance. In this chapter, we will show you the tools you need to keep your VPN healthy and running at peak performance—before if it tries to go belly-up. We will also push training a little harder here because it deserves it. There will be a section on doing periodic checkups to discover adverse trends before they become major *Gotchas!*

You will find a number of appendixes following the summary in Chapter 12. For example, we will compile acronyms and their definitions into one handy reference point you can either dog-ear or put a sticky-note to hold the place. There will also be an appendix of VPN vendors in case you get a hankering to shop for VPN hardware and software. We will sort through more than 2,500 Request for Comments available in the various Internet archives, and give you a list of those related to VPN in one of the appendixes. We will devote Appendix D to compiling checklists that you will need for planning, installing, configuring, managing and maintaining your VPN. Finally, in Appendix E we will give you our selection of recommended reading material so you can expand your knowledge base beyond our modest offering.

We intend to support this book on our Web site, **www.sldenterprises.com,** for as long as it is in print and then a little longer. Visit us with questions or comments as often as you like. We will try to post new stuff as we discover it.

Sincerely,

*Casey Wilson (**Casey@sldenterprises.com**)*

*Peter Doak (**PDoak@sldenterprises.com**)*

# Chapter 1
# VPN, What's It All About?

*Key Topics:*

♦ *What VPN is*

♦ *Networking history*

♦ *Some of the pros and cons*

♦ *General predictions*

The shortest way to define Virtual Private Networking is to say that it is a scheme for using the Internet as a *backbone* for computer networks. On the surface that doesn't seem like much, but when you dig in, it offers tremendous potential. Some enterprises could save tens of thousands of dollars over what they are now paying for leased lines for existing networks. But use of VPN doesn't require the sites to be located around the world, or across the country, or on the other side of the state—they could be, but they could just as easily be on the other side of *Your Town*, U.S.A. In fact, the tools and techniques that make up VPN technology could be applied to a Local Area Network (LAN) right in your building.

## History

For nearly a decade, the Internet has been reasonably calm—a period almost of catching its breath, getting its second wind. The only real significant change has been in the number of users coming aboard. For the past couple of years, the tide has been welling up, gathering energy. It is about to sweep in and it is bringing *Virtual Private Networking* with it.

### 1866—A Peek At The Beginning

Networking took a tiny step forward way back in 1866, when the first cable—2,700 miles long—was strung across the Atlantic Ocean between Ireland and Newfoundland. For the intrepid pioneers of communications, the cable meant that instantaneous messages could be sent between continents for the first time. Owing to the success of that daring venture, more cables were strung and the information age began.

1

Well, sort of. The only power available for the telegraph systems was from batteries—the invention of a power station would lag a few years. The data format was based on a variation of Morse Code, combinations of marks and spaces representing characters similar to the series of dots and dashes devised by Samuel Morse.

Telegraph operators translated messages into holes punched into a streaming paper tape according to a system devised by Sir Charles Wheatstone. The paper tapes were then passed into a telegraph transmitter that sent the information across the cable at the speed of light.

Well, sort of. The electrical pulses traveled at the speed of light, but the data rate was only 100 words per minute. *Teleprinters*, also known as *teletypewriters* or sometimes just *teletypes*, wouldn't come around until the turn of the century—the typewriter had to be invented first.

Cable communications continued unrivaled for 36 years, until a young inventor named Marconi sent his first transatlantic wireless message from Nova Scotia to England. That event shifted the information age into a higher gear.

Well, sort of. Weather had a considerable influence on wireless transmission. The equipment was all handmade and very expensive. Most people looked on it as gadgetry.

## 1880—Hollerith And The Tabulating Machine

Between the laying of the cable and Marconi inventing the wireless, an American mathematician named Herman Hollerith was busy inventing a tabulating machine. Charged with compiling the census of 1890, Hollerith developed a machine that would read holes punched in a card. The machine compiled information, depending on the settings of various switches.

Hollerith didn't invent the first computer. The abacus predated it by centuries. What he did do was invent a machine that, after programming the switches to produce the desired information, merely required the operators to turn a crank. In fact, *computers* were people defined by a job description.

## 1945—ENIAC

Communications via cable and wireless had grown from transatlantic to intercontinental.

It was also in 1945 that engineers and physicists stuffed almost 20,000 vacuum tubes, 1,500 mechanical relays, and hundreds of thousands of resistors, capacitors, and inductors into various cabinets in a 30- by 50-foot room at the University of Pennsylvania's Moore School of Electrical Engineering. Lashed together with miles of copper wire bonded together with hundreds of pounds of solder, the final construct was named the *Electronic Numerical Integrator and Computer* (ENIAC).

Hidden away from the public, ENIAC was a U.S. government top-secret research tool. Initially used to calculate ballistic trajectories of artillery rounds, ENIAC could do in 30 seconds what consumed 20 hours of a trained mathematician's time using the most modern calculator of that day.

In 1946, on the heels of its brilliant success, ENIAC gave way to the *Universal Automatic Computer* (*UNIVAC*). The entrepreneurs were Dr. J. W. Mauchly and a university graduate student, J. P. Eckert. These two, principals in ENIAC, had a vision that they could do better. Their first customer was none other than the Census Bureau, which fronted the UNIVAC enterprise with $300,000 in 1946.

Mauchly and Eckert were much too optimistic. Basic research consumed double the estimated time on the calendar. Actual work on the contract was delayed into 1948; the government refused to allot more funds. By the time census takers were on the street in 1950, Mauchly and Eckert were considering bankruptcy.

## 1951—Enter Remington Rand

The corporate visionaries of the electric shaver company took a gamble and by April 1951, the first UNIVAC arrived on the doorstep of the Census Bureau. It cost almost a million dollars to deliver and the government refused to pick up the tab for the overrun, sticking to the $400,000 cap in the original contract.

UNIVAC was a technical marvel. The number of vacuum tubes was cut by more than a third. The system was packaged in much smaller, even attractive, cabinets. Remember Hermann Hollerith, the guy who made punched cards so popular with the Census Bureau? His 80 column cards could be read directly into the UNIVAC. Better still, the information from the cards could be transferred to magnetic tape, resulting in an even higher computation speed. Scientists and engineers had thought ENIAC's 1 KHz clock rate an astounding feat. Imagine their delight when UNIVAC rocketed along at a blistering 2 MHz.

In 1952, UNIVAC was used to predict the election of Dwight D. Eisenhower to the presidency of the United States. Journalists across the country shunned UNIVAC's output; some said the race was too close to call, but most of them were just reluctant to have a machine show them up. After the election results were tallied, the accuracy of the prediction stunned the political pundits.

The word "computer" was gradually removed from job descriptions and the label stuck on machines. IBM—Big Blue—joined in, and an industry was born. No one then could conceive what the next short decades would bring.

## 1957—ARPA Is Born

Bill Gates was two years old when the Union of Soviet Socialist Republics launched Sputnik. Reacting to the Soviet initiative in getting into space and the implied missile capabilities, President Eisenhower launched the *Advanced Research Projects Agency* (*ARPA*). Its mission was simple: Bring the United States back into the lead in military science and technology. The green flag was dropped on the space race.

More than the mundane job of calculating trajectories of artillery rounds, computers were being tasked with aiming ballistic missiles—delivery systems for doomsday weapons. Orbital and suborbital dynamics were the meat of a geek's vocabulary. Wide-bed, 132-column printers devoured cartons of z-fold paper every hour.

More and more government facilities were being equipped with computers. Universities began installing them. Data was being exchanged between government sites and the universities. Most of it went by *sneaker net*; armed couriers carried the classified stuff over the longer distances where U.S. Mail couldn't be trusted.

Small groups of eclectics were figuring out how to link computers together to share information and the information age was getting ready to shift gears—again.

## 1962—ARPANET Goes Into Operation

Fearing that a nuclear attack on the United States might disrupt vital communications links, the Air Force commissioned the Rand Corporation to conduct a survivability study. The problem, posed in 1962, was how to establish a decentralized network so that if one site or path was demolished, command and control of nuclear bombers and missiles would continue.

Among the several alternatives was the idea of *packet switching*, breaking the data down into chunks at the originating computer and sending the data over existing telephone lines or via radio. The packets, each containing a discrete address and part of the final message, would be reassembled by the destination computer. If the communications link between sender and destination was disrupted, the router would select a different path. If a packet was corrupted or lost, the receiver would shoot a message back to the originator to resend it. Retransmitting a packet meant saving time over putting the entire message out again.

In 1968, ARPA awarded a contract to Bolt, Beranek, and Newman (BBN) to link four computers: SRI at Stanford, the University of California at Los Angeles and at Santa Barbara, and the University of Utah. Most of the early time was spent debugging crashes. Eventually, the early pioneers worked it out and developed the first significant protocol, called *Network Control Protocol* (NCP). ARPANET went into operation at 56Kbps, ostensibly as a research resource. Only a few knew the real reason.

The following year, Neil Armstrong and "Buzz" Aldrin landed on the moon. The computer they carried in the Lunar Excursion Module (LEM) plagued them on descent to the moon's surface with nearly constant alarms warning of *executive overloads*. It barely had enough power to perform the myriad tasks required of it.

## 1972—ARPA Changes Names

Several events occurred in 1972. The ARPA was shifted to the U.S. Defense Department and promptly renamed *DARPA*. The number of host computers increased to 24. The most significant event was triggered by Ray Tomlinson of BBN; he stuck an @-sign into an address and created email.

The following year, Vinton Cerf from Stanford and Bob Kahn from DARPA began working on a new protocol. The name they selected for it was *Transmission Control Protocol* (*TCP*). In a paper on TCP, Cerf and Kahn coined the term *Internet*. The increased number of users on ARPANET and the requirement for communications among different platforms led to refinement of TCP into TCP/IP, the *Internet Protocol Suite*.

## 1976—TCP/IP Enters Service

The number of computers connected to the ARPANET topped 100 and the Department of Defense mandated TCP/IP as the system protocol. The same year, Satellite Net (SATNET) went online connecting the United States with Europe. The CERN European Laboratory for Particle Physics headquartered in Switzerland stepped into the lead in Europe about this time with CERNET, a fast file transfer service among a huge number of mainframes and minicomputers using a 2Mbps serial line and packet switching. This was a significant improvement over the existing system of hundreds of *dumb* terminals connected via twisted-pair and RS-232 ports.

We're going to leave CERN and the Europeans and come back to the United States. However, it is an indication that the information age wasn't totally a parochial venture. We'll visit CERN again in a few years.

In 1977, a little company called Commodore went to market with the *Personal Electronic Transactor*, or *PET*. This would be followed by the VIC-20, then the Commodore C-64. One computer historian estimates that more than 20 million C-64s were built and sold.

The development of UNIX-to-UNIX Copy Protocol (UUCP) led to the creation of Usenet and newsgroups, which entered the arena in 1979.

## 1981—Enter The PC

What some entrepreneurs thought the world needed then was a better mousetrap—it was on its way.

Big Blue hit the market with the IBM PC in 1981. Within a couple of years the IBM XT was being delivered. These were technological marvels of the time. Taking up hardly any footprint on the desk, the machines had 10MB of hard drive and RAM could be expanded to 2MB.

The competition heated up in two years when Steve Jobs introduced the Apple Macintosh (Mac). The Mac bit huge chunks out of the market with its user-friendly operating system. Instead of requiring laborious keyboard entries to launch an application, then opening a file to work on it, Mac users merely clicked their mouse over an icon and the machine did the rest.

Both the XT or the Macintosh could have computed circles around the computer carried to the moon by Armstrong and Aldrin.

## 1984—The Numbers Begin To Grow

With the support of the National Science Foundation (NSF), the next five years would see the advent of Because It's Time NETwork (BITNET), Computers and Science Network (CSNET), Military Network (MILNET), and more. The Internet Activities Board (IAB) was formed. The most dramatic step of this period was the upgrade of CSNET to use T1 lines allowing data speeds to jump from 56K to 1.5Meg. Users numbered about 1,000 or so that year and 2,000 the next.

## 1988—Population Explosion

By 1988, the Internet population topped 56,000. These were for the most part private connections. The NSF had banned commercial use of the Internet, but it was just a matter of time before the barrier would be broken and e-commerce would begin in earnest.

Businesses were wiring in. LANs wound their way through corporate offices on snaky yellow cable. *Appletalk* and *Ethernet* were spoken languages of the geeks. Medical facilities transferred patient information without lugging charts around the building. You could stop into any branch of your favorite bank and check your savings account balance or pay a credit card bill. Insurance companies shared actuaries where they were needed. The list of potential network applications stretched to the limits of imagination.

Private bulletin boards like Fido Net created a way to connect people together from all over the world. For a couple of bucks a month, you could exchange ideas with people you'd never have a chance to shake hands with. Pick any topic and you could find it behind the *conference door*. All this popularity spawned serious competition among the modem makers to see who could be the first to reach 2400 baud over standard telephone lines.

## 1992—Enter The World Wide Web

Remember those guys over in Switzerland at CERN? When they released the *World Wide Web* in 1992, domain names were almost ten years old. That is the same year the number of registered hosts hurdled over the one million mark.

So far we have tracked a small but very significant growth of the Internet. It would not be possible for this or any other book to chronicle the enormous tide that was to follow.

Innovations—these ideas are the stuff the Internet is made from. *Email* was the first; it led to *imagery*, *telephony*, *chat rooms*—a plethora of gimmicks and gadgets. A new language evolved: *cyberspace*, *connected*, *virtual world*, *netheads*, *netizens*, and *geeks*. One dialect spoke of *bridges*, *routers*, *switches*, and *encryption*.

Just a couple years after the creation of the Web, the National Science Foundation released the commercial restrictions it had placed on the Internet. The action caused a virtual explosion. Commerce didn't just stick its toe in the door, it shoved it wide open, and then proceeded to cut more portals.

By then, ARPANET had long since been retired. And what happened to the first transatlantic cable—the one that started it all? The last message over the Great Transatlantic Cable was sent three decades back and the building was turned into a museum.

According to one industry source, the Internet hosted more than 74,000,000 domain names at the end of 1998.

## Now—Giant Leap

Within this cyberspace of connectivity is what this book is all about—*Virtual Private Networking*. While the Internet was developing into a huge commercial venture and millions of individuals were connecting their home computers, thousands of businesses were also wiring in. Software and hardware developers—3-Comm, Novell, Microsoft, Cisco, and others—saw the need to focus on VPN.

For nearly a decade, the Internet has been reasonably calm—a period almost of catching its breath. The only real significant change has been in the number of users coming aboard.

The next major event is going to be Virtual Private Networking, and that is what this book is all about. VPN has been like an automobile coasting downhill with the clutch pushed in, gaining momentum but reserving the power—heading for the next hump in the road. VPN is creating a new dimension to the Internet. New protocols have been written for it. New equipment has been designed and more is on the drawing board. VPN has been around for a couple of years waiting for its turn to lurch into the interest lead.

Now is its chance. Pop the clutch.

# Advantages And Disadvantages Of VPN

According to the pundits, if a business can use Virtual Private Networking, it is going to win on the bottom line, and every business—large or small—can use VPN in one form or another.

One important advantage of VPN is its ability to transmit data across different platforms without worrying about proprietary equipment and its associated protocols.

I asked Howard Myers, business development manager for Fortress Technologies, if he could think of any class of business or enterprise, disregarding its size, that should not use a VPN. "Any business that doesn't want to save on [telephone company] costs and/or that isn't concerned about security!" he answered. He went on to say, "In reality, VPNs today aren't quite ready for extremely large installations requiring enormous bandwidth. Today, they typically perform best for modem through T3 speeds, although that will quickly change."

## But Is It Right For Everybody?

There are scenarios where VPN might just not show a positive return on an investment by an enterprise. Take the case of a company with a dial-in network already up and running. If all the traffic is local, not requiring long-distance toll charges, then VPN doesn't make a lot of sense.

With the same network equipment, but only a limited number of short-haul connections, as in a Local Access Transport Area or LATA, the Information Technology manager needs to do a comprehensive analysis and see how long it would take to amortize the investment in VPN technology.

How VPN is implemented and how much the savings will be is based on making the correct decisions. It won't be the same in every case. Myers believes that VPN may not be practical for very small firms with only one or two persons dialing in and no in-house network expertise.

While you are reading, keep in mind that advantages for some VPN users could easily be ho-hum circumstances and maybe even disadvantages to others. How any business implements this burgeoning technology will depend on how the Information Technology (IT) manager is charged to allocate the available resources.

The point is, the IT manager must determine what and where the advantages are, while keeping away from the morass of potential disadvantages. The IT manager must not fall into the paradigm trap. He or she must evaluate the available VPN technology and figure out how to make it work in his or her environment. There is nothing wrong in looking at the way another company implemented VPN, as long as you make sure its approach will work for you.

## Implementation

There are three levels of VPN implementation. On one end of the scale is the option of calling up an *Internet Service Provider* (*ISP*) and passing the task over to the provider completely. Opposite that, the IT manager merely buys a dial-in service connection and provides all the elements of VPN within the corporate boundaries. The third set of options is to outsource part of the job and keep the remainder. As we will see in following chapters, this can be done in varying degrees.

In the first case, the IT manager and the business enterprise are fully dependent on the ISP, because all the aspects of VPN discussed in this book are turned over to the ISP. On the other hand, keeping all of the VPN operation in-house gives the enterprise complete control.

When the ISP does all the work, it will usually make some guarantees regarding connectivity and the quality of the connections. The business is freed of overhead required for staffing management and maintenance functions, such as training and periodic seminars to stay abreast of the technology. Another benefit is the transparency of hardware and software changes. When it comes time for the ISP to upgrade its system, you, the customer, may never be aware of changes being made. The ISP generally has another advantage—especially if it is a major telephone company to begin with. If a T1 line starts acting up, the ISP can quickly change the lines to ensure top level service.

We shall also look at different approaches to implementing VPN if the decision is made to keep part or all of the control within the enterprise. One IT manager, for example, may choose to perform all VPN functions through software, whereas another may decide on a mix of software and hardware; still another may opt for a total hardware capability.

## VPN For Intranet Applications

By the way, VPN technology is not necessarily used only for extranet communications. It can be used within a company's walls to allow employees access to certain data but restrict them from others.

Take the case of a medical health care facility: A clerk in the billing department may have a need to know what procedures were followed during Joe Doak's physical examination, but should not be privy to the cholesterol level determined by the blood tests.

That same clerk might be allowed to peek into his or her personal records kept by the human services department of the medical facility, but restricted from looking at the records of co-workers.

What an IT manager should be prepared to do is exploit the technology to best suit his company.

## Applications Unlimited

Telecommuting is growing more popular every day. Businesses no longer are restricted by geography in hiring the best person to do a job. An employee can work out of the home and the company benefits from reduced overhead. Using cellular telephones, a real estate brokerage can use VPN to forward data to its field representative. Those same cell phones can be used to track cargo in the trucking industry. A combination of telephone and satellite communications could extend VPN to cover cruise ships on any body of water covering the planet.

## Starting Down The Decision Trail

If you decide to retain some or all of the VPN within the enterprise, you will next have to choose between hardware or software systems and firewall-based VPNs or standalone VPN application packages.

Using an existing internal router and loading in VPN software is a quick and relatively inexpensive way to get started. The downside is that a pure software VPN solution uses processor cycles. Increasing the number of users steals more cycles. The processor is charged with not only its current chores, but also with the additional tasks of authentication and encryption.

Another problem is that it may be difficult to scale up the equipment. As the popularity of VPN calls for more and more users on the system, the processor just might run out of room to handle them. The critical period is generally when a large number of users are attempting to log in at the same time, such as early morning when all the telecommuters are connecting to work.

As an evaluation tool and to learn how VPN works, a software-based system might be an economical learning tool for you. If you find weak spots in the system, you can upgrade to a hardware solution.

We will be discussing this in more depth as we proceed through the book, and a list of vendors will be provided in Appendix C with information on how to contact them on the Web or through snail mail.

## The Hardware Solution

The opposite extreme to the software solution involves vendors who offer a turnkey approach to VPN operation. Their devices are single boxes that will handle your entire VPN concerns. Authentication, cryptography and key management, routing, housekeeping, and logs are all packed together in one compact unit—plug it in and go. However, you need to perform some operations; for example, like all equipment, you have to load in your operating parameters and access databases.

One thing to consider as an offset to the cost of the turnkey device is that they require little or no training or maintenance. Occasional supervision is generally all that is necessary. The cost of a maintenance contract may be less than the overhead cost of an employee.

Most all-in-one VPN systems give you an option of starting with a minimum number and adding on as your VPN usage grows. For example VPNet Technology, Inc., founded in October 1995 and based in San Jose, California, offers a device that starts with the ability to serve 1,000 and can be scaled up to 2,000, then 5,000. The company says the system "...combines standards-based encryption, authentication, key management, and compression technologies to provide VPN support to large enterprises, small- to mid-sized businesses, branch offices, and remote sites."

### Mix And Match

Another scenario is the mixed bag approach, in which the IT manager adds on some equipment to handle part of the VPN workload and assigns some of it to existing hardware.

However you implement the Virtual Private Network, approach the job with an open mind and good resources. In the rest of the book, we will do the best we can to help you make the most intelligent choices.

# A Peek Into The Millenium

Size and shape preclude including a crystal ball within the pages of this book. We canvassed any number of vendors and will—without revealing proprietary secrets—tell you how they are gearing up to bolt into the new millennium. Hang onto your hats, it's going to be an e-ticket ride.

Like we said earlier, the Internet has been fairly quiet for the last several years. Virtual Private Networking is going to change all that. You only have to look at what the major telephone providers are doing to get a hint.

AT&T, MCI, Sprint, GTE, Atlantic Bell, PacBell, and Southwestern Bell are all jockeying for a piece of the action. The money being invested by these and other traditional telephone service companies can't be considered small change. The full service VPN ISP is a reality today, and tomorrow it will capture more and more new businesses.

Novell, Microsoft, and others are in the VPN marketplace today with new and improved software. Tomorrow will bring software that will handle more traffic at increased security.

Today, you can buy VPN hardware from Cisco, 3Com, Fortress Technologies, Internet Dynamics, Assured Digital, VPNet Technologies, and others. Tomorrow will see venture capital outlays to still more hardware companies as the development pace picks up. Alliances and partnerships are being formed as VPN vendors compete for the top of the hill.

The tide is pushing Virtual Private Networking in the direction of business enterprises and, like the mighty oceans send waves up the beach, the Internet is going to build up speed as it broaches. The more timid entrepreneurs will dash away to keep their feet dry, whereas those with their eyes on the prize will stand their ground and feel the tingle and excitement and thrill of the new rush.

## Growth

According to the Internet Industry Almanac (**www.i-i-a.com**), more than 327 million people will use the Internet by year-end 2000—up from 100 million Internet users at year-end 1997. The United States is projected to have more than 139 million Internet users, or 40 percent of the total by year 2000. These numbers include business, educational, and home Internet users.

The IIA isn't the only research group predicting growth. According to survey figures from INTECO Corporation (**www.inteco.com**), 76 million Internet users can access it from home, 51 million have access from work, 22 million have access from a friend or relative's house, and 24 million have access from other locations, such as a school, library, or community center. The research also showed that 39 percent of Internet users are 18 to 34 years of age, and 38 percent are 35 to 49 years old.

INTECO sampled 16,500 nationally representative U.S. households in December 1998 and determined that nationwide, 108 million adults—about 55 percent of the adult population—had accessed the Internet at least once in the previous 30 days. The December 1998 figure was an increase of 38 percent from 78 million in May of 1998, and up 71 percent from 61 million in September of 1997.

According to another report from INTECO, PC banking households blossomed from 3.8 million in the third quarter of 1997 to 7 million by the end of 1998. Two factors are responsible for driving the explosive growth in online banking, according to George Barto, Senior Financial Services Analyst for INTECO. One is the 68 percent rise in the number of U.S. households with access to the Internet (up from 22 million in the third quarter of 1997 to 37 million by the end of 1998). The second is the *build it and they will come* approach taken by financial institutions.

You can see one example of the growth in Table 1.1. The data comes from Network Wizards located in Menlo Park, California (**www.nw.com**). They have been in business since 1990, specializing in products relating to computers and communications. The company designs and sells unique hardware and software products, both directly and through resellers and OEMs.

**Table 1.1   Top fifteen domains on January 1, 1999, compared to 1991.**

| Domain | Category | 1999 | 1991 |
|--------|----------|------|------|
| com | Commercial | 12140747 | 181361 |
| net | Networks | 8856687 | 4109 |
| edu | Educational | 5022815 | 243020 |
| jp | Japan | 1687534 | 8579 |
| us | United States | 1562391 | 127 |
| mil | U.S. military | 1510440 | 27492 |
| uk | United Kingdom | 1423804 | 18984 |
| de | Germany | 1316893 | 31016 |
| ca | Canada | 1119172 | 27052 |
| au | Australia | 792351 | 31622 |
| org | Organizations | 744285 | 19117 |
| gov | Government | 651200 | 46463 |
| nl | Netherlands | 564129 | 12770 |
| fi | Finland | 546244 | 11994 |
| fr | France | 488043 | 13011 |

### How Does This Relate To VPN?

Let's take a look at telecommuting. FIND/SVP, a New York based research and consulting firm (**www.findsvp.com**) reports that the number of telecommuters in the United States jumped from 8.5 million to more than 11 million, a growth rate of more than 15 percent, in just the two years up to January, 1999.

"Many companies, both large and small, have discovered the benefits of allowing employees to work from home part of the time," says Thomas E. Miller, FIND/SVP vice president, who directed the research. "Growth of email, voicemail, and the Internet, combined with a renewed emphasis on work results rather than workplace appearances, have encouraged managers to recognize that employees working part-time down the road are no more distant than employees working down the hall. What matters most is whether or not the job is getting done."

FIND/SVP's survey established that 35 percent of today's telecommuters use the Internet, including 31 percent who use it regularly from home, totaling 3.4 million home users. This number reflects more than a 50 percent average annual growth in telecommuters who are linked to offices.

Telecommuter Central (**www.tcentral.com**) reports increased employee productivity and morale as the top two company benefits. They also cite easier employee recruitment and increased retention as benefits.

What do the employees think about telecommuting? TC said that people also ranked improved personal productivity at the top, followed by reduced commuting time and quality of life. Flexible work hours and flexibility in managing dependent care also ranked high, reflecting in the company's perception of increased morale.

Telecommuting produces additional company benefits in the reduction of overhead costs; these include facility maintenance and energy consumption.

## Voice-Over Internet Protocol

*Voice-Over Internet Protocol* (*VoIP*) has established a toehold and will spread. Voicenet, an ISP based in Pennsylvania, offers Internet telephone services for homes and businesses utilizing conventional telephones for local and long distance calls over the Internet.

"Voicenet has changed the face of communications by offering this revolutionary new way to make low-cost, high-quality telephone calls using the latest Internet technology," said Dante Mattioni, a Voicenet corporate client. "The digital quality is exceptional and the savings are astounding," he added.

In a VoIP seminar conducted over the Internet in January, 1999, John Minasyan, a digital signal processing expert for Texas Instruments, said, "It's [VoIP] certainly still emerging, and in the early stages of market development. But with the advances in the technology—both software and hardware now allowing you to have essentially total quality voice on a controlled packet network—we are seeing incredible interest from corporate or enterprise customers."

The Yankee Group (**www.yankeegroup.com**) projection for the VoIP world-wide market is more than $1.6 billion in 2002. That is based on $193 million in 1998, and an estimate of $310 million in 1999. These numbers are based on the changeover from direct-dial long distance service to local dial-in and VoIP to go cross-country.

Hardware companies like Cisco (**www.cisco.com**) are marketing VoIP systems and pitching their products all across the United States. The implication is that VoIP, coupled with VPN as either a parallel or integral part, makes a lot of sense for business.

# Summary

Virtual Private Networking is not a coming attraction—it is here and it is here to stay. Commercial enterprises, as well as government entities, are already using it, and more are getting online with it every day. New hardware and software are being developed, and improvements are being written and fabricated into existing equipment.

VPN has the potential for saving an individual 40 to 80 percent over the cost of a standard dial-in, depending on implementation. It is up to the IT managers to make the determination.

The Internet is growing faster than anyone could have imagined back when ARPA funded the first studies for networking. From the original four users back in the 1960s, the numbers have grown to more than 150 million—and they are connecting at the rate of one more every 1.75 seconds.

Commerce over the Internet will reach into the billions of dollars by the time the clock ticks once in the year 2000.

# Chapter 2
# A Review Of Local Area Networks

**Key Topics:**

♦ *Standards and their influence*

♦ *Network models*

♦ *Protocol suites*

♦ *Network transmission media*

♦ *Physical devices—hardware*

♦ *Logical devices—software*

In this chapter we are going to limit our discussion to a review of local area networks, LANs. A discussion of the WAN, or wide area network, follows in the next chapter.

Local area networks are complicated entities and a complete discussion of everything about them gets away from the real purpose of this book. However, it is necessary for everyone to understand some fundamental principles that apply to all networks. If you are a network support person working in a support position, and you feel comfortable about your knowledge of how your local network works, feel free to skip this chapter and go on to Chapter 3. On the other hand, if you feel your knowledge may have some missing parts, then this chapter will help fill in some of the blanks.

## What Is A LAN?

Networks are defined by using protocols developed by *standards organizations*. We will look first at some of these organizations. In order to simplify explanation of the processes within the standard, standards organizations create *models*; we will take a brief look at the LAN models developed by three key players in the world of network standards:

♦ The ISO/OSI model for networks

♦ The IEEE 802 Committee model for networks

♦ The Internet protocol suite, as developed under a grant from ARPA

The standards organizations decide what rules define how networks implement the processes necessary for communication between entities. These rules, known as *protocols*, define when, where, why—and most important—*how* the network performs its given tasks. The protocols are implemented in some combination of hardware and software. It's a logical progression then, that we move from protocols to hardware, and from hardware to software.

# Architecture

Almost any computer sold today can be configured to operate on a LAN. Surprisingly enough, most of the less-expensive computers with just a basic operating system will work quite well on a small workgroup–size LAN. This was not always the case. In the early years of personal computers, each manufacturer built its brand of machine to match its idea of what the architecture should be. Trying to connect those early PCs into a LAN led to serious problems, because not everyone agreed on what a PC should be, much less how information would be shared among them.

This situation changed starting in the early 1980s, with the release of the IBM PC. IBM was such a force in the computer industry that when they released their PC, almost the entire PC industry followed suit. It was not until IBM changed their architecture to the IBM PS-2 that the industry decided to break the grip IBM had on it. By then, IBM PC architecture had become a *de facto* standard.

## Enter The Architectural Standard

The PC industry collectively realized that if they were going to be successful in the market, they had to manufacture products designed to real, not *de facto*, standards. Thus was born the Industry Standard Architecture or ISA, and Enhanced ISA or EISA, for personal computers. By manufacturing personal computers to standard architecture, other products that interface with them have a reasonable chance of succeeding. These standards do not happen by accident; they are developed through a long process of consultation, investigation, and testing.

Two examples of standards organizations are the International Organization for Standardization, otherwise known as ISO, and the Institute of Electrical and Electronic Engineers, the IEEE. The IEEE primarily sets standards for electrical and electronic devices.

While these two organizations set standards for a large number of devices and areas, we are primarily interested in the standards they have adopted relating to the computer network industry. The ISO is an international organization, represented in this country by the American National Standards Institute, ANSI.

Other standards and related organizations exist, and their standards are no less important to the industry than those of ISO and IEEE. We will introduce them as needed through the book.

# Open Standards—Public Domain

Standards developed by various organizations generally become public domain, and are known as *open standards*. Manufacturers can make products that conform to these open standards without having to pay royalties.

An example of an open standard is the venerable Transmission Control Protocol/Internet Protocol (TCP/IP). Because TCP/IP development was funded by a grant from the Defense Advanced Research Projects Agency, DARPA, a United States government agency funded by tax dollars, it has always belonged to the general public in a category known as *public domain*. After the DARPA grant was completed, TCP/IP was released by the Department of Defense and was adopted as an open standard.

One thing you should note about open standards is that once an open standard is adopted, manufacturers design and build their products to conform to the standard. Consequently, significant resistance arises to changing an adopted standard. Even if a proposed change is a great improvement, that change could cause much confusion in the manufacturing sector. Instead, when an improvement needs to be implemented, a totally new standard is adopted. It may incorporate many or all features from a previous generation, but it is nonetheless a separate and complete standard. This procedure allows designers and manufacturers to implement improvements in existing products without invalidating or destroying the existing structure.

# *De facto* Standards

Sometimes a company develops a product that it has either patented, copyrighted, or for any reason decided to keep within the corporate proprietary realm. When such a product is so successful because of its marketwide acceptance and successful sales, it becomes a *de facto standard*. An example of this is Microsoft's Windows operating system, or Novell's NetWare network operating system.

*De facto* standards, however, have pitfalls and problems. Suppose Company ABC develops a new and exciting technology component based on a *de facto* standard established by Company XYZ. XYZ may—under proprietary law, at its discretion—levy a licensing fee on ABC. XYZ did, after all, expend engineering and production forces with their associated overhead to create the *de facto* standard. ABC will, in almost every case, pass the cost of the licensing fee on to the end user. The net result? Increased costs to the consumer.

Another problem that arises from *de facto* standards is XYZ's freedom to change the design of its product at any time. If the *de facto* standard product is in widespread use and dominates the technology, end users may have no choice but to go along with the change and purchase new software or hardware upgrades to stay at the leading edge of the technology—or, at the least—to remain competitive.

Not all *de facto* standards become successful in the long run. IBM found that out when it made the decision to stop manufacturing the IBM-PC with its open architecture, and start manufacturing the IBM-PS2 with *Microchannel* architecture. The general public rejected the *Microchannel* architecture. Analysts lay the cause of the PS2's lack of success and eventual demise on its increased costs, some of which were proprietary licensing fees.

# Network Models

In an effort to simplify the complexity involved in defining networks, standards organizations have developed diagrams known as *models*. These models define the structure of network systems in a logical manner. Both ISO and IEEE have developed models for networks. However, these two models are not exactly alike and do not cover the same areas of the network structure.

## The OSI Model For Computer Networks

By the mid-1970s, several mainframe computer manufacturers, including IBM, Digital Equipment Corporation (DEC), and Burroughs, had developed mainframe computers supporting hundreds of users. Each mainframe manufacturer had areas of strength and weakness.

In this type of environment, the architecture of each company could be viewed as being a *virtual* network system; only one central processor unit existed, but it serviced sessions for multiple users. Each manufacturer had its own architectural model, and each was proprietary to that manufacturer.

That was okay for an enterprise company that wanted to invest in a single manufacturer's products. If, on the other hand, a company wanted to purchase products from two or more different manufacturers to take advantage of the strengths of each, the information technology manager encountered some problems trying to pass data among the different components.

These problems led to the formation of several organizations whose common goal was to produce standards for interfacing among the diverse computer systems. The list includes, for example, the following:

♦ International Telecommunications Union (ITU)

♦ Institute of Electrical and Electronic Engineers (IEEE) 802 Committee

♦ Electronic Industries Association (EIA)

♦ International Organization for Standardization (ISO)

Starting with this chapter, we'll take a brief look at their results and see how the various organizations interacted. Then, throughout the book, you will see close cooperation between the agencies.

In another effort to alleviate the connectivity problems caused by incompatibility, the ISO formed a subcommittee in the late 1970s to develop data communication standards for multivendor interoperability.

Meanwhile, IBM was by far the leading computer manufacturer in the mainframe computer industry. During this epoch of computer growth, Big Blue released its preferred *Systems Network Architecture*, which came to be known as SNA throughout the industry (see Figure 2.1). The SNA architecture is still valid throughout the world.

The ISO subcommittee continued working towards the final development of its open standard for networking and finally released the finished version of the *Open Systems Interconnection* (*OSI*) standard in 1984. The release was closely followed by development of a reference model to illustrate the standard. Because of IBM eminence in the computer industry, the OSI model closely resembled the IBM model for the SNA.

Although SNA is still valid throughout the world, the OSI model serves as today's standard architecture for computer networking. It divides communication tasks into layers and defines each layer based on the protocols that govern the operation that takes place at that point. Figure 2.2 shows each of the layers in a stack. We will dissect the model layer by layer and explain the various functions of each layer. Keep in mind that the OSI model defines the operation of all parts of the network, from top to bottom. In a complete network system, capable of full data communications, each separate entity or station on the network must be capable of implementing most, if not all, the defined tasks.

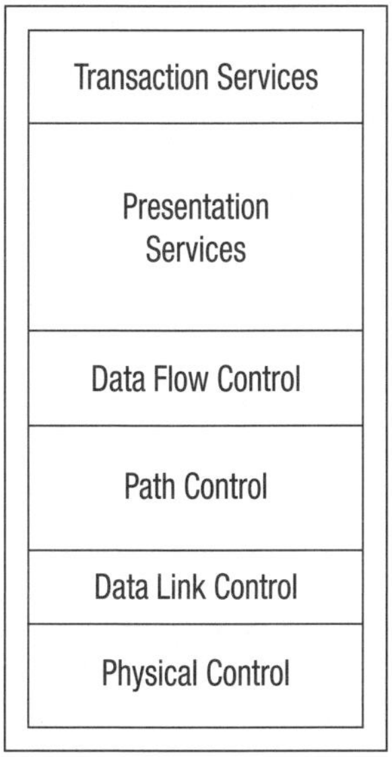

| Transaction Services |
| Presentation Services |
| Data Flow Control |
| Path Control |
| Data Link Control |
| Physical Control |

**Figure 2.1**
The IBM model for Systems Network Architecture.

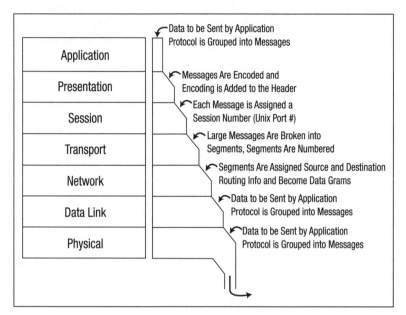

**Figure 2.2**
The model for the Open Systems Interconnection standard released by the International Organization for Standardization in 1984.

## A Closer Look At The OSI Model

The OSI model consists of seven layers; each one is defined based on the operations that take place within its control. It is important to note that layers on two separate systems are considered peers. That is, a layer on one machine communicates directly with the same layer on another machine, without regard to the other layers in the stack, as shown in Figure 2.2. Conventionally, layer 1 is on the bottom, 7 on the top. We shall see that not all layers are critical for the LAN, but they are still there.

### Physical Layer

When data are being transmitted to the network, the *physical layer*, or bottom layer, is responsible for converting data from the form of logical bits and placing it on the network media (or cable) in the form of electrical signals. When the physical layer is receiving, it is responsible for taking electrical signals from the media and converting them into bits of data. For this reason, the physical layer defines the electrical characteristics and connections necessary to interface with the network. The physical layer is also responsible for establishing timing between entities and for low-level accuracy. As a part of maintaining data accuracy, this layer is responsible for detecting when to transmit, when not to transmit, and for determining if someone else transmits at the same time.

At the physical layer, data are handled in the form of logical bits. If a computer has more than one *network interface card* (NIC), more than one instance of physical layer protocol implementation will occur.

### Data Link Layer

The *data link layer* (DLL) is responsible for converting *frames* into bits to be handed to the physical layer for transmission. Its converse function is taking received bits from the physical layer and converting them back into frames. The DLL is also responsible for establishing and maintaining a reliable link between two entities or nodes, especially on noisy or troublesome network media. In order to perform this task, the DLL protocols must define how different nodes are identified on subnetworks. A *subnetwork* is a small part of a larger network separated into distinct parts. Each subnetwork has its own network number. The DLL must be able to establish a reliable channel between the node it exists on and the node at the receiving end of the data stream. The data link layer is responsible for recognizing multiple nodes on the same subnetwork.

It is important to know that the data link layer handles data in the form of frames. If more than one network interface card exists, or if more than one frame *type* is defined for a single NIC, then one implementation of the DLL protocols for each defined type will exist for each NIC.

### Network Layer

The *network layer* is responsible for routing information between networks. Where the DLL is responsible for reliable delivery of information between entities on the same local network, the network layer is responsible for reliable delivery of information between entities on different networks. In a LAN with only a single media path, the network layer is not used often. We do need, however, to understand its functions within the OSI model.

The network layer handles data in the form of *packets*. If a computer has more than one NIC, or more than one frame type assigned to a single NIC, then more than one data stream is defined. In this case, the network layer is responsible for identifying which data stream a particular group of data has been received from, assigning a session identifier to that data stream, and routing the transmitted data for the same session back to the correct data stream. The network layer protocols perform this function by reading the network address of the originating network in the headers assigned to the packets as they are received, assigning the same network address to transmitted data for the same session, and routing the transmitted data for that process back to the proper data stream for that particular network address.

### Transport Layer

The *transport layer* in the middle deals in data units known as *datagrams*. This layer is responsible for guaranteeing error-free connections from one host to another host across the network. In so doing, it more or less hides the complexity of the lower three layers from the upper three layers. Its primary function is to assure reliability from end-to-end.

Another task of the transport layer is to break up large groups of data—complete messages for example—into smaller units called *packets*. These smaller units are then transmitted through the communications network. On the receiving end, packets are reassembled by the transport layer protocols and reconstructed into messages. The transport layer monitors transmission and reception activity from one end to the other to assure that the data packets are reassembled correctly.

### Session Layer

The *session layer* deals in data units known as *messages*. Its primary task is to establish and terminate communications between host processes. While the session is established, the session layer is responsible for monitoring what is going on, as well as performing synchronization and translation between name and address databases.

### Presentation Layer

The *presentation layer* also deals in data units known as *messages*. At this point the model performs any necessary translation of the data. If translation is not required in the LAN, the presentation layer is still there. Keep in mind the bi-directional function of all the layers; what all the layers do to the transmitted data, they do in reverse to the received data. Translation may be in the form of code conversion (that is, EBCDIC to ASCII), data compression, and encryption.

### Application Layer

Again, the *application layer* deals in data units known as *messages*. The application layer is the common interface with the user. Here is where such functions as file transfer (FTP), electronic mail (SMTP), and remote access (Telnet) are performed. Applications, as used here, should not be confused with standard user applications, such as word processing, spreadsheets, and so forth.

### All Together Now

When receiving data, each of the upper layers depends upon the lower layers to perform their tasks and prepare the data before passing it up. Likewise, when transmitting data, each of the lower layers depends upon the ability of the upper layers to process the data before passing the data down the pipe.

As an example, let's use FTP for an application and wend our way through a typical transmission process. The data (in this case a filename or groups of filenames) to be processed is located and queued up by the application layer protocol. The data is then passed to the presentation layer.

The presentation layer performs any other required services, such as data compression or data encoding, and adds information to the data to identify these services. The data is then passed to the session layer.

The session layer adds information to the data to identify which session or process originated the data (the system is designed to handle several sessions/processes at the same time) and passes it on to the transport layer.

The transport layer checks the size of the data and, if necessary, breaks it into packets. This layer assigns a sequence number to each packet, then passes the packets to the network layer.

At this point, the network layer assigns each packet the address of the destination network—provided the destination is outside the local network subsystem—and places the address of the originating network in the packet. From here, the network layer then shoves the packet into the proper data link layer interface based on the destination address.

The data link layer then breaks the packet into frames and places the destination node address in the header of each frame. From here, the DLL passes the frame to the physical layer in the form of bits, one bit at a time. The physical layer establishes the proper timing with the physical network media, and at the proper time places the bits on the media in the form of electrical signals.

Somewhere down the line, at the receiving end, one nanosecond-per-foot later, the whole process goes into reverse. Starting at the bottom and going to the top, each layer performs its specific task until the data is presented in the form of a request for file transfer.

### Now It's Time To Move On To Another Exciting Venue, IEEE 802 Committee

The IEEE 802 Committee was formed in 1980 in response to the proprietary architecture of the mainframe computer manufacturers. The committee released its first standard, *IEEE 802*, in 1985. Like the ISO standard, IEEE 802 provided a model, but in this case, it was aimed at network computer architecture. Keep in mind that the IEEE is concerned with the electrical signals that eventually represent the ones and zeros of logical data.

As other standards were released by the IEEE, each was numbered as a subpart of the basic IEEE 802. Each covers a specific network implementation (*topology*). The IEEE 802 Committee remains active to this date. As technologies change, a new subcommittee is formed to study the new technology and adapt a standard that meets industry requirements. Thus, the IEEE 802 standard continues to evolve. Table 2.1 shows the complete IEEE 802 LAN standards.

**Table 2.1   The IEEE standards.**

| Standard | Purpose |
| --- | --- |
| 802 | Overview and architecture |
| 802.1 | Higher layers and Internetworking |
| 802.2 | Logical Link Control (LLC) |
| 802.3 | Carrier Sense Multiple Access with Collision Detection (CSMA/CD) |

*(continued)*

**Table 2.1**    **The IEEE standards** *(continued).*

| Standard | Purpose |
|----------|---------|
| 802.4 | Token passing bus |
| 802.5 | Token passing ring |
| 802.6 | Metropolitan Area Network (MAN) |
| 802.7 | Broadband Technology Advisory Group |
| 802.8 | Optical Fiber Technology Advisor Group |
| 802.9 | Voice/Data Integration on LANs |
| 802.10 | Standard for interoperable LAN security |
| 802.11 | Wireless LANs |
| 802.12 | Telecommunications and information exchange between systems |

Each standard can have modifications that add to the standard or correct deficiencies within it, for example, 802.12a, b, and so forth. For more information, you can find abstracts of all IEEE standards at **www.standards.ieee.org** on the Internet.

## A Comparison Of The IEEE And ISO Models For Networking

Unlike the ISO model, the IEEE model for networking does not cover all the parts of the network system. But then, it was never intended to—the IEEE model deals primarily with electrical signal levels, signal timing, and node identification. In other words, it deals with how the signal gets from the device to the media, and from the media to the device, as shown in Figure 2.3. Note that the IEEE standards deal with only the bottom layers.

It is, nonetheless, possible to do a reasonable comparison of the two. The IEEE 802 model encompasses the functions found at the ISO/OSI physical and data link layers. Instead of two layers, the IEEE 802 model has three. They are as follows:

♦ Physical layer (PHY)

♦ Media access control (MAC)

♦ Logical link control (LLC)

The IEEE 802 physical layer includes protocols that implement the following functions:

♦ Physical topology

♦ Cable and connector types

♦ Transmission rates

♦ Signal encoding

♦ Synchronization

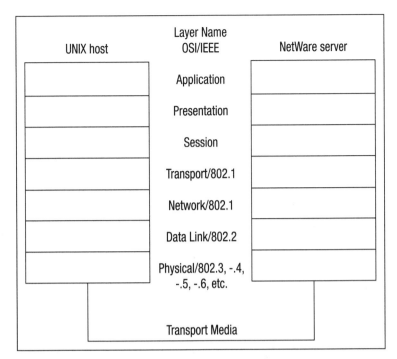

**Figure 2.3**
This is the IEEE 802 model for peer level communications by similar protocols.

The IEEE 802 media access control layer includes protocols that implement the following functions:

♦ Logical topology

♦ Access to the transmission media

♦ Frame format definition

♦ Node addressing

♦ Reliability or frame check sequence

The IEEE 802 logical link control layer includes protocols that implement the following functions:

♦ Managing the data-link communication

♦ Link addressing

♦ Defining *Service Access Points* (SAPS), which are logical interfaces between the LLC and higher layers

♦ Sequencing

### *IEEE 802.3 Subcommittee*

An essential part of the IEEE 802 Committee is the IEEE 802.3 subcommittee. The 802.3 protocol defines the methods used for the transfer of data bits to the network media as electrical signals and vice versa. As part of this important standard, the IEEE 802.3 subcommittee defined a process known as *Carrier Sense Multiple Access with Collision Detection*, or *CSMA/CD*. This protocol is modeled after the original Ethernet network standard developed by DEC, Intel, and Xerox. Since its adoption as an IEEE standard, this network topology is dominant in LAN architecture today.

In defining 802.3, the subcommittee adopted terminology that specifies the network transmission rate in Mbps—whether the topology uses baseband or broadband signaling—and the maximum length of a segment between repeaters measured in meters. Table 2.2 presents a list of the standard topologies.

> **Note**
> *Before moving on, I would like to make an observation: The IEEE 802 Committee was concerned with the lower-level protocols of the network model and chose to leave the rest to others. This does not mean that the upper layers do not exist.*

## The Internet Protocol Suite

Under the guidance of the DARPA, a complete model for networking had been developed by the time the IEEE 802 Committee protocols were adopted. The original DARPA grant was funded by the DoD for the development of a suite of protocols that would implement the logical functions necessary to provide a reliable nationwide data communications network. The two best-known protocols in the suite are Transmission Control Protocol and Internet Protocol. Today this set of protocols is named the *Internet protocol suite* and commonly referred to as *TCP/IP*.

Like the OSI and IEEE 802, the Internet protocol suite has a model; see Figure 2.4. If you compare this model to the OSI model in Figure 2.2, you can see the protocols in this suite somewhat map the OSI model. What is interesting is the way that the Internet protocol

**Table 2.2   The standard topologies of IEEE 802.3.**

| Topology | Description |
|----------|-------------|
| 10base5 | 10Mbps rate, baseband signaling, 500 meters per segment (coax) |
| 10base2 | 10Mbps rate, baseband signaling, 185 meters per segment (coax) |
| 10baseT | 10Mbps rate, over twisted-pair cable |
| 1base5 | 1Mbps rate, baseband signaling, 500 meters per segment (twisted-pair) |
| 10broad36 | 10Mbps rate, broadband signaling, 3600 meters per segment (coax) |
| 10baseF | 10Mbps rate, over fiber-optic cable |
| 100baseTX | 100Mbps rate, over Category 5 twisted-pair cable |
| 100baseVG | 100Mbps rate, over audio grade twisted-pair cable |

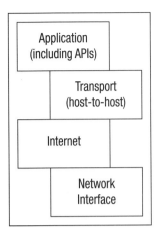

**Figure 2.4**
The Internet protocol suite model.

suite maps the upper layers of the OSI model, whereas the IEEE 802 protocols map the lower layers of the OSI model.

This shows that when you combine the Internet protocol suite and IEEE 802, you implement all the functionality of the OSI reference model. All that remains is to implement these two protocols in one actual product. The Unix operating system developed by AT&T Bell Labs did exactly that and became one of the most popular networking systems around.

What we see is the implementation of a complete network system accomplished in three parts:

♦ The physical aspects of signal management, standardized by the IEEE 802 Committee, a part of which is based on the Ethernet standard.

♦ The logical aspects of network routing, session management, reliability and error control, and upper level application interface, which comes from the TCP/IP protocol suite.

♦ A network operating system that includes software code that would incorporate each of these parts at each entity.

Looking at it in this light, you can understand why Unix, TCP/IP, and the Ethernet network are tied so closely together that they seem inseparable. Each version of Unix is in fact a network operating system, which uses TCP/IP for its protocols and Ethernet for transmitting the signals to the media. This came about not by accident, but by design.

## Selected Network Protocols—A Closer Look

So far, we have discussed the development of protocol suites and the various models they define for networking. Before moving on, let's take time to look more closely at a few selected protocols and see what implementations they define.

First, let's look at the physical media specifications necessary to allow signals to be passed back and forth between the device and the network in general. These protocols, from the 802.2 Committee, are primarily concerned with electrical characteristics and timing. They are used only in passing the data from the device to the network, and from the network back to the device.

One main consideration of these protocols (802.3, -.4, and so forth) is their ability to identify each device on the network as unique; that is, different from all the other devices on the network both logically and physically. Once the signals are sent from the device, or received from the network, this set of protocols is no longer involved in the communications process. Because the Ethernet 802.3 protocol is dominant in the network industry, we will limit our study to it.

The second set of protocols (802.2 or DLL) deals with the specifications for establishing a path for communications between different logical and physical entities on the network, concerned with the accuracy and reliability of the transmitted information. Once this path is established, data can be transmitted. These protocols deal with session make up and tear down, data transmission and accuracy, error detection and correction, and rate of transmission.

Currently, four protocols deal with the logical exchange of data between entities on a network: TCP/IP, Internet Packet Exchange/Sequenced Packet Exchange or *IPX/SPX*, NetBIOS Extended User Interface or *NetBEUI*, and *EtherTalk* (the Apple Macintosh implementation of AppleTalk, using Ethernet network protocols). Of these four protocols, only one is considered an open standard—TCP/IP. The rest are considered proprietary, and may or may not be *de facto* standards, depending on who you ask.

## Ethernet—The Transport Protocol Of Choice

As I mentioned earlier, the IEEE standardized the Ethernet protocol and since then, Ethernet has gained large acceptance with the general public. The protocol itself is primarily concerned with moving signals between physical devices. The actual implementation of Ethernet is a book in and of itself, and several good books have already been written on this topic. However, a quick review of Ethernet standards is important.

The Ethernet standard was developed by DEC, Intel, and Xerox. Later on, the IEEE 802.3 subcommittee used this as a pattern for defining a variety of physical layer options.

Under the Ethernet protocol, information is passed from a device to the network and from the network to a device using a system known as *Carrier Sense Multiple Access with Collision Detection* (CSMA/CD). This method is also known colloquially as *Talk and Listen*. Under this protocol, the information to be transmitted is grouped into data frames. Each frame is annotated with a header stating the address of the device the information is going to, the address of the device the data is coming from, and a special checksum designed for error control. This frame of data is placed in a buffer within the network interface card. A special circuit on the NIC, called a *transceiver* (for transmitter and receiver), listens on the network media to see if any other signals are present. If none are, the data is moved from the buffer to the transmitter and streamed out over the media, one bit at a time. When the data is sent out over the media, its status changes from a bit to an electrical signal, and vice versa. If there are other signals present, the data is held for a period of time specified by the Ethernet protocol and the process is repeated.

No fixed controls determine when devices are allowed to transmit data. Also, no hierarchy is present that gives any one device precedence over another. Each device on the network media is equal to all others on that network. Because there are no controls over when devices may start transmission, it is possible—and frequently happens—that two devices will start transmitting at the same time. When this common occurrence happens, the data from the two devices will have a *collision*. This brings us into the second part of the protocol, *collision detection*.

Each NIC in a device is equipped to detect collisions. This is because at the same time they are transmitting, they are listening on the media to the data they are sending. They compare what they hear with what they send, and if it is not the same, they assume that a collision has occurred. If a collision is perceived, the protocol assumes that all data sent since the last good frame is corrupt. The circuitry in the NIC will then reload the data back to the last known good frame and wait a specified period of time before starting the process all over.

The CSMA/CD protocol is good at what it does. It is easily implemented in hardware, and relatively inexpensive. CSMA/CD makes for a good, low cost, and reliable network system.

### On The Down Side
Some drawbacks exist. First, because no controls determine when each device can transmit, collisions can and do happen. The more devices on the network, the greater the chances of collisions. Because of collisions, Ethernet cannot take advantage of the full bandwidth capacity of the network. Maximum throughput on an Ethernet network segment occurs at about 45 percent of maximum allowable bandwidth capacity. Stick on more users and the actual throughput drops off as more and more collisions occur. The network segment becomes completely saturated at about 55 to 60 percent of maximum bandwidth, with only collisions occurring and not much usable data being passed.

## A Note On Bandwidth
You have probably heard the term *bandwidth* discussed before. Most people in the industry seem to agree that bandwidth is something they never seem to have enough of. Unfortunately, some of the same people do not have a good understanding of exactly what bandwidth means. Books have been written about bandwidth, and I am not about to try to make this book another one. However, some general information about bandwidth is necessary.

For the absolute purists among us, bandwidth is defined as a range of frequencies located on either side of a center frequency at which the sustained signal strength is at least 73 percent of the maximum signal strength.

So what, exactly, does that mean to us computer geeks? Most people associated with networks tend to think the higher the bandwidth, the faster the signal travels. Sorry, wrong answer. The signal travels at the same velocity, approximately one nanosecond-per-foot, no matter what the bandwidth is. In networking, bandwidth is a quantification of traffic volume. The higher the bandwidth, the larger the volume. Lower the bandwidth and you lower the volume. What a higher bandwidth really equates to is a larger volume of traffic.

For a better understanding, let's drop the technical aspects for a moment, and use an analogy. Consider the network cable to be a freeway, except for some very inflexible physical laws. When our data packet automobile gets on the cable freeway, it accelerates nearly instantaneously to the speed of light. No slowing down occurs; autos have only two speeds on our cable freeway: light-speed or stopped.

Check your physics book; this is the way electrons flow on a conductor. Because of these fixed laws, autos can travel on our cable freeway very close together, but when they reach the point at which they are bumper to bumper, our freeway has reached saturation. When that occurs, if one car stops, all the other cars behind that one stop—immediately.

For the sake of discussion, let's make our cable freeway six lanes wide so we can say we have six units of bandwidth going in one direction. At rush hour the autos pile in until the freeway reaches saturation, and no more autos can fit. Remember, once they get on the freeway, they go the maximum speed. At this point, our imaginary freeway can handle six lanes of autos all traveling at the speed of light.

Great, hey? Well, sort of. Let's suppose the autos come to a point where the freeway pinches down to three lanes (every good freeway has road construction, especially during rush hour). For our purposes this region limits us to three units of bandwidth.

What happens? The autos from all six lanes suddenly have to start switching to the three available lanes; we call this *multiplexing*. Because all six lanes in front of the bottleneck are full of autos—saturated—this causes some delays. And because all six lanes are full, all traffic in each lane stops and waits until the autos are switched over to one of the three available lanes.

Somewhere down the road, the autos are being snatched off at off-ramps—lets call them receiving nodes—making room at on-ramps to the transmitting nodes. So, traffic is still moving, but the volume has been reduced to three lanes, half our original bandwidth. Those packet autos that are able to switch to the three available bandwidth lanes keep moving at the speed of light, but because it is rush hour and the traffic is at saturation level, a delay in the overall system is unavoidable.

Now consider the same situation, only it's 2:00 A.M. and very little traffic is present. We still go light speed down the six-lane freeway. Our traffic does not get there any faster in that respect, but because it is early in the morning and not much traffic is out, the autos are spaced farther apart (we are not using up the entire available bandwidth). Before we get to the point where the bandwidth narrows to three units, the packets merge; they are closer together but still traveling at full speed. The data continue the trip with no delay.

What this example demonstrates is that bandwidth has very little effect on signal speed, but a lot of effect on the amount of traffic a network can carry.

## Back To The Ethernet

I mentioned a while back that we were going to limit our discussion to the Ethernet protocol. In this protocol, currently three bandwidths are widely accepted. (Others exist, but their acceptance is limited and we are not going to discuss them here.)

The first in our discussion is standard Ethernet, which has a bandwidth of 10Mbps. This was considered adequate for many years, but in the last three to five years we have seen a great increase in the amount and type of network traffic. The 10Mbps bandwidth is considered by most, myself included, to be inadequate for the traffic demands of tomorrow's network systems.

The next version of Ethernet to be released was 100Mbps; it originally had two versions and both survive today. One version is the standard defined by the IEEE 802.12 subcommittee and is known as *100baseVG*, sometimes called colloquially *AnyLAN*. This implementation uses Ethernet frame type, implemented at a bandwidth of 100Mbps, over voice-grade (that's where the VG comes from) twisted-pair cable. It is not a true Ethernet, however, because the media access method is not CSMA/CD. This implementation is used today, but does not have a large market.

The other 100Mbps implementation of Ethernet is an addition of the IEEE 802.3 subcommittee, and is known as *Fast Ethernet*. The original standard subcommittee was IEEE 802.3u, but in 1998 this standard was incorporated into the IEEE 802.3 standard. This is a true Ethernet implementation using CSMA/CD as the media access method and is the current standard today. In new installations, Fast Ethernet is the protocol being implemented the most.

The newest version of Ethernet is *1Gbps Ethernet*, or *1000baseT*. This is being implemented in larger networks, primarily for switched backbone systems. This standard is being studied by the IEEE 802.3ab subcommittee and, as of the date we wrote this book, is available from the IEEE only in draft form. This means the standard has not been officially finalized. However, manufacturers are making products based on the draft proposal, and this promises to be a very stable and well-mannered system, delivering the high bandwidth required by future applications running on LAN and WAN systems.

The nice thing about all three Ethernets is that they operate over most of the transmission media in place today, especially if that media is rated Category 5 or better. (More about categories later.) A drawback of the Ethernet standard is that because of the manner in which the signal is placed on the media, you never get full use of the maximum bandwidth of the media, as we discussed earlier. Remember, Ethernet is limited to a maximum of about 65 percent of the bandwidth of the media, with a more realistic figure being 45 percent.

# Each Device Is Different—Physical Addressing

In a network system it is critical that each device on the network have a unique address. The United States Postal Service probably delivers thousands of letters to the wrong address every day across the United States because someone left "N" or "S" off a street address, and more than one homeowner is plagued with mail that belongs on the other side of town. To make sure data is delivered to the correct address on the network, the Ethernet protocol standard states how different physical devices are identified.

Under the standard, each NIC or device is assigned a unique hex number. This number is rather large, 48 bits, and is divided into three parts. The first part identifies the manufacturer of the product, the second part identifies the specific product model number, and the third part provides a unique number for each different NIC or device within the realm of the first two parts.

This number is an integral part of the hardware and is almost always burned into the firmware of the NIC or device. It identifies that particular device as being unique from all other similar devices in the world. (I told you it was a big number.)

When the component with this unique number is installed in a network device (a computer), it becomes a part of that system, and the physical identification number becomes the *Node ID*. This way, different devices on a local network cable segment are identified and the LAN system can route information to each independently.

The Node ID is very important because other devices use this number for identifying which devices are connected to a particular network segment. Another name used in place of Node ID is *Media Access Control*, or *MAC* address.

# Which Media Are We Using?

Another important function of the IEEE 802.3 subcommittee was to define the different media types. Five media types are in use today. Take a look at Table 2.3 for a description of the media.

**Table 2.3   Network transmission media.**

| Specification | Description |
| --- | --- |
| 10base5 | 10Mbps rate, baseband signaling, 500 meters per segment. This specification uses RG-8 or RG-11 coaxial cable, known as *Thick Ethernet*. It is commonly used in backbone systems. |
| 10base2 | 10Mbps rate, baseband signaling, 185 meters per segment. This specification uses RG-58 coaxial cable, known as *Thin Net* or *Cheaper Net*. This is used in linear bus cable systems. |
| 10baseT | 10Mbps rate, over twisted-pair cable. This specification uses twisted-pair cable, and has a maximum distance of 185 meters between repeaters. Twisted-pair cable has different ratings, each of which specifies a different maximum bandwidth. This is the most common of all the media types. |
| 10baseF | 10Mbps rate, over fiber-optic cable. This specification uses fiber-optic cable as the media. |
| 100baseTX | 100Mbps rate, over Category 5 twisted-pair cable. This specification is the same basic specification as 10baseT, but it only runs over Category 5 twisted-pair cable and the specifications concerning the number and type of repeaters and hubs is different. |

Recently the IEEE 802 Committee has developed new standards for Ethernet media, particularly for 100baseTX and 100Mbps Fast Ethernet, 10baseFL and 100baseFL, and 1Gbps Ethernet. Keep in mind that the IEEE adopts a new standard rather than changing the specifications for an existing standard, because all are open standards and—as I said before—changing an open standard can have a disturbing effect throughout the industry.

# Logical Devices—The Other Protocols

Now that we have a little understanding of how physical devices are defined on the network, we need to look at how logical devices are defined. Several protocols have been generated throughout the networking industry. One of the earliest was TCP/IP, created back when engineers were scratching their heads and asking, "Is there a better way to do this?" Interestingly enough, TCP/IP proved to be very successful. But, like all good engineers, some of them figured they *could* do it better. Although not all of their endeavors were grand successes, some good successes survived and are in wide use today. We'll talk about a few of the better logical devices as we go along.

But, first...

### TCP/IP, The Venerable Master

The development of TCP/IP closely follows the development of the Internet. It is after all *the* Internet protocol suite. It follows then, that a discussion of TCP/IP can easily become a discussion of the architecture of the Internet. The Internet as we know it today grew out of a grant sponsored by the Defense Advanced Research Projects Agency (DARPA). The original network was known as the *Advanced Research Projects Agency Network*, or *ARPANET*, and its purpose was to test and determine the viability of a communication technology known as *packet switching*.

DARPA developed ARPANET by instituting a process called *request for comment*, or *RFC*. In this process, the initial protocol for TCP/IP was developed by committee and the resulting documentation was distributed throughout the interested community. Other parties commented on the document and made suggestions about how the protocol might be improved. As the process continued, changes were either discarded or approved by DARPA and implemented into the document. After the RFC had passed through this process a number of times, it was then adopted as a standard.

During the early stages of development, the number of organizations allowed access to the protocols was limited. One activity of the IAB was to manage the publication of RFCs that were released into the public domain. This allowed other organizations to construct network systems based on the research done under the DARPA project, and the number of parties involved in the RFC process increased.

Among the new networks that were developed using DARPA protocols was the network funded by the National Science Foundation known as *NSFNET*, and another by the Computer Science Network known as *CSNET*. Finally, in 1990, the ARPANET was dismantled by the Department of Defense. In 1995, the NSF turned over control of the Internet to the private sector, and the rest is history.

The architecture for this technology consisted of three types of physical devices. The first is a number of *hosts* that transfer data between each other in the form of message *packets*. These hosts are connected to a medium of transportation known as a *network* or *network media*. Notice that the network media are treated as separate entities and not part of any host.

The network media tied the hosts together and allowed exchange of information between hosts in the form of packets of data. The network media was in turn tied together by *interface message processors (IMPs)*. These IMPs were special computers designed for the sole purpose of routing the packets of data between different network media.

This concept led to the development of what became the most troublesome single component of any TCP/IP network: The model sees the network media as one entity and the hosts as another. This means that each entity must be identified separately and at the same time linked together. What grew out of this concept was a method for giving each network media an address, and at the same time, giving each host and IMP connected to the network media a different address. This address is more commonly known as the *IP address*; we will talk more about this in a little bit.

The model for this architecture is shown in Figure 2.4 and is divided into four parts. Before we dive into that, I would like to point out—if you haven't already guessed—that the IMPs grew up to become what is known in today's network systems as *routers*.

Starting from the bottom, the first part of the model is labeled the *network interface layer*. This layer comprises the physical link between the device and the network media. This layer must exist on all hosts and IMPs that connect the network media to other network interface layer devices. The network interface layer is analogous to the OSI physical and data link layers combined, because it converts packets of data into bits, and then the bits of data into electrical signals that are placed on the network media.

The *network interface layer* is logically connected to the *Internet layer*. The Internet layer was developed because DARPA required that the hosts be able to connect through a variety of network media, including coaxial cable, twisted-pair cable, and radio-relay equipment (they would have included optical fiber cable, but it hadn't been invented yet). In order to provide this capability, it is necessary to provide some insulation of the hosts from network-specific details. To provide communications capability at the NIL, it was necessary to develop a protocol that would provide end-to-end service. The data units used at this level were known as *datagrams*; units of data with all the information necessary for successful delivery included. The protocol developed to provide this service is called the Internet Protocol or IP. The Internet layer is analogous to the OSI network layer, and must exist on all hosts and IMPs.

The NIL is logically connected to the *host-to-host layer*. The *HHL* is necessary because, whereas the Internet layer with its Internet protocol provides for delivery of data, it does not guarantee that delivery. In other words, IP establishes a circuit with another device, transmits the data, but does not provide any way of acknowledging that the data was actually received. The HHL is also known as the *service layer*, because its purpose is to provide whatever level of service is required. In order to do this, two protocols were developed. The first was Transmission Control Protocol, or TCP; it is used whenever the level of service requires reliable end-to-end guaranteed delivery (that is, each and every packet transmitted is guaranteed to be delivered, or that packet will be retransmited).

The second protocol developed for use at the host-to-host layer was the *User Datagram Protocol*, or *UDP*; it is used when reliable end-to-end service is required but delivery does not have to be guaranteed. The connection is considered reliable because the software checks to see if the complete message was received. If not, the system retransmits the entire message.

Both protocols required some communications between sending and receiving devices in order to keep track of packets and datagrams. To provide this communications capability, a third protocol was developed, called *Internet Control Message Protocol*, or *ICMP*. The host-to-host (or service) layer is analogous to the OSI transport layer, and must exist on hosts and IMPs.

The structure of the TCP and UDP protocols makes it possible to create different entities, known as *services*, within a single logical device. Under the TCP and UDP protocols, this is allowed by using what is known as a *port number* to identify the different services. It is therefore possible to have a single logical device performing several different services. For example, a single computer could function as an email server, a Web server, and an FTP server all at the same time, by assigning each different service a unique port number. The email server would use port 25, the Web server port 80, and the FTP server port 75. Incoming and outgoing traffic are thus routed to the correct service by the TCP/IP protocol.

The HHL is logically connected to the *process/application layer*. In the DARPA model, the process/application layer is the highest layer and only exists on hosts. This layer provides a number of processes or applications (each process is a separate protocol) that gives the network its functionality. Among these are: an application to transfer files from one host to another (File Transfer Protocol or FTP, which uses TCP), a remote terminal application (Telnet, which uses TCP), and an application for sending messages between hosts (Simple Mail Transfer Protocol or SMTP, which uses UDP). Many other protocols exist at the top layer of the DARPA model. The process/application layer is analogous to the combined OSI session, presentation, and application layers.

As I said earlier, no other part of the TCP/IP protocol suite has caused more frustration with network administrators than the configuration and administration of network IP addresses. You would think this would be an easy task; after all, each different device on the network has a physical address known as the *Node ID*, or MAC address. However, one of the problems involved with using the MAC address to identify entities on the network is that it only allows a device to be identified as a single entity. In some cases, it is desirable to have a single physical device identified as two or more different logical devices or entities. When physical devices are operating under the TCP/IP protocol, each physical device can be represented by one or more logical devices or entities. Each of these entities can be assigned a logical or network IP address.

The TCP/IP protocol suite defines the make up and structure of these logical addresses. This logical addressing scheme is made up of a group of four binary numbers called *octets*. Each octet consists of an 8 bit number in the range of 0 through $255_{10}$. When all the bits of the address are combined, a total of 32 bits exists. This address has been commonly called the IP address. Under the rules for the protocol suite, each physical device on the network must have an IP address, but remember, a physical device is allowed to have more than one IP address.

The 32 bits of the IP address are divided into two parts. The first part identifies the network system or network address where the device is located. The second part identifies the physical device, or host address, on that network. Unlike the Node ID, the IP address is not fixed, and under the rules defined by the protocol, the IP address for a host can change even when the network address remains the same.

IP addresses are divided into classes A through E. The class that the IP address falls into depends on the number of bits used to make up the network address, compared with the number of bits that are used to make up the host address. The different classes of IP addresses are identified by the first three bits. The most common is the Class C IP address; this is most generally given to businesses.

### No Two Hosts On The Same Network Can Have The Same IP Address

Here is an important rule: No two hosts on the same network can have the same IP address at the same time, and no two networks connected together in the same Internet can have the same network address at the same time. This can become a real problem, because a limited number of IP addresses is available, whereas a virtually unlimited number of entities exists.

Not surprisingly, the world is running out of IP addresses. In an effort to help, network vendors have come up with systems that allow the connection of a large number of entities to the Internet through the use of a single, or small number, of IP addresses. This process is known as *Network Address Translation* (*NAT*). This is a very important concept, and as we shall see, a form of this has been adopted for use when implementing Virtual Private Networks.

The assignment of IP addresses on the Internet was originally controlled by the Internet Registry, which was for some time located at Government Systems, Inc., in Chantilly, Virginia. In 1995, when the NSF ceased funding for the Internet, control of much of the infrastructure in place then was acquired by the private sector—by for-profit enterprises. Since then, the Internet Registry services have been acquired by Network Solutions located in Baltimore, Maryland.

One other protocol we need to look at is the *domain name system*. Under the IP address protocol, each entity on the Internet is assigned an IP address. Keeping track of all the IP addresses can become a real nightmare. This is especially true when the person using a host computer is not really sure of the location of the destination host. In order to ease this situation and make it more people-oriented, the *Domain Name System* (*DNS*) was adopted.

Under the DNS, each host on the Internet is assigned a *host name* by which it is known from that point on. Each network on the Internet is also assigned a name that becomes the *domain name*. These are registered with the Internet Registry or InterNIC, and assigned to a *top level domain* category. Originally a few top level domains existed, such as *edu* for educational domains, *gov* for government domains, and *mil* for military domains. Today, virtually every country has its own top level domain name; France is *fr*, Switzerland is *ch*, and so on.

The registered domain name was appended to the top level domain, separated by a period; thus the University of Houston becomes *uh.edu*, and the National Aeronautics and Space Administration becomes *nasa.gov*. Commercial enterprises also have a top level domain type called *com*.

As an organization split its network into smaller parts, each of the parts could be given a name, and that name could be appended to the domain name and top level domain type. Following this protocol, Johnson Space Center in Houston became *jsc.nasa.gov*, and the University of Houston campus at Clear Lake, Texas, became *uhcl.uh.edu*. Finally, an individual host name can be appended to the combination of *subdomain.domain.top_level_domain* so that a particular machine at any site anywhere on the Internet can be identified. Thus, a particular mail server with the host name *mailone*, located at the University of Houston, is identified as *mailone.uhcl.uh.edu*.

Under the DNS protocol, these names are stored in database systems located on computers that run the DNS name service. Each local host name is stored in the local DNS server, with the IP address of that particular host listed. Each host on the network has a host service, part of the DNS protocol, known as a *resolver*. When the TCP/IP protocol is configured on the host machine, the information about the IP address of the DNS server is loaded into the resolver. This way, each host knows where to go to resolve local host names to IP addresses.

If the host name is not local; that is, it's on a different subdomain, the DNS server can identify this because the subdomain name is different from the local domain name. In this case, the DNS server hands the request for resolving the domain name up one step to the next higher DNS server. If this DNS server is on the same subdomain, it resolves the domain name and hands the IP address down to the local DNS server, which then passes it to the local host. If the second level DNS server is unable to resolve the domain name because it is on a different domain, then that DNS server hands the request up to the next level domain name server.

The process is repeated until the request is handed to the top level domain type server. At this point, if the name cannot be resolved, it is assumed not to exist and an appropriate error message is returned back down the ladder to the local host that made the request in the first place.

Implementation of the domain name system is, in fact, a fairly complex process, and in this simplified description I have left out several other aspects. This is an overview of LAN and the intent here is only to give a picture of the basic operation. In actual operation, from the user's standpoint, the operation is seamless and is one of the most reliable protocols in use in the Internet today. This is especially true when viewed from the standpoint of the explosion in growth the Internet has experienced in the past five years, and the addition of dozens of new top level domain types, including, as I said earlier, a top level domain type for most of the countries in the world.

As you can see, the TCP/IP protocol suite is very complex. This short discussion has hardly brushed the surface. To do so would go beyond our intentions here. However, it is important that you remember the points we discussed—they have a direct bearing on Virtual Private Networks.

# Novell NetWare—IPX/SPX

The TCP/IP protocol suite is not the only protocol suite in use today. In fact, as already stated, it is not even the most common. We need to mention three other proprietary protocol suites because of their popularity in the network industry.

The most common protocol suite in use today is *Internet Packet Exchange/Sequenced Packet Exchange (IPX/SPX)*. This protocol was originally developed by Xerox. Then Novell® got hold of it, made a few modifications, and started marketing it heavily.

Comparing IPX/SPX to TCP/IP reveals that the IPX part of the combined protocol covers most of the same functions as the IP. Similarly, the SPX covers most of the same areas as the TCP.

Until the release of NetWare® version-five by Novell in 1998, all Novell NetWare systems used IPX/SPX as their native protocol suite. While Novell NetWare before NetWare 5 can, and does, support TCP/IP, it does so only after converting from IPX/SPX. Because the NetWare native protocol is IPX/SPX, data that is sent and received using TCP/IP protocols over the network is converted to IPX/SPX for processing internally within the server.

One of the features that made the IPX protocol suite so popular with the networking community is the way it handles assigning network logical addresses. IPX/SPX differs from TCP/IP in that the logical network address is not developed separately from the Node ID. With IPX/SPX, the network address is made up of the network number assigned by the network administrator and either the Node ID or MAC address, which is normally assigned by the manufacturer of the NIC or other device. Once the administrator has assigned the network number, the network address for each physical device is generated automatically when the network software is loaded.

What this means to the administrator of the network is that it is not necessary to worry about assigning a logical network address to every physical device. This is accomplished automatically when the network operating software is installed. We will add some more detail about this later. This type of network is easily installed and, because it will operate over almost all topologies with a wide range of protocols including Ethernet, IPX/SPX has had great success in the market place.

### Trade-Offs

However, the advantages of IPX/SPX are not without trade-offs. Because the network address is not assigned by the user or administrator, each physical device can have only one logical device. Under some conditions this is considered a limitation. In the IPX/SPX protocol suite, a number of different services can exist on certain—but not all—machines within the network. In other words, under IPX/SPX, not all machines are treated equally on the network. Again, we'll delve deeper into this later in the chapter. For now, let's understand that this has a direct effect on the capabilities of each machine within a NetWare network and that affects how we implement VPN.

## Microsoft Windows: NetBEUI

No discussion of computer-related products is complete without a discussion of Microsoft Windows. Starting with version 3.11 and going through Windows NT, the native protocol suite for Microsoft Windows is NetBEUI. This is an enhanced NetBIOS protocol suite and is easily implemented. NetBIOS allows connections of Windows computers in what is known as a *peer-to-peer* network system. That means that all machines on the network are equal in capability, at least in terms of network operations. However, NetBEUI is somewhat limited in its capacity, and peer-to-peer networks can become somewhat unmanageable as they get larger.

Because of these limitations, Microsoft developed a TCP/IP protocol suite that can be implemented with Windows known as *Winsock*. Because of the wide acceptance of Windows in the marketplace, Winsock has become a *de facto* standard. The Winsock TCP stack allows computers equipped with Windows to use most of the protocols found in TCP/IP.

Windows machines running Winsock are allowed to have several services going at the same time, but each physical machine running Windows 95 or 98 is allowed only one logical network IP address. Microsoft has made the APIs for their Winsock generally available, and today almost every application layer protocol for TCP/IP (FTP, Telnet, SMTP, HTTP, etc.) is available in one form or another for Windows. One protocol in particular that is not a part of the TCP/IP standard is *Point to Point Tunneling Protocol* (PPTP). We will deal heavily with PPTP in a later chapter.

## The Apple Implementation—AppleTalk And EtherTalk

Apple Computer created the AppleTalk protocol suite in the early 1980s, when the company made a decision to offer the Apple Macintosh computer with network capabilities. In 1989, AppleTalk Phase 2 was released; this increased the potential size and complexity of AppleTalk networks and allows AppleTalk to coexist on large complex networks, thus allowing the AppleTalk protocol suite to scale up to enterprise networks.

The AppleTalk protocol suite was developed after the OSI Reference model development was under way. Because of this and some other design considerations, the AppleTalk protocol suite can be mapped fairly well to the OSI model. One of the more interesting developments of the implementation of the AppleTalk protocol suite is the use of Ethernet topology. In order to keep naming conventions consistent, Apple Computer chose to name this implementation *EtherTalk*, or *EtherTalk Link Access Protocol* (ELAP).

AppleTalk is a good, user friendly, and robust protocol suite. However, in today's world, if you want to use the Internet, you are going to have to use the Internet protocol suite and that certainly means using TCP/IP. With this thought in mind, Apple Computer developed a TCP/IP stack for the Macintosh named *MAC IP*; this allows a Macintosh Computer on an AppleTalk network to access hosts on a TCP/IP network. The actual implementation of this is rather complex and goes beyond the scope of this chapter. If you need more information, you can find books on the subject.

# Hardware

Now that we have looked at the definitions for network systems, we need to take a look at the physical devices that make up the system. We will divide these physical devices into three areas:

♦ Computers and other physical devices that can be configured as entities on the network.

♦ Physical media that is used to transport data in the form of signals from one device to another.

♦ Devices that bind the media together, otherwise known as hubs, concentrators, and switches.

## Computers

Not all computers are made equal. They have different amounts of memory, different storage and video capabilities, and so forth. In any case, for a computer to operate on a LAN, it must be capable of some basic operations and of some means of extending that capability. Almost all digital PCs made today follow the same basic architecture shown in Figure 2.5.

The core part of this architecture consists of a central processing unit, connected through metal paths (printed circuits or wires known as *buses*), to the other sections of the computer system. These other sections can include memory, input/output, and peripheral interfaces.

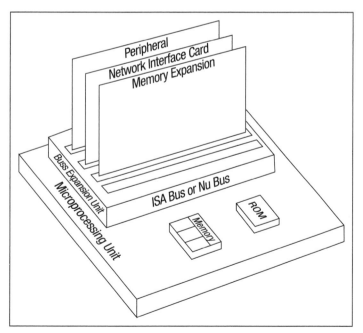

**Figure 2.5**
Basic computer architecture for a networking PC.

In the world of PCs, we refer to the CPU as a *microprocessing unit*, or *MPU*. Several companies manufacture MPUs, such as Intel, AMD, Cyrix, and Motorola. While many MPU manufacturers can and do make computers, most of the popular computers on the market today are *not* manufactured by the same company that produces the MPU. Examples of this are the Apple Macintosh, which uses an MPU manufactured by Motorola, and the Compaq, which uses an MPU manufactured by either Intel, Digital Alpha, Cyrix, or AMD.

### Expanding The Hardware

In order to allow greater versatility in the computer system, a method of expanding the hardware capabilities of the computer is generally included as a part of the computer architecture. This expansion capability is usually a part of the peripheral interface and on newer computer systems is implemented in two ways.

The first—and most common implementation—commonly known as a *bus expansion unit* or *bus slot*, has been around for a long time. Two examples of this capability are the ISA bus architecture found on PCs and the NuBus architecture found on Macintosh computers. In an effort to further standardize the industry, a fairly new interface known as *PCI bus* has been adopted. The PCI bus architecture will work with both PC and Macintosh computers, although very few cards are available that will work with both.

The second interface that allows expansion of the computer system is the universal serial bus interface found on newer PCs and Macintoshes. Other devices are being developed that will work on either type of platform.

The memory section contains some type of *bootstrap* or *boot* program. Modern PCs and Macs have volatile memory; when you turn the machine off, it becomes as stupid as a brick and it stays that way until a few milliseconds after the power switch is flipped back to on and the system reboots. The boot is usually burned into the *read-only memory* (ROM), and has the task of getting the computer started and loading the operating system into *random access memory* (RAM). Once this is accomplished, the CPU jumps to the start of the operating system and pretty much everything we're interested in happens from that point on.

Different computers have different operating systems. A large number use some version of Microsoft Windows, but this is not the only operating system out there. Other computers may use Unix, and Apple Macintosh computers use some version of Apple's operating system known as OS-x. The latest version of the Mac operating system, at least as late as the writing of this chapter, is OS 8.5.

### Proprietary Business

Some computer manufacturers have tried to keep the computer and operating system under their total control; for example, Apple Macintosh. Few operating systems other than those supplied by Apple will run successfully on the Macintosh. On the other hand, Intel and

Microsoft have pooled their resources for years, supporting the proliferation of Intel processor–based computers comprising myriad IBM PC clones on the market, referred to commonly as the PC. Microsoft Windows is not the only operating system that will run on a PC or its clones; in fact, several other operating systems, such as some versions of Unix, Linux, DR DOS, and others, will also run on a PC.

## Connecting A Computer Into A Network Is A Two-Part Process

Unless the machine was purchased as a *turn-key* system, there is a two-part process required to make a computer ready to connect into a LAN. The components are readily available and generally easy to install.

The first part is to extend the capabilities of the hardware to allow it to connect to the network media. This extension of the hardware is usually accomplished by inserting a printed circuit board in a bus interface slot. This board must also have the proper connector to mate with the network media. These printed circuit boards are called *network interface cards*, or NICs. For the computer to properly connect with the network, the NIC must match the standards for both the type of physical interface and the physical aspects of the network protocol to be used to pass signals back and forth over the network media. The NIC is also the device that includes the MAC address and identifies a particular computer as unique from all the other computers on the network.

The second part of this process is to extend the capability of the computer's operating system to include software that can make decisions about the needs of the user. This software extension must have the capability to determine if the information the user needs is located locally within the computer itself or externally somewhere out on the network. If the computer operating system is Unix or Linux, it is called *host*, otherwise this software is known as *client*. When added to the operating system, it allows the computer to attach to the network and exchange information with other properly configured computers. The difference between client and host computers on a local area network is not always clear, and the two terms are often used interchangeably.

Once the computer hardware is properly expanded to include the capability of connecting to the network and the operating system has been expanded to allow the computer to act as a client on the network, the computer is ready to function as a network entity and exchange data with other entities on the network.

## Now How The Heck Do We Do That?

We must have some means of connecting the computers together to allow information to be exchanged. You can do this in three ways: the first—and most popular method—is to use copper cable; the second method is to use optical fibers; and the third is wireless or radio link.

Each of these methods has their strong and weak points; we'll discuss the most important aspects of each method.

### Copper Cable

The most common way computers are connected together is through the use of copper wire bundled into cables. The use of copper cable in local area networks is standardized in this country by two organizations: the Electronics Industries Association and the Telephony Industries Association. These two standard-setting organizations have developed EIA/TIA 568 A and B, which defines the type of cable used, the type of connector used, and other factors concerning the use of copper cable for wiring networks within commercial buildings.

Several types of cable are in use in networks today, but the two most common are *twisted-pair* cable (by far the most common) and *coaxial* cable. Twisted-pair cable comes in different types, sizes, and grades. In case you're wondering, the advantage of twisting the pairs of wire together is a reduction of induced electrical noise.

The most common type of twisted-pair cable *Plain Old Telephone Service* (POTS) cable. When networkers started using POTS for transmitting data, it became apparent that some deficiencies existed, so engineers started doing their thing to develop higher-grade data versions. These evolved into *unshielded twisted-pair* (UTP), and STP, not the gasoline additive, but *shielded twisted-pair*. That in turn lead to *category* conventions so different grades could be lumped together under a standard.

POTS, UTP, and STP come in different sizes, based on the number of pairs enclosed in each cable housing. The standard for wiring offices is the 4-pair cable shown in Figure 2.6 (Editor's Note: The following figures in this chapter are from Novell course number 801, and used courtesy of Novell, Inc.). Between offices in a typical enterprise, you will find large multipair cables, usually up to 100 pair. Larger numbers of pairs in each cable are available and are typically used to provide service between the phone company central office and customer site. With twisted-pair cable, one pair transmits information and the other pair receives it. However, unless the cable is used with equipment specifically designed to do so, the information is not transmitted and received at the same time.

Today, the most common data cable categories are Category 3 and Category 5. Category 4 has virtually disappeared. All other things being equal, the higher the category of the cable, the more traffic it can support. Today, the standard cable for new network installations is Cat 5—in 4-pair for individual cable runs to desktops or larger, and up to 100 pair for runs between offices and/or buildings. Between UTP and STP, UTP is by far the most common selection for data installations today.

Of all the specifications that make up any category standard, probably the most important is impedance. The TIA/EIA standard for Category 5 is, for example, 100 Ohms. This factor is determined by the output and input circuitry of the devices at each end of the cable; they must be identical within very close tolerances. If the impedance of the cable does not match

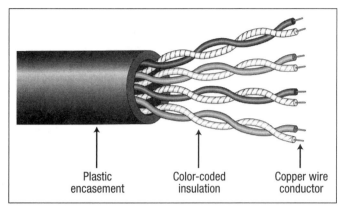

**Figure 2.6**
Typical 4-pair network cable.

the circuit impedance, some of the energy transmitted into the cable is reflected back to the source, causing interference waves. The result is a loss of energy at the receiving end. The worse the mismatch and/or longer the mismatched cable, the more significant the losses.

Coaxial cable is not as common as twisted-pair, but still found in many installations. It is generally more expensive to manufacture, install, and maintain than equivalent twisted-pair. This type of cable has two conductors instead of two or more pairs. One conductor is centrally located (hence the name *coaxial*) within a metal shield made of braided copper wire; see Figure 2.7. The metal shield also serves as an outer conductor in the cable; insulating material is used to keep the two conductors separated. The spacing of the inner conductor from the shield is very important and the insulator is designed to maintain that dimension throughout the length of the cable. The disadvantage is that any kink that crushes the insulator will degrade the cable's data transmission performance, even if it is not shorted.

Like twisted-pair cable, coaxial cable comes in different sizes and types, which affect the ability of the network to function correctly. For this reason, you should always be careful

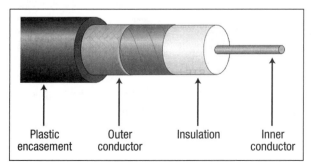

**Figure 2.7**
Coaxial cable.

about using the correct coaxial cable for the job. With coaxial cable, the same conductor is used for both sending and receiving data; consequently, the cable cannot be used to transmit and receive information at the same time. However, this does not mean that coaxial cable is slower than twisted-pair, because the same rule applies to twisted-pair cable, unless the equipment is designed for full-duplex operation.

One last point about coax: It comes with solid or multistrand center conductor. The multistrand is more flexible and, in some cases, easier to install. On the other hand, the solid strand is less expensive. Arguments exist that you should not mix the two in the same network but, in my opinion, they are not valid. If the electrical characteristics between RG-58 and RG-58U are the same and the manufacturer meets required standards, the electrons whizzing down the wire are not going to stop and read the label on the outer insulating sheath.

### A Typical Installation

A typical installation for a Local Area Network using copper cable starts from a point generally in or near the computer room. In large installations of this type, the cable originates and terminates at devices known as *punch-down blocks*. This device makes a good, semi-permanent, mechanical and electrical connection point between large-pair cables strung between offices and buildings and the smaller 4-pair cables going to each desktop. The place where the cable terminates is usually referred to as a *wire closet* or *data cabinet*, although it may in fact be inside a cabinet or frame. The cables are terminated at the punch-down block with the use of a special tool known as a—yes, you guessed it—*punch-down tool*. Because cable connections on a punch-down block can be changed with minimal effort, the LAN can be reconfigured as the need arises.

From the wire closet, the cable is run to the desktop using smaller, generally 4-pair cable. The standard terminator for twisted-pair cable at the desktop is the *RJ-45* connector, shown in Figure 2.8. This is an eight conductor modular connector, similar to that used on telephones. The RJ-45 comes in both male and female versions, and on smaller installations is often used in place of punch-down blocks for termination in the computer room and wire closet. In order for twisted-pair cable to work well (and to ensure a quality installation), the termination must be done with care and precision according to manufacturer's instructions.

The EIA/TIA 568 standard defines the specifications for termination of twisted-pair cable, both on punch-down blocks and RJ-45 modular connectors. It is especially critical to the proper operation of Category 5 cable that this standard is followed.

Often, the wire closets on large installations will be connected together by a single *backbone* cable. The backbone is usually a coaxial cable, RG-8 or RG-11 (sometimes called *ThickNet*), or fiber-optic cable, and is run around the building from wire closet to wire closet, connecting the office subnetworks into one large LAN. In large installations this is the primary use for coaxial cable.

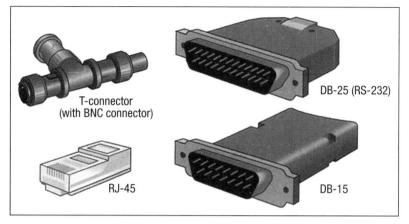

**Figure 2.8**
Various network media connectors.

Coaxial cable may be run directly to the desktop in smaller networks. When used this way, the cable is a different type, such as RG-58; this is smaller and more flexible than the RG-8 or -11 when used for a backbone.

On older installations that use coaxial cable to go the desktop, you may find some RG-62 cable. This cable was very popular for use in Attached Resource Computer Local Network (ARCNet). If you have any of this cable at your site, and you do not have any equipment using ARCNet, your best bet is to replace it as soon as possible; it is not compatible with Ethernet standards.

Fiber-optic cable is not used as much as copper wire in LAN installations. Its use is primarily for long distances between wire closets or major distribution centers. Fiber-optic cable closely resembles coaxial cable in the way it is constructed, as shown in Figure 2.9. Three characteristics identify different types of fiber-optic cables. The first of these is the optical characteristics of the fiber core, either multimode or single-mode. Second is the diameter, measured in microns, of the fiber itself. Third is the physical construction, either single fiber break-out cables, or multifiber, gel-filled cables.

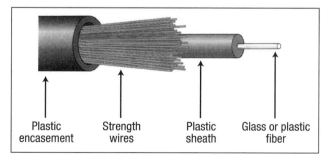

**Figure 2.9**
Fiber-optic cable schematic.

Starting at the center is a fine fiber, which is actually in two parts: the center core, which is a fine glass or high grade translucent plastic, and the outer cladding that surrounds the core. It is the core that carries the actual signal information in the form of a modulated light-wave carrier.

Depending upon the type of glass fiber used, data transmission occurs in one of two ways. In *multimode*, some of the light energy travels directly down the core, and some bounces off the cladding and is reflected back into the core. Because the light wavefronts travel over a complex path, the maximum distance that multimode fiber can run before the signal needs to be regenerated is relatively short compared to other types of optical fiber cables. However, the advantage of multimode fiber cable is that it can support signals where the wavelength of the carrier is not constant. This allows the use of light generated by inexpensive sources, which are used a lot on NICs in relatively less critical fiber hubs and repeaters.

The second type of fiber-optic cable is characterized as *single-mode*. This type of cable does not bounce the light off the inside of the cladding. Instead, the light travels in a very closely controlled monochromatic wavelength and goes straight down the center of the cable. Because of the way the light travels, single-mode cable is good for long runs, such as between towns and cities.

The trade-off between single- and multimode is the expense of the equipment needed to generate the closely controlled carrier wavelength. For this reason, you are most likely to see single-mode cable used in WANs, where long distances must be covered, and multimode cable used in LANs where the distance traveled may only be to the next wiring closet.

You can also purchase multifiber cables, where the make-up is a combination of single-mode and multimode fibers. Some signals will operate acceptably only on single-mode fiber, regardless of the length of run. In this case, the use of multifiber cable with both types of fibers is a good, cost-effective solution.

Because the fiber core itself is rather fragile, two methods of construction are used in fiber optic cable. If only one fiber exists per cable, the fiber is generally surrounded by a plastic or rubber sheath. This sheath, in turn, is surrounded by Kevlar (yep, it's the same thing they make bullet-proof vests of) or some similar type of material. This gives the fiber bundle a strength member to pull on when installing the cable. The Kevlar is surrounded by an outer protective rubber or plastic coating. All these pieces together make up what is known as a *break-out cable*. Break-out cables can be purchased individually, or together, in one large protective casing.

Like the number of pairs of wires in twisted-pair cable, each fiber optic cable can contain more than one fiber. When this is the case, the manufacturer must take a different approach in manufacturing. The fiber is not only in danger of being broken by pulling on the individual fibers, but also—as the cable is routed around bends and corners—the fibers near the middle tend to bunch up. This can cause some problems. In order to get around this,

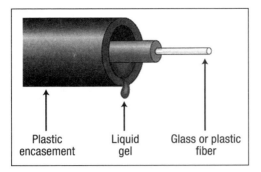

Plastic encasement  Liquid gel  Glass or plastic fiber

**Figure 2.10**
Detail drawing of gel-filled fiber-optic cable.

manufacturers make what is known as *gel-filled* fiber-optic cable, as shown in Figure 2.10. The individual fibers are all run together in the center and are surrounded by a semi-fluid gel, thus keeping the fibers suspended and at the same time allowing the diameter to change when the cable is pulled around corners.

Manufacturing costs have decreased significantly for optical fibers in the last five years. Today, if it were just the cost of the fibers involved, this could be a cost-effective solution for runs all the way from desktop to desktop. However, you should consider other costs when installing fiber. Optical cable termination is nothing like soldering or crimping onto copper. The fiber must be terminated on the ends using special ST or FDDI duplex connectors. Both are expensive and require that the cable end be polished after the connector is installed. That drives the cost of optical fiber cable higher. For all these reasons and more, most fiber cable installed today is still used for runs between wire closets and distribution centers and very little is used at the desktop level.

With all this added cost and complexity, what makes fiber so attractive? The answer is simple: super bandwidth. Most twisted-pair cable installed in LAN sites today is Category 3 or Category 5, which has maximum bandwidths of 20 and 100Mbps. New twisted-pair cable is being developed that promises to reach higher bandwidths than this, and in the future, we will see this change. Meanwhile, the bandwidth of optical fiber cable *starts* at 100Mbps and goes up. The high end of the bandwidth is still in the theoretical range. In real terms, no high end exists. This promises to open up networks built on fiber backbones to huge amounts of network traffic. What this means is that if you are installing or replacing your network infrastructure today, optical fiber is a good investment that you will not outgrow for many years.

### Wireless Communications

Wireless communications media uses modulated electromagnetic energy in the infrared and radio spectra. Both have a place and fill certain needs within their respective limitations.

Both radio and infrared can be transmitted over tight beams or broadcast omnidirectionally. And, using technology available today, most wireless systems, except broadcast infrared, are capable of supporting standard Ethernet bandwidths.

On the down side, from a security perspective, all wireless communication is susceptible to eavesdropping. If the information on your network is confidential, you should not use wireless technology without some other means of safeguarding your data. The safeguards usually involve some form or another of encryption.

You've seen the light-beam pointers that are in vogue for doing presentations in front of large audiences. Those are actually low-powered lasers in the helium-neon or $H_eN_e$ spectrum and produce a very bright, very red dot. If you have one of these $H_eN_e$ gadgets, point it at a wall and press the button twice, one short pulse and one long pulse. Congratulations, you just transmitted the letter "A" in Morse code. Significantly, you did it in a tight beam or *point-to-point* mode. Only a receiver at the place where the dot hit would have picked up the signal. In contrast to that, go over to the light switch on the wall and flip the switch in the short-long sequence; that is *broadcasting*, and everybody in the room knew when it happened. Now, replace the $H_eN_e$ source with a $GA_s$, gallium-arsenide, source, and the beam would be in the very-near infrared spectrum and invisible to the eye. This is the source most often used for wireless data transmission.

Point-to-point wireless equipment works best where you have relatively long distances to cover, across a manufacturing shop floor for instance, or where a lot of electromagnetic noise is present, such as a large welding shop, that would wreak havoc on electrical signals in a wire bundle.

The broadcast system works very well in an open office environment or perhaps on the sales floor of a department store. In this type of system, a reflector is located at a point where it can be seen by all of the units connected to the network at that location. Each unit has a receiver and transmitter connected to the NIC in the computer. The transmitter aims a laser source at the reflector. The modulated beam is reflected to each of the receivers within the work area. Usually these transmitter and receiver units are built into a small enough package to allow it to sit on top of the PC or at some other convenient position. Setup is simple and the devices work well where cabling is a problem.

---

### Avoid Eye Damage

Caution: The laser pointer is very low power and eye damage would require a very long exposure period. Other lasers, perhaps the kind used to transmit between buildings, are significantly more powerful and can cause damage at significantly shorter exposure times. Compound that with an invisible beam, and lasers can be dangerous under some circumstances.

---

### Radio Frequencies

When using radio frequency energy as a transmission media, the same fundamental methods are used as with infrared light. Radio communications in a local area network have little or no practical use, so we'll just leave that here and come back to it in the next chapter.

## Concentrators, Hubs Switches: The Glue That Binds

So far, we have covered the hardware used to allow computers to connect to the network media and the different types of media itself. The last part of the picture as far as hardware is concerned is that some device is necessary to connect all the media together. Several devices have been developed for this purpose and they generally fall into two device categories: switched and non-switched.

Before we look deeper into these devices, we need to clear up one or two points. In networking terminology some devices are known as *hubs* and other devices as *concentrators*. For a number of years, the major differences between a hub and a concentrator depended on what type of network system you used. For example, if your network was ARCNet, you used a hub (either passive or active) to tie ARCNet machines together. If your network was Ethernet, you used a concentrator located in the wire closet to connect your Ethernet devices together. The actual difference between the two is more technical than that, but this was one difference that was fairly common at one time.

ARCNet systems have long since lost their market to Ethernet. However, the term "hub" is used today with Ethernet topology to describe a device used to connect several network devices together. At the same time, the term "concentrator" is also used to describe what appears to be the same type of device. In an effort to simplify this, just for the purpose of this book, unless I am talking about a specific product distributed by a specific manufacturer, I will use the term "hub" to connect devices on the network together. The purist may argue that I am not technically correct, but I'm going to do it to cut down on the confusion. Just remember, however, that the term "concentrator" could—and often does—mean the same thing. Not all networks use hubs. Some Ethernets use coaxial cable as the media and are sometimes called *cheaper net*. This is a recognized industry standard, and the technical term is *10base2*. If your network is Ethernet and you are using coaxial cable, the chances are you will not have a hub.

In Ethernet segments that use coax, the devices are tied together by using a *BNC Tee* (see Figure 2.8). This is a tee device with special connectors on it that allows the NIC to tie directly onto the coaxial cable. The cable is then routed from one device to another. At the end of the cable, where the connection is made to the last device on the cable, the cable is terminated using a special resistor that matches the cable impedance and prevents ghost signals from reflecting back down the cable. All signal energy reaching the end of the cable is absorbed by the terminating resistor.

This method of using coaxial cable to connect devices together is known as a *linear bus*. When one device outputs its signal to the network, every other device on the network receives the signal exactly as it is, with no regeneration or conditioning. The 10base2 standard is very convenient for connecting devices in a small installation.

## Ethernet Concentrators And Hubs

Ethernet systems that use media other than coaxial cable in 10base2 configuration have a central location where the signals from each device are collected. The device located at this central point is known as a *hub*. The most common type of Ethernet hub is used to connect twisted-pair cables together in a 10baseT logical network segment.

Certain Ethernet hubs can convert the electrical signals to light energy for transmission over optical fiber cable according to 10baseFL. From the standpoint of network administration, the difference between 10baseT and 10baseFL installations is insignificant, so we will not elaborate further.

Ethernet hubs can be connected together from one to another in a *daisy chain*, but the protocol limits the number and type of hubs that can be connected this way. It is also possible to connect Ethernet hubs using coaxial cable. When used in this manner, the coaxial cable may be used as a backbone cable, carrying the signals to each concentrator on the network. Rules within the standards define the method and number of Ethernet hubs allowed to be connected within a network system.

Some Ethernet hubs can be connected together, or stacked, in a manner that makes all the hubs in a stack appear to the network as a single device. This type of hub is known as a *stackable hub*. Each hub is responsible for performing several operations on data working around the LAN, including signal reception, processing and regeneration, and transmission. Received signals are processed to filter out any unwanted noise and restore the signal to optimal levels. After this processing, the signal is retransmitted to all the ports in the hub.

Under certain conditions, such as a faulty NIC, an Ethernet device may start generating large amounts of noise—garbage, if you will. Because all devices at a hub are connected together, this noise could be retransmitted to all, including other hubs. Under these circumstances, the entire network segment and, in some cases, the entire network, will fail. It only had to happen a few times before the engineers and technicians jumped on the problem. Now, most modern Ethernet hubs are equipped with electronic circuits designed to quickly disconnect the trashy port and allow the rest of the network to continue functioning.

## Managed Network Devices

One family of Ethernet hubs, called *manageable* or *smart* hubs, can be monitored and controlled remotely. These hubs use a protocol known as *Simple Network Management Protocol* or *SNMP*. Every time a change takes place within a device on a managed network, a special type of message, called a *trap*, is generated. This trap signal is transmitted to a monitoring station on the network. For instance, when a managed hub encounters a noisy port, it disconnects it from the rest of the network, generates a trap signal, and sends it to the monitoring station.

Usually the monitoring station is running some type of *network management software*. When the monitoring station receives the trap signal, it interprets the signal and generates an error message. Needless to say, the electronics in managed types of devices is a lot more complex, not to mention the management software package. The disadvantage is that this increased complexity almost always drives the price of a managed network up. Some of the increased operating cost is in payroll overhead. After all, an error message is of no value without someone to read and act upon it. The payoff is in better knowledge of what is happening to the network, which reduces down time.

## Ethernet Switches

As the size of a LAN grows, the number of users passing information across the network increases. As this happens, the percentage of total bandwidth used increases. As we have already seen, when the percentage of total bandwidth used reaches about 45 percent, the network is carrying about all the traffic it can handle. If the use of the network continues to move upward, the result will be more collisions and less traffic overall.

### Backbone Routers

This problem can be corrected in several ways. One way is to use two NICs in some of the computers to form a separate subnet that functions as a backbone, thus dividing the large network into smaller elements, isolated from each other. If a user on one subnet needs information from a machine on another subnet, the network will route just that request and information across the backbone. This way, a heavy user load on one subnet does not impact the bandwidth on the others.

This type of system has advantages and disadvantages. From a hardware standpoint, the machines that have two NICs in them are actually acting as routers. As we shall see in the next chapter, routers can add great flexibility and increase functionality to a network system. However, they are not without problems. Because the network is now divided into several parts, administration becomes much more complicated. This is especially true if the protocol being used is TCP/IP, in which case the administrator must manage IP addresses. This makes the choice of implementing a backbone system one that requires some thought and planning.

### Building Bridges

Another way of improving the performance on an overcrowded LAN is through the use of *Ethernet bridges*; these are special repeaters placed at strategic points within the structure of the LAN. When used correctly, a bridge will learn the Node ID of all devices connected on either side of it. If a device on one side of the bridge communicates with a device on the same side of the bridge, the bridge looks up the Node ID for both devices. Because they are on the same side of the bridge, the bridge will keep all the signals on that side.

If a device on one side of the bridge starts communicating with a device on the other side, the bridge will look up the Node ID of both devices, determine that they are on opposite sides, and pass the traffic across. This effectively isolates the network into smaller segments, thereby reducing the overall traffic on all parts of the LAN.

Bridges operate at the MAC layer of the IEEE 802 network model. That means that no interface exists with the network layer where the routers operate. Simply stated, it is not necessary to assign a complex subnet strategy with associated IP addresses. This makes network administration much easier.

### Ethernet Switches

It makes sense to combine the concepts of hubs and bridges together, to produce a *switching hub*. That is exactly what some network technology manufacturers have done. Rather than have a backbone made from a subnet, the latest technology uses a *collapsed backbone* concept to implement the backbone in a switching hub. The switching hub is capable of learning all the Node IDs for all the devices connected to each port in the hub. Traffic that is addressed to a device on another port in the switch is allowed to pass through; all others are blocked at the switch port. By implementing this type of switching hub, an overcrowded LAN can be divided into segments. Each segment is designed so that its available bandwidth is capable of sustaining the maximum number of users on that segment.

The development of switching technology did not stop there. Switching hubs have now reached the capability of providing full-duplex transmission to a server. By placing two NICs in a server and connecting them both to the same hub, it is possible to set up one NIC card to send data from the switch to the server, and the other NIC to receive data from the server and pass it to the switch. By combining full-duplex transmission and segmenting busy LANs into smaller elements, it is possible to push the internal bandwidth of a switch configured for use in 10Mbps and 100Mbps LANs to 700 Mbps. This high bandwidth is what is typically required in today's graphics intensive network environment.

# Network Operating Systems—The Software

All the hardware in the world are just so many paperweights without software. Then too, software is just so many lines of ink on paper without something to execute it. The point is that we need to delve into software and find out where it came from and how it makes a LAN successful.

# Novell NetWare

This is as good a place to start as any. Novell started developing network software in the early 1980s. Its original software products were sold as Network Operating Systems, or NOS. The primary network operating system developed by Novell today is called *NetWare*. First introduced in the early 1980s as NetWare 86, it has gone through three major revisions. The first was brought about by Intel's development of the 80386 CPU. When this occurred, Novell released the next version of its product as NetWare 386. From the name, this doesn't sound like much of a difference, but in reality, it was based on new architecture and was a major departure from the previous version.

Then Intel released the 80486 CPU in rather short order, before Novell was near ready with a new NetWare release. That pushed Novell to stop naming its products in line with the Intel chip numbers; instead, Novell renamed the next version of its product NetWare 3. About that same time, Novell was ready to release an upgrade for NetWare 286 and decided to call it NetWare 2 to conform to their new naming conventions. NetWare 3 went through a version release as NetWare 3.1, and then a minor revision as NetWare 3.11.

NetWare 3.11 has become the most popular network operating system in the world, having spanned almost 15 years with only one other minor version upgrade to NetWare 3.12. Today, 15 years after its initial release, and in spite of everything Microsoft and Novell have developed, use of NetWare 3.1x is so strong in the market that Novell has released yet another new version, NetWare 3.2, which is Y2K compliant.

Novell did not stop with the success of NetWare 3.1x. In the early 1990s, the company released a major new version, NetWare 4. The new software was once again based on a new architecture, and was as radical a change from NetWare 3.x as NetWare 3 was from NetWare 2. NetWare 4 was the first network operating system that created a *logical object* for every entity attached to the network and stored all these objects in a *directory tree*. Novell named this directory system *Novell Directory Services*, or *NDS*, and for large networks with thousands of objects, having a directory system makes managing the network much easier.

The radical differences in NetWare 4.x appeared, for some customers, too big of a step function, regardless of improvements. Just the added complexity of dealing with NDS caused many companies to wonder if the gain was worth the pain. That, combined with several problems in the software itself, caused the new system to be not well received by the market. Novell went into high gear and released NetWare version 4.1. This was a much more robust and stable network operating system designed to eradicate the bugs that slipped by in the parent release. While it still had the added complexity of NDS, Novell found ways to make the transition less painless and easier to live with in their release of NetWare 4.11.

### Along Comes—You Guessed It—The Internet

With the huge public acceptance of the Internet and Internet applications, Novell added several Net-related applications to its catalog. At first, it sold them as separate products, but betting on the market, the company combined the Internet stuff with its then-popular NetWare 4.11 NOS and called the resulting product *Intra-NetWare*.

The latest release of the NetWare 4.x series, released in early 1999, is called NetWare 4.2; it was released for two main reasons, one of which is Y2K compliance. The other reason we'll get to shortly.

### Look Back At The Beginning

The next major release from Novell was NetWare 5. Like releases 3 and 4, NetWare 5 is based on new architecture. Before we look inside this new release, we need to look inside previous versions of the NOS.

From its inception in the early 1980s, the architecture of Novell NetWare has resembled that of an earlier network system called XNS, developed by the Palo Alto Research Center, PARC, of Xerox Corporation. NetWare NOS is based on a *server-centric* model. This model has workstations, or *clients*, attached to the network that obtain *services* (that is, database file, print, message, and other applications) from one or more high-end computers. These high-end computers are known as *servers* and provide the network system with appropriate services. In certain ways, this model more closely resembles a mainframe computer model. The primary difference is that the processing power is distributed throughout the network to all the individual workstations.

Early NetWare servers operate with their own independent operating system; they did not need DOS, Windows, or any other operating system loaded in order to operate. With versions of NetWare up through 2.x, the operating system was compiled and a *cold boot loader* created during the installation process. This type of system requires that when changes are made to the server hardware, a new operating system has to be compiled.

With the release of NetWare 3.x, all that changed. Instead of compiling a new system each time a change is made, NetWare 3.x servers use some version of DOS to start up and initialize the computer. Then, the NetWare server kernel *server.exe* is loaded as a DOS executable file. This kernel reads two configuration files called *startup.ncf* and *autoexec.ncf* and configures the NetWare environment based on these configurations. After the NetWare kernel is loaded, the DOS is removed from memory, leaving the NetWare network operating system to run on its own.

This approach allows the development of software modules called *NetWare Loadable Modules*. These NLMs can be added to the kernel as they are needed; they can be added with a load command or removed with an unload command. This allows the network operating system to be changed without shutting down the server or interfering with network users. This modular approach has been used in all versions of NetWare through NetWare 5.

### Let's Deal With The Clients

Because workstations are considered a different type of entity on a NetWare network, they must have their own operating system. The most common workstation operating system is

Windows, although NetWare also supports Apple Macintosh, Unix, DOS, and Windows NT workstation software. The workstations require a software driver known as *client software* to make a logical connection with the network. Over the years, Novell's client software has undergone several major architectural changes.

The early versions of NetWare used a client driver known as a NetWare *shell*. This was a *terminate and stay resident* (*TSR*) program called *NetX* that was loaded into the PC at startup. NetX loaded along with a driver provided by the manufacturer of the NIC called a *Multiple Link Interface Driver* or *MLID*, and an IPX/SPX protocol stack named *IPXODI*. The combination of these drivers allowed the PC to interface with the network and provided the protocols necessary to provide communications between workstation and server. This suite of drivers was developed by Apple and Novell, and was known collectively as the *Open Datalink Interface* or *ODI*.

### Novell Peeks In The Window

The ODI interface and NetX worked well with all versions of NetWare 3 and PC workstations running some version of DOS. When Novell released NetWare 4 and Microsoft released Windows 3.1, it was necessary to produce a network client interface that would provide better peer level communications between the lower layers of the OSI model components.

Novell responded to the challenge with the release of what came to be known as *The DOS Requestor*. This client interface included the same ODI interface as the original NetX product at the lower levels, but replaced the netx.exe NetWare shell with a series of drivers collectively labeled *Virtual Loadable Modules* or *VLMs*. The ODI interface provided the same functionality as before at the physical, data link, and network layers, while the VLMs provided the enhanced connectivity required by Microsoft Windows at the upper levels. This allowed a much better interface between NetWare servers and Microsoft Windows, and remained the norm until the release of Windows 95.

Once Windows 95 landed on software shelves, Microsoft was seriously looking to compete with Novell for the network market, and the once casual Microsoft attitude toward networking and associated products tightened up considerably. When Microsoft released Windows 95, it provided a driver to interface Windows 95 workstations to NetWare servers. Interestingly, while Novell NetWare works fine with the Microsoft Client for NetWare with versions of NetWare that do not include NDS, the Microsoft Client for NetWare does not support versions of NetWare that do support NDS. That means some users were left out in the cold.

### Expansion Of The Client Driver Suites

In order to take advantage of the features offered by the Novell Directory Services, Novell developed and released a series of drivers for Microsoft Windows 95 that have become known as *NetWare Client 32*. The Client 32 adapts many features of the NetWare servers to the client workstation, and implements most of the protocols found in all seven layers of the OSI model. With the development of the Client 32, Novell moved away from the ODI interface, and today, the only area remaining where ODI is used is in the NetWare Client for DOS and Windows 3.x. Today, NetWare Client 32 driver interfaces are available for Microsoft Windows 3, 3.1, 3.11, 95, 98, and NT, the Apple Macintosh, IBM OS2, Unix, Linux, and any of several versions of DOS.

### NetWare Adapability

The ability to allow interconnection with a large number of different platforms and operating systems is one feature that makes NetWare so popular.

Another thing that helps NetWare's popularity is the ease with which networks can be assembled from readily available parts. Very little, if any, network configuration has to be done to build a NetWare network. Another factor that relates to this ease of administration is at the core of all the versions of NetWare through NetWare 4.x—they all use IPX/SPX as their native protocol.

Remember what we said earlier: In IPX/SPX protocols the mechanism for identifying and locating individual entities on the network system; that is, assigning network addresses does not have the same complexity as TCP/IP. That decreases the administrator's workload. With the IPX/SPX protocol, the network administrator assigns only two numbers to each server on the network. The first number identifies a virtual network that resides inside the server and is known as the *IPX internal network number*. That unique number identifies the logical server that exists inside the hardware. Novell maintains a list of internal IPX network numbers, and customers can register their IPX network number with them. This helps assure that no two Novell servers anywhere in the world will have the same number. Because the number of servers on a network is fairly small compared to the number of users, IPX/SPX networks are fairly easy to set up and administer.

The second number, known as the *network number*, identifies a cable segment where a particular network card in the server is connected. The network number only identifies a cable segment, not the server or servers. All servers connected to the same cable segment use the same network number.

Unlike IBM's NetBEUI protocol, the IPX/SPX protocol was designed to handle both small and large networks. For this reason IPX/SPX is fully routable, robust, and reliable. A model of the protocol was developed and, as we have shown earlier in this chapter, it maps reasonably well to the OSI model for networks.

### A Proprietary Problem, And A Shift In Influence

IPX/SPX is not without its faults. For one thing, it is proprietary, and while it has long been recognized as a *de facto* standard, it is not an open standard. Because of that, no central location outside of Novell exists where network numbers and IPX internal network numbers are recorded and maintained. Many see this a potential cause of problems.

Another potential problem is the lack of network management tools that have been developed for IPX/SPX. When you combine these potential problems with the large acceptance of the network world for the open standards of TCP/IP in last few years, you can see why IPX/SPX has just about reached the end of its growth into new areas—and why TCP/IP will soon be the dominant leader.

### Back To NetWare 5

Novell had been studying the potential problems with using IPX/SPX, and, in answer to the challenges, released the newest version of NetWare, 5, in late 1998.

NetWare 5 is the first version of NetWare to run TCP/IP as its native protocol. This required major changes in the software, but only minor changes in architecture. Like its predecessors before it, NetWare 5 is a modular-based system and incorporates Novell Directory Services. It uses DOS for initial startup and two configuration files, *startup.ncf* and *autoexec.ncf*.

Because NetWare 5 supports TCP/IP, the workload for configuration and administration of networks increased. To make the transition as painless as possible, Novell developed a large number of tools for the administration of TCP/IP, especially through the use of the directory. That step required architectural changes in the design of the directory tree, so Novell made those changes. Today, Novell Directory Services can support very large trees with up to one billion objects in a single tree. This is truly an amazing feat.

Another new feature of NetWare 5 is the inclusion of Java and the *Java Virtual Machine*. The JVM is an imaginary computer implemented by emulating it in software on a real machine. Because NetWare 5 now comes with a JVM as part of the NetWare kernel, Java applets and Java applications execute quickly on NetWare 5. This allows development of a *Graphical User Interface (GUI)* for the server that takes up only a small percentage of the server resources. As we write this, this particular GUI, called *Console One*, is in the proof of concept stage, with the goal of being able to access it from a browser anywhere on the network and using it to configure the server.

Even though NetWare 5 is based on TCP/IP, it has not abandoned support of the IPX/SPX protocol. It does this in a manner similar to the way previous IPX/SPX versions of NetWare supported TCP/IP, by encapsulation or *tunneling*. Because NetWare 5 supports both TCP/IP and IPX/SPX, transition from previous versions of NetWare need not be an all-or-nothing event.

Still, some companies are reluctant to give up on a proven protocol like IPX. I mentioned a while back that Novell released a new version of NetWare, version 4.2. I also mentioned the two reasons for this, one of which was Y2K compliance. The other reason for NetWare 4.2 is for those companies that want the latest features, but do not want to give up on IPX; these companies can keep NetWare 4.x and run IPX as their native protocol.

Since its initial release, NetWare 5 has been well received in the market. It is proving to be reliable, robust, and versatile, and shows promise to be the best version of NetWare ever.

## IBM And OS2

The decade of the 1980s saw a tremendous rate of development in the PC industry. Many companies and corporations were born and thrived, or starved and disappeared in short order. By the end of the 1980s, three companies grew to the point at which it could be said that they dominated the PC industry. It is to no one's surprise that all three of these giants collaborated on the same product line. These companies are IBM, Intel, and Microsoft— and the product they all had a part in was the IBM PC.

It is worth noting that prior to the development of Windows, Microsoft developed the operating system used on the IBM-PC, known as *IBM PC DOS*. The IBM PC was so well-received in the market that imitations, the *PC clone*, started invading shelves all over the country, and Microsoft released a generic version of PC DOS and called it *MS DOS*. The two operating systems were very much alike, primarily because they had the same ancestry.

When Intel came out with the 80386 CPU, IBM made a competitive decision to stop further development of the PC and introduced a new architecture called *Micro Channel*. The primary operating system for the Micro Channel Architecture was called *OS2*. Some insider hints claim that OS2 development started with Microsoft, but the finished product was delivered by the software engineers at IBM. OS2 was, and still is, a multitasking (meaning it can run more than one application at a time), multiuser (meaning it can support more than one user at a time) operating system that could also support network functions.

Engineers at IBM had been developing network software for some time before the introduction of the PC. When IBM started production of the personal computer, it was natural that work should start on a software product to allow networking operations between machines. One product that grew out of this development was a protocol to support networking on the Intel CPU. This protocol was known as *Network Basic Input/Output System* or *NetBIOS* for short. To provide still more network functionality, IBM enhanced its NetBIOS protocol and called it *NetBIOS Extended User Interface* or *NetBEUI* for short. We shall take a closer look at NetBEUI shortly, but for now let's jump over and see what Microsoft was doing all this time.

## Microsoft And Windows

Along about 1984, shortly after Intel introduced the 80286 CPU, Microsoft introduced a graphical user interface in its Windows operating system. Modeled somewhat after the Apple Macintosh GUI, the product was named Windows 286 and, while it wasn't exactly a flop, it was not very well received.

With the introduction of the 80386 CPU by Intel, software engineers at Microsoft had a chip that could provide a reasonable degree of power, and shortly introduced the Windows

3 GUI operating system. This was received somewhat better and when the next version, Windows 3.1, rolled into the marketplace, it was blessed as a success. As it came out of the box, the Microsoft Windows 3.1 GUI was considered, at least by some, to be multitasking but not multiuser. Microsoft solved this with the introduction of Windows 3.11, otherwise known as *Windows for Workgroups*. As it came out of the box, Windows 3.11 was capable of supporting network features. The interesting thing about that is that the software engineers at Microsoft did not develop their own protocol for network operations. Instead, because of their close association with Big Blue, they adopted the IBM network protocol, NetBEUI, from OS2.

Like Novell NetWare, Microsoft collaborated to produce an interface driver for the network connection. In the case of Microsoft, the interface is named *Network Device Interface Specification* or *NDIS*. Developed in a cooperative effort between 3Com and Microsoft, NDIS today remains the primary driver set for interfacing versions of Microsoft Windows with network interface cards.

The NDIS interface contains two parts. First is a Media Access Control or MAC layer driver that interfaces the software with the NIC. The second part is a protocol stack that interfaces with the software at higher layers. This combination effectively shields the software at the higher levels from the network hardware and prevents software developers from having to concern themselves with programming at the network connection.

NetBEUI was envisioned by the software engineers at IBM as being a small high-speed network protocol, designed specifically for workgroups of 2 to 200 computers. Since it was never intended for use on large networks, the protocols necessary for routing between different subnets were left out. This produced a product that performed well, but only on small networks. The Microsoft implementation of this protocol in Windows 3.11 was a peer-to-peer network system, in which users shared resources on their local machines with others on the same network.

When Microsoft released Windows 95, and later Windows 98, they chose to stay with the NetBEUI protocol as the native, out of the box, protocol for networks. However, NetBEUI is not versatile enough to perform on a large, global network such as the Internet. This was obvious from the very start, and the software engineers at Microsoft soon developed a TCP/IP protocol suite for Windows. As has already been mentioned, this was introduced as an upgrade for Windows 3.11, and is now known as Winsock.

Winsock has since gone through several version releases, and is a *de facto* standard in the industry. Today, almost all of common application layer protocols are available for Windows xx. For this reason, Winsock, or TCP/IP, is the preferred protocol for building large networks with Microsoft Windows products.

### Microsoft Windows NT, One Level Up

While Microsoft Windows xx provides some network capabilities out of the box, it was evident that those capabilities would never equal the speed and versatility required for acceptance by major corporations.

Microsoft introduced a network operating system known as *LAN Manager*, but it was never a great success in the market. In an effort to improve their competitive position, Microsoft introduced a new version of its Windows GUI system named *Windows NT*. Unlike Windows versions 3.1 through Windows 98, Windows NT is a total 32-bit operating system. NT does not support all the previous software bases developed for the Intel platform. What this means is that for a software program to run successfully on Windows NT, it must be designed for Windows 9x or Windows NT.

The benefits of this are readily evident. Because it is a 32-bit system, Windows NT does not have to perform 16- to 32-bit conversion and vice versa. This gives it a speed advantage over Windows 9x, and speed equates power. Windows NT uses a new file storage architecture, which greatly improves disk access time, adding still more power. The multitasking/multiuser capabilities of Windows NT have been significantly enhanced over those of Windows 9x, allowing operation of many more sessions by a much larger number of users, hence still more power. Many other benefits exist, but as you can see, Windows NT was introduced as *the* software product developed by Microsoft for large enterprise networks.

The Windows NT network system user interface is based on a similar design to Windows 9x, but the architecture is completely different. Windows NT has two versions: NT Server and NT Workstation, and both versions are capable of supporting workgroup-size networks. It is only when the network requirement grows beyond the workgroup, by the requirement for services other than simple file and printer sharing, that the NT Server product comes into its own.

Microsoft does promote a server-centric network philosophy, but it is possible, and frequently happens, that the server is used as a workstation to run applications. Microsoft considers this capability to be a feature, and touts the ability to run applications directly on the server instead of having to be loaded over the network to a workstation as one of the strong points about Microsoft NT.

At the same time this, can cause problems. Many an NT network has been brought to a standstill because the server utilization went to 98 percent when someone started a 3D–screen saver running as an application on an NT Server.

### NT Domains

In the Microsoft NT network design, groups of users having similar tasks in common can be placed into logical organizations called *domains*. Each domain can have one or more NT servers and users can access services on each server within the domain. Each server in a domain can be configured to perform as either a *primary domain controller* (PDC), or as a *backup domain controller* (BDC).

If a domain has only one server, that server is the PDC. If the domain has more than one NT server, only one can be designated as the PDC. The PDC stores information about all users in that domain and allows users to log onto a domain and access resources on all servers within the domain without having to log onto each server as a separate operation.

Microsoft NT allows the creation of one or more BDCs in the same domain. These are NT servers that can take the place of the PDC in the event the PDC is not available. If the server is installed in a domain with more than one other server and is not configured as a PDC or a BDC, then it is considered to be a *simple server*.

### The Native Transport Protocol

For Microsoft Windows NT, the native transport protocol is NetBEUI. However, because of the limitations of NetBEUI, the *preferred* protocol for Microsoft Windows NT is TCP/IP. When Microsoft Windows NT is combined with the TCP/IP protocol suite, it is possible to produce very large, complex enterprise network systems. This comes at a price—because of the domain design architecture for Windows NT networks, with the use of PDCs and BDCs, administration of an NT network system may become complicated. Add to this the further complexity of administering a TCP/IP network system, and you can see that administering Microsoft Windows NT is not exactly a piece of cake.

**Note**
*Microsoft intends to fix that percevied problem with the Active Directory included in Windows 2000.*

## Novell NetWare And Microsoft Windows NT

Microsoft Windows NT has been very well received and enjoys a share of the network market on par with Novell NetWare. Contrary to what many people believe, Novell NetWare and Microsoft Windows NT can both run on the same network system. Many people today also assume that most business enterprises are making decisions to go with either Novell NetWare or Microsoft Windows NT. Sorry to disagree with them, but this is not the case. What many companies are doing today is supplementing their NetWare networks with the application server capabilities of Microsoft NT.

Recognizing the comingling of the two diverse systems, and based on its experience in development and implementation of NDS, Novell developed and is marketing a version of NDS for Windows NT. By using NDS for NT, entities in an NT network become objects in the directory tree and can then be managed by the administrator. This makes administration of NT a lot easier.

Today enterprises are incorporating Novell NetWare 4.x or NetWare 5.x with NDS capability into existing Microsoft Windows NT networks, thus using both products, each in the areas where it is strongest. This means enterprises are no longer using only one network operating system. Today, large companies are using combinations of products that best meet the requirements of their particular needs. This is especially true, as we shall see in the next chapter, on large enterprise *Wide Area Networks* (WANs).

# Security Issues

The biggest threat that any enterprise faces is penetration of its security. Operators of small LANs, especially those with no dial-in capabilities, tend to let their guard down, thinking that all too much emphasis is placed on security. Administrators of large enterprise networks tend to hand the issues off to turnkey approaches.

The simple fact is that security is an issue, regardless of size. Security is the preservation of a company's information. That includes, but is not limited to, the incursion of a hacker—the biggest perceived threat. It also includes, for the small enterprise, apathy toward protecting passwords. On a visit to a local ISP, I observed a list of passwords taped to the side of a terminal back in the maintenance room. I asked what they were and was told it was a list of all the technicians' passwords. It was put there so they could use each other's accounts.

Another threat to security, when defined as preservation of a company's information, is the importation of viruses. I let my guard down one time and didn't check a floppy disk from a major nationwide organization. From it, I collected the Concept virus and infected 93 files before I discovered it was there. Most of the 93 were manuscript files.

Because security at the LAN is nearly identical at the WAN, we are going to defer to the next chapter for a comprehensive study of the issues. Then, later on in the book, we will talk about VPN security, and still farther we'll devote an entire chapter to the preservation of information.

# Chapter 3
# *Wide Area Networks*

**Key Topics:**

♦ *Network differences*

♦ *Various telephony services*

♦ *WAN architecture*

♦ *Protocols for the WAN*

♦ *WAN hardware*

♦ *Introduction to security*

In the previous chapter we looked at components that make up a LAN. In this chapter we will expand the LAN to the next level, a *Wide Area Network* (WAN). Some other terms are worthy of mention here: the *Metropolitan Area Network* (MAN), the *Enterprise Network*, and the *Global Area Network* (GAN). Like Chapter 2, this chapter is a review of the technology used by the industry.

The expansion of LAN architecture to a WAN can increase the complexity of the network by many factors. This is especially true if the resulting WAN is global in scope and depends on telephony service providers for links between sites. For the most extreme case we need look only at the Internet, which has grown so large that its size and complexity simply boggles the mind.

If your job requires interfacing with counterparts that provide telephony services for your Wide Area Network, you may find the information in this chapter quite useful. We'll define the standards and protocols used to interconnect a LAN with telephony service providers and to build a WAN. If you don't know what telephony services are available, then you will definitely find this chapter useful.

## What Makes The Difference?

Similar equipment is used to construct the various types of networks. The real differences are the amount of equipment used, the geographic coverage of the network, and the use of some additional protocols.

MANs are usually considered to be contained within a metropolitan environment, including its suburbs, whereas a WAN is considered to be much larger.

Think of an enterprise network as a network on the physical scale of a WAN, but including several different types of computer systems, including *mainframe, mini-,* and *micro-computer* systems, and running mission critical applications. The term *mission critical,* referring to applications, implies that if the system fails, the result will cause great financial or physical harm to the customers that depend on the system.

Global Area Networks are relatively new and reasonably self-explanatory. WANs have been around longer and many cross borders into other countries, so it's not a good idea to get hung up on the terminology.

As previously stated, each of these networks, MAN, WAN, enterprise, and GAN, includes the same genre of equipment. The physical size of the network is what makes the principal difference between them. For this reason, and to avoid confusion, we will lump all three types of networks the one term—Wide Area Networks.

## WAN Architecture

The architecture of a WAN closely follows the architecture of a LAN. Recall that a LAN is made up of two or more entities that need to share information, and some means of allowing them to communicate. The means include network interface cards, media connecting the entities, concentrators or hubs, routers, and a variety of protocols.

If we change the scale upwards, a WAN is composed of two or more networks, as shown in Figure 3.1, that need to share information, and some means of allowing them to communicate. For now we have bundled all the interconnecting hardware, software, and protocols into the interface boxes. The networks on the WAN can be of the same type, that is, IPX/SPX on both, or they can be two different types, such as IPX/SPX on one and AppleTalk on the other, or they can be a hodgepodge.

Implementing WAN technology requires three elements, each with a set of open or *de facto* standards and a set of protocols to implement those standards. The first element we covered in Chapter 2 in the discussion of LAN technology. Obviously, if you are going to construct a WAN consisting of two or more LANs, you must have two or more existing LANs.

The second element is an infrastructure capable of supporting WAN technology. In most of the industrialized world, this infrastructure is provided by telephony service providers, in the form of either *public switched telephone networks (PSTN)* or *public data networks (PDN)*. The standards for telephony services have been under development for many years, and new development is an ongoing process. In this chapter we will look at a few of these standards.

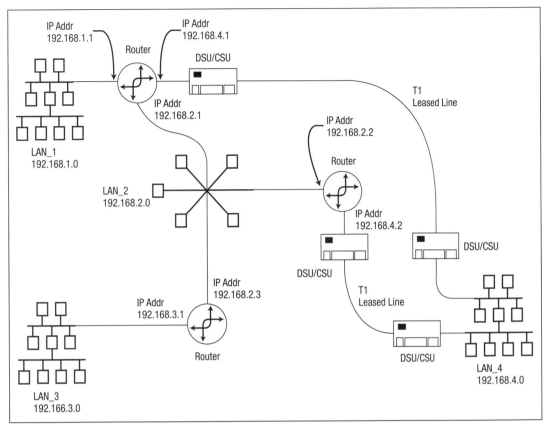

**Figure 3.1**
A simple Wide Area Network.

Finally, the third element is a means of connecting the LAN architecture to the WAN architecture so that reliable transmission of data between two networks can take place. To accomplish this, a special type of computer known as a *router* is used. Router technology is one of the most difficult and competitive areas in the network industry. In this area, protocols exist that have been in place for a relatively long period of time. Also, new open protocols and proprietary protocols are being implemented, and we shall take a look at some of them.

## Let's Map Out The Chapter

In our investigation of WAN architecture, we will take the same approach that we did with LANs. We'll dig into the media that can be used to connect our networks. Then we'll look at how the standards organizations define Wide Area Networks and delve into implementation of these definitions in major protocols. Next, we will take a look at some examples of physical hardware used to make up a WAN. After that, we will see how some software vendors have implemented this WAN architecture into their products.

## Security

Finally, we will introduce a new topic in this chapter—*network security*. If you recall, we invited you to skip Chapter 2 and we expect a few of you have. For that reason, we chose not to bring up network security in Chapter 2, and introduce it here instead. Security is no more or less important on a LAN than it is on a WAN. In fact, the implementation of security follows the same basic principles, regardless of size. It is fair, however, to say that security becomes more fragile as the number of users increases.

# WAN Service Providers, AKA POTS, AKA Plain Old Telephone Service

Unlike LANs, WANs almost always cover a geographical area exceeding the maximum distance specified by the standard for the topology connecting users to a LAN. When this happens, the network administrator, IT manager, or MIS manager must decide on what method to use to connect the network together. In some cases, the owner of the LAN may decide to bear the cost of wireless equipment to provide this service. In other cases, the owner of the LAN may decide to use services already in place for use by the general public by using *Plain Old Telephone Service* (POTS).

Existing telephone networks provide data and voice service for the general public, including enterprises. Current convention in the telephony industry separates POTS into two groups: one carries voice signals primarily and another carries data signals primarily.

## Public Switched Telephone Network

When viewed as a single service, the system that is used as a primary carrier of voice signals is the *public switched telephone network* (PSTN). The PSTN is the largest network in the world—much larger than the Internet. After all, the majority of the Internet is carried by the PSTN and many more telephones are hooked up than modems. PSTN has also been in existence for many years—long before the Internet was a gleam in ARPA's eye—and is reliable to a fault, providing virtually instantaneous communications with any point in the world by simply dialing a series of numbers or pressing a series of buttons on a touchpad.

It may come as a surprise, but PSTNs were using digital communications long before computer networks needed them. Way back then, digital circuits provided better quality, with greater capacity, over longer distances than analog circuits. The first use of digital voice circuits was implemented in Chicago, Illinois, in 1962.

We are not going to provide a detailed explanation of PSTN operation. Suffice it to say that PSTN is primarily concerned with providing analog voice service through a series of switched-circuit lines and, because a connection must be made before any information can be exchanged, the services provided by the PSTN are considered to be *connection-oriented* services. Of particular importance to the network administrator is that access to PSTN services is completely unrestricted and available to the general public at large.

## Public Data Network

The second group of services available to the owner of a LAN is the *public data network* (*PDN*). Unlike PSTN, PDN is primarily concerned with carrying data, although it still is able to carry voice. When compared with PSTN, this service is newer; however, it is the fastest growing segment of the communications industry and analysts are predicting that PDN service will soon pass PSTN in traffic volume. Like PSTN, PDN is available to the general public; often the same service provider owns the infrastructure that provides both. The use of PSTN and PDN services is often referred to as using *land lines*, a holdover from the early days of computer technology.

## Standards And Standards Organizations Revisited

The services offered by PSTN and PDN are collectively known as *telephony* services. Like all complicated systems that have to work with different types of equipment, standards exist to define their characteristics. The standards for telephony services are written by a different group of standards organizations from those discussed in previous chapters. In some cases, standards have been borrowed from one side and rewritten with a different moniker. Such is the case with the IEEE RS-232 standard, which is also published as the V.24 standard by the International Telecommunications Union (ITU).

The (ITU) is a United Nations agency, headquartered in Geneva, Switzerland, that enjoys world-side recognition for developing international telecommunications standards (**www.itu.org**). The ITU-T standards are the international standards developed by the Telecommunication Standardization Sector (formerly CCITT) of the ITU. They are the result of studies carried out on technical, operating, and tariff questions with the aim of ensuring world-wide interconnectivity and interoperability, including radio systems in public telecommunication networks, and setting the level of performance required for these interconnections. More than 2,600 ITU-T standards are in force today; the majority are new or revised standards that have appeared since the 1988 *CCITT Blue Book*.

## Standards For Wide Area Networks

The ITU has adopted many standards for telephony services. Primary among these are two groups of standards known as the *X-series* (for example, X.25, pronounced X-dot-25) and *V-series*. Partial listings of X- and V-series standards are shown in Tables 3.1 and 3.2. Many more are in force today, but these tables list the ones we are most likely to encounter in the WAN.

**Table 3.1  Partial listing of X-series standards from the ITU.**

| Standard # | Function |
| --- | --- |
| X.7 | Technical characteristics of data transmission services |
| X.21 | Interface between data terminal equipment (DTE) and data circuit-terminating equipment (DCE) for synchronous operation on public data networks |
| X.21 *bis* | Use on public data networks of DTE which is designed for interfacing to synchronous V-Series modems |
| X.25 | Interface between DTE and DCE for terminals operating in the packet mode and connected to public data networks by dedicated circuit |
| X.28 | DTE/DCE interface for a start-stop mode data terminal equipment accessing the packet assembly/disassembly (PAD) facility in a public data network situated in the same country |
| X.29 | Procedures for the exchange of control information and user data between a PAD facility and a packet mode DTE or another PAD |
| X.34 | Access to packet switched data transmission services via B-ISDN |
| X.35 | Interface between a PSPDN and a private PSDN that is based on X.25 procedures and enhancements to define a gateway function that is provided in the PSPDN |
| X.200 | Information technology - Open Systems Interconnection - Basic Reference Model: The basic model |
| X.207 | Information technology - Open Systems Interconnection - Application Layer structure |
| X.300 | General principles for interworking between public networks, and between public networks and other networks for the provision of data transmission services |
| X.328 | General arrangements for interworking between frame relaying public data networks and ISDNs |
| X.340 | General arrangements for interworking between a Packet Switched Public Data Network (PSPDN) and the international telex network |
| X.400 | Message handling system and service overview |
| X.500 | Information technology - Open Systems Interconnection - The Directory: Overview of concepts, models, and services |
| X.800 | Security architecture for Open Systems Interconnection for CCITT applications |
| X.802 | Data link layer aspects |
| X.803 | Information technology - Open Systems Interconnection - Upper layers security model |
| X.810 | Information technology - Open Systems Interconnection - Security frameworks for open systems: Overview |

**Table 3.2  Partial listing of V-series standards from the ITU.**

| Standard # | Function |
| --- | --- |
| V.2 | Limits power levels of modems used on phone lines |
| V.6 | Standard synchronous signaling rates - leased lines |
| V.7 | List of modem terms (in English, Spanish, French) |

*(continued)*

**Table 3.2  Partial listing of V-series standards from the ITU** *(continued)*.

| Standard # | Function |
| --- | --- |
| V.24 | (Known as EIA RS-232 in the USA.) V.24 defines only the functions of the circuits. EIA-232-E (which is how the current version of the standard is designated) also defines electrical characteristics and connectors. The 232-equivalent electrical characteristics and connectors are defined in ISO 2110. |
| V.28 | Electrical characteristics for V.24 |
| V.32 | 9600/4800bps FDX modems |
| V.32bis | 4800, 7200, 9600, 12000, and 14400bps modems and rapid rate renegotiating |
| V.33 | 14400bps (and 12000bps for 4-wire leased lines) |
| V.35 | 48Kbps 4W modems (The industry no longer recommends the use of this standard. It was made obsolete by V.36.) |
| V.36 | 48 KBPS 4W modems |
| V.37 | 72 KBPS 4W (V.36 and V.37 are not really "4w modems." They are group band modems, which means they combine several telephone channels.) |
| V.90 | A modem serial line protocol allowing download speeds of up to 56Kbps with upload speeds of 33.6Kbps. V.90 modems are designed for connections that are digital at one end and have only one digital-to-analog conversion. |
| V.100 | Interconnection between PDNs and PSTNs (Public Data Networks, Public Switched Telephone Networks) |
| V.110 | ISDN terminal adapter |
| V.120 | ISDN terminal adapter with statistical multiplexing |
| V.230 | General data communications interface, layer 1 (The suffix "bis" designates the second version of a particular standard.) |

Early WAN use consisted primarily of connecting remote terminals to mainframe computers over land lines. In order to provide this service, a standard was needed to define the interface between the computer system and the telephony service. Keep in mind that the purpose of standards was to assure uniformity between different proprietary systems.

The standards published by the ITU to deal with the interface between a computer system and telephony services are: X.21, X.25, X.28, and X.29. These standards apply primarily in the slower modem range, generally below 64Kbps. The exception is X.25, which defines interfacing with packet switched (the same as Internet) and bit synchronous (high speed serial interface) networks. The X.2n series of standards loosely correlate with the physical, data link, and network layers of the OSI model.

## Then, The Internet Came Along

With the development of the packet switched data network known as the Internet, the ITU had to write standards to define the interface between packet switched networks. They did it with the publication of the X.75 standard that allowed connection of networks at higher speeds than the original X.2n series of standards.

As the Internet expanded, a larger number of entities joined in. This led to a need for connecting a hodgepodge of heterogeneous network systems—mainframe, mini-computers, PCs, Unix systems, et al.—including a definition of a public or private international electronic mail and message-handling system. The ITU's answer was folded into two additional groups of standards: X.400 and X.500. So far the X.500 group is up to X.586.

## Digital To Analog And Back Again—The V Series

The X-series series of standards established a uniform interface between the equipment used on the network and the equipment used by providers of telephony services. However, in connecting a LAN to the PSTN, another interface needs to be addressed. Computers process data in the form of digital signals and the PSTN deals with voice transmission, which is analog in nature. To connect a network to telephony services, the digital data signals have to be converted to analog for transmission then back to digital on the receiving end. To fill this need, the ITU published standards known as the V-series.

The conversion of digital to analog is performed through a process called *modulation*. Conversely, the conversion of analog to digital is performed through a process called *demodulation*. To perform this conversion a hardware device called a *modem* (MOdulation/DEModulation) was developed.

Early modems did not use standards developed by the ITU. The first commercially available modems used an RS-232 interface defined by the IEEE for connection to the computer, and a transmission process developed by AT&T Bell Labs (before the breakup of AT&T) known as the Bell 212A. By today's standards this early equipment was extremely slow, operating at speeds of 120bps (yes, that's 120 *bits per second*) all the way up to 1200bps.

With no particular desire to reinvent the wheel, the ITU adopted the IEEE RS-232C interface, made a few changes, and published a new interface as the V.24 standard. At the same time, modem technology improved enough to increase the speed to a whopping 2400bps. That was really sailing to the geeks of the time.

## The Race Was On

The next modem standard published and generally accepted was developed to increase speed. The ITU's V.32 standard defined modem transmission at the rate of 9600bps. That was followed in short order by V.35, which defined transmission rates up to 48Kbps. As of the writing of this book, the newest published standard is V.90. Modems that incorporate V.90 standards are capable of transmission at rates up to 56Kbps. However, tariff regulations in the United States prohibit data transmissions over standard land lines at this speed, so the transmission speed of these devices is limited to 54Kbps.

## Meanwhile, Back On The PDN

All of the V-series standards described so far provide a standard interface for computer network systems using dial-in equipment to connect to the analog circuits of the PSTN. What about the PDN? It is a digital network that operates at much higher speeds than PSTN; we cannot ignore it.

The PDN employs several protocols and standards that we will discuss directly. For now, we need to single out one, the *high-level data link control* (HDLC) protocol used for high-level synchronous connections to X.25 packet based networks. V.32*bis* is the ITU published standard that defines in-band dialing on HDLC bit-synchronous serial lines.

As I mentioned earlier, the telephony services developed digital voice circuits ahead of digital data circuits. Different methods are used to implement the two signals.

### *Voice*

Digital voice circuits are not as picky about the accuracy of the individual bits received. When they are translated back to analog, slight differences in information will average out of the reproduced signal. On the other hand, they are sensitive to timing. If the transmitted signal stops, then restarts, the receiver cannot speed up to make up for the delay and the signal will be disrupted.

To transfer digital voice signals, the PDN system uses *synchronous* technology wherein the devices at both ends of the circuit are cued to the same clock pulse. This method avoids delay in receiving a transmitted signal and prevents the voice from "breaking up" at the receiver. If the data received encounters some errors, they will be averaged out in the receiver or appear to the listener as static.

### *Data*

Digital data is not so picky about timing, but very picky about accuracy. Digital data uses a method known as *asynchronous* technology. In asynchronous transmission, the devices on both ends are controlled by different clocks on the ends of the circuit. The clock frequencies are closely controlled and it is relatively easy to start and stop the clocks. The data is separated into frames and each frame is transmitted as an individual segment, complete with error checking. This method provides a high degree of accuracy.

## Leased Lines From POTS

Telephony service providers provide digital data lines to network owners in what is known as a *point-to-point leased line*. The leased line is reserved for the exclusive use of the network and the cost of this line is based on the distance between the two ends and the speed of the line.

A *Data Service Unit/Channel Service Unit* (DSU/CSU) device is installed at the connection between the network and the phone line. The DSU/CSU provides the interface between the network and the leased line; one must be installed on each end. In addition to interface, the DSU/CSU provides diagnostics and protection for the network and leased line.

### Defining Leased Line Standards

Several standards define leased lines and, in some cases, the standards differ between countries. In the United States, leased lines are referred to by what is known as the *T-series* standards, in which different leased lines are defined by the letter "T" followed by a number: the higher the number, the higher the bandwidth of the line. See Table 3.3.

The most common leased line used for business in the United States is a partial T1, for transmission of 56Kbps, or a full T1. Europe uses a similar naming convention, substituting "E" for "T". The European specifications are shown in Table 3.4. Remember, these lines were used initially to carry voice traffic, thus the listing for the number of voice channels. Existing technologies using processes known as *multiplexing, demultiplexing,* and *inverse multiplexing* that make it possible to combine different combinations of these standard channels to provide a larger range of services than just the three or four listed. Thus the telephony service provider can provide circuits with larger or smaller bandwidth allocations to tailor the digital circuit to the needs of the customer.

### Time Out For Some Definitions

Multiplexing combines several signals for transmission on some shared medium (for example, a telephone wire). The signals are combined at the transmitter by a multiplexer

**Table 3.3   The general characteristics of T-series leased lines.**

| T-series | Operating Speed | Number of Voice Circuits |
|---|---|---|
| Partial T1 | 64Kbps | 1 |
| T1 | 1.544Mbps | 24 |
| T1C | 3.156Mbps | 48 |
| T2 | 6.312Mbps | 96 |
| T3 | 44.736Mbps | 672 |
| T4 | 274.1Mbps | 4,032 |

**Table 3.4   The general characteristics of E-series leased lines.**

| E-series | Operating Speed | Number of Voice Circuits |
|---|---|---|
| E1 | 2.048Mbps | 30 |
| E2 | 8.448Mbps | 120 |
| E3 | 34.368Mbps | 480 |

(colloquially called a *mux*) and split up at the receiver by a demultiplexer. Now, *inverse multiplexing* is splitting a higher capability into equivalent units of smaller capability, such as taking a T-2 line and making 4 T-1 lines (see Table 3.1). Multiplexing can be performed different ways: *time division, frequency division,* and *code division.*

### Trunks And Trunk Lines

The T-series standards provide a point-to-point circuit between two network connections. What about providing a connection between two points within the telephony service provider's facilities? Telephony service providers identify these point-to-point connections between their facilities as *trunks* or *trunk lines.* Because trunk lines must carry more traffic, the bandwidth has to be considerably higher.

To assure quality service, the Exchange Carriers Standards Association (ECSA) developed a set of standards known as the *synchronous transport signal* (STS). The higher data rates associated with some STS standards requires the use of optical fiber cable in place of copper cable. For this reason, each of the STS standards has a corresponding *optical carrier* (OC) standard as shown in Table 3.5.

Like the T-series standards, the STS series standards can be combined in ways that provide more available bandwidths than those listed. However, if an STS or OC line is not to be made available for multiplexing or inverse multiplexing, then it is identified by adding the suffix "C". Thus an STS-3C circuit cannot be inversely multiplexed down to three STS-1 circuits.

The STS or OC standards define the characteristics of the circuit, but not the characteristics of the transmission. To do that, a different set of standards has been published, known as *synchronous optical network* (SONET) in North America. In Europe these same standards are known as *synchronous digital hierarchy* (SDH). The SONET and SDH standards provide information, such as how the data are framed and what type of procedures are used for multiplexing lower bandwidth circuits together onto a higher bandwidth STS circuit.

### Local Subscriber Loops And ISDN

The use of leased lines for data communications is widespread throughout the world today. They are expensive, especially when the cost is borne by an individual and not a business.

**Table 3.5   Specifications of STS and OC standards.**

| Synchronous | Optical | Speed | Number of Voice Channels |
|---|---|---|---|
| STS-1 | OC-1 | 51.840Mbps | 810 |
| STS-3 | OC-3 | 155.520Mbps | 2430 |
| STS-12 | OC-12 | 622.080Mbps | 9720 |
| STS-24 | OC-24 | 1,244.160Mbps | 19440 |
| STS-48 | OC-48 | 2,488.320Mbps | 38880 |

A line put in by a telephony service provider to an individual or business for regular dial-up voice service is called a *local subscriber loop* (LSL). Telephony service providers have been looking for ways to increase the bandwidth available to the LSL and, at the same time, lower the cost. One of the first standards developed to meet the requirements for higher bandwidth and lower cost was *Integrated Services Digital Network* (*ISDN*). ISDN provides digital voice and data to the LSL, while at the same time using the same copper phone cable at the analog voice circuit. See Figure 3.2.

### The ISDN Interfaces

The entry level ISDN circuit available for subscribers is known as a *basic rate interface* (BRI). The next step up in capabilities and performance is the *primary* rate *interface* (PRI), followed by *broadband ISDN* (B-ISDN). B-ISDN, at the time of this writing, was still in

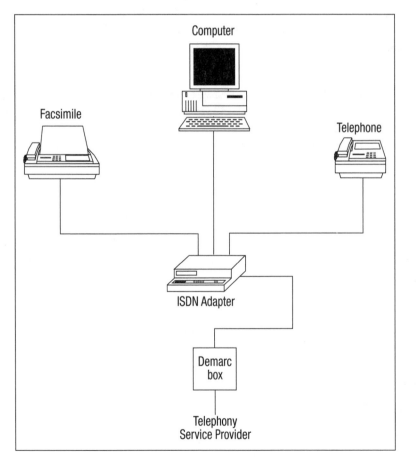

**Figure 3.2**
Basic ISDN scheme.

development and early reports suggest it will be dependent on an optical fiber network. Voice and data are carried on ISDN over *bearer* (64Kbps) and *delta* (16 or 64Kbps) channels, called *B-* and *D-channels*. Another *H-channel* is available for *higher* bit rates. Table 3.6 is a summary of ISDN specifications. One single ISDN BRI will support a much higher throughput with greater reliability than a 56Kbps modem.

### Deregulated ISDN Charges

However, the increased performance is paid for by higher rates. How much a business or personal subscriber pays can vary wildly.

In Florida, as of February 1, 1997, subscribers to one major service could sign up for either business or residential service at either a flat rate or metered usage. After paying $200 for the installation, a business would pay $118 per month under the flat rate for the first 400 channel hours and 2.5 cents per minute for extra time. For the metered service the monthly charge goes down to $59.90 and the 2.5 cents per minute starts with the first minute. (These figures are based on rates published by Oasis Technology at **www.oasistech.com/isdngte.htm**.) Another company in Florida offers the first 400 minutes for $70 per month and provides free ISDN installation. After 400 minutes of channel time the rate is 2.5 cents per minute.

Business subscribers in some parts of California can get ISDN service for a $70.75 one-time line installation charge, plus a $125 one-time ISDN installation charge, plus $28.82 monthly service for each B-Channel used. That does not include the tariff charges and sales taxes.

### ISDN Add-Ons

ISDN connection will not require ripping up your sidewalk and punching new holes in the side of your business. The tried and true POTS already running into your home and business is all the wiring you'll need outside.

Inside is a different matter. You will have to invest in some new hardware, like a *network terminator* (commonly called an *NT1*). The NT1 performs the demultiplex and branches the 2-wire POTS into 4-wire ISDN. Prices vary for the NT1, depending on the bells and whistles attached. A basic "add-a-box" NT1 can be had for $150, and a Rolls Royce model can go as high as $6,000. Because ISDN is digital technology, you will need a digital telephone ($300 and up) or an adapter for your analog telephones ($100 and up). One more item: Depending on the distance from the POTS point-of-entry to the NT1, a *network interface* (NI) box may be required. The cost is roughly equivalent to the NT1.

**Table 3.6   Specifications for ISDN channels.**

| Interface | #B | #D | #H | Total Bandwidth |
|-----------|-----|-----|-----|-----------------|
| BRI | 2 | 1 | | 144Kbps |
| PRI | 23 | 1 | | 1.544Mbps |
| B-ISDN | ? | ? | ? | 150Mbps (design goal) |

Some shareware entrepreneurs have developed monitoring kits that will track your ISDN usage. Depending on the features and the shareware costs, these utilities can provide an operations log and perhaps trip an alarm if a channel has been open for some time, but no data has passed over it.

### *Another Technology—The DSL*

A newer development in LSL technology is *digital subscriber line* (*DSL*). One version of DSL, the *asymmetric digital subscriber line*, or *ADSL*, uses a method of differentiating between the data going *downstream* to the subscriber, and the data coming *upstream* from the subscriber. By doing so, the allowable bandwidth for the downstream channel can be higher than the bandwidth for the upstream channel. This in turn allows faster downloads for subscribers connected to the Internet. The maximum bandwidth allowed for the downstream channel is 6.144Mbps, whereas the maximum bandwidth allowed for the upstream channel is 640Kbps.

Those are the maximum allowable bandwidths. Actual use will be slower because an ADSL downstream channel may at times be shared and a 64Kbps control channel using bandwidth on the upstream channel is mandatory. Despite this, ADSL promises to provide local subscribers with high speed communications links to the Internet. As we shall see later in the book, this high speed communications channel to the Internet can be a very important factor in implementing VPN technology.

Several more standards have been recently adopted or are in the process of being finalized. This field is very exciting because it promises to finally create communications channels that will operate all the way to the end of the LSL.

# WAN Protocols

We can implement only published standards, and to do that we need once again to look at rules defining how all this is going to take place. So the next step is to develop some WAN protocols.

As we stated earlier, the documents defining how the standards are implemented are collectively known as *protocols*. These are the rules for how transmission devices must operate if they are to work together. We will look at four major WAN transmission protocols:

- X.25 (revisited)
- Frame relay
- FDDI
- ATM
- Dynamic Packet Transport (Cisco proprietary)

# X.25 Revisited

It would seem that the networking industry should have replaced the X.25 years ago, but this versatile standard doubles as a protocol and remains alive and healthy. As a standard, X.25 defines the characteristics of the connection between the PSTN and a packet switching network. When viewed as a protocol, X.25 defines how the connection is made and how the packets are transmitted through the PSTN. As a protocol, X.25 defines specific devices used in a WAN.

One group of devices are DTEs that deliver data to a PSTN. This includes terminals, computers, and routers. X.25 defines another group of devices, the DCEs, that act as a connection point on the PSTN. DCEs include modems and other ports. We can say the X.25 protocol defines synchronous connection between DTE and DCE devices.

The X.25 protocol has been around since the mid-1970s and is considered a mature protocol. However, it is not without faults. The X.25 protocol was developed at a time when the quality of most phone lines in the world left much to be desired. For that reason, major emphasis was placed on error detection and correction. Today most X.25 networks run virtually error free, but the additional requirement of the data detection and correction requires a fairly large investment in packet overhead that slows down the amount of useful data transmitted.

Another factor affecting the overall performance of the X.25 protocol is the transmission method used known as *store and forward*. This requires that transmitted data be stored in memory before being forwarded to the opposite device. This method of transmission can cause noticeable delay and, in many camps, is not considered adequate for high speed data transmission.

# Frame Relay

To overcome perceived shortcomings of the X.25 protocol, particularly in the area of speed, designers removed some error detection and correction routines, increased the amount of actual data per packet, and adopted a new method of transmission to replace the store and forward technology. The result was a new protocol known as *fast packet switching*, more commonly known as *frame relay*.

The frame relay protocol defines the transfer of data in units called *frames*, which transport up to 8K of data each. Frame relay was designed for the primary task of connecting two LANs together over a high speed (4Mbps to 100Mbps) synchronous data line. It achieves higher data rates because it does not have the error detection and correction overhead of X.25 and has a much larger data-to-packet ratio.

Frame relay does not include the instructions necessary to build up and tear down connections on the fly and must maintain a *permanent virtual circuit* on each end of the transmission medium. The virtual circuit requires the use of a permanent digital link on both ends, similar to a leased line. Although frame relay is designed for high speed data links, usually in the range of 10Mbps or higher, it is not uncommon to see operation over lines with bandwidth more in the range of T1 lines.

# FDDI

In our discussion of LANs we did not mention token-passing protocols, such as the IBM Token Ring. We did this because the token ring is a proprietary protocol owned by IBM, and Ethernet is the most widely used LAN protocol in the world. However, one token-passing protocol has gained enough acceptance in LAN and, more importantly, in WAN architecture to warrant discussion. That protocol is *Fiber Distributed Data Interconnect* (*FDDI*). This protocol is a published protocol that, interestingly enough, in this country has been adopted by the ANSI.

FDDI is based loosely on the IBM Token Ring protocol, because it consists of a number of computers connected in a point-to-point configuration to form a ring, or closed loop. A special data packet called a *token* is passed repeatedly from one computer to another around the ring. This token can also be referred to as *permission to transmit*, because only the system in possession of the token is allowed to transmit.

At first glance this might seem to be an awkward, complicated, hard-to-use system. However, the complexity is only in the setup; in actual use token-passing networks perform very well, especially in areas of high network use with large amounts of traffic. Because only one entity on the network can transmit at a time, the result is no contention and no collisions.

With no collisions allowed, the bandwidth utilization can reach its maximum and token-passing networks can handle large volumes of traffic. IBM Token Ring architecture offers other benefits, especially in the area of reliability, but in an effort to keep from coming across as a sales person for IBM, I think I'll leave that for a different book.

### The Down Side Of Token Rings

With all they have going for them, you might expect token-passing architectures to shove the rest out of the network picture. That is exactly what IBM thought when they developed the IBM Token Ring in the mid-1980s. The down side is that the architecture is complicated. Setup and implementation require a higher level of expertise than other architectures, particularly Ethernet. All this combined to keep the cost of implementing an IBM Token Ring network relatively high, which in turn, kept acceptance relatively low.

### Back To FDDI

With the advent of optical fiber technology in the 1980s, the allowable bandwidth compared to copper took one giant step up. With the highly available bandwidth of optical fiber cable and the high bandwidth utilization of token passing architecture, it was natural that an effort would be made to develop a protocol designed primarily for backbone systems.

The IBM Token Ring architecture had been proven to be very reliable, and optical fiber cable had been proven to support a bandwidth of 100Mbps. From there, the advent of FDDI architecture was a natural.

### FDDI Architecture

True FDDI architecture consists of two rings, known as *counter rotating* because data are passed over both rings in opposite directions. See Figure 3.3. A *dual attachment station (DAS)* connects individual rings together. A *single attachment station (SAS)* connects individual computers into the ring. The NIC used in a computer connected to a FDDI network is usually an SAS, whereas the concentrator can be either an SAS or a DAS.

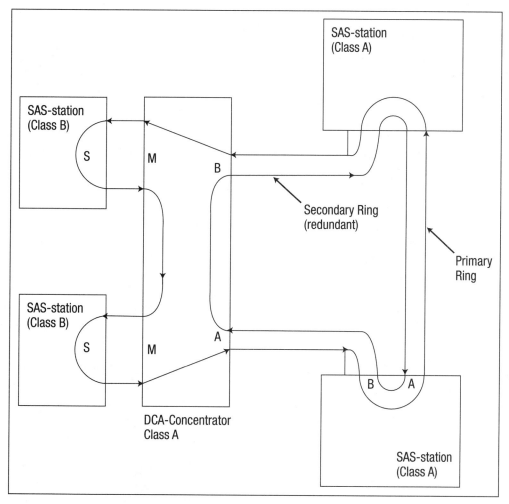

**Figure 3.3**
An example of FDDI architecture.

Why two rings? In the event of a failure (either cable fault or computer fault), the DAS can reconfigure the cable so that the ring bypasses the failed component or branch and restores network services to the remainder of the users. That means the reliability factor is increased dramatically.

Although FDDI was envisioned as a LAN backbone protocol, it found its real growth area in MANs. With FDDI technology, enterprises could build a ring around a metropolitan area (a campus, for example), reliably connecting all its branches to the main office with a relatively low cost per connection. At the same time, the combination of 100Mbps bandwidth and high utilization of token passing architecture would provide a significant increase in overall useful throughput. Today, FDDI is widely accepted and finds a high degree of use.

## Asynchronous Transfer Mode (ATM)

Networking pundits predict that the future of data communications is the ATM. Development of ATM protocols started in the early 1990s with a consortium of industry representatives known as the *ATM Forum*. This unique protocol is designed to solve many of the problems currently encountered in LAN and WAN architectures, especially those dealing with transmission of digital voice, high-quality video, and messaging systems.

To resolve the perceived problems, ATM incorporates several technologies that were not available to early protocol developers. Primary among these new technologies is the implementation of optical fiber technology coupled with gigabit-bandwidth layer-3 and layer-4 switches. We shall see that the use of this ultra high transmission technology allows the development of other new and exciting technologies defined within the ATM protocol.

### The Packet Problem

As mentioned earlier in this chapter, a problem arises when transmitting voice or high quality video over digital links using older protocols. If data packets are delayed in transit, the receiver has no way of speeding up to replace lost information back into the data stream going to the destination. What this means to the user is a break in either the voice or video message.

The problem is further aggravated by the ability of X.25, frame relay, and Ethernet protocols to transmit data packets that are not consistent in size. The inconsistent size makes synchronization of transmission and reception extremely difficult, sometimes impossible. This problem was well known to the engineers working on the development of ATM. To overcome the problem, they decided that all ATM protocol packets would be fixed-length.

That led to the next problem of what size to make the packets. The answer is made more difficult to find because of the nature of the problem we are trying to solve. Remember the goal: to design a protocol that will transmit voice, video, and data equally well over the same digital network. These needs are mutually exclusive.

### The Packet Length Solution

Voice and video require relatively small packets delivered at specific intervals to achieve the highest accuracy. Data circuits, on the other hand, require relatively larger packets and are not a concern with delivery timing.

The solution was to evolve a fixed-length packet technology that included two new protocols. All ATM packets have the length fixed at 53 bytes (one byte meaning 8 bits, or one octet). The packet includes 48 data bytes and 5 header bytes. One change to ATM was the ability to establish a *virtual channel* with a specified bandwidth allocated for exclusive use by this channel only. The other change was to specify the *quality of service* (QOS) for the virtual channel. The combination of virtual channel technology, combined with the ability to specify a QOS, formed a reliable circuit that can deliver voice and high-quality video over a digital data link.

### What About The Data?

Recall that a high-speed data link requires almost the opposite of a voice or video link. It required large data packets, and is not overly concerned about packet timing. In order to resolve this disparity, the designers included the ability for data transmission to request an *available bit rate*, or *ABR* connection. This is a compromise made possible because of the ultra-high-speed implementation of layer-3 and layer-4 switches that use optical fiber technology and gigabit bandwidth. The higher speed of that technology more than makes up for the smaller packet size.

### The ATM Bottom Line

ATM promises to deliver good solutions to the problems it is designed to solve. It is, however, a new technology and has not yet reached the stage where it can be considered mature. Many manufacturers implement ATM technology using proprietary equipment, which will not interface with equipment manufactured by others. No small factor in making an ATM decision is cost. As with any new technology, the cost is still relatively high compared to equipment that has been around for a while. As with all new stuff, the cost will drop as manufacturing methods are improved and the popularity grows.

As we write this book, ATM is the most promising new technology and new standard for the future. Because ATM is designed to be easily implemented by hardware (rather than software), faster processing speeds are possible. The prespecified bit rates are either 155Mbps or 622Mpbs, and one Ohio State University research paper reports that speeds on ATM networks are expected to reach 10Gbps.

### Dynamic Packet Transport (DPT)

Cisco Systems, one of the many manufacturers of computer network–related products, has found a unique spot in the computer industry. Cisco manufactures network routers, switches, and remote access products designed for use only in WAN installations. Its strategy has garnered it the role as the leading provider of routers and routing equipment for the Internet. It is an innovative company, constantly seeking new ways to make its products more efficient and more effective.

Cisco's innovations center around a five-phase plan for the implementation of a totally integrated network system. The new system will combine data, voice, and video technologies into a cell or packet-based network infrastructure. The technology will be based on industry standards and open APIs. According to Cisco literature, implementation will begin with two phases of WAN integration followed by addition of the following features:

♦ Multiservice gateway

♦ Campus/metropolitan-area network (MAN) integration

♦ Directory linkage to policy-based end-to-end call management.

According to Cisco, in each phase Quality of Service (QOS), call management, infrastructure integration, and infrastructure management capabilities are added.

Our discussion of hardware routers requires a corresponding discussion of routing protocols. Cisco routers are capable of implementing all the standard routing protocols we shall discuss, but Cisco's real strength has been in the area of proprietary protocols designed for Cisco products. According to Cisco (as we were writing this), the company is in phase four of a five-phase plan for implementing a completely optical routing system. The new schema are designed for ISPs to link multiple *points of presence* (POPs) together using high speed optical fiber in a MAN.

As a part of this new system, Cisco is introducing a proprietary WAN protocol called *Dynamic Packet Transport* (DPT). It is not the purpose of this book to act as a public relations agent for Cisco and it is not the purpose of this chapter to dig really deeply into the inner workings of a proprietary protocol. However, because of Cisco's prominence in the router market and the high performance history of their proprietary protocols, any innovation like DPT is worth at least as quick a look as we have given others.

DPT is a performance-oriented protocol that, according to documents from Cisco, can be implemented over new fiber installations. It will allow the use of several new Cisco protocols, or existing ring-based architectures such as FDDI, implemented over high-speed SONET optical fiber. Just like ATM, DPT is designed to support virtual channel and quality of service features that will, hopefully, allow high quality video, VoIP, and virtual networks to be implemented.

Several DPT protocol features are interesting and merit mention here. For example, according to Cisco, when DPT is implemented in a point-to-point dual-ring topology, it uses one ring for sending data packets only, and the other for sending control packets. Cisco claims this gives almost double the bandwidth over current protocols, such as FDDI. Another interesting feature of DPT is the *Spatial Reuse Protocol* (SRP).

When SRP is implemented in a point-to-point ring, the packets are removed when they get to the station they are addressed to. That, according to Cisco, allows two or three different communication events to take place each time the token goes around the ring. If implemented properly, this greatly increases the effective bandwidth of the whole network.

Several innovative features in this overall protocol (such as the two just mentioned), when taken together, make DPT look very promising. However, keep in mind that to get full benefit from DPT you must use Cisco equipment exclusively throughout your entire network. If your company is a large ISP covering a large metropolitan or state area, this may be practical. However, if your company is a small ISP dependent on a PDN service provider to implement T1 access to your POPs, then it may not be practical.

Last, but certainly not least, I mention DPT here also because, along with all the other good things it promises, it also promises to deliver a *secure virtual channel* over an *insecure public network*. As we draw closer and closer to our final target, you'll see that that is what is truly needed to establish a VPN.

# Physical Components

As mentioned earlier, a WAN is two or more LANs connected together over a large territory. Each network entity comprising the WAN can use the same or different protocols. The method of connecting the networks together requires special hardware, some of which we have seen before.

## Bridges

In Chapter 2 we looked at a *bridge* to connect together networks using different protocols. Bridges operate at the data link layer (DLL) of the OSI model or, if you prefer the IEEE model, at the media access control (MAC) layer. Bridges are often called *MAC layer devices*. In its most basic state, a bridge divides two network segments by learning the MAC addresses of all devices connected to either side of the bridge. Once this has been accomplished, the bridge looks at the destination address of the packet and, if that address is on the opposite side, it passes the packet across the bridge. If the address is not located on the other side of the bridge, it prevents the packet from crossing.

When a bridge is used to connect two networks that are using different protocols, it follows the same basic principle for the network on either side of the bridge. The bridge follows the protocol of the network that it is connected to. This is illustrated in Figure 3.4, where a bridge is used to connect an AppleTalk network to a Novell NetWare network.

On the NetWare side of the bridge a combination of the *link support layer* (LSL) and *Internet Packet Exchange* (IPX) protocols is used, and on the AppleTalk side of the bridge *AppleTalk Address Resolution Protocol* (AARP) is used. For packets that are passed from one side of the

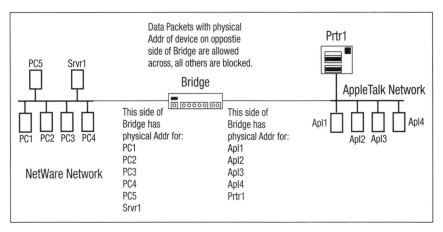

**Figure 3.4**
Connecting AppleTalk to Novell NetWare using a bridge.

bridge to the other, the bridge provides *protocol conversion* from one protocol to the other. (A more detailed discussion of these protocols will follow later in this chapter.)

The key to remember here is that the operations performed never get above the MAC layer and, in the scope of operations as a whole, are not overly complicated. Bridges that are used to connect networks with different protocols are special devices designed to perform that specific task.

### A Problem Case

A problem arises when the network scenario of Figure 3.5 is presented. In this case we see two NetWare networks, NW-1 and NW-2, each of which is connected to an AppleTalk network, Apple-1. The problem here is that Apple-1 is between NW-1 and NW-2, and all three are connected together by two bridges, bridge-1 and bridge-2. Suppose a user on NW-1 originates a packet for another user on NW-1. The information goes directly to that user and the bridge blocks that packet from exiting its parent network.

Now, let's have a user on NW-2 make a request for data from one of her chums on Apple-1. The bridge sees that the address is not on its side of the bridge, does a quick check, and finds it next door. The packet is then dropped onto the connection and sent across to the Apple-1 bridge where it is delivered to the AppleTalk network.

So far, so good.

The trouble starts when a packet originates from a user on NW-1 that is addressed to a user on NW-2, or vice versa. To get there, the packet must cross both bridges, and therein lies the problem.

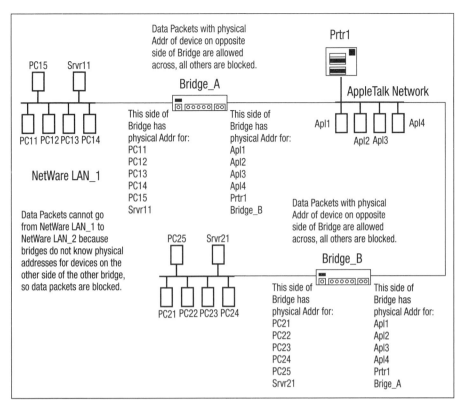

**Figure 3.5**
A problem connection.

The bridge on NW-1 knows only the MAC addresses of the devices connected to the AppleTalk network via the Apple-1 bridge; it is totally ignorant of the NW-2 bridge and whatever entities may reside on NW-2. When the NW-1 bridge peeks into its address file, it cannot make a match for the destination address and, therefore, blocks the packet from leaving NW-1.

In other words, when three networks are connected together as shown in Figure 3.5, each bridge is allowed to pass traffic across to an adjacent network, but no farther. It's obvious from this example that a better process is needed.

## The Glue That Binds: Routers

As we saw from the simple example on bridges, when the number of LANs connected is greater than two, and entities on each network wish to be able to communicate with all the other networks, then a means other than node IDs or MAC addresses must be implemented. In order to accomplish this, we need to move beyond the physical address of a device on a single network.

Remember, each different entity on the network has a node ID *and* a network ID. Usually the network ID is a combination of two addresses: One identifies the entity and the other identifies the network. The most common protocol in use in WANs is TCP/IP, so I will use this protocol for my example.

When implemented in a WAN, TCP/IP is actually a combination of several lower level protocols and can be implemented in several different network systems, on several different types of computers. For the purpose of this section, I am going to use the implementation in the Unix operating system. Surprisingly enough, the Unix implementation is much simpler than most of the others. That is because all the entities are treated equally by the network and are given a *host name*, or host (they may not be equal in fact, but with the Unix operating system the network doesn't know that).

### IP Addressing, Revisited

We covered IP addressing as it refers to LANs in Chapter 2. In this chapter we will take a second look and add a bit more information, but first a short review is needed.

In the TCP/IP protocol, each different entity is assigned a unique designator called an *IP address*. This address is made up of four groups of decimal numbers, each number in the range of 1 through 255, and is usually written in what is known as *dotted decimal notation*, in which the numbers are written as decimal numbers separated by a period. Each group of decimal numbers is known as an *octet*, because they are 8-bit binary numbers. For our tutorial we will use 192.168.0.75 as an example IP address.

Other things about this address (such as *Class A*, *Class B*, and *Class C* addresses, and public verses private network addresses) are important to anyone setting up a TCP/IP network. But that goes beyond what we're trying to accomplish here, so I won't go into them any further than necessary to demonstrate how routers work. Our example address is considered to be a *Class* C IP address. One other thing—in case you haven't noticed, it is common practice in the industry to refer to a TCP/IP address as simply an *IP address*.

Some network and host addresses have special meaning in the TCP/IP protocol:

♦ If the network address is all zeroes, the protocol interprets it as *this network*.

♦ If the network and host addresses are all zeroes, the protocol interprets it as *this host on this network*.

♦ If the network and host addresses are all ones, the protocol interprets it to mean *send to all hosts* within the local network.

Now, about that network address. As we mentioned before, the IP address for an entity on the network is divided into two parts. In our example address, 192.168.0.75, the first three octets identify the network, and the last identifies the host on the network. So in this case the network number is 192.168.0.X and the host is X.X.X.75.

# The Routing Process, Part One

So far we have an IP address assigned to our local host and we know it is divided into two parts, the network number and the host number. The next thing we need to add is a *network mask*. This is an important element in the TCP/IP routing protocol. If it's not there or, even worse, not correct, the IP routers are going to have serious problems routing packets to their correct destinations.

## Masking

The network mask is so important to the operation of TCP/IP that default masks have been established for all the classes of IP addresses. What this means is that if the administrator does not specify a network mask, the TCP/IP protocol will. Unfortunately, most network administrators do not have a really good understanding of what the mask really does. To understand how the mask functions, you have to understand two things: *relationship* and *digital logic operation*.

### Relationship

Relationship refers to how numbers in $base_{10}$ relate to numbers in $base_2$ or—to put it another way—the relationship between decimal and binary numbers. The binary number 0000 0000 is equal to the decimal number zero and the decimal number 255 equals the binary number 1111 1111. In our example IP address, the decimal number 192 is represented in binary as 1100 0000.

### Digital Operator

The one critical logical operator you must know is the **AND** function. If you don't know how this operation works, and you really do want to understand how address masking works, don't despair. Stick a bookmark here and grab that dusty textbook off the shelf or head down to your favorite bookstore and find a small (yes, you can really find a small book) text on digital logic. Make sure it covers the logical operations **OR** and **AND** to your satisfaction; buy it, read it, and study it. Then come back here and finish this chapter.

But be warned, once you do that, you will understand how network protocols decide when to look for the destination on the local network, and when to pass the message to the router, and the magic will be gone forever.

### So What Is A Network Mask?

Simply stated, the *network mask* is a binary number that identifies how many bits of the host IP address are the *network number* and how many bits are the *host number*. If we change to the binary number system for a brief time, it is easier to understand.

In the network mask, the bits representing the network number are all ones, and the bits representing the host number are all zeroes. So, for our example host IP address, the network mask would be:

255.255.255.0

and the binary representation would be:

1111 1111 . 1111 1111 . 1111 1111 . 0000 0000.

Still with me so far? We almost have all the tools we need. Let's add the final two elements: *default gateway* and *Address Resolution Protocol* (ARP).

## Default Gateways

We need the IP address of a special machine on our local network that connects our network to other networks, wherever they may be. This machine is identified by different server names, depending on whose convention you are using. The convention we will use is the *default gateway*, called this because if the protocol can't locate the destination address any other way, this is where it will forward the data packet. In a nutshell, the default gateway is the doorway to the world.

## ARP

The final piece we need is a protocol that performs the process of determining where the destination host is, or failing in that, determines where to forward the message. In TCP/IP the protocol that performs this service is known as the ARP.

The actual process is known as *resolving* the address. The implementation of ARP is required on all computers that use the TCP/IP protocol, even on a LAN. In all probability, the actual program that performs the process will have different names on different operating systems. In Unix it is known as a *resolver*.

## Resolver Functions

For each packet (or group of packets) transmitted, the resolver performs the following steps:

1. Determine if the destination host is on the same network as the local host.
2. If the destination host is on the same network as the local host, identify the MAC address of the destination host. (More about this later.)
3. If the destination host is on a different network, look at a *host table* to see if a path exists to the destination host.
4. If the destination host is on a different network, and an entry exists in the host table for the destination, identify the MAC address of the machine on the local network that is the *gateway* to the destination host.

5. If the destination host is on a different network from the local host and *no* entry exists in the host table for the destination, identify the MAC address of the default gateway.

To work properly, the resolver must know, as a minimum, each item we have listed so far. These are the following:

♦ IP address for the local host

♦ Network mask for the local host

♦ IP address for the destination host (either on the same network as ours or a different network)

♦ IP address of the default gateway

Resolvers have greater capability than this simple example, but for our purposes this will suffice. In an effort to keep things simple, we will not go deeply into all the intricacies of the resolver.

## Making The Mask Work For Us

Now that we have all the parts and pieces, let's look at an example and see how it works. To step through the example, we will have to convert the IP address (written in dotted decimal notation) to binary number form. This will make it a lot easier to follow. Assume that the local host IP address is 192.168.0.75, and in the first example I want to send a packet to another machine on the same network at address 192.168.0.55. Remember also that the subnet mask for our local network is 255.255.255.0. Putting all the pieces together looks something like Table 3.7.

First, the resolver must determine if the destination host is on the same network as the local host. To do that, the resolver performs a logical **AND** operation between the subnet mask and the destination IP address given in Table 3.7, then subtracts the result of that operation from the IP address of the local host. This operation is shown in Table 3.8.

**Table 3.7    Elements of address masking.**

| Host | Decimal Address | Binary Address |
|---|---|---|
| Local | 192.168.0.75 | 1100 0000 . 1010 1000 . 0000 0000 . 0100 1011 |
| Destination | 192.168.0.55 | 1100 0000 . 1010 1000 . 0000 0000 . 0011 0111 |
| Subnet mask | 255.255.255.0 | 1111 1111 . 1111 1111 . 1111 1111 . 0000 0000 |

**Table 3.8    Boolean AND function of addresses and masks.**

| Host | Decimal Address | Binary Address |
|---|---|---|
| Destination | 192.168.0.55 | 1100 0000 . 1010 1000 . 0000 0000 . 0011 0111 |
| Subnet mask | 255.255.255.0 | 1111 1111 . 1111 1111 . 1111 1111 . 0000 0000 |
| logical **AND** | | 1100 0000 . 1010 1000 . 0000 0000 . 0000 0000 |
| local host | | 1100 0000 . 1010 1000 . 0000 0000 . 0100 1011 |
| Subtract **AND** result | | 1100 0000 . 1010 1000 . 0000 0000 . 0000 0000 |
| Final result | 0.0.0.55 | 0000 0000 . 0000 0000 . 0000 0000 . 0100 1011 |

Notice that as a result of these two operations, the network number is 0.0.0.0 and the host number is 0.0.0.55. Referring back to the special cases described earlier, if the network number is all zeroes, then the destination is considered to be on the local network. Because the destination host is on the same network as the local host, the resolver does not look in the host table for a route to the destination, nor does it forward the data packet to the default gateway. The resolver program resolves the IP address of the destination host to a MAC address, and forwards the packet to that address.

To resolve the IP address of the destination host to a MAC address, the resolver transmits a special type of data packet to all the hosts on the local network. This type of transmission is known as a *limited broadcast*, limited because it goes only to the local network. The special data packet contains the host number for the destination host. Each host on the local network subtracts the host number for the destination host from its own host number and looks at the result. If the result is all zeroes, then, according to the information in Table 3.8, the result equates to this host on this network; in other words, it's a match. In that case the host will transmit its physical node ID (MAC address) to the originator and establish communications between the two machines.

Why do we have this added step? Why not just use the MAC address to begin with? This is exactly what is done in the IPX/SPX protocol used by Novell NetWare versions prior to NetWare 5.X. The problem is that it limits us to *one* host address only per machine. The TCP/IP protocol uses logical instead of physical addresses and allows assignment of more than one host number to a physical MAC address. That is very desirable when we have machines that provide many different services for the network.

### Points Worth Repeating

As we have seen, the process used by the ARP is simple but effective. It is worth noting that all routable network protocols have similar processes to determine the same type of information. And don't forget that the resolver functions are part of the TCP/IP Address Resolution Protocol. This protocol operates at the Internet layer of the DARPA network model, which is roughly equivalent to the network layer of the ISO/OSI network model.

Routing, and functions related to routing, take place at the *network layer* of the OSI model, unlike bridges, which operate at the *data link layer* of the OSI model. As we shall see, routers are much more versatile than bridges.

### Internet Control Message Protocol

It is worth mentioning here that the process using the special data packet in a *limited broadcast* environment is a part of another protocol known as *Internet Control Message Protocol* (*ICMP*). The ICMP defines several special data packets used for different purposes, including those used by the ARP for resolving IP addresses on local host machines to MAC physical addresses.

# The Routing Process, Part Two

Our network IP address example worked so well that you probably want to see another one. We are going to give it to you, but before we jump into it, I want to point out some things that might not have been obvious the first time around.

I showed that the network mask is a number with the same binary length as the host IP address and can be written in the same dotted decimal notation format. In the mask, the bits assigned to the network number are set to 1 and the bits assigned to the host number are set to zero. Under those conditions, any time the logical **AND** operation is performed between the mask and host IP address, the result will yield the network number, and only the network number. The host number will always be zero. The reason I emphasize this is to show that *routing* operations are concerned only with *network* numbers. The host number is not important until the data packets arrive at the destination network.

## Routing To A Different Network

Let's do the drill again, only this time send a data packet to a host on a different network. Once again my local host IP address is 192.169.0.75, and this time the IP address of the destination host is 192.169.10.55. The subnet mask is the same as it was, 255.255.255.0. Our information looks something like Table 3.9.

As in the first drill, the resolver's task is to determine if the destination host is on the same network as the local host. The resolver performs a logical **AND** operation between the subnet mask and the IP address of the destination host and subtracts the result from the IP address of the local host, as shown in Table 3.10.

The result is definitely *not* zero. This number has special significance, but we don't care about it at this point. All we were interested in discovering was that the destination host is

**Table 3.9  Routing information for different networks.**

| Host | Decimal Address | Binary Address |
|---|---|---|
| Local | 192.168.0.75 | 1100 0000 . 1010 1000 . 0000 0000 . 0100 1011 |
| Destination | 192.168.10.55 | 1100 0000 . 1010 1000 . 0000 1010 . 0011 0111 |
| Subnet mask | 255.255.255.0 | 1111 1111 . 1111 1111 . 1111 1111 . 0000 0000 |

**Table 3.10  Resolver function to determine IP address of destination host.**

| Host | Decimal Address | Binary Address |
|---|---|---|
| Destination | 192.168.10.55 | 1100 0000 . 1010 1000 . 0000 1010 . 0011 0111 |
| Subnet mask | 255.255.255.0 | 1111 1111 . 1111 1111 . 1111 1111 . 0000 0000 |
| Logical **AND** | | 1100 0000 . 1010 1000 . 0000 1010 . 0000 0000 |
| Local host address | 192.168.0.75 | 1100 0000 . 1010 1000 . 0000 0000 . 0100 1011 |
| Subtract logical **AND** | | 1100 0000 . 1010 1000 . 0000 1010 . 0000 0000 |
| Resolved address | 255.255.246.55 | 1111 1111 . 1111 1111 . 1111 0110 . 0100 1011 |

on a different network than the local host. Our resolver will ignore Step 2 of its assigned duties. It is not necessary to resolve the host number to a MAC address if the destination is not on our local network.

Resolver Step 3 calls for a peek at the host table to see if a route exists to the destination resolved in Step 1. (The host table is a list of routes to other networks that is maintained by the system administrator.) The routes maintained in the host table this way are also referred to as *static routes*, because they are very seldom changed.

The resolver compares the result of the logical **AND** operation with each entry in the host table. If it finds a match, it will have a route to the network where the destination host is located. In this case the resolver reads the IP address of the host machine acting as the gateway to the network on which the destination host is located. The resolver program then attempts to resolve the IP address to a MAC physical address. It does this in a similar manner as discussed earlier, using ICMP special data packets. When the host machine acting as the gateway responds with its MAC address, the resolver hands this MAC address to the IP protocol, which establishes communications between the two machines.

In the case of our example, let's suppose the host table has no entry matching the resolved destination host network number. The situation then, is that the resolver program has no route to the destination host's network. In this case, the resolver drops down to Step 5 and reads the IP address of the default gateway. Then it uses the logical **AND** trick to resolve the IP address to a MAC physical address (remember, the default gateway is located on the same network). Once the MAC address of the default gateway is determined, the resolver program hands it to the IP protocol, which then establishes communications between the two machines.

We know now that the resolver protocol will attempt to resolve every valid IP address it is given to a corresponding MAC physical address on the local network. The ARP must be able to do that in order for the IP protocol to establish communications between the two machines.

# The Routing Process, Part Three

Now we shall venture into the arcane realm of actual WAN routers. This area is quite complex and covers a large variety of different equipment, protocols, and implementations. Other authors have devoted entire books to the exquisite details of just WAN routing protocols, hardware, and software. I am going to take a very simplistic view of the subject at hand. If your appetite for WAN is not sated here, I encourage you to dig into any of the many RFCs and books already been written on the subject. To that end I have compiled a list of some of my favorites and put it in an appendix. Having said that, let us move on.

### A Few Wrapup Points

Some host tables can be updated *dynamically* by the software. On another note, once the resolver program has resolved an IP address to a MAC address, it will keep the MAC address in memory for a while. If another data packet comes along addressed to an IP address in memory, the resolver does not have to use ICMP data packets to resolve the MAC address. These enhancements will work as long as the route to a different network doesn't change and IP addresses of all the host machines remain the same. We shall discover that some protocols are designed specifically for these conditions.

# Gateways

In a WAN, the term *gateway* describes a computer used to connect your LAN to another network. If that other network also has a gateway to still another network, it should be possible to send data information packets from a local host on your local network to any other valid destination host, on any other network, via multiple gateways.

The first step is to send the data packets from your local host to the gateway on your local network. Let's assume the data packets arrive at the gateway and are stored there for a short period of time. If we change our perspective from the local host to the gateway, then the gateway assumes the role of local host, and the process of figuring out what to do with the data packets is repeated, only this time the packets are shunted to the network next door. What we are actually doing is following a route through the networks to deliver data information packets to a specified destination host machine on a specified network. In this respect the terms *gateway* and *router* mean the same thing. In fact, on some System5 UNIX flavors like Sun Solaris, there is a file under /etc called "defaultrouter" that contains the default IP gateway of the system. The differences between the two machines are more a matter of semantics than of physical or logical processes.

Building on this logic, we can develop a definition for the terms *router* and *gateway* (remember in our simplistic view, the two terms mean the same thing). Essentially then, a *router* or *gateway* is a computer connecting two separate, different, physical and logical networks together. The router has two tools for doing its work: an interface connected to each different physical network system, and software that forwards the data packets to the appropriate logical network. The real magic in routers comes from the manner in which they can find a path through the maze of interconnected networks to the final destination.

Enabling routers to find paths through the labyrinthine internetwork system requires implementation of several different protocols. Once again, for our purposes we will limit the discussion to only a few of these protocols. Where to begin?

## Router Tables

All routers have a *router table* created in one of two ways. A basic router table of *static entries* can be created and maintained manually on a small WAN without too many routers. The advantage here is that the administrator can pick the routes through the network based on external circumstances. The down side to static router tables is that they must be maintained, and each time a change is made to the network, the entries must be updated.

A better way of implementing router tables is to put in only the basic information, including at least the default gateway entry. When the router is brought online, it will heuristically learn routes to various networks from the data packets it processes. Over a period of time, the router will amass a very large router table holding many entries and routes through the internetwork. This is the preferred way to update router tables.

Specific information in router tables varies from one routing protocol to another, but in essence the tables must all contain some basic information. At a bare minimum this includes:

♦ The network number of the destination network

♦ The interface on the router that is used to get to that network

♦ A cost, or metric, used in calculating which interface to use

♦ A time stamp indicating when this entry was made in the router table

♦ A second time stamp indicating the last time this entry was used to route a data packet

The first two items are old hat for us now, and we needn't devote any time to them.

The metric is used when more than one route exists through an internetwork to the destination. In that case, the router must make a decision about which interface to use. In its simplest form, the cost is based on the number of routers the data packet has to go through to get to the final destination. This is often called the *hop count*—the number of hops.

However, other factors are also important here. For example, a destination network could have two routes available. One route has a metric of two hops and the other route has five. At first glance the route with two hops would look more promising. Closer inspection of the routes shows that on the route with two hops, one of the links used is over a T1 line with 1.44Mbps bandwidth. At the same time, on the route with five hops the link speed is 10Mbps or better all the way. In this case the route with five hops would be the preferred route, because the bandwidth is so much higher. As you can see, it is important to look at all the factors, not just the hop count.

The last two essentials in the router are necessary for calculating a *time-to-live* for the router table entry. Many routers stay online for long periods of time. Some have been in operation for years with minimal maintenance. During that time they have handled millions of data packets and learned routes to thousands, perhaps hundreds of thousands, of networks. If some means of carving out old routes is not available, a busy router would soon gobble all available memory and storage building an enormous table.

To prevent plugging the resources with obsolete information, the router protocol assigns a *time stamp* to the table entry at the time it is created. Each time the entry is used, the router makes a second entry or updates the original entry with a new time stamp. Entries that have not been used within a deadline specified by the network administrator in the router setup are purged from the table, thus maintaining an orderly efficient router.

# Routing Protocols

Now that we have determined more specifically what a router is and what it does, and what it needs to perform those tasks, let's take a look at two specific types of routing protocol implementations. Keep in mind that several routing protocols are in use today, but we are only going to discuss two of them

### *RIP*

The *Routing Information Protocol* (*RIP*) is defined in several RFCs. RIP is a *distance vector* routing protocol. The decision on which route to take to the destination network is based on the best path to the destination. Often this is based on the number of hops the packet must make to get to the final destination.

The RIP is implemented in several different network operating systems. Occasionally, an implementor may make minor changes to the RIP in an effort to enhance the protocol for specific equipment or needs. Therefore, each implementation may be a little different. To avoid problems caused by the differences, the standard warns that you implement RIP according to the Internet Standards detailed in RFC 1058.

*Distance vector* means that the tables in RIP routers are periodically updated by transmitting data packets using *multicast* addresses. These data packets contain information about the entries in the routing table of each RIP router in the network system. The RIP protocol assumes that all the devices on the network, routers, and hosts have a routing table that, as a minimum, includes the following:

- IP address of the destination
- Route metric to the destination
- Address of the next router in the route to the destination
- A flag bit indicating if the entry has been recently updated

The RIP protocol is not without faults and Internet RFC 1058 acknowledges several of these, including the following:

- A maximum hop count of 15 from the sender to the destination.
- Routing loops are possible on large networks because of the time required to update routing tables across a large network.
- Metrics used to calculate the best route to the destination are fixed and do not allow for changes in the network caused by faults and outages.
- The RIP protocol is unable to include subnet mask information in its router table updates and, therefore, cannot inform other RIP routers of the existence of subnets within the network.
- Because RIP uses multicast packets for updating routing tables on all the routers, it can cause excessive traffic on a large-scale WAN. For that reason RIP is considered best used as a gateway, or *Interior Gateway Protocol* (*IGP*).

In spite of its shortcomings, RIP is implemented in a large number of networks—primarily because, in small- to medium-size networks, it is robust, mature, and easily implemented. Also worth noting here is that a relatively newer version of RIP, *RIP II*, is available. RIP II is a distance vector routing protocol like the original RIP; however, it includes enhancements to overcome some of RIP's shortfalls. At the top of the enhancement list are the abilities to include subnet mask information in the update multicast packets and to include information of variable subnet masks.

### OSPF

The *Open Shortest Path First* (OSPF) is a different breed of routing protocol. OSPF uses *Link State Protocol* functions to keep its router tables updated. Link state does this two ways: first, by using information from the header of each IP packet to gather information about network addresses; and second, by transmitting special *hello packets* containing information about neighboring routers. By using these two methods, information about router table entries can be passed between neighboring LSP routers without generating large amounts of network traffic.

Another feature of the link state routing protocol is its ability to build router tables of information about hierarchical network topologies. OSPF can do this because the information contained in the router tables can be used to calculate multiple minimum-cost routes to the same destination while using network and route loading to balance the loads. OSPF is also capable of faster dynamic updates on actual network conditions, allowing it to reconfigure router tables in the event of a fault.

Putting all of these characteristics together makes LSP routers ideal for very large and complex internetworks with large numbers of routers. However, like RIP, OSPF is not without its down side. OSPF is more complex—involving different types of routers, depending upon their location within the network system. This means that expertise is required in order to set up and maintain an OSPF router–based internetwork system.

# The Routing Process, Part Four

Routers can be used to create an internetwork system that contains several *subnetworks*. I will take us through this process, but first, a word of caution. The coverage of the TCP/IP protocol suite and IP addressing has, so far, been intended only to demonstrate how routers work. This book is not intended to demonstrate how to set up and subnet a Class C IP address.

In the example that follows, you may think I did not cover the material well enough earlier in the chapter. If this happens, you have two choices. First, get copies of RFC 950, "Internet Standard Subnetting Procedure," and RFC 1118, "The Hitchhiker's Guide To The Internet." Second (which I don't recommend), is to accept what I've said at face value and move on.

**Table 3.11  Allocation of workstations and servers per division.**

| Division | Workstations | Servers |
|----------|--------------|---------|
| E&D | 350 PC's | 5 |
| M&S | 150 PC's | 2 |
| Admin | 100 PC's | 2 |

Also, several excellent books that cover IP addressing are available at real space and cyberspace bookstores. Okay, let's attack Part Four.

## A WAN Paradigm

For our example, assume an engineering design company named P&C has about 600 employees. The employees are divided into three divisions: engineering and design (E&D), marketing and sales (M&S), and administration (Admin). Table 3.11 breaks down the number of workstations and servers in each division, and we lay the company out in Figure 3.6.

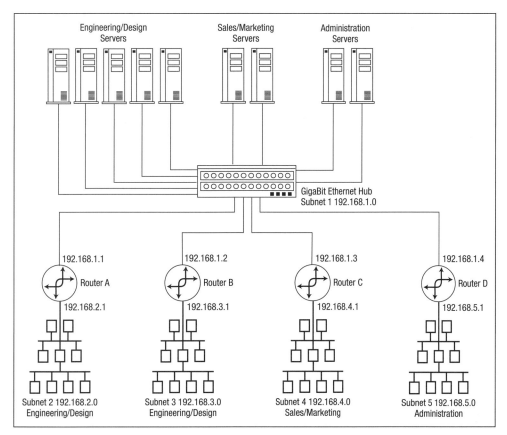

**Figure 3.6**
The P&C company paradigm.

The E&D group uses a sophisticated computer aided drafting (CAD) program, along with high-end math and structural analysis software. M&S relies on a client tracking and presentation package. Admin's work requires an accounting system that includes a work-in-process tracking system. Finally, the company has a connection to the Internet through a T1 digital leased line that is provided by the local PSTN and goes to an ISP located in the same city.

The MIS manager for P&C decided to use TCP/IP for the network system protocol. For the network software you, the reader, can act as consultant and recommend Novell NetWare 5, Microsoft Windows NT, Unix, or Linux. The ISP has assigned five Class C IP addresses and registered them with INTERNIC, along with our domain name. In setting up the network, the boss (P of P&C) placed major emphasis on ease of installation, reliability, and cost and longevity, in that order of priority.

After huddling with the techies for a couple of days sweating over the management requirements, the MIS manager decided to:

♦ Use Ethernet as the transport protocol throughout the network, based on its ease of installation and low cost.

♦ Solve the reliability issue by implementing the network infrastructure as a series of subnetworks, tied together by a backbone system with each server connected directly to the backbone.

♦ Answer the longevity issue with a 100Mbps Ethernet on each subnet and a 1Gbps Ethernet backbone.

After a quick consultation with both P and C, the MIS manager assigned the IP addresses as follows:

♦ *192.168.1.0*—Backbone subnet

♦ *192.168.2.0*—Half of E&D

♦ *192.168.3.0*—Second half of E&D

♦ *192.168.4.0*—M&S

♦ *192.168.5.0*—Admin

The connection to the Internet will be made from the backbone and all connections between subnetworks will be made using hardware routers.

The final layout looks like Figure 3.6. We see the backbone network with the Internet connection made through a CSU/DSU. All the servers are attached to the backbone. The routers each have two connections, one to the backbone and one to its subnetworks.

## What's Wrong With That Picture?

As an example of how to use routers to create an internetwork system, look at Figure 3.6. As a real-life example of an actual installation, it leaves much to be desired. Close inspection will find many faults with this network system, but three things show up right away:

♦ *Too many routers*—This network design requires the use of four routers, one for each subnet and one for the Internet connection. Later on, I'll show you how to combine some of the routers into one physical device.

♦ *No redundancy*—The servers were placed on the backbone in order to allow the highest speed (1Gbps) access. However, if one router fails, it will isolate that subnet from the backbone, preventing access to the server and effectively shutting down that subnet.

♦ *Total waste of valid IP addresses*—This is certainly the biggest problem. We use 5 Class C IP addresses, a total of 1,275 IP addresses, to provide access for only 600 users. This is a little less that 50 percent of the total IP address use. Although it is true that the system has plenty of room for future growth, it is also true that not too many ISPs are going to unload five Class C IP addresses willingly.

These are but three problem areas that need to be addressed in our Figure 3.6 model. As I said earlier, closer inspection will uncover more. Keep in mind that although this design was done to demonstrate using routers to create an internetwork system, it is still not good practice to leave this design with obvious faults.

There ought to be a better way—and there is. Read on.

## Brouters And Switches

So far, we know bridges connect two segments of the same network together at the physical and data link layers of the OSI model. They do their job by learning physical, or MAC layer, addresses for each device connected to either side of the bridge. Bridges are concerned with only physical or MAC addresses and cannot identify a logical network. As such, both of the segments must be a part of the same logical network and have the same network number or address. Because of that, bridges can divide an overloaded network into smaller logical segments to reduce the overall network load.

We know that routers connect two or more networks together to form an internetwork or—depending on your viewpoint—intranetwork. Routers do for network addresses what bridges do for physical addresses. If your router uses the link state instead of the distance vector routing protocol, it performs its task in much the same manner as bridges.

In Figure 3.6 the network infrastructure comprises several subnets connected by routers. The system uses a handful of protocols, including: TCP/IP, IPX/SPX, and NETBEUI. Because IPX/SPX and TCP/IP are routable protocols, data packets used to transport information with them will pass through the routers with no problems. However, NETBEUI is not a routable protocol, and its data packets will be hung up at the routers.

To fix this problem, hardware manufacturers developed a combination bridge and router, a *brouter*, if you will. Brouters can be used to connect logical networks together using routable protocols such as TCP/IP. In the event of a non-routable protocol, the *brouter* acts as a bridge, learning MAC layer addresses on either side, and passing non-routable protocols, such as NETBEUI, across.

This may seem a strange implementation, but it is quite common. Brouters, when used as routers, can network addresses throughout the internetwork, and forward traffic as needed. When the brouter is used as a bridge, it passes data packets across as long as the physical MAC address is known to be on the other side. Just like the bridges we studied earlier, if the physical MAC address is not directly on the other side of the bridge, the brouter cannot identify the destination and will not allow the data packet across. That means brouters can be used only on directly adjacent segments of the network.

## Switches Revisited

If you will recall, a switch can be thought of as a device that provides the same capabilities as a hub or concentrator, but at the same time has the ability to segment the network into smaller sections through bridging.

If the functions of a bridge and a router can be combined to produce a *brouter*, how about making a *swouter* by adding the functions of a router to a switch? Except for the name, the design engineers make the combination. The result is actually known as a *layer-3 switch*. The term comes from the OSI model where routing functions are performed on layer-3, the network layer.

What about the layer-4 switch? Where does that term come from? Hang on, let's take one step at a time.

Layer-3 switches combine high-speed switching and bridging functionality of a switch with the ability to learn routes through an internetwork system as routers do. This is one of the newest developments available on today's market and provides reliable high-speed connections between different subnetworks within an internetwork structure. Layer-3 switches maintain the equivalent of a router table in memory. The switch's router table is acquired in the same way that traditional routers develop their tables. When a layer-3 switch is implemented using link state routing protocol, it is amazingly efficient and highly versatile.

By using layer-3 switches instead of routers, the MIS manager can redesign the previous network to look like Figure 3.7. The new design replaces the backbone routers with a layer-3 switch, thus collapsing the backbone down into the switch. The switch now takes care of routing between each of the subnets and the servers. Internally the switch performs at the speed of the interface it is using at the time, so no appreciable loss of speed occurs. Notice also that we have now readdressed the IP address of the servers to the network address of the group they are serving. This eliminates the Class C IP address that was assigned exclusively to the backbone. Just like a bridge, the switch can logically pass data packets through to the proper subnet and at the same time implement router functions to pass data packets from other subnets to the appropriate server.

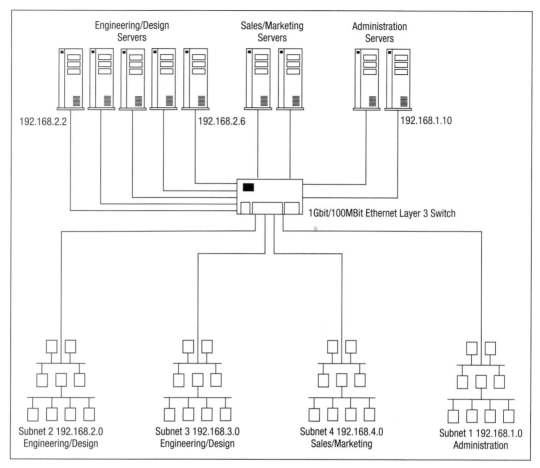

**Figure 3.7**
A more practical WAN model for the P&C company.

Layer-3 switches are a huge improvement in the arena of speed and versatility in subnetworks. Today's cost is the only real drawback with the layer-3 switch. Like all other items of hardware, the cost will come down when the demand decreases or competition heats up. Then we will see a lot more layer-3 switches in use.

## Layer 4 Switches; Virtual LANs And QOS

If layer-3 switches are so good, what more can we do? Well hang on, you ain't seen nothin' yet! In discussing some of the protocols and their features, I mentioned two terms that you may or may not be familiar with: *quality of service* (QOS), and *virtual LAN*.

I deferred in-depth explanation at the time because although I needed to introduce the subjects, I didn't want cloud the issue with a long treatise. Now that you have a fundamental understanding of routing and bridging functions and how they are implemented in switches, it's time for more detail.

### Virtual LANs

With the advent of layer-3 switches, one switch can handle the functions of passing data packets to a network segment, regardless of whether it is bridged or routed. If you replace all the network hubs with layer-3 switches, it is possible for the switches to learn the physical MAC address of devices connected to the switch, all the way down to a single machine connected to a single port. Keep in mind that all the hubs and concentrators in the network must be replaced with layer-3 switches—all the way down to individual items of equipment located on the desktop.

Once we know the MAC address of all the equipment, it is possible, using routing technology available today, to assign a specific user to a specific item of equipment. After that, we can group users into logical subnetworks, or *virtual LANs*, with each group of users assigned a different subnet. The physical location of the user's equipment within the network structure does not matter because the layer-3 switch will take care of routing the data packets to the appropriate port on the appropriate switch, all the way to the desktop. You can see this scheme in Figure 3.8.

This has the dual benefits of more efficient network addressing and bandwidth. A side benefit is the ability to provide each user a guaranteed level of service.

### Quality Of Service, Layer-4 Switching

The term *quality of service* describes a network connection that provides the user *guaranteed bandwidth*. Here is one example. By today's standards, to stream full motion video at a reason-able quality of resolution requires a bandwidth of 20Mbps. This is, actually, down from 68Mbps five years ago and, if you get the bandwidth up to 100Mbps, the resolution becomes fantastic.

In most current network structures, streaming full motion video is out. Why? Because most networks today cannot guarantee 20Mbps bandwidth to a single user—unless, of course, that user is the only user on the network.

Layer-4 switches allocate higher bandwidth to some ports and lower bandwidth to others. This requires implementing a newer protocol, such as ATM or Cisco's DAT. As you will recall, these protocols selectively guarantee a channel's bandwidth. This capability is implemented at the transport layer of the OSI model, or layer-4, which gives the switch its name. This ability is referred to in the industry today as QOS.

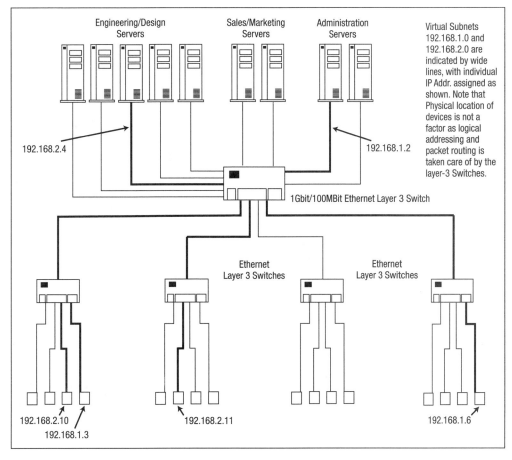

**Figure 3.8**
Schematic diagram of a routing and switching example.

Combining the virtual LAN functions of layer-3 switches with the QOS capability of layer-4 switches assures users the ability to perform the tasks required for their job.

Could anything be better? Yep.

## The Next Step, Directory Services

The only drawback to the system design at this point is that the virtual LAN and QOS are tied to individual workstations on desktops. However, this will not always be the case. By using the transport layer, layer-4, to define the QOS, it is possible to use an identifier or *label* to identify the quality of service required by an individual user.

With a *directory service*, like Novell's NDS, available to the network administrator, the properties assigned to each user can be extended to include the user's QOS label. What if layer-3 and layer-4 switches were designed to support directory service features?

At Novell's spring, 1999, Brainshare Conference in Salt Lake City, Utah, I watched a demonstration of Novell NetWare 5, Novell NDS V8, and layer-3/layer-4 switches from Nortel.

Here's the way they work: When the user logs in to the network from any machine at any location within the internetwork system, the directory service assigns the QOS label to all ports connected between the user's machine and the network servers that provide the resources the user needs. In short, the switches will create a *virtual channel* connecting the user to the resources needed, and implementing a guaranteed QOS. When the user logs out of the network, the virtual channel will be torn down, and the network will await the next login sequence for that user.

In the demonstration, the Nortel switches used Novell NDS features and performed exactly as I have described. Cisco said its new products will support Novell's NDS—as well as Microsoft's Active Directory—in a similar manner. This will eventually extend QOS capability to the Internet. The ability to create a virtual channel and implement a guaranteed QOS is a major step towards establishing a reliable VPN capability.

## Network Routers: Some Final Thoughts

I couldn't help making a few last comments about routers and router technology. By nature, I am a conservative person who likes to look at things from different points of view before deciding on the actual value. That's what this closing section on network routing is all about. (If you want, feel free to skip over it.)

Like the difference between gateways and routers, some questions arise about the use of *software routers* (network operating systems running on standard computers and performing routing functions) versus *hardware routers* (dedicated hardware devices running specific programs that only do routing). Technically speaking, the difference could be said to be one of semantics. Routing is a process that is performed by a program that runs on a computer.

The program can be separate from the computer, such as a program located on a CD-ROM disk. When loaded on a computer designed to perform a multitude of tasks, the program will implement routing as one of these processes. An example would be a Novell NetWare server that has more than one NIC installed. Each NIC would connect to a separate network cable segment, and the server could be configured to route data packets between the two network segments. In this case, the router would be considered a *software router*.

On the other hand, the program can be encoded in ROM, and run on a computer enhanced to perform only routing operations. Because the hardware is to be used for only one purpose, it can be enhanced and the architecture of the system can be designed with every possible performance advantage included. Although the purist will argue the difference between the two systems as being only one of semantics, the realist will notice significant difference in performance between the two.

I mention this because the network industry is very competitive, with companies always trying to figure out ways to improve their products, and convince you that their product is better than the competition's. For example, a representative from one company tells you about dedicated hardware routers that act as gateways and routers on the Internet. Another company representative speaks glowingly about using Windows NT to perform the same process.

Which is better? The answer to that depends on what you need. You don't need a $5,000 to $15,000 Cisco router to connect an office network with 10 users to an ISDN Internet connection. On the other hand, $2,500 worth of Pentium II with 128Meg of RAM won't hack it in a system connecting a network of 3,000 users to a T3 Internet pipe.

One final thought, then we move on. We started out with simple routers and software routers that can easily fill most of the functions in that arena. We ended up with layer-3 and layer-4 switches that can implement virtual channels and quality of service to individual ports. Obviously, the ability to perform the latter functions is entirely in the domain of the hardware router. I doubt if any NOS developers will ever try to duplicate the capabilities of a layer-3 or layer-4 switch in pure software.

# Remote Access For Users

Another important feature of WAN technology is allowing remote users to access the network through dial-in modem connections. *Remote access* is commonly implemented through one or more modems installed in *modem banks*. This type of connection differs from a WAN link that uses a digital leased line such as a T1 or 56K leased line (see Figure 3.9). Typically, remote access users gain access through the PSTN voice lines, which are analog in nature. Because of this difference, a different set of protocols is employed for remote access.

The majority of dial-in users on WANs remotely initiate a connection to the network through the use of a serial connection to either a router or a computer equipped to establish dial-in access. The most common interface in both cases is the IEEE standard RS-232C interface for serial communications. This standard has been around for many years, and is considered mature and robust. Although the RS-232 standard is used in the majority of operations, it does suffer speed restrictions. If a higher-speed serial line interface is required, the user must use the IEEE RS-422 interface. This higher-speed serial interface is not used often for modem connections.

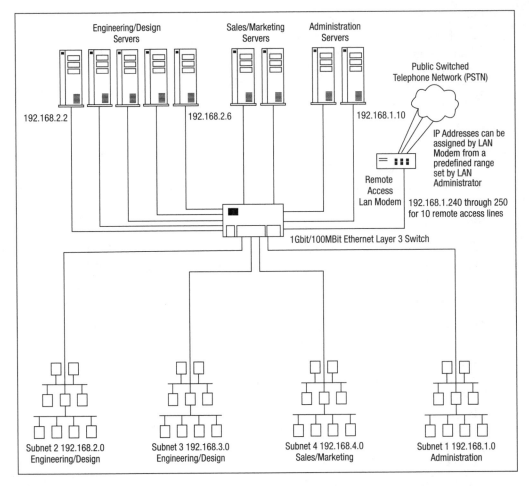

**Figure 3.9**
Remote access.

Several protocols are imbedded in the TCP/IP protocol suite and are available for remote user access. Two of the most common are:

♦ Serial Line Internet Protocol (SLIP)

♦ Point to Point Protocol (PPP)

Although both are common protocols and can pass TCP/IP packets to remote users via a modem connection, significant differences exist between them.

## SLIP

When using SLIP, you must know the IP address assigned to you by the network administrator, and the IP address of the remote system you will be dialing in to. When the connection is being made to a modem bank or dial-in access router, this may not be a problem. However, if your installation uses *Dynamic Host Configuration Protocol* (DHCP) to assign IP addresses to remote users, SLIP won't work. Another shortcoming of SLIP is its inability to handle multiple services or threads concurrently. This SLIP weakness shows up when using services like the World Wide Web, which performs much better if multiple threads can be created.

## PPP

SLIP protocol has been around for a number of years and has provided reliable, though limited, service. Over the past few years SLIP has gradually been replaced by PPP. PPP is similar to SLIP only in appearance. In functionality it is a much enhanced protocol and makes up for many SLIP shortfalls by supporting many capabilities not available in SLIP. Those capabilities include the following:

♦ *Operation not limited to just TCP/IP*—For example, Microsoft's implementation of PPP supports IPX/SPX, NETBeui, and AppleTalk protocols on the same connection at the same time.

♦ *Support of DHCP*—Allows network administrators to assign IP addresses on an as-needed basis.

♦ *Support for IP header compression*—Allows faster data transmission.

These improved capabilities make PPP a better choice for establishing dial-in connections with remote users.

# Implementations Of WAN Protocols By Selected Software Vendors

Now that we've gone on about hardware, it's time for a discussion about software. In and of itself, a computer is a stupid, even moronic machine. Arthur C. Clarke's (in)famous HAL-2000 took decades of programming and billions of lines of code. Lines of code—software—that's the real brains of a computer. We can't discuss all the code writers, so I choose these major players:

♦ Microsoft

♦ Novell

♦ Unix and Linux

# Microsoft

Microsoft offers a WAN system in their Windows NT Version 4. The product is available in both server and workstation, with the server enhanced to provide a larger, faster file service, better print services, and true multiuser/multitasking capability. Windows NT 4 server makes an ideal platform on which a large number of remote applications can be run. Microsoft is expected to release its new network offering, Windows 2000, in the final quarter of 1999.

While we are waiting for Windows 2000, Microsoft suggests using Windows NT and the TCP/IP protocol suite. NT supports all the standard TCP/IP protocols we have mentioned in this book and includes some proprietary designs to enhance its use as a WAN operating system.

Microsoft's network concept has users with a requirement for similar network services and security joined into logical groups. The groups, identified as domains, are joined together to form internetworks. The concept of domains, when implemented on a large scale using NT, does cause some administration problems. Microsoft hopes to solve the problems with the release of Windows 2000 and its *active directory*.

Active directory will give the network administrator the capability of creating a database of objects, logical and physical, on the network. Having done this, administration of the network through the use of the directory will be much easier.

For the future of WAN connections, Microsoft has been partnering with Cisco to implement Cisco router products into the active directory structure. The network administrator will then be able to manage Cisco routers through the directory tree.

Windows NT does not support the TCP/IP protocol stack natively, because it does not fit well with the Windows interface. That's why Microsoft implemented TCP/IP in their proprietary Winsock protocol stack. Winsock has since become a *de facto* standard, and is supported throughout the industry. By using the Winsock protocol stack, Microsoft NT servers implement the full range of routing functions, including both distance vector and link state. When more than one NIC is installed in a Microsoft NT server and the appropriate protocol is implemented, NT does an admirable job as a software router.

# Novell NetWare

For a number of years, Novell relied on its proprietary IPX/SPX protocol for implementing WAN services. This protocol supports both distance vector and link state in a similar manner as those used in TCP/IP. In this respect, IPX/SPX is a fully routable protocol stack, easily adapted to WANs. In addition, all versions of NetWare, going back to NetWare 3.x, have been capable of implementing support for TCP/IP and are fully capable of routing TCP/IP packets throughout Novell NetWare LANs.

With the release of Intranetware, Novell added a new feature that is of interest—an IPX/IP gateway that performs IPX to IP conversion, keeping track of users' IPX address numbers and using a single IP address to access Internet services. Intranetware is still a viable product used in many networks.

Of special interest to us here is that NetWare servers can create an *IPX tunnel* that allows tunneling IPX protocol packets through an IP network such as the Internet. The IPX packets can be encrypted before tunneling, thereby creating a *Virtual IPX Network* system over the Internet. Does that ring a bell? The concept came in very handy when Novell made the decision to implement VPN into its product family.

### Novell's NDS

When Novell introduced NetWare 4 in 1993, it was the first network operating system to offer a directory service, called *Novell Directory Services* (NDS). Since its introduction, Novell has steadily improved NDS and increased the schema to incorporate more features. By the time this book finds it way to the shelves, Novell will have just released Novell Directory Services, Version 8—NDS V8 for short.

I was introduced to NDS V8 running in beta 3 (final beta) at Novell's 1999 Brainshare Conference. It appears that with its new V8 directory product, Novell has made some truly remarkable accomplishments in WAN management. NDS V8 makes it possible to manage all the network services, including active DHCP, DNS, NIS servers, network print servers, and network file servers, entirely through the directory. With major ISPs as the target, Novell showed off an actual NDS V8 directory tree with more than one *billion* objects running on a Compaq server with NetWare 5. This astounding product could give an ISP such as AT&T Worldnet or GTE Net the capability of managing its entire WAN network from one location anywhere in the world.

Novell has been partnering with some major players in the WAN network area (IBM, Compaq, Dell, Nortel, Bay Networks, and Cisco) to implement NDS capability into its products. Because WANs are very seldom made up of products produced by only one vendor, each of these agreements means that the administrator's job managing a WAN that uses these products will be a little easier.

The importance of directory services has pretty well been established, but we must mention the ability of NDS to create virtual channels based on properties listed for each user. The ability to enlarge the schema, or properties list, of the users to include new tags like the QOS label will eventually allow assignment of virtual channels, and QOS tags to individual users, regardless of their login point.

IPX/SPX has always been fully routable. Earlier versions of NetWare supported routing through proprietary protocols like RIP and Service Advertising Protocol (SAP), based on the distance vector routing protocol. With the introduction of NetWare 4, Novell introduced *NetWare Link State Protocol* (NLSP), modeled after the link state routing protocol. Today these protocols continue to be available in NetWare. A Novell NetWare server equipped with two or more NICs in the same machine and configured appropriately will operate very well as a software router.

In 1998 Novell released NetWare 5, its newest version. NetWare 5 is dramatically different because it is the first Novell NOS in the history of the company to use TCP/IP as its native protocol. That means that Novell is in a position to support all current and future protocols (those under development) for TCP/IP. This move towards open standards and protocols assures that Novell is willing to become a very active player in the Internet structure and has several new products designed to enhance the operation and expand the use of the Internet under development.

One of the nascent products is of particular interest in relation to the subject of this book—Novell's involvement in VPN services. We shall have more to say on that subject.

## Unix, Linux, And TCP/IP

Unix and Linux both use TCP/IP as their native (and often only) protocol suite. They implement the full range of open standards and protocols associated with TCP/IP. What this means in real terms is that when more than one NIC is installed in either a Unix or Linux machine, they are both capable of acting as network routers, using either the distance vector or Link State Protocols as required.

In partnering with companies like Cisco and others, the commercial versions of Unix—for example, SCO Unix—probably have an advantage over Linux. This is because Unix enjoys a much higher proportion of commercial installations, and the Unix kernel is considered more capable of WAN and enterprise routing functions than that of Linux. However, the new Linux kernel was released in mid-1999 and promises to overcome previous shortfalls. Linux is showing a definite push to gather momentum in the enterprise and WAN network area.

Right now, neither Unix nor Linux has a native directory service. That doesn't mean they are left out in the cold when it comes to providing directory service capabilities. Several major vendors, including Netscape, have developed large-scale directories that will run quite well on Unix machines. One version of Linux, from Caldera Systems and SCO Unixware, offers support for Novell NDS.

So, the future for WAN architectures across major platforms looks very bright. However, if we open the window of our network to the Internet, we need to be sure that we can let the fresh air through and keep the bugs out. Especially the stinging bugs.

# Network Security, It's Everyone's Concern

An entire chapter near the end of this book is devoted entirely to security, but we should introduce one or two items up here near the front. Security and convenience are opposite poles and the ultimate security measure (I'll repeat this later) is to pull the power plug out of the wall.

## Security Concerns With Dial-In

The discussion so far relating to remote users has centered around the user dialing in to equipment, either computers with modems attached—or remote access routers with modems attached—and establishing a connection directly to the network. The use of modems, and therefore the use of PSTN services, causes a definite security concern. In an effort to alleviate this problem, two other protocols have been developed, both related to establishing secure connections. These are:

◆ Challenge Handshake Authentication Protocol (CHAP)

◆ Password Authentication Protocol (PAP)

When using CHAP, the node on the network receiving the incoming connection initiates a series of data packets called a *challenge sequence*. The caller then modifies the challenge sequence through an algorithm and sends them back, which becomes the *handshake*. If the handshake is satisfactory, the remote user is considered to have passed the challenge and is authenticated by the network.

PAP uses a different procedure to perform essentially the same function. In PAP, a series of ID/password pairs from the remote user are compared against a list of authorized ID/password pairs. If a match is found, the incoming call is validated and the remote use is allowed.

Both protocols are designed to allow remote user authentication before allowing access to the network. However, the network administrator should keep in mind that any time PSTN or PDN services are used to access the network, they are open to the general public at large. This can lead to dangerous situations, especially on sensitive information networks. It is important in those cases to implement a system of encryption of all data packets sent over the network, especially user names and passwords.

## A Taste Of Virtual Private Networks

In today's information age environment, the majority of remote access users dial in to an ISP and make a PPP connection to the Internet. At the same time, a growing number of businesses have a connection of some type to the Internet from their LAN or WAN.

Would it not be a good idea if the remote users could access the company LAN or WAN directly from the Internet? This, of course, is the idea behind Virtual Private Networks.

However, before you jump off and make your network available for your remote users all over the world, you want to make sure you have taken every possible precaution to keep every *hacker* in the world out. That's what this book, hopefully, is going to help you do.

# What Is Network Security?

If you ask that question to different 15 network administrators, chances are you will get 15 different versions of what makes up network security. My version will, in all probability, be version number 16.

### Security Isn't All About Hackers

Network security involves many different areas, most of which overlap each other. Unfortunately the terms "easy to use" and "secure" are at times mutually exclusive. No such thing exists as a secure network that is easy for the users to use and for the administrator to administer. Nevertheless, most network administrators must implement some level of security, and see that this is maintained to the best degree possible.

Everyone is aware that in some network systems data and information are stored that the company considers private—perhaps they are personnel records, perhaps they are proprietary fabrication methods. If someone wants to gain access to that sensitive information, either for personal gain or malicious intent, this is considered to be a security risk.

Another area that comes under the general umbrella of security is making sure that the data is secure to the point that in the event of catastrophic failure, the data would not be lost. How many network administrators can truthfully say that if a fire wipes out the entire computer room, the data can be restored because the backup tapes are stored in a different location?

### Firewalls

Many companies with an Internet connection are installing *firewalls* at their connection point. Sometimes called *proxy servers*, these devices are expected to provide protection for the network by logically removing the network from the services provided over the Internet.

Firewalls are very effective at what they do. If the data stored in your network system is highly sensitive, then you should have some type of firewall protection in place. As the use of the Internet continues to grow, the dangers present on the Internet will grow in proportion. A good firewall, properly maintained, will help to prevent problems associated with Internet access. The key words in the last sentence are "help to prevent." Firewalls are not the end-all cure for security concerns.

# Chapter 4
# *Development Of VPN Standards*

**Key Topics:**

- *Request for Comments*
- *RFC authorship*
- *VPN defined*
- *Encapsulation and tunneling*
- *Internet security*
- *Cryptokey management*

We spent the last two chapters together organizing a common understanding of the concepts necessary to develop and maintain LANs and WANs. We knowingly left out lots of detail—you can't cover something as complex as computer based networking in two chapters. The goal was to brush up on the commonalties that will let us take a closer look at specific areas defining Virtual Private Networks.

## The Venerable TCP/IP Protocol Suite (Yet Again)

The TCP/IP protocol suite came into existence in the 1970s as a means of defining standards and processes for a packet switched network. If we choose 1975 as a release date for the TCP/IP protocol suite version 0, and assume you purchased this book somewhere around late 1999 or early 2000, then this venerable protocol suite is about 25 years old while you are reading this. That means TCP/IP has probably been around longer than some of our readers.

Now, I stated somewhere earlier in the book that I am, by nature, a conservative person. I don't jump out and buy the latest and greatest whatever just because it is new. But even I know better than to buy something for my computer systems that is 25 years old.

In the computer industry that's not just old, that's downright ancient. Surprisingly, in an industry where 12 to 24 months is the average life time of a product, TCP/IP not only survived, but it actually got stronger as it got older. (My editor won't like clichés, so I must stay away from fine wine similes.) TCP/IP gained so much popularity that it surpassed every other network protocol suite in the world. So, how did TCP/IP survive for 25 years? The answer is in the process that produced TCP/IP and the rest of the Internet standards in the first place. And that process is certainly worth a closer look.

# How Internet Standards Are Developed

We've mentioned Requests for Comments (*RFCs*) several times in the past chapters, leaving a trail of clues but never really saying what they are, why we need them, where they come from, or what you're supposed to do with them. I apologize. That was really unkind of me, because the process of RFCs is what made the TCP/IP protocol suite and the Internet the real powerhouse products that they are. It is, also, that same process that will push the Internet beyond the realm of our imaginations.

## The Process Of RFCs

RFCs are a collection of notes, gathered together in the form of documents and presented to the networking community for review, comment, and suggestions. And, in some cases, they just disseminate information or report on an event.

The process of developing RFCs began in 1969 for the purpose of discussing information relating to the ARPANET. If you stuck with us to this point, you know that the original ARPANET was born as an experiment to link four university computers and grew up to become the Internet.

Today, RFCs number more than 2,500, dating back 30 years, for the purpose of discussing information related to the Internet. Most, but not all, RFCs are written in technical jargon. Some are quite humorous. A few die an ignominious death. Still others take a rather profound look at what this industry is now—and what it hopes to become.

---

### RFC Trivia

♦ The first RFC was created by UCLA and released on April 7, 1969.

♦ More than 2,051 RFCs reside on the active list.

♦ Security is the most popular RFC subject. In one two-month period (February and March 1999), more than 90 RFCs mentioned it.

♦ More than 80 RFCs refer to tunneling. The first one was in March 1997.

♦ The first VPN RFC was #2194, released on September 14, 1997.

♦ As of April 17, 1999, only 10 RFCs directly relate to VPN.

---

### RFC Authorship

A formal process exists for developing and publishing an RFC. Who does the creation? Who does the approving? Are you ready for this? *Anyone* can write an RFC—anyone. However, as you knew there would be, there's a slight catch: You must follow certain rules that we'll discuss shortly.

Although anyone can write an RFC, almost all of them are written by electrical and software engineers in the Internet industry. It is common for an RFC to be co-authored by several people and normal practice for the author(s) to list their employer's company on the RFC documents. The inclusion of a company's name on an RFC is not necessarily an endorsement by the community—nor is taking umbrage with an RFC considered castigation of the company. It does, however, provide a useful tool for contacting the author.

### Genesis

An RFC starts out as an *Internet Draft* (I-D) and must be written to certain standards following a specific format. The information on the standards and format is readily available to the general public in RFC 2223. RFCs can be located in several indices on the Web; my favorite is **www.faqs.org/rfcs/**.

If you have an idea for material to be considered as an RFC, you should send it via email to the RFC Editor will review the I-D to make sure it meets the proper specifications and format; if it does email to **rfc-editor@rfc-editor.org**, it will be distributed and made available for comment.

### Comment Cycle

Who makes the comments? I-Ds are read and commented on by the *Internet Engineering Task Force* (IETF) and its *Internet Engineering Steering Group* (IESG). Over a course of about six months, the IESG will make comments concerning the I-D. As it becomes older, it goes through several steps, until it finally reaches the level at which it is either rejected, merged with a similar I-D in the same area, or approved for adoption as an RFC.

> **Tip**
>
> *Once a document is approved for publication as an RFC, the author is notified and has 48 hours to review the document and make any minor changes or corrections. After that, the document is published as an RFC. For historical reasons, once the document is published as an RFC, it is not changed, ever. I guess you better get it right before it gets to that point.*

As I mentioned, this process began in 1969 and has continued through to this day with only a few changes reflecting different RFC editors. By using this process, the Internet and the Internet Protocol suite (TCP/IP) can be updated with new standards and protocols as they become available. This means that the Internet Protocol suite is not a finished product, but instead is under constant and ongoing new development and change. Looking at it in this light, it could be said that the TCP/IP protocol suite is a *living document* because it hasn't been finished yet.

By this time you might be asking yourself why we waited until this point in the book to discuss the finer details of RFCs. If you think about it, a tremendous amount of information is being made available in the form of RFCs. One of the newest areas that is being developed is *Virtual Private Networking* (VPN). I thought it appropriate that we show how the process works that produces the standards and protocols relating to VPNs, at the same time giving you, the network administrator, some specific VPN terminology related to it.

So, having gone on a short tour of LANs, WANs, and the RFC process, let's jump in the soup and learn to swim.

# Virtual Private Networks—A Definition

As we've done in previous chapters, we will look first at the standards and protocols—in this case those related to defining a VPN. We will rely more on RFCs in this chapter than we have in the past chapters. However, RFCs can get pretty dry, and casual reading of them is not exactly what I would do for fun. So, I'll pick out the meaty parts, and leave the rest for those of you with a deeper interest than the usual network administrator. In the last part of the chapter, we'll dig a little deeper into the security issues related to VPN and the Internet.

Surprisingly enough, the list of stated definitions for the term Virtual Private Network is short. Whereas volumes of rhetoric have been written about the virtues of VPNs and the wonderful possibilities that exist because of VPNs, not too many people have stated a definition.

Most definitions given are overly simplistic. For example, *Novell's Encyclopedia of Networking* defines a VPN as: "A private network implemented over the Internet." I hate to disagree with an otherwise excellent book and author, but to me the terms *private network* and *the Internet* are mutually exclusive. At best this definition is vague, at worst it is an oxymoron. VPN technology is being used in both LAN and WAN configurations without striking out onto the Net.

Other definitions give a more complete, and therefore a (slightly) better definition. An example is given in Douglas Comer's excellent text, *Computer Networks and Internets*, published by Prentice Hall. In this text, Professor Comer states: "A Virtual Private Network combines the advantages of private and public networks by allowing a company with multiple sites to have the **illusion** [author's emphasis] of a completely private network, and to use a public network to carry traffic between sites."

Professor Comer's definition is more complete, but it still leaves the reader with the thought: "How do we create the illusion?"

Because the purpose of this book is to help network administrators implement a VPN, and any definition ought to include all the parts, I am going to throw in my two cents' worth. I define a VPN as a virtual channel that:

♦ Is used to connect two private networks.

♦ Has been made secure, and therefore private, through means of a reliable encryption technology.

♦ Exists as a part of a public network system *like* the Internet.

In my definition you can see the need for the two preceding chapters where we demonstrated the technology required for creating private and public networks. Also in those chapters, especially Chapter 3, we demonstrated the technology required to create *virtual channels* within an existing network system.

Now we will discuss the technology required to put all the pieces together, and answer the question left hanging from Professor Comer's definition, to wit: *How do we create the illusion?*

# Standards Relating To VPN

It is interesting to note that few RFCs relate directly to VPN terminology. In fact, as this book is being written, only 10 RFCs include the term *VPN* as a part of the document. RFC 2194, released on September 14, 1997, is the first that mentions VPN directly. This, more than anything else, shows that VPN terminology is relatively new, even though the technology needed to accomplish it has been around for some time.

How does a *standard* differ from a *protocol?* In the early part of this book I mentioned that standards are conceptual in nature.

## Standards Vs. Protocols

Standards set down specific details that one vendor's product must meet in order to work with another vendor's product. Protocols, on the other hand, define the specifics of implementation; "*this is how we do it…*" type of documents so other technologists are aware of what's going on inside the engine.

In fact, the differences between them are not well defined. One example is Point to Point Tunneling Protocol, or PPTP. Its very name implies it is a protocol, yet many in the industry include PPTP in their list of VPN standards. To avoid the accusation of being argumentative, I will trade technical correctness for rhetoric and refer to the accepted protocols for VPNs as standards.

According to software vendors, the VPN industry uses four standards:

♦ Layer Two Forwarding Protocol (L2F)

♦ Layer Two Tunneling Protocol (L2TP)

- Point to Point Tunneling Protocol (PPTP)
- IP Secure (IPsec)

The group appears to be different—each somehow using a different process to do the same thing. L2F and L2TP look about the same and imply some relationship to the layered model for networks we looked at in earlier chapters. L2TP and PPTP seem to relate through something called *tunneling* (maybe a new buzzword). Finally, it looks like IPsec relates somehow to security.

Go back and reread my definition of a VPN. It may surprise you to learn that, in actual fact, three of the four standards are pretty much the same, at least in concept. IPsec, a new standard for IP, is substantially different from the others. Let's use my VPN definition and inspect the other three more closely, and then we'll deal with IPsec. The first part of the definition is that a VPN is a *virtual channel*. One method of creating a virtual channel is using a process known as *tunneling*, so let's deal with it first.

## Tunneling Through Cyberspace

The process of *tunneling*, as it relates to packet switched data networks, has an interesting history. The initial use of tunneling had quite a lot to do with making the Internet work, but very little to do with VPNs. The concept was first proposed in RFC 791 back in September 1981, as a method of encapsulating *Multicast* data packets for transmission to specific routers within the Internet. Research indicates the term tunneling was not defined until November 1988 when RFC 1075 was published. This RFC further defined and detailed a process that has become known as *encapsulation* (more about this later).

> **Tip**
>
> *All datagrams are broadcast to all entities on a cable segment because they are all connected in parallel. In a multicast datagram the IP address is all ones, so all the entities accept the datagram. In a unicast datagram the host bits are set to the IP address of the intended receiver and only that receiver will accept it; all the others drop it in the bit bucket.*

Follow-on RFCs detailed more enhancements of the tunneling process to pass data packets from different protocol stacks through an IP network. Such was the case in June 1991 when RFC 1234, written by Don Provan of Novell, was published, detailing a protocol for tunneling IPX data packets through an IP network. This technique was developed independently by Schneider and Koch (S&K) and by Novell, but Novell gets credit for the RFC.

In July 1991, RFC 1241, *A Scheme for an Internet Encapsulation Protocol: Version 1*, was published. This is historically significant because, prior to this RFC, no standard protocol for tunneling had existed. The RFC details were adopted by the industry and became Version 1 of the tunneling protocol. In a short time, the tunneling process became a standard protocol.

We're going to skip down a couple of hundred RFCs to RFC 1504. This notable document was published in August 1993, and detailed how the tunneling protocol could be enhanced to transport AppleTalk data packets through an IP internetwork. This RFC is particularly noteworthy because not only did it detail how to tunnel AppleTalk data packets through the Internet, it was the first document that mentioned creating *point-to-point* tunnels, a subject that is very important to VPN.

### VPN Is Born

Every now and then, a significant milestone occurs in an endeavor not because the persons involved knew what they were creating, but more because they simply needed to solve a problem and used the best tools at hand. That happened during the period from October of 1994, to the same month in 1995. Watch closely or you'll miss the significance.

In October 1994, RFC 1700 was published with the unassuming title: *Assigned Numbers, STD 2*. The authors defined a method of tunneling which they called *The IP in IP Encapsulation Protocol/Payload Number 4*. That same month, RFC 1701 was born as *Generic Routing Encapsulation* (GRE) and further defined the processes RFC 1700.

Then, almost exactly a year and 150 RFCs later, number 1853, *IP in IP Tunneling*, was published as an Informational RFC by William Simpson, with the intention of keeping the Internet community informed of (then) current uses of existing technologies. It detailed activities used by a group called the Packet Radio Relay League (PRRL) for transmitting data packets across radio relay links using existing methods from RFCs 1700 and 1701.

Prior to all this buzz, the data were being transmitted over an open media called *radio relay* and were thus subject to eavesdropping by anyone with the proper receiving equipment. To protect the information, the PRRL people decided to use an *encryption algorithm* on the packets as they were being transmitted.

So what was the big deal? What does that have to do with VPNs? Simply, this is the first detailed description I can find of the combination of tunneling (to create a virtual channel) and encryption (to make the data secure). In other words, it's the earliest documented account of a true VPN.

Many RFCs helped define the protocols and establish the standards used in implementing that VPN. The Internet community developed the technology and protocols over a long period of time and, in most cases, the goal was to solve problems basic to the operation of the communications system—not create VPN. As I mentioned earlier, the first published RFC that uses the term VPN was published in September 1997, almost two years after Simpson wrote RFC 1853. So far, VPN has gone through a long gestation period, but this is almost always the way it is when you live on the leading edge.

## Shoring Up The Tunnels

Since number 1853, more than 700 RFCs have been published, most of them building on an earlier document, with a few pointing the way to new and exciting innovations. Remember the canons of the system; once an RFC is published, it is not changed. A new implementation of an existing protocol requires a new RFC—no matter how small the change.

With the increased interest engendered by VPN, a corresponding increase in tunneling technology has occurred. Since March 1997, more than 80 RFCs make reference to tunneling in one way or another, but not all have a direct bearing on the tunneling protocol. Table 4.1 is a list of the more significant tunneling references. Appendix B contains these and several more RFCs, along with their abstracts. If you care to read the text, use the search engine at **www. faqs.org/rfcs** for the applicable number.

# Tunneling, Part Deux

Earlier in this chapter, we went to a great deal of trouble to follow the trail that led to the development of VPNs. A key part is the creation of virtual channels through the Internet. Network administrators create virtual channels through a process called *tunneling*. We did not, however, provide much detail about what tunneling is, or how it is implemented. Let's go there now for a closer look—for the light at the end.

**Table 4.1   Requests for Comments involving VPN tunneling protocols.**

| RFC# | Title |
| --- | --- |
| 1075 | *Distance Vector Multicast Routing Protocol* |
| 1234 | *Tunneling IPX Traffic Through IP Networks* |
| 1241 | *Scheme For An Internet Encapsulation Protocol: Version 1* |
| 1504 | *AppleTalk Update-Based Routing Protocol: Enhanced AppleTalk Routing* |
| 1853 | *IP In IP Tunneling* |
| 2002 | *IP Mobility Support* |
| 2003 | *IP Encapsulation Within IP* |
| 2004 | *Minimal Encapsulation Within IP* |
| 2005 | *Applicability Statement For IP Mobility Support* |
| 2194 | *Review Of Roaming Implementations* |
| 2341 | *Cisco Layer Two Forwarding (Protocol) "L2F"* |
| 2344 | *Reverse Tunneling For Mobile IP* |
| 2356 | *Sun's Skip Firewall Traversal For Mobile IP* |
| 2473 | *Generic Packet Tunneling In IPv6 Specification* |

## A Reminder

Before we jump to the next section, I want to make a few comments about how RFCs affect the system administrator. I may have convinced some of you to run out and buy a high speed laser printer and ten reams of paper so you can print out all the RFCs and take a year or two to try and figure out what's important on your own. I certainly hope not.

You purchased this book so I could do the grunt work for you. Does that mean system administrators never need to read an RFC? Maybe, maybe not. Occasions may arise when you just can't seem to get a straight answer to an important question. If that happens, remember that anyone can access the entire RFC library. They are not classified, and no *secret documents* hide within the list. Instructions on how to find and download any RFC are in Appendix B.

Most technically competent system administrators can understand an RFC. There's no magic in them, but you will find new terminology. Most people (with the exception of the true geek) will find them to be quite boring. Jump in and get your feet wet.

I will add a caution—sometimes finding the answer to your questions is like navigating the bayous of a Cajun swamp. Except for the root documents, almost all RFCs refer to previous RFCs. You will find (as I did) that a search for one simple answer often requires that you page through parts of as many as five to ten RFCs. To help you avoid the 'gators, I also included a few search tips in Appendix B.

# Where Does Tunneling Start?

Tunneling is accomplished through a process known as *encapsulation*. To better understand it, we need to take a closer look at the structure of the data packets used in the IP protocol. At this level, the data packets are more commonly referred to as *datagrams*. In the TCP/IP suite, the transport layer protocol is the *User Datagram Protocol* (UDP) and the data packets are referred to as *user datagrams* made up of groups of bits called *octets*. If you remember back to the discussion of IP addressing, you will recall that an octet is 8 bits. Figure 4.1 is the way I visualize a UDP datagram.

## RFC 1075

Now that we understand a little more about the terminology used, lets take a look at the development of the tunneling (that is, encapsulation) process. Early tunnels were developed as a means of transporting multicast datagrams through an IP internetwork. Multicast

**Figure 4.1**
User datagram packet structure.

datagrams are special packets of information delivered to several entities within a group or subnet address. They are not normally passed through routers to networks outside of the originating, or source, computer.

### Transmission Problem

A problem occurred in which computers (or entities) in different subnetworks, or different networks within a larger internetwork, needed to receive the same multicast datagrams. Because some routers would not forward the multicast datagrams, they could not reach their destination reliably.

To overcome this problem, a method was developed known as "...a weakly encapsulated normal multicasted datagram." What that mouth full of words, quoted from RFC 1075, means, is the complete multicast datagram consisting of headers, checksum, and payload is converted (encapsulated) into a *source route IP datagram*. The source route IP datagram has a different header structure, and can accommodate the complete multicast datagram without losing the proper bit alignment. Once encapsulation has taken place, the IP addresses of the final destination and source routers are inserted into the datagram header.

**Tip**

*Keep in mind that if the proper bit alignment is not maintained, the router will fail to recognize the incoming data as meaningful and, instead of forwarding it through the Internet, will simply drop it in the bit bucket.*

The datagram is then transmitted using the algorithms applicable to the IP protocol being used and is forwarded by each router along the way until it gets to the final destination router. Each router the datagram goes through can now forward the datagram because the destination in the header is the IP address of the destination router instead of a multicast destination IP address.

When the packet arrives at the final destination, it is *decapsulated*; the source route header is removed and the IP address is replaced with the original multicast IP address. The datagram is then delivered to the proper host(s) in the destination network.

Keep in mind three main points:

1. Because encapsulation and decapsulation take place at the *routers*, the originating and receiving hosts are not aware of the tunnel's existence.
2. The process requires that the routers doing the encapsulation and decapsulation are aware of the tunnel and the address of the final destination router. This requires some maintenance by the administrator, and a special algorithm for encapsulation and decapsulation. In other words, it requires a special *tunneling router*. When this process was first published as an RFC, no standard for datagram encapsulation existed. This was a work-around that was developed as a solution to an existing problem. In fact, the authors of RFC 1075 said, "We consider tunnels to be a transitional hack."

3. Finally, although this method works in most cases, it requires the originating router to be aware of the makeup of the networks between the source and destination. This is not very feasible if we are going to use the modern Internet as a place to create our VPN tunnels.

### RFC 1241

The importance of Internet standards cannot be overemphasized. Without them, communicating on the Internet would be like a planet-wide Tower of Babel. Bearing the imposing title *A Scheme For An Internet Encapsulation Protocol: Version I*, RFC 1241 defines, according to its authors, "...an Experimental Protocol for the Internet Community."

In the early days of tunneling, no standard existed and creating tunnels depended on *hacking* the existing protocols to accomplish the desired results. Although this approach was doable, it did not work in all cases, and reliability suffered as a result. RFC 1241, the standard for encapsulation protocol, would resolve many of these issues.

The first step in resolving the problem was a complete study of the problem culminating in several proposed solutions. The best solution, according to the Internet engineering gurus, was to develop a standard encapsulation protocol.

The next step was the design of an architecture to accomplish the desired operation that would operate within the existing internetwork structure. To allow maximum compatibility with existing equipment, the new encapsulation protocol would have to use the existing IP header format. Using this format, the source router would not be required to know any specific information about the networks between it and the destination router.

Developing the architecture required adding new terminology, or at least new definitions, to geek-speak. The jargon uses about sixteen new terms defined in RFCs, but for our purposes we need only look at six:

♦ *Encapsulator*—"...the entity responsible for mapping a given user space datagram to the encapsulation space, encapsulating the datagram, and forwarding the encapsulated datagram to a decapsulator."

♦ *Decapsulator*—"...the entity responsible for receiving an encapsulated datagram, decapsulating it, and delivering it to the destination user space."

♦ *User space*—"...the address and routing space within which the users reside."

♦ *Encapsulation space*—"...the address and routing space within which the encapsulators and decapsulators reside."

♦ *Clear datagram*—"...the unmodified IP datagram in the user space before encapsulation."

♦ *Encapsulated datagram*—"...the datagram consisting of a clear datagram prepended[sic] with an encapsulation header."

*Encapsulators and decapsulators can be either gateways or routers, and the function can be combined with its counterpart in the same physical machine, although it exists as a separate entity in the internetwork.*

A diagram of the architectural model for the encapsulation standard is shown in Figure 4.2.

### How Does It Work?

Encapsulators and decapsulators have IP addresses in the user and encapsulation spaces to which they belong. An entity with an IP address in the same user space as the encapsulator transmits a clear datagram into the user space. The clear datagram looks like the user datagram in Figure 4.1. This clear datagram is received by the encapsulator that makes the determination (based on the destination IP address) that encapsulation should take place. When the decision is made that encapsulation is necessary, the encapsulator uses an algorithm to create an encapsulation header, appended to the front of the clear datagram. When this operation is completed, the clear datagram becomes an encapsulated datagram. An example of an encapsulated datagram is shown in Figure 4.3.

The encapsulator forwards the datagram to a decapsulator, the IP address of which is determined by the same algorithm that is used to create the encapsulation header. The generation of the encapsulation header is rather complex, and a description of the bit patterns and

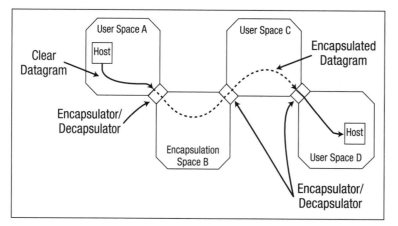

**Figure 4.2.**
RFC 1241 encapsulation architecture.

| Encapulating IP Header (32 bits) | Encapulation Protocol Header (32 bits) | IP Header Fields (96 bits) | Source IP Addr (32 bits) | Dest. IP Addr (32 bits) | IP Options (32 bits) | Data (up to 64K Octets) |
|---|---|---|---|---|---|---|
| | | | | | | |

**Figure 4.3**
Encapsulated datagram packet structure.

definitions for the bit patterns would serve no useful purpose here. If you just have to know all about it, chase down a copy of RFC 1241 and go for it.

When the encapsulated datagram reaches the decapsulator, the process is applied in reverse: The encapsulation header is converted back to a clear header, and the datagram is delivered to the destination.

If you followed the process to this point, you may have noticed the following small points:

♦ The source and destination entities are not aware of the existence of any tunneling.

♦ Using this process requires that two new entities, the encapsulator and the decapsulator, exist at the two endpoints of the tunnel (or virtual channel). This is a very important fact, as we shall soon see.

♦ The encapsulator and decapsulator must be aware of each other, but need not know any specific details about the networks in between (remember, the encapsulation header uses the standard IP header format).

## The Tunneling Process, Part III (Later RFCs)

Of course, progress on tunneling did not stop with RFC 1241. Research continued and, following tradition, more than 80 tunnel-related RFCs have been published since then. As VPN matures, new terms are coined and new RFCs are published defining them. Two recently evolved terms are *Mobile User* and *Roaming User*. The age of the mobile user arrived with the development of true laptop computers, not just notebooks. It was natural for enterprises to want to extend the corporate intranet to the mobile user, and the term *VPN* was used more and more.

### Mobile Users

A *mobile user* can be loosely defined as a user that moves from one physical location to another but requires the use of the same IP address in all locations. Mobile users produce an entirely new set of problems, some of which we will address in another chapter of this book.

When the mobile user wants to have only one specific ISP, their *Home ISP*, perhaps for billing purposes, the mobile user evolves into a roaming user and creates yet another set of inter-ISP-related problems concerning location, tracking, and billing. To resolve these issues, several RFCs have been published. Among these are the following:

♦ RFC 2002—*IP Mobility Support*

♦ RFC 2003—*IP Encapsulation within IP*

♦ RFC 2004—*Minimal Encapsulation within IP*

♦ RFC 2005—*Applicability Statement for IP Mobility Support*

♦ RFC 2194—*Review of Roaming Implementations*

♦ RFC 2356—*Sun's SKIP Firewall Traversal for Mobile IP*

### *The ISP Enterprise*

A new enterprise consists of ISPs offering turnkey VPN services to their customers. That led to publication of RFC 2341 for Cisco's L2F Protocol. In fact, Cisco has written RFCs that cover two of the protocols (or *standards*) used in VPNs: L2F and L2TP. Both of these RFCs use existing tunneling protocols as we have described, but move the implementation process to the ISP instead of the corporate intranet.

The list goes on and on. Yet in all the implementations proposed to date, the primary method of reliable datagram delivery remains encapsulation based on the foundation developed in RFCs 1075 and 1241. The fundamental process used in encapsulation has not changed since, except for the size of the headers and the information in them.

# A Look At The Development Of Two VPN Protocols—PPTP And L2F/L2TP

All existing implementations of VPNs rely on tunneling. In RFC 2194, the authors state "...*via a Virtual Private Network (VPN), enabled by tunneling protocols such as PPTP, L2F, or L2TP.*" This further demonstrates how closely related each of these protocols are to each other and recognizes that they are, in fact, the means of creating tunnels through Internet cyberspace.

## Point-To-Point Tunneling Protocol

The *Point-to-Point Tunneling Protocol* (PPTP) is an extension of the *Point-to-Point Protocol* (PPP) protocol. Whereas an RFC specifically defining PPTP does not exist, an IETF Draft titled "Point-to-Point Tunneling Protocol" is in the works (draft-ietf-pppext-pptp-10.txt). The draft went to the IETF in June 1996 from a consortium of companies known as the PPTP Forum. The forum includes Microsoft, Ascend Communications, 3Com/Primary Access, ECI Telematics, and US Robotics. To understand the basics of PPTP we must go back and take a closer look at the PPP Protocol.

### *First, PPP*

RFC 1171 and its associated configuration document, RFC 1172, were published in July 1990. RFC 1171 states that the PPP is a product of the Point-to-Point Protocol Working Group of the Internet Engineering Task Force (IETF) and that PPP was developed because of the large growth in the number of hosts supporting TCP/IP. As it turned out, very few hosts were connected using point-to-point (that is, serial) links. Several reasons were given for this lack of point-to-point TCP/IP host connections, but the primary reason seemed to be the lack of a standard encapsulation protocol.

The PPP resolved this and several other issues by providing a standard method for transmitting IP datagrams over serial point-to-point links. In doing this, PPP operations are provided by three functions. These are as follows:

- A method for *Encapsulating IP Datagrams* over serial links.

- An extensible *Link Control Protocol* (LCP).

- A family of *Network Control Protocols* (NCP) for establishing and configuring different network-layer protocols.

RFC 1172 defines the PPP configuration parameters. Of interest here is the *Password Authentication Protocol* (PAP). According to RFC 1172, PAP is used to authenticate a peer by verifying the identity of the remote end of the link. PAP is intended for use primarily by hosts and routers connected through switched circuits or dial-up lines to a PPP network server. The PPP network server is sometimes called a *Remote Access Server* (RAS). Interestingly, RFC 1172 states clearly that PAP is *not* a strong authentication method. Passwords pass over the circuit in clear text without protection from repeated trial and error attacks.

### A Quick Brush Past Security

Neither RFC 1171 nor RFC 1172 mention encryption. That means PPP and PAP do not apply any encryption algorithm to the data or the headers. To shore up the weakness, a new authentication protocol was developed and published in RFC 1994, in August 1996. Titled *PPP Challenge Handshake Authentication Protocol (CHAP)*, RFC 1994 does not redefine the PPP protocol. In fact, it relies heavily on PPP to handle housekeeping chores such as establishing the connection and encapsulating the datagrams. What RFC 1994 does define is a method for *authentication* when using PPP.

CHAP periodically verifies the peer's identity using a process the RFC refers to as a *3-way handshake*. According to the RFC, the authentication process is performed upon initial link establishment and repeated whenever necessary. The process is as follows:

1. After the link establishment phase is complete, the authenticator sends a *challenge* message to the peer.

2. The peer responds with a value calculated using a *one-way hash* function.

3. The authenticator checks the response against its own calculation of the expected hash value. If it matches, the process continues. If not, no connection is established.

4. At random intervals, the authenticator sends a new challenge to the peer and the process jumps to Step 2.

At this point the authentication method depends upon a *secret* known only to the authenticator and a particular peer. We will see where this is implemented in a surprising manner directly. Also, since CHAP may be used to authenticate many different systems, name fields may be used as an index to locate the proper secret in a large table of secrets. We will also see how this is used in a different protocol. And finally, although this RFC does not specifically state which hashing algorithm should be used, it does mention MD5.

## Generic Routing Encapsulation Protocol

We've taken a good look at the encapsulation process but only from the standpoint of *generally* how it works but not *specifically* how it works. Let's dip into that cauldron and see what's brewing.

### RFC 1701

Unfortunately for the software engineer, the *specifically* part is downright complex. Each different protocol and each different frame type adds to the level of complexity. Striving to simplify the procedure, a Network Working Group put together RFC 1701 defining the *Generic Routing Encapsulation Protocol* (GRE) in an attempt to provide a simple, general-purpose mechanism which reduces the problem of encapsulation. The RFC states that GRE protocols may not be applicable to all situations. But they will work in many cases, and one is the implementation of (drum roll and fanfare, please maestro) PPTP.

## Finally, PPTP Defined

You might say that, in the process of getting to this point, we covered so much along the way that there's not too much left; well, almost. By now you should have a little understanding of PPP, PAP, CHAP, and GRE. Don't you just love acronyms. These four protocols form the foundation for PPTP.

You can download a Microsoft PPTP definition white paper at **www.microsoft.com/ NTServer/commserv/techdetails/prodarch/understanding_pptp.asp**. The document says PPTP architecture uses three processes:

1. PPP connection and communication.

2. PPTP control connection that establishes a connection to a PPTP server on the Internet, and creates a virtual tunnel.

3. PPTP data tunneling, in which the PPTP protocol creates IP datagrams containing encrypted PPP packets which are then sent through the PPTP tunnel.

The second and third are dependent on successful completion of each previous process. If any one fails, the entire process must be repeated.

The Microsoft white paper makes the following points.

♦ Initial dial-in authentication may be required by an ISP, and if so it is not related to Windows NT–based authentication.

♦ Having a secure password model in place is critical to successful deployment of PPTP.

For data encryption, PPTP uses the RAS *shared-secret* encryption process deriving an encryption key from the hashed password stored on the client and server. The RSA RC4 standard creates this 40-bit session key based on the client password. Remember, we said earlier that CHAP authentication depends upon the existence of a shared-secret known only to the authenticator and its peer. Microsoft's *MS-CHAP* uses the password as the shared-secret, and bases the entire encryption algorithm on that password.

Some inconsistencies appear in the Microsoft document; most are minor, but one jumped out very quickly. Microsoft states that in the PPTP protocol the data is encrypted using the methods found in the PPP protocol. We can find nothing that states that PPP uses *any* encryption. This is probably an oversight by Microsoft. However, if you study the white paper you may also puzzle over it.

# RADIUS

All the protocols mentioned so far will provide good service when the number of users is small; however, some corporations have thousands of remote users. To allow access by these large numbers of users, RFC 2058 defines a protocol named *Remote Authentication Dial In User Service* (RADIUS). In the strictest terms, RADIUS is a remote access protocol, not a VPN protocol. The two are very closely related, and as we shall see in Chapter 5, some vendors use RADIUS features in their VPN implementations.

### *RFC 2058*

RFC 2058 describes RADIUS as a protocol "for carrying authentication, authorization, and configuration information between a *Network Access Server* (NAS) which desires to authenticate its links and a shared *Authentication Server*." The following are particularly important points about RADIUS:

♦ The Network Access Server operates as a client of RADIUS.

♦ RADIUS servers are responsible for receiving user connection requests, authenticating the user, and then returning the necessary information for the client to deliver service to the user.

♦ A RADIUS server can act as a proxy client to other RADIUS servers of other kinds of authentication servers.

By now, you may have noticed that the NAS and the authentication (or RADIUS) server are not the computers used by the remote or dial-in user. The RADIUS protocols forward the authentication, authorization, and configuration information through the Internet—to the remote user's home network. Forward in this case has significant meaning.

Remember, with CHAP the name fields may be used as an index to locate the proper secret in a large table of secrets. This is one of the primary features of RADIUS. It uses a database system to maintain a list of users. This database contains information that is used for authentication and configuration.

---

## Quality Of Service

In addition to user names and passwords, the database contains information concerning the type of service to deliver to the user. This is a direct lead into identifying the *quality of service* (QOS) which, as we have already seen, plays a significant role in the type of connection and service allowed.

---

The authentication process used by RADIUS is very similar to that used by CHAP. But unlike the Microsoft implementation in PPTP, RADIUS authentication gives the user *an unpredictable number*. The user is then challenged to encrypt the number and give it back. The encryption algorithm is based on a special device, such as a *Smart Card*, or a software product.

### Microsoft Modifications To RADIUS

Microsoft made specific changes to the RADIUS protocols to operate with its products such as Windows NT 4. To allow third parties access to these specific changes, RFC 2548 was published in March 1999 outlining the vendor-specific RADIUS attributes. The document also details *Microsoft Challenge-Handshake Authentication Protocol* (MS-CHAP).

## Cisco Systems

Cisco Systems views the Internet from a different perspective than most vendors. Their perspective is from the inside looking out. It is natural, then, that Cisco is interested in protocols that work within the structure of the Internet, and see the remote or dial-up user as their primary user.

### Layer Two Forwarding (L2F)

To meet its goals, Cisco published RFC 2341, *Cisco layer Two Forwarding (Protocol) "L2F,"* in May 1998. The primary emphasis of L2F is to move above the physical layer protocols to the link layer, and allow transport of the link layer and higher protocols through the fabric of the Internet. The physical layer protocols remain within the dial-up connection to the ISP.

---

### RADIUS And The World

RADIUS is used to carry authentication, authorization, and configuration information between Network Access Servers and Authentication Servers—it may not have been very clear, but the NAS and RADIUS servers could be located on opposite sides of the world. The RADIUS protocol is designed with this type of environment in mind. We shall see in Chapter 5 that Cisco took this one step further. By adding accounting features in the mix, Cisco developed protocols to pass *Authentication, Authorization, and Accounting* information through the Internet. Cisco calls this information AAA, and uses this as one cornerstone for Cisco VPNs.

---

Once the connection is established, L2F forwards the datagrams containing the information for Authentication, Authorization, and Accounting through virtual tunnels within the Internet keeping the location of the initial dial-up server invisible. The user only sees the network where the connection is terminated, the Corporate LAN.

L2F also addresses the issues of IP addressing and accounting, offering recommendations and laying the foundation for handling both in a reliable manner. L2F defines new terminology, including:

♦ Home Gateway

♦ Home LANs

♦ Remote User

♦ ISP network access Server (similar to the NAS mentioned before, except owned by the ISP)

### Connection, Authentication, And Encapsulation

For the initial connection to the ISP, L2F will work with standard PPP or, if necessary, several proprietary versions. L2F will work with standard CHAP or some modifications thereof for authentication. For encapsulation, L2F specifies the protocols necessary to encapsulate the entire PPP or SLIP packet in an L2F datagram. This L2F datagram is then forwarded through the Internet to the Home Gateway. The initial intent is for as much of this as possible to be transparent to the user.

### TACACS And The Daemon

In developing L2F, Cisco used an earlier protocol known as *Terminal Access Controller Access System* (TACACS) originally designed by the Defense Data Network as a means of restricting access to terminal access controllers. Cisco enhanced TACACS several times, eventually evolving it into TACACS+. The final version improved on its predecessors by providing the capability to separate the functions of authentication, authorization, and accounting, and by encrypting all traffic between the NAS and the running process. The TACACS+ running process is known as a daemon.

### L2TP—The Best Of Both Worlds?

Though technically about the same, vendors and users alike will perceive significant differences between PPTP and L2F. PPTP is favored by Microsoft, which has the vast majority of the desktops in the world, and L2F is favored by Cisco, with the vast majority of the Internet in its back pocket. Despite the fact that both PPTP and L2F use encapsulation and encryption, the two are not mutually compatible. It would seem natural that someone would want to take the best of both products and build a third protocol.

### Enter The Layer Two Tunneling Protocol

The IETF is proposing an industry standard combining the best parts of PPTP and L2F and calling it the *Layer Two Tunneling Protocol* (L2TP). As of May 1999, L2TP is still in development, but some parts of it are being implemented by Cisco and Microsoft.

Will the promises of L2TP bear fruit? We really can't say. Another new kid moved into the neighborhood. His name is IPsec and he looks bigger and badder.

**Note**

*In our discussion to this point, we gracefully mangled the terms standard and protocol. We didn't do it on purpose, but rather by necessity, because the marketing department of major software vendors insist on calling protocols standards when in fact they are not.*

# Making IP Secure, IPsec

The IETF tackled the IPsec project as a working group. RFCs defining specific IPsec protocols started showing up in 1995. The list of RFCs consigned to obsolescence grew as newer ones were written, often under the same title and distinguished only by number and publication date.

At the time this book was written, three RFCs defined the IPsec core:

1. RFC 2401, *Security Architecture for the Internet Protocol*, November 1998, defines the implementation of IPsec.

2. RFC 1827, *IP Encapsulating Security Payload (ESP)*, August 1995, defines the encapsulation protocol used to create virtual tunnels through the Internet.

3. RFC 2402, *IP Authentication Header (AH)*, November 1998, defines the construction of the authentication header.

These three reference several preceding RFCs that define various protocols and algorithms. Primary among the referenced RFCs are encryption and encryption key management algorithms. The IETF working group incorporated the protocols defined by all these RFCs into IPsec.

According to the authors of RFC 2401, IPsec was designed to provide "interoperable, high quality, cryptographically-based security for IPv4 and IPv6." IPv4 is the current version of the Internet Protocol and v6 is being developed as its replacement.

IPsec is a relatively new standard, but is so important to the continued successful growth of the Internet that it has become one of the predominant subjects in RFCs for the past two years. The IPsec standard is a means of implementing reliable security at the IP protocol level of the Internet. The complex standard deals with many topics, including VPN. Two important concepts woven into the fabric of the Internet at the IP level are:

- *Confidentiality*—This implies that information sent out over the Internet can be made—and kept—confidential in a reliable manner.

- *Authentication*—This implies that when the data is received by the destination entity, a method exists for verifying that the data originated from the proper entity and was not tampered with en route.

To implement these concepts, IPsec uses two groups of protocols, defined as *traffic security protocols*:

- *Authentication Header (AH)*
- *Encapsulating Security Payload (ESP)*

The IPsec protocol suite allows implementation of the preceding two groups in several different ways, often using different concurrent combinations. This could easily become a management nightmare. To ease the management end of things, IPsec uses a group of *key management* protocols with the imposing title "Internet Security Association and Key Management Protocol with a subset of the Oakley key exchange scheme," or *ISAKMP/Oakley* for short.

# IPsec, Part I: The Need For Security

Before we jump into the details of IPsec, let's take a look at why so much emphasis is being dumped into the arcane pot of security. The original developers of ARPANET did not place much emphasis on security—not by design, but for necessity. Like any new endeavor, more emphasis was placed on developing reliable operation than on establishing security. After all, they were the only ones in town with the new toys. Who could afford an IBM 360 to hack in and mess things up?

After reliable operation was established, the Internet community was still relatively small and was not open to the general public. Most of the members knew each other by first names and trust went a long way. Based on trust, the decision by ARPA was to leave the Internet open from a security standpoint, which allowed for much greater exchange of information.

The tunneling process was devised fairly early on as a means of solving a problem. As mentioned earlier, tunneling was considered to be a *hack*, or a means of circumventing established rules (another term for protocol is *rule*). Most of the original *hacks* were experiments for which time was of the essence and eventually became the subject of new RFCs and perhaps later were turned into legitimate protocols. Security continued to shuffle along behind convenience.

## *Foresight*

I truly believe the early developers of the ARPANET standards and protocols knew they were working on the next epoch of global communications among individuals, corporations, and governments. I think they knew and looked forward to the time when the developments they were fostering would change the way the world operates. I also think they had the foresight to see the future downsides and put in place mechanisms for changing the structure to meet the needs as the Internet evolved. The RFC process, the *Internet Activities Board* (IAB), and the *Internet Engineering Task Force* (IETF), are examples of their foresight.

Equally farsighted commercial enterprises jumped in to fill the gap when the National Science Foundation and other government agencies stopped funding the Internet. Virtually overnight, Internet access rules and the restrictions of use (like advertising and e-commerce) changed dramatically. The globalization of the Internet took off and hasn't stopped yet, and all of it is related to the RFC process.

I think the speed at which the Internet has grown has surprised most of the original developers of the ARPANET. On the other hand, I don't think the amount of malicious intentional damage and destruction caused by opening the Internet to the world has surprised them in the least. When you open your door to the world, you also open your door to every individual, anywhere in that world that for whatever antisocial, psychotic reason has it in for civilization in general and a few entities in specific.

If the Internet is to become the next standard for global communications for individuals, corporations, governments, and nations, it can no longer be an open, unsecure enterprise. Thus the need for IP security. Recognizing this need, the IAB and IETF started work on IPv6, an evolved form of *IP New Generation* (IPNG). Several new enhancements were added to the IPv6—which we will look at directly—and some of them were retrofitted into IPv4.

IPsec includes encapsulation protocol enhancements. The fundamental process is the same, but the layout of the headers and fields was modified to incorporate improvements. Like the security features, most of the encapsulation protocols are, to a certain degree, backwards compatible and would work with IPv4.

## IPsec Part II, Encapsulation

Because encapsulation (tunneling) is a fundamental part of VPN, and is implemented as a protocol in IPsec, let's take a close look at this operation. The IPsec Protocol uses the more descriptive term *encapsulation* for the concept of tunneling. Fundamentally, they mean the same thing.

The tunneling protocol for IPsec starts with RFC 1827, *IP Encapsulating Security Payload (ESP)*, which defines a versatile method of datagram encapsulation. At the time this RFC was published, tunneling was part of IPNG development. As I said earlier, RFC 1853, published in October 1995, described tunneling and encryption to transmit IP datagrams over radio relay links. Although the PRRL efforts did the trick and is the first documented tunneling/encapsulation work, it left lots of room for improvement. Since then, the ESP concepts and protocols detailed in RFC 1827 have become the preferred encapsulation method for use with IPsec.

ESP is designed to provide integrity and confidentiality to IP datagrams. According to the authors of RFC 1827, ESP may be implemented in a standalone manner, separate from IPsec. When used this way, ESP does not require the use of an authentication header.

ESP may also provide authentication—if the proper algorithm and mode are used. If authentication is desired—remember, it is not required—it is implemented in the form of an *Authentication Header* (AH). This means ESP can provide three basic operations:

♦ Confidentiality and Integrity of IP Datagrams only

♦ Authentication only

♦ Both Authentication, and Confidentiality and Integrity of IP Datagrams

Which one of the three choices is implemented is driven by the choice of algorithm and algorithm mode.

**Tip**

*When ESP is implemented as a part of the IPsec protocol suite, the Authentication Header or AH is always implemented.*

### Confidentiality And Integrity

ESP provides confidentiality and integrity by encrypting data to be protected (the payload) and placing it in the payload portion of the IP encapsulating security payload. When tunnel-mode ESP is selected, the original IP datagram is placed in the encrypted portion of the ESP and the entire ESP frame is placed within a datagram having unencrypted IP headers. This process is slightly different from previous encapsulation protocols in that, when using the original datagram, including headers, it is encrypted and becomes the encapsulating security payload. Earlier encapsulation protocols added a special IP header to the original datagram, but pretty much left the original IP header intact.

Another difference between ESP and its predecessors is the ability to encapsulate and encrypt TCP, IGMP, and ICMP, transport-layer segments, as well as IP datagrams. Recall from Chapters 2 and 3 that these segments are necessary to transport control messages from different layers of the protocol stack and provide reliable communications between the end points. If necessary, the segments can also be encrypted, but because encryption algorithms place more demand on system resources, the transport-layer segments can be encapsulated and tunneled without being encrypted.

The system administrator can choose from a number of different encryption algorithms when using ESP. It is possible to enable a number of tunnels, each using ESP and each using a different encryption algorithm to encrypt the data. Datagrams can be padded by inserting null characters before encryption and is useful in defending against a security attack known as *traffic analysis*. The default cipher for IPsec is 56-bit DES-CBC and guarantees at least minimal interoperability between IPsec entities.

### IP Authentication Header—I'm Me, Who Are You?

Here is a question every network administrator should be able to answer: How do you know your mobile users are who they say they are? Conversely: How do the mobile users know who or what they are connected to? If you don't know the answer, and your network incorporates confidential or proprietary information, you need to be concerned about the question.

*Security association* (SA) is a key to successful IPsec and in a little bit, we'll prove it. But first, it is necessary to take a quick look at the other traffic security protocol implemented in the IPsec standard, the Authentication Header (AH).

*Sniffers* are devices used to monitor data packets transported through the network. They play an important role in checking to make sure the network is healthy and operating within standards. The bad news is a that sniffer can be used to capture data packets anywhere between two end points of a network. Using the IP protocol suite, a hacker can modify the IP headers of captured data packets and transmit the packets back to the originator. Done properly, the modified data packets trick the originator into establishing a covert communications link with the hacker in the middle, instead of point-to-point with the real user on the other end. Network jargon calls this a *Man in the Middle* attack, and it should be a concern of all network administrators.

The authors of RFC 2402 designed the AH Protocol to provide some defense against the man in the middle and, although 2402 defines the whole protocol in exquisite detail, RFC 2401 succinctly defines the AH services as follows:

♦ Connectionless integrity

♦ Data origin authentication

♦ An optional anti-replay service

Like ESP, AH has two modes of implementation: transport or tunnel mode. When AH is implemented in transport mode it provides protection primarily for upper layer protocols where the datagrams are not encrypted. When AH is implemented in tunnel mode, the protocols are applied to tunneled IP packets.

ESP does not protect the outer IP header in front of the ESP payload but, on the other hand, the AH Protocol protects as much of the outer IP header as possible. It is not possible to protect the entire outer IP header because some parts change as the datagram is routed through the Internet and the originator has no way of knowing what those changes will be. In the datagram, the AH is placed between the ESP and the outer IP header. Figure 4.4 shows how a datagram AH is made up of several fields:

♦ *Next Header*—This indicates the higher level protocol following the AH, for example ESP or TCP.

| Next Header Field | Payload Length Field | Reserved Field | Security Parameters Index (SPI) | Sequence Nr. Field | Authentication Data Field |
|---|---|---|---|---|---|

**Figure 4.4**
Authentication Header (AH) structure.

- *Payload Length*—An 8 bit field specifying the size of the AH.

- *Security Parameters Index*—Reserved for this connection.

- *Sequence Number*—An incremented number for each packet sent with a given SPI.

- *Authentication Data*—A digital signature for this packet.

IPsec requires specific algorithms for implementing ESP and AH. These *minimum requirement* algorithms guarantee minimal interoperability between IPsec entities. All IPsec implementations must support HMAC-MD5 and HMAC-SHA1 for the AH.

## The Internet Security Association Key Management Protocol With Oakley Key Exchange

To provide reliable *secure* transport operation, entities at each end of an IPsec implementation must know what happened or is going to happen on the other end—that proper authentication is done and the correct methods for encapsulating and decapsulating are in place. In addition, datagrams must meet all the standards for traditional IP protocols. To provide this service, a *security association* (SA) is established between the origin and destination. When you consider all the different algorithms and protocols involved in IPsec, you should begin to understand why we said earlier that SA is fundamental to the operation of IPsec.

### Security Association

The initial description of SA came out in August 1995 in an RFC (1825) titled *Security Architecture for the Internet Protocol.* You might have noticed the dates for RFC 1825 and RFC 1827 are the same and that they are authored by the same person, R. Atkinson of the

---

### Hashing Message Authentication (HMAC)

*Hashing Message Authentication (HMAC)* is a mechanism for message authentication using cryptographic hash functions. HMAC can be used with any iterative cryptographic hash function, for example, MD5 and SHA-1, in combination with a secret shared key. The cryptographic strength of HMAC depends on the properties of the underlying hash function. You can get the details from RFC 2574.

---

Naval Research Laboratory. But it gets even better: RFC 1825 was superceded in November 1998, by RFC 2401 with the same title and authored by (ready for this?), R. Atkinson of the Naval Research Laboratory. It makes you think he has some interest in security, doesn't it? It is also an indicator of how the RFC system works.

According to 2401 and 1825, SA is a simplex virtual connection that provides security services to the data. Unlike the ESP and AH where either one or both protocols can be used, in the SA scheme, security services can be provided by either AH or ESP, but not both. Because both AH and ESP can be applied to a traffic stream, two SAs must be established when both AH and ESP are implemented.

Establishing secure duplex (bi-directional) communications between two security gateways requires that a SA be established for each direction. In the current implementation of IPsec, SA management mechanisms are defined only for unicast SAs. This means that today, current SAs can be established only for point-to-point communication. Future enhancements will allow point-to-point and point-to-multipoint communications.

Each SA is uniquely identified by three components:

♦   A Security Parameter Index, or SPI

♦   An IP Destination Address

♦   A security protocol, either AH or ESP

As previously noted, two types of SA modes are defined: transport and tunnel. A *transport mode SA* is a security association between two hosts. A *tunnel mode SA* is an SA applied to an IP tunnel. If an SA is made between two security gateways, or between a security gateway and a host, then that SA must use tunnel mode. VPN will, for reasons we will establish in the following chapters, use tunnel mode SA.

You can combine SAs to provide multiple levels of security, as well as transport or encapsulation capabilities. When SAs are combined, we call the result an *SA bundle*; this is a sequence of security associations through which traffic must be processed. Each SA in the bundle is placed there by the system administrator to satisfy a requirement of the total security policy.

In actual implementation, the system administrator develops the SA bundles during installation and configuration. Only in the rarest of cases should it be necessary for the administrator to get down to the code or configuration file level. However, a knowledge of the final outcome helps to make the configuration process more understandable.

### IP Headers

When tunnel mode SA is used, the datagram contains *inner* and *outer* IP headers. The outer IP header specifies the IPsec processing destination, such as the security gateway at the destination network, and the inner header specifies the ultimate destination for the packet. Internet routers may change a datagram's outer header as it is passed through the Internet and scant protection is afforded it. Conversely, the inner IP header will not change, and is securely protected by AH and ESP. An *authentication header* (AH), a third header, is placed between the inner and outer headers. The AH contains information for the destination entity to use in processing the received datagram.

We said that an SA is identified in part by its security protocol and that only one protocol, AH or ESP, can be assigned to a unique SA. If AH is the assigned protocol and the SA is tunnel-mode, portions of the outer (IPsec processing destination) header are protected, as well as all of the inner header and the tunneled IP datagram.

If, however, the assigned protocol is ESP for a tunnel-mode SA, protection is afforded only to the tunneled IP datagram, and not to the outer header. An example of an encapsulated IP sec datagram is shown in Figure 4.5.

### Payload Padding

In a similar manner, ESP *payload padding* is used (according to RFC 2401) to make data packets appear to be of uniform size, belying the actual content of the datagrams. Padding is useful in situations where a mobile user uses a dial-up connection and receives an IP address dynamically. The user then establishes an ESP SA to the enterprise security gateway for passing datagrams. This is an implementation of VPN.

# Key Management Protocol (KMP) With Oakley Key Exchange

RFC 2411 by Rodney Thayer (Sable Technology), Naganand Doraswamy (Bay Networks), and Rob Glenn (NIST), and RFC 2412 by Hilarie Orman (Department of Computer Science, University of Arizona), are two excellent informational RFCs dealing with encryption.

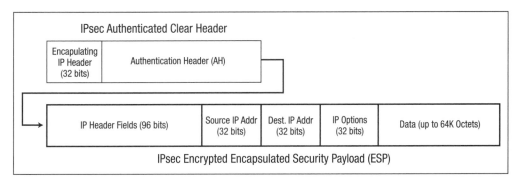

**Figure 4.5**
IPsec AH/ESP datagram packet structure.

Without a doubt, the best method of implementing security on the Internet today is encryption. Unfortunately, the best way of creating a hole in security is through improperly maintained encryption.

How do we make a system *reliably secure?* The secret is to maintain the security features we enable. Put another way, the secret is through good management. That's what *Key Management Protocol* (*KMP*) is all about.

## About Encryption, The (Real) Short Version

Almost every network user is familiar with passwords—those neat cryptic words that only you know that allow you to gain access to the network: your spouse's birthday written backwards; the model name of your mother-in-law's second car (was it Nissan or Sentra?); the first and last three digits of the dollar bill framed on the wall over your desk.

The best passwords are not words at all. The best passwords are made up of groups of characters (letters *and* numbers), randomly selected from the set of 96 printable ASCII characters. Not all the printable ASCII characters can be used in passwords. Some have special meaning to most operating systems. If these characters are used for passwords, the computer may do something different than you really want.

The problem with passwords is remembering them. Everyone forgets their password now and then. When that happens, what do you do? Let me guess. You open the middle drawer of your desk and look at the list taped to the bottom of the drawer. No one in the entire world would ever think to look there, would they? The password is fine as a means of authentication to the network, but how good is the maintenance? How long has it been since you changed your password?

The more critical question is: "How long ago did a cracker steal it?"

## Ciphers And Keys

The numbers produced in the encryption process are known as *ciphers*. However, in this country, the term cipher is not used often, and is not very common. As we said, ciphers are generated by applying sets of numbers to a predefined mathematical process, or algorithm. The more commonly used term for the sets of numbers used to generate a cipher, is *key*, or *keys*. A key is nothing more than a number, the larger the better, used in the encryption algorithm. In the world of encryption we find two types of keys: *public* and *private*. Let's cover private first.

### Private

A private key is a large group of numbers that is known to one person only or to a selected group of individuals. A well-maintained private key encryption system is without a doubt very secure. Notice I keep saying *well maintained*. The problem with private key encryption is maintenance. This is especially true if more than one person is involved. As the number of people involved in the encryption algorithm increases, the chances of a compromised key increase exponentially; the more people involved, the higher the likelihood of someone writing the key down to be discovered by someone without authority.

The problems are compounded when the group is spread across the city, county, or country. If you don't have a trusted system, and you want to keep the key private, the only way to inform the others about a change in the key is by getting everyone together at the same time in the same place. What fun, we all get to take a trip to the home office every Monday to get the new key. Add up the number of people, multiply by the hours used, and multiply again by the general and administrative overhead rate from the accounting department—it can be serious bucks.

Private key encryption is fine if you have only one or two individuals involved—more than that becomes a problem. It doesn't take long before the problem negates the benefits of encryption. A better way ought to exist, and it does—it is called public key encryption.

### Public

Today the most dominant form of public key encryption is the RSA *Public Key Cryptosystem*, named after its developers, Rivest, Shamir, and Adleman (RFC 2459, by Russell Housley, et al.). RSA encryption is based on the same principal as private key encryption, using very large numbers as keys that are manipulated through a mathematics algorithm. The difference between public key and private key encryption is the existence of two keys, one public, and one private. Both keys are generated by the same algorithm. Either key can be used to encrypt or decrypt the cipher. However, if one key is used to encrypt the cipher, the other key can only be used to decrypt it. In other words, if the public key is used to encrypt the data, the private key is the one that can only be used to decrypt the data, and vice versa.

The public key encryption scheme can be used by itself for encrypting and decrypting data sent between two individuals. However, when combined with AH and ESD, reliability and security are increased dramatically. When a connection is made between two endpoints, the endpoints are authenticated, and then a public/private key pair is generated or selected from a secure database of reliable key pairs. After the endpoints are authenticated so each end knows who is on the other end, one of the keys is sent to the other end. When both endpoints have a key, they can encrypt outgoing data and decrypt incoming data.

## Final Notes About VPN Protocols

We made a point that the architectural model for datagram encapsulation requires two new types of network entities, encapsulators and decapsulators, and that all VPN protocols perform some type of data encryption. When a VPN is initiated in a LAN, these services are usually performed by a computer other than the client workstation. In the next chapter, you will find that the computer systems providing the encapsulation, decapsulation, and encryption services have many different names. For the moment I'll call them, collectively, *security gateways*. An example of a simple implementation of the VPN protocols in a network system would probably look like Figure 4.6.

Figure 4.6 reflects only the encapsulation process and not the security features implemented in the IPsec protocol suite. In a properly implemented IPsec protocol suite, most of the protocols will be transparent to the network administrator. Even more important, all the protocols will be transparent to the user—that's what really counts.

The encapsulation and encryption protocols and processes place a considerable burden on system resources. This is especially true in the case of encryption. Exactly how large the burden is depends on several factors, but the primary factor is the WAN link speed to the Internet. If the WAN link is a 56K modem, the security gateway won't work nearly as hard as it would with two or three T1 links or a 10 MB/Sec frame relay.

When VPN protocols are implemented between two networks that are using security gateways to provide encapsulation and encryption, the resources can be sized to fit the required need, and in some cases provide other services (firewall, Web proxy, and so forth).

A laptop or notebook computer required by a remote or mobile user may not have the resources required to perform the tasks of a security gateway and its intended job. Granted, very powerful laptop computers are on the market today, but lots of older laptops that won't make the grade are still in use. If a remote user works on a laptop, implementing VPN may require an upgrade on that end.

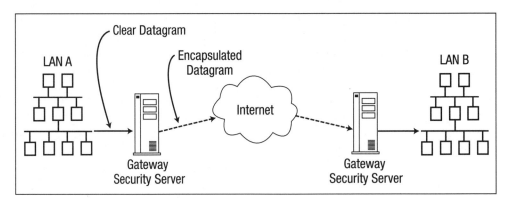

**Figure 4.6**
Encapsulation architecture applied to a WAN structure.

# Wrap Up

The purpose of this chapter was to investigate the development of the Request For Comments and how the RFC process is used to make the Internet the powerful ever-evolving information and communication resource that it is. For threading through the treatise, we looked at some of the protocols used in the creation of a VPN. That is, after all, what we are all about here.

One example followed a thread through the RFCs to give you a better idea of what tunneling is, and how it was developed, as well as to show you how the RFC process works. We saw that although most of the RFCs are for creating standards and protocols, some are just for information—to inform others in the networking community of how groups such as the Packet Radio Relay League are using the technological resources available and how serendipity can play a part in technology growth.

We've worked hard not to create any *de facto* endorsement and to stay independent of any manufacturers, except in areas where to do so would have rendered the discussion meaningless. In some cases deciding which RFCs to include or not to include was difficult. Surely, we left out an RFC or a protocol (perhaps more that one) that you feel should be here, perhaps as a better example. But we only have so much room in this book, and we got first pick.

As we found out in this chapter, IPsec is much more than a simple application or protocol. In fact, IP is an entirely new architecture for Internet Protocol. Among other things, IPsec provides authentication, encryption, encapsulation, and key maintenance protocols. Each of these protocols can be implemented in several different ways, so that the level of security can match the needs of the users. IPsec provides such reliable and secure communications that almost all the current implementations of VPN use it now, recommend it, or are in the process of adopting it.

This chapter discussed how the protocols used to implement VPNs work. The requirement for more resources has brought about several different implementations of the VPN architectural model. In the next chapter we will see how some selected vendors implement VPN. As usual, each vendor has their own approach and, of course, states unequivocally that their implementation is the best. As always, the definition of *best* is like beauty—it is mostly in the eye of the beholder, or so the saying goes.

# Chapter 5

# How Manufacturers Are Implementing VPN Standards

*Key Topics:*

♦ *Vendor profiles*

♦ *Various architectures*

♦ *VPN protocols*

♦ *Vendor interoperability*

♦ *VPN directions*

This chapter will describe how manufacturers implement Virtual Private Network (VPN) standards in their network products. It will tell what protocols and encryption methods are being used. It is beyond the scope of any book, this one included, to include all the manufacturers that are currently producing products for the Virtual Private Network market. The following manufacturers will be targeted initially:

♦ The PPTP Forum (Microsoft, Ascend Communications, 3Com, ECI Telematics, and US Robotics)

♦ Novell

♦ Cisco (Independent ISPs)

♦ Indus River Software

## Seeking A Common Ground— Caveats And Disclaimers

We contend that you don't discuss religion, politics, or network operating systems unless you want to start an argument. To say the network industry is competitive is like saying the space shuttle converts fuel to noise. Everyone—unless they can't bend their elbow when scratching the end of their nose—has a favorite vendor and favorite products.

We are no different. The fact is, the co-authors of this book occasionally share disagreements on what's best. But it is not our intention to do a sales pitch for any specific product, so we will do our absolute best to keep our personal opinions from overflowing into the text. All of our examples will be taken from off-the-shelf products, *not* those promised tomorrow, next week, or months from now—regardless of how super the sales department's claims. If it is not on the shelf as we write this, it won't be in this book.

As of May 1999, several companies have VPN products on the market; more than we can cover in our page budget. That means some will be left out of the discussion in this chapter, perhaps your favorite. To those players we extend our apologies, and a compromise—in Appendix C you will find a listing of every VPN vendor (including contact mechanics) that we could locate when we finished this chapter.

Some of the companies we approached, perhaps worrying over divulging proprietary information, declined to participate with us. We respect their decisions and have included their names in Appendix B. We choose not to reveal which of the collection are in that category.

Now, having told you of our attempts to get as much information from vendors as possible, our concerns about the players that we are leaving out, and about this book becoming a sales pitch for a particular vendor, we fully expect our email box will overflow with flame-email, wondering why we didn't say *this* about *that*. You have our sincere promise that all flames will be cheerfully ignored.

# Who Is Using What?

VPN manufacturers are roughly grouped into three camps depending on preferred protocols. Microsoft, 3Com, and a few others all use one form or another of PPTP. Cisco and a very few others are bent on L2F. (The IETF is working towards consolidating PPTP and L2F into L2TP—or L2FP if you prefer.) The rest, including Novell—and to a certain degree Cisco—are jumping on the IPsec bandwagon. The information you get here comes from manufacturers over a general cross section of the three philosophies.

We tend to think they will all eventually use IPsec, just as every major network vendor now supports IP in one form or another. To prove the point, Microsoft said, in a paper on its not-yet-released Windows 2000, that users should implement IPsec for increased security in VPN installations.

# Firewalls

Implementation of a VPN requires serious consideration of some type of security. In many cases this security will include some type of firewall protection. Recall from Chapter 4 that the encapsulation protocol used to create tunnels required special equipment to perform the function of encapsulation and decapsulation. In Chapter 4 we called these machines *security gateways*.

The location of the security gateway with respect to the firewall is important, and any discussion of VPN implementation has to include firewall terminology. IT managers and network administrators are faced with several choices in throwing up a firewall to protect their enterprise. Adding to the confusion are new terms being invented in geek-speak. To make sure we are all using the same terminology, let's have a short discussion of firewall concepts.

# Three Firewall Concepts

When firewalls are implemented in the network structure, they are generally placed at the point at which the intranet connects to the Internet. Although several different methods of implementing firewalls exist, we will discuss three common methods.

### Screened Host Gateway

A firewall is combined with a gateway to provide filtering protection between the Internet and intranet. In this method, a proxy server is placed in the intranet, as shown in Figure 5.1.

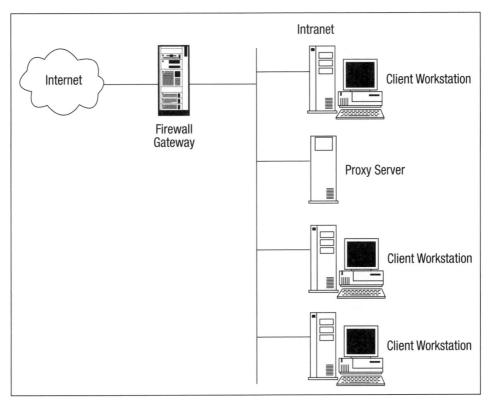

**Figure 5.1**
Screened host gateway.

With this type of implementation, the equipment used as the firewall may be provided by the ISP or the owner of the network.

### Screened Subnet

Here the intranet is separated from the Internet by a subnet aptly known as the *demilitarized zone* (DMZ). This requires two firewall gateways, one on each side of the DMZ subnet. The proxy server is placed in the DMZ subnet, as shown in Figure 5.2.

Note that the equipment used as the firewall between the DMZ subnet and the Internet is often called a *boundary router* and is configured for filtering. These components are sometimes provided and maintained by the ISP. The equipment used as the firewall between the DMZ subnet and the intranet is provided by the intranet owner. Here, the proxy server is located *outside* the firewall.

### Dual-Homed Proxy Host

This method is similar to the screened subnet, except that the internal firewall gateway and proxy host functions are combined. Like the screened subnet above, this method includes a DMZ subnet, as shown in Figure 5.3.

Also like the screened subnet, the equipment used as the DMZ firewall between the subnet and the Internet is often provided by the ISP, and the firewall/proxy server equipment is provided by the intranet owner.

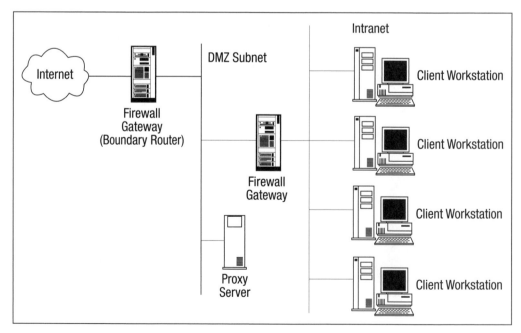

**Figure 5.2**
Screened subnet.

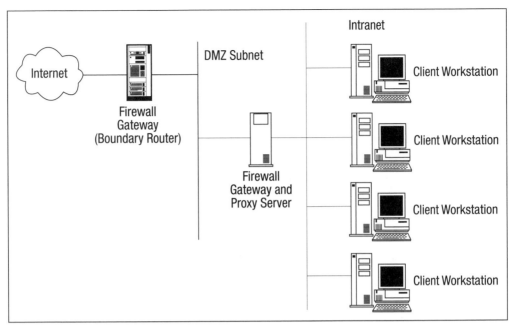

**Figure 5.3**
Dual-homed proxy host.

### So What?

What difference does it make how the firewall is set up? Isn't a VPN a VPN? As we shall see, the answer is: *most definitely not*. The method used to implement the firewall protection will have a lot of impact on the implementation of the VPN. As we discuss the different methods of VPN implementation, we will use these three basic diagrams a lot.

So, now that we're all on common ground, at least as far as terminology goes, on with the show.

# (Some) People That Make It Work

This section will peek into what networking solutions are offered by some vendors and see how they implement VPN protocols. In doing this we will cover the following areas for each vendor.

♦ A (very) short history of each vendor (in case we uncover a vendor you don't know).

♦ A look at their overall approach to networks (yes, they are different, and the difference affects how their network products work).

♦ VPN implementation architecture, or how each vendor's hardware and software fits within the network structure.

♦ Which protocols are implemented in the VPN process.

# Microsoft *Et Al.,* The PPTP Forum

A person would have to live in the deep backwoods of a very small third world country not to have heard of Microsoft. You can agree or disagree with Microsoft's statements about its software products, its marketing practices, and even its ongoing problems with the Department of Justice—but no one can disagree with its successes in the PC industry.

Microsoft budgets enough to tell the world what Microsoft software is, how it works, and what it does. We choose not to let this book become a forum for the continuation of that rhetoric. Instead, we're going to look at a group of companies (some of which could be labeled industry giants; you may not recognize the name of others) that agreed to develop a method allowing remote access to Microsoft Windows NT through the Internet.

## A (Short) History Of The PPTP Forum

Two years after Novell's 1983 presentation of NetWare, Microsoft ventured out with a network operating system dubbed *MS-NET*, based perhaps on the Microsoft LAN (MILAN) that tied the corporate computers together.

The next Microsoft network product was a slight improvement. Called *LAN Manager*, it was a moderate success in the market, and stayed around for a number of years. But LAN Manager had a problem: It was text based, not *graphical user interface (GUI)* based. By this time Microsoft had invested serious effort to become the GUI leader with a brand new concept called *Windows*.

Serious network system design began in 1988 when Microsoft lured David Cutler and some of his colleagues away from Digital Equipment Corporation to try and catch up. It took another five years for that crew to polish and present Microsoft NT. The one driving requirement for the new network system? It had to use the Windows GUI interface. Today, two separate products are available: the original NT, now known as *NT Workstation*, and the *Windows NT Advanced Server*.

Network administrators can install Windows NT on a desktop and use it as a workstation or client, but to configure a machine into a serious server to handle more than a handful of computers in a branch office requires the second package.

Because Windows NT was touted as an enterprise WAN system, on a scale with Unix, Microsoft had implemented the ability for users to access the NT server from remote sites. This was possible through an additional module named *NT Remote Access Server*, or *RAS*. By using RAS, users could dial-in through banks of modems, and extend the network out to their remote site. It didn't matter if the remote site was a branch office, home office, or a hotel room.

Somewhere along this same time-line, the Internet exploded. Suddenly people all over the world could exchange information with other people instantaneously through this mysterious entity called the Internet. It wasn't long before someone at Microsoft suggested an add-on for the RAS server, one that would allow connection through the Internet. In providing this service, Microsoft was faced with the same problem everyone else was—security, or in better terms, a lack of security through the Internet.

We don't know the exact date when Microsoft decided to take on the problem. We do know it was prior to June 1996. Microsoft proposed a partnering agreement to several companies with the objective of enhancing the existing protocols to allow remote users to connect to Windows NT networks and servers through the Internet. We feel fairly certain that at the time, the term Virtual Private Network was not in common use, though the concepts of VPNs were in the minds of several people. The result of this partnering agreement was submitted as a draft titled "Point-To-Point Tunneling Protocol" (PPTP), draft-ietf-ppext-pptp-10.txt.

The companies initially involved in the project were:

♦ Microsoft, **www.microsoft.com**

♦ Ascend Communications, **www.ascend.com**

♦ 3Com, **www.3com.com**

♦ ECI Telematics, **www.telematics.com**

♦ US Robotics (now part of 3Com)

These companies are listed as authors of the original draft. If other companies were involved, please believe that we did not leave them out intentionally—we just can't find any record of them. Of the five, Microsoft is the only one that develops only software. Three of the remaining four offer primarily hardware-only solutions, and one company, Ascend Communications, markets hardware and software solution products.

The purpose of the partnering agreement was to develop enhancements of existing protocols to allow secure connection to Windows NT network servers on the Internet. At the time, the popular tunneling protocol used IP datagram encapsulation. The goal was to enhance that protocol to include the multiprotocol features found in PPP and the result was PPTP. Because it had its origins in the original PPP protocol, PPTP could encapsulate other datagram protocols (such as IPX [Novell NetWare], NetBEUI [IBM OS-2, and Microsoft Windows], and AppleTalk [Apple Macintosh]) within IP headers and tunnel them through the Internet.

This held out some real promise for the future. Unfortunately the future is a fickle thing. If we could only see into the future, we would all be rich. The same holds true for the original players in the forum. PPTP soon found itself under attack from two different areas.

### Cisco And L2F

Cisco was either not invited or chose not to participate in the PPTP Forum; it developed its own standard and named it *Layer Two Forwarding*, or L2F. Microsoft, with a 90 percent share of desktops, was using PPTP. Cisco, with an 80 percent share of the routers, was using L2F. The two were different and interoperability between them was nil. That led to an IETF proposal to take the best features of both products, combine them, and create yet another new protocol, named *Layer Two Tunneling Protocol* (*L2TP*). Today L2TP is supported by a number of providers in the VPN market, including most of the original members of the PPTP Forum. The other protocols necessary to provide the complete VPN architecture, such as authentication, authorization, and encryption, are commonly shared between PPTP and L2TP.

### Then Came IPsec

We covered IPsec in the last chapter and won't bore you with the details again. We will say this: It looks as if IPsec is going to be the future protocol suite for VPN software. As of the time this is being written, every provider of products for the VPN market has either announced products that support the IPsec protocols, or has announced plans to incorporate the IPsec protocols in their future products—including Microsoft, Cisco, Novell, and the original companies that comprised the PPTP Forum.

**Note**

*Since the original partnering agreement that developed the PPTP Forum, two of the companies involved, 3Com and US Robotics, have merged. At the present time US Robotics is a subsidiary of 3Com. Also, ECI Telematics has had a slight name change. It is now named ECI Telecom.*

## The PPTP Fourm Approach To Networks

If you take a look at the mix of products available from the member companies of the PPTP Forum, they pretty much have the network system covered. Yet at the same time they offer products that operate at different points within the WAN structure. A look at each company individually produces the following:

♦ *3Com and US Robotics*—3Com initially produced high-end LAN interface cards, hubs, switches, and routers incorporating multiprotocol capability—including PPTP—into its Netbuilder and SuperStack II product lines. With the acquisition of US Robotics, 3Com extends their WAN capability to the remote user by providing a complete line of modems and remote dial-in/dial-out products. 3Com/US Robotics offers a complete line of modem servers designed specifically for ISPs.

♦ *ECI Telecom*—Uses slightly different terminology, so its product literature will mention *Virtual Private Dialup Networks* or VPDN, instead of VPN. Also, product documentation refers to *Network Access Servers* (*NAS*), instead of Remote Access Servers. It primarily targets ISPs. We shall see that it is not the only company to take this approach. Its primary product is a line of Internet access routers, which have been enhanced to provide high speed VPDN operations, at the ISP, not at the corporate site.

♦ *Ascend Communications*—Offers a complete line of VPN solution products. Ascend Communication products implement every phase of a VPN solution, from the software to the

Internet router. Ascend is an old line company that has been around a long time and continues to market innovative leading edge products.

♦ *Microsoft*—Primarily concerned in finding efficient, cost-effective ways to allow users to connect NT networks through the Internet. Its Windows 9x and Windows NT have built-in support for PPTP protocols and VPN.

The five companies have the WAN structure pretty well covered.

## VPN Implementation Architecture

Because the members of the PPTP Forum have such a diverse range of products, it is difficult to target a single implementation architecture. However, they all share some similarities:

♦ *Authentication*—Before creating a VPN tunnel, users must follow clearly defined authentication procedures. This almost always is based on CHAP, or the enhanced MS-CHAP, and usually incorporates the *shared secret* key encryption.

♦ *Authorization*—If necessary, users can be assigned policies to allow for different levels of authorization. If authorization is implemented, it is usually provided by policies stored within a database, usually on a separate server; in this case, RADIUS.

♦ *Data encryption*—Before data is transmitted over the Internet, it should be encrypted to prevent intercepted data from being read by unauthorized clients on the network.

♦ *Key management*—Creates and refreshes encryption keys for servers and clients.

♦ *Multiprotocol support*—Allows heterogeneous clients to communicate over the VPN.

## VPN Protocols Used With PPTP

We've been over it enough so that by now you know PPTP and L2TP have all the abilities to meet the requirements just listed. For VPNs using NT 4, Microsoft has staked its security bid on PPTP as its native protection suite. VPN connections are made with initial 40-bit or 128-bit encryption keys depending on the end unit's country of origin.

**Note**

*With a few notable exceptions like Canada and some privileged concerns, United States government policy restricts the distribution of 128-bit technology.*

When used in NT 4, PPTP depends on two proprietary protocols, Microsoft Challenge Authentication Protocol (MS-CHAP) and Microsoft Point-to-Point Encryption (MPPE), to protect user data. Some initial weaknesses showed up in implementing PPTP, but Microsoft says they have developed patches to shore them up.

## PPP Hacker Attack

At the time of this writing, at least one issue remained unresolved—*PPP negotiation spoofing* (gaining access to a network by faking an Internet address). It is possible in a PPP session for an adversary to spoof by inserting or modifying packets. Microsoft says they intend to address this and other problems in a future release by redesigning the PPTP control channel.

For a review of layer-2 protocol features, let's look at an excerpt from **msdn.microsoft.com/ workshop/server/feature/vpnovw.asp**:

♦ *User authentication*—Layer 2 tunneling protocols inherit the user authentication schemes of PPP, including the EAP methods discussed later. Many Layer 3 tunneling schemes assume that the endpoints were well known (and authenticated) before the tunnel was established. An exception to this is IPSec ISAKMP negotiation, which provides mutual authentication of the tunnel endpoints. (Note that most IPSec implementations support machine-based certificates only, rather than user certificates. As a result, any user with access to one of the endpoint machines can use the tunnel. This potential security weakness can be eliminated when IPSec is paired with a Layer 2 protocol such as L2TP.)

♦ *Token card support*—Using the Extensible Authentication Protocol (EAP), Layer 2 tunneling protocols can support a wide variety of authentication methods, including one-time passwords, cryptographic calculators, and smart cards. Layer 3 tunneling protocols can use similar methods; for example, IPSec defines public key certificate authentication in its ISAKMP/Oakley negotiation.

♦ *Dynamic address assignment*—Layer 2 tunneling supports dynamic assignment of client addresses based on the Network Control Protocol (NCP) negotiation mechanism. Generally, Layer 3 tunneling schemes assume that an address has already been assigned prior to initiation of the tunnel. Schemes for assignment of addresses in IPSec tunnel mode are currently under development and are not yet available.

♦ *Data compression*—Layer 2 tunneling protocols support PPP-based compression schemes. For example, the Microsoft implementations of both PPTP and L2TP use Microsoft Point-to-Point Compression (MPPC). The IETF is investigating similar mechanisms (such as IP Compression) for the Layer 3 tunneling protocols.

♦ *Data encryption*—Layer 2 tunneling protocols support PPP-based data encryption mechanisms. Microsoft's implementation of PPTP supports optional use of Microsoft Point-to-Point Encryption (MPPE), based on the RSA/RC4 algorithm. Layer 3 tunneling protocols can use similar methods; for example, IPSec defines several optional data encryption methods that are negotiated during the ISAKMP/Oakley exchange. Microsoft's implementation of the L2TP protocol uses IPSec encryption to protect the data stream from the client to the tunnel server.

♦ *Key management*—MPPE, a Layer 2 protocol, relies on the initial key generated during user authentication, and then refreshes it periodically. IPSec explicitly negotiates a common key during the ISAKMP exchange, and also refreshes it periodically.

♦ *Multiprotocol support*—Layer 2 tunneling supports multiple payload protocols, which makes it easy for tunneling clients to access their corporate networks using IP, IPX, NetBEUI, and so forth. In contrast, Layer 3 tunneling protocols, such as IPSec tunnel mode, typically support only target networks that use the IP protocol.

You might have noticed that the Microsoft white paper refers to some security topics we haven't said much about, like *smart cards* and *token cards*. We'll pin those down in Chapter 10 when we wrap up all the security issues.

### Interoperability

Interoperability is a big factor in the design of Microsoft products and has been a hotly debated issue in the Internet community. No company, even the giants like Microsoft, IBM, Novell, Cisco, and others, can turn their back on the heterogeneity of the Internet. The Information Technology managers have preferences—they all prefer one product over another, and unanimity will forever be a dream from Mount Olympus.

That very thought demands attention by Microsoft. Not only must data be communicated through diverse networks, in some cases devices must be operated at remote sites—the simplest example is remote access of a printer. With this thought in mind, Microsoft has announced that future support for IPsec will be available in the upcoming Windows 2000 release (more about this in a bit).

# RedCreek

If your schedule can't wait, or you don't want to upgrade to Windows 2000 yet you still would like to implement IPsec with Windows NT 4, a third party solution exists. A company named RedCreek Communications (**redcreek.com**), offers a complete line of software and hardware products to provide an IPsec solution for Windows NT 4.

RedCreek Communications has taken an innovative approach to the implementation of IPsec with Windows NT 4. You are probably aware that NT 4 requires considerable resources to operate and that the IPsec protocol suite also requires quite a bit of horsepower to give an adequate level of performance. The RedCreek solution to this is to implement the IPsec protocols in a combination of hardware and firmware on the NT server. This solution is in the form of a PCI add-in card that fits in an open PCI slot in the NT server. This essentially offloads the overhead presented by the IPsec protocols from the NT server to the PCI card, and frees up the NT server processor(s) to perform other tasks. On the client end of the tunnel the requirements are not quite so bad, as the need for authentication and authorization are removed, and only one tunnel, not hundreds, require support. Thus, the IPsec protocols are implemented as a software product that runs under Windows 9x or Windows NT at the remote site. The RedCreek implementation of IPsec under Windows NT allows a much greater degree of interoperability than has been possible in the past.

## Windows 2000

The replacement for NT 4 was originally named NT 5, but it has been renamed and is now called Windows 2000 (W2K). This book and that software are in production together. The changes that could come about in the software before it is released to the public is the number one reason we have decided not to use it between our covers.

Like NT, network administrators will be faced with buying W2K for starters and, if they want the server, buying W2K Server edition. From our perspective, the most exciting promise being made about W2K (and Server) is the Active Directory Services.

## Summary

The original PPTP Forum was formed with the intent of providing a tunneling protocol that could be used to allow access to Microsoft NT networks by remote users through the Internet. As noted, the PPTP protocol has been joined by Cisco's L2TP, and both share many of the same protocols for the purpose of authentication, authorization, encryption, and encapsulation. Both PPTP and L2TP enjoy a substantial portion of the market today, but as VPN's implementation becomes more common, the driving force is interoperability.

Industry experts are predicting that the IPsec protocol suite will become the predominant standard for VPN implementation. For this reason, every VPN manufacturer today either already supports IPsec, or has plans for supporting IPsec in future releases of their products.

# Novell

Founded in 1983, the corporate headquarters of Novell is maintained in Provo, Utah, with worldwide connections, alliances, and strategic partnerships. You can find them on the Web at **www.novell.com**.

## History

Novell® produces a network operating system known as NetWare®. Contrary to rumors, Novell is very much alive and doing quite well with their flagship product, NetWare 5. The company also produces a large number of network-related products, including VPN, as part of a suite of Internet-related features.

Novell has the most experience when it comes to tunneling protocols. Because early NetWare products relied on the IPX/SPX protocol stack, a method of tunneling packets through networks with IP protocol has been in use for a number of years.

Novell's philosophy has always been to develop the highest level of security possible for NetWare. NetWare encryption dates back to version 3.11. NetWare clients always encrypted their passwords before transmitting them over the network. Starting with NetWare 3.12, Novell developed a protocol using the equivalent of SA and packet signing on individual packets for protection against the *man-in-the-middle* attack.

Novell considered IP inherently unsecure because the Internet protocol suite used open architecture and, until recently, based their products on the IPX protocol. Two events changed the way they thought in Provo. First, with the explosion in growth of the Internet, for better or worse, the world jumped on the IP bandwagon. The wonderkids in Provo (some of which have gray hair) saw the writing on the wall: *Switch to IP or go the way of the dodo bird*. The second event was development of IPsec, which made it possible to implement a high level of security over an open architecture network. Novell wisely embraced IPsec as the mechanism for implementing security within the NetWare architecture.

## Novell's Approach To Networks

From the very start, networking, and network-related functions, have been the primary product at Novell. In developing NetWare, Novell set down the priorities for a network operating system in the following order:

♦ Ease of use

♦ Security

♦ Reliability

♦ Speed

### Ease Of Use

Novell's theory is that network administrators don't use the network, they keep the network alive for the users, and Novell provides a number of GUI-based tools designed to make the network administrators life a little easier. The most significant is *Novell Directory Services*—the ability to have all the network objects in a single database and assign properties based on needs takes some strain out of the administrator's job.

Users use the network, and to them the process should be no more difficult than operating the computer. So Novell's implementation employs a high-end computer to provide services to the network, not the user. Other than the login procedure and the availability of a lot more drive letters, users on a Novell network should not notice any difference before or after the network is installed. For the users, the server is only an electronics-filled box sitting in the network administrator's office with a *Do Not Touch* sign dangling from it.

### Security

In developing its approach to security, Novell emulated the manufacturers of mainframe computers and has what we believe is the highest level of security in the network industry. We will discuss permissions and trust in greater detail in Chapter 10, but for now accept the premise that Novell views the network as a closed system. New users have access to only the bare essentials necessary to prevent them from crashing the system. From there on, everything the user has access to is explicitly granted by the network administrator based on need.

### Reliability

This should speak for itself. It doesn't matter how fast or how good the product is, if it doesn't work reliably, no one will want it. All software has bugs, and Novell software is no different from any other vendor's product. Most of them are caught during the *beta test* process, some make it out to the world, and some are never found. Products live or die on customer satisfaction. If you don't believe that, look back at OS-2.

### Speed

Speed is the name of the game. Novell knows this and makes every effort to continue to improve the speed of its products. In this respect Novell is no different from all the other vendors, who are all slaves to technology.

## Novell's VPN Architecture

From an architectural standpoint, NetWare is a *server-centric* network operating system. It uses PC computers equipped with major resources to provide clients on the network with a large list of network services.

Although individual clients can communicate with each other on an individual basis, NetWare NOS is not considered a peer-to-peer system. Clients cannot easily share their individual workstation's resources with others. Based on this architecture, establishing a VPN using Novell NetWare requires two distinct parts: one part client-based, and the other part based at the Security Gateway.

Novell NetWare has long been implemented as a WAN architecture. WANs developed using NetWare as the primary NOS used the traditional concept of a private network at distributed locations, tied together with WAN links (T1, Frame Relay, ISDN, etc.). Novell places a great deal of emphasis on giving the network administrator the responsibility of establishing and maintaining the highest level of security possible. It is natural then that Novell's approach to establishing a network connection between the private network and the Internet requires maintaining the LAN/WAN administrator's security expectations.

To meet the requirement, Novell developed a suite of interrelated network services under the name *Novell BorderManager*™ that acts as the security gateway. Although Novell's primary goal is to make it possible for current NetWare owners to establish secure manageable connections to the Internet, the company also offers the BorderManager suite as a standalone product. As a standalone product, BorderManager includes a *runtime* version of NetWare installed on the server.

One final note: the BorderManager server can be implemented as a gateway or as a proxy server.

## Gateway

As a gateway, the server operates with one network connection to the DMZ subnet and another network connection to the intranet. This way, the BorderManager server is the same physical equipment as the firewall proxy host, shown in Figure 5.3. This is Novell's recommended implementation in order to take advantage of the entire range of features provided by the BorderManager Server.

## Proxy

As a proxy server, BorderManager uses one network connection and can be placed inside or outside the firewall. When installed as a proxy, the BorderManager server is the proxy host shown in Figures 5.1 and 5.2, and will provide reliable and secure proxy host and VPN capability. On the down side, the user cannot take advantage of the full range of features possible with the BorderManager server.

## Master/Slave Configuration

Network administrators can install BorderManager on more than one machine within a corporate intranet. In that case, one server must be configured as the *Master* and any others within the same intranet must be configured as *Slaves*. This configuration allows establishing VPNs *within* the corporate intranet as shown in Figure 5.4. This type of IntraVPN is desirable in many cases.

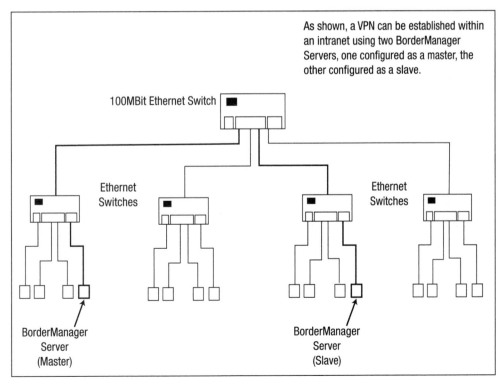

As shown, a VPN can be established within an intranet using two BorderManager Servers, one configured as a master, the other configured as a slave.

**Figure 5.4**
VPN within the corporate intranet.

# VPN Protocols Implemented With BorderManager

Novell first offered VPN capability with BorderManager 2.1 using a proprietary protocol based on RFC 1234. The protocol established site-to-site tunnels, through encapsulation, over the Internet, or within an intranet. Version 2.1 uses encryption with public key cryptography to provide and maintain confidentiality and integrity. With the release of Border-Manager 3 in May 1999, Novell shifted to VPN protocols based on the open standards of IPsec and away from proprietary protocols.

### Version 3

BorderManager Release 2.1 did not directly support the implementation of client-to-site VPN tunnels. The capability to provide this service was not implemented until the release of Version 3. To allow NetWare implementations without BorderManager (or with version 2.1) to establish client-to-site VPN's, Novell NetWare Client includes support of the PPTP protocol. A Novell white paper details how to establish a PPTP VPN from a remote user to the corporate intranet using the combination of Windows 9x and NetWare Client 32.

Novell improved its VPN architecture with BorderManager 3. Version 3 is based on the IPsec protocol suite. For the real security minded—we hope that's the majority of our readers—here is some information about the standards Novell has adopted in the BorderManager 3 that apply to VPN:

♦ Simple Key Exchange Internet Protocol (SKIP)

♦ IP Security (IPsec) based on:

  ♦ Authentication Header (AH) RFC 1826

  ♦ Encapsulated Security Payload (ESP) RFC 1827

♦ Key/data encryption (domestic version) based on:

  ♦ 128-bit RC2

  ♦ 128-bit RC5

  ♦ 64-bit DES

♦ Authentication (domestic version) based on:

  ♦ 128-bit keyed MD5 128-bit HMAC MD5

  ♦ 160-bit keyed SHA 160-bit HMAC SHA

Don't get too excited about the encryption terms above if you are not familiar with them. You will see them explained in Chapter 10. Also, we only listed domestic encryption and authentication algorithms; the key and data encryption algorithms are different from the export versions.

### Tunnels

BorderManager 3 provides site-to-site tunnels through the Internet and intranet and, unlike its predecessor, also provides *client-to-site* encrypted tunnels using PPP through an ISP or NetWare Connect. Also like 2.1, version 3 uses the NetWare Client 32 with Windows 95/98 to establish a VPN connection, except the client architecture has been enhanced to make the process more transparent to the user.

Remember from Chapter 4 that earlier versions of NetWare were based on IPX/SPX protocols and could tunnel IPX packets through an IP network. The VPN capability provided by BorderManager 2.1 is probably a modification of IPX/SPX and is the most likely reason why Version 2.1 does not support client-to-site implementation. However, BorderManager 3 architecture has been designed for TCP/IP. Now, even though BorderManager 3 provides VPN capability based on IPsec, Novell did not turn their backs on the large number of networks still using older NetWare using the IPX/SPX protocol; BorderManager 3 suites provide tunneling and encryption protection for both IP and IPX packets.

### Compatibility With Other Software

Because Novell developed BorderManager 3's VPN capabilities using published open standards, some degree of interoperability with other vendor's IPsec compliant products should be possible. Interoperability between different vendors products becomes more and more important as more and more companies move toward establishing VPN's between corporate intranets. It is important that Unix systems can talk to NetWare, Microsoft, or anybody. We'll deal with that problem in Chapter 6.

### The Novell Directory Services Connection

We mentioned earlier in this section that having a directory system containing all the entities in the network could make administration a lot easier. We also mentioned a movement inside Novell to step closer to open published standards and away from proprietary standards. With the release of NDS Version 8, Novell made significant improvements in the move towards this goal. NDS V8 has a much better interface with the *Lightweight Directory Access Protocol* (*LDAP*).

### So What Does This Mean In Real Terms?

You will be hard pressed to find anyone in the network industry (with the notable exceptions of marketing departments) not agreeing that the authentication provided by NDS is one of the best in the industry. It allows the network administrator to assign properties to a user or user interface that include virtual channels, QOS, and CAs. These are all part of the AH and SA implemented in the IPsec protocol suite.

In short, you can set up entities and assign VPN properties to that entity. Using the improved LDAP interface, you can update those properties through the Internet from a distant location. Add to this the interoperability provided by the open IPsec standard, and you can establish a VPN with a non NetWare site and maintain a reasonable degree of manageability and administrative control over the connection.

## Wrap-Up On Novell

BorderManager 3 provides an enhanced means of implementing VPN as an addition to an already existing NetWare network, or a standalone to whatever network system you have. As we have shown, the BorderManager Server can be implemented as a gateway at the connection point to the Internet, or a proxy server inside or outside the firewall. BorderManager 3:

♦ Implements the security of IPsec over a public network like the Internet or a private intranet.

♦ Supports site-to-site and client-to-site tunnels.

♦ Protects either IP or IPX packets. Client-to-site tunnels are established using the PPP protocol when connected through an ISP or NetWare Connect.

# Cisco Systems

After shipping its first product in 1986, Cisco now claims to sell its products in approximately 115 countries. Cisco has headquarters in San Jose, California, and major operations in Research Triangle Park, North Carolina, and Chelmsford, Massachusetts. On the Web, it can be found at **www.cisco.com**.

## History

Cisco claims that 80 percent of the hardware routers in use on the Internet came from its plants. The company catalog includes a wide range of products and has become the number one leader in providing routers for use in WAN and Internet systems. As with all manufacturers in the computer industry, some software products are included in the Cisco catalog, but its forte has always been the WAN router market.

Unlike vendors sporting a broad range of product offerings in several areas of computer operations, Cisco seems content with a smaller niche. Its products are designed to work quietly in the background, providing services that users at the keyboards never realize. Although Cisco does, and will continue, to sell its products to corporations and other organizations for WAN infrastructures, its primary markets are not the corporations, companies, or end users—they target the service providers.

## Cisco's Approach To Network Architecture

Cisco depends on ISPs as the primary implementers of their network products and has developed a range of service offerings for them, including the following:

- Quality of Service
- Manageability
- Reliability
- Scalability
- Security

### Quality Of Service (QOS)

QOS, according to Cisco philosophy, addresses two fundamental requirements: predictable performance and policy implementation. Policies assign resources in a prioritized way. In pursuit of predictable performance, Cisco implements protocols that prioritize service classes, allocate bandwidth, avoid congestion, and link Layer 2 and Layer 3 QOS mechanisms.

### Manageability

Cisco provides an integrated set of products for service planning, operations, and accounting through the *Cisco Service Management System* (CSM).

### Reliability

The product line is designed with a provision for backup paths if a link or device fails.

### Scalability

Cisco claims that VPNs based on Cisco's *MultiProtocol Label Switching* (MPLS) technology can be scaled up to support tens of thousands of VPNs.

### Security

Cisco VPNs are built around Authentication, Authorization, and Accounting (AAA), data privacy, and integrity, and use a broad range of protocols for the tasks.

## Partnership Approach

When offering these services to ISPs, Cisco proposes a partnership with them and encourages the ISPs to partner with their customers. This allows enterprises to grow their business intranet and extranet capabilities by relying on the capabilities of the service providers, which are in turn backed by Cisco Systems.

Such an arrangement provides a small- to medium-sized business the capability to establish and maintain high-end services, such as VPNs, without a significant investment in new hardware or increased personnel requirements—perhaps an attractive offer for many businesses, especially those that have only small LANs or intranets.

## VPN Implementation Architecture

Cisco promotes implementation of three types of VPNs:

- ◆ *Access VPNs*—Handle remote-access connectivity for mobile users, telecommuters, and small offices.

- ◆ *Intranet VPNs*—Link remote offices using the Internet.

- ◆ *Extranet VPNs*—Allow suppliers, customers, partners, and communities of interest to form a virtual network across the Internet.

From a physical standpoint, Cisco views VPNs as originating at the ISP's router because it views the implementation as the responsibility of the ISP. An exception is a major corporation with the resources to implement Cisco equipment (routers, etc.) as a part of their *customer premises equipment* (CPE). The firewall is provided usually by the LAN owner, and any VPN implemented through services provided by an ISP on Cisco hardware and software would most likely have the security gateway located outside of the firewall. In Figure 5.2, the security gateway could be combined in the same device used as the firewall gateway between the Internet and the DMZ subnet.

Because Cisco products tend to concentrate around hardware, using routers, switches, and hubs, they mostly deal with the lower levels of the OSI model although its management software products work at all layers up through the Application Layer. Cisco products work exceptionally well—when interfaced with other Cisco products. This high degree of performance has been known to drop off when another vendor's product lies on the other end.

## VPN Protocols

Cisco considers the ISP a major segment of its market and the company leans heavily on protocols designed to locate a particular *home* router out of the thousands of devices located on the Internet. Cisco's VPN offerings also lean heavily on AAA derived primarily from the basic TACACS+, RADIUS, and CHAP protocols with, of course, modifications to improve performance. Cisco implemented these protocols as a part of their *Layer Two Forwarding (L2F)*, and continued the implementation under the new *Layer Two Tunneling Protocol (L2TP)*.

Along with L2TP, Cisco offers products implementing IPsec, GRE, and MPLS protocols. Cisco's implementation of IPsec uses *Encapsulating Security Protocol* (ESP) and the *data encryption standard (DES)* to protect encapsulated payloads passing through the Internet. Cisco uses the implementation of MPLS to build virtual circuits that can be implemented with a guaranteed QOS.

Cisco markets these protocols through a combination of software and hardware. The primary VPN software product is *CiscoSecure Access Control Server* (ACS). ACS software is implemented on Cisco hardware. Not all of the protocols we've listed are implemented in every Cisco product. Cisco, like other manufacturers, tends to implement the higher level protocols in their high-end products.

# Management Systems

Cisco prefers the term *management system*, rather than directory services. Like their other products, the Cisco *Service Management System* (CSM) is targeted primarily at ISPs. Although CSM might not provide the depth and extensibility of other directory services, it provides the ISP with seamless management of WAN switches, routers, firewalls, and Cisco IOS software. The CSM is a suite that includes these Cisco programs:

♦ Planning Center

♦ Netsys

♦ WAN Service Administrator

♦ Provisioning Center

♦ User Control Point

♦ Info Center

♦ Accounting Center and Data Collectors

When applied and used together, this suite of management tools arms the ISP with an integrated set of products for service planning, provisioning, operations, accounting, and billing.

# Collaborations

With Microsoft working to include Active Directory in its new Windows 2000 product and Novell's NDS looking for industry-wide acceptance, Cisco has signed partnering agreements with both companies to keep its Internet routers abreast of the fast-paced developments.

# Summary

Since 1986 Cisco has enjoyed the number one position as the preferred provider of hardware routers, switches, and remote-access products. The company focuses a wide range of products and support options on its primary customer, the ISP, and encourages the ISP to target large, medium, and small enterprises with the same products.

Cisco VPN services, either direct or through ISPs, are based on AAA incorporating several different protocols, including L2F, L2TP, and IPsec. The products offer dedicated virtual channels with guaranteed QOS, combined with the scalability into the tens of thousands of virtual connections. Because Cisco creates partnerships with ISPs and encourages ISPs to do the same with their customers, VPN services can be made available to businesses without substantial increases in equipment and personnel.

# Indus River Software

Indus River Software, located in Acton, Massachusetts (**www.indusriver.com**), is unlike any company we've discussed so far. It is an emerging enterprise, founded in 1996 and financed by U.S. venture capital firms. There's nothing wrong with that; in fact almost every major company in this industry, including a few we have mentioned in this book, started out with venture capital. What makes Indus River stand out from the rest is its stated mission: "...to develop new technologies and solutions for enterprise-class VPNs."

VPN is what the staff, scientists, engineers, and technicians at Indus River do; it's the only thing they do and they've been at it since they opened the doors. Their focus on VPNs has given them a great deal of insight into the market, with some surprising results. The people at Indus River Software strike me as being very good at what they do and their emphasis is where it really needs to be—on the user.

## Indus River Approach To Networks

Like other players in the VPN market, Indus River Software sees the Internet as a tool that provides the mechanism through which virtual channels, or tunnels, are created to move encrypted IP datagrams from one location to another. As with the other vendors, Indus River Software places lots of emphasis on speed, reliability, and at the same time on being user friendly. Their white paper—**www.indusriver.com/pro/pro_dnld.htm**—lists three key features needed for a successful VPN:

- ◆ Scalability
- ◆ Manageability
- ◆ Simplicity

### *Scalability*

Designed primarily for remote-access VPN systems, Indus River Software is based on a highly-scaleable, turnkey solution to fill the requirements of large corporate users, and is marketed under the trade name RiverWorks. The architecture is based on the concept of providing three distinct services, each being a separate operation, but able to operate together when required:

- ◆ Provide an intuitive, simple user interface at one end of the tunnel (the remote user), and a high-speed dedicated tunnel endpoint processor at the other end. Encapsulation and encryption take place at the tunnel endpoints.
- ◆ Provide a separate authentication server so the authentication and authorization processes do not interfere with the operation of the tunnel processors.
- ◆ Provide a set of comprehensive management tools.

### Managability

The Indus River concept of a remote access VPN system consists of five main components:

♦ *RiverWorks Tunnel Server*—A proprietary tunnel processor providing high-speed scalable tunnel processing for up to 2,000 simultaneous connections per server. If more than one tunnel server is required, they can be added to the enterprise network in one of two ways: grouped together in a cluster or distributed at different sites throughout the enterprise network. Regardless of which method is used, the River Works Tunnel Server can be located on either side of the firewall.

♦ *RiverWorks Management Server*—One proprietary server inside the firewall for end-to-end management of the VPN tunnels and users. The management server contains the database of users, passwords, and policies if this feature is implemented.

♦ *RiverMaster Management Application*—A PC-based software application used in conjunction with the Management Server to perform network management activities on the RiverWorks VPN(s).

♦ *RiverPilot Universal Access Manager*—An easy-to-use client access tool combining Internet and traditional dial access methods to ensure that the user is connected through the most efficient ISP.

♦ *RiverWay Subscription Service*—An up-to-date database of current ISP access numbers, rate tables for both ISPs and carriers, and system diagnostics files.

### Simplicity

With all the emphasis on remote access VPN, Indus River has placed extra effort into making the VPN as fast as possible while at the same time easy to use. Two examples are as follows:

♦ The remote user environment is a highly intuitive GUI interface based on the concept of cellular telephony. When the user initiates a connection, two software services are enabled transparently: *TollSaver Connection Manager* (an on-board database of ISP and carrier rate tables to make a decision on the best link available) and the *Prescriptive Diagnostics Engine* (which detects and corrects connection faults by consulting an on-board Prescriber database, selecting a diagnostic script from that database, and executing it).

♦ After the connection is established, RiverWorks enhances performance using protocol extensions, such as channel learning, that set the size of the protocol window based on the actual round-trip time for packets and selective retransmission of lost packets.

These two examples demonstrate the degree of thought that the software engineers at Indus River Software have put into the development of their VPN solution.

## RiverWorks VPN Protocols

In designing the RiverWorks VPN product, the software engineers at Indus River took a page from Microsoft philosophy manuals. When an existing protocol did not deliver a required level of performance for specific goals, the protocol was enhanced. The result has been a highly scaleable product with an acceptable degree of interoperability and low burdens on the user.

The RiverWorks VPN solution encounters the same difficulties as all other existing VPNs. These can be divided into the following areas.

♦ Tunneling

♦ Authentication

♦ Encryption

### Tunneling

RiverWorks' primary tunneling protocol, *Indus River Tunneling Protocol* (IRTP), is proprietary and few details are available. IRTP probably started out as PPTP and has been enhanced to improve performance required to meet the goals. Primary among these enhancements were:

♦ Compression prior to encryption

♦ Adapting the transmission window to use the actual Internet *round-trip time* (RTT)

♦ Reducing packet loss and retransmission of only lost packets

### Authentication

RiverWorks employs several different schemes for implementing authentication. Like Microsoft, they can use the native database password as a *shared secret* known to both ends of the VPN and implement it with CHAP. In addition, RiverWorks can implement RADIUS to maintain remote user policies, names, and passwords.

A stronger authentication method known as *two-factor authentication* is also supported. This method is based on the remote user supplying two factors:

♦ Something the user knows, such as a password.

♦ Something the user has, such as a hardware-based token card (SecurIDR from Security Dynamics is a good example), or a software-based algorithm keyed to a specific machine.

The stronger two-factor authentication method can also support the RADIUS protocol.

A key feature of RiverWorks architecture is authentication using a separate *management server* to maintain a database comprising users, passwords, and policies. This database is customized and extended in the form of a *TollServer Database* and distributed to the remote user as a part of the RiverPilot software.

### Encryption

Several protocols can be used for encryption. Among them are:

- *RC-4*—Uses either a 40-bit or 128-bit key.
- *DES*—Uses a 56-bit key.
- *Triple-DES*—Uses a 128-bit key.

Like the authentication process, encryption can use a shared key algorithm based on the password as the shared key, another key known to both ends, or a public key algorithm. Another option is the selection of a key management protocol and the use of digital certificates and CAs. When used together, these combine to provide a *public key infrastructure*.

So you see that a large number of protocols can be used with the RiverWorks VPN solution. The choice of protocols is at the discretion of the network administrator following his or her company's security policy.

## Summary

Indus River Software is a relatively new company in the computer industry and is content at the time to focus its resources on the relatively new technology called VPN. Interoperability is one of Indus River's important long-term goals. They also look for IPsec to emerge as the standard protocol suite for IP (including VPN) security. Indus River software engineers are mapping out a long-term future strategy based on that foresight.

# Chapter 6

# *Incorporating VPN Into An Existing Network*

## Key Topics:

- ♦ *Network access and use policy*
- ♦ *Training*
- ♦ *Technical support staff*
- ♦ *Design notes*
- ♦ *Hidden cost considerations*

I want to caution you about skipping this chapter. In some previous chapters we said words to the effect that if you are familiar with the information, you can feel free to skip to the next chapter. We explicitly withdraw that suggestion in this case. We start this chapter by looking at the impact of VPN implementation on users and support staff. Implementing a VPN solution may have some effects you don't expect or plan for.

Your company may be implementing a VPN solution between a central location and a number of branch offices in order to reduce the cost of supporting a stable of T1 lines. Given this case, you may think that users perceive no difference in the appearance or operation of the network. So why should you have to review existing network access and use? Later in this chapter I will create a small scenario that could easily be applied to any company. This scenario demonstrates that in sharing a limited resource between the users' perceived needs and the needs of the company, everyone is involved in some way.

As in the preceding chapters, we will make some basic assumptions. First, you currently have an existing network of at least LAN proportions and you may also have a WAN with one or more branch offices and one or more traveling or remote users. Presuming that your business is related to supply or manufacturing, we assume that you might also be moving towards setting up an extranet with some of your suppliers, vendors, or some of your customers.

# The Human Factor

As we shall see, all of these are valid applications for installing a VPN system. What you will also see is that the larger and more complex the system, the greater the need for a cohesive plan that is as well structured as possible.

It was not too many years ago that the first step in implementing a network system was to make a plan. Groups of individuals—usually managers—from the different enterprise divisions gathered together and negotiated compromises based on what was theoretically possible versus what could realistically be implemented. The problem today is that few network plans adequately describe the types and variety of implementation methods possible with existing technology.

Why? The reason is simple—the technology has outgrown the scenario where a bunch of people from different divisions, who all know each other by their first names, can even keep up with what is available. Otherwise we wouldn't have an MIS department with information technologists and network administrators.

None of that relieves an enterprise from the absolute requirement of adequate planning. But plans are only part of good network operations. Anyone starting out now and hoping to still be on the same track in three to five years must have a policy.

## Policy Planning

Several years ago, it would have sufficed for a network to be designed and built around a single basic plan. Today, because of the vast improvements in technology, companies looking to implement new network systems find it necessary to design a plan for each user on the network. Probably no other area of network implementation requires this more than the VPN. With such a daunting task facing you, where or how do you start? For large corporations or small enterprises with ambition to grow, the answer is obvious: the plan must be based on the accepted *policies*.

*Policy*, as applied to networks, is one of those buzzwords. Lots of people talk about it; it must feel good rolling off the tongue. But how many people really know what a good network access and use policy is? Just to be sure we are talking about the same thing, let's take a quick look and see if your definition and my definition are the same. As with everything else, we'll start with some history first.

### *Does Your Company Currently Use Policies?*

You may not be aware of it, but everyone working for (or somehow connected with) a company has a set of policies they follow. The most common policies are administrative: rates of pay, holidays, vacation allowance, and so forth. Today, IT managers and network administrators are defining new types of policy—guidelines for computer and network usage.

Not too many years ago, when most network systems were based on mainframe computers, the MIS department at most enterprises was given the responsibility to allow users access to the computer system. Generically speaking, the network administrator created a user account, set up access to data files needed, and implemented procedures defining what that user was allowed to do with those files. All the procedures were based on the tasks the user was required to perform. When protection was necessary, the MIS department issued passwords, specifying the length of the password and its expiration date—usually some regular interval. Keep in mind, the password allowed the user to log onto the *mainframe* computer.

Starting in the 1980s, the NetWare network operating system appeared. From the start, Novell decided that the same level of security available for mainframe computers would be available for network information accessed by PCs. This security specified which sections of the file system the user had access to, which programs the user could run, which data files the user could access, and to what level the user could make changes. This information was stored on the file server in a special database, the *Access Control List (ACL)*. Novell's only concern was controlling user's access through the network, including the NetWare servers; it did not try to implement any type of security on the PC workstation itself.

In the mid-1980s Microsoft introduced Windows 3. This operating system was very versatile, and users soon discovered they could change a large number of items to suit themselves. On occasion, such changes did more harm than good and MIS or Computer Technical Services (CTS) was called on to restore system operation. With the release of Windows 3.11 and peer-to-peer networking, users were cabled together into workgroups, allowing them to make changes not only on their local machines, but also on other users machines as well. Microsoft had a philosophy at that time that restricting what a user could and could not do with their computer was considered to be *old world* technology, certainly not the *new technology* they were planning for the NT release.

A third factor entered the picture. The computer industry was developing new products for the Windows environment. In most cases the new stuff was great, and solved problems some enterprises didn't know existed. As a result, the computer industry grew by leaps and bounds. Two particularly noteworthy products are digitizing flatbed scanners and multimedia video and sound software and hardware. As we will show you later on in this chapter, these two items alone can shoot holes in *any* network plan.

Windows NT improved on a concept present in almost all multiuser network operating systems, but primarily found in Unix systems. In Unix systems, the configuration information for the environment of the computer—outside of the core operating system or kernel—is stored in several text files. When Microsoft developed Windows 3.x, they followed this basic concept and stored the user's configuration information in text files, primarily WIN.INI and SYSTEM.INI. You can edit these text files with any text editor, and software and hardware developers were encouraged to follow this same model and either make entries in existing *.INI files or develop clones.

With the release of Windows 95 and NT, Microsoft raised the concept of configuration files to the next higher level. The software changed the configuration information from text files to a *registry database* containing all the information pertaining to the configuration of that specific computer. Later, with the release of Windows 98 and Windows NT 4, the registry was enhanced and enlarged and, more importantly, could contain information about the configuration of the computer for *each different user* of that computer. The registry contained information on what changes the user could make, what programs and data files the user could access, and to what level the user could make changes on that data.

The registry is not just a text file, it is a *database* file modified with tools designed for that function and the administrator determines who has access to the tools. Every change a user or administrator makes to the Windows Desktop is recorded in the registry, including granting or revoking trusted relationships on the network. The registry is the users' configuration storehouse and determines what authority each user has over the system data files.

Then came the *directory*—the binding force—containing information on all objects known to the network. Properly configured, the directory is linked to the registries that are customized for individual users. Working in the directory, the network administrator can use one tool to establish uniform corporate policies on all users throughout the entire system. Users can move freely about the corporate workspace and log onto any PC that meets the company policy on minimum hardware requirements. It matters not if they are sitting at their assigned desk, on the manufacturing floor, or in a hotel room in Cut-N-Shoot, Texas.

Well, at least that's the way it's supposed to work. Remember that original network plan I talked about a while back? I made the point that most of the time the plan is a compromise between what is theoretically possible and what can be realistically implemented. Using Microsoft terminology, users are given access to network services based on *trusted relationships* implemented by the system administrator based on the company's policies. The term *policies* has become the buzzword used to describe an enhanced version of what the MIS department has done for many years in the mainframe environment—that is, to grant users' rights to programs and data files based on trusted relationships. The big difference today is the amount of details that must be defined and the amount of information that must be known—some of which has to come from a crystal ball—in order to establish a good policy for network access and use.

### *Should You Consider Implementing Policies?*

If your company has more than two employees and does not have written policies in place to adequately describe network access and use, finish this chapter, then pick up the phone and call your boss. It's time to get to work on a policy. Was an existing policy taken under serious review the last time changes were made to the network? If the answer is no, reach for the telephone and start the review process.

Is the company considering a change in its network, a greater degree of Internet dependence, or perhaps investing in VPN? (Why else would you have bought this book?) The time for policy development is now, because it will have direct influence on planned modifications.

Eventually, when a company grows large enough—and we hope yours does if it is not there already—the network access and use policy will reach a time when it is under constant review and continuous development.

### What Items Should Be Detailed In Policies?

The number of differences in individual networks, equipment, and procedures, coupled with different attitudes of management at different plants combine to make this a nearly impossible question to answer. What is the company's attitude toward accessing the Internet to play interactive games, like contract bridge? Are proprietary documents filed away on the engineering design staff's computer? How well do you want to protect the personal records of the employees?

WWWWWH is an old journalist's key for Who, What, Why, When, Where, and How. Who do you want to allow access to what files, subnets, extranets, VPN? Why do they need them and what can they do with them once attached? When can the files be accessed, and by whom? Where must the users initiate access or contact and how do they go about it? WWWWWH serves only to open Pandora's Box.

Like the Internet itself, a discussion of what should and should not be included in a good network access and use policy could rapidly grow to become the focus of this book. Fortunately, several good sites exist on the Web and you can read their policies. Here are three sites for you to peruse:

♦ **www.stonehill.edu/technology/networkpolicy.htm**

♦ **www.uel.ac.uk/1_the-university/university-services**

♦ RFC 2196

One item that should be mentioned here is especially important if you are switching a number of remote users from traditional dial-in access to Internet VPN access. Contrary to what a few ISPs would have you believe, access to the Internet is not unlimited. As with any resource, the Internet has physical limits; making a change in one area often causes unexpected changes in other areas.

Your traveling or remote users have necessary tasks for the performance of their jobs and will depend on a minimum guaranteed level of Internet access to succeed. I mentioned two technological marvels that could wreak havoc on a network: scanners and multimedia. The reason I mentioned these two in particular is because they take up a tremendous amount of storage on the system and moving these files from one location to another places a real strain on available resources. If one of the tasks your remote users do routinely is to stream video or audio in real time, you need to take this into consideration when developing and implementing your network access and use policy.

Nothing works better than a plausible scenario—in this case, a fictional company named Specialty Training, Incorporated. The company's claim to fame is developing specialized multimedia-based training for manufacturers in industries with groups of 20 to 40 employees. Specialty Training has an in-house staff to develop and present unique training based on the customer's needs. In some cases, this training includes proprietary information that the customer entrusts to Specialty Training; however, the customer wants the information protected. Sounds like a pretty neat company, eh?

Specialty Training employs 100 people. Fifteen are outside sales staff that travel all over the world marketing the company's training products. One of the employee benefits is a stock option plan in which every employee is vested. The rest of the crew work in the home office where most of them have desktop PCs connected via an Ethernet LAN with—according to company policy—unrestricted Internet access across a T1 line. The boss, George M., thinks this is a good idea, as it keeps the employees up-to-date on current events and boosts moral. Nobody remembers how far back it was, but a Web channel that presented streaming video and audio from the Internet propagated from PC to PC until just about everybody had the ability to "tune in" to stock market prices, weather, and news.

In the past, no one has experienced any noticeable problems using these capabilities. Today, the stock market is taking a dive. Employee pensions are in jeopardy. Every 90 seconds, the boss glances over to his terminal, watching to see if his stake is being depleted. Harry, down in the stockroom, is busily updating the inventories, and Marcie, in the human relations office, is preparing the quarterly report on sick leave. On their machines the audio is turned down as the market report scrolls across the bottom of their screens.

Specialty Training began its enterprise operations following conventional formats. The training products were developed in-house, copied onto a digital format (usually one or more CD-ROMs), and delivered to the customer. When the customer requested a change, the process of editing in the changes, burning a new set of CDs, and delivering them consumed time, a commodity always in short supply. The enterprise, like all other industries, is competitive, and Specialty Training is always on the lookout for faster and less expensive ways of developing and delivering its products to the customer.

What sets Specialty Training apart from its competition today is its development and use of remote access links through dedicated dial-in ISDN connections to deliver its product. This shortens the development delivery cycle and, because each circuit is in effect an extension of Specialized Training's private network, allows a degree of protection for the manufacturer's proprietary information. To reduce the cost of maintaining several dial-in ISDN lines, Specialized Training decided to implement a VPN with its location on one end of the tunnel and its customer's network system on the other end.

Laura D., ST's top salesperson, has taken advantage of new world technology to set up a sales pitch to a client that has been especially hard to catch. The contract promises to be very lucrative—if the new prospect can be convinced to sign it. Laura has arranged a presentation for the prospective customer's top management and has everything in place for 10:00 A.M., Central Time. One of the goals is to show ST's ability to communicate in real time. George will do a short welcoming talk about the company, complete with pictures and illustrations, and turn it back to Laura, who will access image files and sound bites from the sales department subnet back at headquarters.

The plush conference room at the Hilton is ready; Laura has been there since 7:00 A.M., making sure. Carafes of fresh coffee and trays of pastries have been delivered and early arrivals are helping themselves. A projection screen has been lowered at one end of the room so everybody can get a good view. The laptop computer is connected through its modem to a local ISP and the VPN link back to ST headquarters has been established. The laptop is delivering formatted video from the headquarters to the compact LCD projector on the conference table and the ST logo is onscreen. At the same time, a small discrete camera is relaying images of the conference room back to George M.'s desk.

ST's president is sitting at his desk watching the conference room image on his computer terminal, waiting for his cue from Laura. He isn't exactly watching the picture of the conference room; his eyes are on the streaming "ticker-tape" stock report scrolling across the bottom of the screen looking for ST's corporate symbol. The New York Stock Exchange has been open for two hours and the Dow Jones Average has dropped alarmingly.

At this point, just as Laura switches on her microphone and begins to talk, more than 60 of the 85 PCs in the headquarters building are logged onto the Internet. Everyone is deeply concerned. Each one of those channels back home requires a bandwidth of at least 50 Kbps, which gives an overall bandwidth requirement of 60x50=3,000 or about 3 Mbps. This is about double what a T1 will support. In effect, the T1 is now delivering less bandwidth per user than a 56K modem connection.

What do you suppose is going to happen to the presentation that is just starting for that potentially lucrative customer? Have I made my point about the need for network access and use policies?

# Security

Your search for VPN solutions has probably netted you as many different schemes as you have tallied up different vendors. Each claimed to be a little different from its neighbor, and each says that difference makes them perform better than any of the others—a good example of circular logic. However, all VPN solutions, almost without fail, have two common threads: first, a claim of high dependability; and second, a claim of achieving a certain level of security. After a while, you begin to get the feeling that VPN and security almost mean the same thing. And to a certain degree, that assumption may be right.

We are going to devote all of Chapter 10 to security, but, because this chapter deals with how the implementation of a VPN solution will affect local and remote staff, as well as support staff, we think a short discussion on what to expect is in order.

### How Much Security Is Enough?

This is a question you should continue to ask yourself and bring up at every system review meeting. We can't answer it; we don't know what your company's policies and security posture are. Sometime back I pointed out that the higher the level of security on a network (any network), the more difficult it becomes to use the network to move data. The level of security you should implement is of course dependent on the type of data that you are using your network to process. Even though it is not my intent for you to use this book as a guide for establishing and implementing network security, I will keep waving the flag that says you need to be aware of security-related issues.

### Should You Increase Your Existing Security?

When you implement a VPN solution as a part of your network system, the answer to this question is probably going to be yes. This does not mean, however, that you will have to increase existing security in all areas of your network system.

Extending your private network to the Internet exposes several areas that warrant close attention to security. We will discuss them in detail in Chapter 10, but three issues beg early attention here because they have direct effects on the users, administrators, and support staff:

♦ *Remote user passwords*—New passwords must be created for your remote users, especially if you go with a solution using PPTP protocol with a shared secret encryption method. In this case the choice and protection of passwords becomes much more important.

♦ *Proprietary data and information*—Hark back to the Specialty Training scenario. If your plan is to use your VPN as a transport mechanism for another company's proprietary information, you need to be aware of it and establish safeguards. In many cases liability issues may be involved.

♦ *Extending your private network (extranets) to your suppliers and customers*—If you plan to eventually extend your VPN to include connections to your suppliers and customers, you will have to coordinate your procedures with these parties. Security implementation should be one of the major areas covered.

**Note**

*I mentioned in a previous chapter that security works only when it is properly maintained. You cannot simply implement an improvement in security and presume it will be forever adequate. Security, like all elements of your network, must be reviewed on a regular basis, and constantly monitored.*

# Training

Training is every bit as important as security. Ask the accounting department of any major corporation what the single biggest expense in the network area is, and the answer will be too much training. Ask any computer support staff for a major corporation what their single biggest computer-related problem is, and the answer will be not enough training.

### Why Is This?

The reason is simply that each user is different and views everything from a different perspective, with different priorities and goals. For example, a group of people is involved in a conversation and one individual makes a statement. Take two people at random from the group and ask them what was said. Chances are, you will get two different answers.

To most people, computers are complex, frightening, and prone to failure. If you are an administrator or on the support staff, you may think this is not true; but if you are a user, you know it is.

### User Training Needs

The required level of end-user training depends on many factors. Among these are the following:

♦ The type of VPN you are implementing—Internet, Extranet, Remote User Access, or a combination thereof.

♦ Does your existing network already support traveling or remote users through the use of dial-up remote access? If you are currently supporting remote users, does your existing solution use RADIUS authentication?

♦ The type of VPN solution you choose.

In the following sections we will look at these issues as we detail some training needs.

### How To Use The Workstations

If you are replacing several existing branch office connections with a VPN solution, then the end users' perspective will probably not change, especially if the network system uses a Directory Service, such as Novell NDS, or the Active Directory in the soon-to-be-released Windows 2000. In both cases the users are authenticated to the directory, and the actual operation of the network is transparent. Some things in life really are great.

This is true also in the case of implementing a VPN solution for the purpose of establishing an Extranet with vendors and clients. In this case the users must be made aware of the new facilities and proper procedures for establishing a connection. Once again, the directory service makes the operation transparent.

On the other hand, if you are implementing a VPN to provide access for your remote users, some training will be required for the new interface. Except for setting up a remote access system from scratch, your users should already be familiar with how to use Windows Dial-up-Networking to connect to the corporate site, especially if you are currently using some form of RADIUS authentication. In many cases the users will also be familiar with how to use the same dial-up interface to connect to an ISP. For VPN, the users will have to know a two-step process: first, connecting to the ISP, and then using the network client software (either Microsoft or Novell) to connect and authenticate to the corporate network.

Some VPN providers have gone to great lengths to make the interface as user friendly as possible. One of these is the Indus River RiverWorks VPN. If your requirements fall into the category of a major corporate VPN, you may want to download a demo of this interface at **www.indusriver.com**.

Finally, consider the case of a VPN solution provided through an ISP. Chances are very good that in this case the engine behind the VPN solution will be from Cisco Systems. In this case, the user will follow the same basic procedure as the two-step process outlined previously: First establish a connection to an ISP, then authenticate to the corporate network.

### How To Find An ISP In Cut-N-Shoot, Texas

Believe it or not, Cut-N-Shoot is a real town in Texas, just northwest of Houston, off I-45 (**www.positiveimage.com/trailer/**). It's not very big, and doesn't have a large industrial base, and I doubt if a road warrior will ever have to spend the night there. But traveling users will spend the night in other places that are just as remote. If they are expected to use the VPN to connect to the corporate network every night, someone had best come up with a plan on how to find the nearest ISP, and train the user how to do this.

The problem has several solutions—here is my pick for the best three:

♦ *Use an ISP that provides global coverage.* Several ISPs provide multisite coverage; two that come to mind are AT&T Worldnet (**www.att.net**) and GTE Net (**www.gte.net**).

**Note**

*Both of these provide global, as well as national access. In addition, both have 800, 888, or 877 numbers you can call when local access is not available. But beware, these may appear to be toll-free, but both companies will tack a premium onto your service bill for connecting to their modem banks.*

♦ *Set up a database of available ISPs in the areas where your remote users travel, then train them to look up ISPs in their area.* It will be necessary to keep the database updated and train the users in the procedure for uploading the database when they authenticate to the corporate network. You can create a script to upload automatically the ISP database in the background. Building and maintaining this database will put more workload on the support area. This needs to be taken into consideration. An interesting thought: Indus River Software maintains this database already. It may be possible to purchase this as a separate service, or other companies may exist where you could purchase a similar service.

♦ *Keep at least one remote access dial-up line available for use when an ISP is not available.* When all else fails, the road warrior can always "back up 10 yards and punt." In other words, have a contingency solution available.

These are but three possible solutions. Regardless of how you provide the solution, the problem is very real, and will not go away.

### What Do I Do When It Doesn't Want To Work?

In working with something as complex as computers and data network systems, it is not a question of *will it fail* but more likely *when* will it fail? Sooner or later the system is not going to work as advertised. The result can be very costly and compound user frustration.

What you do when a problem arises depends upon the level of support possible from the computer support group. This, in turn, is directly related to the size of the company or corporation. Major corporations probably already have some type of computer support available 24 hours a day, 7 days a week. For a small company, the cost of 24/7 support is probably beyond the resources of the company. In both cases the company can implement some fundamental steps. If you are already supporting remote users through dial-in access, you probably have some or all of these in place:

♦ *A simple, easy to follow, guide for the user*—In developing a guide, avoid acronyms. When the guide is finished and tested, print it on paper. Acronyms only add to an already frustrated user's confusion, and lower the credibility of the guide. The hard copy is important, so don't put the guide on the computer in some form of help screen. Users may not be able to access it in the first place, and an on-screen guide adds to the frustration by making them switch back and forth between screens. Make sure each user has a copy handy.

♦ *Evaluate your support staff*—Train one or more persons to have an in-depth knowledge of the operations of the VPN and remote client software, then have a meeting with the remote users and decide on a schedule of times when that person will be available. Make it known to the users that help will be available during these times. This may require changing or extending the normal work hours, but in the long run it will be well worth the trouble.

♦ *Make your support proactive instead of reactive*—This is the really hard one. How do you do it? One step is to emphasize the necessity of everyone—users and support staff—keeping accurate logs of problems as they arise. Set up a form on the users' computers that they can easily fill out to record connection errors, then develop a simple script to upload this file each time the user authenticates to the network. This will build a performance baseline, and help you spot problems before they occur. Of course, someone must review the logs and, when appropriate, take action. In the short run, this adds to the load—in the long run, it will cut down on problems and increase the efficiency of the system.

### Support Staff Training Needs

Obviously you must train your support staff on the VPN software. If you are not already supporting remote access dial-in, you may find it necessary to change the normal hours that your support staff is available. Once the VPN is installed and the usual start-up bugs have been found and eliminated, support of the VPN should not be any more difficult than the normal support of an Internet access. Most companies already have an Internet connection of some type by now, and are basically familiar with support issues related to that service.

Once your support staff gets over the VPN software learning curve, the major support issues arise in helping the remote users. I have not mentioned it to this point, but one of the most helpful items you can have in this regard is a *help desk service*.

### Do You Have An Existing Help Desk In Place Now?

If you already have a help desk support service in place, it is a simple matter to change the software database used by the help desk to include the VPN. If you don't have a help desk support service in place, investigate the possibility of creating one. Help desk software and manning the help desk will add to the operational costs, but is well worth the tradeoff in lower user frustration. Again, in the long run the payback is increased efficiency overall. Help desk software is readily available from several sources, and is easily implemented.

If you are just beginning the plans for installing VPN, now is the time to perform a complete evaluation to see if the cost of implementing a help desk can be justified.

**Tip**

*Even though it's a bother, impress upon everyone in your support staff the importance of keeping records of everything they do. Compile these into a time log, which can be used to demonstrate the cost of supporting the users to management. This will go a long way to helping justify the cost of adding a help desk support staff.*

### How Much Support Is Enough?

In any new implementation, the steepest part of the learning curve is always encountered early and a VPN solution is no different. Each different company or corporation has its own idea of how much support is enough. Ideally, every time a user has a problem, immediate help is available and problems are fixed in a matter of minutes. Unfortunately, such a high level of support is usually not possible, but we can come close.

As a guide I offer you a two-part proposal. In the first part of this chapter I show some areas that will be impacted by the implementation of a VPN solution. I also made some suggestions about keeping logs and tracking problems to produce a *baseline* of support operations. Show this chapter to your management, director, or team leader. Do it now, before you get too far into the implementation of VPN, and make this proposal:

♦ *First, and most important, if your organization has been operating with its network for longer than a year, you should have reached a point at which the level of support offered to the users is now considered adequate.* It doesn't matter what that level of support is. If you have been using basically the same network system with the same basic suite of software applications for longer than a year, you have reached a point at which the level of support is considered to be the highest available support for the users that the company can afford. On the other hand, if you have not been using your network for at least a year, then I don't think you have had enough time to trap all the bugs and eliminate them—in other words, you're still on the learning curve.

♦ *Now you are going to make a change by implementing a VPN solution of some kind, either intranet, extranet, or Remote Access.* By now you should have made an evaluation to see if your support needs are going to change. The second step is to implement the VPN solution, and wait six month's (yes, I know that is a long time). Before six months goes by, you might find that your level of support is so critical that you must increase your support staff. If this is the case, then by all means do so. When you reach the point where your VPN solution has six month's longevity, develop a new baseline of support operations. As a bare minimum, the level of support available six months after you implement a change should not be any lower than it is right now.

Support is a difficult option to justify and requires documents to back it up. Many problem areas can develop in any VPN implementation. I hope that I have given you some tips on what to watch for, and what to do about them when they do pop up.

# Design Consideration

In this section we shall look at factors affecting the overall VPN design. The existing network we now have will be the primary consideration, and we'll look at how best to fit the VPN solution into that structure.

## Current Architecture

We discussed network architectures in Chapters 2 and 3 to help everyone get on a level playing field with the terminology. Feel free to go back through them if you skipped them and need a refresher.

For our purposes in this section, existing network architectures can be divided into two groups. First are LAN installations—this includes network systems in which the number of computers may range anywhere from a few up to several hundred, but have only one physical location with no wide area network (PSTN or PDN) links other than a connection to the Internet. The physical site may include more than one cable segment tied together by bridges, switches, or routers. We make the assumption that the LAN has some type of Internet connection through a firewall. See Figure 6.1.

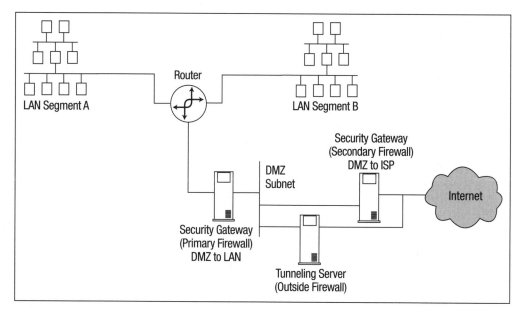

**Figure 6.1**
LAN with demilitarized zone (DMZ) subnet Internet connection.

The second group includes WAN installations. This category includes everything in the LAN category mentioned previously, except it is located on more than one physical site connected together by some type of PSTN or PDN links, and may include one or more RASs providing access to your network for users outside the boundaries of the environment. A diagram of this type of network in depicted in Figure 6.2.

Please note that the Internet connection firewalls in Figures 6.1 and 6.2 use two security gateways with a DMZ subnet between them. If your Internet connection fits this scenario, and you are adding a separate tunneling server to perform the encapsulation and encryption functions, I recommend that you locate the server outside the firewall, in the DMZ subnet, as shown in Figures 6.1 and 6.2. A properly configured VPN tunneling server installed this way provides excellent protection for your network against attacks from the Internet.

Your Internet firewall may consist of only one security gateway as pictured in Figure 6.3. If this is the case, and you do not wish to change your existing Internet connection architecture, you can place the tunneling server inside the gateway as shown in Figure 6.3, but you must configure your existing firewall server to forward IP datagrams utilizing the correct IP port number for VPN service. We'll show you how to do this in the next couple of chapters.

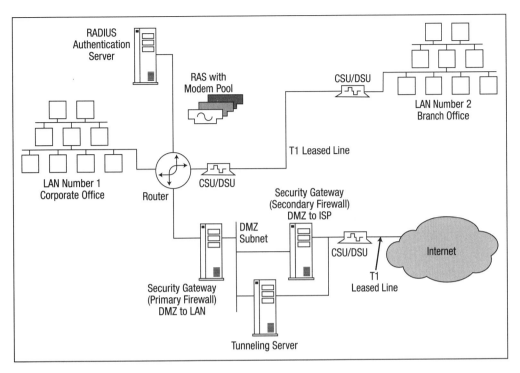

**Figure 6.2**
WAN with DMZ subnet Internet connection.

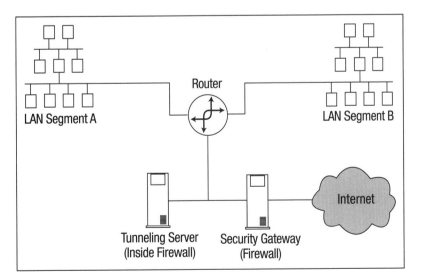

**Figure 6.3**
LAN with single firewall Internet connection.

If your WAN architecture is similar to Figure 6.2, you may have enough remote users to take advantage of the authentication services provided by RADIUS. You may already have a RADIUS authentication server currently installed, or are considering implementing RADIUS. The installation of a VPN does not replace or invalidate the benefits gained by using RADIUS. The two products can be configured to work quite nicely together. It does, however, require a higher level of configuration. Installing and configuring a VPN to work with RADIUS will be covered as a special case in Chapter 9.

Earlier we looked at VPN architectures, and listed three distinct types of VPN:

♦ *Internet*—The traditional VPN concept, which allows remote users to access the LAN in a secure manner using the Internet as a transport mechanism.

♦ *Intranet*—Uses the encryption capabilities of the VPN architecture to pass IP datagrams through your existing LAN in what could be considered an *Ultra-Secure Tunnel*.

♦ *Extranet*—Allows connections to be established with vendors and customers, using the Internet as a transport mechanism.

Let's start with the traditional Internet VPN solution.

### Should I Change From What I Have Now To Something New?

The change from one LAN architecture to another is not an easy undertaking and will encounter political resistance. I have always been a proponent of gradual changes over time, rather than a major rebuilding effort. The only exception I would make is if your existing network was rather small and the change does not inflict a great deal of retraining or other hardship on the users. My advice is that if the network as a whole is operating in a satisfactory manner, and the only change you are making is the implementation of a VPN, make every effort to adapt the VPN solution to the existing network architecture.

The same basic philosophy holds true in the case of the network operating system you are currently using. Both Microsoft NT and Novell NetWare have a VPN solution available. Additionally, third-party VPN solutions that will operate quite well with both Microsoft and Novell network products wait just around the cybercorner.

Cisco's VPN solution is primarily designed for implementation by the ISP industry and enterprises that base their Internet access on Cisco products. The operation of a Cisco VPN solution is transparent to Microsoft NT or Novell NetWare.

If Unix or Linux is your network bag, third party products, including Cisco's VPN solution, will do the trick. The primary concern here is the client software package that will run under either Unix or Linux.

In short, if you like the way your existing networking software product is performing, it fits an old technician's canon: *"Don't fix what ain't broke."* If your current network software is either Microsoft NT or Novell NetWare, you will want to take a really close look at the available solutions offered by these companies before making a decision not to implement their VPN solution.

### *How Much Help Should I Expect From My ISP?*

In implementing a VPN solution, get your ISP involved at the beginning, as early in the planning stage as you possibly can. Several of the VPN protocols use routing techniques and routers that require specific protocols. Your ISP must be informed of your VPN plans to make sure both sides are compatible for the tasks required.

Chances are, your ISP will be more than willing to work with you in establishing a satisfactory VPN solution. You are, after all, its customer and it depends on your business, just as you depend on your customers for your company's continued success.

You will depend on your ISP to provide services at a stated level of Internet access. Often this level of service is detailed in an agreement known as *Terms of Service* (TOS). In some cases, the TOS for the level of service you are currently receiving may not include the capability of forwarding IP datagrams required by specific protocols in a specific VPN solution. This is especially true if that solution includes implementing policies that establish a specific QOS. In that case, you must revise your TOS to a higher level.

In the worst case, your ISP may be incapable of providing the TOS your VPN plan requires. If it comes to that, you must choose between a different VPN solution and changing ISPs. This is an excellent reason for bringing your current ISP into the early planning stages.

I know from experience in dealing with vendors that it always works better for both sides when you deal with only one vendor rep. With most ISPs, it will be your account representative. If you haven't met that one person, it's time to get on the phone and introduce yourself. If you think more than one person is involved, lean on the ISP to narrow it down to a single person; this will definitely improve communications. Barbara is not going to remember what Sam didn't write down.

After you have made a decision on which VPN solution you are going to implement, you should contact the ISP rep and let him or her know which solution you are going to implement. That way they can pass this information on to their engineers and assure that everything concerning your account has been implemented at their site.

Your ISP must be told if you decide to implement the Cisco VPN solution direct from Cisco. If this is your decision, and you are partnering with your ISP in the implementation, your ISP account representative should already be aware of what is required.

# Compatibility

Unless you have made plans to implement a major change to your existing network system at the same time you implement your VPN solution, the issue of compatibility is of critical importance. Some issues dealing with compatibility rate more than a cursory glance.

### *Will It Work With My Existing System?*

This is one of the key issues that must be addressed. I mentioned this before, but you may have skipped that chapter. All current VPN solutions require the TCP/IP protocol suite for proper operation. The most common transport protocol for TCP/IP is Ethernet, even though TCP/IP has been implemented, and runs quite satisfactorily over Token Ring and FDDI transport protocols as well.

Remember, as I mentioned earlier, some routers cannot handle encapsulated IP datagrams. Read the specifications or check with the manufacturer to verify this important compatibility function. If you are not sure which routers in your network may be required to perform this routing task, check them all. Worry about a specific router being in the VPN path only when you know that it is not capable of providing the required service.

All the VPN solutions we studied have two primary components.

♦ *Encapsulation server*—The component that performs encapsulation and encryption. In cases where a separate authentication server, such as RADIUS, is not in place, this machine will probably perform authentication and authorization services also.

♦ *Client software*—At the client end, the computer must have enough power to perform encapsulation and encryption and still be portable. In a VPN, this computer must have client software compatible with the platform (Microsoft/Intel, Unix/Linux).

Let's take a closer look at these issues, first from the standpoint of the encapsulation server. In Novell NetWare and Microsoft Windows NT, encapsulation and encryption is performed by a module loaded on an existing platform. In the Novell solution, the platform is an Intel-based server running Border Manager. In Microsoft, the platform is an Intel server running NT 4.

In a Cisco implementation, a specific router, located either inside or outside the firewall or at your ISP, performs encapsulation and encryption tasks. This router must be fully compatible with all the existing devices in your network.

All other third-party solutions use a dedicated processor-based platform to perform the tasks of encapsulation and encryption. Based on these examples, compatibility between your existing network system and the tunneling server should not be a significant problem as long as the IP datagrams are unencapsulated at or near the firewall.

From the standpoint of the client computer, we may not be quite so lucky. The tunneling servers available with or for the majority of VPN solutions available today will work with almost any network operating system—that's the lucky part. The unlucky part comes on the client end. If your clients are using Intel platforms with Microsoft Windows 9x or NT, then almost all the VPN solutions will work with your client's computer operating system. If, on the other hand, the client's computer is Unix, Linux, Apple OS 7.x, or 8.x— or a different processor from Intel Pentiums—then your choices of VPN solutions is substantially diminished.

Many Intel Pentium processor-based laptops have the intrinsic capability of sustained operation at the required level of performance to handle the workload. For the most part, you will be pleased to learn that most of today's VPN solutions are compatible with the majority of client operating systems operating on Intel Pentium laptop computers—including Windows 9x, Windows NT 4, Unix, and Linux.

# Expansion

The fuel that has fed the growth of networking industries in the last 10 years has been the rapid proliferation of affordable computer systems. That same affordability, placing computers on virtually every desk and in every home, has paved the Internet into the so-called *Information Superhighway*. So, here we are at the cusp—enter the VPN.

### Internet VPN

Throughout this chapter we've made this the primary type of VPN. The traditional Internet VPN performs one of two basic functions:

♦ *Remote user connection*—The remote or traveling user connects to the corporate LAN or WAN using the encapsulation and encryption capabilities of VPN software applications to establish a secure virtual connection through the open unsecure public Internet.

♦ *Corporate LAN to LAN*—The encapsulation and encryption features of VPN use the open unsecure public Internet as a transport medium to connect multiple LANs in a secure environment.

It is natural to assume that once enterprises prove that VPN is reliable and trustworthy, the use will escalate. In some cases, this increase in use will not change the basic architecture; it will still be implemented as a traditional Internet VPN connecting remote users to the corporate network, or multiple corporate LANs together.

These issues notwithstanding, two other possible growth areas warrant a closer look.

### Intranet VPN

The intranet VPN is implemented to create virtual private channels *within* a corporate intranet. This type of VPN never extends beyond the border of the intranet to public access. At first glance, this may seem useless, but a closer look will show potential advantages to the valuable features of intranet VPNs.

Investigative agencies have for years reported that the great majority of cases of industrial espionage have been, to quote a theatrical cliché, inside jobs—the machinations of employees within the enterprise, not external attacks from the Internet. Consider, for example, a manufacturer or developer of leading edge technology products with a WAN connecting four corporate facilities in a moderate size city in southern California. Knowing the vulnerability of intercept, the MIS manager's policy dictates that data can move only between the research and development and engineering departments via sneaker net because a project was compromised not too long ago. It doesn't matter that the culprit was discovered and subsequently fired; the company lost a critical technology edge and a significant share of the market. Now we have a new-millennium corporation resorting to 1940 networking techniques by hand-carrying data files across town between departments.

An intranet VPN would create a virtual tunnel between the two departments. That way, confidential information would be encrypted and thus protected from internal intercept by unauthorized persons. Many existing VPN solutions available today, including products from both Microsoft and Novell, allow this type of configuration.

In the case of expanding an existing Internet VPN to include intranet capabilities, the questions of compatibility issues are negligible, provided the equipment destined for use as the intranet VPN is of the same type, or capability, as the equipment used in the Internet VPN solution.

### Extranet VPN

Suppliers and distributors, in fact any enterprise involved in direct sales to its customers, can benefit from an extranet VPN. Some formats of encryption are being commonly used over the Internet already. Extranet VPN is a considerable step above that. In this case, we are talking about connecting one company's LAN directly to another's. By implementing this type of configuration, information concerning prices, orders, shipping dates, and delivery schedules could be maintained practically in real time.

Perhaps your company is already doing this using leased lines or dial-in. If that's the case, you have a natural setup for extranet VPN to improve delivery schedules, reduce stock levels, and provide a more efficient operation. However, a downside to this type of implementation lurks in the shadows. Even though the VPN solution will provide encapsulation and encryption capabilities, and by doing so keep sensitive data secure, it requires a minimum level of *interoperability* between the VPN solutions that each company has deployed.

Today, the VPN technology relies on three main protocols and that can lead to some interoperability problems. Also, some problems exist between different vendor's implementations of protocols, particularly IPsec, mainly because of different philosophies in the emerging technology. As more and more VPN vendors employ the IPsec open standard, interoperability problems will diminish. But for the time being, interoperability is a valid issue that must be addressed.

If you think an extranet VPN is a real possibility in your company's future, you should start talking with your suppliers and customers now to prevent problems further down the road.

# Hidden Costs And Other Considerations

So many variables exist in determining costs related to implementing a new technology-based solution that it is impossible for us to even make a guess at what your particular VPN solution will cost. What we can do as a service to you is help you with the foresight to include everything in the planning. Going back to your boss for extra bucks to buy something you didn't know you'd need can create tension you don't need, especially when you've already put in a lot of evening hours and the switchover date is only days away.

From the beginning, this book was intended for network administrators and support technicians. Quite often, when a new solution for an old problem appears on the market, such as VPN, and a decision is made to implement that solution, the network administrators and support technicians have little control over which product or suite to implement. The network administrator and support staff are usually tasked with implementation and support after the decisions have been finalized. About this time all the *hidden costs* start coming to the surface.

Maybe we can help by pointing out some of those hidden costs. What I propose to do is develop a checklist of items you will need to implement a reasonable degree of support for a basic VPN. Our paradigm is a traditional Internet VPN, used to establish a secure virtual tunnel with either a remote user or a LAN at another site. As with everything else, the exact equipment needed at your site will vary based on your individual needs. You can, however, take the items listed and expand them, based on your experience, to suit your particular enterprise.

Keep in mind that this equipment is for a single support site, centrally located within the corporate enterprise. If you have more than one support site, consider the equipment needs for each site separately.

## Hardware

You will need at least one administration computer. You probably already have an administrator's workstation set up. Still, you should keep the following thoughts in mind. Almost all the VPN products recommend an Intel platform running either Windows 9x or Windows NT for the administrator workstation. Even though VPN products with administrator software packages must exist that will run under Unix on a Sun Solaris workstation, I have not come across them, and none that I have found list an administrator's software package to run on the Apple Macintosh.

It is also a good idea to have a laptop computer handy, configured for use as a VPN tunneling server. This can be useful on large networks for checking the operation of the VPN from wire closets and hubs, and on opposite sides of routers.

## Software

You will need the administrators support software for the VPN product you are implementing. Here are some software products that will prove helpful in troubleshooting a VPN:

♦ *Protocol analyzer*—VPNs depend on encapsulation and encryption algorithms. They also depend on the routers' abilities to forward encapsulated IP datagrams through the network. An analyzer software package—and a technician trained to use it—can go a long way in locating problems related to these two fundamental operations.

♦ *Internet performance monitoring*—With any VPN solution, you are moving your remote access infrastructure from traditional PSTN or PDN provided lines to the Internet. Where before you were guaranteed a certain amount of bandwidth on a dedicated digital line, such as a T1 line, for example, with the VPN you are dependent on the bandwidth available from your ISP to the Internet. Do you have any idea what the peak times for Internet use are? How do you determine that? Software packages exist for tracking Internet bandwidth use and provide you with a graph of Internet activity over a 24-hour period. One such program is Chariot, from Ganymede Software (**www.ganymede.com**).

♦ *Performance metrics*—Several factors affect the total throughput of any network system. *Latency* and the number of *dropped packets* are two. Ask your VPN vendor how to monitor these two statistics for your installation and implement this as a regular procedure. This tool will allow you to adjust the transmission window and tune your VPN for peak performance.

♦ *WAN emulation and testing software*—Wouldn't it be nice to see how well a particular software implementation will perform under given conditions? A software product called Cloud can be acquired from Shunra Software (**www.shunra.com**) that allows users to emulate a WAN network system. By injecting typical real world performance—taken from actual performance metrics—you can see how the network operation is affected. Other software packages are capable of similar operations as well.

# Training

The most expensive part of any technology undertaking is training. After having been in the PC computer industry since the early 1980s, I am a firm believer in that statement. Training must be a major factor in the educated decisions about VPN startup. Remember that training falls into two arenas: technical support staff and end users.

## Technical Support Staff

Even if you have the vendor provide everything necessary for the installation and initial configuration, the technical support staff are going to have to support the VPN solution implemented. Regardless of which vendor's solution you implement, you will have to get at least one, and preferably two, technicians trained to support the product. The only exception is outsourcing your VPN solution completely to your ISP. As a part of the training for technicians, emphasize the following points:

♦ *Help for the technicians*—What procedures does the vendor have in place to provide your technicians with a *reasonable* degree of help in a *reasonable* period of time? Use your own experience to make a determination on what can be considered reasonable.

♦ *VPN performance metrics*—How do you go about recording and storing performance metrics related to the operation of the VPN?

- *Firewall changes*—Depending on where you locate the tunnel server, you may need to make changes to your current firewall server. Find out what changes, if any, will need to be made to the firewall to incorporate the new VPN solution.

- *End user training*—If your end user training is to be outsourced, make sure that at least one person from the technical support staff attends the end user training. This will help to prevent any misunderstandings at a later date.

### End User Training

This is not nearly as complicated as the training required for the technicians. However, in regard to training, the users outnumber the technicians and the end-users will almost always have a more difficult time learning to use the new product. Training the end user will incur the highest training costs. We mentioned some of the following points in the earlier section on training but they are worth listing again, because they can be hidden costs in a new implementation.

The users must be trained on what to do when the VPN system just won't work. Always have a contingency plan in place, and make sure your remote user knows what that plan is. This should be a part of the written procedures for remote users. If nothing else, leave at least one dedicated dial-in line for remote access as a backup.

Your ISP can help train the users on how to find the nearest ISP for the locations your road warriors are apt to find themselves in. If your software maintains a database of ISPs and rates, then you need to be concerned with how best to update that database. The remote users can access the database through the remote dial-in if it becomes necessary, but they need training on how to do that.

When you change from dedicated dial-in connections to using the services of a local ISP, your users will, in all probability, start getting more errors. Many of these errors will go away if the user waits a short period and then tries the call again. If possible, a nice laminated sheet with common errors and solutions would be nice. But you need to make this a part of the end user training.

### Note
*Even though both areas of training are equally important, you should remember that the end users will encounter the largest number of problems—and be the first to find fault with new technology.*

## Support

Once you get the product installed and technicians and end users have been trained, the job changes from the implementation stage to the support stage. As with training, the support stage operations fall into two categories: technical and end-user operations.

### Technical Operations

This is the behind-the-scenes action required to keep the system running. Quite frequently you will find that problems occurring in this area tend to be long-term debugging procedures. Even though solving problems here will help improve performance and reliability in the long term, they are not critical because end-users can continue to function. Operations in this area can be divided into different issues and each area can be assigned to a specific technician. Here is a list of the most common issues:

♦ *Vendor related*—You should make every effort to establish a good relationship with the vendor of your VPN solution. If possible, it is generally a good idea to find one technician at the vendor's site that you can deal with and assign the communicaton task to one technician on your end at the same time.

♦ *ISP related*—Your dependence on your ISP is now going to move into the area that could possibly be termed *critical operations*. You must establish a good working relationship with your ISP. Keep your ISP informed of changes at your facility, and encourage your ISP to reciprocate. It is a good idea to study the TOS provided by your ISP so you know what level of service to expect your ISP to provide.

♦ *In-house related*—This is where the majority of problems arise. One of the most important steps you can take in this area is to develop and implement procedures for monitoring and recording statistics that reflect the actual operations of your network. Once you have these in place, you can establish a process in which these statistics are reviewed at regular intervals and a baseline of network operations established. Once you have a baseline, a regular review process will flag areas where corrective action can be made before the drips become floods. This is the key to making support proactive versus reactive.

### End-User Operations

End-user operations are critical to the successful deployment of any network service. A VPN solution is no different from any other network service in this respect. Several procedures can be implemented that will go a long way towards establishing successful end-user operations:

♦ *Network access and use policy*—We mentioned before the importance of having a network access and use policy. If the end users know what they may and may not do with their computers, it will go a long way in helping the support staff not to mention security.

♦ *Regularly scheduled training*—Technology is constantly changing and, because VPN is relatively new, lots of changes are coming. Computers are getting faster and more powerful, and the Internet is growing every day. Your network system is, in all probability, going to evolve. It is important that you schedule regular end-user training, and inform the end users of these changes.

♦ *Establish a help desk*—Setting up and maintaining a good help desk is a lot like implementing a new accounting system. During the initial setup you will wonder if the end result will be worth the trouble. After you get it set up, it must be updated regularly; requiring procedures for regular reviews of problems that will surely crop up. I can assure you that within a year of implementing a well staffed and supported help desk, you and your end users will wonder how you ever got along without it. If your network supports more than 50 users, I consider the establishment of a help desk to be almost critical in the area of end-user support.

## Words Of Wit And Wisdom

Often when we get into the midst of a major project, we tend to lose sight of the forest because we can't see past the trees. Quite often the technical support group gets so wrapped up in getting the new network service running that they forget the real purpose of the network is to provide end users with access to the services they need to do their jobs. However, like all good end users everywhere, they won't let the techies forget the purpose of the network for long.

## Summary

In this chapter we considered some things you should be aware of when you implement a VPN solution in your existing network. In doing so we have drawn upon experience gained in supporting and troubleshooting conventional LAN and WAN networks and extended these procedures to cover that area of VPNs. We also have used numerous comments provided by vendors and users that have had solutions in place for a relatively long period of time—considering the short amount of time that VPN solutions have been available. One thing you should remember is that the concept of VPN is itself a relatively new network service, and in reality everyone is still somewhat on the upsweep of the learning curve.

I think we have talked about everything related to VPNs that needs discussing. So, in the following chapters we will, finally, cover the actual implementation process itself. Hang on tight, I think we're about to get started.

# Chapter 7
# *Basic NetWare VPN Model*

**Key Topics:**

♦ *Implementation checklists*

♦ *Network access and use policies*

♦ *BorderManager theory of operation*

♦ *Site-to-site VPN*

♦ *Master and slave configuration*

In this chapter we are going to demonstrate the process for installing and configuring a basic VPN between two LANs. In the first part of the chapter we will look at the architecture of an existing WAN system. Next, we cover the steps in developing a plan for moving to a VPN solution using Novell® NetWare 5® and Novell BorderManager™. Then, in Chapter 8, we'll do essentially the same job, but we will configure the VPN software using solutions available in Microsoft NT 4.

Although connecting the two LANs in our paradigm together with a VPN is not really going to save the company enough to pay for a corporate Lear Jet, you should keep in mind that the most complex WAN can be isolated down to connecting two LANs. This is the core. With that thought in mind, we should approach the implementation of a new architectural solution from the simplest possible concept.

Skipping this chapter is at your own peril. As we did in Chapter 6, we withdraw any implied invitation to jump ahead. We are going to break new ground here, perhaps even revealing stuff one or two of the big software guys didn't even know they could do.

## Simplified System With Limited Capability

In this model implementation, we will start with a WAN comprised of two LANs. We presume the WAN is mature and fully operational. Our model system has limited capability. For example, it does not provide support for remote users nor does it provide support for extranet VPN clients, such as suppliers and customers. Nevertheless, this implementation covers the majority of the implementation and configuration procedures for a VPN. The only problem is that of a classic nature—the company is a success. It is growing and as it grows, the seams of its network are straining closer and closer to the bursting point.

# Architecture

We need a model company, so let's invent one named Vintage Air, Incorporated; see Figure 7.1. The primary business of the company is to provide a fleet of aircraft for static display, movie production, air shows, and promotional events—anywhere for any reason. Our company is relatively small. It has a flight museum, maintenance, and display facilities located at Scholes Field (GLS) in Galveston, Texas, and a maintenance, restoration, and storage facility located at Hobby Airport (HOU) in Houston, Texas. Minor maintenance is performed at GLS, and major maintenance, such as overhauls, is handled at HOU. Business operations are conducted at the Galveston facility.

## Architecture Of The Existing WAN

The WAN architecture of the existing network for Vintage Air is pictured in Figure 7.2. As you can see, the company has its two LANs, one at Scholes Field in Galveston (GLS) and the other at Hobby International Airport in Houston (HOU). The two facilities are connected together through a T1 leased line. In addition, each facility has a T1 connection to the Internet.

The company has established a network access and use policy, and limits employees' access to the Internet during business hours. WAN service is adequate at each facility where speed and bandwidth are concerned. A key company employee is the network administrator, J. V. Hackley, who is familiar with the network operating system, and has configured the network so that users at either facility can access information they need, regardless of where the information is located. For the most part, these operations are transparent to the users. The LAN architecture of each facility is pictured in Figure 7.3. The LAN consists of one

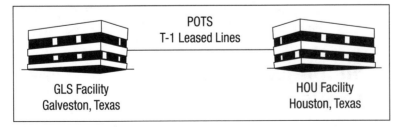

**Figure 7.1**
Vintage Air, Inc.

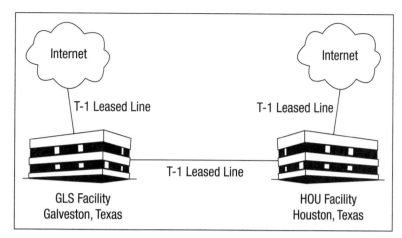

**Figure 7.2**
WAN architecture for Vintage Air, Incorporated.

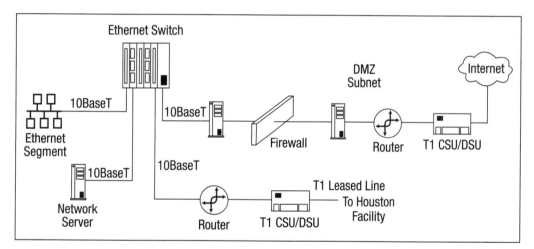

**Figure 7.3**
Vintage Air—LAN architecture.

Ethernet segment connected to a 10Mbps switch and has one primary network server connected to its switch. In addition, one port from the switch goes through a router to a CSU/DSU, and then to the T1 leased line to the other facility.

Another port from the switch goes to the Internet firewall security gateway. The firewall system that is being implemented is a *screened subnet* with a DMZ subnet between the two security gateways. As long as it is properly maintained, this system provides a fairly high level of security.

The Galveston facility is larger than the Houston facility, and serves as the home office.

# Traffic Patterns

Because our main intent is to implement a solution to replace WAN links with a VPN solution, it is certainly worth our time to investigate how Vintage Air utilizes those links.

Three types of data are crucial to the operation of Vintage Air. During the past five years, the enterprise has evolved the following functions:

♦ Scheduling and flight information

♦ Corporate office reports

♦ Maintenance reports

## Scheduling And Flight Information

Remembering that the primary business of Vintage Air is providing vintage aircraft for air shows, movies, and special events, it is easy to see that scheduling and flight information is of critical importance. Altogether, Vintage Air has 54 different flying machines divided up between the two facilities. It is important for the operations officer to know what assets are available in the hangars, which aircraft are committed to flight schedules, and exactly where each aircraft that is out on a mission is at any given time.

The office most concerned with this information is the sales department. These are the folks who are meeting commitments to customers, as well as scouring the Internet for leads to prospective clients. Repeat business is a staple for Vintage Air, but the sales staff must continue scouting for new prospects in order for the company to grow while it is replacing the occasional lost customer.

## Corporate Office Reports

Middle- and executive-level management reports such as employee information, information on leads, revenue, operational expenses, and other reports necessary for the smooth operation of the company are passed across the WAN links as needed. Because these reports are generally rather small in size, the Vintage Air IT manager has imposed no restriction on when the reports may be transmitted. These reports are generated at each facility and stored in a specific directory on the local server. Upon request by any employee, a copy of an individual report is attached to an email addressed to the proper recipient.

## Maintenance Reports

At the end of each week, current status of all aircraft, as well as pending maintenance, is transmitted to the Galveston facility. There it is archived and stored for future reference.

# Vintage Air On The Internet

In addition to acting as a transport mechanism for business reports, the Internet connection provides two services that Vintage Air management considers beneficial to company success: email and mindshare.

## Email

Email has become a very important part of the operations of the company; so much so that it is now considered critical to the proper exchange of ideas and operation of the company. All email is stored and archived. The company does have a policy concerning proper use of the email system as a part of its network access and use policy.

## Mindshare (Information Exchange)

With the rapid growth of the Web, Vintage Air management realizes that the company can now reach a considerable market, which was not affordable before. The company established a Web site hosted by a service provider, and pays an agency to maintain it for them. The company also uses the Web on a regular basis for locating information. Employees are allowed to access the Internet, including the Web, within the guidelines of the network access and use policy.

# Network Access And Use Policy

For the most part, the employees willingly try to stay within the guidelines of the network access and use policy. Due the large amount of junk and garbage email, and the large number of email viruses on the Internet today, the network support staff (one techie at HOU and two at GLS) have reported that email alone could rapidly overcome the bandwidth available in the T1 links between the two facilities. For this reason, email policies have come under close observation from executive management.

# Future Plans

Vintage Air is aware that unauthorized intruders may attempt to penetrate their system to gain access to their network, and have implemented a reasonably good firewall system. To date, no one has broken into the Vintage Air network system from the outside and the employees have all been loyal and trusted, protecting the corporation from the inside.

The company is also aware of the unsecure conditions that exist within the Internet itself, and have studied several possibilities for overcoming these conditions with the establishment of a VPN solution between the two facilities. This would change the architecture of their network to that shown in Figure 7.4. The company initiated a study to research the implementation of this VPN, from the standpoint of both benefits to the company, and considerations of possible trouble areas.

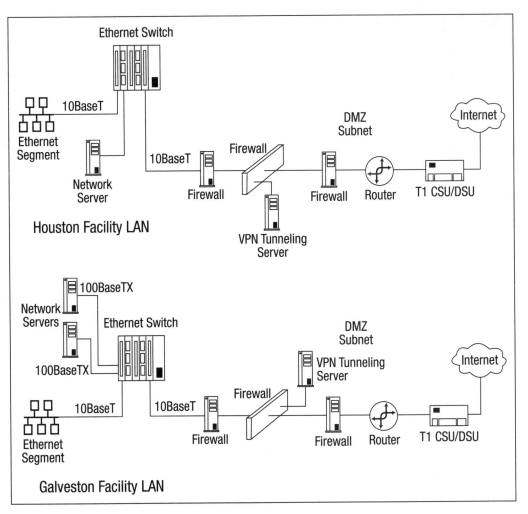

**Figure 7.4**
VPN LAN-to-LAN implementation architecture.

# Benefits And Considerations Of Implementing VPN Solution

In order to do a proper evaluation of the two different network systems, we need to refer to the LAN architecture in Figure 7.4. In comparing the diagrams of the existing LAN architectures to the proposed WAN architectures, the following benefits stand out:

♦ The number of T1 lines has been cut in half. T1 lines are expensive so this is going to save some bucks.

♦ The same T1 lines used for the regular Internet access will be used for the VPN.

♦ The number of routers and CSU/DSU units has been reduced. The only cost savings (unless Vintage Air holds a garage sale on surplus computer equipment) will be the reduced admin and tech support.

♦ Once the VPN solution is in place at the Galveston facility, it will include room for expansion in the future with little or no additional equipment or WAN links required.

This is not to say that Vintage Air is getting off without some potential problem areas. Consider the following:

♦ The exchange of data between facilities will now be taking place over the Internet. This will put the speed and reliability of the link in the hands of people that the company may or may not be able to influence.

♦ The Internet is plagued with hackers and crackers who search for network vulnerabilities with the intention of disrupting the operation or stealing the information contained therein.

♦ Because the number of T1 lines and associated equipment is reduced, those savings may be offset by requirements for new hardware and more than likely some new flavors of software.

♦ The VPN will require some support staff. The geeks that do the maintenance today will charge some training time to climb up the learning curve. As necessary as it is, and as beneficial as it will prove out in the future, training time will appear to be nonproductive in the short-term viewpoint.

Other benefits and costs can be gleaned from Vintage Air's proposed new system, as well as the proposal you are developing for your company's VPN solution. The point here is to establish a process for evaluating the merits of any change and to look for the options with the most advantage for the system life cycle.

## Planned Phased Approach

The WAN example used in this chapter might seem rather small, but it does provide a good starting point. Your personal situation might be similar to Vintage Air in concept, if not in actual market, or it may be quite a bit more complex. In either case, my suggestion is to develop a plan, with reasonable time lines. On the time lines, schedule the implementation in phases, allowing time to correct any problems that pop up unexpectedly.

Software is available to help you develop Gantt and PERT charts for the project. In no particular order, here are four packages available on the Web:

♦ *SureTrak Project Manager 2*—**www.crownsys.com.sg**

♦ *Power Planner*—**www.sphygmic.com/pplan.htm**

♦ *Quick Gantt for Windows*—**www.ballantine-inc.com/software/charts.htm**

♦ *Microsoft Project*—**www.microsoft.com/office/project/**

Obviously, I can't list all the particulars for your time-line plan, but I can point you at some of the information you'll need when you start putting it together:

♦ Start date for the implementation

♦ Block diagrams for subnet entities

♦ Acquisition lead times for hardware and software

♦ Installation of hardware and software

♦ Implementation phases

♦ Training

♦ Target completion date

Some of the elements will be dependent on others. For example, you are not going to implement anything until you get the hardware and software. Also, both the implementation and acquisition can be broken down into chunks and spread out over time. Still another factor is the subcharting that can be done. For instance, on the master chart, training can be spread from start to finish, but on a subchart it can be divided into different blocks corresponding to departments. Figure 7.5 is one example of a typical Gantt chart for project planning.

Another way of displaying the same information is the PERT chart shown in Figure 7.6.

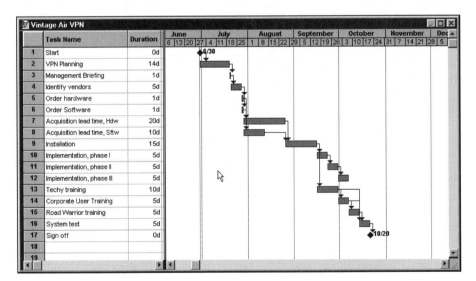

**Figure 7.5**
Vintage Air VPN planning chart in Gantt format.

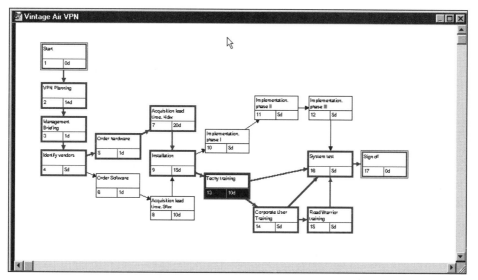

**Figure 7.6**
Vintage Air VPN planning chart in PERT format.

# Installation And Configuration Items Related To The New VPN Model

So far we have invested a large amount of resources covering LAN, WAN, and VPN fundamentals. In all probability, some of you already had a pretty good knowledge of the topics covered. It was not my intent to try to reteach something you already know, but more to make sure that everyone that has reached this point in the book has at least a fundamental understanding of what is involved. In our examples of Vintage Air, Incorporated, in the first part of this chapter, we have all the elements that make up a typical VPN between two entities. At the same time, the parts of the network that will become the VPN are reasonably straightforward and easy to follow. What we need now is to take a look and see what's really involved.

## Developing The Procedure

Call up a couple of acquaintances and ask them how to level a lopsided table and odds are you will get more than one suggestion. When you work with computers, software, and data communications devices, it doesn't take long to figure out more than one way to do something—just ask more than one geek. Implementing a VPN solution is no exception to this rule.

You can always find more than one way to implement any change. Depending on who is making the appraisal, some are good, some are not bad, and some are unacceptable. My goal is to help you develop a process for implementing whatever changes are necessary to bring about a VPN at your enterprise. It is important to remember that we don't know what your specific system requirements are and therefore can only deal in generalities. That means we are going to: (1) give you information about some stuff you don't need and won't use; and (2) leave something out that will require you to figure it out for yourself using your skills and knowledge of your network system. In-between those two extremes, we shall poke a lot of information into the bag.

Take the generalities given in the book, and modify them based on your experience. I am going to suggest one process that I personally like. If you decide, based on your experience, that my process doesn't fit your specific area, by all means, modify it to suit yourself.

## A Vendor Independent Plan

You will discover several ways of dealing with vendors. In many cases the vendor takes a very active roll in the setup and implementation of the product. In some cases the vendor delivers what is known as a *turnkey* solution—the vendor provides everything, up to and including training.

In dealing with something as complex as a LAN or WAN system, this approach might be the only way that an overworked, short-staffed computer services gang can implement a change. In this instance, it is a very good, though somewhat pricey solution.

On the other hand, for various reasons this may not be the best solution. It may be neither possible nor desirable for a vendor to get involved in the project past the stage of supplying the required equipment. If the staff has the resources to invest in implementing the solution, then this approach also is not at all bad.

The problem here is that unless you have participated in networking installation and configuration a time or two before, and are good at working under pressure—lots of pressure—it is real dicey sorting out configuration problems over the telephone. If you are faced with a do-it-yourself implementation, this book will be more than some minor assistance. This book will be of some assistance even if you decide to go with the vendor for a turnkey solution, because it will be solid gold in the planning stages as well.

As we have stated previously, many VPN solutions are available in the market today. Many of those solutions are based on proprietary or semi-proprietary products. For us to cover the installation and configuration of all of them in this book is simply not possible. Suffice it to say that, depending on your choices, you may have to depend on the vendor for a great deal of assistance. Other VPN solutions, especially those from Novell and Microsoft, are based on more open or *de facto* standards and those two network giants have a plethora of technical assistance aids. These VPN solutions can be implemented with little or no assistance from the vendor that delivered the products.

In the latter case, you will find that you have to develop a plan and implement the solution *independent of the vendor*. In reality, even this is not 100 percent correct. As in every other venture in the world of networking, you will find that you need to contact the vendor to iron out small details of configuration. You will also find that you need to contact your ISP (who is really a vendor) and assure that their equipment will operate properly with your VPN. This is expected, in all probability by the vendor, if not by you. As we will see later, it is important to work this into your plan. So in reality we end up saying that our plan is as *vendor independent* as we can make it, and still get the system installed, configured, and running.

## The Checklist Approach

Implementing any solution involving something as complex as digital communications equipment requires establishing a system to assure—as much as possible, anyway—that you don't miss anything. Implementing a VPN is definitely in that category.

In the following pages we will implement some vendors' solutions employing basically the same equipment and software. Only the implementation procedures will differ from one vendor's product to another. The end result in all cases will be a VPN, we promise.

Although you can use several procedural processes, the checklist approach is in my experience the most comprehensive and most reliable. Start off by establishing a master checklist covering the entire process—call it a checklist of the checklists, if you will. As with any major system, if you implement the system correctly, you will never reach a *final* step. You will reach the point where the process evolves into maintenance and evaluation. That checklist will be evolved and photocopied, *ad infinitum*.

Later we will develop more checklists, but let's get the master list out of the way first.

❏ *Equipment Required*—A list of all equipment and software required for completing the project. This will include test and maintenance items also.

❏ *Support Needs*—Resources to tap for assistance on installation and configuration of hardware or software.

❏ *Pre-Implementation*—The parts and pieces you should have up, running, and configured before you start ripping the guts out of your existing network.

❏ *Implementation*—A step-by-step sequence, including any testing sequences, for rolling the VPN into the system.

❏ *Post-Implementation*—A few temporary patches and hacks will typically be installed to hold things together while you are doing the implementation. This is the point where you yank them out to free up the drive space and unburden the bandwidth.

❏ *VPN Management, Checklistus Immortalus*—The maintenance and procedures to be performed on a regular basis. This will include evaluating logs and appraising system performance.

❏ *Future Planning*—Now that you have your VPN up and running, what steps do you need to take to assure the solution will meet future demands?

Following a checklist requires discipline. Often when a step is completed, the next step is right in front of you, begging to be accomplished—then the next one and the next one. Sometimes an out of sequence step presents itself, begging: "Do me. Do me next." This is where discipline is essential. When each checklist step is accomplished, stop, pick up your pencil (or hammer and chisel if you are working in the non-Pentium stone age), and deliberately mark that step off. This accomplishes two things: First, when you are interrupted by that danged telephone, you know exactly where you left off when you come back. Second, this is a good time to go over what you did in your mind, a chance to develop that warm fuzzy feeling that things are going well. If you don't get the warm fuzzies, something is probably wrong with what you did.

Here's another thing: If you do something and don't like the results, undo it and figure out what's wrong. Just because it is on the checklist doesn't mean it is correct. You will be sorely tempted to leave out a step or two here and there, because *you already know something*, or *you already did that*. This could be something as simple as writing down the name and phone number (including extension) of your contact at the ISP.

After spending a few years troubleshooting computer problems over the telephone, it has been my experience that many case history problems developed because the person performing the implementation and configuration missed a step. In some cases they didn't really miss a step; they simply skipped over it because they were sure *they had already performed it*. It is difficult enough to troubleshoot problems using a two-way communication, such as the telephone; it's impossible to troubleshoot them in only one dimension—like this book.

So what am I trying to say here? I strongly suggest that you follow the checklist and do it with immaculate discipline. We have included all of the checklists in Appendix D and you can find them on our Web site **www.sldenterprises.com**. You have our permission to make copies of the checklists for your own personal use. If you sell copies, however, you need written permission. By the way, you gotta split the take with the authors and the publisher. You can find the publisher's address in the front matter.

Follow your checklists with the discipline we suggest and you will find more than a casual chance for your system to come up running when you get finished—leaving you with only some fine tuning for optimum performance.

# Implementing Novell NetWare VPN

In the following sections we will implement a VPN solution using NetWare 5 and BorderManager. The procedure will be in the form of checklists, with comments, figures, and suggestions that detail information we think is important for particular steps. You will find the checklists, *sans* explanations, in Appendix D. Keep in mind that in this example we are implementing a basic VPN between servers on two existing networks.

The Novell implementation of VPN is supplied as part of a suite of products designed to be implemented at the border of your LAN and the Internet. The BorderManager VPN product was originally designed to use the Internet for making direct connections between LANs; its use is transparent to the clients.

If you already have BorderManager services, and have installed the BorderManager server as a security gateway, you don't need to purchase a separate computer for a tunneling server. The VPN is implemented on the same server as the other BorderManager services, as shown in Figure 7.7.

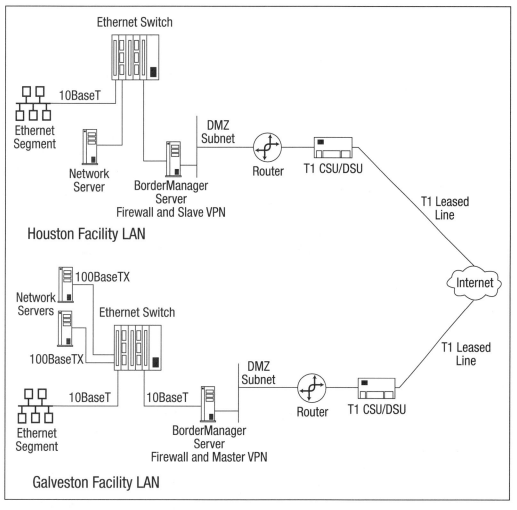

**Figure 7.7**
LAN-to-LAN implementation using Novell BorderManager.

If you are not currently using BorderManager, you will have to install it within your existing LAN structure. The BorderManager product is designed to sit, as the name implies, at the border of your existing LAN and the Internet and act as a security gateway, and I recommend you install it that way.

If the Internet access policy at your facility requires a separate firewall, the BorderManager server will work quite well installed in parallel with another existing firewall server—that is, outside the firewall—or implemented as a part of your LAN using only one Network Interface Card (NIC)—that is, inside the firewall. See Figure 7.8 for some examples.

*NetWare Directory Services* (*NDS*) is a key feature of NetWare. The BorderManager server is an integral part of NDS and must be placed within the directory tree. The exact location of the BorderManager servers within your directory tree is dependent on the tree's complexity and scope. Keep in mind that VPN users are not required to log onto the BorderManager server and the BorderManager server does not have to be in the same container as the users that will benefit from its services.

Because the VPN implementation is so closely tied to BorderManager, we will partially cover the installation and basic configuration of the Novell BorderManager Services product. We are going to cover the configuration of BorderManager only with respect to the VPN capabilities and accept the defaults—as they come from Novell—for the remaining features and services. Consult the Novell documentation if you need more information about configuring the remaining features.

We make the assumption that you, the network administrator, are reasonably familiar with Novell NetWare, and know how to configure a service. You must also be prepared to enter the information necessary to configure routing through the NetWare server. We will look at this a little more in depth shortly.

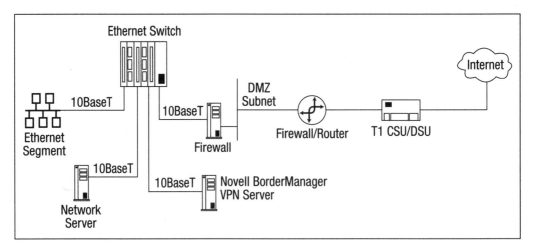

**Figure 7.8**
Examples of using a BorderManager server inside or outside a firewall.

Here's an interesting trip on the merry-go-round—Novell has developed a Java-based GUI with a look and feel similar to the Unix X-Windows interface for you to use when installing and configuring BorderManager. For years Novell shied away from the GUI in favor of text-formatted entries. It was a distinctive difference between Novell and Microsoft when it came to network operation and administration. How does the saying go? "What goes around, comes around." In the next chapter, you'll find that Microsoft has some sections that abandon the GUI in favor of going into DOS mode to make some entries.

However, as of the time this is being written, not all the NetWare configuration utilities have been replaced with their GUI equivalent. So, some configuration steps remain to be accomplished using text-based configuration utilities. The two installation and configuration utilities we will be using the most are the Internet configuration program INETCFG.NLM, and NetWare Internet access services configuration program named NIASCFG.NLM.

When it comes to installing services on NetWare, Novell expects you to do the actual installation of the new software at the server, but very little actual configuration and implementation. This philosophy holds true with the implementation of BorderManager VPN. After BorderManager is installed and the VPN is initially configured, the remaining tasks for implementation and management of the VPN end points are performed through the NWADMIN (network administration) program, with the BorderManager *Snap-In* installed. This program runs on a Windows 9x/NT workstation, Unix, and some Linux machines.

## Theory Of Operation—BorderManager VPN

The VPN implementation provided with Novell BorderManager is versatile, and can be implemented in any of several different ways. It is based on the IPsec protocol, versatile in its own way. As you are probably aware, the tradeoff for versatility is complexity.

Although Novell has made the process of installation, configuration, and implementation both logical and painless, and provides excellent documentation, it still doesn't hurt to take a look at what the terms mean and at some of the capabilities of the software. In this section of this chapter we'll continue with the basics, connecting two LANs together, and build on that as we move ahead.

Before we jump into the actual implementation, let's take closer looks at the two underlying foundations of this type of VPN: encapsulation and encryption (Where have we heard those terms before?). Then we'll get to the step-by-step procedures.

### Why Two Servers?

Why are we connecting two servers together when it is the clients that need to exchange information? Well, remember that the idea behind the VPN is to *connect two LANs together* using the Internet as the network media. The problem is that the GLS network located in Galveston has a completely different IP address than the HOU network located fifty miles away in Houston. Recall our discussion about the relationship among IP addresses, networks, and subnets back in Chapter 3. I stated in that chapter that all devices operating on the same subnet need to have the same network number, but a different host number. Logic tells you that if the IP addresses are different, the IP networks are going to be different also. How can we connect the devices located on two networks together when they have different IP addresses, and therefore different networks?

The answer lies in the ability to use a network router to transfer IP datagrams between two different networks by changing the IP address to that of the next-hop router in the IP datagram header. In this case, we want to transfer the IP datagram between a real network and a virtual network—or tunnel, if you will allow us to interject a VPN term here and there. This is the basic process of encapsulation. If we have two or more routers, all belonging to the same virtual LAN, they form virtual tunnels and can pass IP datagrams through those tunnels.

What type of machine can do the routing? One choice is some type of network server, and this is where the BorderManager server comes into the picture. During the configuration procedure, you assign both real (public) and virtual (private) IP addresses to the BorderManager servers, and they then route data packets from the real network to the virtual network in the encapsulation process. They will be able to route traffic between the end points of the virtual network—through the tunnel—by using the real media of the public network—in this case, the Internet.

To do that, you have to configure a BorderManager server on each real LAN, and assign to it both real and virtual IP addresses. The virtual address makes that specific computer part of the virtual LAN. The virtual IP addresses assigned to the VPN on each BorderManager server must conform to the IP addressing requirements that we wrote about in Chapter 3. In other words, all BorderManager VPN servers, masters, and slaves, must be in the same virtual IP subnet and have different virtual IP host numbers. That way, you create a virtual subnet that is in reality scattered all over the Internet. Traffic is passed between the VPN servers to the real destination LAN using the Internet as the transport media. Pretty spiffy, eh?

One other thought—because these devices are going to form a virtual network, in reality separated by hundreds or thousands of miles of rather complex Internet structure, it works best when some type of control system is in place. In answer to that, Novell developed the concept of the *master* and *slave* VPN servers. On any virtual network implemented with Novell BorderManager, you can have lots of slaves, but only one master VPN server. Those are the rules as decreed by the wizards of San Jose.

So, looking back at Figure 7.7, we see that we have two LANs connected to the Internet, and a virtual subnet that transverses through the Internet to allow traffic to be passed from one end to the other.

### Some Thoughts About Encryption

If you recall from Chapter 4, in which we discussed the development of IPsec and the authentication and encryption that takes place within the protocol, you can use several types of encryption techniques. IPsec primarily uses *public key* encryption methods, and for this reason a public key needs to be generated and distributed.

The BorderManager VPN uses the same type of public key encryption method as IPsec. As a part of installing the BorderManager VPN, you select which of the VPN servers will be the master server. The master will then generate a key, using a random seed chosen by the network administrator. This is the public key, and the network administrator must deliver it to the slave server's site. When the slave is set up, the public key is applied against an algorithm and a *message digest value* is generated. This value is compared to one created at the master. If both values are identical, you can presume that no one has tampered with the public key and the slave server installation can proceed.

When the VPN master server configuration has been completed, the server is automatically added to the VPN. When the VPN slave server configuration is completed, the slave must be added to the VPN using the NW Admin NetWare administration program, running on an administrator workstation. After the master and slave VPN servers are on the same virtual subnet, they will perform a synchronization procedure. Part of the synchronization is a mutual agreement between the two servers, based on the requirements for authentication and encryption entered by the network administrator. If you do not enter any specific requirements for authentication and encryption, the BorderManager VPN will use a set of default parameters. Among other things, these parameters establish the frequency for generating and exchanging new keys.

### Putting It All Together

That about wraps up the theory of operation. The next step is the actual implementation. I do need to remind you of one more thing. At the beginning of this chapter I went to quite a bit of detail about some basic things you should do before you start the actual implementation. Just because we didn't go over the same things again doesn't mean that I'm suggesting you don't do them. They are every bit as important for the installation and configuration of the Novell BorderManager VPN as they were for Windows NT. In other words, you still need to do your homework first, before you get to this point. Now, on with the show.

## Checklist Number One: Equipment Required

To determine the amount and type of equipment required to implement your VPN, you need to draft an exact plan and detailed drawings of the network changes to implement. The drawing should include all IP addresses and anything else you think is important. The network administrator for Vintage Air made a decision to have a separate drawing for each LAN like the GLS facility details in Figure 7.9.

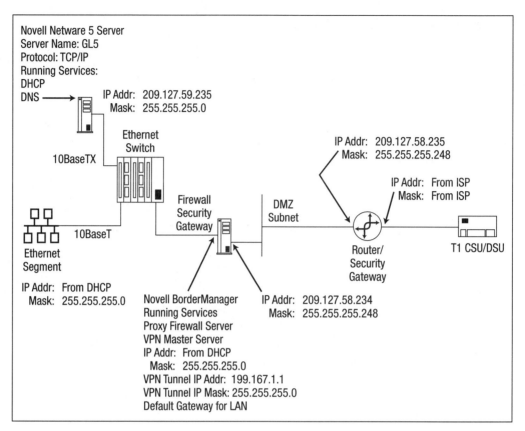

**Figure 7.9**
GLS network drawing.

The next item I would recommend is a configuration form for the new equipment required. As a minimum, you will need one for each of the two BorderManager servers (if your facility does not already have them installed). The network configuration form in Table 7.1 will work fine for this.

Finally, you need a list of items you will require to complete the project. Although we cannot make a determination about your exact needs, we can offer a suggestion that as a minimum the list will include the following:

♦ A computer capable of running Novell NetWare 4.11, 4.2, or 5, and capable of supporting Novell's BorderManager. A high-end Pentium II or Pentium III with a minimum 128 Mbytes of RAM will do the job you need.

♦ [For our example] Novell NetWare 5, and Novell BorderManager Enterprise 3.

♦ One or more client computers, either Windows NT 4 Workstation, or Windows 98. One of these will be used as the administrator's workstation.

♦ WAN equipment, including ISDN interface adapters, DSU/CSU, and WAN routers.

**Table 7.1    BorderManager server network configuration.**

| Property | Value |
|---|---|
| NIC 1 | Model # |
| NIC 2 | Model # |
| NIC Protocols | TCP/IP |
| NIC Protocols | IPX/SPX |
| DHCP | Do not use |
| *TCP/IP Properties* | |
| NIC 1 IP address | 209.127.59.234 |
| NIC 2 IP address | 209.127.58.234 |
| VPN IP address | 199.167.1.1 |
| Mask (both) | 255.255.255.0 |
| Gateway (both) | Default |
| DNS properties (both) | Default |
| Enable IP forwarding (1) | Yes |
| Enable IP forwarding (2) | N/A |
| DHCP relay (both) | No |
| Services for bindings | Default |

**Note**

*In many cases the router shown between the DMZ subnet and the CSU/DSU is a hardware router supplied by your ISP. If this is the case, and you need to make changes to this router, who will be responsible for (re)programming them?*

In all probability, other items of equipment, hardware, and software will be required for your particular implementation. This is a recommended minimum list, not by any means a complete list.

## Checklist Number Two: Support Needs

The following are suggestions of who you may need to contact for help resolving problems with your installation and configuration.

♦ NetWare software vendor, especially if they are a Certified Novell Service Center.

Name: _____

Company: _____

Phone: (_____)_____

♦ Hardware vendor:

Name: _____

Company: _____

Phone: (_____)_____

♦ Internet Service Provider:

Name: _____

Company: _____

Phone: (____)_____

♦ PSTN or PDN provider:

Name: _____

Company: _____

Phone: (____)_____

♦ Other support options:

Name: _____

Company: _____

Phone: (____)_____

**Note**

*Before we dive into the actual implementation process, make sure everything up to here is completed and in place. Go back one more time and see that each item is up, running, and configured—before you start.*

## Checklist Number Three: Pre-Implementation

If it is at all possible, set up a test network and go through the implementation process using the test network first, before committing to the live network. If you can't do that, then this list becomes all the more important:

♦ Create a contingency plan—preferably with a time line and point-of-no-return established.

♦ Notify users, especially those directly involved with the VPN, that you are working on the network and service may be interrupted from time to time.

♦ Verify that the PSTN/PDN carrier has signed off connectivity.

♦ Verify that add-on (new) hardware is functional and, if necessary, upgraded to meet specifications required:

   ♦ Hard drive space

   ♦ Network interface cards

   ♦ RAM

   ♦ Transport media (cables—UTP and fiber-optic)

   ♦ Other

- Verify that all rollover (existing) hardware is functional and, if necessary, upgraded to meet specifications required:
  - Hard drive space
  - Network interface cards
  - RAM
  - Transport media (cables—UTP and fiber-optic)
  - Other
- Complete diagnostics tests on Uninterruptible Power Supply (UPS).
- Verify that you have enough registered IP addresses available for new added Internet connections.
- Check your detailed drawing and make sure that you have assigned an IP address to the network connection on each new item of equipment.
- Physically locate any new hardware equipment and install any and all new cables.
- Power up the new equipment and assure yourself that it is all functioning correctly.
- You should perform the following five steps before you take down your existing WAN link between the two sites. This is necessary in order for the directory tree to synchronize between the two sites with the new equipment located in the tree.
- If necessary, install the Novell NetWare 5 operating system on the computer designated for the BorderManager server. Run VREPAIR on the NetWare SYS: volume to assure that no volume errors have cropped up.
- Determine that all equipment involved in the implementation has the proper protocols assigned, proper addresses assigned, and that routing has been established between subnets.
- If you haven't already done so, upgrade the version of DS.NLM on all servers to the latest recommended by Novell. The latest version of DS.NLM is available by download from **support.novell.com**.
- When you install the NetWare 5 system on the servers, you should also install them at their appropriate locations in the NDS directory tree. If your tree is relatively small, my recommendation is that you place the BorderManager servers in the same container. However, this may not always be possible.

**Note**

*The next step is very important because BorderManager makes full use of Novell Directory Services.*

- Make sure that the directory is fully synchronized and no directory-related problems exist. Run DSREPAIR on all servers that have a replica of the partition that will contain the BorderManager VPN servers.

*Synchronization*

When you configure and restart the master VPN server, the packet filters activate and only VPN packets will pass through the interface connected to the public network. If this is the only connection with the BorderManager computer on the other end (that is, the slave server), the master and slave will lose contact. This is normal and will remain this way until you configure the slave and install it in the VPN. After the slave installation, the master and slave will synchronize using the VPN virtual subnet, and communications will resume.

♦ Install and configure the TCP/IP protocol and set up initial routing functions.

*Note*

*Even though NDS and DHCP have been moved close together—to the point that when DHCP assigns an address, it makes an entry in the DNS table in the directory—I strongly recommend that you assign the IP address for the NICs in the BorderManager server statically. This will allow you to use IP addresses instead of domain names when configuring the VPN, and greatly simplify the VPN configuration and troubleshooting.*

Most of the preceding steps apply to the servers at both ends of the VPN. If your technician resources are limited, you can install, configure, and test one server at a time. The exception is the addition of the slave VPN server into the virtual network.

# Checklist Number Four: Implementation

The following procedure comprises the implementation of a site-to-site VPN using BorderManager: (Each procedure's configuration utility is shown in parentheses.)

♦ If you have not already done so, run INETCFG.NLM on the NetWare servers that will house the BorderManager software, and copy all the network-related load and bind commands over to the appropriate files that are maintained by the INETCFG program.

♦ Install BorderManager software on the NetWare servers (GUI Install).

♦ Install BorderManager Snap-In for the NetWare administrator utility: Windows 9x/NT, BorderManager Setup.

♦ Configure the master server (NIASCFG.NLM).

♦ Configure the slave server (NIASCFG.NLM).

♦ Add the slave server to the VPN (NWADMIN).

*Note*

*When you install the BorderManager VPN, you must extend the schema in the directory tree. To do that, you must be logged in as a user with administrator rights at the root of the tree.*

*Caveat*

Novell BorderManager Enterprise 3 is a full suite of products, each serving a unique function when the BorderManager is used as a gateway to the Internet. As we go through the installation of BorderManager, I want to emphasize the following points emphatically:

According to Novell,—and I agree,—when implemented properly, BorderManager is a complete firewall solution for your Internet connection.

This document is *not* a complete installation and configuration document for BorderManager. The VPN implementation and configuration covered here is only a part of the overall suite of products, and when implemented by itself will not provide firewall protection for your LAN.

What you find is that most businesses install and configure BorderManager to get the firewall and filtering security that is afforded by that product, then add the VPN solution as needed. If you are adding BorderManager as a VPN solution, be sure you perform the proper configuration to enable the firewall protection that comes along with it.

## Run The INETCFG.NLM Program

You may have already run INETCFG. In that case, skip to step 5. If you are not sure, start with Step 1. If the necessary commands have already been copied, the information dialog box will *not* appear, and you can continue with Step 5:

1. At the server console, Figure 7.10, type "INETCFG" and press Enter. This will load the Internet configuration program and, if this is the first time this utility has been run, open an information box, as shown in Figure 7.11. (Editor's Note: All screenshots that follow in this chapter are used courtesy of NetWare, © 1983–1998, Novell, Inc.)

2. The information dialog box will inform you that all load and bind commands will be copied to the configuration files maintained by INETCFG, and that all future configurations must be done using INETCFG. Select Yes and press Enter to copy the necessary configuration information and change the dialog box to look like Figure 7.12, asking if you want to restart the computer.

**Figure 7.10**
Administrator's console calling for Internet configuration screen.

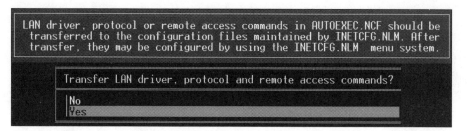

```
LAN driver, protocol or remote access commands in AUTOEXEC.NCF should be
 transferred to the configuration files maintained by INETCFG.NLM. After
 transfer, they may be configured by using the INETCFG.NLM  menu system.

      Transfer LAN driver, protocol and remote access commands?
     |No
     |Yes
```

**Figure 7.11**
Internet configuration screen asking for transfer authority.

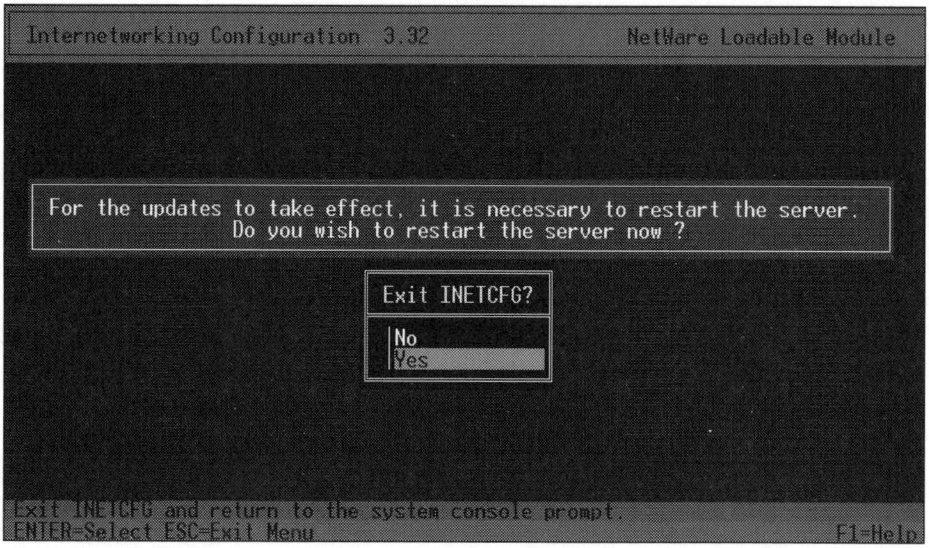

```
 Internetworking Configuration  3.32              NetWare Loadable Module




     For the updates to take effect, it is necessary to restart the server.
                 Do you wish to restart the server now ?


                       Exit INETCFG?
                      |No
                      |Yes




Exit INETCFG and return to the system console prompt.
ENTER=Select ESC=Exit Menu                                       F1=Help
```

**Figure 7.12**
Internetworking Configuration dialog box requesting exit.

3. Select No and press Enter. The dialog box will change, as shown in Figure 7.13, asking if you wish to use the Multiprotocol Router Fast Setup method.

4. Select No, use the standard method, and press Enter to go to the INETCFG opening screen shown in Figure 7.14.

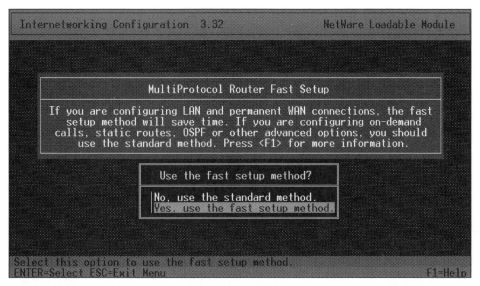

**Figure 7.13**
Multiprotocol Router Fast Setup dialog box.

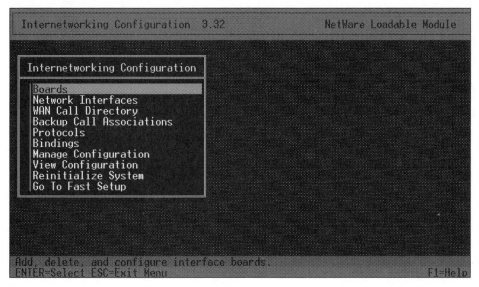

**Figure 7.14**
Standard method selection.

**Figure 7.15**
Exit INETCFG utility.

5. Press Esc and an information box will display, as shown in Figure 7.15, confirming that you want to exit the INETCFG utility.

6. Select Yes and press Enter to exit INETCFG and return to the server console.

## GUI Install—BorderManager Software

To install the BorderManager services on a NetWare 5 server, use the following procedure from the NetWare server console:

1. Insert the BorderManager CD in the CDROM drive and mount the CD as a NetWare volume by typing CDROM at the server console and pressing Enter. A slight delay will occur while the server locates the CD-ROM index. At that point, the CD will be mounted as a NetWare volume, as shown in Figure 7.16.

2. If the GUI interface is not loaded, type "STARTX" at the server console and press Enter. You should end up with the screen shown in Figure 7.17.

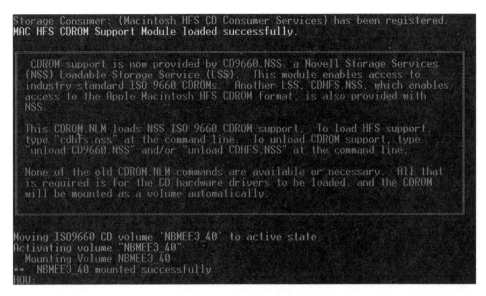

**Figure 7.16**
Mounting NetWare software distribution volume.

**Figure 7.17**
GUI interface screen.

3. Click the Novell logo in the lower left corner of the screen for a pop-up menu, as shown in Figure 7.18.

4. Click on Install. A window will display, as shown in Figure 7.19, listing the currently installed products.

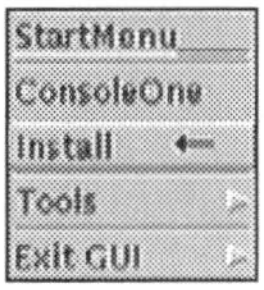

**Figure 7.18**
Novell pop-up menu.

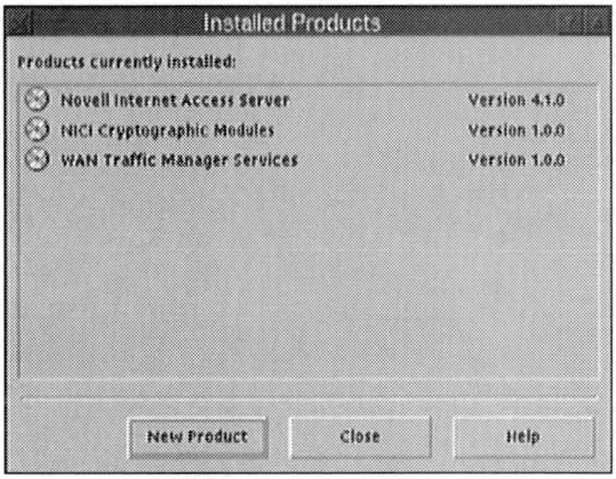

**Figure 7.19**
List of installed products.

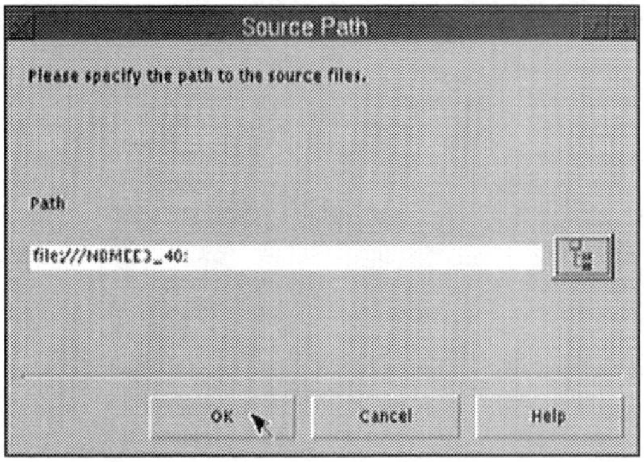

**Figure 7.20**
Source Path dialog box.

5. Click on New Product and the Source Path dialog box, shown in Figure 7.20, will open.

6. Replace the default path A:\ with the path to the CD-ROM drive. Alternatively, you can click on the *Browse* icon to open the screen shown in Figure 7.21 and browse to locate the CD-ROM drive. When you have the correct path entered, click on OK to open the BorderManager Services Installation program, as shown in Figure 7.22.

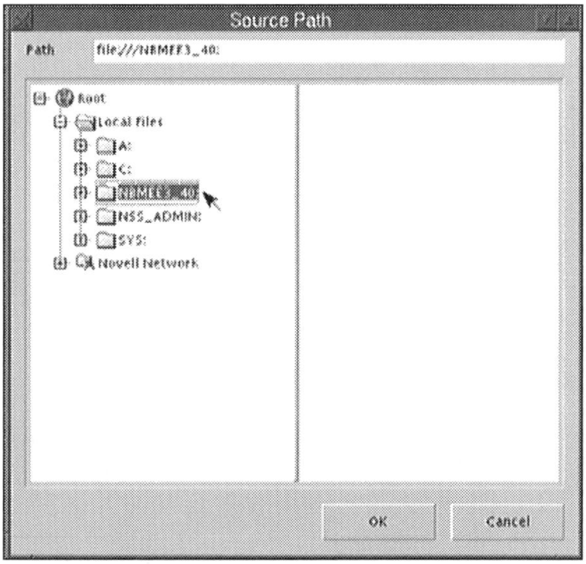

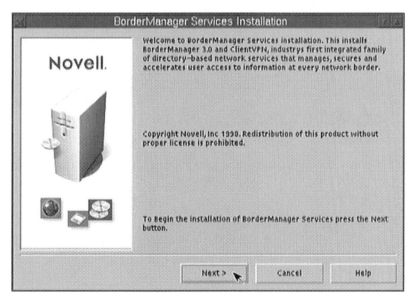

**Figure 7.21**
Insert the path to locate the CD-ROM drive.

**Figure 7.22**
BorderManager Services Installation window.

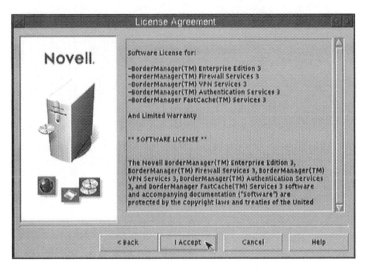

**Figure 7.23**
License agreement.

7. Click on Next to begin the installation. This will open the window shown in Figure 7.23, presenting the license agreement.

8. After you have read the license agreement, click on I Accept. A window will open, Figure 7.24, allowing you to use the license diskette or license file, or enable trial licenses for all services. In addition to these options, you can use the NetWare Administrator to install product licenses after the installation.

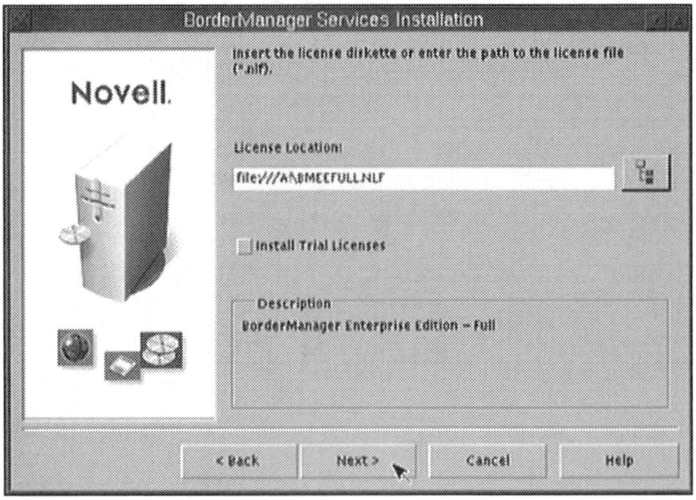

**Figure 7.24**
Choices for license selection.

**Note**

*We assume you will install the BorderManager license from a floppy diskette.*

9. Insert the license diskette. Enter the path to the disk drive if the default path is incorrect. Click Next. If more than one license is available on the disk, an information dialog box will display, as shown in Figure 7.25, informing you that a browser will open allowing you to select the license you wish to install.

10. Click on OK. The Select License to Install browser will open, as shown in Figure 7.26, displaying the available licenses, and allowing you to choose the license you wish to install.

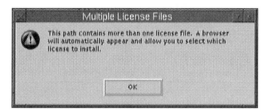

**Figure 7.25**
License information dialog.

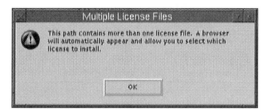

**Figure 7.26**
Select license to install.

11. Select the license you wish to install and click on OK. The Select License to Install browser will close, and the BorderManager Services Installation dialog box will open, as shown in Figure 7.27, displaying information on the licenses to be installed.

12. Review the license display. You can click Back to go back and make changes. When you are satisfied with the license(s) to be installed, click Next. At this time, a warning dialog box may open, as shown in Figure 7.28, informing you that the current version of Novell Internet Access Server™ will be overwritten, but the configuration will be retained.

13. When you are satisfied with the license selection, click Next. That will open the login screen shown in Figure 7.29, prompting you to login to NDS.

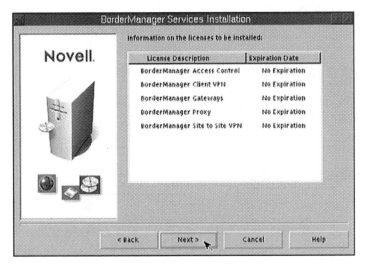

**Figure 7.27**
Services installation dialog box.

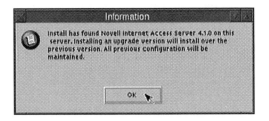

**Figure 7.28**
Overwriting warning box.

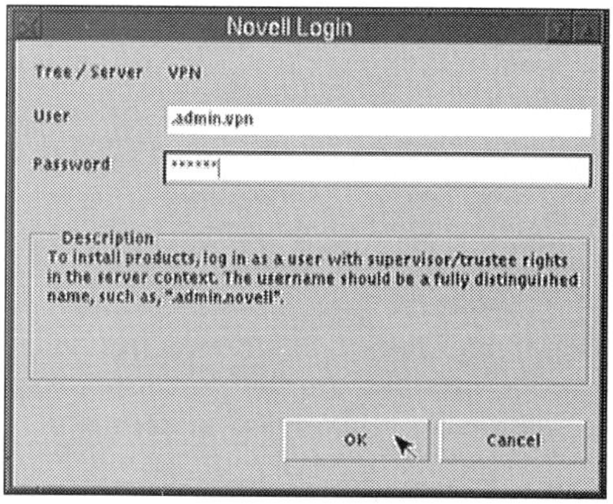

**Figure 7.29**
NDS login screen.

14. Enter your fully distinguished user name. Press the Tab key—or click on the password entry line—and enter your password. Press the Enter key—or click on OK—to close the login screen and open a window displaying the NICs installed and configured in this computer. See Figure 7.30.

**Note**

*You must log in as a user with administrator rights at the [ROOT] of the tree for administrator rights at the container level in which the server object is located. Administrative rights are required to extend the NDS schema and configure the NICs.*

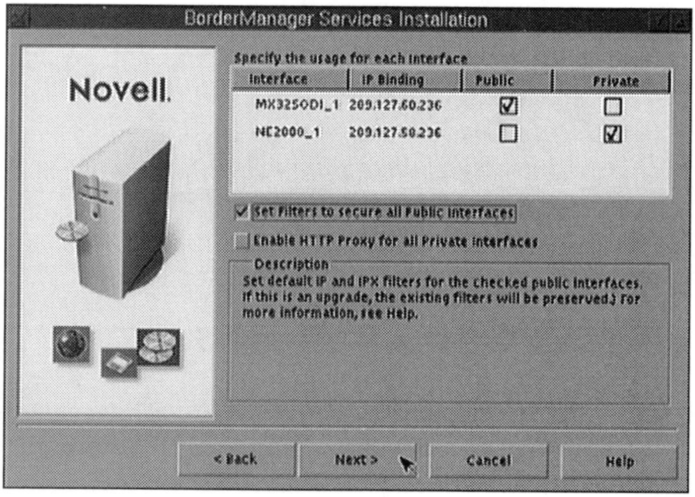

**Figure 7.30**
Configuration screen for installed network interface cards.

15. Review the list of NICs and their IP bindings. Each interface must be specified as public (the Internet), private (your LAN), or both public and private. One selection is required for each network interface.

    ♦ Specifying a public interface activates the Set Filters to Secure All Public Interfaces option. After you have selected the public interfaces, check this box to establish default IP and IPX filters for all public interfaces. (For more information about setting IP and IPX filters, see the Novell documentation.)

16. Specifying a private interface activates the HTTP proxy for All Private Interfaces option. The next checkbox enables access control restrictions for Web browsers. I recommend you leave it *un*checked. (For more information about the HTTP proxy, see the Novell Documentation.)

17. Click on Next, and the BorderManager Services Installation window, shown in Figure 7.31, will open, prompting you to enter a unique DNS domain name for your network.

18. Click on Next. The BorderManager Services Installation window will change, as shown in Figure 7.32, and you will be prompted to enter the IP addresses for up to three DNS servers.

19. Click on Add to open a dialog box allowing you to enter the IP address of at least one, and up to three, servers. The search order will be the order you list the DNS servers. You can change the listed order, moving them with the Up and Down arrows. When the search order is as you want it, click on Next. The BorderManager Services installation screen will change, as shown in Figure 7.33, to display a list of product options for you to install. In this case, there is only one option available.

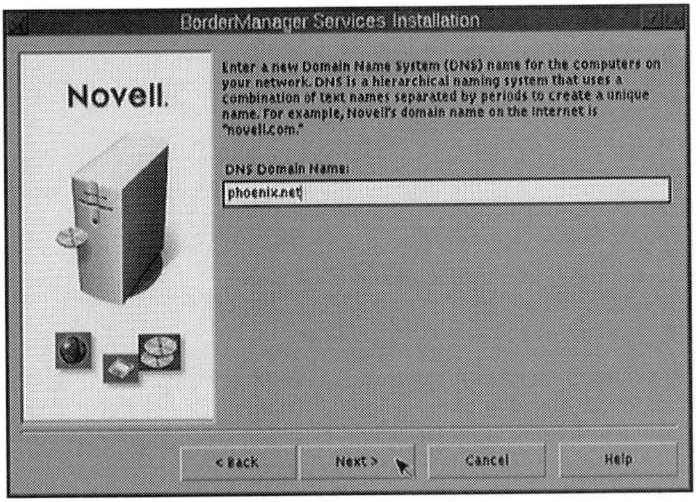

**Figure 7.31**
Domain name prompt.

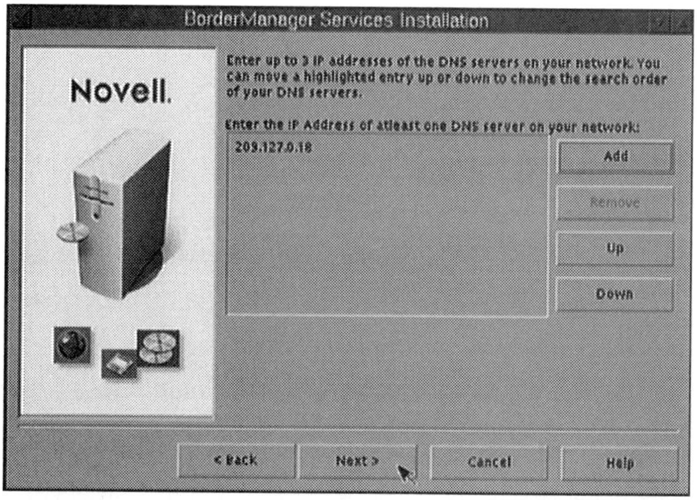

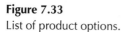

**Figure 7.32**
Prompt to enter IP addresses for DNS servers.

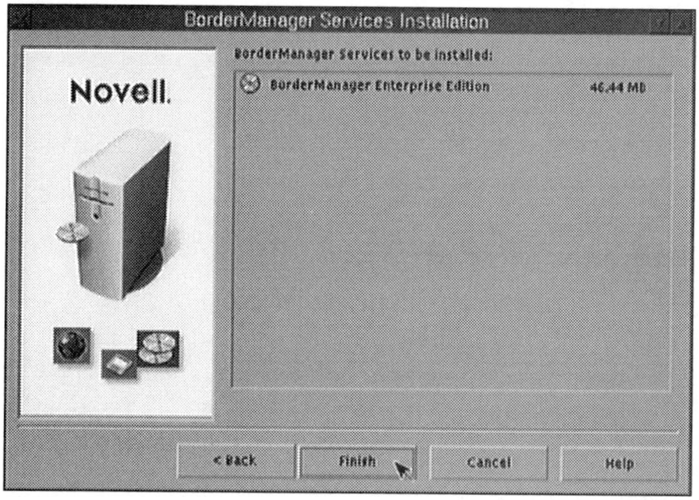

**Figure 7.33**
List of product options.

20. Select the products for your installation, verify that they are correct, and then click on Finish. That will open the information window shown in Figure 7.34 and display the installation progress.

**Figure 7.34**
Installation progress display.

During the installation process, if the server encounters a possible conflict, such as copying a file off the CD-ROM that is older than the existing file on the server, the installation process will stop. An information box informing you of the possible conflict will open, and the server will wait for your input as to how to proceed. This is a normal part of the installation process.

When the installation is complete, another information window will open, as shown in Figure 7.35, telling you to reboot the server for the changes to take place. You also have the option of viewing the README file at this time.

21. Click Reboot, and restart the server.

You have now completed the installation of the BorderManager services. Don't forget that you have to complete this process on the servers on both networks.

## Adding The BorderManager Snap-In Utility

Sooner or later, if it isn't already in your computer, you need to modify the NetWare administrator utility called *NWADMIN* by adding *Snap-In* so that you can administer BorderManager services. If you are not familiar with how to reconfigure the NWADMIN with use of snap ins, don't worry—the process is a sn...; it's painless. We could wait until after we configure the master and slave VPN servers, but this is a good place to change

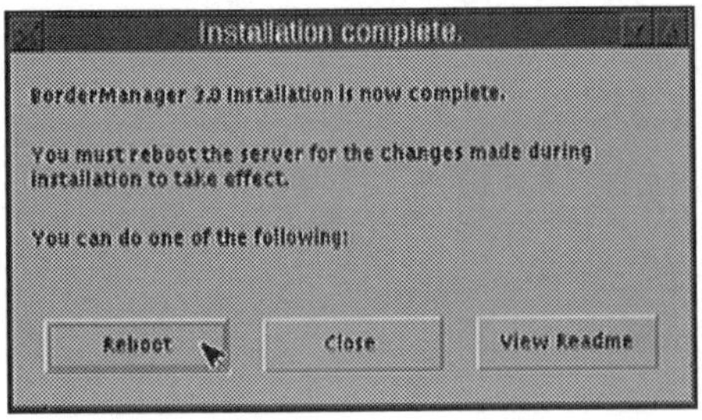

**Figure 7.35**
Option to reboot server.

directions for a while. By the way, if you have been using BorderManager for other services already, there's a good chance the Snap-In has already been added.

We make the assumption that you are using a Windows 9x/NT workstation to perform this procedure. Here are the steps for adding the BorderManager Snap-In:

1. Log in to the directory tree as a user with admin rights at the root of the tree or container level where the master VPN server will be located.

2. Click on Start; then point to Run and click again. The Run Programs dialog box will open, as shown in Figure 7.36, prompting you to enter the name of the program to run.

3. Type in the path to the SYS:\PUBLIC\BRDRMGR\SNAPINS\SETUP.EXE file, and click Next. (You could click on Browse, and use the browser to locate the program.) The setup program will load, and the Installing BorderManager screen will open, as shown in Figure 7.37, with the appropriate information.

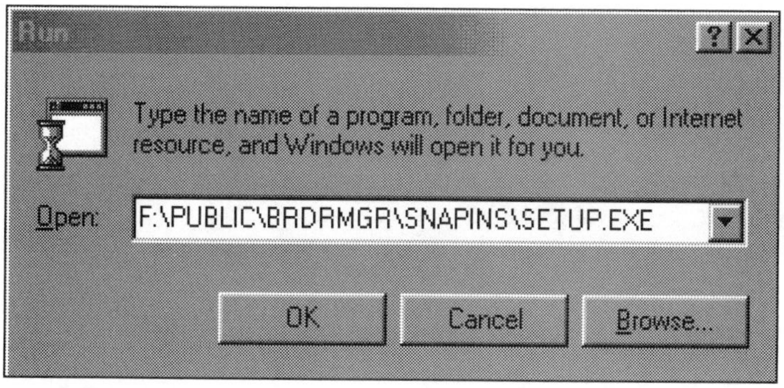

![Run dialog box with Open field showing F:\PUBLIC\BRDRMGR\SNAPINS\SETUP.EXE and OK, Cancel, Browse buttons]

**Figure 7.36**
Run Programs dialog box.

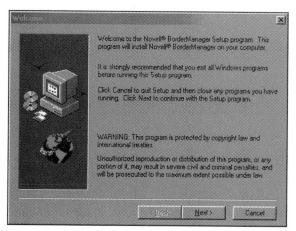

**Figure 7.37**
Installing BorderManager screen.

4. Click on Next. The setup program will search for the directory that contains the NWAdmin.exe program. When it has located this program, the Choose Destination Location dialog box will open, as shown in Figure 7.38, prompting you to choose the destination for the installed files.

5. Click on Next to stick with the default, or follow the instructions on the setup screen as appropriate for your specific configuration. The setup program will proceed with the chore of copying and configuring the necessary files. When the setup is complete, an information dialog box will open, as shown in Figure 7.39, asking if you wish to view the README file at this time.

6. If you wish to view the README file, click Yes; otherwise click No. If you click No, the information dialog box will close, and another information dialog box will open, as shown in Figure 7.40, informing you that the BorderManager files have been installed, and asking if you want to launch the NW Admin utility now.

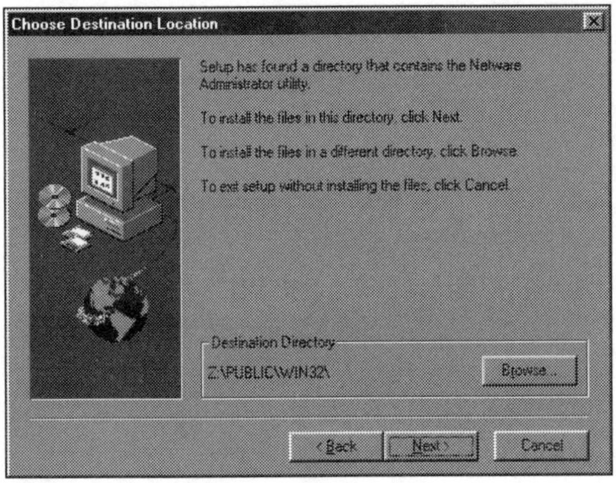

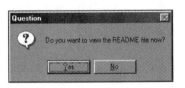

**Figure 7.38**
Choose Destination Location dialog box.

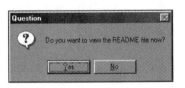

**Figure 7.39**
README request panel.

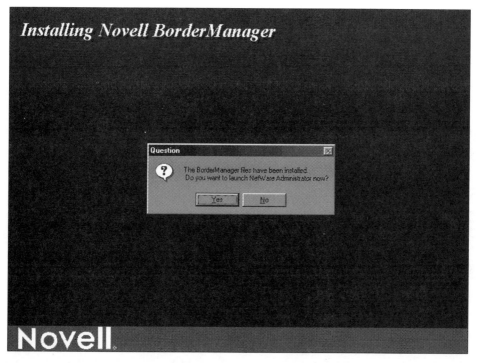

**Figure 7.40**
Installation notification and launch request.

7. If you wish to launch the NW Admin utility, click Yes. If you do not wish to launch the
   NW Admin utility at this time, click No. If you click No, the setup screen will close
   and the Windows Desktop will become the active screen. That's all there was to that,
   now let's get back to work.

## Configure The BorderManager Master VPN Server—NIASCFG.NLM

The next step is to configure the master VPN server. During this configuration you will
select the encryption methods you wish to use and generate the public key. This configuration is performed at the server console—on the server that will be the master VPN server.
Here we go:

1. At the server console type "LOAD NIASCFG" and press Enter. This will load the
   NIASCFG configuration utility, and the server screen will look like Figure 7.41. If this
   is the first time you have run NIASCFG, you will see an information box informing you
   that all load and bind commands will be moved to the NETINFO.CFG file.

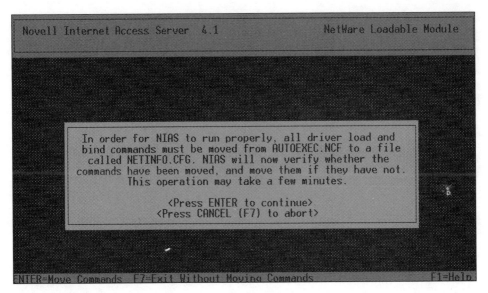

**Figure 7.41**
Load and bind information screen.

2. Press Enter to continue. The NIASCFG utility will verify that the appropriate commands have been relocated to the correct file. A new information box will open, shown in Figure 7.42, informing you that you must restart the server before any new changes will take place.

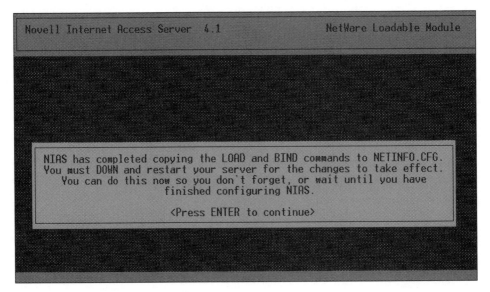

**Figure 7.42**
Restart request screen.

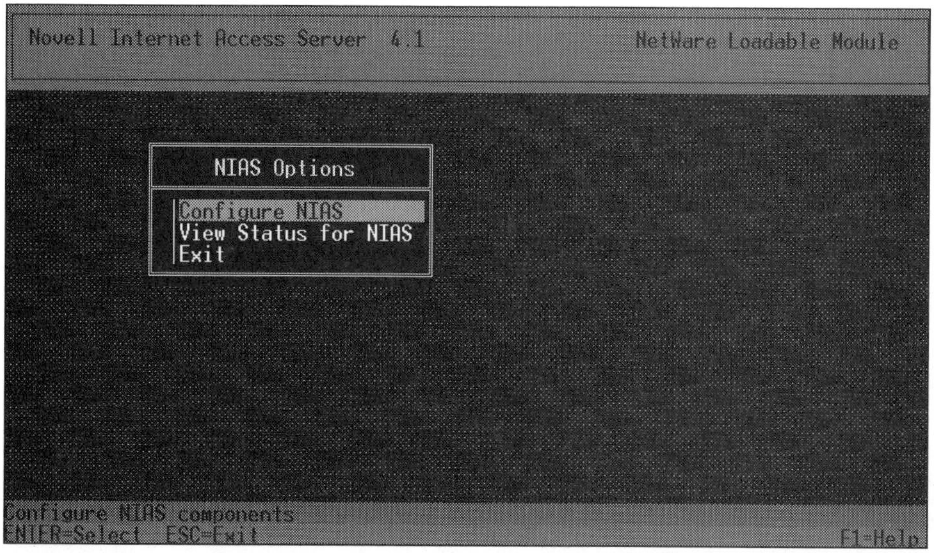

**Figure 7.43**
NIASCFG opening screen.

3. Press Enter to continue. The NIASCFG utility opening screen will appear, shown in Figure 7.43.

4. Select Configure NIAS, and press Enter. The Select Component to Configure box will open, as shown in Figure 7.44.

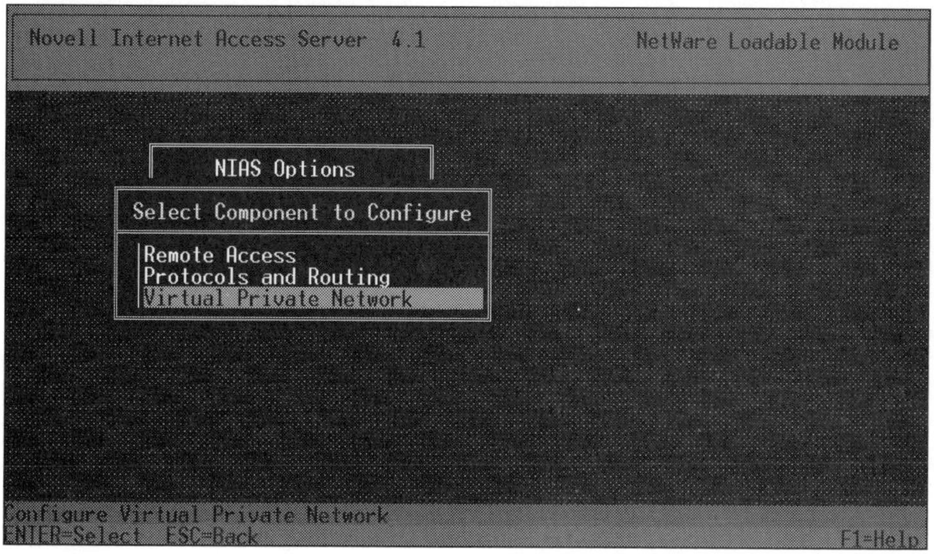

**Figure 7.44**
NIAS component configuration.

5. Select Virtual Private Network, and press Enter. If this is the first VPN Server (either master or slave) you are installing in the tree, the directory schema will have to be extended. In this case, the VPN Configuration dialog box will open, as shown Figure 7.45, and the following substeps will be performed, one time only:

5a. You will be prompted to login to the NDS tree as a user with administrative rights at the root of the tree—usually this is the ADMIN user. Enter the fully distinguished name of the user and press Enter, enter the password, and press Enter again to log in to the directory. After NDS has authenticated the user name and password, the directory schema will be extended to include the new VPN objects. An information dialog box will open, shown in Figure 7.46, informing you that the extension has been done.

5b. Press Enter. The information dialog box will close, and the VPN Configuration screen, Figure 7.47, will display.

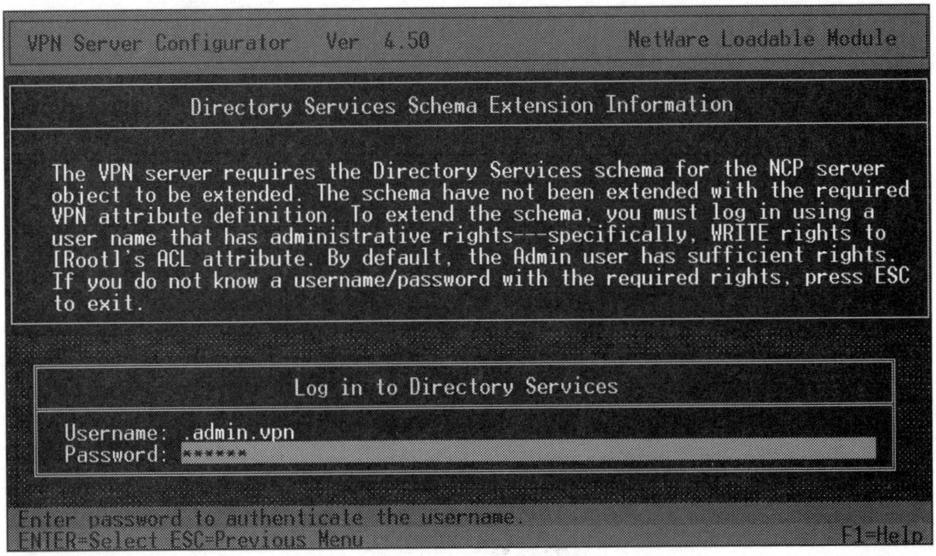

VPN Server Configurator Ver 4.50
NetWare Loadable Module
Directory Services Schema Extension Information
The VPN server requires the Directory Services schema for the NCP server object to be extended. The schema have not been extended with the required VPN attribute definition. To extend the schema, you must log in using a user name that has administrative rights---specifically, WRITE rights to [Root]'s ACL attribute. By default, the Admin user has sufficient rights. If you do not know a username/password with the required rights, press ESC to exit.
Log in to Directory Services
Username: .admin.vpn
Password: ******
Enter password to authenticate the username.
ENTER=Select ESC=Previous Menu
F1=Help

**Figure 7.45**
VPN configuration screen.

VPNCFG has successfully extended the Directory Services schema with the VPN attribute definition.
<Press ENTER to continue>

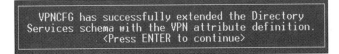

**Figure 7.46**
Notification that extension of the directory was completed.

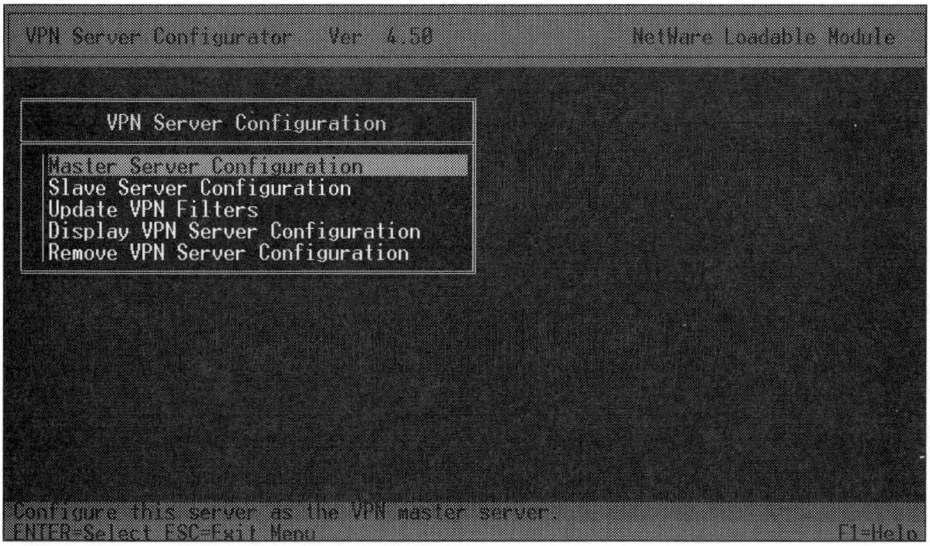

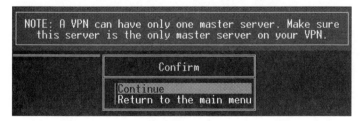

**Figure 7.47**
VPN configuration after directory changes.

6. Select Master Server Configuration, and press Enter. An information dialog box will open, shown in Figure 7.48, informing you that each VPN can have only one master VPN server, and asking you to confirm that this is the only master VPN server for this VPN.

7. Select Continue and press Enter. The Master Server Configuration menu box will open in the VPN server configuration screen, shown in Figure 7.49.

8. Select Configure IP Addresses, and press Enter. The Configure IP Addresses dialog box, shown in Figure 7.50, will open.

**Figure 7.48**
Confirmation of master server for the VPN under configuration.

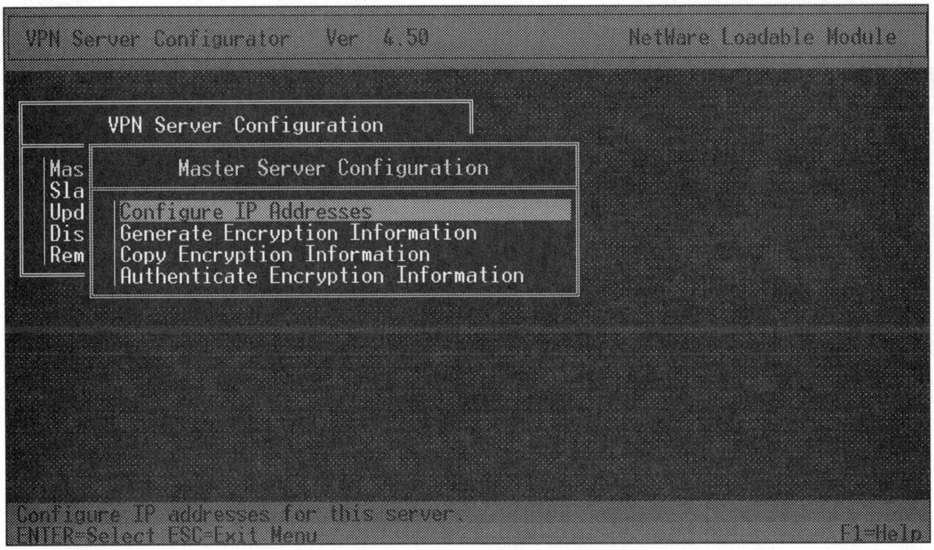

**Figure 7.49**
VPN Server Configuration menu.

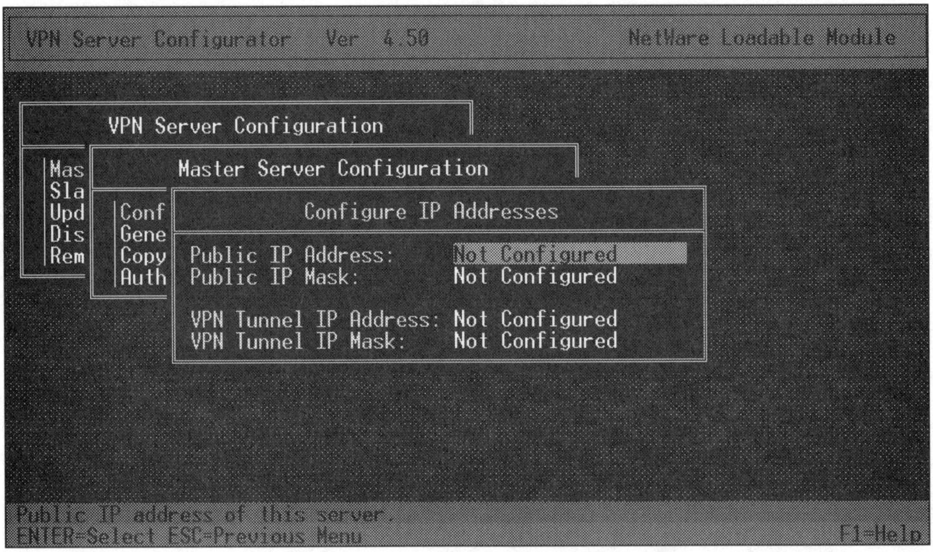

**Figure 7.50**
IP address configuration dialog panel.

9. Enter the public IP address for the VPN master server. This will most likely be an address in the range of addresses assigned by your ISP. After you have entered the public IP address, press Enter, then enter the IP net mask for the master VPN server public IP address. When you have entered the mask, press Enter.

10. Enter the VPN tunnel IP address. This address should be unregistered, as it will never be seen outside your private network. (Remember that all VPN servers in the same VPN must be in the same IP subnet.) Press Enter, and then enter the IP net mask for the master VPN tunnel IP address. A dialog box similar to Figure 7.51 will appear.

11. When the IP address information is correct, press Esc. A confirmation dialog box will open as shown in Figure 7.52, asking you to confirm that you want to save the new IP addresses.

12. Select Yes, and press Enter. An information dialog box will open, as shown in Figure 7.53, informing you that the VPN packet filters were successfully added.

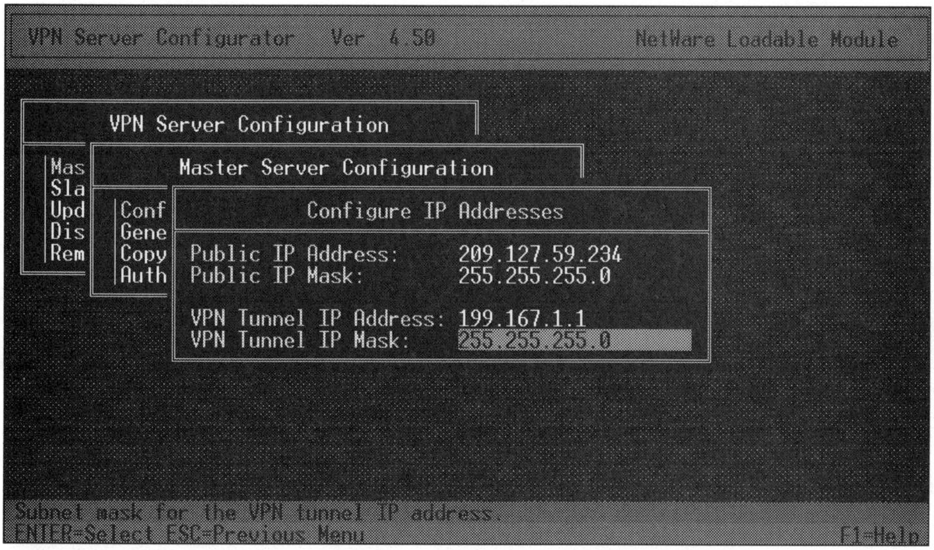

```
VPN Server Configurator   Ver 4.50              NetWare Loadable Module

        VPN Server Configuration
   Mas      Master Server Configuration
   Sla
   Upd  Conf         Configure IP Addresses
   Dis  Gene
   Rem  Copy   Public IP Address:    209.127.59.234
        Auth   Public IP Mask:       255.255.255.0

               VPN Tunnel IP Address: 199.167.1.1
               VPN Tunnel IP Mask:    255.255.255.0


Subnet mask for the VPN tunnel IP address.
ENTER=Select ESC=Previous Menu                          F1=Help
```

**Figure 7.51**
IP address configuration screen after entering the net mask.

**Figure 7.52**
IP address confirmation screen.

**Figure 7.53**
VPN packet filters have been added.

13. Press Enter. The information dialog box will close, and you will be returned to the Master Server Configuration menu box shown in Figure 7.49.

14. Select Generate Encryption Information and press Enter. The Enter Random Seed dialog box will open, shown in Figure 7.54, prompting you to enter a seed for the encryption algorithm.

**Note**

*The value you type in as the random seed serves only to provide a more random selection value to start the process of generating the encryption public key. You will not need it again, so don't worry about remembering the random seed number you invent.*

15. Type in any combination of up to 255 characters and press Enter. An information dialog box will open, shown in Figure 7.55, informing you that the encryption information has been generated successfully.

16. Press Enter to continue. A new information dialog box, shown in Figure 7.56, will inform you that the VPN attributes have been successfully updated.

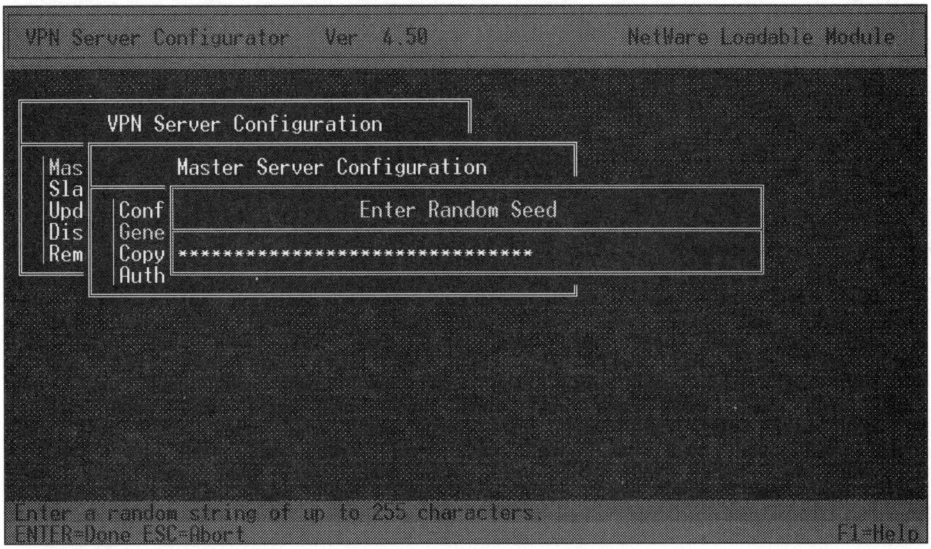

```
VPN Server Configurator   Ver 4.50              NetWare Loadable Module

        VPN Server Configuration
 Mas        Master Server Configuration
 Sla
 Upd    Conf        Enter Random Seed
 Dis    Gene
 Rem    Copy  ********************************
        Auth

Enter a random string of up to 255 characters.
ENTER=Done ESC=Abort                                    F1=Help
```

**Figure 7.54**
Random seed entry prompt.

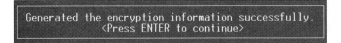

**Figure 7.55**
Encryption information report.

```
The VPN attributes have been successfully updated in Directory Services.
                     <Press ENTER to continue>
```

**Figure 7.56**
Updated VPN attribute report.

17. Press Enter to continue and you will return to the Master Server Configuration menu box shown in Figure 7.49.

**Note**

*At this time the VPN public key resides in the master encryption information file, named MINFO.VPN. You will need to send this file to the slave VPN server site where it will be required for configuring the encryption algorithm there. It is advisable to copy this file to a floppy diskette. This is the next step in the configuration process.*

18. Select Copy Encryption Information, and press Enter. A dialog box will open, as shown in Figure 7.57, prompting you to enter the path to the disk drive where you will copy the encryption information. (The destination can be a floppy diskette or the hard disk.)

19. Enter the path information, and press Enter. When the process is complete, an information dialog box will open, as shown in Figure 7.58, telling you the action was successful.

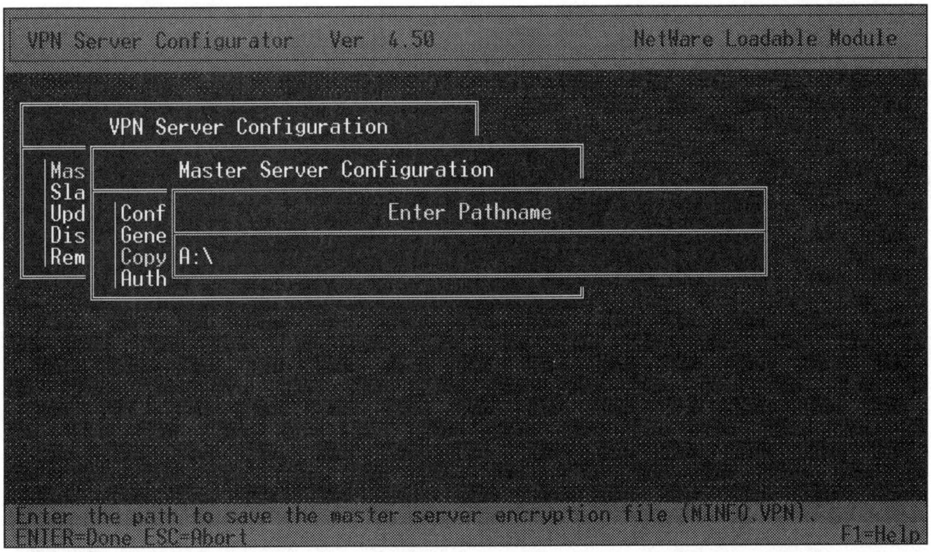

```
VPN Server Configurator   Ver  4.50              NetWare Loadable Module

        ┌─ VPN Server Configuration ──────┐
   ┌────┤   VPN Server Configuration      │
   │Mas │  ┌─ Master Server Configuration ──────────┐
   │Sla │  │                                         │
   │Upd │  │Conf │  ┌─ Enter Pathname ──────────────┐│
   │Dis │  │Gene │  │                               ││
   │Rem │  │Copy │  │A:\                            ││
   │    │  │Auth │  └───────────────────────────────┘│

 Enter the path to save the master server encryption file (MINFO.VPN).
 ENTER=Done ESC=Abort                                          F1=Help
```

**Figure 7.57**
File path prompt.

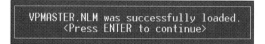

Copied the encryption information successfully to the specified path.
<Press ENTER to continue>

**Figure 7.58**
Successful file storage report.

VPMASTER.NLM was successfully loaded.
<Press ENTER to continue>

**Figure 7.59**
Notification of successful load of VPMASTER.NLM.

20. Press Enter to continue. A different dialog box will open, shown in Figure 7.59, informing you that the VPMASTER.NLM—this is the master VPN server core program—has successfully loaded.

21. Press Enter to continue and you will be returned to the Master Server Configuration menu box, shown in Figure 7.49.

22. Press Esc repeatedly until a confirmation dialog box opens, as shown in Figure 7.60, asking you to confirm that you want to exit from this NLM.

23. Select Yes, and press Enter. The NIAS configuration utility will close, and you will be returned to the server console.

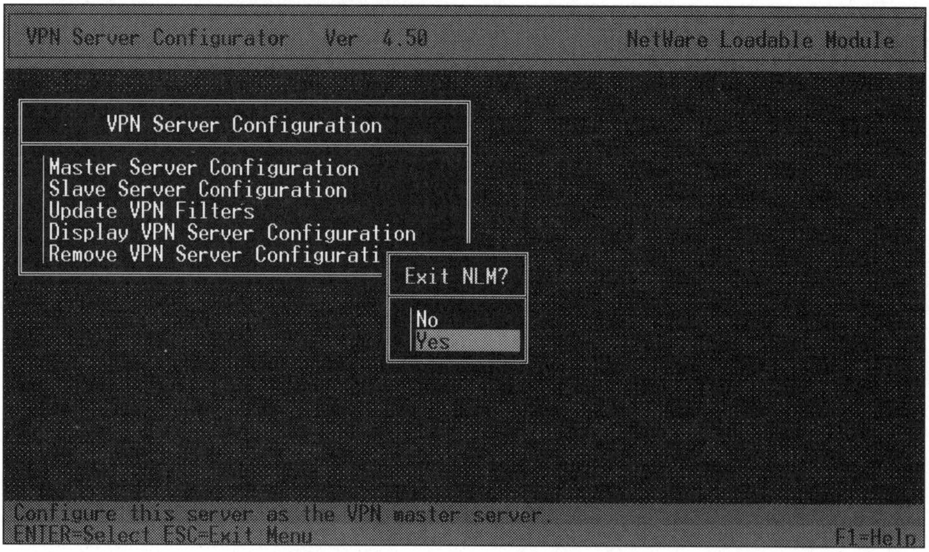

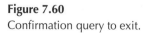

```
VPN Server Configurator  Ver 4.50              NetWare Loadable Module

      ┌───────────────────────────────────┐
      │       VPN Server Configuration     │
      ├───────────────────────────────────┤
      │ Master Server Configuration        │
      │ Slave Server Configuration         │
      │ Update VPN Filters                 │
      │ Display VPN Server Configuration   │
      │ Remove VPN Server Configurati┌──────────────┐
      │                              │ Exit NLM?    │
      │                              ├──────────────┤
      │                              │ No           │
      │                              │ Yes          │
      │                              └──────────────┘

 Configure this server as the VPN master server.
 ENTER=Select ESC=Exit Menu                              F1=Help
```

**Figure 7.60**
Confirmation query to exit.

This completes the configuration of the master VPN server. Label the floppy disk with the encryption information and store it in a protected location. You will need it to configure the slave VPN server.

## Configure The Slave Server—NIASCFG.NLM

Configuring the slave server is very similar to the process of configuring the master server. The primary difference in the installation process between the two is that during the master server configuration process, the encryption algorithm was seeded with a random character string. This encryption algorithm then generated a Master Encryption Information File (MINFO.VPN), which you saved on a disk. During the process of configuring a slave VPN server, the MIFO is used to seed the slave server encryption algorithm, and a Slave Encryption Information File is generated.

As a part of the slave configuration process, you must verify the file authenticity by using the encryption algorithm to generate a *message digest value* at the master and slave. The value must be identical on both servers in order to verify that the MINFO.VPN file has not been tampered with.

To configure the slave VPN server, perform the following procedure:

1.  At the server console type "LOAD NIASCFG" and press Enter to load the NIASCFG configuration utility. The server screen will look like Figure 7.61. If this is the first NIASCFG run, an information box will tell you that all load and bind commands will be moved to the NETINFO.CFG file.

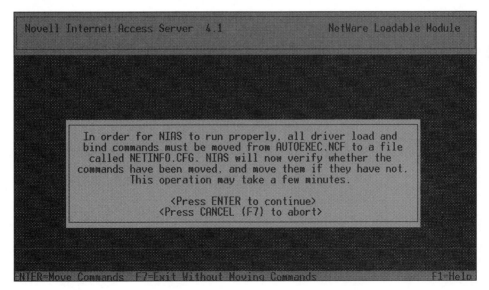

**Figure 7.61**
Slave server load and bind commands.

2. Press Enter to continue. The NIASCFG utility will verify that the appropriate commands have been relocated to the correct file and a new information box will open, as shown in Figure 7.62, telling you to restart the server before any changes will take place.

3. Press Enter to continue. The NIAS options dialog box will open, as shown in Figure 7.63.

4. Select Configure NIAS and press Enter. The Select Component to Configure box will open, as shown in Figure 7.64.

5. Select Virtual Private Network and press Enter.

If you have already configured the master server, this should be the second VPN server in the tree and the following substeps should not apply. However, if this is the first VPN Server—master or slave—to be installed in the tree, the directory schema will have to be extended. In that case, the VPN Configuration dialog box will open, as shown in Figure 7.65, and you will perform the following substeps. You will be prompted to log in to the NDS tree as a user with admin rights at the root of the tree (ADMIN is the most common user for this purpose).

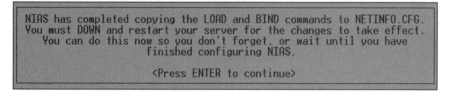

```
NIAS has completed copying the LOAD and BIND commands to NETINFO.CFG.
You must DOWN and restart your server for the changes to take effect.
   You can do this now so you don't forget, or wait until you have
                 finished configuring NIAS.

                    <Press ENTER to continue>
```

**Figure 7.62**
Slave server information box for command relocations.

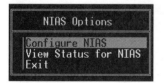

```
       NIAS Options
Configure NIAS
View Status for NIAS
Exit
```

**Figure 7.63**
Slave server NIAS options dialog box.

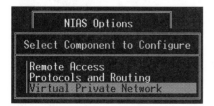

```
        NIAS Options
Select Component to Configure
Remote Access
Protocols and Routing
Virtual Private Network
```

**Figure 7.64**
Slave server select component panel.

```
 VPN Server Configurator   Ver  4.50            NetWare Loadable Module

   ┌─────────────────────────────────────────────────────────────────┐
   │           Directory Services Schema Extension Information         │
   │                                                                   │
   │  The VPN server requires the Directory Services schema for the NCP server │
   │  object to be extended. The schema have not been extended with the required │
   │  VPN attribute definition. To extend the schema, you must log in using a │
   │  user name that has administrative rights---specifically, WRITE rights to │
   │  [Root]'s ACL attribute. By default, the Admin user has sufficient rights. │
   │  If you do not know a username/password with the required rights, press ESC │
   │  to exit.                                                         │
   │                                                                   │
   │   ┌─────────────────────────────────────────────────────────┐    │
   │   │              Log in to Directory Services               │    │
   │   │  Username:  .admin.vpn                                  │    │
   │   │  Password:  ******                                      │    │
   │   └─────────────────────────────────────────────────────────┘    │
   └───────────────────────────────────────────────────────────────────┘
 Enter password to authenticate the username.
 ENTER=Select ESC=Previous Menu                              F1=Help
```

**Figure 7.65**
Slave server VPN configuration panel.

6. Enter the fully distinguished name of the user, press Enter, type in the password, and press Enter again to log in to the directory. After NDS has authenticated the user name and password, the directory schema will be extended to include the new VPN objects. An information dialog box, Figure 7.66, will open, informing you that this has been done.

7. Press Enter to close the information dialog box and open the VPN Server Configuration menu, as shown in Figure 7.47.

8. Select Slave Server Configuration and press Enter to open the menu box shown in Figure 7.67.

9. Select Configure IP Addresses and press Enter; the Configure IP Addresses dialog box will open, as shown in Figure 7.68.

```
 ┌─────────────────────────────────────────────────┐
 │  VPNCFG has successfully extended the Directory  │
 │  Services schema with the VPN attribute definition. │
 │           <Press ENTER to continue>             │
 └─────────────────────────────────────────────────┘
```

**Figure 7.66**
Slave server Directory Services information panel.

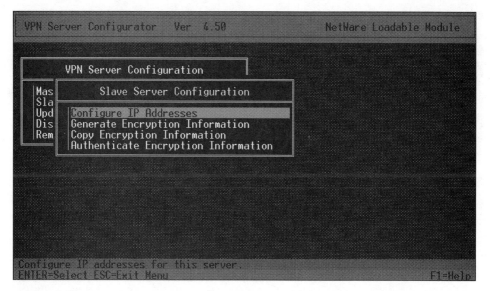

**Figure 7.67**
Slave server configuration menu.

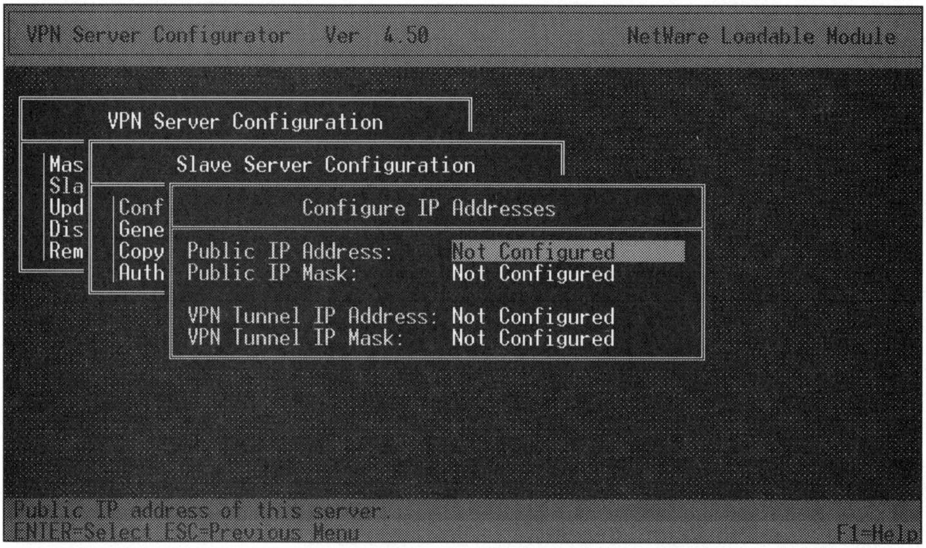

**Figure 7.68**
Configure IP Addresses dialog box for slave server.

10. Enter the public IP address for the VPN slave server, press Enter, type in the IP net mask for the slave, and press Enter.

11. Enter the VPN tunnel IP address—this address should be unregistered, as it will never be seen outside your private network. Remember that all VPN servers within the one VPN

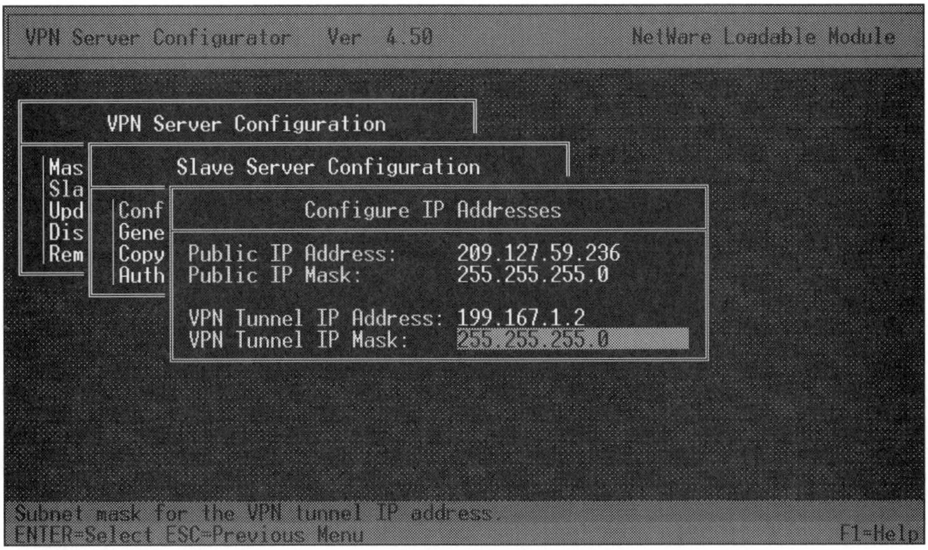

```
VPN Server Configurator   Ver  4.50              NetWare Loadable Module

      VPN Server Configuration
   Mas        Slave Server Configuration
   Sla
   Upd   Conf            Configure IP Addresses
   Dis   Gene
   Rem   Copy  Public IP Address:      209.127.59.236
         Auth  Public IP Mask:         255.255.255.0

               VPN Tunnel IP Address:  199.167.1.2
               VPN Tunnel IP Mask:     255.255.255.0



Subnet mask for the VPN tunnel IP address.
ENTER=Select ESC=Previous Menu                           F1=Help
```

**Figure 7.69**
Entry point for IP net mask for tunnel address.

must be in the same IP subnet. Next, press Enter and type in the IP net mask. After you enter the net mask, the dialog box should appear similar to the one shown in Figure 7.69.

12. After verifying that the IP address information is correct, press Esc to open a confirmation dialog box, as shown in Figure 7.70. Select Yes and press Enter. The information dialog box in Figure 7.71 will open to tell you that the VPN packet filters were successfully added.

13. Press Enter to close the information dialog box and return to the Slave Server Configuration menu box shown in Figure 7.72.

```
Save IP Addresses?

 No
 Yes
```

**Figure 7.70**
IP address confirmation request.

```
VPN packet filters were successfully added.
        <Press ENTER to continue>
```

**Figure 7.71**
Notification of successful operation.

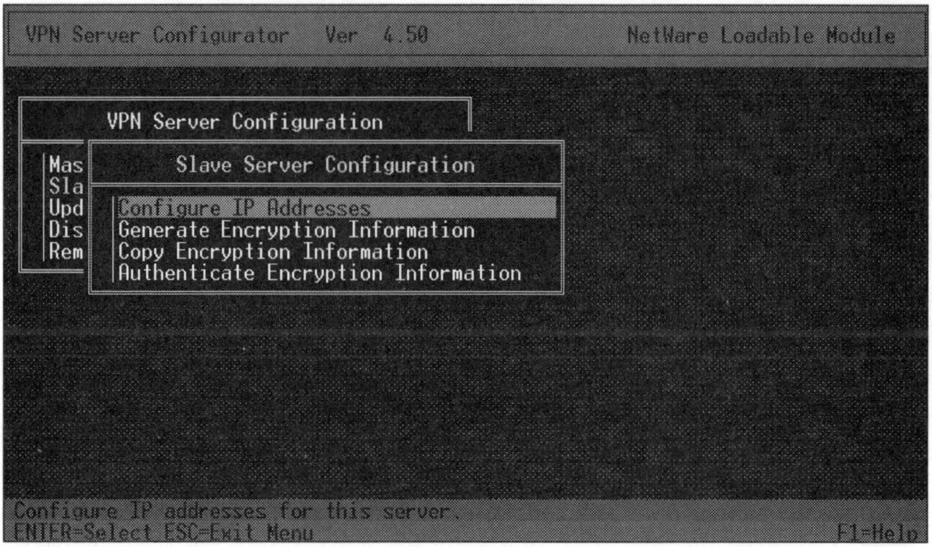

**Figure 7.72**
Slave server configuration menu.

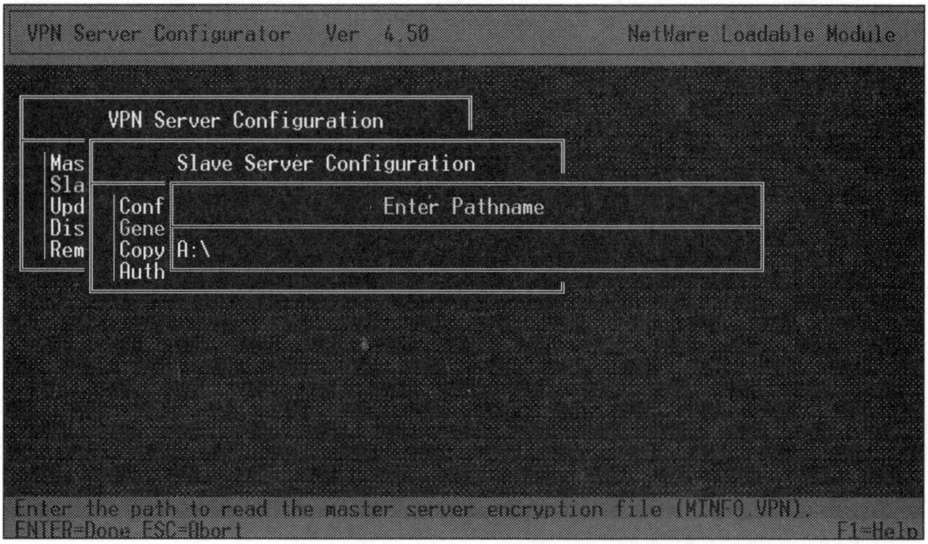

**Figure 7.73**
Entry point for encryption information.

14. Select Generate Encryption Information and press Enter for the Enter Pathname dialog box shown in Figure 7.73, prompting you to enter a path to the encryption information file, MINFO.VPN.

15. If you have not already done so, insert the disk containing the MINFO file in the floppy disk drive, confirm that the path listed is correct, and press Enter. An information dialog box will open, like Figure 7.74, displaying the message digest value.

16. At this point you need to verify that the message digest value generated at the slave VPN server matches the message digest value generated at the master VPN server. If the message digest values match, select Yes and press Enter. The Enter Random Seed dialog box will open, as shown in Figure 7.75.

17. Type in any combination of up to 255 characters and press Enter. The information dialog box shown in Figure 7.76 will open to inform you that the encryption information has been generated.

18. Press Enter to continue and a new information dialog box will open, shown in Figure 7.77, to inform you that the VPN attributes have been successfully updated.

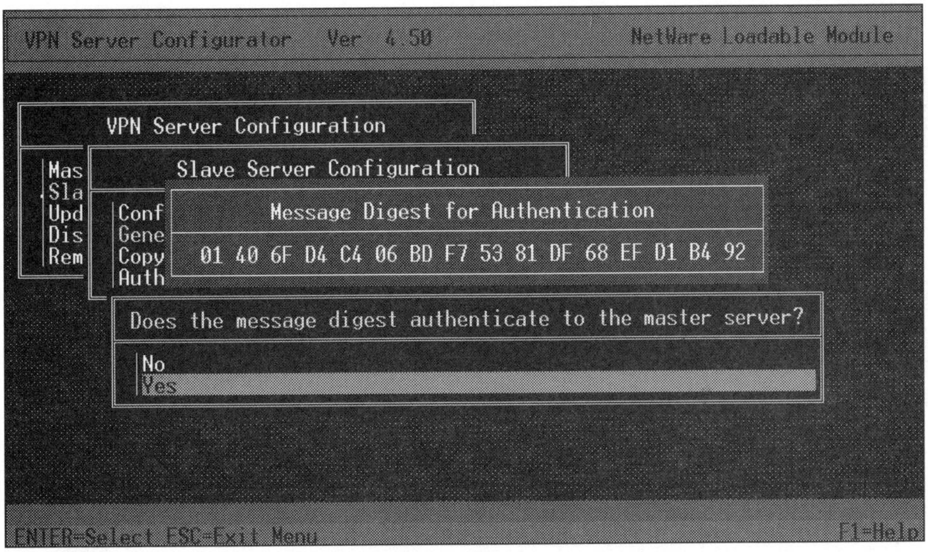

**Figure 7.74**
Message digest value.

```
VPN Server Configurator   Ver  4.50              NetWare Loadable Module

         ┌─────────────────────────────────┐
         │    VPN Server Configuration      │
    ┌────┤    ┌──────────────────────────────────────┐
    │Mas │    │   Slave Server Configuration          │
    │Sla ├────┤   ┌──────────────────────────────────────┐
    │Upd ││Conf│        Enter Random Seed               │
    │Dis ││Gene│                                        │
    │Rem ││Copy│                                        │
    │    ││Auth└──────────────────────────────────────┘
    └────┴────┘

 Enter a random string of up to 255 characters.
 ENTER=Done ESC=Abort                                   F1=Help
```

**Figure 7.75**
Random seed request.

```
┌─────────────────────────────────────────────────┐
│ Generated the encryption information successfully.│
│          <Press ENTER to continue>                │
└─────────────────────────────────────────────────┘
```

**Figure 7.76**
Successful report for generating encryption information.

```
┌──────────────────────────────────────────────────────────────┐
│ The VPN attributes have been successfully updated in Directory Services.│
│               <Press ENTER to continue>                         │
└──────────────────────────────────────────────────────────────┘
```

**Figure 7.77**
VPN attributes information.

19. Press Enter to return to the Slave Server Configuration menu box, shown in Figure 7.78.

Now the VPN public key exists in the slave encryption information file, named SINFO.VPN. You will need to copy this file to a floppy diskette and send it to the master VPN server administrator. Here is how to make the copy:

20. Select Copy Encryption Information and press Enter to open a dialog box like the one in Figure 7.79, prompting you to enter the path to the disk drive where the encryption information will be saved. You can copy the information to a floppy diskette, or to a specific location on the hard disk drive. In this case, you should choose the floppy so you can send the information back to the master location.

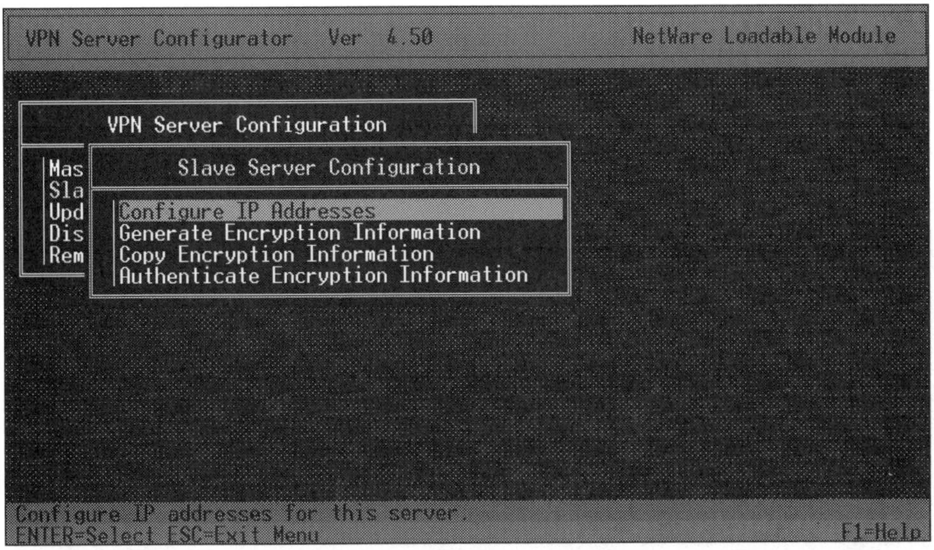

**Figure 7.78**
Slave server configuration menu.

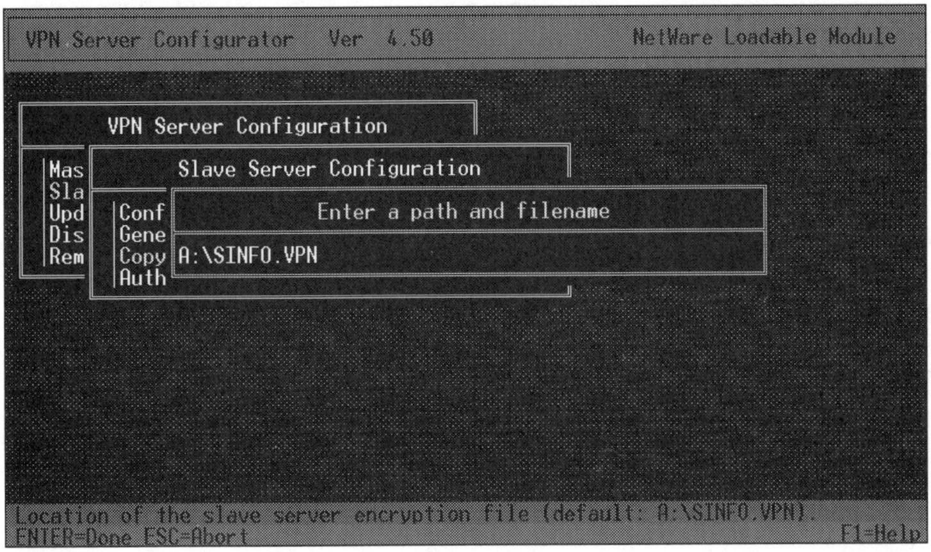

**Figure 7.79**
Selection menu for copying the encryption information.

21. If the default value shown in the dialog box is not correct, type in the appropriate path information and press Enter. After the encryption information has been copied, an information dialog box like the one depicted in Figure 7.80 will inform you that the encryption information has been successfully copied.

```
┌────────────────────────────────────────────────────────────────┐
│ Copied the encryption information successfully to the specified path. │
│                    <Press ENTER to continue>                     │
└────────────────────────────────────────────────────────────────┘
```

**Figure 7.80**
Success report for copying encryption information.

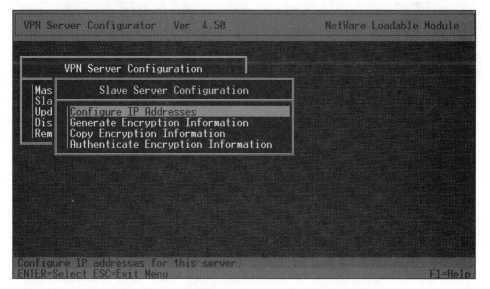

**Figure 7.81**
Slave server configuration menu after copying encryption information.

22. Press Enter to close this information dialog box and return to the Slave Server Configuration menu box shown in Figure 7.81.

23. Press Esc to close this menu and an information dialog box will open, as shown in Figure 7.82, informing you that VPSLAVE.NLM—the slave VPN server core program—has loaded successfully.

24. Press Enter to continue. The information dialog box will close, and you will be returned to the VPN Server Configuration menu box, as shown in Figure 7.47.

25. Press Esc repeatedly until the confirmation dialog box shown in Figure 7.83 asks if you really want to exit from this NLM—like you haven't had enough fun.

26. Select Yes, and press Enter. The NIAS configuration utility will close, and you will be returned to the server console.

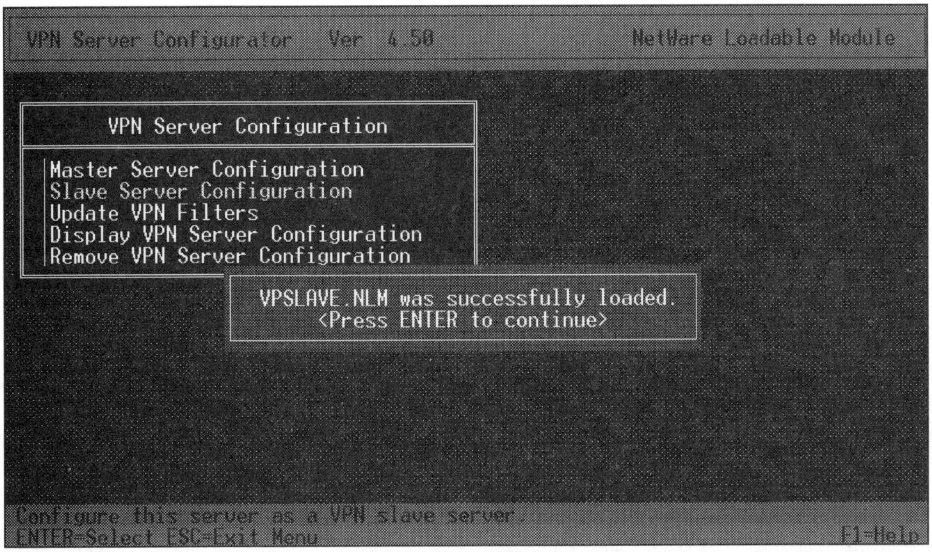

**Figure 7.82**
Success report for loading the slave VPN server core program.

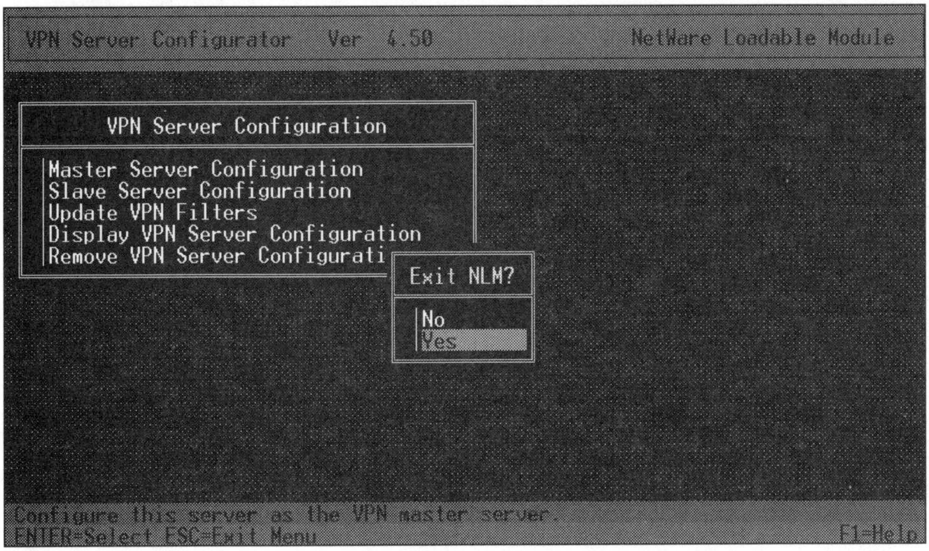

**Figure 7.83**
Exit confirmation panel.

One more time with the drum-roll and fanfare—you have completed the procedure for configuring the slave VPN server. But before the slave can communicate with its master, you must add it to the Virtual Private Network with the NetWare network management utility NWAdmin32. Take a break for a few minutes. I'll have the procedure ready for you when you get back.

## Add The Slave Server To The VPN

After you completed the NIASCFG procedures, the master server was automatically added to the VPN. The slave is different. We have to do that, and here's how:

1. Log on to the directory tree as a user with Admin rights at the root of the directory tree or the container level where the master VPN server will be located.

2. Click on Start, point to Run, and click again. The Run Programs dialog box will open, as shown in Figure 7.84, prompting you to enter the name of the program to run.

3. Type in the path to the SYS:\PUBLIC\WIN32\NWADMIN32.EXE file, and click Next or Browse, then use the browser to locate the program. The NWADMIN program will load, and the directory tree will open, as shown in Figure 7.85.

**Note**
*What your actual screen looks like depends on where your last context was, and what the configuration of your tree is like.*

4. Navigate to the container that has the object representing the master VPN server, and double-click. The details dialog box for the server object will open, as shown in Figure 7.86.

5. Click on the BorderManager Setup Page button. The BorderManager setup page will open, as shown in Figure 7.87.

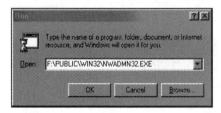

**Figure 7.84**
Run Programs dialog box.

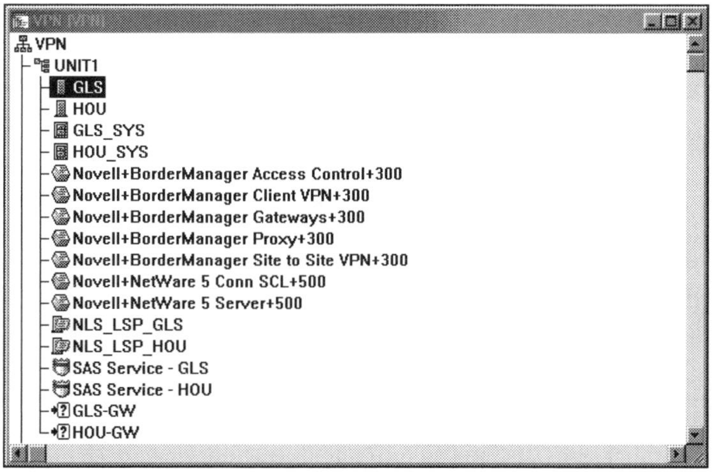

**Figure 7.85**
The directory tree information panel.

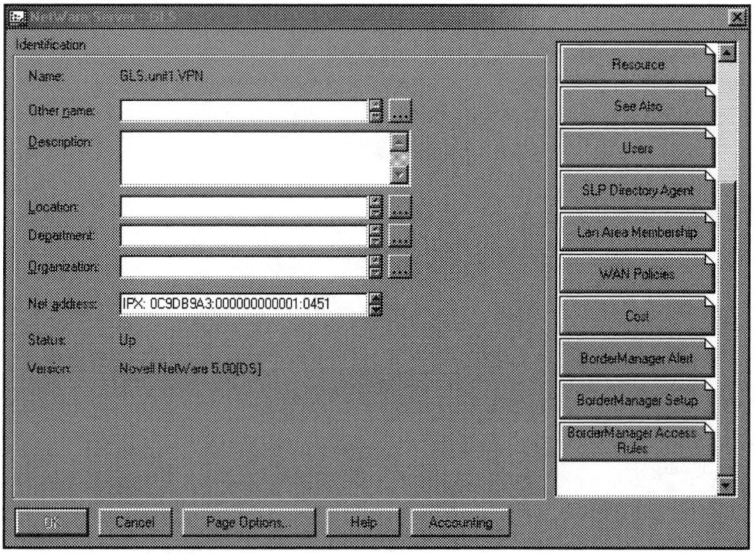

**Figure 7.86**
Details dialog panel for the slave server.

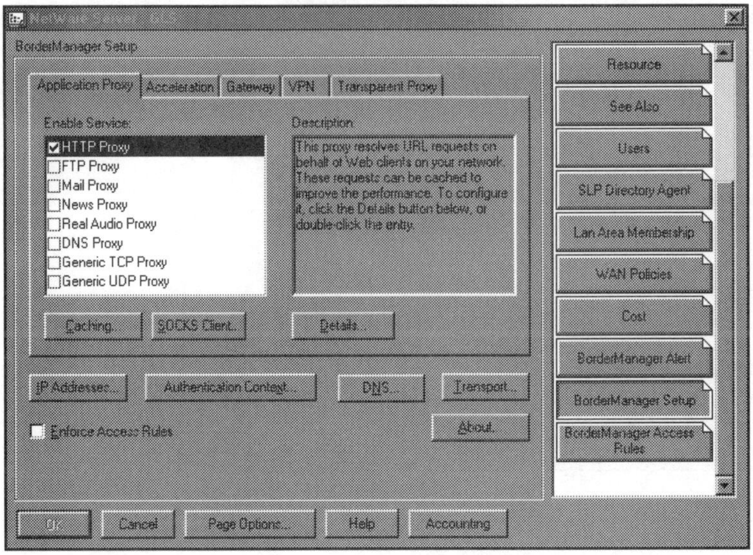

**Figure 7.87**
BorderManager setup page.

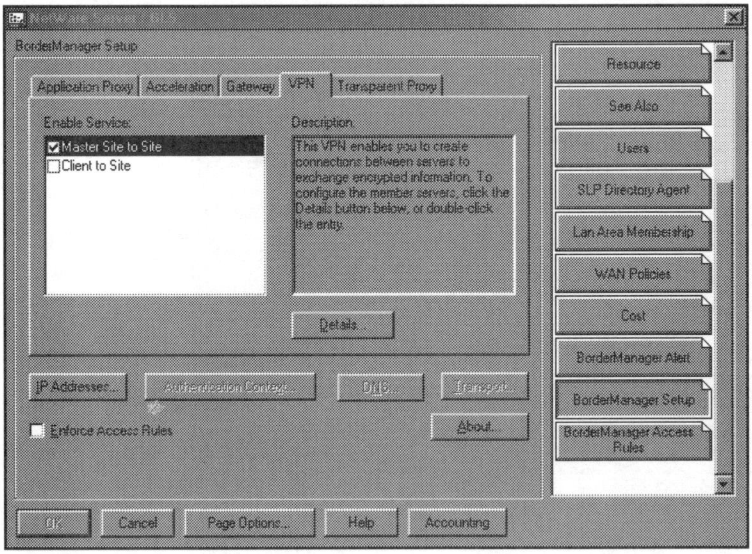

**Figure 7.88**
VPN dialog page.

6. Click the VPN tab to open the VPN dialog page, as shown in Figure 7.88.

7. Under the Enable Service window, double-click the Master Site-to-Site listing. This will open the dialog box shown in Figure 7.89.

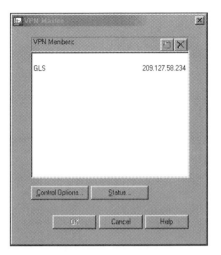

**Figure 7.89**
Master Site-to-Site dialog.

8.  Click the Add icon—the left one of the two in the upper right hand corner of the list box shown in Figure 7.90. This will open the File Open dialog box, as shown in Figure 7.91, prompting you to enter the location of the encryption information file (SINFO.VPN) for the slave server you wish to add.

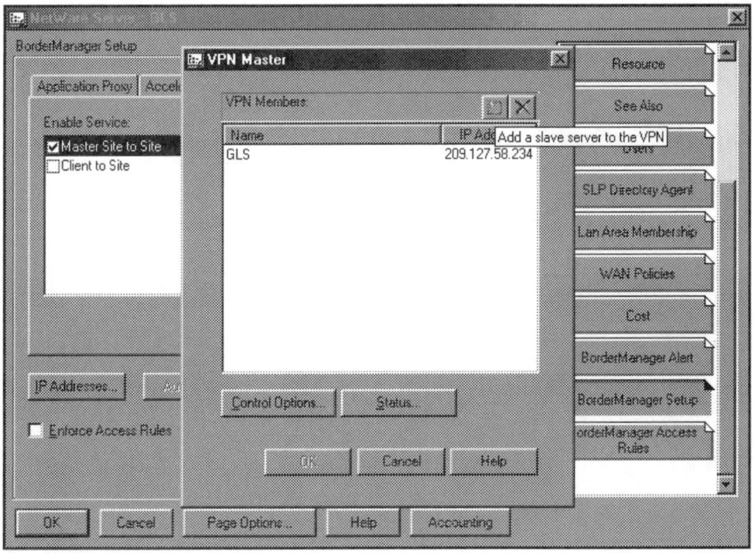

**Figure 7.90**
Detailed view of the list box.

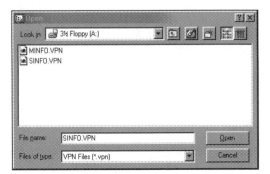

**Figure 7.91**
Request for encryption file information.

9. If you have not already done so, insert the disk with the encryption information file in the disk drive on the computer on which you are running the NWADMIN program. Type in the path to locate the encryption information file for the server you want to add or, if the file is stored on the master VPN server, enter the path to the location of the file. Click Open to open and read the file, and the master VPN server will use this information to calculate a message digest value. An information dialog box will open displaying this value, as shown in Figure 7.92.

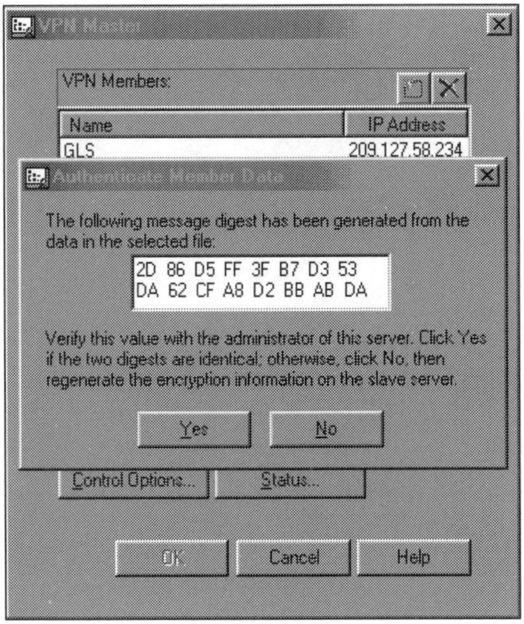

**Figure 7.92**
Information dialog showing the message digest value.

10. Contact the slave server administrator and compare the value of your message digest with the one generated at the slave server console. If the two are equal, click Yes; otherwise, click No. When you click Yes, an information dialog box will open, as shown in Figure 7.93, informing you that the slave server has been added to the VPN. This same dialog box will prompt you if you want to add to the list of protected networks and hosts on this VPN accessible through the slave server.

11. Click Yes. The protected IP Networks and Hosts dialog box will open, as shown in Figure 7.94.

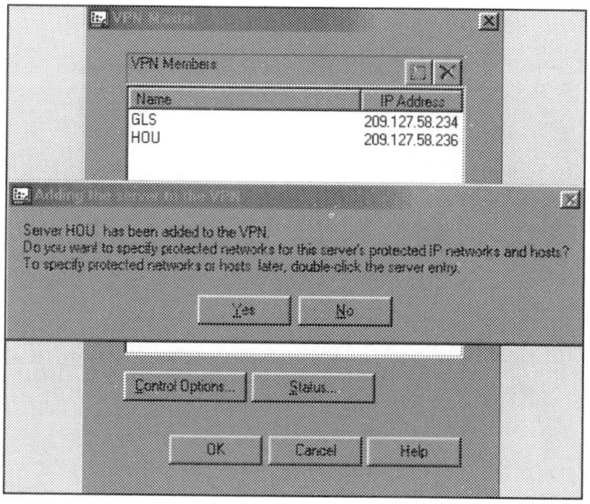

**Figure 7.93**
Report of slave server addition to the VPN.

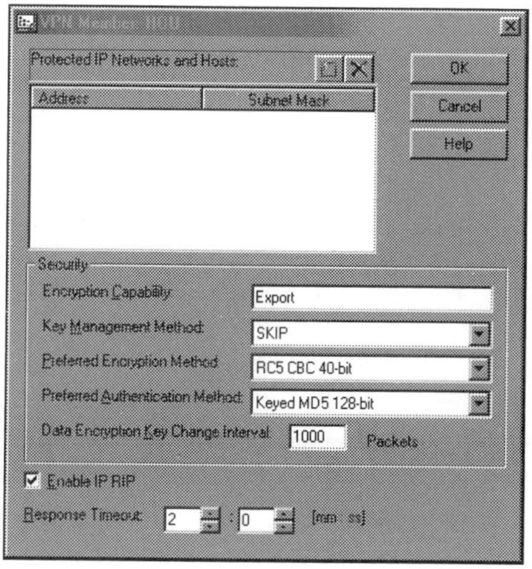

**Figure 7.94**
Protected IP Networks and Hosts dialog box.

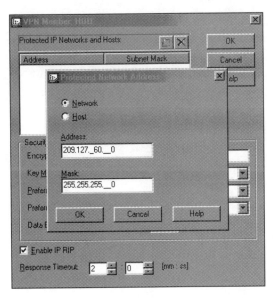

**Figure 7.95**
Add Protected Network input box.

12. Click on the Add icon. The Add Protected Network input box will open, as shown in Figure 7.95.

13. Enter the IP address and network mask, for the network or host connected to the slave VPN server. When you have the information correct, click on OK. The Add Protected Network input box will close, and the new network or host will be listed in the Protected Networks and Hosts list box.

14. Click on OK. The Protected Networks and Hosts list box will close, and the Master Site-to-Site dialog box will become active. The newly added slave VPN server will now appear in the list, as shown in Figure 7.96.

15. Click the Status button. The Synchronization Status dialog box will open, as shown in Figure 7.97.

16. Click Synchronize All. The status of the VPN servers will change to Configuring. After a short time they should show a status of Up-to-Date. At this time the slave and master servers will synchronize, and a virtual tunnel will be created between them.

17. If the two servers lost communication when the master VPN server was configured, a new communications channel will be established through the VPN tunnel, and within a short time communication between the two servers should be established.

**Note**

*We covered only the configuration of one slave VPN server in this chapter. If you have configured more than one slave VPN server, you will have to perform this process for each of the slave servers you want to be a part of the VPN.*

**Figure 7.96**
Master Site-to-Site dialog box.

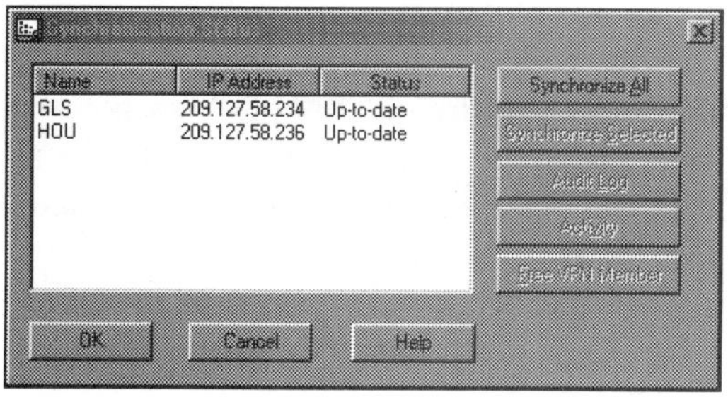

**Figure 7.97**
Synchronization Status dialog box.

18. Click on OK until you exit from the BorderManager Setup page.

19. Close and exit from the NWADMIN Utility.

Well, there you have it. You have added the slave VPN server to the virtual network.

## Post Implementation

Well, we're almost there. Here are some other things you'll need to do now:

♦ Check all the replicas of the NDS tree, and make sure that they are all synchronized, and that no NDS errors are flagged. For that you can use DSREPAIR.NLM, or your favorite Directory Service diagnostics program. How fast the directory is synchronized depends on how many replicas you have, their locations, and the size of your directory tree. In extreme cases, it may take as long as 24 hours for the directory to sync up.

♦ Make sure all the servers are communicating with each other and that the time is fully synchronized across the complete WAN.

♦ When you are satisfied that the directory is in good shape and all the servers are communicating with each other, take down the existing (old) WAN link. This will force the two networks to start using the VPN, which they should already be using, (more about that later). At this time, you should see no difference in the operation of the network, the directory, or communications between existing servers on either network.

♦ If you have a protocol analyzer, you can capture some packets destined for the network on the other side of the VPN and decode them. The data in the packets should be encrypted, and you should not be able to recognize any information.

♦ Notify all the users that they are now operating on the VPN and ask them to report any problems they may encounter. Start a trouble log and log all problems reported.

♦ Remove any temporary restrictions, or other implementations you may have put in place on a temporary basis.

♦ In configuring the NetWare Server to support BorderManager, Novell assumed the server would be used as a firewall and that users would not log onto the server. For the most part this is correct; however, an exception can happen when using the newly released BorderManager VPN Client for a secure connection from the BorderManager server to your remote user's computer. In this case change the set parameter on both the master and slave VPN servers to: SET REPLY TO GET NEAREST SERVER = ON, and login to the BorderManager VPN server using the VPN Client.

## VPN Management

Kick the tires and light the fires, then take it out for a test. Not quite ready for that yet? Why not? Okay, so it's not an F-117 Stealth Fighter. So flip the switches and push the keys—in any case it's a good idea to sit down at a user's position now and wring the system out thoroughly. If you have a second copy of the system drawings, try and communicate with every application, workstation, and device you have—and do it from both ends.

# M & M (But Not The Candy Kind)

Once you have satisfied yourself that things are operating as expected, it is time to look at some management strategies and think about the M words: *management* and *maintenance*. We're going to change our approach at this point. In the previous parts of this chapter we pretty much told you what you could do and then told you how to do it. In this section we're going to tell you *what* you can do (the *how to do it* will come later, in Chapter 11).

## Maintenance Operations

As we went through the setup, we took the default settings whenever we could, for two reasons:

♦ For the most part, we figured just going through the installation and configuration would keep you busy enough without making you worry about setting this parameter or that access time.

♦ Usually you will find that the system comes up reliably and runs rather well with the default settings.

After you have the VPN up and running, you can then go back and finetune the VPN based on needs determined by the type and amount of usage applied to the VPN. This is all a part of regular maintenance and will become evident from the logs you keep on system performance.

You should make changes to any network system in a systematic, planned manner, leaving time between each change for the network to go through at least one complete operational cycle. What is an *operational cycle*? It is the time it takes to perform all the operations that normally occur within a network system. Some examples include:

♦ Accounting systems usually close the books at the end of the accounting cycle. This is either every four weeks, or once per month—and, yes, there is a difference.

♦ If your network system performs a partial backup every day and a complete backup every week, then your backup operational cycle is weekly.

Get the picture? Okay, remember that. If possible you should make one change at a time, and wait one complete cycle between changes. Fair warning—take one variable at a time.

Among other things, the following maintenance operations apply specifically to VPNs:

♦ *Adding a server to a VPN*—Remember that each VPN can have only one master VPN server, but any number of slaves. Remember that before a VPN server can be added to an existing VPN, it must be configured using NIASCFG.NLM.

♦ *Selecting network protocols used by the VPN*—The BorderManager VPN can be configured to use both TCP/IP and IPX/SPX protocols.

♦ *Specify networks protected by a site-to-site VPN*—Otherwise known as adding static routes to the router table. One big difference is that, in order for a VPN to know of a static route, the route *must* be added using the NetWare administrator NWADMIN. If the routes are added using the NIASCFG.NLM server utility, the master or slave VPN servers will not recognize them.

---

### Caution

Novell says, and once again I agree with them, that the default settings provided in Novell products are designed to provide optimum performance for the largest group of users. Changes to improve performance in one area often have the opposite effect in another area.

---

♦ *Configuring data encryption and data authentication methods*—Using the NetWare administrator program, NWADMIN, you can select a preferred encryption method, and specify a value for the Data Encryption Key Change Interval.

♦ *Selecting the VPN topology*—Using the NetWare administrator program, you can select a preferred VPN topology from the available options of Mesh, Star, or Ring. Setting this parameter allows more efficient operation, because the VPN does not have to look for duplicate router entries to get the best route to a network.

♦ *Selecting whether the connection is initiated from one side or both sides*—This option allows for more efficient operation by controlling if the VPN works in simplex or duplex operation.

♦ *Removing a slave server from a VPN*—Those are the steps required to disconnect a slave when it is no longer used and remove traces of its existence from the master.

## Managing Your VPN

To a large degree, the VPN is a part of the larger WAN. Any day-to-day administration tasks performed should, as a matter of course, be applied to the VPN and will not be covered here. Some areas of management apply specifically to the VPN structure, and we will discuss them here.

You can perform most of the administration tasks related to the VPN from a Windows NT/ 9x computer using the NetWare Administrator, NWADMIN. These tasks include the following:

♦ *Selecting the VPN server response time*—This parameter determines how long the server will wait, without receiving any data packets, before it tears down the connection. A shorter setting will give faster response on a high-speed link that is usually always busy. A longer setting will wait longer before tearing down the connection, and that is desirable on slow-speed links.

♦ *Tuning master-slave server synchronization*—The master and slave servers communicate with each other over the VPN. By adjusting the master-slave server synchronization, you control the Update Interval, Connect Timeout, and Response Timeout parameters. This should be done slowly, over a longer period of time, so that reaction to changes can be plotted and maximum performance gained.

♦ *Synchronizing VPN servers*—When you make a change on a VPN, the master server will need to update the slave servers with the new information using the synchronization function. Normally, synchronization takes place at regular intervals; however, the network administrator can force a synchronization to take place at any time through the NetWare administrator program NWADMIN.

# Monitoring VPN Statistics

As a normal part of operations and maintenance, you should set up a system of checking and monitoring statistics relating to the VPN. This is especially true during the first few weeks of operation. Regular monitoring and recording of statistical information will help make your support operations *proactive* instead of *reactive*.

We will cover monitoring statistical information in greater detail in Chapter 11, where we also cover troubleshooting. For now, a brief overview of the kinds of information you can monitor is more appropriate. As I mentioned earlier, BorderManager relies on NetWare as the transport mechanism moving data through the network. Even though it is a virtual network, NetWare treats the VPN as simply another network connection. Because of this, it is possible to monitor all of the statistical information NetWare normally retains for any type of network connection.

Those of you that have been working with NetWare for a while know that a wide range of statistical information is available about the operation of various objects within the network. You may also feel that this information is found usually by using various monitoring programs on the NetWare server. In the case of the VPN, you are in for a surprise. The VPN is a virtual network, fabricated and controlled by the directory tree. Statistical information on the performance of the VPN is available directly from the tree. What do we use to maintain and administer the directory tree? That's easy: We use the NetWare administrator utility, NWADMIN.

The statistics available on the operation of the VPN can be divided in four basic groups:

♦ VPN server activities

♦ VPN server audit logs

♦ VPN realtime monitoring

♦ VPN client connection status

Each of these groups has several different types of statistics that can be monitored; we will look at specific details in Chapter 11.

You can use either of two methods to monitor the VPN server activities and the VPN server audit logs. Both require the use of the NetWare administration program NWADMIN. In the one case, you can view the statistics for any of the VPN servers. In the other case, you can view the statistics for only one slave server.

What makes the difference is the VPN server object you choose to view the statistics from. If you double-click the VPN master server object, you can view the statistics for any of the VPN servers. To do that, follow these steps:

1. Log in to the tree as a user with admin authority at the root of the tree, or the container level where the VPN master server is located.

2. Load the NetWare administrator program, NWADMIN.

3. Double-click on the VPN master server object in the tree.

That will allow you to view these statistics for any VPN server, either the master or any of the slave servers.

On the other hand, if you change the last step and double-click on the slave server object, you can view the statistics for that server only. This is a useful feature in two ways:

♦ As a troubleshooting procedure, it may be necessary to see if the other end of the VPN is receiving the packets originating at one end of the VPN. Using the slave server object will allow you to do that.

♦ If you have your network administration distributed, with an administrator responsible for the network located at each site, using the slave server object allows the administrators at branch office sites to monitor the slave VPN server at their site, without giving them the authority to monitor every site.

To do this, load the NetWare administrator program, NWADMIN, and double-click on the server object that represents the particular slave server you wish to get information on. This will allow you to view the statistics for that server only.

## Monitoring The Internet

Do those three words make you laugh? No one can monitor the Internet, right? Well, for the most part that's correct. Why would anyone want to? But from this point on, the performance of your network is now related to the performance of the Internet and that means you need to be able to do at least some types of statistical monitoring of the beast.

### What Do You Need To Look At, And How Do You Look At It?

Earlier in this book we named some software packages you could use to monitor the Internet and gather information about various statistics. To a certain degree, your ability to do this may be limited. Your site is, after all, just an extension of your ISP's router. This is where a good relationship with your ISP will come in handy. Most ISPs monitor the Internet for overall performance and percentage of bandwidth used. This is valuable information, and your ISP should be willing to make this available. We would never suggest a bribe, but talking to your ISP provider about this over lunch isn't a bad idea, especially if your boss will pick up the tab.

On a more local scene, your particular interface can monitor the following statistics:

♦ Latency

♦ Number of dropped packets

♦ Overall application throughput

♦ Typical route through the Internet for a data packet

I know of two useful programs for gathering this type of information. One is named Cloud, from Shunruai Software; the other is named Chariot, from Ganymede Software. Either will prove useful for gathering information on latency and the number of dropped packets.

The typical route through the Internet for a data packet may not be as easy to get. One utility you can try is called *Traceroute*. Under normal circumstances this program sends a data packet from one location to the other, and at every router along the way it sends back an ICMP message packet. However, this may not work very well with a VPN, because the Traceroute packet itself may be encapsulated and sent to the other end. If that happens, you may have to drop back and rely on a protocol analyzer to provide better information.

Okay, that's a quick glance at the two M words, maintenance and management. As I said, we'll come back and take a more detailed look in Chapter 11.

## Last Checklist: Future Planning

Now that we have the VPN up and running, it will never need improvement. (If you believe that statement, I have a room full of 40Mg hard disk drives I'll make you a really good deal on.) The time to start looking at the future is today.

So, what are some things you need to be watching out for? As with all other questions like this, we don't have an exact answer. But at a minimum you should be watching for change, usually in the form of an increase in demand, in the following areas:

- Network expansion:
    - User population
    - Connect time
    - Bandwidth utilization
- VPN capacity:
    - Tunnel server capacity
    - Supporting systems capacity
    - Bandwidth use
- Longer term network growth:
    - Remote users
    - Accessibility to client sites (extranet)
    - Accessibility to vendor sites (extranet)
- Future interoperability issues

I've listed only a few items that I think will eventually effect the overall operation of your VPN. It's up to you to add more specific items that apply to your specific installation.

# Wrap Up

This has been a big chapter, and we have covered a lot of ground. I hope that with the foundation we put in place in the early part of the book, you didn't find this chapter too intimidating. In the next chapter we're going to do this same thing again. Only this time we'll look at the products produced by that company in Redmond, Washington. See you there.

# Chapter 8

# *Basic VPN Using Microsoft Solutions*

*Key Topics:*

♦ *Implementing VPN with Windows NT 4*

♦ *Implementation checklists*

♦ *Encryption and authentication*

♦ *Configuring Windows 98 Client*

If you skipped over Chapter 7 in a rush to get to the Microsoft stuff, please go back and read the first part. We took some time there to establish a paradigm company called Vintage Air, Incorporated, and used it as the basis for implementing a VPN. We could have copied all that stuff to here, but we're using enough trees for this project already. Stick a bookmark back there so you can find it easily as we develop this VPN using Windows NT.

Besides our model company and its networks, you can find some other good stuff in Chapter 7 that applies to establishing a VPN regardless of what solution you pick. It has to do with the philosophy of planning. We figure the quickest way to jump into the cooking pot with the goose is to start fiddling with your network without adequate planning.

So, just presume that everything in Chapter 7, from the beginning until we start delving into the section titled "Implementing Novell NetWare VPN," belongs to the front of this chapter equally as well.

## VPN Using NT 4 With PPTP Protocol

In technical article Q154091 (last reviewed July 2, 1999), Microsoft engineers define the ability of a server to receive a dial-up call and initiate a tunnel on the caller's behalf as *compulsory tunneling*. The article then makes a point that "Windows NT RAS does not presently support [compulsory tunneling]." Furthermore, we reviewed the release notes for Windows NT 4 Service Pack 4 and did not find that the addition of compulsory tunneling is a new feature to the RAS server.

So what does all that mean? Although Microsoft says you can use Windows NT to connect NT servers on two different LANs together, the intent seems more toward dial-in users—that is, VPN communications between client and server, not server and server. Microsoft does state that several of their partners, among them 3Com and ASANTI, produce VPN software based on the PPTP protocol suite that does support compulsory tunneling, and recommends that if you need to implement a server-to-server VPN using the PPTP protocol you investigate one of these companies.

However, if Microsoft says you can do it, we will. We can accomplish our goal of establishing a secure connection between the two LANs using the Internet as our transport medium and use NT 4 to do it. We just have to use a roundabout method of connecting the two LANs together. Watch us.

## The Scheme

When using the Microsoft implementation of PPTP, the secure connection is made from each individual client workstation to the PPTP server located on the LAN where the data you wish to access exists. Although our VPN implementation relies on some unusual procedures (using dial-up networking to make a connection to the LAN, for example), once you understand the concepts, the operation is straightforward.

The VPN solution used in this section does not involve individual remote or dial-in users, but each facility has lots of users (or clients) that need access to the information in each network. In this respect it serves as a good basic starting point. An example of the implementation in a typical network system is shown in Figure 8.1.

Several items in Figure 8.1 beg for additional comment:

♦ Not counting security gateways, each network has only one Windows NT server in place before the addition of the NT RAS. Our goal is simplicity, and at first glance, keeping the number of servers to a minimum would certainly appear to reduce the complexity. However, as we detail shortly, the *best* solution is to use two NT servers, one exclusively for RAS.

♦ Microsoft NT 4 bases its security solutions on trusted relationships among computers and users organized into logical domains. In this respect the domain model used by Microsoft can range from fairly simple, where everything shares one domain—to very complex, with multiple domains that have multiple trusted relationships.

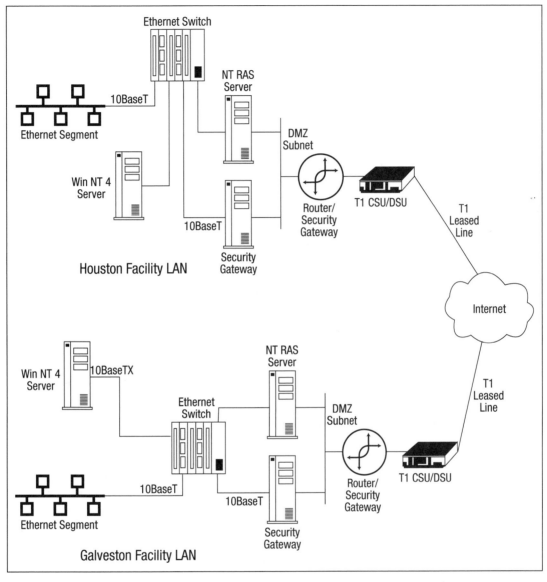

**Figure 8.1**
LAN-to-LAN implementation MS Windows NT 4.

## Domain Controllers In Windows NT

Two types of servers can exist within the domain: a *Primary Domain Controller* (*PDC*) and a *Backup Domain Controller* (*BDC*). An NT server can also be installed in a domain as a *Member Server*, which has no control functions. All administrative changes that are made to the users on the network are first made in the PDC, and then propagated to the BDCs. This requires a permanent connection of some type with all the servers within a domain. A connection is made in this implementation between the two networks only when someone is actually logged on a server located in the remote LAN. Even then, because of PPTP filtering, the packets used to communicate amongst servers are not allowed to pass from the Internet to the server. It is therefore important that each site have an independent domain with its own PDC and BDC servers. Users that take advantage of the VPN to access the other domain must log on to the NT servers in the remote domain.

♦ Additionally, we will discuss the implementation of the VPN without regard to the domain model you have on your network. We will mention domains only to the extent that it is necessary to implement the VPN, and assume that you, the network administrator, are familiar with how to accomplish the required tasks.

♦ Each network of our Vintage Air system initially has only one Windows NT server. When implementing a VPN solution using Windows NT, you may find, as I did, that it is less complicated and more versatile to add a second NT server to each network, rather than try to implement VPN tunneling and encryption functions on existing equipment. This adds a RAS between the switch and the DMZ subnet on each LAN. Here are my justifications for the additional cost and complexity:

  ♦ For security reasons, the network should accomplish PPTP filtering on the tunneling server. According to Microsoft, PPTP filtering can only be implemented on LAN adapters, not on dial-up or ISDN WAN link devices installed in the NT server. That requires you to implement an Internet connection using a DMZ subnet, such as a screened subnet or dual-homed firewall. Remember that security is an important issue when dealing with the Internet.

  ♦ Once you install PPTP filtering on the tunneling server, only PPTP data packets are accepted; all other data packets are rejected. That effectively shuts down your Internet access if you are using only one NT server with one NIC connected to the Internet. To prevent that from happening, it is simpler (as I found), albeit more expensive, to use two NT servers: one for regular Internet access, and the other as a dedicated RAS.

♦ The Windows NT-PPTP servers are used as routers. To implement routing functions, each server requires at least two network interface cards. One connects to the LAN, the other to the DMZ subnet. I choose to put the RAS in parallel with the inner security gateway in the screened subnet firewall, as in Figure 8.1.

For the most part, the discussion and walkthrough will deal with the procedural steps for implementing a VPN between the two networks involved. When we are required to perform some steps differently on either end of the VPN, we will make those differences clear. Okay, that about covers the finer details of the general procedure. Now, let's get started. Just as we did in Chapter 7, we will follow the master list here.

## Rehearsal Hint

Although we will list each step for installing and configuring the RAS, we make the assumption that you, the network administrator, are familiar with configuring an NT server. We also assume that you understand the concepts involved in routing between two different networks using the Microsoft implementation of TCP/IP. The task may involve modifying the Registry on the NT server, as well as the addition of static routes to the NT router table. If you have never performed this type of operation, it's a good idea (if possible) for you to set up an NT server with two NICs and rehearse the steps involved in implementing routing functions.

Later we will develop more checklists, but let's get the master list out of the way first.

❏ *Equipment Required*—A list of all equipment and software required for completing the project. This includes test and maintenance items also.

❏ *Support Needs*—Resources to tap for assistance on installation and configuration of hardware or software.

❏ *Pre-Implementation*—What parts and pieces you should have up, running, and configured before you start ripping the guts out of your existing network.

❏ *Implementation*—A step-by-step sequence, including any testing sequences, for rolling the VPN into the system.

❏ *Post-Implementation*—A few temporary patches and hacks typically will be installed to hold things together while you are doing the implementation. This is the point where you yank them out to free up the drive space and unburden the bandwidth.

❏ *VPN Management, Checklistus Immortalus*—The maintenance and procedures to be performed on a regular basis. This includes evaluating logs and appraising system performance.

❏ *Future Planning*—Now that you have your VPN up and running, what steps do you need to take to assure the solution will meet future demands?

Following a checklist requires discipline. Often when a step is completed, the next step is right in front of you, begging to be accomplished—then the next one and the next one. Sometimes an out-of-sequence step presents itself, begging: "Do me! Do me next!"

This is where discipline is essential. As you accomplish each step: stop, pick up your pencil (or hammer and chisel if you are working in the non-Pentium stone age), and deliberately mark that step off. This accomplishes two things. First, when you are interrupted by that danged telephone, you know exactly where you left off when you come back. Second, this is a good time to go over what you did in your mind, a chance to develop that warm fuzzy feeling that things are going well. If you don't get the warm fuzzies, something is probably wrong with what you did. Here's another thing; if you do something and don't like the results, undo it and figure out what's wrong. Just because it is on the checklist doesn't mean it is correct.

You will be sorely tempted to leave out a step or two here and there, because *you already know something*, or *you already did that* someplace else. This could be something as simple as writing down the name and phone number (including extension) of your contact at the ISP.

After spending a few years troubleshooting computer problems over the telephone, it has been my experience that many case history problems developed because the person performing the implementation and configuration missed a step. In some cases they didn't really miss a step; they simply skipped over it because they were sure *they had already performed it*. It is difficult enough to troubleshoot problems using two-way communications such as the telephone; it's impossible to troubleshoot them in only one dimension—like this book.

So what am I trying to say here? I strongly suggest you follow the checklist and do it with immaculate discipline. We have included all of the checklists in Appendix D and you can find them on our Web site **www.sldenterprises.com**. You have our permission to make copies of the checklists for your own personal use. If you sell copies, you need written permission. By the way, you gotta split the take with the authors and the publisher. You can find the publisher's address in the front matter.

Follow your checklists with the discipline we suggest and you will find more than a casual chance for your system to come up running when you get finished—leaving you with only some fine tuning for optimum performance.

## Checklist Number One: Equipment Required

First, you need to develop an exact plan, with detailed drawings, for the network changes you will implement. The drawing should include all IP addresses that you will need at both ends. The network administrator for Vintage Air made a decision to have a separate drawing for each LAN. The GLS facility is detailed in Figure 8.2.

Next, you should construct a configuration form, Table 8.1, for the new equipment. This will require a form for each new RAS.

Next, you need a list of the items required to complete the project. Once again, we can't guess at your exact needs, but at a minimum they should include the following:

♦ One computer capable of running Microsoft Windows NT Server version 4 and supporting Windows NT RAS

♦ Microsoft Windows NT 4 Server software package, *and* Microsoft Windows NT Service Pack 4

A note about the Windows NT 4 Service Pack. Even though you may have already installed the Windows NT Service Pack 4, according to Microsoft, if you install any new services or system programs, you must reinstall the Service Pack 4 again. You'll also need:

♦ One or more client computers with your choice of Windows NT 4 Server, Windows NT 4 Workstation, or Windows 95/98 installed

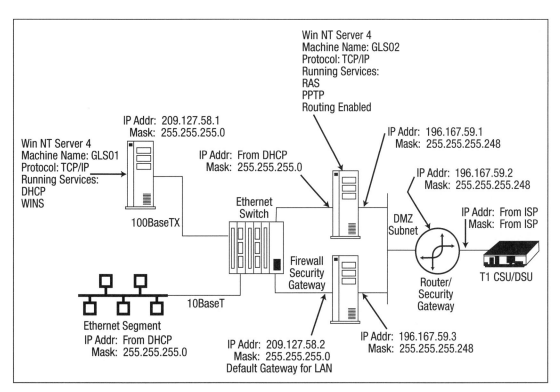

**Figure 8.2**
Galveston facility LAN.

**Table 8.1 Windows NT Server network configuration.**

| Property | Value |
| --- | --- |
| Connection to network | Wired to Network |
| IIS | Do Not Install |
| NIC 1 | Model # |
| NIC 2 | Model # |
| NIC Protocols | TCP/IP |
| Services | Default |
| DHCP | Do not use |
| **TCP/IP Properties** | |
| NIC 1 IP Address | 209.127.59.234 |
| NIC 2 IP Address | 209.127.58.234 |
| Mask (both) | 255.255.255.0 |
| Gateway (both) | Default |
| DNS Properties (both) | Default |
| Enable IP Forwarding (1) | Yes |
| Enable IP Forwarding (2) | N/A |
| WINS Server Addr (both) | 209.127.59.236 |
| DHCP Relay (both) | No |
| Services for Bindings | Default |

**Note**

*Dial-Up Networking for Windows 95, in its original form, does not support the PPTP protocol, but Microsoft has released an upgrade, Dial-Up Networking 1.3, to fix that. Third-party companies offer software products to support PPTP on client machines with operating systems other than Windows.*

- ISDN terminal adapters
- DSU/CSU
- WAN routers

**Note**

*Another consideration: If you are using hardware routers, who will be responsible for (re)programming them?*

## Checklist Number Two: Support Needs

The following are suggestions of offices you may need to contact for help resolving problems with your installation and configuration.

- Software vendor for Windows NT 4, especially if it is a Microsoft Certified Solutions Provider (MCSP):

Name:_____

Company:_____

Phone: (____)_____

- Hardware vendor:

Name:_____

Company:_____

Phone: (____)_____

- Internet Service Provider:

Name:_____

Company:_____

Phone: (____)_____

- PSTN or PDN provider:

Name:_____

Company:_____

Phone: (____)_____
♦ Other support options:

Name:_____

Company:_____

Phone: (____)_____

**Note**

*Before we dive into the actual implementation process, make sure everything up to here is completed and in place. Go back one more time and see that each item is up, running, and configured, before you start.*

## Checklist Number Three: Pre-Implementation

If at all possible, set up a test network and go through the implementation process there first, before committing to the live network. If you can't do that, then this list becomes all the more important.

♦ Create a contingency plan, preferably with a time line and established point-of-no-return.

♦ Notify users, especially those directly involved with the VPN, that you are working on the network and that service may be interrupted from time to time.

♦ Verify PSTN/PDN carrier has signed off on all connectivity issues.

♦ Verify that add-on and all rollover (existing) hardware (especially if used) is functional and upgraded, if necessary, to meet required specifications. The important factors are the following:

   ♦ Hard drive space

   ♦ Network interface cards

   ♦ RAM

   ♦ Transport media (cables—UTP and fiber-optic)

   ♦ Other

   ♦ Run the diagnostics tests on your Uninterruptable Power Supply (UPS).

♦ Verify that you have enough registered IP addresses available for Internet connections.

♦ Assign an IP address to the network connection on each new item of equipment.

♦ Verify installation of NT 4 Server operating system on the RAS.

> **Note**
>
> *If your existing network has only one domain, and you have room within that domain for additional servers, I suggest you make the RAS a BDC within the same domain. If your LAN has more than one domain, and you have trusted relationships established among domains, then the choice of which domain to use is up to you.*

When you perform the NT 4 installation, NT may not auto-detect the two NICs. If this is the case you will have to provide the drivers for the NICs, either from the manufacturer's diskette, or download them from the Internet. After the NIC drivers have been installed, you can install the TCP/IP protocol. If your network uses DHCP and WINS services, you will probably want to use DHCP to provide the IP address for the NIC that connects to the private LAN.

If you are using DHCP and WINS on your network, you need to keep in mind two facts when setting up the PPTP server:

♦ You cannot use DHCP to supply the address of the NIC connected to the DMZ subnet. This address must be assigned statically.

♦ According to Microsoft, when the client starts to establish a VPN tunnel to the RAS, it must enter either the IP address of the PPTP server or the computer name for the same server in the dial-up networking dialog box.

---

### Security

If you use the computer name, the network must use the WINS service to resolve the name to an IP address. Keep in mind that the primary reason for setting up a VPN is to avoid opening up your network to potential problem sources on the Internet. If you use WINS to supply the IP address for the PPTP server, a connection must be established through the Internet to query the WINS server and determine the IP address of the PPTP server. This takes place before the PPTP tunnel is established. This is a potential security breach. For this reason, I feel that using DHCP to assign this IP address overly complicates the situation and creates unnecessary network traffic, as well as a potential security breach. I suggest that you assign this IP address statically.

You should configure the trusted relationships with the other NT servers and/or domains in the network. Add the users or groups that will need to administer the RAS server and perform any other configuration steps you feel are necessary.

---

Most of the preceding steps apply to the servers at both ends of the VPN. It is better to install both servers at the same time. Notwithstanding, if your manpower resources are limited, you can install, configure, and test one NT server at a time.

## Checklist Number Four: Implementation Procedure

Now we install the PPTP software on the Windows NT server. I have taken the liberty of dividing the process into the following three-part operation that differs slightly from the *normal* routine suggested by Microsoft:

♦ Install PPTP and select the number of VPN devices.

♦ Add the VPN devices as RAS ports, configure encryption and authentication options, and configure the RAS Server.

♦ Configure the RAS for routing and enable PPTP packet filtering.

**Note**
*These steps cover only the server installation—client installation is covered as a separate operation later in the section titled "Configuring Windows 98 Client."*

### Step One: Installing PPTP On A Windows NT Server

To install the PPTP protocol on a Windows NT 4 Server, perform the following steps:

1. Open the Windows NT Control Panel by clicking on Start | Settings | Control Panel.

2. Double-click on the Network icon; see Figure 8.3.

**Figure 8.3**
Windows NT 4 Control Panel.

3. Click on the Protocols tab; see Figure 8.4.

4. Click on Add; see Figure 8.5.

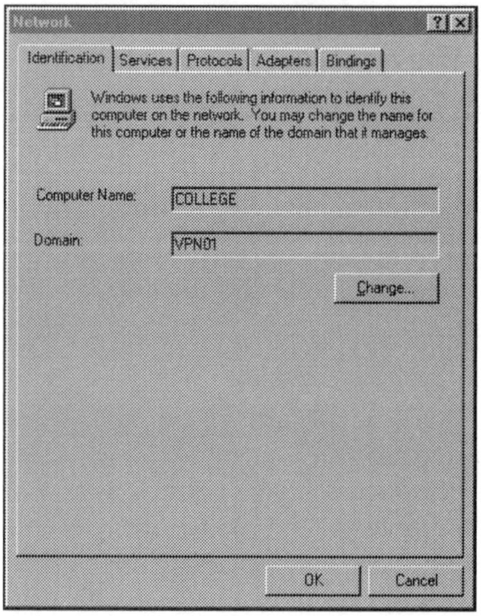

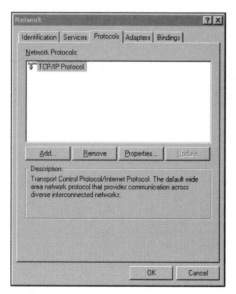

**Figure 8.4**
Networking properties panel.

**Figure 8.5**
Protocols tab.

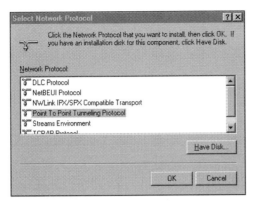

**Figure 8.6**
Select Network Protocol panel.

5. Select Point-To-Point Tunneling Protocol, as shown in Figure 8.6.

6. If the default location listed in Figure 8.7 is not correct, type in the location of the NT Server Version 4 Installation Files and click on Continue. (If the files are being copied from the CD, don't forget to insert the CD at this time.) At this point the software will copy PPTP files and load them into the server.

7. When the file copy procedure is complete, the PPTP Configuration dialog box will open, as shown in Figure 8.8.

8. Enter the number of VPNs you want this server to support by clicking on the drop-down arrow for the Number of Virtual Private Networks. Click the increase or decrease arrows until the correct number is indicated. You can also highlight the figure in the box and type in a number.

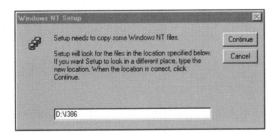

**Figure 8.7**
File selection panel.

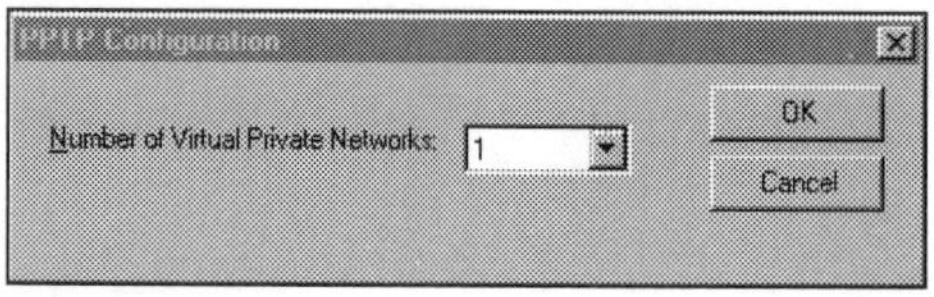

**Figure 8.8**
PPTP configuration dialog box.

**Note**

*The default is one, and you will need at least one connection for each concurrent network connection. If the number of users that will access this part of the network from the Internet is small, you can have one connection for each user.*

9. Select the correct number and click on OK.

The Setup Message information box will open, as shown in Figure 8.9.

10. Click on OK.

The Windows NT Server configuration process will create the number of VPN Devices you specify. When the configuration process is complete, the Remote Access Service dialog box will open, followed immediately by the Add RAS Device dialog box, shown in Figure 8.10.

**Figure 8.9**
Setup Message information box.

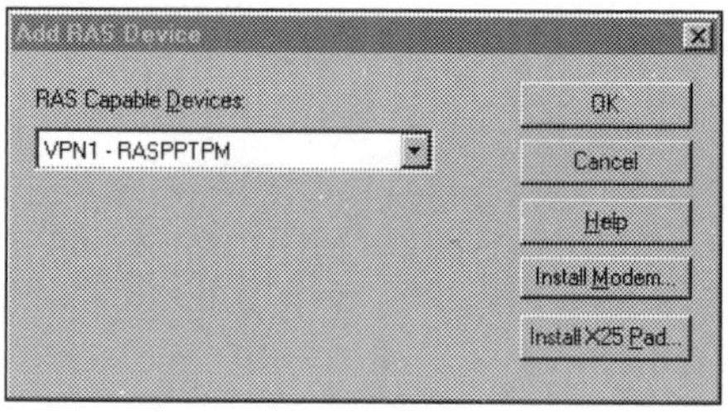

**Figure 8.10**
Add RAS Device dialog box.

At this point you have completed the process of installing the PPTP protocol on a Windows NT server; however, the changes will not take effect until the server is shut down and restarted. You have the option to shut down now and restart, or continue and add the VPN devices to the Remote Access Server (RAS). I recommend that you continue. If you choose to continue, skip down to the step follow the next note; otherwise:

1. Click the Cancel button in the Add RAS Device dialog box to go to the Remote Access Setup Properties dialog box.

2. Click the Cancel button. A Remote Access Setup information box opens, informing you that changes made to the Remote Access Server will not be saved.

3. Click Yes. The Network control panel becomes active.

4. Click the Close button. This opens a Network Settings Change information box, informing you that the changes will not become effective until you restart your computer, and asks if you want to restart your computer now.

5. Remove the CD from the CD-ROM drive and click on Restart.

After the NT server has restarted, and you have logged back on, it's time for...

### Step Two: Adding VPN Devices As RAS Ports, Configuring Encryption And Authentication, And Configuring TCP/IP For The VPN Tunnel

If you chose not to shut down and restart the Windows NT server after completing the setup of the PPTP in the previous section, do not perform the first six steps of this section, but skip to the step following the next note.

When the NT server restarts, if you log on as the same user, the control panel will open. If the control panel is open, skip the first step of this procedure. Otherwise, proceed as follows:

1. Open the Windows NT Server Control Panel, shown in Figure 8.3, by clicking on Start | Settings | Control Panel.

2. Double-click on the Network Icon.

3. Open the Remote Access Setup Properties dialog box by performing the following substeps:

   a. Click the Services tab to open the Services Page, then click Add to open the Select Network Service dialog box shown in Figure 8.11.

b. Select Remote Access Service and click on OK. At this point the Windows NT Setup dialog box opens, as shown in Figure 8.7, prompting you for the location of the Windows NT Installation Files.

c. If the default location listed is not correct, type in the location of the files (if you chose to restart the server after the installation of the PPTP Protocol steps, you will have to insert the CD at this time). Click the Continue button. The Remote Access Server files are copied, then the Remote Access Service dialog box opens, followed immediately by the Add RAS Device dialog box, as shown in Figure 8.10.

### Note

*If you chose not to restart the NT server after completing the installation of the PPTP protocol, this is where you continue the installation procedure.*

When you installed the PPTP protocol, you specified the number of VPN devices this server will have; the setup program then created them. Now, you need to add these devices as RAS ports by performing the following substeps for each VPN device:

1. The Add RAS Device dialog box shown in Figure 8.10 should already be open. Point to the RAS Capable Devices list arrow and click to display the VPN devices that must be added.

2. Select a VPN device and click on OK. That device is added to the RAS, the Add RAS Device dialog box closes, and the Remote Access Setup panel shown in Figure 8.12 opens.

3. If you have more VPN Devices to add, Click on the Add box to open the Add RAS Device dialog box.

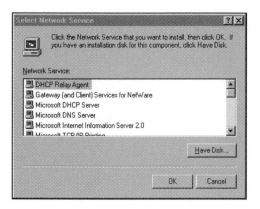

**Figure 8.11**
Select Network Service panel.

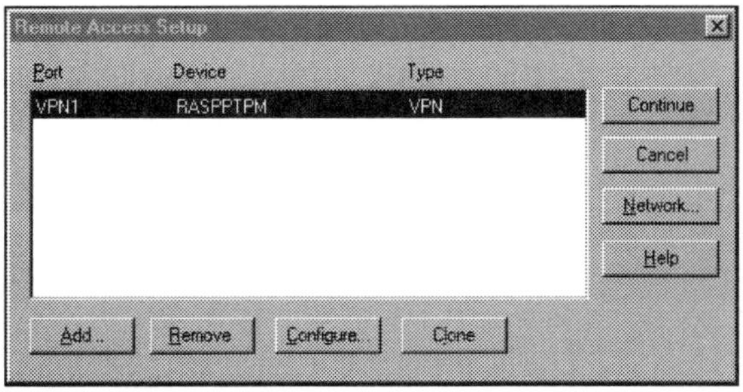

**Figure 8.12**
Remote Access Setup panel.

4. Go back to Step 1 and continue, repeating each step until you have added all the VPN devices to the RAS server.

Repeat the preceding four steps for each VPN device you created. When you have completed adding the VPN devices as RAS ports, the Remote Access Setup dialog box will look like Figure 8.13, except it will contain your information. Each VPN device listed in the window is now a RAS port.

5. Verify that all the added VPN devices are configured for Receive Calls Only by performing the following substeps for each new VPN device.

*Note*

*According to Microsoft, when you add a VPN device on a Windows NT server, the device should be configured automatically for Receive Calls Only. For safety, you should verify that it did indeed happen.*

a. Select a VPN port and click on Configure.

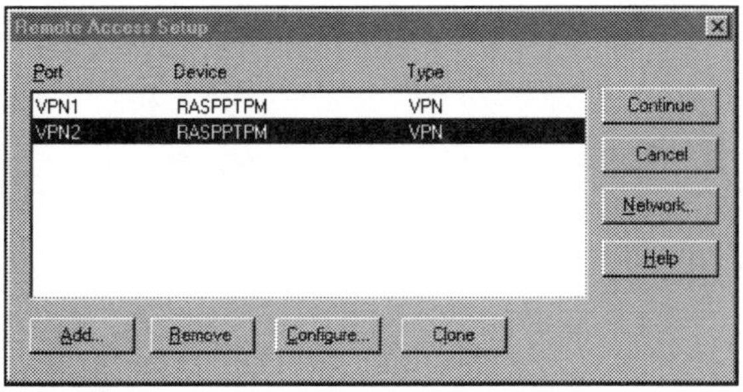

**Figure 8.13**
RAS dialog panel.

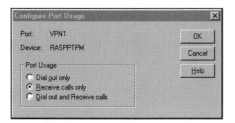

**Figure 8.14**
Configure Port Usage dialog box.

> b. The Configure Port Usage dialog box for that device will open, as shown in Figure 8.14.
>
> c. Verify that the Receive Calls Only Radio Button in the Port Usage dialog box is selected.
>
> d. Click on OK to return to the Remote Access Setup Properties dialog box.

**Note**

*Remember to repeat this operation for each of the VPN devices you have created.*

> 6. Configure the network for the VPN Device by selecting the encryption and authentication options. To do this, click on the Network button (located in the Remote Access Setup Properties dialog box) to open the Network Configuration dialog box shown in Figure 8.15.
>
> a. Verify that only TCP/IP is checked in the Server Settings.
>
> b. Verify that the Require Microsoft Encrypted Authentication radio button is selected.

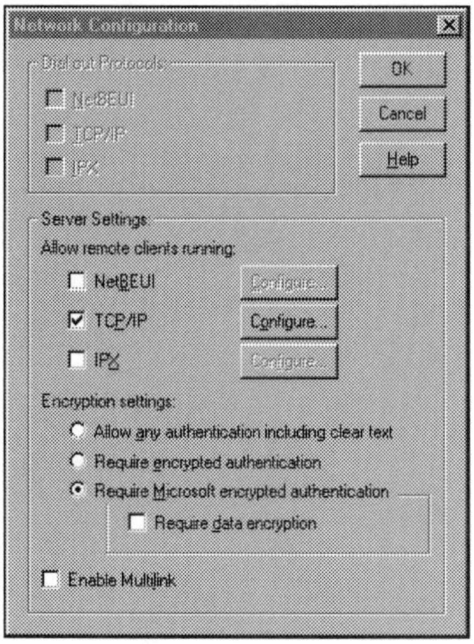

**Figure 8.15**
Network Configuration dialog box.

c. Check the Require Data Encryption checkbox.

d. Click on OK. This opens the RAS Server TCP/IP Configuration dialog box shown in Figure 8.16.

At this stage you will supply information the RAS uses to configure the TCP/IP protocol for the VPN tunnel:

7. Verify that the Allow Remote TCP/IP clients to Access the Entire Network Radio Button is checked.

8. Check the Use Static Address Pool radio button.

9. Type in the beginning IP address you have selected.

10. Type in the ending IP address. All addresses must be in the same subnet, they must be contiguous, and you must add at least one more than the total number of RAS ports you have configured.

11. When all the information is correct, click on OK. The RAS Server TCP/IP Configuration dialog box closes, and the Remote Access Setup Properties dialog box opens.

12. Click Continue to install the RAS. When this operation is complete, a Setup Message information box opens to inform you that the Remote Access Server has been successfully installed.

13. Click on OK to return to the Network window.

14. Click Close to close the Network window. This opens a Network Settings Change information box, informing you that you must shut down and restart your computer before the new settings will take effect.

15. Click Yes to restart your computer.

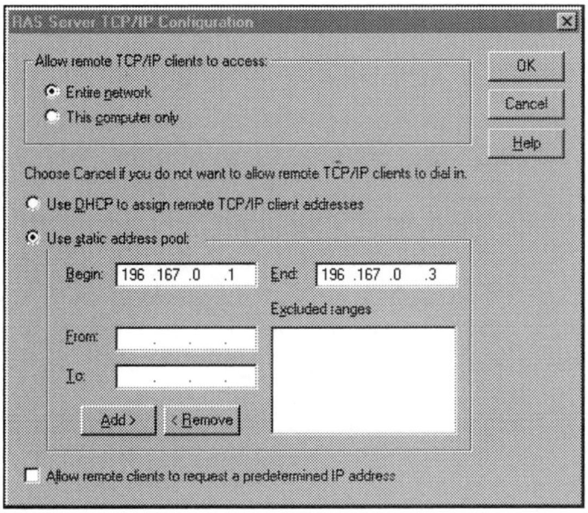

**Figure 8.16**
TCP/IP Configuration dialog box.

**Note**

*If you copied the installation files from the CD, remove it now.*

### Step Three: Configure The RAS Server For IP Packet Routing

The RAS must be configured for IP packet forwarding so those PPTP packets from the Internet will pass through the server to your network. Enabling IP forwarding is a simple step, and we will get to that in a moment. Of more importance is assuring that the NT RAS can route the packets in the direction we need them to go. This procedure will require two steps:

1. Make an entry in the Registry to prevent the server from building a default route.

2. Make the correct entries as static routes in the routing table, pointing to the correct subnetwork.

### A Closer Look At Routing Tables

Any computer configured to use TCP/IP has a table of IP information called the *routing table*. You should recall from Chapter 3 that a routing table is a database used by the TCP/IP protocol to locate the proper path for IP data packets. In the Microsoft implementation of TCP/IP, each record has the following fields:

♦ IP address of the destination machine or destination network

♦ Network mask

♦ IP address of the machine acting as the gateway to the destination machine

♦ IP address of the interface on the local machine that the packet should be passed through to get to the gateway

♦ A cost, or metric, used in calculating the best route

The routing table is used to expedite packets between networks. It is also used to locate the local machine's interface card for route discovery packets—to locate unknown IP addresses. In the initial installation and configuration of Microsoft's implementation of TCP/IP, a

---

**Caution**

Read this section very carefully, and proceed only if you have problems traceable to incorrect entries in the routing table. Performing the steps in this part of the configuration requires that you make changes to the Windows NT Registry, a process that, if done incorrectly, can cause severe complications with the NT server. I strongly suggest that if you do not need to make these changes—*don't*.

---

default entry of 0.0.0.0 is automatically created in the routing table for each NIC when it is installed in the machine. In Chapter 3, we found out that the IP address 0.0.0.0 is used to indicate *this network*, or the *local network*. If no other entry for the destination IP address exists in the routing table (that is, the IP address is unknown), the TCP/IP looks for the unknown IP address in the local network.

In some cases, like when two or more NICs have been installed in the same computer, the automatic creation of a default route entry of 0.0.0.0 can cause improper operation of the router, and a subsequent failure to properly route packets to the correct destination. So then, what is a well-mannered TCP/IP supposed to do?

This is where you step in and save the day. First, you are going to make an entry in the Registry to disable creation of the default route 0.0.0.0. You'll make this registry entry for each NIC in the machine being used as the router. Once a logical entry is made in the Registry, the router will no longer create defaults. That, in turn, means that entries will have to be made statically, one entry for each computer or network destination to which you want to route packets. As you can see, this can lead to a lot of work, and I strongly recommend you investigate your particular installation closely before performing this operation.

A final note. Table 8.2 lists three of several good technical documents available from Microsoft that offer detailed information on configuring and maintaining routing using Windows NT Server 4. You can access these articles, and others, at **technet.microsoft.com.**

### Adding The Registry Entry

Before you start, make a note of the Registry entry names for the NICs installed in your computer. These names may not be exactly what you think they should be, and you may have to get some help to locate the NIC Registry entries.

**Note**

*Making modifications to the Windows NT Registry can cause problems with the NT operating system. If you are not familiar with making these modifications, I advise you to perform these steps on a noncritical computer until you feel comfortable with the task.*

**Table 8.2   A list of technical articles about routing.**

| Article Number | Subject |
| --- | --- |
| Q140859 | "TCP/IP Routing Basics for Windows NT" |
| Q169790 | "How to Troubleshoot Basic TCP/IP Problems in Windows NT 4" |
| Q154091 | "Microsoft Windows 95 Dial-Up Networking 1.3 Upgrade Release Notes" |

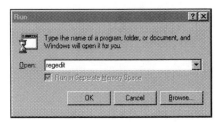

**Figure 8.17**
Program Run dialog box.

We are going to add an entry in the Registry called *DontAddDefaultGateway*, and assign a hex number value of 0x01 to it. Here's how to do it:

1. Click on Start and point to Run, then click. This opens the Run dialog box shown in Figure 8.17.

2. Type in "regedit," and click on OK. This opens the Registry Editor shown in Figure 8.18.

3. Click the plus (+) sign next to the following folders as they appear:

   ♦ HKEY_LOCALMACHINE

   ♦ SYSTEM

   ♦ CurrentControlSet

   ♦ Services

At this point the Registry Editor dialog box should look similar to Figure 8.19.

4. Scroll down through the *service* entries until you find a NIC to change or investigate. Click on its plus sign, then click on Parameters and TCP/IP. The Registry information for this NIC appears in the right-hand window of the Registry Editor dialog box shown in Figure 8.20.

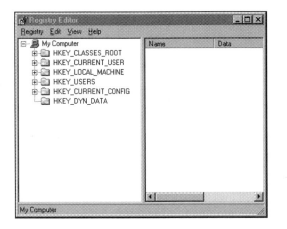

**Figure 8.18**
Registry Editor dialog box.

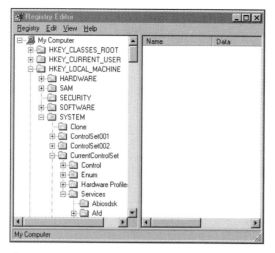

**Figure 8.19**
Expanded Registry Editor dialog box.

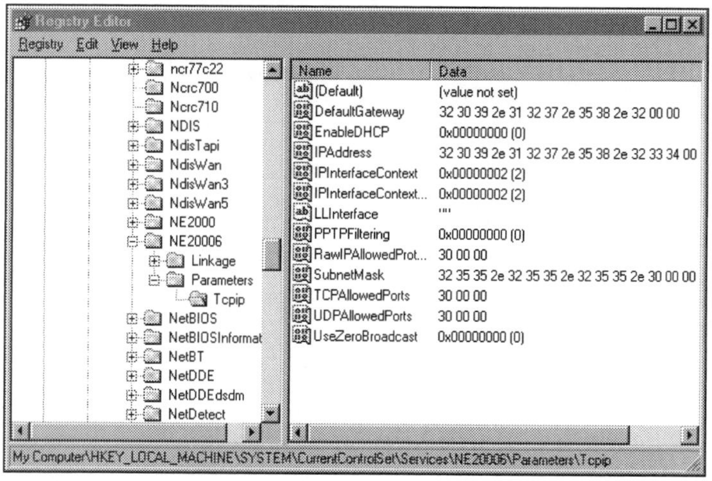

**Figure 8.20**
Registry Editor dialog box.

5. Click on Edit to open the drop-down menu, then select New➡DWORD Value, and click to create a space for a new entry in the *Properties* window on the right side, as shown in Figure 8.21.

6. Type in the following name for the new entry: "DontAddDefaultGateway" and press Enter. This adds the DontAddDefaultGateway entry, with an initial value of 0x00, into the properties for the NIC card entry, as shown in Figure 8.22.

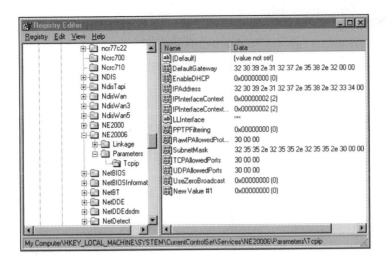

**Figure 8.21**
Editor panel ready for entering new value.

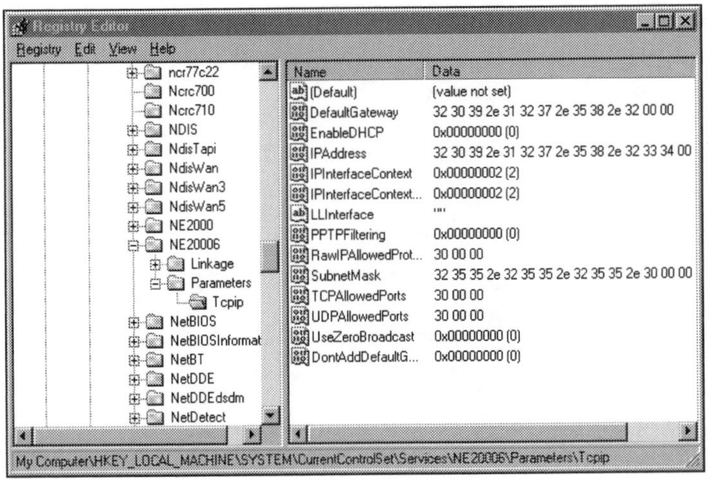

**Figure 8.22**
Editor with new values entered.

7. Now change the value of this entry to 0x01. To do this click on Edit to open the edit drop-down menu, then click on Modify. This opens the Edit D WORD Value dialog box, shown in Figure 8.23.

8. Verify that the value name is *DontAddDefaultGateway* and the hexadecimal radio button in the base section is selected, then type "01" in the value data section. If all this is correct, click on OK. The Edit D_WORD Value dialog box closes, and the Registry Editor becomes active again. The entry for the DontAddDefaultGateway property now has a value of 0x00000001 (1), as shown in Figure 8.24.

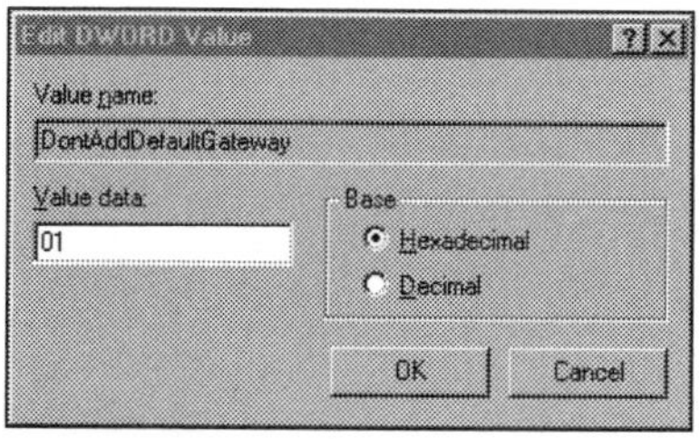

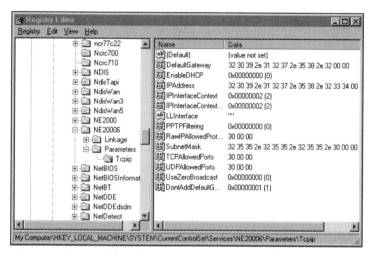

**Figure 8.23**
Editor drop-down menu for adding data.

**Figure 8.24**
Completed Registry Editor panel.

9. Finally, click on the Close button in the upper right hand corner of the Registry editor. After making the change in the Windows NT Registry, restart the computer to have the change take effect. Also keep in mind that you may have to perform this procedure once more for the other NIC installed in the computer.

### Making Static Entries In The Router Table

Now that you have made an entry disabling the creation of a default route for the router table, you need to make some static entries there. Do this with the DOS **route** command, with the syntax *route add*. If you have routes you want to add each time the server is restarted, you can put the entries in a DOS batch file and load the file using autoexec.bat. You can also make the route entries permanent by adding the -p switch to the route command.

For more information on the syntax for the route command, open a DOS window and type "route /?" to display a help screen with all the syntax listed. For more info on using the **route** command, refer to the technical articles listed in Table 8.3.

**Table 8.3** **List of Microsoft technical articles on the subject of using the DOS commands.**

| Article Number | Subject |
|---|---|
| Q140859 | "TCP/IP Routing Basics for Windows NT" |
| Q141383 | "'P' Switch for Route Command Added in Windows NT" |
| Q157025 | "Default Gateway Configuration for Multihomed Computers" |

To add static routes to the router table use the following procedure. In this example you will add a route entry to find the NT server GLS01 located at IP address 209.127.58.1 on the Galveston Facility LAN, Figure 8.2:

1. Click Start | Programs | Command Prompt. This opens a virtual MS-DOS session window, shown in Figure 8.25.

2. At the DOS prompt, type the following: "route -p add 209.127.58.1 209.127.58.234" (without the quote marks) and press Enter. This makes a static entry in the router table identifying the interface for routing data packets to the computer with IP address 209.127.58.1.

Adding static routes to router tables can rapidly become complex and time consuming, and we could use up a large amount of space in this book discussing static routing. If you need more information on adding static routing entries, including the function of the –p switch, please refer to the technical articles listed in Table 8.2, as well as the Windows NT reference manuals.

### *Configuring IP Packet Forwarding*

Now that you have made the appropriate entries in the Windows NT Registry and entered your static routes in a batch file or as persistent entries, you need to configure the RAS for IP forwarding. This is a straightforward configuration step.

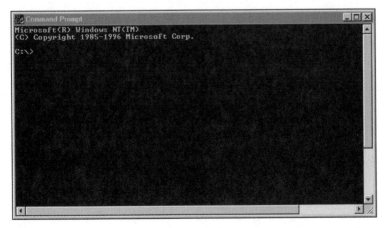

**Figure 8.25**
Virtual DOS command window.

To implement IP packet forwarding on the RAS Server, use the following procedure:

1. Click Start | Settings | Control Panel to open it, as shown in Figure 8.3.

2. Double-click the Network Icon to open the Network control panel, as shown in Figure 8.4.

3. Click the Protocols tab to open the Protocols panel, select TCP/IP, and click on the Properties button to open the TCP/IP Properties dialog box.

4. Click the Routing tab to open the Routing page, as shown in Figure 8.26.

5. Check the Enable IP Forwarding checkbox, then click on OK. This closes the TCP/IP Properties Routing Page, and the Network control panel becomes active.

6. Click on OK to close the Network control panel. This opens a Network Settings Change Information box, informing you that changes made will not take effect until the computer is restarted.

7. Click Yes to restart the computer. The Windows NT server shuts down and the computer restarts.

### Enable PPTP Packet Filtering

If you placed your PPTP server in the network according to the suggestions in this book, then it is parallel with your Internet firewall, with one side facing your private network and the other side facing the DMZ subnet. I mentioned earlier that this is acceptable because a properly installed and correctly maintained PPTP server is every bit as secure as any Internet firewall.

One step that Microsoft recommends is to enable PPTP filtering on the NIC that faces the DMZ subnet. That effectively prevents the server from accepting any non-PPTP packets. From a security standpoint, this is exactly what you want. However, the catch—as you

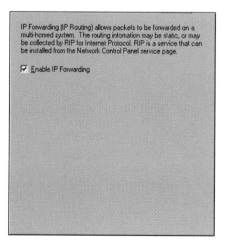

**Figure 8.26**
Microsoft TCP/IP Properties panel.

might expect—is that you *can't* use such valuable tools as *Ping* and *Traceroute* to trouble-shoot suspected TCP/IP problems that might crop up on that NIC. Of course, you can always turn the PPTP filtering off, provided you can find a way to access the Windows NT server running on the machine, especially if the machine is in another location.

Okay, you get the point I'm trying to make. Set up the system, do all the debugging and checking and proving that it works—*first*. Then, enable PPTP filtering. Just keep in mind during this installation and debugging that this computer is sitting at the Internet boundary with very little in the way of high level security implemented. Got the picture? You are vulnerable to Internet attack during that time. Enough said about that.

To implement PPTP packet filtering, perform the following procedure:

1. Click Start | Settings | Control Panel.

2. Double-click the Network Icon to open the Network control panel.

3. Click the Protocols tab to open the Protocols panel, select TCP/IP, and click on the Properties button to open the TCP/IP Properties dialog box.

4. Click the IP Address tab to open the IP Address dialog box, then click Advanced to open the Advanced IP Addressing dialog box, as shown in Figure 8.27.

5. Click the Network Adapter drop-down arrow and select the adapter connected to the Internet. Click the Enable PPTP Filtering checkbox.

6. Click on OK to close the Advanced IP Addressing dialog box, and drop back to the TCP/IP Properties dialog box.

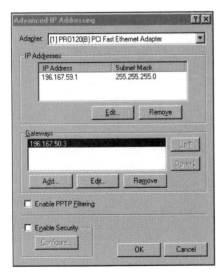

**Figure 8.27**
Advanced IP Addressing panel.

7. Click on OK to close the TCP/IP properties dialog box and the Network control panel displays. Click Close to get a Network Settings Change information box, informing you that changes will not take effect until the computer is restarted. Click Yes to restart the computer. NT server shuts down and the computer restarts.

**Note**

*Do the previous procedure only on the NIC that connects to the Internet.*

You have now completed configuration of a server to act as a PPTP tunnel server. We need to do something less stressful for a change—so let's set up a client.

## Installing And Configuring PPTP On Windows 98

Setting up PPTP with Windows 98 can be divided into three procedures:

♦ Verify that the VPN networking routines have been installed from the Windows 98 CD or install them as necessary.

♦ Install the Microsoft Virtual Private Network adapter.

♦ Create and configure a Dial-Up Networking icon to make the connection to the PPTP Server.

First things first. Normally, when Windows 98 is installed with the standard components, it does not install the Microsoft Virtual Private Networking adapter. You need to verify if the adapter was installed; if not, then we must do the installation manually. For now, we are going to assume that nothing is installed. If you find everything is in order, then chalk this one up to a confidence check. Here is the procedure:

1. Click Start | Settings | Control Panel. The panel in Figure 8.28 displays. How you have the preferences set determines whether the HTML format displays on the left side of the screen as shown in the Figure 8.28; however, that's not critical. The main stuff is in the icons on the right.

2. Double-click on the Add Remove Programs icon and your screen will look like Figure 8.29.

3. Click on the Windows Setup tab to open the Properties page, as shown in Figure 8.30.

4. Use the scrollbar to move through the available components window, and select Communications. Then click on the Details Button to open the Communications components dialog box shown in Figure 8.31.

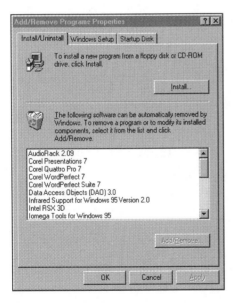

**Figure 8.28**
Windows 98 Control Panel.

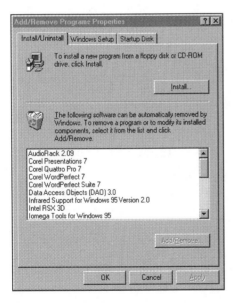

**Figure 8.29**
Add/Remove Programs Properties control panel.

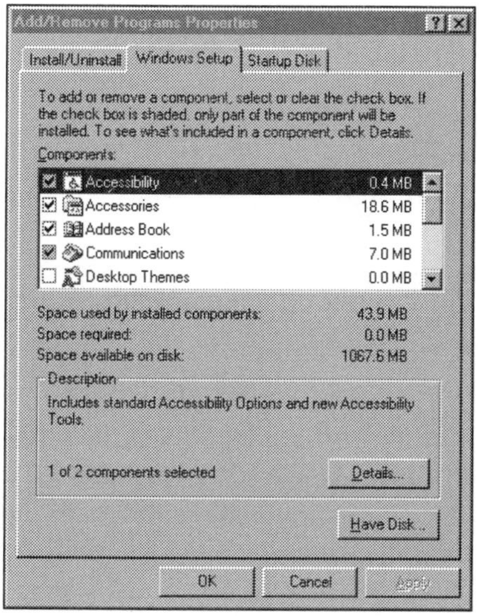

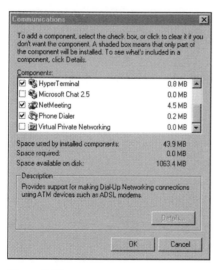

**Figure 8.30**
Add/Remove Programs Properties control panel showing the *Windows Setup* tab selected.

**Figure 8.31**
Communications components dialog box.

5. Using the scrollbar, look through the available components until you locate Virtual Private Networking. If it is not there, check the checkbox for Virtual Private Networking. Click on OK to close the details window and return to the Add/Remove Program Properties Control Panel, as shown in Figure 8.30. Click on OK to close it.

**Figure 8.32**
Disk request panel.

At this point, if you had to add a checkmark to the box for Virtual Private Networking in Step 5, an Insert Disk Information Box opens, as shown in Figure 8.32, informing you that you need to insert the Windows 98 CD. Otherwise, you can skip down to the section on installing the Microsoft VPN adapter.

6. Click on OK and open a Copying Files dialog box like the one in Figure 8.33. If the default path shown for the location of the Windows 98 installation files is not correct, type in the correct path. If you are copying the files from the Windows 98 CD, insert the CD in the CD-ROM drive at this time and click on OK. The file copy procedure will start.

After the first of the files have been copied, a Dial-up Networking Setup information box opens, as shown in Figure 8.34, informing you that after the Add/Remove Programs has completed you will need to restart your computer before proceeding with the dial-up networking configuration.

7. Click on OK and the remaining files will be copied. After the file copy procedure has completed, the Add/Remove Programs Properties window closes and the Control Panel becomes active. Remove any diskettes or CDs and restart the computer.

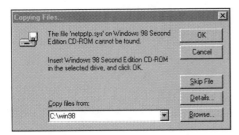

**Figure 8.33**
Copying Files dialog box.

**Figure 8.34**
Dial-Up Networking Setup information box.

### Installing Microsoft VPN Adapter

You have now either installed or verified that the Microsoft Virtual Private Networking components are active in your client machine. The next step is to install the Microsoft Virtual Private Network Adapter supplied with Windows 98:

1. Click Start | Settings | Control Panel. Double-click on the Network icon as shown in Figure 8.28 to open the Network control panel shown in Figure 8.35.

2. Click the Add button to open the Select Network Component Type dialog box, shown in Figure 8.36.

3. Select Adapter, then click Add. This opens the Select Network adapters dialog box, as seen in Figure 8.37.

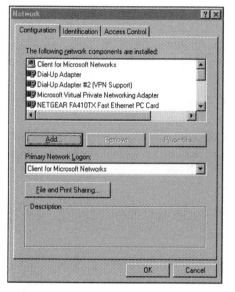

**Figure 8.35**
Network control panel.

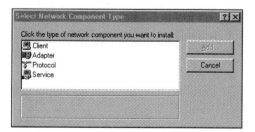

**Figure 8.36**
Select Network Component Type dialog box.

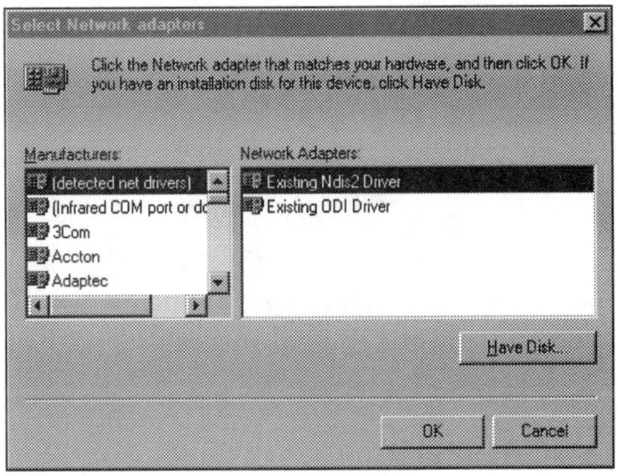

**Figure 8.37**
Select Network adapters dialog box.

4. Using the scroll arrows for the left-hand window, scroll through the list of manufacturers until you find Microsoft; then click on it. This opens the list of Microsoft Network Adapters in the right-hand window, as shown in Figure 8.38.

5. Select Microsoft Virtual Private Networking Adapter in the right-hand window, then click on OK to return to the Network control panel. Click on OK to close the Network control panel. This opens a System Settings Change information box, as shown in Figure 8.39, informing you that the settings will not take place until the computer is restarted. Click on Yes to restart the computer.

This completes the installation of a Microsoft Virtual Private Networking Adapter for Windows 98.

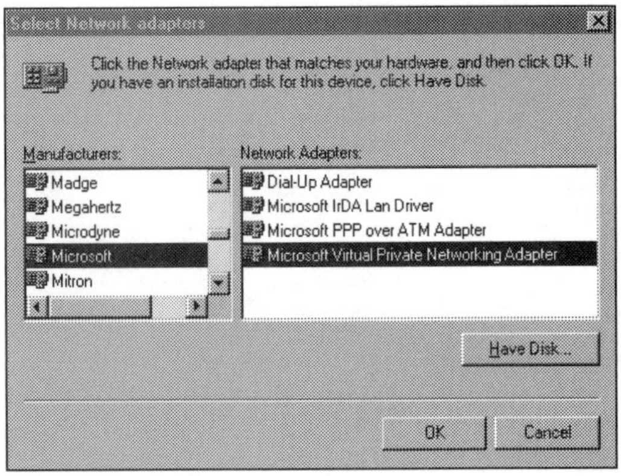

**Figure 8.38**
Selecting Microsoft as manufacturer and VPN as adapter.

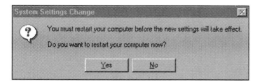

**Figure 8.39**
System Settings Change information box.

## *Dial-Up Networking Icon*

The next few steps will lead you through the procedures to create and configure a dial-up networking icon.

1. Click on Start | Programs | Accessories | Communications | Dial-Up Networking. This opens the Dial-Up Networking group, as shown in Figure 8.40.

2. If you have no dial-up connections at this time, the Make New Connection dialog box automatically opens, as shown in Figure 8.41. If you already have one or more dial-up connections configured, then double-click on the Make New Connection icon to open the new connection dialog box.

3. Type in any name you want to use to describe the connection. We could be cryptic and use just VPN-1 or verbose and name it Vintage Air, Galveston Facility. Use whatever name you want—I think it would help if it is the name of the network or computer on the other end of the VPN tunnel. After you've entered the name, press the Tab key to move the cursor to the Select A Device data area. Click the drop-down arrow to the right of the data area, then point to Microsoft VPN Adapter, and click again. The Microsoft VPN adapter should be selected in the data area, as shown in Figure 8.42.

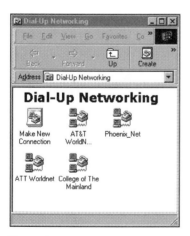

**Figure 8.40**
Dial-Up Networking group.

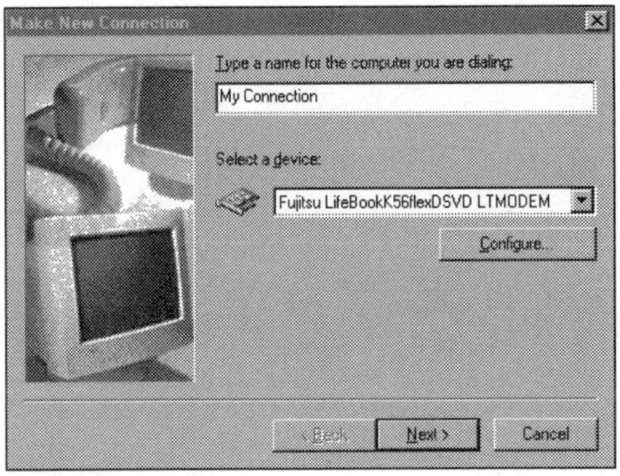

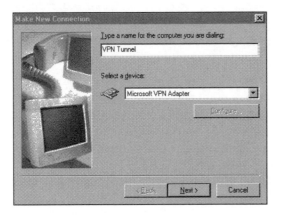

**Figure 8.41**
Make New Connection dialog box.

**Figure 8.42**
Dial-up computer and device selected.

4. Click on the Next button to open the Host Name or IP Address data entry area as shown in Figure 8.43.

5. Type in the IP address of the computer you are making a connection to on the other end of the VPN tunnel. If you have made a DNS entry for the *host name* for that computer, you can enter that. When you have the IP address or host name entered correctly, click on Next. This opens the Make New Connection information screen, shown in Figure 8.44, telling you that a new dial-up networking connection with the name you assigned has been created.

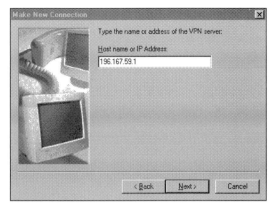

**Figure 8.43**
Host name or IP address entered.

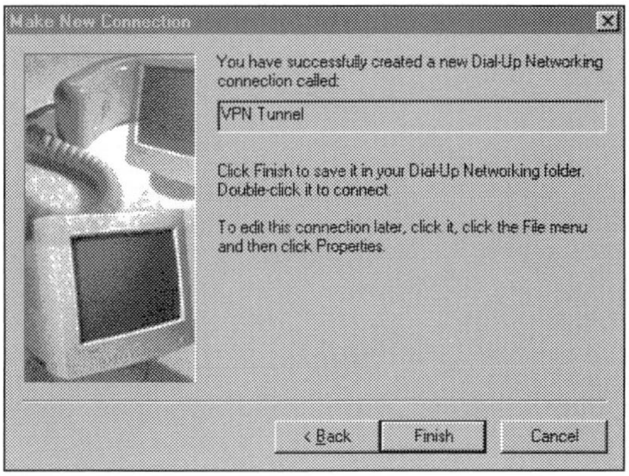

**Figure 8.44**
New connection is complete.

6. Click on Finish to close the Make New Connection dialog box and open the Dial-Up Networking group window in Figure 8.45, showing the new connection.

### *Configuring The Dial-Up Connection Icon*

The next few steps will guide you through the procedures for configuring the VPN dial-up connection icon.

1. Point to the VPN Dial-Up Connection you created, and right-click. Click Properties to open the dialog box for the connection you have created, as shown in Figure 8.46.

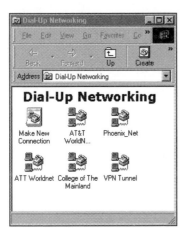

**Figure 8.45**
VPN tunnel connection added to dial-up networking.

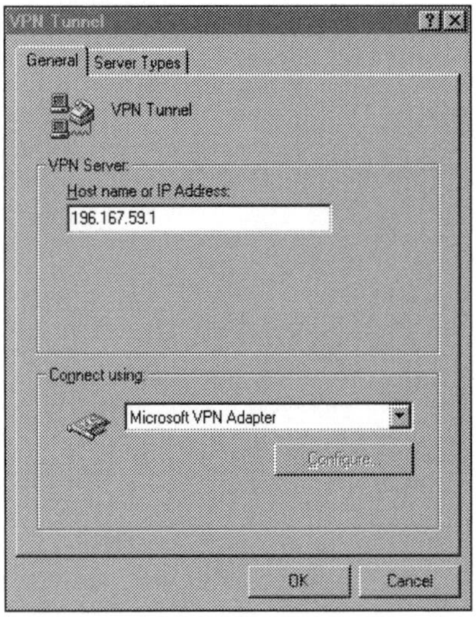

**Figure 8.46**
Entering connection properties for VPN.

2. Click on the Server Types tab to open the server types dialog box, as shown in Figure 8.47.

3. In the Advanced Properties Area, make sure the Require Encrypted Password and Require Data Encryption checkboxes are checked—the rest are optional.

4. In the Allowed Network Protocols Area, make sure that the TCP/IP checkbox is checked. The other checkboxes in the allowed Network Protocols area are optional, but TCP/IP is required for PPTP. Click on the TCP/IP Settings button to open the dialog box shown in Figure 8.48.

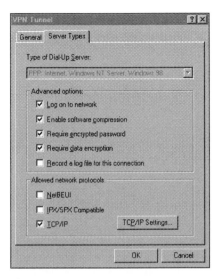

**Figure 8.47**
Server Types tab dialog panel.

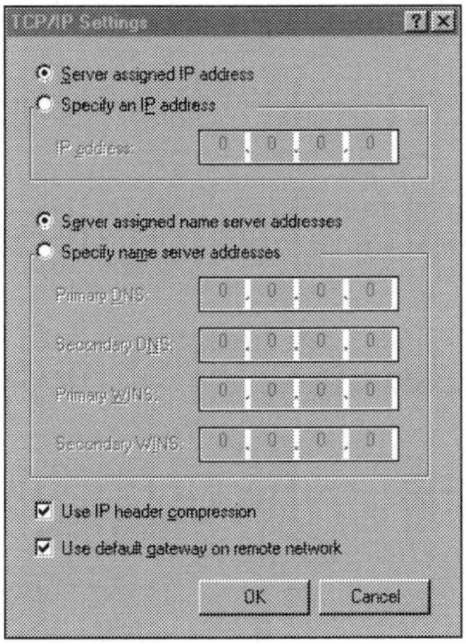

**Figure 8.48**
TCP/IP Settings dialog box.

5. If you want the PPTP Server to assign an IP address, then verify that the Server Assigned IP Address radio button is selected. If you want to assign an IP address, select the Specify an IP Address radio button and enter a valid address. (Remember that if you specify an IP address, the address must match the range of addresses you entered when you configured the TCP/IP protocol settings on the PPTP server.)

6. If you want the PPTP server to assign an address for the name server, then verify that the Server Assigned Name Server Address radio button is selected. If you want to use a specific name server address, select the Specify Name Server Address radio button and enter the IP address of at least one DNS or WINS server that will be accessible to this computer.

7. If your system can support IP Header compression and you want to use the default gateway on the remote system, leave the appropriate checkboxes selected. When the TCP/IP configuration is correct, click on OK to return to the server types dialog box and click on OK to return to the Dial-Up Networking Group window.

At this point you have created and configured a dial-up interface to connect to the PPTP server.

## Take It For A Drive

Now that we have PPTP installed on the NT server and on the Windows 98 client, we can take the system for a test drive. The operation is fairly straightforward. As always, before you try anything new, like making your first VPN connection, check and make sure that all the equipment is operating correctly. If you run into a glitch, at least you will have taken that many fewer variables into the troubleshooting and debugging process.

Use the following procedure to connect your Windows 98 client computer to the Windows NT server using the PPTP Virtual Private Network:

1. If the Dial-Up Networking window is not open, click on Start | Programs | Accessories | Communications, and click on Dial-Up Networking to open the panel in Figure 8.40.

2. Double-click the icon for the VPN connection you created in the Dial-Up Networking window. This opens a Connect To dialog box, shown in Figure 8.49.

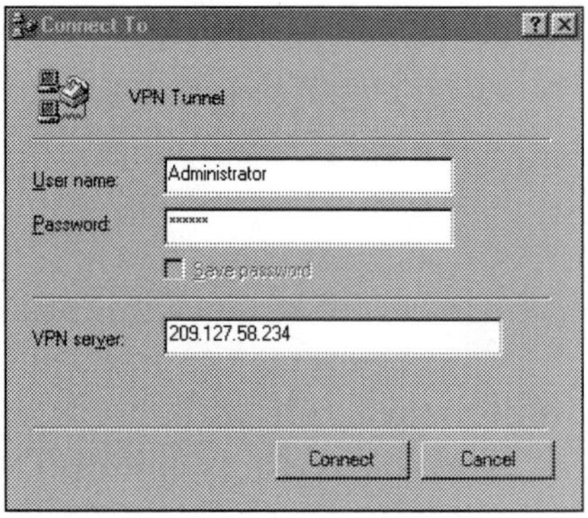

**Figure 8.49**
Connect To dialog box.

3. Enter your user name and password, make sure the IP Address or Host Name is correct, and click on Connect. An information window saying Connect To VPN Device will appear.

4. After a short period the Microsoft Client Logon Screen opens, prompting you to enter the network password. Type in the correct password and click on OK. The Microsoft Client logon screen closes, and (fanfare and drum roll, please, maestro) you will be connected to the NT server.

At this point you should be able to perform any tasks appropriate for the type of user you are logged on as. While you are here, try every possible AP you can think of.

## Checklist Number Five: Post-Implementation

Well we're almost there. Some things you need to do now:

♦ Make sure all the servers can communicate with each other, and that no apparent incorrect configurations exist, especially in establishing static routes.

♦ When you are satisfied that everything is in good shape, all the servers are configured correctly, and the necessary client workstations have been configured with the dial-up VPN adapter, take down the existing (old) WAN link. From this point on your users will have to start using the VPN via the dial-up adapter. At first this additional step may be a bit awkward, but given time to adapt to the new interface, the users should see no difference in the operation of the network.

♦ If you have a protocol analyzer available you can capture some packets destined for the network on the other side of the VPN and decode them. The data in the packets should be encrypted, and you should not be able to recognize any information.

♦ Notify all the users to be sure and report any problems they may encounter. Start a trouble log and log all problems reported.

♦ Remove any temporary restrictions, or other implementations you may have put in place on a temporary basis.

## Checklist Number Six: VPN Management

As we said in the previous chapter, kick the tires and light the fires, then take it out for a test. What this really means is that you should do a through evaluation test of as many different standard—that is, day-to-day type stuff—operations as possible. I have found that it is usually better if someone from the computer support group finds a problem than if a user finds the problem. So flip the switches and push the keys—in any case it's a good idea to sit down at a user's position now and wring the system out thoroughly. If you have a second copy of the system drawings, try and communicate with every application, workstation, and device you have—and do it from both ends.

Once you have satisfied yourself that things are operating as expected, you can then start to look at some management strategies and think about the "M" words; Management and Maintenance. We're going to change our approach at this point. In the previous parts of this chapter we pretty much told you what you could do, then told you how to do it (providing as many illustrations as possible). In this section we're going to tell you what you can do, but the *how* will wait for later.

### Maintenance Operations

As we went through this set up, we took the default settings whenever we could for two reasons:

♦ For the most part, we figured just going through the installation and configuration would keep you busy enough without making you worry about setting this parameter or that access time.

♦ Usually you will find that the system comes up reliably and runs rather well using the default settings.

After you have the VPN up and running, you can go back and fine tune the VPN based on needs determined by the type and amount of usage applied to the VPN. This is all a part of regular maintenance.

### Caution

What we said in the previous chapter about the Novell defaults applies equally well when it comes to the Microsoft defaults. That is, the default settings provided with products are designed to provide optimum performance for the largest group of users. Changes to improve performance in one area can and sometimes do adversely affect another area. You should make changes to any network system in a systematic, planned manner, leaving time between each change for the network to go through at least one complete *operational cycle*; that is, the time it takes to perform all the operations that normally occur within a network system. Some examples:

♦ Accounting systems usually close the books at the end of the accounting cycle. This is either every four weeks, or once per month (yes, these are different).

♦ If your network system performs a partial backup every day and a complete backup every week, then your operational cycle for your backup is weekly.

Get the picture? You should make one change at a time, and wait one complete cycle between changes.

## VPN Maintenance

Among other things, the following maintenance operations apply specifically to VPNs:

♦ *Selecting network protocols used by the VPN*—The PPTP VPN can be configured to use both TCP/IP and IPX/SPX protocols. If you have any need to support IPX/SPX protocols, you can do this quite easily.

♦ *Add static routes to the router table*—In this case, using Windows NT, you need to open a virtual DOS session and use the **ROUTE ADD** command.

♦ *Configuring data encryption and data authentication methods.*

## Managing Your VPN

To a large degree, the VPN is a part of the larger WAN. Day-to-day administration tasks performed should be applied to the VPN as a matter of course, and will not be covered here. Some areas of management apply specifically to the VPN structure, and we will discuss them here. You can perform all of the administration tasks related to the VPN from the Windows NT server. These tasks include the following:

♦ Selecting links

♦ Tuning for optimum performance

♦ Monitoring statistics and bandwidth usage on the NICs

## Monitoring VPN Statistics

As a normal part of operations and maintenance you should set up a system of checking and monitoring statistics relating to the VPN. This is especially true during the first few weeks of operation. Regular monitoring and recording of statistical information helps make your support operations proactive, as opposed to reactive.

We will cover monitoring statistical information in greater detail in Chapters 9 and 11 and deal even more heavily with troubleshooting in Chapter 11. For now, a brief overview of the kinds of information you can monitor is more appropriate.

**Note**

*The same monitoring information is available in both NetWare and Windows NT. However, you may have to look in different areas for it.*

A wide range of statistical information is available about the operation of various objects within a network. This information is found by using various monitoring utilities in the Network Administration subgroup that can be found in the administration tools of Windows NT Server. VPN statistical information can be acquired with that bag of tools also.

## Monitoring The Internet

Do those three words make you laugh? No one can monitor the Internet, right? Well for the most part, that's correct. Why would anyone want to? But from this point on, the performance of your network is now related to the performance of the Internet. So that means you need to be able to do at least some types of statistical monitoring of the beast.

### *What You Need To Look At, And How*

Earlier in this book we named some software packages you could use to monitor the Internet and gather information about various statistics. To a certain degree, your ability to do this may be limited. Your site is, after all, just an extension of your ISP's router. This is where a good relationship with your ISP will come in handy. Most ISPs monitor the Internet for overall performance and percentage of bandwidth used. This is valuable information, and your ISP should be willing to make this available.

On a more local scene, your particular interface could monitor the following statistics:

♦ Latency

♦ Number of dropped packets

♦ Overall application throughput

♦ Typical route through the Internet for a data packet

Earlier we mentioned two programs that are useful in gathering this type of information. One is named Cloud, from Shunrua Software **www.shunra.com**; the other is Chariot, from Ganymede Software. Either program will prove useful for gathering information on latency and the number of dropped packets. The typical route through the Internet for a data packet may not be as easy to get. One thing you can try is using Traceroute. Under normal circumstances this program sends a data packet from one location to the other, and at every router along the way it sends back an ICMP message packet. However, this may not work very well with a VPN, because the Traceroute packet itself may be encapsulated and sent to the other end. If this happens you may have to drop back and rely on a protocol analyzer to provide better information.

That's a brief glance into maintenance and management, the nonchocolate version of M&M. As I said, we'll come back and take a more detailed look in Chapter 11.

## Last Checklist: Future Planning

If you believe that because your VPN is up and running and you gave it a really good wringing out, it will never need improvement…then I have a room full of 40MB hard disk drives I'll make you a good deal on.

The time to start looking at the future is today. So what are some things you need to be watching out for? As with all the other questions like this, we don't have an exact answer. But at minimum you should be watching for change—usually in the form of an increase in demand—in the following areas:

♦ Network expansion

    ♦ User population

    ♦ Connect time

    ♦ Bandwidth utilization

- ◆ VPN capacity
  - ◆ Tunnel server capacity
  - ◆ Supporting systems capacity
  - ◆ Bandwidth use
- ◆ Longer term network growth
  - ◆ Remote users
  - ◆ Accessibility to client sites (extranet)
  - ◆ Accessibility to vendor sites (extranet)
- ◆ Future interoperability issues

We've listed most of the items that will eventually effect the overall operation of your VPN. You can tailor the list by adding more specific items that apply to your network.

# Wrap Up

You may have noticed that not as much seems to be involved in establishing the PPTP VPN using Windows NT as with implementing the IPsec VPN using BorderManager The tradeoff might be that, especially from the users' standpoint, the PPTP VPN may seem more cumbersome in operation.

In my opinion—when used to connect two LANs together as we have done in this and the previous chapter—BorderManager probably provides the better out-of-the-box solution. Microsoft readily admits that their VPN solution is not designed to provide this type of service. However, third party providers make PPTP-based products designed to operate in a similar manner as the BorderManager VPN, except that they use Windows NT as the platform and PPTP as the protocol. If your needs fall in this area, we have listed some of these companies in Appendix C. Also, you can check our Web site, **www.sldenterprises.com,** for the latest list of PPTP VPN providers.

In the next chapter we are going to expand our small scale VPN out to the remote user, the territory where the PPTP VPN was designed to be used.

# Chapter 9

# *Expanding The VPN*

**Key Topics:**

♦ *VPN Client installation*

♦ *Novell BorderManager Client*

♦ *Windows NT PPTP Client*

♦ *Remote user administration*

♦ *Troubleshooting*

In the previous two chapters you followed the installation and configuration of the VPN software to allow you to connect two LANs together. This type of arrangement is commonly known as a *site-to-site* VPN. Now that the VPN is in place connecting the Galveston and Houston sites, it's time to expand the network and allow a user with proper rights to access it from anywhere a connection to the Internet is available—in essence, anywhere a user can find a telephone connection. This type of connection is commonly referred to as a *client-to-site* VPN. However, remember that the connection must be secure to protect the networks from unauthorized access.

## Why's And Where's—Some Basic Theory

In the client-to-site VPN installation, we will use Windows 98 as the operating system for the basic client and build on that. The procedures are similar between the Windows PPTP VPN client installation and the Novell BorderManager™ IPsec client installation. Both clients require the use of the Windows dial-up networking interface to establish a connection to the Internet through an *Internet Service Provider* (*ISP*). Because of those similarities, it is my choice to deal with the installation and configuration of both the Windows PPTP and the Novell BorderManager IPsec clients in a single chapter. The differences and similarities will be noted and, when it becomes necessary, discussed in greater detail.

## Differences Between Site-To-Site And Client-To-Site

The differences between site-to-site and client-to-site VPNs are more than just cosmetic. In extending the VPN to allow connection by remote clients, we must expand the architectural model to include ISPs and they can be located anywhere. This expanded model will resemble the plan shown in Figure 9.1. This opens up a new world of possibilities, and also invites a new world of potential problems. How these problems are resolved can make the difference between a successful implementation and a never-ending series of problems.

From a conceptual standpoint the operation of the client-to-site VPN is straightforward. At the end of the VPN tunnel located at the facility headquarters, we install and configure a tunneling server. This procedure is nearly the same as in the previous chapters. At the client end the client workstation is equipped with the necessary software to perform the encryption and encapsulation functions. In other words, we make the client machine the equivalent of a tunneling server. The last step is to equip the client machine with the software to allow a connection to the Internet from a remote location. This is usually done through the services of an ISP in the remote area.

To initiate the VPN, a tunnel must be created between the two endpoints of the expected tunnel. The LAN site already has a connection established to the Internet with a tunneling server configured and online. At the client end, the usual procedure is to establish a connection to the Internet first, usually through the Windows dial-up networking adapter (or the equivalent if your operating system is not Windows), as shown in Figure 9.2.

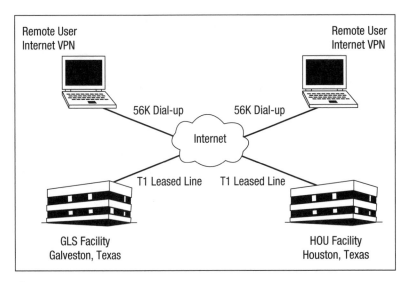

**Figure 9.1**
An expanded VPN model.

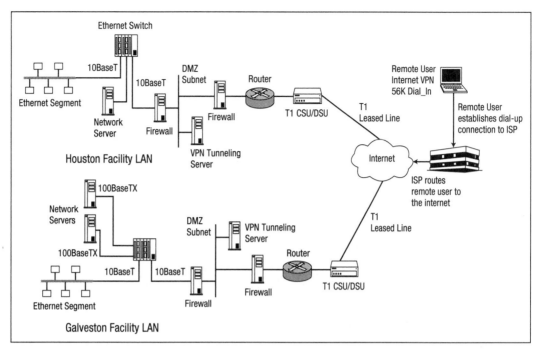

**Figure 9.2**
Step one, client-to-site VPN implementation.

Once the Internet connection has been established, the software that will create the equivalent of the tunneling server is started on the client computer. This is usually an enhanced version of the client software for the particular network operating system you are using. When you start the tunneling software at the client end, it establishes communications with the LAN site tunneling server and creates a VPN tunnel between the two end points, as shown in Figure 9.3.

The single greatest difference between a site-to-site and a client-to-site VPN is the Internet connection. In a typical LAN environment, you establish the connection to the Internet in an area with limited access by the public—in a closely controlled environment such as a computer room, wire closet, or telephone POP. However, a client-to-site VPN requires connecting the remote client to the Internet from locations that are about as different from the LAN environment as they can be. As I said earlier, the dial-up-networking adapter (if your client is Windows 98) typically makes the connection through a local call to an ISP—that's what VPN is, after all, about.

Often a road warrior will do this from a hotel room, using the hotel's preferred public switched telephone network (PSTN) to make a connection to what is hoped will be a reliable ISP. Of course, this is all guaranteed to work every time, right? I am going to stress this point as we make our way through this and the following chapters. I am firmly convinced that the key to a successful client-to-site VPN implementation is good proactive

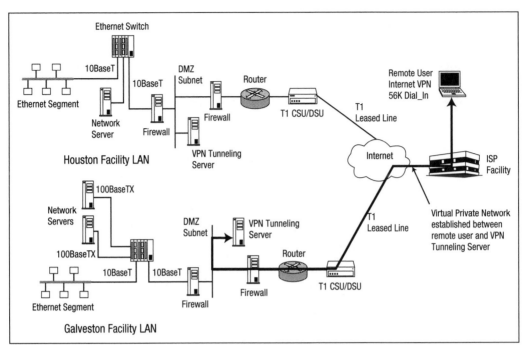

**Figure 9.3**
Step two, client-to-site VPN implementation.

troubleshooting, end user training, and world-class support. That, folks, requires solid planning and maintenance.

### Building The Tunnel

Once the client has established a connection to the Internet via an ISP, the next step is implementing a VPN tunnel back to the headquarters. This brings up another difference between a site-to-site and a client-to-site VPN: the equipment for the two endpoints of the VPN tunnel—in other words, the encryption and encapsulation (or tunneling, for short) server. In the case of the client-to-site VPN, the workstation the client is using, often a laptop computer takes on the task of encrypting and encapsulating the outgoing packets, and decapsulating and decrypting the incoming packets. In other words, the laptop becomes the tunneling server. Depending on the type of encryption used, this can place a great demand on the resources of the laptop computer. In some cases the users may find that their performance is greatly affected.

Although the two differences we talked about so far are not by any means minor, they are primarily architectural in nature. As such, it is possible to implement changes in the software to incorporate these and all the other architectural differences into an enhanced software product. This enhancement will allow incorporation of the new features brought about by the change in the architecture.

### One More Difference

Another difference between the site-to-site and client-to-site VPNs exists that is not quite as easy to overcome. In fact, recognizing and managing this difference will make your VPN implementation either a success or a problematic, worrisome failure. It is based on the fact that, sooner or later, the remote user is going to have a problem.

In extending the VPN to the remote user, it becomes necessary to extend some of the support of the computer services group to the same location. This implies that if the remote user is a traveling user, then some of the computer services support group must go along. I don't mean this in a literal sense, but instead in a logical sense. If we are going to expect the remote user to establish a connection with the LAN, using something as complex as a VPN encryption and encapsulation server, then the computer support group had better be prepared to support that remote user. In the latter parts of this chapter I will address this in greater detail.

## The ISP Interface

As I said earlier, a major difference between site-to-site and client-to-site access is the necessity of first making a connection to an ISP. As we shall see further on, this is the one area that offers the greatest chance for problems. This requires the use of a dialer installed in the operating system on the remote computer. As I mentioned before, for the purpose of this chapter, we will cover the installation and configuration of the Windows 98 dial-up-networking adapter. This is by no means a suggestion that Windows 98 is the only operating system that can be used. The simple fact is that the page budget for this chapter simply will not allow us to cover the installation and configuration of the equivalent software product for every possible operating system. If your system is something other than Windows 98, for example Mac OS-8x, or Linux, you will need to refer to the user's manual for the product you are using for instructions on installing and configuring the software necessary to establish a connection to the Internet through an ISP. Also, in case you are using Linux, you must refer to the software manual for installation of the product you are using for installation and configuration instructions for either the PPTP or IPsec software products.

Installing the dial-up-networking is just one part of the picture. You may be required to set up the TCP/IP protocol stack more commonly known as *WinSock*. Microsoft made the WinSock installation and configuration about as straightforward as it can be, but it is still not a simple click-of-the-mouse operation. Generally speaking, you will only have to set up WinSock one time. After that, barring any significant changes in overall operation, the TCP/IP settings should not require any modifications. Unfortunately, this may or may not be the case with the dial-up-networking adapter.

### Murphy's Laws

Murphy's Laws are the foundation for all the things that can go wrong if you don't plan for every possible event. Murphy's first law says, "If anything can go wrong, it will—and it will go wrong at the worst possible time."

A computer support group can analyze a given situation for potential problems, develop plans for fixing them, and establish procedures for implementing the plans, but they cannot account for every possible situation that may occur. Murphy will take care of that. Much to your dislike, sooner or later, your remote users won't have a dial-up connection in their laptops for their locale. In that event, they are going to use the dial-up-networking to create a new connection all by themselves. If Murphy's laws hold true to form, they will do this alone, in a dark hotel room, in the thriving metropolis of Cut-n-Shoot, Texas, where the definition of reliable phone service is two tin cans and some string. What else could possibly go wrong?

One possible solution is to establish a plan, and then establish a backup plan, then an *if all else fails do this* plan. This is proactive as opposed to reactive support. Later on, we will look more closely at establishing a proactive plan, with systematic steps that go from the best to worst to the *if all else fails* situation. The goal is to make the level of support the highest it can possibly be given the resources available to you.

After the road warrior establishes a connection to the Internet through a local ISP, the next step is to load the VPN client and set up a tunnel through the Internet. This gives rise to an interesting problem area that is important enough to warrant a closer look. Windows 98 is a good multitasking, multiuser operating system. If your user has Windows NT Workstation on their PC that's even better, because Windows 98 is capable of creating several concurrent sessions, some of which use the same software package to perform two seemingly separate sessions on the same platform. One example is the client who wants to access the LAN site using a secure VPN and, at the same time, access the Internet in a normal manner.

A close look under the hood of the laptop will show that when a connection is made to the VPN tunnel, a concurrent connection to the Internet poses real security issues. If a computer is used to establish an Internet connection for a Web browser or email and at the same time to establish a connection to a VPN tunnel, the TCP/IP protocol will create two logical interfaces within the TCP/IP protocol stack, one for each of the connections. Surprisingly enough, it does not take a great deal beyond this capability for the laptop to become a software router and start routing IP datagrams from the Internet through the VPN tunnel. That greatly increases the risk of compromising the tunnel by allowing the laptop to be used as an unsecure gateway. Needless to say, this is not a good thing.

## The VPN Tunneling Server Interfaces

Let's discuss two types of server interfaces:

♦ LAN

♦ Client

### The LAN (Site) Server Interface

In Chapters 7 and 8 we covered the use of Windows NT and Novell BorderManager to establish a site-to-site VPN between two LANs, so we need not cover the full installation and configuration of the software again. With some minor exceptions, no difference exists in the installation and configuration of the tunneling server located at the LAN site, regardless of its application as a site-to-site or client-to-site VPN. Also, Windows NT PPTP and Novell BorderManager IPsec tunneling servers can both concurrently support site-to-site and client-to-site VPNs.

One aspect of the LAN server that we did not cover is its use as a *Remote Access Server (RAS)*. A RAS is a computer that is configured to allow a WAN link connection between two LANs or to allow remote users to dial in and establish a connection directly to the LAN. In the first case, this implementation requires the use of one or more dedicated high-speed WAN links—such as a T1 or partial T1. In the second case, the implementation requires using one or more banks of modems, each with their own dial-in access line.

The normal implementation of a VPN uses the Internet as the transport medium, eliminating the need for several T1 lines between sites and the maintenance of modems with their associated POTS lines. The reason I mention this here is because the Windows NT PPTP and the Novell BorderManager IPsec tunneling servers can be configured to allow the computer to act both as a VPN tunneling server and as a RAS. This way, remote users can dial directly into the VPN server and establish a VPN tunnel through direct connection. This method eliminates the necessity of using the Internet, but increases the telephone toll-charges. For you to use the server this way requires an additional configuration that will be discussed later in this chapter.

### The Remote (Client) Server Interface

The next step is to load the client-to-site VPN software on the remote user's computer for the encryption and encapsulation process. For Microsoft Windows 98 and Novell NetWare® the software is provided in the form of an enhanced client software package.

In the Windows 98 VPN the PPTP tunneling server software is a logical network adapter named, appropriately enough, the Microsoft VPN network adapter, and is installed as an adapter in the *network neighborhood properties*. The user configures the Microsoft VPN network adapter through the Dial-Up Networking group. The steps to perform the installation and configuration of the Microsoft VPN network adapter were already been covered in Chapter 8, but we will spend some time going over them again.

In its BorderManager VPN product, Novell provides the IPsec tunneling software in the form of an enhanced version of the NetWare Client 32 designed specifically for remote VPN connections. Client-to-site VPNs make up the only requirement for this package and this is the first time you'll see it.

# Product Comparisons

Before we can delve deeply into this aspect of VPNs, we must first do some comparisons between our two major candidates and drop in some words about other products as well. As you will see, you can always find more than one track leading to the final destination.

## Similarities Between The Products

Many VPN products show noticeable similarities because they share a common operating system and platform architecture, primarily because they share the Windows 98 operating system and the Intel platform. This is, not surprisingly, especially true when implementing Windows NT (with its PPTP) and Novell's BorderManager (with IPsec).

You have already seen that both products use the Windows 98 dial-up network interface to establish a connection with an ISP. This is an absolute first step that cannot be ignored and that is true for most of the VPN products currently on the market. If your client operating system is not Windows 98, it must provide you with the equivalent software application to establish a connection to the Internet through an ISP.

### Indus River

Indus River's VPN product sports an interesting adaptation of the Windows 98 dial-up-network interface. It is a custom dialer interface displaying a graphic image of a cellular telephone on the screen. The road warrior uses the logical cell phone to recall numbers from a phone book or key in the number one digit at a time. It is a very intuitive and easy to use interface, and is well thought out. For a closer look, go to **www.indusriver.com** and download a demo version of the company's VPN software.

### Microsoft

Because its products are designed primarily for remote user access, Microsoft developed a logical VPN adapter—to enhance Windows 98 and NT—for the user to install as an adapter through the network properties. The user configures the adapter to work with the Microsoft Dial-Up Networking interface to establish a secure connection with an NT server configured for tunneling.

### Novell

Novell follows a similar approach, except it developed an enhancement for NetWare Client 32. If you are familiar with Novell's NetWare products, you probably already have some knowledge of the NetWare Client 32 for Windows 9x and Windows NT. Rather than follow in Microsoft's footstep and develop a logical VPN adapter, Novell enhanced the NetWare Client 32 for Windows 98 and Windows NT. You establish a secure connection through this enhanced client to a BorderManager tunneling server. You can use the standard NetWare Client 32 and the VPN Client 32 on the same machine, provided the standard Client 32 is version 2.2 or greater.

If you followed us through Chapter 7, you know that the BorderManager uses two types of VPN servers—master and slave. If your VPN connects two LANs together, one server must be a master, and all the others are slaves. If you allow remote clients access to the LAN through the VPN, they can connect to either a master or slave. In some cases this makes administration less complicated.

### More Similarities

You can see more similarities in how the tunneling servers are identified within the structure of the Internet. To beef up security, BorderManager and Windows NT recommend that you use IP addresses for the tunneling servers rather than the DNS or WINS names when configuring the VPN clients. When you configure a computer to act as a VPN server and provide the tunnel interface, you quite naturally want to set filters that will not allow any IP data packets except those packets that meet the specific protocol of your VPN to be accepted by the interface. The simplest way to establish a connection to an interface that has these types of filters set is to use the IP address. Then, the tunneling interface will not accept any other method.

Also, even though it obviously is not feasible to establish a network connection to the Internet and expect it to remain a closely guarded secret, it is not a good idea to advertise it to the whole world. If you use host names and make DNS entries in name servers for the VPN tunneling server, you provide another opportunity for hackers to locate the tunnel end point. Within reason, you should make every effort to keep the IP addresses of the tunneling servers as secure as possible.

## Differences Between The Products

If all the VPN products were the same, they would all come with the same wrapping. But we don't know of any company that is named Novcisindusoft, so let's look at the major differences between two products: Microsoft and Novell.

### Microsoft

You have probably noticed throughout the book that Windows NT VPN is designed primarily to allow remote users access to Windows NT networks—this is the basic implementation of a client-to-site VPN. In Chapter 8 you saw that Windows NT VPN does not surrender gracefully to a site-to-site implementation. In fact, the only way to do it is to use a modification of the client-to-site VPN. As you will see, the Windows implementation of the PPTP lends itself to remote clients in a much more workable manner.

### Novell

Novell designed BorderManager VPN to allow users to connect two LANs in an almost transparent manner. But as you have seen, it is a bit more difficult to set up and configure than the Windows NT VPN. This doesn't mean BorderManager doesn't lend itself to remote users. Novell's thought along this line is that the interface to the network should be as similar to the standard network interface as possible, and still allow encryption and encapsulation to take place. Because Novell encourages its users to adopt the Novell Client 32 interface for network users, it has developed an enhanced version of the software specifically for the BorderManager. It's very similar to the standard Client 32 and can coexist on the same computer with the standard Client 32, provided that the standard Client 32 is version 2.2 or higher.

# VPN Client Installation Procedure

As we have done in the other chapters where we covered installation and configuration steps, we are going to use the checklist approach. We'll start off with a master checklist, then proceed with the individual steps. If you skipped Chapters 7 and 8, I recommend you go back and read them. Even if you are installing a product other than Windows NT VPN or Novell BorderManager VPN products, you will find useful information about establishing logical procedures in those chapters.

## The Checklist Approach

Later we will add more details to each of the checklists, but let's get the master list out of the way first. Because we are just expanding the VPN to the remote user, the master checklist is not going to cover all the areas that were included in the previous chapters. The master checklist for the VPN expansion is reduced to five checklists, dropping off the last two. We will finish up the chapter with sections on remote user administration and troubleshooting. Those will be more in the form of discussion and suggestions than a checklist approach.

By installing and configuring a client-to-site VPN, you are really expanding your network to the world. Where have you heard that before? Think about that. You will have implemented all the equipment, processes, and procedures that are required at your LAN at the client site—wherever that is. The only difference is, the client doesn't need quite so much of it.

Let's get the master checklist out of the way, first:

❑ *Equipment Required*—A list of all equipment and software required for completing the project. This includes test and maintenance items also.

❑ *Support Needs*—Resources to tap for assistance on installation and configuration of hardware or software.

❑ *Pre-Implementation*—What parts and pieces you should have up, running, and configured before you start ripping the guts out of your existing network.

❑ *Implementation*—A step-by-step sequence (including any testing sequences) for rolling the VPN into the system.

❑ *Post-Implementation*—A few temporary patches and hacks will typically be installed to hold things together while you are doing the implementation. This is the point where you yank them out to free up the drive space and unburden the bandwidth.

As with the checklists in the other chapters, you need to follow the checklist with discipline and pay attention to details to assure successful implementation.

## Checklist Number One: Required Equipment

This is a slight modification of the equipment checklist from the previous two chapters. In this case you are concerned only with the equipment required for the client computer. We are going to use as our example an Intel Pentium-based laptop computer. This should not be interpreted as meaning that you could only install the client software on laptop computers. In some cases—for example, Helen the telecommuter—you may want to install the software on a conventional PC platform. You still want a high-grade Pentium with no less than the amount of RAM suggested by the VPN product manufacturer and maybe a little more.

First thing on the list is a configuration plan:

♦ Which of the VPN tunneling servers will this client attach to if you have configured a site-to-site VPN connecting two LANs? At a minimum you will need information such as IP addresses for the tunneling server. If you use a network diagram, it is not a bad idea to update the drawing, adding the remote client and associated information. An example is shown in Figure 9.4.

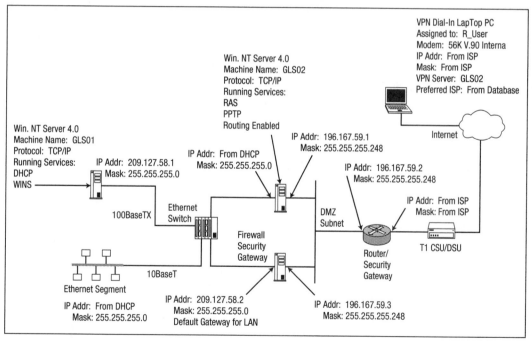

**Figure 9.4**
GLS facility LAN with a remote user.

- List the protocols to be sent over the VPN tunnel (TCP/IP, IPX/SPX etc.).
- Determine what applications are needed, such as email, word processing, spreadsheet, and so forth.
- If your VPN is Novell NetWare based, you should record the location of the user in the tree.
- Next, you should fill out a configuration form for the client equipment. (I advise you to use a separate form for each new client.) As with the previous forms, you can feel free to add any information you feel might be useful, but as a minimum I recommend that you include at least the information shown in Table 9.1.

You need a list of items you require on the workstation to complete the installation and configuration of the VPN software. This may change depending on the type of computer you have and the VPN product you are using. As a minimum this should include the following:

- A computer capable of running Microsoft Windows 98 or your favorite client operating system reliably. Make sure that this computer has a sufficient amount of RAM (64MB recommended), and a Pentium processor (166 MHz or better recommended).
- Microsoft Windows 98, or your favorite client operating system, installed. If you did not install Windows 98 yourself, verify the installation of dial-up-networking. This is the default, but it never hurts to check.
- A high-speed modem (56K V.90 recommended). The modem can be either internal or external, depending on the preferences and capabilities of the user and the computer. The modem should be installed, tested, and working reliably.
- The computer should have a CD-ROM drive or a NIC installed and tested.

**Table 9.1    VPN Client Information Form.**

| Property | Value |
| --- | --- |
| Mfg. | Fujitsu |
| Processor: | Pentium 233 w/mmx |
| RAM: | 32 Meg |
| Operating system: | Win 98 Rel 2 |
| Type of modem: | Internal/Rockwell Chipset/28.8 V.34/(supplied with PC) |
| Modem init string: | Windows default |
| **ISP info (this info must be available for all the ISP's this client will use)** | |
| Access phone Number | 713-860-2898 |
| Interface type | PPP |
| IP address: | From DHCP |
| Mask: | From DHCP |
| Gateway: | Default |
| DNS properties: | PRI Name Server IP Addr: 209.127.0.18 |
| | Sec Name Server IP Addr: 209.127.0.19 |
| Domain name: | Phoenix.net |

# Checklist Number Two: Support Needs

Remember that famous quote from Yogi Berra? "...deja vu all over again." This is the same list we put in Chapters 7 and 8. It is just as important here and you need one for each remote access client.

♦ Software vendor for Windows NT 4, especially if it is a Microsoft Certified Solutions Provider (MCSP):

Name: _____

Company: _____

Phone: (____)_____

♦ Hardware vendor:

Name: _____

Company: _____

Phone: (____)_____

♦ Internet Service Provider:

Name: _____

Company: _____

Phone: (____)_____

♦ PSTN or PDN provider:

Name: _____

Company: _____

Phone: (____)_____

♦ Other support options:

Name: _____

Company: _____

Phone: (____)_____

**Note**

*Before we dive into the actual implementation process, make sure everything up to here is completed and in place. Go back one more time and see that each item is up, running, and configured before you start.*

# Checklist Number Three: Pre-Implementation

You either read Chapters 7 and 8, and you have your VPN servers configured correctly or you don't—we sure hope you did and do. Although the number of items in the pre-implementation process for the client installation is not as involved as for the servers, it is every bit as important. Installing a client is much easier than installing a server, but if installing a client-to-site VPN is a brand new experience for you, we recommend taking time out to set up a test network on a spare computer and go through the implementation process there, first.

Enough of that. Let's get on with the list:

♦ Create a contingency plan, preferably with a time line and point-of-no-return established and share it with the user. This is especially important if you are configuring the user's computer, and the user is doing without in the meantime.

♦ Notify users, especially those on the VPN of interest, that you are working on the network and that service may be interrupted from time to time. Even though you are only installing a client, Murphy may toss a glitch into the system requiring you to reboot the server. Telling people ahead of time may reduce the infernal jangling of the telephone when you have both hands full of troubleshooting charts.

♦ Verify that all hardware, new or rollover (existing), on the client computer is functional and, if necessary, upgraded to meet specifications required. Check the following:

  ♦ Hard drive space

  ♦ NICs

  ♦ RAM

  ♦ Transport media (cables—UTP and fiber-optic)

  ♦ Other features/equipment you have that we don't know about

♦ Check your detailed drawing and make sure that you have assigned an IP address to the network connection on each new item of equipment.

♦ Determine that all equipment involved in the implementation has the proper protocols and addresses assigned.

♦ Make sure that all software to be used, especially Novell NetWare, Microsoft Windows NT, and Novell BorderManager, have all had the latest support packs installed per recommendations by either Novell or Microsoft. For the newest list of recommended upgrades check each vendor's Web site.

♦ If you haven't already done so, upgrade the version of the network clients to the latest recommended by the software vendor. Check for the latest clients at the Web sites for either Microsoft or Novell (or any other vendor whose product you are installing).

**Note**
*The next step is very important because BorderManager makes full use of Novell Directory Services.*

♦ If you are installing the NetWare BorderManager VPN, make sure that the directory is synchronized fully and no directory-related problems exist. Run DSREPAIR on all servers that have a replica of the partition that will contain the BorderManager VPN Servers. A Directory Tree that has problems can cause client problems.

♦ Install and configure the TCP/IP protocol and set up initial routing functions.

♦ Power up the equipment, and run some diagnostics tests to assure yourself that it is all functioning correctly. The goal here is to eliminate as many potential problem sources as possible. The more variables you eliminate, the less tools Murphy has to work with.

Most of the preceding steps apply to the workstations. You still have some configuration steps yet to perform on the BorderManager VPN servers.

## Checklist Number Four: Implementation Procedures

Okay, we have looked at some theory about how this is supposed to work and looked at some similarities and differences between the two products we have chosen as our examples—the only thing left is to apply the Nike principle and *Just Do It*.

One last word before we jump in the water. Remember that in this chapter we are expanding the VPN that we built in the previous two chapters. This means that the VPN tunneling servers located at the LAN end of the VPN tunnel have already been installed and configured, and are up and working in a site-to-site environment. The only time we will make any changes to that end is when it becomes necessary to allow remote users to access the VPN.

The two products really are different, so we will divide this section into two installation checklists, the first for BorderManager, and the second for Windows NT. On with the show.

# The Novell BorderManager VPN

In Chapter 7 you installed the BorderManager VPN software on the NetWare servers and configured two computers for a site-to-site VPN, but did not provide for clients to access the VPN from outside your system. You perform that task from a computer configured as an administrator's workstation and that's where you are going now.

## Configuring A Server For User Access Via The Internet

We assume that you are running Windows 98. Log on as a user with Admin rights in the container where the VPN server you want to configure is located. Then:

1. Click on Start | Run. This opens the Run dialog box as shown in Figure 9.5 (Editor's Note: All screenshots that follow in this section of this chapter are used courtesy of Netware, © 1983–1998, Novell, Inc.).

2. Type in the path shown in Figure 9.5; or as an option, you can click Browse and navigate your way through the path to the Nwadmin32.exe file.

3. Click on OK. The NetWare Administrator program will start, as shown in Figure 9.6.

**Figure 9.5**
Windows 98 Run command dialog box.

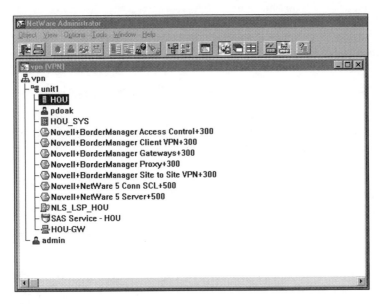

**Figure 9.6**
First Novell network administration screen.

4. Double-click on the server object representing the VPN server. The server property page will open, as shown in Figure 9.7.

5. Click on BorderManager Setup, this will open the BorderManager Setup properties page, as shown in Figure 9.8.

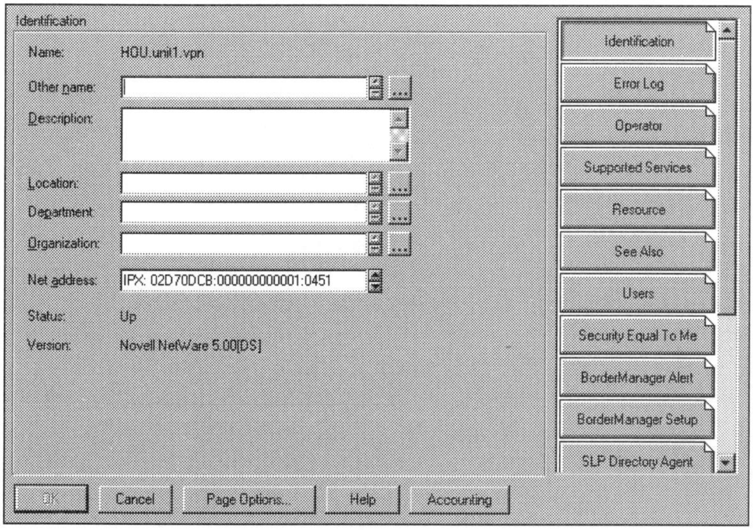

**Figure 9.7**
Server properties page.

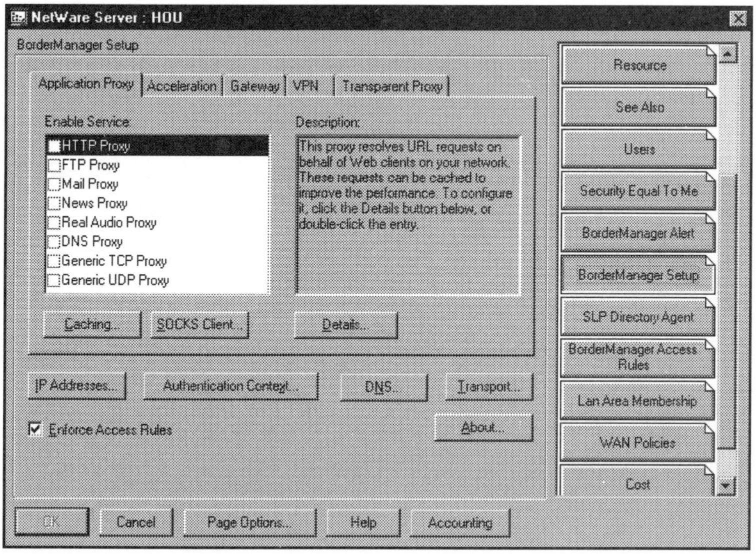

**Figure 9.8**
BorderManager setup screen open to the Application Proxy tab.

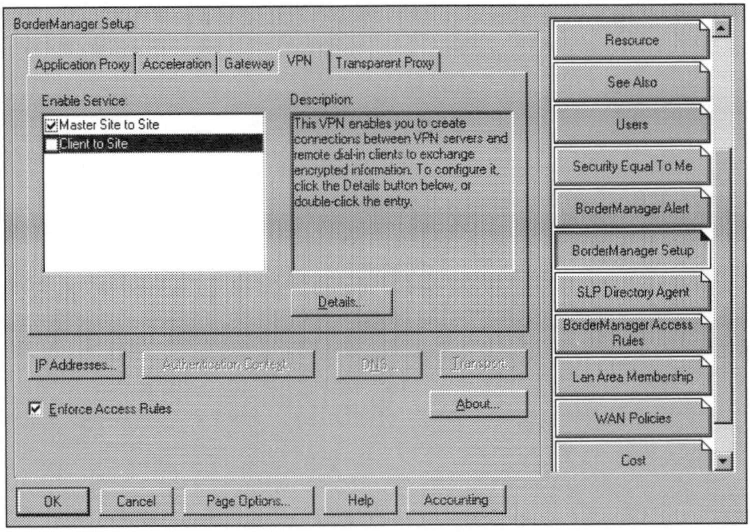

**Figure 9.9**
BorderManager setup screen open to the VPN tab.

6. Click on the VPN Tab. This opens the VPN property page, as shown in Figure 9.9.

7. Place a checkmark in the Client to Site checkbox, and click on Details. This opens the VPN Client details page, as shown in Figure 9.10.

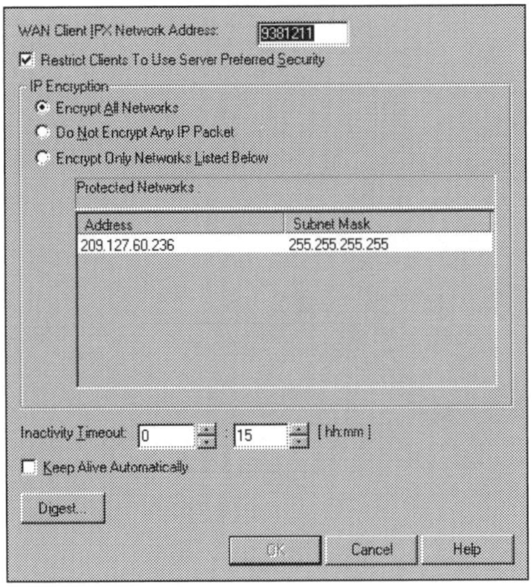

**Figure 9.10**
VPN Client details.

The following configuration items refer to Figure 9.10:

7a. To enable the encryption of IPX data, you must enter a valid IPX network address in the WAN Client IPX Network Address data entry box.

**Note**

*If you enter an address here, it must be a valid, unique IPX address. It cannot be the same IPX address that is already bound to another adapter in the computer. This is the IPX address that will be assigned to the user upon connection to the VPN tunnel. When IPX support is enabled for a VPN client, the client's IPX LAN connection will be disabled when the dial-in VPN IPX connection is established. This is a normal function of the software and also occurs when the dial-up client is not using the VPN.*

7b. If you do not want the client and server to negotiate the data encryption and data authentication methods, you can put a checkmark in the Restrict Clients To Use Server Preferred Security checkbox.

7c. If you want to specify a limited number of networks that the client will be able to access using data encryption, select the Encrypt Only Networks Listed Below radio button. If you select this radio button, you must add the specified networks by clicking the Add icon and entering the specified networks.

**Note**

*By default, IP encryption is enabled for all Networks.*

7d. If you wish, you can select the amount of time allowed before the VPN expires. To do this select the appropriate time in the Inactivity Timeout selection boxes.

7e. If you wish, you can enable the VPN server to send "keep alive" packets periodically. To do this, place a checkmark in the Keep Alive Automatically checkbox.

7f. To view the Information Digest code that is sent to the client, click on the Digest button. You should record this information, as you will need to provide it to the clients for their initial login to this server from a new workstation.

**Note**

*If you are not sure about what configuration to use with any item, I suggest you take the default for now. For the most part, the default settings will work correctly for the largest percentage of users.*

8. When you have configured the VPN client information, click on OK. You will be returned to the VPN property page, as shown in Figure 9.9.

9. Click on the BorderManager Access Rules push button. This will open the BorderManager Access Rules properties page, as shown in Figure 9.11.

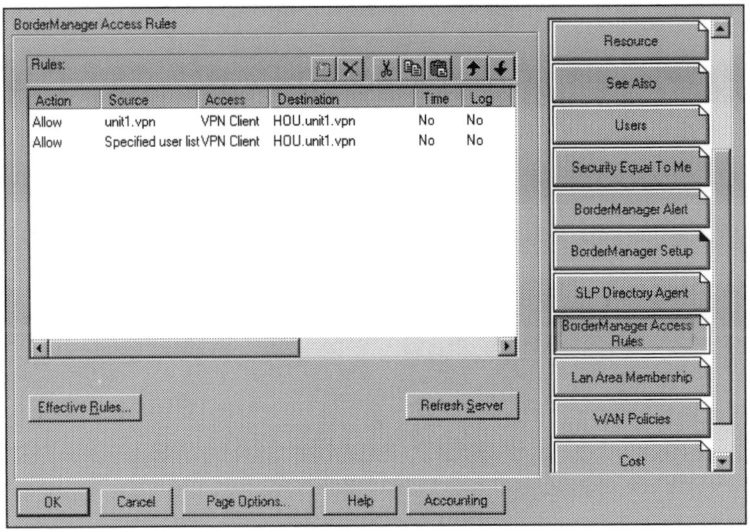

**Figure 9.11**
BorderManager Access Rules properties page.

10. You must now add the users that are authorized to gain access to the network through the VPN. To do this, click on the Add icon to open the Access Rule Definition properties page, as shown in Figure 9.12.

The following configuration items apply to this page. Although you may configure these items any way you wish, our recommended configuration procedure is listed:

10a. Under Action, select the Allow radio button.

10b. Under Access Type, select VPN Client from the selection drop-down menu.

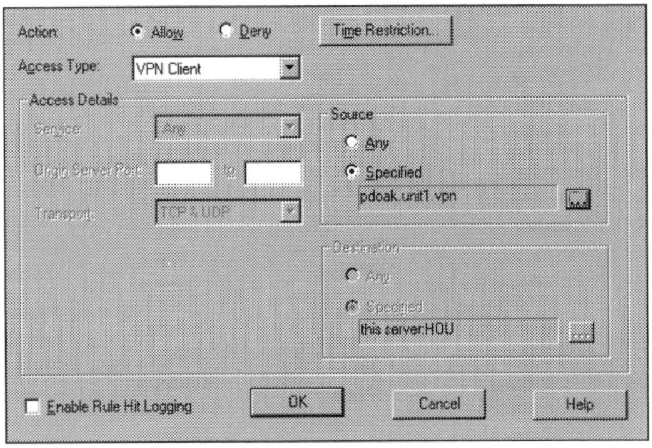

**Figure 9.12**
Access Rule Definition properties page.

10c. In the Source section, select the Specified radio button.

10d. Click on the Browse icon to open the VPN User Specification properties page, as shown in Figure 9.13.

10e. Click on the Add icon to open the Select Object dialog box, as shown in Figure 9.14.

10f. Use the Browse context list to navigate your way through the tree until the object you wish to add is shown in the Available objects window. Select the object you want to add in the Available objects window and click on OK. This returns you to the VPN User Specification properties page, with the object you selected now listed.

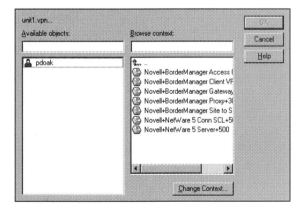

**Figure 9.13**
VPN User Specification properties page.

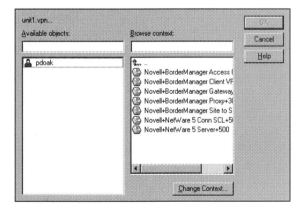

**Figure 9.14**
Select Object dialog box.

10g. If you need to add more objects, repeat the previous two steps until you have all the objects you wish to add. When you have finished adding objects, click on OK. This returns you to the Access Rule Definition property page, with the specified objects listed in the Source dialog box.

10h. When you have completed the Access Rule Definition configuration procedure, click on OK. This returns you to the BorderManager Access Rules properties page, as shown in Figure 9.11, with the new Access Rule listed in the Rules list.

11. When you have completed configuring all the BorderManager Access Rules, click on OK. This activates the new rules at the VPN server, and the screen will return to the NetWare Administrator opening page, as shown in Figure 9.6.

12. Click the Exit icon to close the NetWare Administrator.

You have now completed the procedure of setting up the BorderManager VPN server for client access from the Internet. If you are not the person that will configure the computers that the clients will use, make sure to supply the clients with the following information:

♦ The NDS username and password assigned to each user.

♦ The actual IP address of the VPN server.

♦ If necessary, the Digest of the VPN server security authorization information.

### Installing And Configuring The Client Software

To access the Novell BorderManager Client-to-Site VPN, you must establish a connection to the Internet through an ISP, then load the Novell VPN client. Establishing a connection to the Internet is usually done using Dial-Up Networking Windows 98. In this section we will cover the steps necessary to install the Novell VPN client and create an icon in Dial-Up Networking for connecting to an ISP. This will include the following:

♦ Installing the Novell VPN client

♦ Creating an icon in the Dial-Up Networking group

♦ Configuring Dial-Up Networking

♦ Making the connection

When you installed Windows 98, it included Dial-Up Networking by default.

### Installing And Configuring The Novell VPN Client For Windows 98

To install the Novell VPN Client for Windows 98, use the following procedure:

1. Mount the Novell BorderManager CD in the CD-ROM drive.

2. Click Start | Run to open the Run dialog box, as shown in Figure 9.15.

**Figure 9.15**
Run dialog box.

3. Type in the path as shown in Figure 9.15. As an option you can click Browse and navigate your way through the path to the setup.exe file. Click on OK. This starts the setup program. The Novell Virtual Private Network Client Installation screen will open, as shown in Figure 9.16.

4. Click on Next. The dialog box will change to an information box, as shown in Figure 9.17. Verify that the conditions listed are correct.

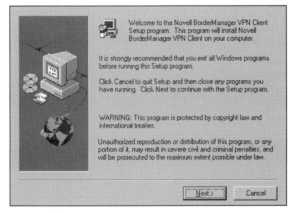

**Figure 9.16**
Novell Virtual Private Network Client Installation screen.

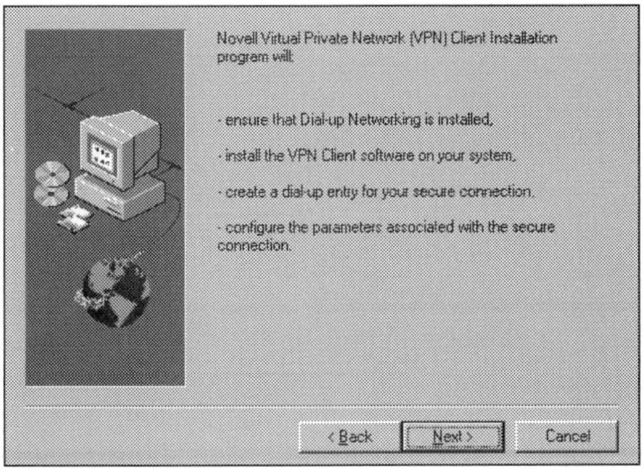

**Figure 9.17**
Installation information screen.

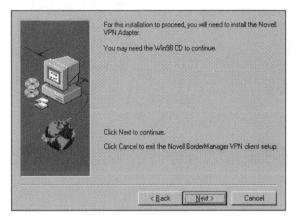

**Figure 9.18**
Notification for need to install VPN adapter.

5. Click on Next. The information in the dialog box will change to that shown in Figure 9.18, informing you that you need to install the Novell VPN adapter, and that you may need the Windows 98 CD.

6. Click on Next. The setup program will perform a file copy operation. After a short period of time an Insert Disk dialog box will open, as shown in Figure 9.19, prompting you to insert the Windows 98 CD-ROM.

7. Click on OK. The Copying Files dialog box will open, as shown in Figure 9.20, prompting you for the path to the Windows 98 files.

8. Enter the path to the Windows 98 files, and click on OK. The dialog box will close, and a new box will open, Figure 9.21, telling you that the VPN client has been installed and you will need to make a new connection in the Dial-Up Networking group.

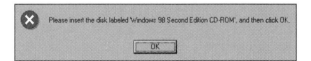

**Figure 9.19**
Request for Windows 98 CD.

**Figure 9.20**
Copying Files dialog box prompting for the path to Windows 98 files.

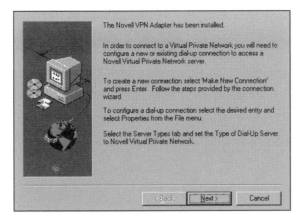

**Figure 9.21**
Novell BorderManager VPN Client Information.

9. When you are ready to continue, click Next. The information dialog box will close, and the Dial-Up Networking group will be opened on the Desktop.

At this point you should proceed to create a Dial-Up Networking icon for the dial-up connection you will use to connect to the ISP. This dial-up connection must use the Novell VPN adapter as the server type.

### Create And Configure A Dial-Up Networking Icon

If you have been following the previous procedures to this point, the dial-up networking panel should be open on your screen and you can skip the next step. Otherwise, click on Start | Programs | Accessories | Communications | Dial-Up Networking. This will open the Dial-Up Networking group, as shown in Figure 9.22.

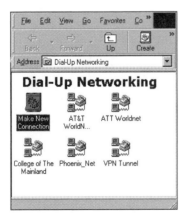

**Figure 9.22**
Dial-Up Networking Control Panel.

With the Dial-Up Networking control panel on your screen follow these steps:

1. If you have *no* dial-up connections configured, the Make New Connection dialog box will automatically open, as shown in Figure 9.23. If you already have one or more dial-up connections configured, double-click on the Make New Connection icon to open the new connection dialog.

2. Type in a name to describe the connection. I don't favor cryptic names, but maybe you do. I would prefer *VPN Link to HOU* over VPN1. After you've entered the name, press the Tab key once to move the cursor to the Select a device drop-down menu. Open the menu and select the modem you want to use for this dial-up connection. The menu will close and your modem will be listed in the Select a device data area, as shown in Figure 9.24.

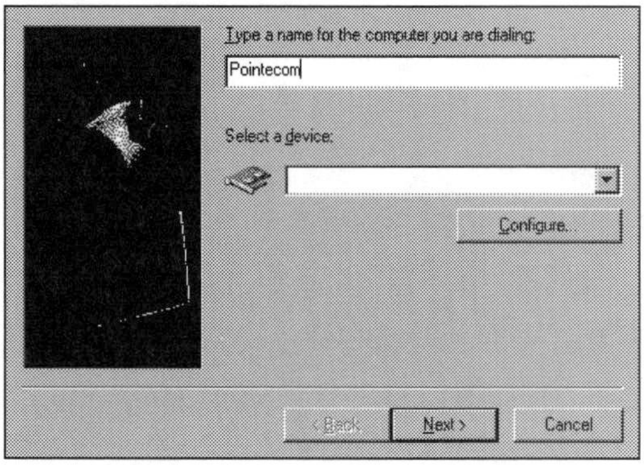

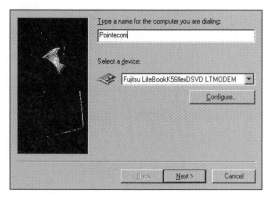

**Figure 9.23**
Make New Connection dialog box.

**Figure 9.24**
Make new connection with device selected.

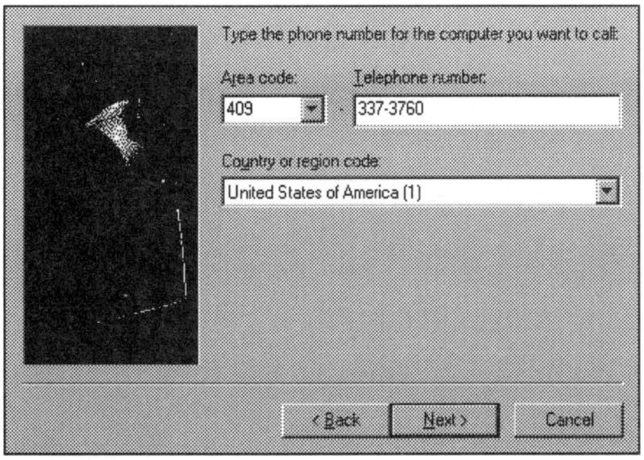

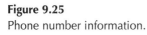

**Figure 9.25**
Phone number information.

3. Click on the Next button to open the Make New Connection dialog box, as shown in Figure 9.25, prompting you for the phone number of the computer you want to call. Don't be confused between the word *computer* and the term *ISP*; in this case they mean the same thing.

4. Consult your ISP information sheet, and fill in the appropriate information. Click on Next. A new dialog box will open, shown in Figure 9.26, informing you that a new dial-up networking connection with the name you assigned has been created.

5. Click on Finish to close the Make New Connection dialog box and return to the Dial-Up Networking group window, as shown in Figure 9.27, and notice that your new connection is now available.

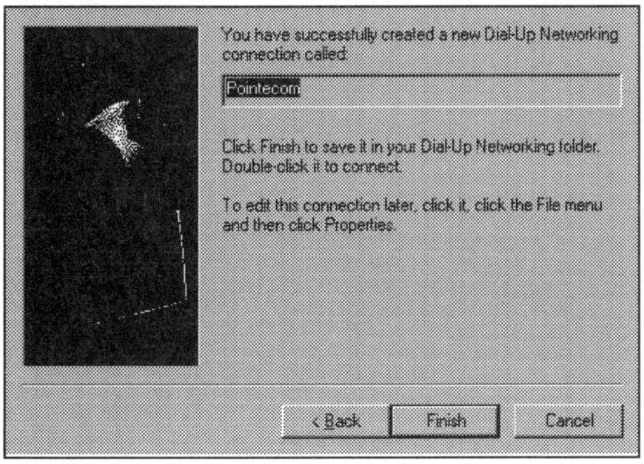

**Figure 9.26**
New connection confirmation.

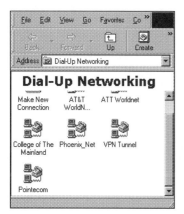

**Figure 9.27**
New connection added to Dial-Up Networking.

**Note**

*At this point you have completed the procedure for adding a new Dial-Up Networking Connection icon, but you still need to configure it.*

### Configuring The Dial-Up Connection Icon

Do this to configure the Dial-Up Networking Connection icon:

1. Point to the dial-up connection you just created, and right-click to open the selection drop-down menu, then left-click on Properties. That opens the Dial-Up Connection properties pages, Figure 9.28, for the new connection.

**Figure 9.28**
Properties pages for new connection.

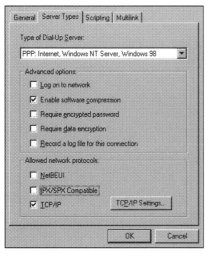

**Figure 9.29**
Server Types properties page.

2. Click on the Server Types tab to open the Server Types properties page, as shown in Figure 9.29.

**Note**

*For a dial-up connection to a BorderManager VPN, the server type must be Novell Virtual Private Network. When you select this server type, all the Advanced Options and Allowed Network Protocols will be grayed out, except for the TCP/IP protocol.*

3. Open the Type of Dial-Up Server drop-down menu, then click on the TCP/IP Settings button to open the TCP/IP properties page, as shown in Figure 9.30.

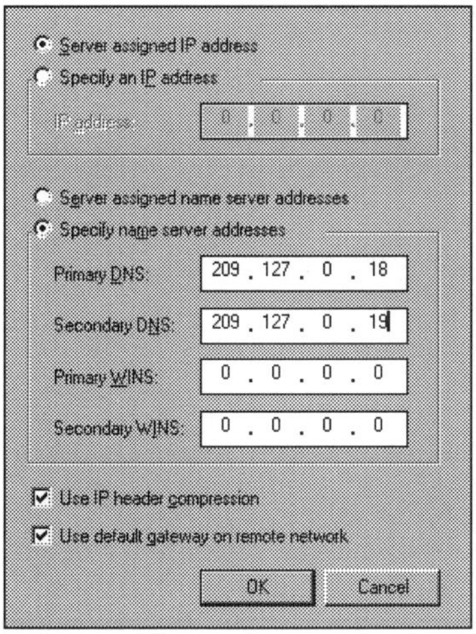

**Figure 9.30**
TCP/IP properties page.

4. Consult your ISP configuration sheet and verify if the called server will assign an IP address. Otherwise, click the Specify name server addresses radio button, and fill in the appropriate information for the primary and secondary DNS servers. Verify that the checkboxes for Use IP header compression, and Use default gateway on remote network, are checked as appropriate. When the TCP/IP properties are filled in correctly, click on OK. This returns you to the Server Types properties page, shown previously in Figure 9.29.

5. Click on OK. The property pages will close and you will be returned to the Dial-Up Networking group, shown in Figure 9.27.

That completes the dial-up-networking configuration.

6. Click on the close box ("X" in the upper-right corner of the dial-up-networking panel) to close the window and return to the Novell Virtual Private Network Client Installation screen, as shown in Figure 9.31.

7. When you are ready to continue, click Next. The Install Novell BorderManager VPN Client dialog box will change, as shown in Figure 9.32, prompting you to enter the type of dial-up connection for the VPN server.

8. Click the Indirect through an ISP radio button to make an Internet connection through an ISP. If you will always be connecting to the same VPN server, consult your configuration sheet and type in the actual IP address for the public interface. On the other hand, if you are going to be using this same configuration to connect to different VPN servers, or you don't have the IP address of the VPN server, you can leave this entry blank, and the software will request an address each time you initiate a connection.

9. When you are ready to continue, click Next. The information in the Install Novell BorderManager VPN Client dialog box will change, as shown in Figure 9.33, and give you the options to View the Readme file and Create a shortcut on the desktop for the VPN login. Both options are selected in the default settings.

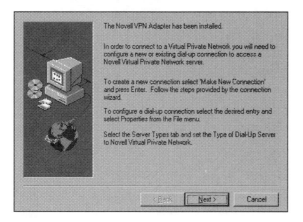

**Figure 9.31**
Novell VPN installation notification.

**Figure 9.32**
Request for connection type.

**Figure 9.33**
This panel is the next to last step in the installation.

10. When you are finished here, click Next to continue and close the box. The Reboot dialog box, as shown in Figure 9.34, displays next, prompting you to restart your computer.

11. To restart your computer, remove any diskettes and/or CD-ROMs from the appropriate drive(s) and click Finish. The setup program will close.

We recommend that you restart before continuing the installation process. (This also is a good time to take a quick beverage break.) If the setup was successful, a Novell Virtual Private Network adapter will appear in the Windows 98 Network control panel when the computer has completed rebooting. Also, if you selected that option, you will have a VPN Login shortcut on the Desktop.

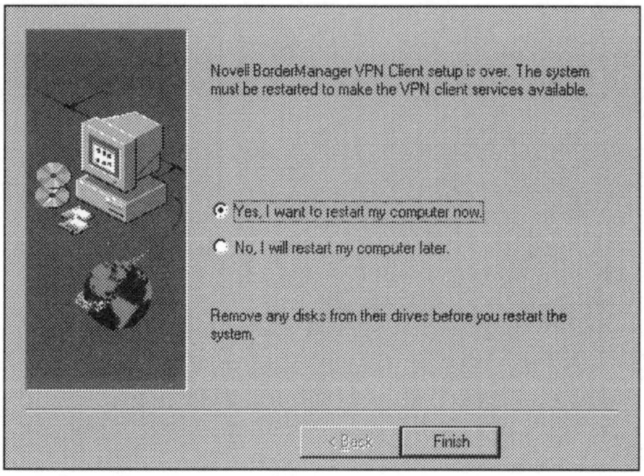

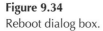

**Figure 9.34**
Reboot dialog box.

Take a bow, you have completed the installation and configuration of the Novell Virtual Private Network Client and the Dial-Up Network configuration!

## Using The Novell VPN Client To Access The VPN Server

I suppose now that you have all this good stuff installed and configured, you are asking what's next. Well, we probably ought to take it for a short ride and see how it works so far. If you have all the proper equipment and you have installed everything up to now as per the instructions, the system should work as advertised.

Access your network with the BorderManager VPN client as follows:

1. Start the Novell VPN Client in one of the following three ways:

   ♦ If you choose to create a VPN Login icon for the Windows Desktop, double-click that icon.

   ♦ Click Start | Programs | Novell | VPN client | VPN Login.

   ♦ Double-click the VPN Dial-Up-Network entry. When the specified connection is established, the Novell VPN Login program is launched.

2. We will assume that you double-clicked the VPN Login icon on the desktop. That action started the VPN Login program and opened the Novell BorderManager VPN Client, as shown in Figure 9.35.

3. Use the information sheet provided from the BorderManager Client Configuration and fill in the following information in the appropriate fields:

   ♦ NDS username

   ♦ NDS password

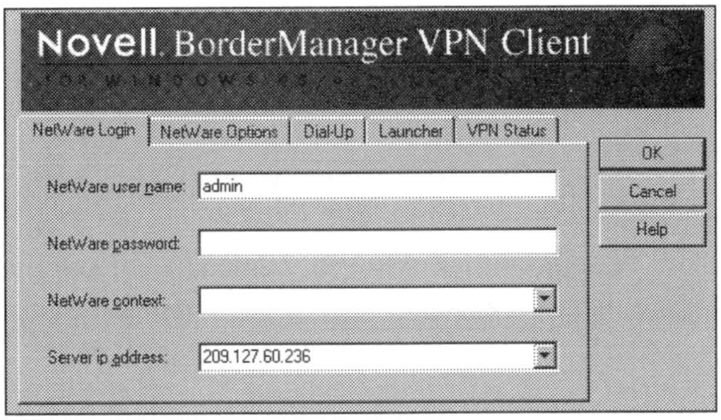

**Figure 9.35**
Opening screen for BorderManager VPN Client.

**Note**

*This username and password may be different from the ISP Internet password.*

- ◆ NDS context
- ◆ VPN server's actual IP address

4. Select the Dial-Up tab and change to the VPN Login Dial-Up property page, as shown in Figure 9.36.

5. Use the configuration information sheet for the ISP and put the following information in the appropriate areas:

- ◆ Name you used when you created a dial-up networking icon.

- ◆ User name assigned by the ISP for the dial-up user.

- ◆ The password assigned by the ISP for the dial-up user. This entry is optional and if used will replace any entry made in a similar area in the Dial-Up Networking entry.

- ◆ One or more phone numbers for accessing the ISP. This entry is optional, and if used, will replace any entry made in a similar area in the Dial-Up Network entry.

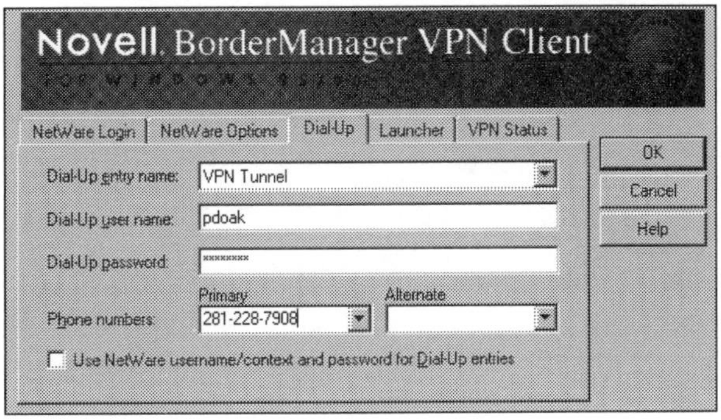

**Figure 9.36**
Entering client dial-up information.

6. If you are using RADIUS to authenticate users, you can automatically use the NetWare username/context and password used in the RADIUS account by placing a mark in the Use NetWare username and password checkbox.

7. When the dial-up property information is correct, click on the NetWare Options tab to open the next page, as shown in Figure 9.37.

8. Here you select from the available options to meet your specific needs. The installation selects all by default. Except for the Enable ipx checkbox, the options are self-explanatory; Enable ipx enables IPX encryption over the VPN. If you don't select this option, you can't use IPX for this VPN session. If you enabled IPX encryption on the VPN server when you went through the configuration process, you should leave this option enabled here.

9. To launch an application after the VPN tunnel is established, you can click on the Launcher tab and go to the Launcher property page shown in Figure 9.38. You can then click the Browse button and navigate through the path and select an application to launch.

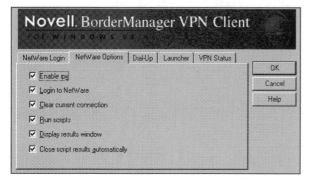

**Figure 9.37**
Properties page for NetWare Options.

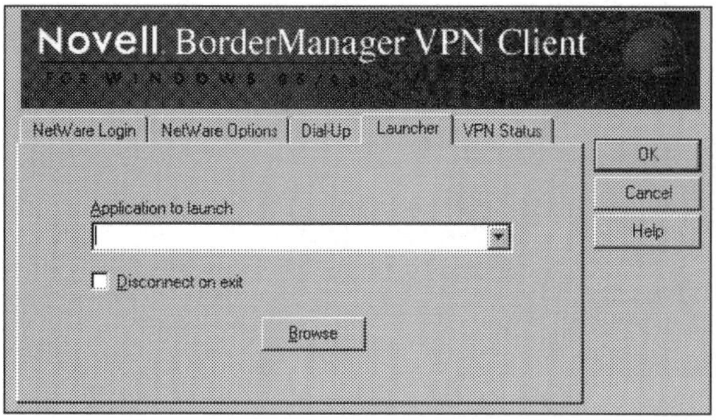

**Figure 9.38**
Properties page for the Launcher.

10. When you have all the information entered correctly, click on OK.

11. If this is the first time that you have connected to this VPN from this workstation, you will be presented with a dialog box containing the digest information from the VPN server. This is the same digest information presented during the VPN server configuration. Hopefully, you recorded the information when you were configuring the server for client access. Verify that it is correct and click on OK.

12. During the initial connection and login process, the Novell VPN Login dialog box will change to the VPN Status tab so you can monitor the progress of the login from this page.

13. After the connection is established and you have logged in to the Tree, the default login script will execute and the VPN Login dialog box will close. The software will create an icon representing the VPN connection and place it in the Taskbar. Double-click on that icon to monitor the VPN statistics.

### BorderManager—The Long And The Slow Of It

The first time or two you make a VPN connection through the Internet you will probably perceive a long delay. Normal operations may seem to take much longer than you would expect. What is happening is that you have just given birth to a new VPN, and the routers between the servers on either end of the tunnel take a while to learn the most direct route from point to point. The delays will diminish; once the route is optimized, the only thing that can have an adverse effect on the operation of the VPN is loading up the bandwidth to maximum and the condition of the routers along the route through the Internet. Give the system at least three days and you'll see the performance improve steadily until it peaks.

Okay, that about wraps up the Novell BorderManager VPN. Let's see what the boys and girls have to offer from Redmond.

# The Windows NT PPTP Connection

A VPN based on Windows NT uses the dial-up network to establish a tunnel even if you're not dialing out using a modem. Because of this, much of the ground we are going to cover in this section has already been covered in Chapter 8 where we installed a site-to-site VPN. The only real difference here is that we are going to set up a dial-up network connection to an ISP, then use that connection to access the Internet. From that point we establish communications with the VPN server and finally create a VPN tunnel.

## Setting Up The Client

Setting up PPTP with Windows 98 can be divided into three procedures:

♦ Verify that the VPN networking routines have been installed from the Windows 98 CD or install them as necessary.

♦ Install the Microsoft Virtual Private Network adapter.

♦ Create and configure a Dial-Up Networking icon to make the connection to the PPTP server.

### Installing The Windows 98 PPTP VPN Client

As we mentioned in Chapter 8, the Microsoft Virtual Private Networking adapter is not one of the standards components when Windows 98 is installed. You need to verify if the adapter was installed and if not, perform the installation procedure. We are going to assume that the VPN adapter is not installed. Follow along with us and if you find you already have a working adapter, skip down to the section titled "Create And Configure A Dial-Up Networking Icon."

If the following steps look familiar, it's probably because you saw them back in Chapter 8 or you've been fiddling with the computer on your own. This is the same procedure as we performed in Chapter 8, so it may look a little familiar:

1. Click Start | Settings | Control Panel. The panel in Figure 9.39 will open on your screen. How you have the preferences set will determine whether you have the HTML format displayed on the left side of the screen as shown in the figure; however, that's not critical. The main stuff is the icon field on the right.

2. Double-click on the Add Remove Programs icon and your screen will look like Figure 9.40.

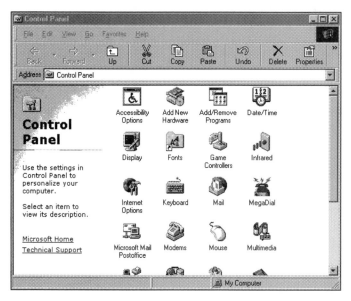

**Figure 9.39**
Windows 98 Control Panel.

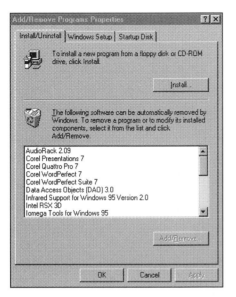

**Figure 9.40**
Add/Remove Programs Properties control panel.

**Figure 9.41**
The Windows Setup tab of the Add/Remove Programs properties Control Panel.

3. Click on the Windows Setup tab to open the Properties page, as shown in Figure 9.41.

4. Use the scrollbar to move through the Components window and select Communications, then click on the Details button. This opens the Communications components dialog box, shown in Figure 9.42.

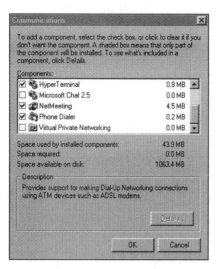

**Figure 9.42**
Communications components dialog box.

5. Using the scrollbar, look through the available components until you locate Virtual Private Networking. If not already checked, check the box for Virtual Private Networking. Click on OK to close the Details window and return to the Add/Remove Program properties Control Panel, shown in Figure 9.41. Click on OK to close it.

6. If you checked Virtual Private Networking, an Insert Disk dialog box will open, as shown in Figure 9.43, informing you that you need to insert the Windows 98 CD. Otherwise, you can skip down to the "Installing Microsoft VPN Adapter" section.

7. Click on OK and open a Copying Files dialog box like the one in Figure 9.44. If the default path shown for the location of the Windows 98 Installation Files is not correct, type in the correct path. If you are copying the files from the Windows 98 CD, insert the CD in the CD-ROM drive at this time and click on OK. The file copy procedure will start.

**Figure 9.43**
Disk request panel.

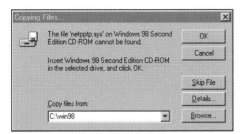

**Figure 9.44**
Copying Files dialog box

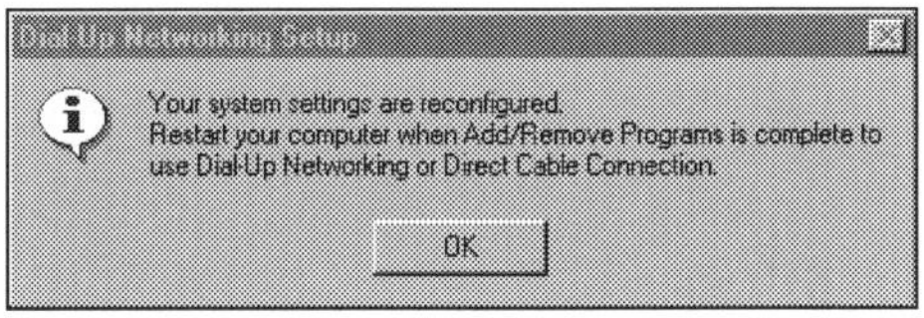

**Figure 9.45**
Dial-Up Networking Setup information box.

8. After the first of the files have been copied, a Dial-up Networking Setup information box will open, as shown in Figure 9.45, informing you that after the Add/Remove Programs has completed you will need to restart your computer before proceeding with the Dial-Up Networking configuration.

9. Click on OK and the remaining files will be copied. After the file copy procedure has completed, the Add/Remove Programs properties window will close, and the Control Panel will become active. Remove any diskettes and/or CDs and restart the computer.

### Installing Microsoft VPN Adapter

You have now either installed or verified that the Microsoft Virtual Private Networking components are active in your client machine. The next step is to install the Microsoft Virtual Private Network adapter, if it isn't already in the system:

1. Click Start | Settings | Control Panel. Double-click on the Network icon (Figure 9.39) to open the Network Control Panel, shown in Figure 9.46.

2. Scroll through the list for Microsoft Virtual Private Networking Adapter. If it is already installed, you can skip the rest of this section. Otherwise, click the Add button to open the Select Network Component Type dialog box shown in Figure 9.47.

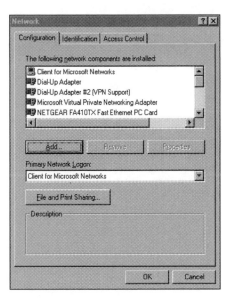

**Figure 9.46**
Network Control Panel.

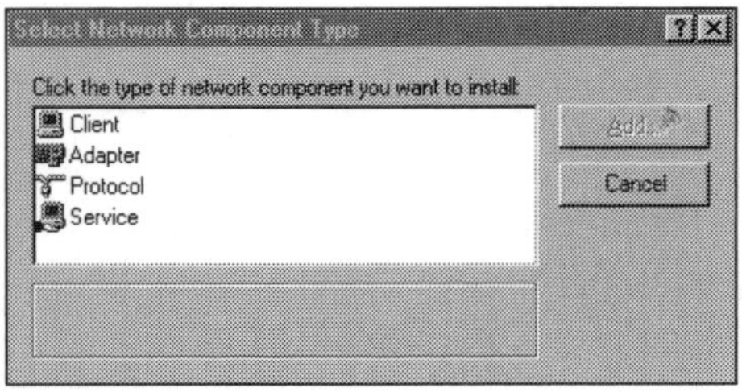

**Figure 9.47**
Select Network Component Type dialog box.

3. Select Adapter, then click Add to open the Select Network adapters dialog box shown in Figure 9.48.

4. In the left-hand window, scroll through the list of manufacturers, then click on Microsoft. This opens the list of Microsoft Network Adapters in the right-hand window, as shown in Figure 9.49.

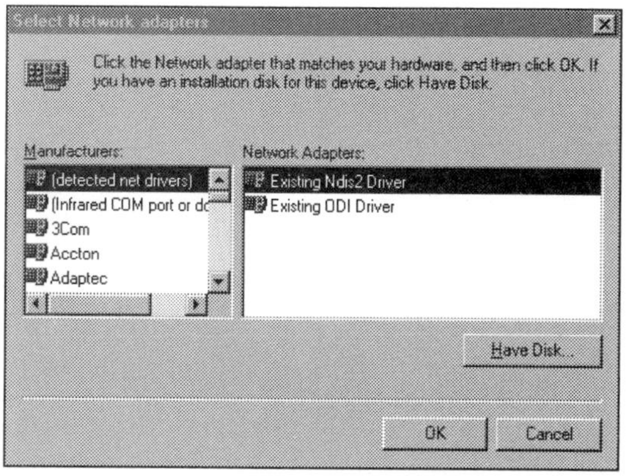

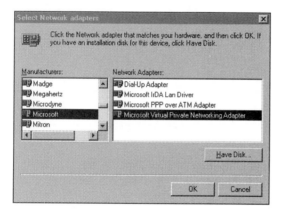

**Figure 9.48**
Select Network adapters dialog box.

**Figure 9.49**
Selecting Microsoft as manufacturer and VPN as adapter.

5. Select Microsoft Virtual Private Networking Adapter in the right-hand window, then click on OK to return to the Network Control Panel. Click on OK to close the Network Control Panel. This opens a System Settings Change information box, as shown in Figure 9.50, informing you that the settings will not take place until the computer is restarted. Click Yes to restart the computer.

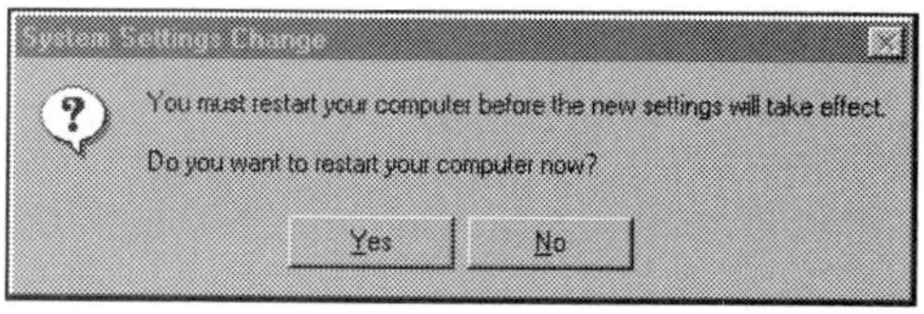

**Figure 9.50**
System Settings Change information box.

That completes the installation of a Microsoft Virtual Private Networking adapter for Windows 98.

### *Create And Configure A Dial-Up Networking Icon*

Are we having fun yet? You are almost there. This section is easy enough, but it does require some thinking on your part:

1. Click | Start | Programs | Accessories | Communications | Dial-Up Networking to open the Dial-Up Networking group, as shown in Figure 9.51.

2. If you have no dial-up connections at this time, the Make New Connection dialog box will automatically open, as shown in Figure 9.52. If you already have one or more dial-up connections configured, double-click on the Make New Connection icon to open the new connection dialog.

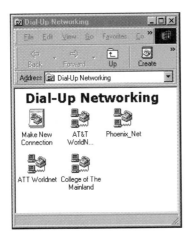

**Figure 9.51**
Dial-Up Networking group.

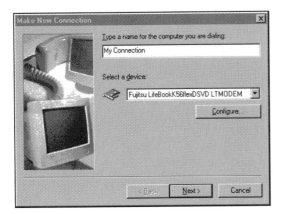

**Figure 9.52**
Make New Connection dialog box.

3. Type in any name you want to use to describe the connection. We could be cryptic and use just VPN-1 or be verbose and name it Vintage Air, Galveston Facility. Use whatever name you want—I think it would help if it were the name of the network or computer on the other end of the VPN tunnel. After you've entered the name, press the Tab key once and the cursor will move to the Select a device data area. Open the drop-down menu to the right of the data area and click on Microsoft VPN Adapter. The Microsoft VPN adapter should be selected in the data area as shown in Figure 9.53.

4. Click on the Next button to open the Host name or IP address data entry area, as shown in Figure 9.54

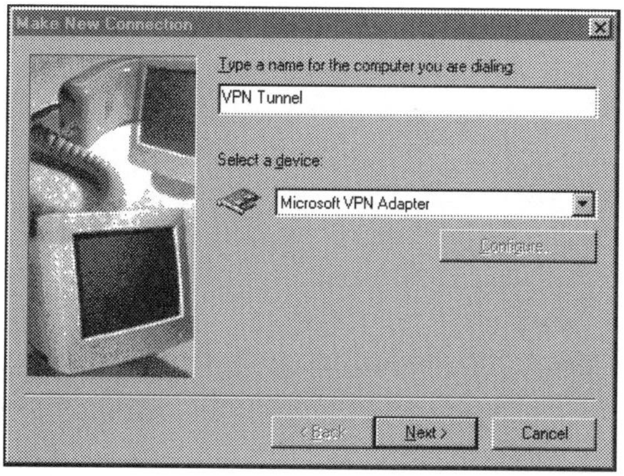

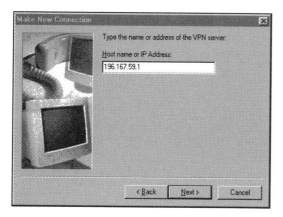

**Figure 9.53**
Dial-up computer and device selected.

**Figure 9.54**
Host name or IP address entered.

5. Type in the IP address of the computer you are making a connection to on the other end of the VPN tunnel. If you have made a DNS entry for the *host name* for that computer, you can enter that, then click on Next. This opens the Make New Connection information screen, shown in Figure 9.55, telling you that a new Dial-Up Networking connection with the name you assigned has been created.

6. Click on Finish to close the Make New Connection dialog box and open the Dial-Up Networking group window in Figure 9.56, showing the new connection.

That was almost too easy. In case you haven't figured it out, you are not restricted to the number of dial-up connections you create.

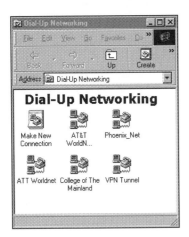

**Figure 9.55**
New connection is complete.

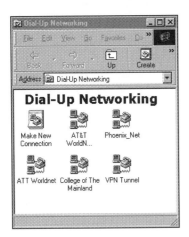

**Figure 9.56**
VPN tunnel connection added to Dial-Up Networking.

## *Configuring The VPN Dial-Up Connection Icon*

Now it's time to deal with the icon and wrap up this Microsoft stuff:

1. Right-click on the VPN Dial-Up Connection you created. Click on Properties; this opens the dialog box for the connection you have created, as shown in Figure 9.57.

2. Click on the Server Types tab to open the Server Types dialog box, as shown in Figure 9.58.

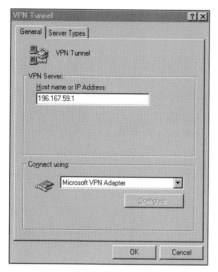

**Figure 9.57**
Entering connection properties for VPN.

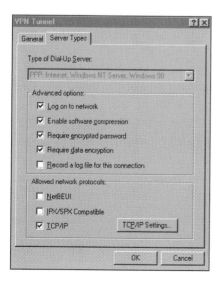

**Figure 9.58**
Server Types dialog panel.

3. In the Advanced option area, make sure the Require Encrypted Password and Require Data Encryption checkboxes are checked—the rest are optional and can be checked as desired.

4. In the Allowed network protocols area, make sure that the TCP/IP checkbox is checked (it is required).

5. Click on the TCP/IP Settings button to open the dialog box shown in Figure 9.59.

6. If you want the ISP to assign an IP address, verify that the Server assigned IP address radio button is selected. If you want to assign a specific IP address, then click or select the Specify an IP address radio button, and enter a valid IP address.

7. If you want the ISP to assign an address for the name server, verify that the Server assigned name server address radio button is selected. If you want to use a specific name server address, select the Specify name server address radio button, and enter the IP address of at least one DNS or WINS server that will be accessible to this computer.

8. If your ISP can support IP header compression and you want to use the default gateway on the remote system (these are the defaults), then leave the appropriate checkboxes checked.

9. When the TCP/IP configuration is correct, click on OK twice.

At this point you have created and configured a dial-up interface to connect to the PPTP server. You can, for your convenience, create a shortcut to this interface and put it on your Windows Desktop.

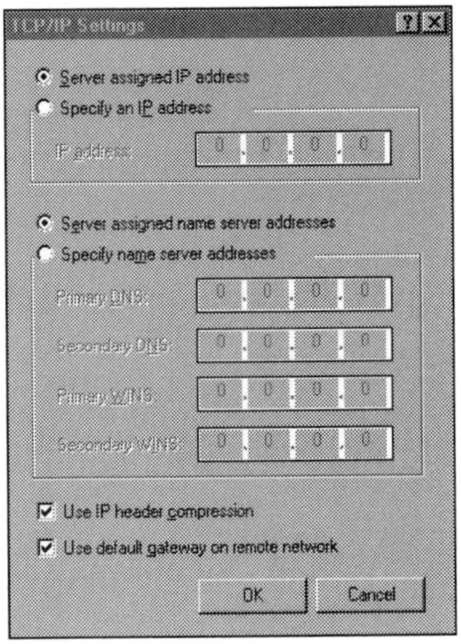

**Figure 9.59**
TCP/IP Settings dialog box.

# Using The Windows VPN Client To Access The VPN Server

Okay, so now that we've got it, how do we use it? Using the Microsoft Windows PPTP VPN is straightforward. Only two steps are required:

♦ Establish a connection to the ISP using the normal dial-up procedure.

♦ Use the dial-up network VPN connection to establish communications with the PPTP VPN server and make a secure connection to the NT network.

## Establish A Connection To The ISP

Do this to establish a connection the ISP:

1. Double-click on the appropriate connection icon in the Dial-Up Network group (or on the Desktop if you have a shortcut) for the ISP you wish to use to initiate the client end of the VPN. This opens the Connection dialog box, as shown in Figure 9.60.

2. Fill in the appropriate user name and password, and change the other information as necessary, then click on Connect. This initiates the connection and starts the modem dial sequence. An information dialog box will open, as shown in Figure 9.61, informing you of the progress of the connection.

3. When a connection has been established, the information dialog box will close and the Connection Monitor icon will appear in the Taskbar.

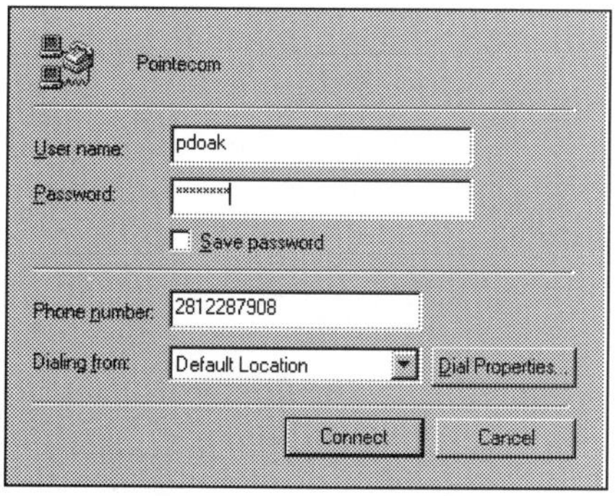

**Figure 9.60**
Connection dialog box.

**Figure 9.61**
Connection status box.

At this point you have established a dial-up network connection to the ISP. Now you will establish communications with the PPTP VPN server. Do this:

1. Double-click on the appropriate connection icon in the Dial-Up Network group (or on the Desktop if you have a shortcut) for the PPTP VPN tunnel connection. This opens the Connect To dialog box for the PPTP VPN connection, shown in Figure 9.62.

2. Verify that the information is correct, then click on Connect to initiate the connection and start the VPN tunnel development sequence. An information dialog box will open, as shown in Figure 9.63, displaying the progress of the connection.

3. With the connection established, the screen will display the profile the administrator has established for you on the Windows NT server. A second connection monitor icon will appear in the Taskbar—the first is for the dial-up connection to the ISP, and the second is for the PPTP VPN connection.

You have now established a secure connection to the Windows NT server through the PPTP tunnel. To disconnect from the PPTP VPN, double-click on the Connection Monitor icon in the Taskbar. An information dialog box will open displaying the statistics of the connection. To disconnect, click on Disconnect.

What you do from here, of course, depends on why you established the connection. Within reason you can perform any tasks. You will need to keep in mind that your connection to the network is now running at modem speed, which will have a drastic effect on the performance of some programs. We will cover this a little more in depth in the troubleshooting section that follows.

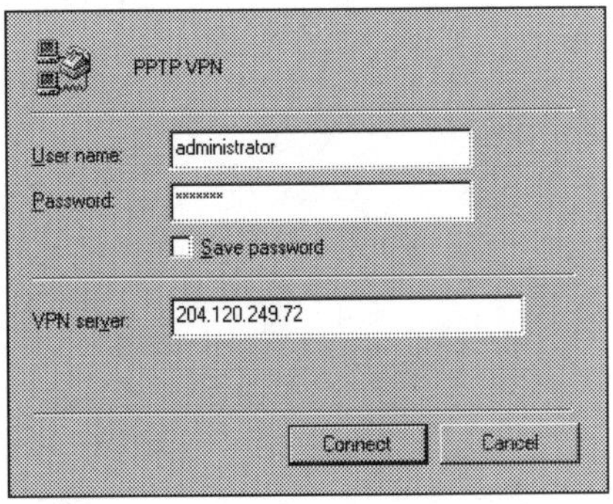

```
                  PPTP VPN

User name:    administrator

Password:     *******

              ☐ Save password

VPN server:   204.120.249.72

                        [ Connect ]   [ Cancel ]
```

**Figure 9.62**
Dialog box for entering connection information.

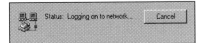
Status: Logging on to network...   [ Cancel ]

**Figure 9.63**
Connection progress report.

## Checklist Number Five: Post-Implementation

Now is the time to go back and undo any temporary patches you may have put in place during the client installation. Some items to remember at this point include the following:

♦ If your operating system is BorderManager running on NetWare, perform a check of the Directory Tree and make sure no problems exist there.

♦ If you have a BorderManager Site-to-Site VPN, as well as a Client-to-Site VPN, run NWAdmin from a workstation and verify that the master server and all slave servers are synchronized correctly.

♦ If you are using Windows NT 4, and you have added any new features on the NT server, go back and reinstall the Windows NT Service Pack 4. This must be reinstalled each time new features are added to the NT server.

♦ If you are using BorderManager and have not done so yet, install the latest Support Pack. Read the technical document for each support pack, and upgrade any other necessary items, including VPN clients and snap-ins for NWAdmin on all the NetWare servers.

♦ Remove any temporary cable patches, temporary hubs, switches, and routers you may have needed for the installation.

♦ In configuring the NetWare Server to support BorderManager, Novell assumed the server would be used as a firewall and that users would not log onto the server. For the most part this is correct; however, an exception can happen when using the newly released BorderManager VPN Client for a secure connection from the BorderManager server to your remote user's computer. In this case change the Set parameter on both the master and slave VPN servers to: SET REPLY TO GET NEAREST SERVER = ON, and login to the BorderManager VPN server using the VPN client.

# Remote User Administration

Now that you have the VPN client software installed and checked out, you need to set up a schedule of administrative tasks to perform on a regular basis. We are going to cover overall administration more thoroughly in Chapter 11, so in this chapter let's discuss the basics for the administrative tasks that apply to the remote users. Rather than put this in the form of a checklist, I am going to make some suggestions based on information that I have picked up over the years.

One thing that needs to be developed, if it's not already in place, is a system of logging problems and complaints—and, of course, the applied fixes. Because your remote users fall into a unique category, it is a good idea to open a separate section of the help desk reporting database just for them. It may not be feasible for your particular installation if you only have two or three telecommuters and road warriors. On the other hand, if you have 15 or 20— one company I know of has 2,000—remote users, a separate service makes perfect sense.

The support staff must understand that they log all problems as soon as they are reported. It's not enough just to log the problems; the entire administrative team needs to develop a habit of checking the problem logs when they first come to work. Make it your first order of business.

Back in the dark ages, the support staff maintained the logs in real paper books. That's not really necessary any more, in fact, much better ways of logging problems are waiting for you at your local software store. Several companies sell good Help Desk software packages to maintain logs of reported problems. You can then use the logs for tracking and statistical analysis to decide on improvements in applications and training procedures. If you do this, you are investing in proactive maintenance, not waiting for the reactive incidents.

## Laptop Computer Issues

Other than the steady diet of restaurant food and the lumpy hotel beds, one problem that road warriors universally share is the need for a laptop computer. The laptop computer presents an entire list of new problems from both the support side and the admin side.

### Software Updates

One of the big problems with laptops is software updates. You won't have problems performing periodic upgrades of the applications software on a conventional desktop—especially if the software is loaded on a server and shared among users. But a remote user with a laptop is a whole new ball game. To begin with, have you ever tried to launch MS Word from a server to a laptop—over a 56K modem? Good luck! Okay, so the remote/traveling users need to carry their apps around on their laptop. That's no problem. Today's laptops come with hard disk storage that is adequate for the task and, except for the user's guides, the applications don't add any weight to the system. They do carry the user's guides with them, don't they? To use as the first reference source when they have problems? They do, don't they?

But what about the latest patch for MS Word that you (the administrator) downloaded from **www.support.microsoft.com**. How do you get this patch to the remote user? Obviously, you need to find out what the road warrior's work schedule is. You (the administrator) are going to need to track down the users, get their schedules, and train them to work closely with the computer support group. Then you can plan on grabbing their laptops on their next trip back to the office. You need to make it a point to everyone, *especially* the remote/traveling user, that upgrades are a vital necessity. Your software must be as user consistent as you can possibly keep it.

### Data Backups

The next big problem with laptops is data backup. Most of the backup software on the market today will back up data from desktop clients as easily as backing up data off file servers. The situation changes when the desktop grows legs and walks out the door to go to

Cut 'N Shoot. The regularly scheduled backup procedure on the LANs doesn't mean much in a motel room several hundred miles away, does it? When you try to back up the hard disk drive in the laptop computer over a 56K modem you encounter the same problem you had when you tried to launch MS Word.

Here's one solution. First, create an area on the file server in which the road warriors can store their data files. I suggest you avoid using their home directory for this, because you will want to go into this area periodically and purge the outdated files. Load a backup software package on the laptop computer and configure it to back up critical data from the laptop to the preassigned storage area on the server. You can write a backup script that assigns a seldom-used drive letter to the user's data storage area and automate the process so the road warrior has only to perform a simple mouse-click on the desktop. *Bingo*—the data is backed up in the time it takes to go down the hall for a soda.

Configure the laptop's backup software to only back up data files that have been changed since the last complete backup. Most of the time, the amount of changed data is very small compared to the total amount of data on the laptop. One last thing, train remote/traveling users to turn in their laptops when they get back to the office so that a complete backup of all the files on the hard drive can be performed. Each time a complete backup is performed, you (the administrator) will purge all the incremental backups that the user performed on the road.

All this may seem like a lot of work, but the alternative of trying to recoup even one day's work because it wasn't backed up... well, think about it. With some good planning, encouragement for the users, and a little practice, backing up the data will become an ordinary event.

### Airport Security Scanners

What about the scanners used at airports to scan luggage? Will they harm a laptop computer? I don't know a single individual who likes to take out their laptop and have it inspected every time they go through an airport. Don't misunderstand me. I'm not saying some security measures are not necessary—they are, and I support them. But do the security personnel really have to inspect laptops separately? Why can't they just trust the baggage scanners?

I get mixed opinions when I ask people about this. The airport security people that run the scanners and the manufacturers of the scanners say that running your laptop computer through a scanner will not harm it or the data in it. Most support technicians I have talked to laugh when I tell them that—most of them say that if their users run their laptops through a scanner they will not be responsible for the results. Then I read one advisory that said although the X-ray machine won't cause any damage, we would be wise to consider the magnetic fields surrounding the motors that drive the conveyor belts. So what's the user to do? I think your company should research the issue and establish its own policy. As some help, I offer this opinion, and it is entirely my own.

Most laptop computers cost between $900 and $4,000. One of us—two co-authors are writing this book—owns a personal laptop that cost $1,700; he's a middle-of-the-road guy. He also knows a bit about physics and electronics. Based on that knowledge and information that we've both read, the manufacturers and airport security people seem to be truthful: Nothing in that scanner will harm a laptop computer. So, when he goes through an airport security point, does he let them scan his laptop? *Absolutely NOT*. He says, "Not until I hear more service technicians say they don't mind carrying theirs through will I put my laptop computer on the belt. Now, I do carry floppy diskettes and Zip disks in my laptop computer case and I put that case through the scanner. To this date I have never had a single problem with any of those floppies or Zip disks."

The other one of us also owns a medium-priced laptop but refuses to pass his machine down the belt for a totally different reason. More than ten percent of all laptop thefts occur at airports. In case you haven't heard of the problem, here's how it works. A pair of thieves marks a potential victim. One thief passes through the security checkpoint and waits on the other side as the second gets in the line immediately ahead of the victim. After the conveyor belt whisks away the victim's laptop into the belly of the scanner, the second steps into the magnetic detector portal with something in a pocket that sets off the alarm. During the ensuing delay, the first thief retrieves the laptop on the other side and quietly wanders away into the crowds. This ploy has worked even in those airports that require you to open the laptop for visual inspection.

A second version of airport thefts doesn't even involve the scanner portals. The road warrior with the laptop stacked on top of his roll-about luggage is the target of a pair of thieves. Once will walk in front of the victim and either stop or collide with him. During the distraction and delay, the second will come up behind and pluck the laptop off the luggage and disappear. And, no, strapping it to the luggage won't protect you—a carton knife will slice through the straps in less than one second. So, what's the answer? You be the judge. What's the value of the data and how can it be protected?

## Maintaining A List Of ISPs

Now we get to the fun stuff. How in the world do you maintain a list of ISPs for those remote users who roam all over the country and maybe even the world? You can face the problem with a few different approaches. We will look at some and hopefully provide you with some necessary information.

### The All-In-One ISP Vs. The Independent ISP

One solution is go with an ISP that has more or less global connections. Two examples are AT&T WorldNet and GTE Net. Both are global service providers with local Internet access through dial-up POPs in almost every major city in the U.S.A. and around the world. If you cannot find a local number, both have toll-free numbers. However, you might be surprised by an additional service charge on your Internet bill for using the *toll-free* service connection. Both AT&T and GTE provide you with toll-free (no additional charge) numbers you can use to find out the access number for the nearest dial-in POP, or you can visit their Web sites and use a search utility to get the information.

But do they support PPTP and IPSec VPNs? Yes and no. Almost any current router will support encapsulated IP datagrams, and the global ISPs have fairly new equipment. The only problem you may encounter is if you want the ISP's router to perform the encapsulation functions. You might have problems also if you want to use the advanced accounting and billing features in Cisco's L2TP software. In some cases you may need to be a little pickier about your ISP. Also, keep in mind that the more bells and whistles you want, the higher the cost.

### The Independent ISP

The Internet has been responsible for the greatest birth of independent small businesses seen in a long time. Almost everywhere you look, small independent ISPs are competing for your business. They all want your business, and they are doing everything they can to give you the best level of service possible in order to capture and keep it. Most independent ISPs have one thing that makes them more attractive than the larger major players: They cost less. Their pricing is very attractive for a company with one to ten users that need Internet access. Where the problems arise is when those users are road warriors, and travel outside the independent ISP's local POP. These problems revolve around issues dealing with gaining local access, tracking billing, and service issues.

### The Access Charge Dilema

The problem with using independent ISPs for Internet access is, of course, that few of them have the resources necessary to provide independently Internet access outside their local POP. Talking with different ISP operators about this dilemma, I learned that the majority of them are members of state, national, or international organizations. ISP members of these organizations are willing to work with each other to provide their clients local access in other cities and provide you with a list of cooperating services. The problem then becomes one of tracking access times and making sure the proper ISP gets paid. Obviously, you are going to pay the independent ISP a fee for this extra service.

For a list of the organizations of ISPs, as well as information on where you might locate an ISP database that may help get you started, check the Web site **www.sldenterprises.com**.

### Building And Maintaining An ISP Database

Regardless of where the information comes from, your traveling users need a database of valid ISP providers. IndusRiver Software has a service that compiles a database periodically of ISP sites, access fees, charges, and access telephone numbers. To my knowledge, this list is available only for use with IndusRiver RiverWorks software. However it would be worth looking into to see what it would take to make this available as a third-party option.

Your network support group can round up a list. The task is to make arrangements with ISPs in different cities, and distribute an Internet access database to the remote users. You trade the extra service fee charged by your ISP for an additional load on your overhead. It is your responsibility to determine which is the most cost-effective solution.

This book is dedicated to real products that are on the shelf and available as we write it. So all I can say is that the rumors give the new software a built-in address feature to acquire ISPs and their access numbers from a database and place it into the BorderManager Client 32. Unfortunately, this new client made it to the public a little too late for a good evaluation, but this promises to be a very nice feature. As mentioned earlier, this new client is available for download from **www.novell.com/download/**.

Of course, someone still has to gather the information to put in that database. Various ISP organizations provide lists of their members that you could convert to a flat-file or even a Client-Server database. However, someone still has to do this. Currently, unless you are using a specific third-party VPN solution, such as an IndusRiver product, that chore must be done by someone on staff or contracted out. I have a hunch that in the near future some hard-charging enterprise will develop a commercial version of the list and market it to businesses with VPN capability.

### Developing A Script That Will Auto Download The Database Update

The other thing that can go a long way toward a successful VPN deployment is a script to download automatically the latest updated ISP database when the remote user makes a connection to headquarters. Windows NT and BorderManager Client 32 can launch a resident program immediately after the connection has been established. You can use almost any scripting language to create a script that will automatically compare the last dates of two files and download the server file if it is the newer one.

If for some reason you can't develop a script of your own, check the Web site at **www.sldenterprises.com.** If you find one there, you have our permission to download it for use in your network or on any of your road warriors' machines.

That about touches all the bases as far as remote user administration goes. Like most things that deal with computer operations, the list of network administration tasks is constantly changing—and, like the Internet itself, it is constantly growing. We have just scratched the surface here, but I think we gave you enough to get you started.

The next stop is also an important one—what you need to plan for in the way of troubleshooting for the remote user; for instance, making sure he or she has user's guides for all their apps.

# Troubleshooting The Remote User

Notice the title of this section is "Troubleshooting The Remote User" and not the remote user's laptop or PC. A saying in the computer service industry goes something like "*The problem's not fixed until the user says it's fixed.*"

It has also been said (mostly by the techies) that troubleshooting computer problems is largely a function of troubleshooting the user. I tend to think both statements are fairly accurate, though I encourage my students not to use them in the company of most users. Of course, PCs do fail, along with all other manner of hardware. Hardware problems are encountered routinely and this is not the place to discuss them. As I did with administration, I would like to use this section to concentrate on those problems that will affect the remote user other than blown memory chips and cranky hard drives. While we're at it, let's discuss how to implement the best level of support possible.

In this section, we are going to lay the foundation for what's coming in Chapter 11. Before I can cover the details, I feel it's important to develop an idea about what type of problem you can expect to find in dealing with the remote users, and what kind of general procedures I think you ought to have in place for dealing with those problems. Then in Chapter 11 we'll look at troubleshooting specific problems.

## Before We Start, Some Troubleshooting Theory

Troubleshooting any type of complex technical system involves three fundamental areas:

- *Knowledge of the product*—To troubleshoot something you must possess a good fundamental knowledge of what you are working with, how it is supposed to work, and how to put it together or configure it. Knowledge of a product is gained only through experience working with that product; reading the books will only get you started. To learn any product, you must work with it.

- *Logical thinking*—The ability to take a process and break it down into the steps necessary to move data from the input stage to the output stage. Many people call it intuition, other call it just plain dumb luck. I call it paying attention to details. Whatever you call it, it is this ability that separates the successful professional techies and network administrators from the wannabes.

- *Good tools*—Tools are used to help you analyze the product to try and show you places where possible problems may exist. The tools you use in troubleshooting technical systems are varied, and not all of them are used by the support tech.

The only time you will see some road warriors is when they drop by the shop to leave or pick up their laptops. A few will call you almost daily with some gripe or another. Fortunately, the greatest majority are in the middle ground. When a user first starts out on the road, you can't expect them to help solve their own problems. But it won't take too many problem calls from hotel rooms before the good users start to understand that they are the ones in the hotel room with a downed system, not you. One of the most powerful tools in your arsenal to help the users overcome their problems is training. As many times as I have mentioned training in this book, you probably have figured out by now that I am a believer in training. I believe that if you don't have a regular training schedule established where you work, you should talk to your boss about getting one started, and the sooner the better.

At the beginning of this chapter I said that one of the things you will need to do is figure out how to move your support site to the remote users site in a virtual sense. This is perhaps the most difficult task in providing troubleshooting service for the remote user. In the rest of this chapter we are going to look at various ways of doing that. We do not by any means profess to have all the answers for troubleshooting remote users. I do have a certain amount of experience, and we do have a certain knowledge of the product we are dealing with. Along the way we are going to mention some of the tools you will find useful.

### Using The Available Help On The Computers

The first troubleshooting tool is the laptop or PC in front of the user. Windows 9x (98 especially), Windows NT, and the Macintosh all provide very good help for resolving problems with OS-associated operations. In addition, Windows and Mac help systems allow the third-party software developers to provide software help files with the same look and feel as the OS. This makes a uniform help system that with a little training is informative, helpful, and easy to use. From the standpoint of the computer support group, here are some suggestions you should think about implementing:

♦ Regularly scheduled training sessions designed especially for the remote user. Use these training sessions to familiarize the remoter user with potential or recurring problems, especially problems taken from the trouble logs. Chalk up another reason for keeping them.

♦ Encourage the users to investigate the help topics supplied with all the software products they will use while on the road.

♦ If your remote users have special areas that are not covered in traditional help topics, consider having some custom help topics developed. It is expensive to have this type of work done, but it can pay back the cost in the long run.

♦ Have a section of your company's Web site dedicated to providing help information for remote users that have problems accessing the network through the VPN. This is especially useful to the user who can't tunnel back but can still access the Internet. The users may be able to resolve the issues on their own.

♦ Train your support staff so they know about and can use all the tools available to help the remote user. Having the help information available doesn't do anyone much good if no one in your support staff knows it's there or can't use it if they accidentally stumble across it.

### How Much Help Can You Build Into The Computer?

Sooner or later, you will reach a point where you must decide whether adding more troubleshooting tools while trying to make the computer more useful is cost effective. Beyond that point either the support technician goes to the customer, or someone brings the computer into the shop. Unfortunately in either case, the remote user is facing an immediate crisis. At this point it becomes necessary to extend the support site logically to the user's location.

Reaching across cyberspace begins with a telephone call and for that you should have a restricted voice phone number just for the users to dial and talk to a real live person. By the time the user reaches this point they will have expended all other options—they badly need help, and this is where you have promised them they will get it.

Before they make the call, it's nice if we can teach them to make a few notes.

### User's Troubleshooting Checklist

We are doing some things that you ought to have the user write down before placing a call to the help desk. But first let me make a suggestion or two. Make up this checklist or one like it with your information, but *do not* put it on the computer. If the user is having problems with the computer, it doesn't take a rocket scientist to figure out that they may not be able to access a checklist that's on the computer.

Here's another suggestion that comes with a little story. It has been said that during World War II, when one or two U.S. soldiers were in England, that the British officers were amazed by the audacity of most of the U.S. soldiers. It seems that most of the time when a U.S. soldier was given some assignment, they always wanted to know why. This seems to be a common thread among U.S. citizens. I told this little story in order to point out that if you give a blank form to a remote user, and tell them to fill in the requested information before calling for help, chances are most of them are going to ask why.

Given that premise, doesn't it make sense to make this one topic for your training session with the remote users? You can discuss each item and explain why it is important. It's certainly a lot easier for them to fill in a blank if they know the rationale behind it.

I'll list some items that I have found are helpful through experience. Feel free to discard any that don't apply to your system, and by all means add anything we missed. By the way, it is not unknown for the troubleshooting list to fix the problem by showing the user a step or operation that was not properly completed. In our example we are going to follow only one path through the decision tree. For example, the answer to the fourth item is presumed to be yes—a no answer would follow down another track.

Here we go. Imagine the user sitting cross-legged on the sagging bed of a motel in Cut 'N Shoot with a defunct laptop getting ready to call back and plead with you to help him. Here is what you want the user to tell you when he calls in:

1. What type of computer is in trouble? If the computer is on the company's plant account list, put space on the form for the barcode or other ID number. When the user calls in for help the help desk operator can look this number up in the database and get a complete list of what's on the computer, both hardware and software. The operator can also find out if this is a recurrent problem and what the last fix was.

2. Are you trying to access the VPN? Not all help problems are related to accessing the VPN; however, at this point I am going to assume the answer to this question is yes. In a full-blown logic tree, this question may lead to an application.

3. Can you make a connection to the Internet? The user may not be able to answer this question. If they can, it will tell us if the problem is with the ISP they are tying to contact, or with the VPN.

4. Can you make a connection to the network through the VPN? Same here as the last one. You are progressing through the logical operations, searching for the specific problem.

5. If you can make a VPN connection to the local network through the Internet, what operation are you attempting to perform that is causing the error? At this point we have the user logged in to the local network from the Internet, so now it's a problem running a program of some type that is on the network.

6. Have you tried more than one time to perform the operation?

7. Does the system stop at the same point each time that you try to perform the operation?

8. When the system stops, what (if any) error are you receiving? (fill in)

   ♦

   ♦

Whoever is sitting at the help desk should have these same questions available and go through them in the disciplined order that they are contrived. This is the start of a good diagnostics plan. Now that we have this information, what can we do with it?

### Some Things Are Just Not Practical

It is just not practical to try and load a new hard drive image into the laptop over a modem, even a top-of-the-line 56K modem. Most hotel and motels don't provide two telephone lines into the rooms so simultaneous talk and test is out of the question. The point is, although you can have your help desk provide lots and lots of suggestions, limits remain.

### Some Things Are More Realistic

So the users have made their way through the help files, filled out the trouble checklist, and called the help desk. Now what? The user reads off the troubleshooting checklist as the techie tracks through the decision trees. Now and then the process will come to a series of diagnostics and the situation reverses for a few moments: the techie will read off procedure steps for the user to perform and report the results.

Don't despair. This sounds like a doomsday task, but in actuality it works pretty well, provided the techie and the user are trained to communicate, talking the same geek-speak and reading off the same page. What happens is that if the problem is not too complex, for example, a step left out or a misspelled password, the user and the help desk can pretty much resolve and fix it.

If the problem is more complicated, especially if some software on the user's computer has to be reconfigured, it may just not be practical to talk the user through it. When you reach this point you have to pass the problem up one notch and use a different set of tools.

### Accessing The Remote Computer From The Support Site

Remote access software is fairly common in the computer support industry today. When you have a situation that cannot be resolved any other way, the answer is to use software and the modem to access the user's computer from the support site. Several good software programs are on the market shelves that will allow a support technician access to the laptop in Blazing Sands, Arizona, from the support site at GLS. When this becomes necessary, here are some tips I think will make the operation easier:

♦ Have a batch file or script on the remote laptop or PC for the user to execute. The module will configure the computer's modem to connect to an incoming call. The techie back home and the user in Cut 'N Shoot agree on a countdown—one minute is at least three times longer than is needed. Then the user hangs up the phone, connects the POTS to the modem, executes the script or batch file, and then sits back to watch.

♦ It's easier if the connection is originated from the support site to the remote location, rather than the other way around. Think about it; if the user can't access the company network, what makes you think she can access the support site?

♦ Keep in mind that during the time that the support site is accessing the remote computer, the connection is *not* secure. Use caution when transmitting data in either direction.

### Back-Up Plan (When All Else Fails, Take Three APCs And Call Back In The Morning)

Okay, the road warrior tried the help files and they didn't help. He called the help desk and they couldn't help. The problem was bumped up to the higher level technical support, but the techies couldn't capture the recalcitrant computer remotely. Now what?

At this point someone, probably you, will be faced with the onerous task of deciding how bad the road warrior needs his or her machine. If the need is not immediate, maybe the most cost-effective solution is to have the remote user return home and bring the computer into the shop for repair. If the remote user needs the computer bad enough, say to close a big contract, the range of options is considerably more narrow:

♦ FedEx a new laptop overnight. Don't laugh, this wouldn't be the first time.

♦ Locate a reliable PC service center in the area where the remote user is, and have the user take the laptop in for repair. This is especially good if the problem looks like bad RAM or a dead battery.

♦ Put the support technician on an airplane and go fix the computer or deliver a spare. When you have a contract that can run into tens of thousands of dollars, the cost of an airline ticket suddenly becomes cost-effective.

♦ Last resort and worst-case scenario, locate a PC vendor in the area where the remote user is located, and have them deliver a new laptop to the remote user's hotel. This may be more cost effective than an airline ticket if the remote user is in a foreign country, like Japan.

*If you do ship or deliver a new computer, you will be sure and load the most recent backup into, it won't you?*

Well, those are just some suggestions for how to administer and support the remote user. It really comes down to how much that remote user needs that laptop, and how badly they need to connect to the company network. In the end you will be the judge of that. Oh, yeah, if you run out of plans and preset alternatives, don't be afraid to use your incentive, you may come up with a great idea.

Before I leave this section I want to jump onto my soapbox and get into one of my rare lecture modes. We need to say a few words about holding the user's hand.

### You Want What? Har, Har! (Holding Hands 3,000 Miles Away)

I should call this section Psych-001. Perhaps even a more apt title would be: "How Not To Treat The Customer."

I made the statement before that when a remote user calls in to the help desk, they have exhausted their options. In spite of what I've heard from some quasi-technicians, I really do believe this to be the case most of the time. The road warrior would much rather fix his or her own problem than admit defeat.

Remember the last time you went into a store or shop and came face to face with an indifferent clerk? Remember saying to yourself, or perhaps even out loud, that it was no way to treat you—you were the customer, after all.

It also doesn't hurt to remember that the user has had just as long a day as you, that it's just as late where the user is as it is where you are. On top of it all, you're probably a lot more comfortable sitting at your work site than the user is in a hotel room. And it also doesn't hurt to remember that that user is, after all, your customer.

Here's another interesting little fact that seems to amaze most support technicians: The great majority of computer users don't make their living configuring software and understanding how computers work. To the great majority of computer users, the computer is a tool like the jet airplane that flies them between cities. To them, that little box is every bit as complicated as that jet. When the jet doesn't work, the airline company doesn't expect the pilot to fix it—he is the operator. Does this sound familiar? If the airplane develops a problem, the pilot reads down through a contingency checklist for possible solutions. When he gets the plane on the ground safely, he climbs out and leaves it for the technicians.

Why is it some technicians expect the user—the operator—to fix the computer and ridicules them when they can't? Most of the time when a remote user calls the help desk, it's late, they're tired, they have already tried the contingency checklists. They just want someone to fix the machine.

Do everyone at your company a big favor: Pass the last few paragraphs around.

# Chapter 10

# *VPN Security*

**Key Topics:**

◆ *Threats*

◆ *Network attacks*

◆ *System defenses*

◆ *Authentication*

◆ *Encryption*

We promised in just about every chapter so far to talk about security. Well, here we are. In order to address properly the subject of security, we will by necessity venture back to the LAN and WAN and work our way out to the VPN. We need to get to the root of the issue. We must understand what security really means and what we are trying to accomplish with all the elaborate schemes available for defending our resources.

Along the way, you need to determine how much is enough. If you are the bank keeping our royalties from writing this book, we want you to have lots of security. On the other hand, if your enterprise has only a handful of employees and the computer is merely something that keeps a few records and establishes an occasional contact with one or two salespeople on the road, or maybe a couple of telecommuters working out of their homes, some basic precautions might suffice; maybe you don't need to worry about it all.

We'll start off by defining security, at least from our perspective, then we'll expose a few of the more common hacker attacks and explain how they work—some of them are surprisingly simple for the devastation they wreak. We'll give some case studies of actual events and add in real-life examples of network attacks going on right at this moment—as you read these pages.

Next comes system defenses. What you, as the network administrator, information technology manager, keyboard thumper, road warrior, or company president can do to enhance your company's security level.

We can't do the job properly without getting into the nuts and bolts, so be assured we are going to spend more than a couple of pages delving into the geeky stuff: Firewalls, gateways, proxies, passwords, authentication, encryption, tunnels, protocols, hardware, software, and anything else it takes to put your Virtual Private Network into cyberspace and survive.

> **Note**
>
> *"Contrary to every other statement you might have heard, one ultimate action will absolutely prevent any loss of electronic data caused by a breach of security—pull the power cords out of the wall socket and throw away the computers."*
>
> *—Casey Wilson and Peter Doak, 1999*

# Security Defined

*Security*—in a nutshell—is protection against unauthorized access of information, protection of data integrity, and assurance of system operation by authorized persons.

## What's It All About, Alfie?

For 99 percent of the recreational computerists, security is a no-brainer. Passwords are an inconvenience inflicted on them; requiring them to occasionally type in their first name spelled backwards. On the other end of the spectrum, the realm of the inveterate paranoids, one percent of computer security specialists refuse to connect their computers to any kind of network whatsoever, be it WAN, LAN, or the guy in the next cubicle. The rest of us inhabit the middle ground. We know risks await us, but we likewise know we can reduce the risks to a manageable level with careful planning and routine maintenance.

### Secrecy

Every enterprise has some information on their computer that, for various reasons, must be kept secret. In some cases—proprietary information, for example—the data are hidden from the public because the boss wants them to be. Or, as in the case of Specialty Training back in Chapter 6, this might be information entrusted to the company with serious liability penalties assessed for inadvertent disclosure. Your own company's manufacturing techniques or the cooking time of maple syrup may be the secret that put it on top and worth taking steps to protect.

### Integrity (Of The Data, Not The People)

*Computer viruses* are, for the most part, clumps of memory taken over by some jerk who has nothing better to do. In the main, they are benign and do no harm. On the other hand, some viruses are devastating. Not long ago, a particularly destructive virus, code named explorer.exe, wiped out hundreds of files, destroying thousands of work hours. Some enterprises were forced to defend themselves by taking entire departments offline. Others were less fortunate and completely shut down their corporate networks.

Viruses aren't the only threat to security. Hackers love to modify your data files, especially the ones relating to finances. They rarely invade a network with the objective to steal anything, just stir it up. (Don't get me wrong, as far as I'm concerned no such thing as a *harmless* prank exists.)

### Convenience

*Denial of service* is the term the security geeks have coined for tying up your bandwidth so you cannot move data across your network. That is the antithesis of what your network is all about. The less convenient your computer is, the more frustrated your users will be.

Viruses are only one mechanism used for denial of service. *Email flooding* is another. Spamming is one. Hackers and crackers can send an undefended port into an endless loop, grinding everything to a halt.

# Threats

Every network administrator should have some concern about security threats related to their network. All threats can be divided into two types:

♦ Unauthorized access of system resources, both from inside and outside the organization.

♦ Attacks against system resources, usually in the form of some type of computer virus.

In addition to the threats, the increased use of electronic media for various types of commerce has brought about another security concern. This concern revolves around the need for positive identification of digital entities before exchanging electronic information. This equates to a sort of *I know who you say you are, but is it really you?* situation.

In the course of this chapter we are going to discuss the unauthorized access first, as it is this type of threat that (at least for now) takes up the majority of the security administrators' efforts.

## Attacks From Within

Here's an interesting bit of information, readily available off the Internet. Research conducted by various organizations, both government and private industry, has shown that the largest majority of unauthorized access to system resources, and a corresponding amount of damage and loss, takes place by attacks from within the corporate system, usually by an employee of the company. Yet the same companies invest the majority of their network security dollars in preventing attacks from outside intruders.

Why is this? In order to get a better handle on this apparent contradiction in terms, we need to get a better understanding of the term *unauthorized access*. Simply stated, unauthorized access means that a user, through some means, gains access to data areas that they have been instructed not to access. In some cases steps have been taken to prevent the user from gaining access to certain areas. In other cases the user has been told, sometimes in rather strict terms, that access to certain areas is not allowed.

In the past few years, with the rapid growth and proliferation of Internet access throughout major corporations, we see the term *unauthorized access* take on a new meaning. Unauthorized access, in the strictest interpretation, can mean getting email on a company computer that is not related to the normal functions of the business. Another example that is a little bit easier for most of us to accept is using corporate assets, the computer system, to download or distribute pornography over the Internet.

Literally hundreds, if not thousands, of incidents fall between the two ends of the spectrum that we just discussed. They include such things as tuning in streaming video and audio from the Internet, carrying on realtime video calls with personal friends and relatives, and so on. How is the network administrator supposed to deal with this new implementation of an old problem? We are going to come back in the latter part of this chapter and try to answer that question.

# The Inside Intruder

The typical inside attack comes about either through an accidental discovery of a system weakness, which is then exploited, or deliberate systematic attempts to breach the system security. Let's look first at the accidental discovery.

*I only left for a moment*—Not surprisingly the most common security breach is the employee that leaves a logged-in computer unattended. Bill is an engineer, working in the research department of a design company. During the day, Bill is logged into the system and working normally. Something comes up that causes Bill to leave his desk and computer system for a moment. Rather than log out, he simply leaves it logged in. While he's gone, another person discovers the system and calmly looks up confidential information that is otherwise inaccessible. Unless the system generates some type of audit trail, it is very likely that no one will ever know that the incident happened at all. This can shortly lead to the next step.

*Impersonation—If I can only get Bill to leave his computer for a few minutes*—If this continues, it is quite possible for the intruder—for that's what he is now—to put in place a plan to get Bill to leave his desk periodically, just long enough for the intruder to search part of the system looking for a particular item of information, but not long enough to cause Bill to log out of the system. Over a period of time the intruder can perform a systematic search of the records on the system, locating and copying information that he or she is not authorized to have. This way, the accidental discovery of a system weakness becomes exploited by the intruder. Over a period of time the intruder may get bolder, and eventually may get caught. On the other hand, this may not happen. We only know of the ones we catch, not the intruders that get away.

*Crackers—While the cat's away*—In most organizations employees are trusted to perform their jobs as well as they can without full-time direct supervision. This allows the deliberate, planned attempt to overcome system security to take place. In this case the employee deliberately and systematically attempts to overcome the security that is put in place to prevent unauthorized access to the system.

For example, on every Unix system that I have ever worked with, an account is created when the system is installed for the *superuser*. This *supervisor*, or *administrator account*, has access to everything in the Unix system, including the ROOT of the directory. An intruder bent on breaking into a Unix system does not have to worry much about which user has access to what information. All they have to do is discover the superuser password and they have access to the entire system.

Let me ask you, in your position as a network administrator, do you have a problem staying awake at night when you should be sleeping? I can help you spend endless hours at night worrying about your system. Suppose I told you that several cracker programs are readily available off the Internet that can crack the superuser password on 50 percent of the installed Unix systems, and do the job in less than 20 minutes.

Now, how good is your network security?

I could mention a few other ways that inside intruders can gain access to the system, but I think you get enough of the picture. I think, instead, you would prefer that I tell you some simple steps you can take to tighten up your system. Unfortunately, you must pay a price. As you increase the level of difficulty for an intruder to crack the system, you also increase the difficulty for your users to access to the system.

Because a good security plan works for attacks from both outside and inside, let's sneak a quick peek at a typical intruder attack from outside, then we'll see if we can't stop both types of attacks.

## The Hacker From Hell, Or The Network Administrator's Worst Nightmare

The rapid growth of the Internet has made possible the exchange of information on a scale that most people could not even comprehend 15 years ago. It has also spawned an entirely new type of devious, insidious creature, bent only on destroying everything they can touch. What is interesting in today's society is the image that these individuals have managed to acquire. In some areas, a cult worship surrounds this group of misfits that call themselves hackers and crackers.

Let me say right up front that I feel this type of person to be the electronic equivalent of the freeway sniper who hides behind a hill taking pot shots at the cars going by. The passengers in the cars are simply trying to get from one point to another and sometimes pay dearly for the attempt.

Following are some methods that this person can use to try and destroy your system.

### Network Attack

Excluding unauthorized access by employees and others from inside the system, the term *network attack* can be generally considered to be an attempt by an entity to do one of the following:

♦ Gain access to your system under conditions that would normally prevent that access.

♦ Disrupt the normal flow of data through the network system, and by doing so disrupt normal operations.

♦ Implant false or bogus information into the system.

Many methods are used for accomplishing these three objectives. However, they can be grouped loosely into the following areas.

♦ *Interception*—In this case, the attacker taps in to the system, sometimes by doing something as simple as plugging a network protocol analyzer into a port on a hub. In other cases, the means of interception may be as complicated as placing a carefully manufactured RF Energy pickup next to an unshielded twisted pair cable. This is an attack on the confidentiality of the data transported through the system.

♦ *Interruption*—Here the attacker destroys or disables a component of the system in an attempt to disrupt the normal flow of information through the system. The range of components can be something as simple as a hard disk drive, or something as sophisticated as a router or network switch.

♦ *Modification*—This is perhaps the most sophisticated method of network attack. It involves interruption of the data signal, then interception and modification of the data, and then retransmitting it on to its original destination. To perform this procedure without being detected requires sophisticated equipment normally beyond the means of the casual hacker. But it is possible to manufacture the equipment given the proper information and motivation.

♦ *Fabrication*—In this case, data is falsely fabricated and implanted in the network system. The final result of data fabrication can range from hardly any to extremely catastrophic, depending on the nature of the industry and the type of data.

Taken individually, each of these methods can be defeated without causing undo hardship and difficulty of operation for the regular users of the network. When these threats are considered as a group, the defense against a coordinated attack can become quite complex, and this in turn can raise the level of difficulty in the use of the network.

### Viruses

The conceptual history of computer viruses can be traced back to the initial proposal that described techniques for the encapsulation of IP datagrams. You may recall from an earlier chapter that the author of that RFC stated that the encapsulation techniques were considered to be a hack of the system. Let's take a closer look at some types of viruses. Towards the end of this section we will mention a particularly nasty type of virus that you really want to be aware of.

In making an effort to describe and categorize the different types of viruses that exist, we can start with two basic categories.

*Viruses that cannot replicate themselves*—Some people would not consider these to be viruses at all. But because I consider a virus to be a section of unwanted programming code that has been planted gratuitously in your system without your knowledge or permission, I will include these here. This type of virus is generally confined to a single system, and in this group we can include malicious programs. *Malicious programs* are those programs placed in a system in deliberate violation of stated policy, with the intent of overcoming the normal system security. This includes such programs as:

- *Backdoor users and passwords*—These are dummy or false users, most often created during system setup, for gaining entry to the system in the event the regular administrative or supervisor passwords are lost or those accounts corrupted. In many cases the person performing the installation views this as a safeguard, necessary to guard against the time when the regular administrator forgets the password, or a similar situation. Although no one may ever use the back door except as a last resort, it is a violation of security.

- *Stealth users*—This is a particular type of user that you can create in Novell Directory Services (NDS). I'm not going to tell you how, but you can create containers with users (commonly referred to as stealth users) in those containers that cannot be seen under normal circumstances. You can use this as a backdoor into the NetWare network. To create this type of user requires Admin rights at the root of the directory tree, so this is not something that the average network user is able to do. (Unless, of course, the network administrator left the ADMIN console unattended for a doughnut and cup of coffee.)

- *Trojan horses*—These are snippets of code compiled into the normal program code and therefore hidden from view. When activated, these Trojan horses perform tasks that range from something as simple as printing meaningless garbage to the screen, to tasks as serious as storing all the passwords in a text file and allowing a specific user to copy the file to another machine. All this happens without the regular user of the computer having a clue as to what's taking place.

- *Time bombs*—These are programs, usually written in a scripting language like PERL, that access the computer clock and measure the time elapsed since the time bomb was reset. The reset can be automatic, such as every time the system goes through a startup or a warm boot, or may require some specific action or entry at the local keyboard. If it is not reset and the preset time is exceeded, the bomb goes off and the script activates. Depending on how vicious the attacker is, the result can be a large amount of systemic damage, usually lost data. Here's a thought to keep you awake: Maybe the bomb planter is an unhappy employee expecting to be laid off or terminated. Who is going to reset the bomb after he or she is gone?

---

### Case History

One ultra-high security facility operated by the U.S. Navy fell victim to a virus plague, even though the facility was not networked internally, much less to the outside world. Discovery of the infestation was a fluke accident. By the time the plague was eradicated, every one of dozens of machines were found to be infected, some of them with more than 100 viruses in a single machine.

---

*Viruses that can replicate themselves*—True viruses are computer code capable of replicating themselves. The authors of earlier viruses wrote them in C, Pascal, or even assembly languages. These early viruses were simply sections of compiled code not linked into an executable file. They depended on being embedded in an executable (*.exe or *.com) file to work. Once the executable file was loaded into the system memory, the virus code section located itself in a specific section of system RAM. Then, depending on the virus's mechanics, it would infect every executable program used during the time the system was running. Because the virus was located in RAM, the virus died when power was turned off. No matter though, because it had replicated itself numerous times and it would spring back to life the very next time the operator used an infected program.

### Spreading The Virus

Early Unix systems provided multiuser capability by using a large computer system as a host that provided its processing power for several users with serial terminals. This system allocated a section of RAM to each user when they initiated a session. In their day these were powerful network systems.

Unfortunately, these early Unix systems, particularly those based on the Motorola 68xxx family of processors, were particularly vulnerable to a specific type of replicating virus. The architectures of the Unix operating system and the C programming language allowed programmers to develop a virus that propagated itself through the Unix system memory by jumping from one user's memory area to another. This was a particularly brutal virus, and could effectively bring down an entire Unix system.

Today's distributed network systems—Windows NT, for example—use the same architectural philosophies as the early Unix systems, even though the internal structure of an NT system is quite different from an early Unix system. Each user that accesses an NT server and starts a session is assigned a section of RAM memory with known delineation.

Although the internal structure of NT has many safeguards in place, including the fact that it runs primarily on Intel processor architecture, the virus programmers have honed their skills to match. The end result is that today, viruses exist that can infect an entire network system, and if allowed to replicate themselves unchecked, will eventually cause a failure of the entire network system.

*Case History*

One of the authors of this book was, himself, twice attacked by a macro virus named "Concept-A." In the first case, the virus arrived on a floppy disk from a *trusted source*—a national organization with division offices in each state and hundreds of branch offices in each division. As I found out later, it is its misfortune that the organization does not have an adequate set of policies in place and the network administrators are not well trained. I have never accepted another assignment from them.

In the second instance, the organization that distributed the virus to me had only just discovered their infestation and passed it on to me before their defenses were in place and the virus cleaned out. Their reaction was immediate and professional and I have no problem with maintaining a good relationship with them.

As an added note: In the first instance, the author was doing an evaluation of virus detectors and had no less than five loaded at the time. At the time, none of them noticed Concept-A.

### Macro Viruses

One important feature software developers added to many PC applications was the ability for the operator to perform small repetitive tasks within the application, such as cut-and-paste or highlight-and-drag. The inventors aptly named these features *macros* and eventually extended the user with the capability of writing their own macros and imbedding them with the applications. For some users, this is a godsend—for example, just by pressing two keys, I can completely change the formatting of a paragraph. With another combination of keys I can write an entire heading for a letter.

Because the macro is in reality a programming capability, eventually some creep figured out how to write a virus using macro programming. These macro viruses become active the first time a user calls some specific function. The virus replicates by attaching a copy of itself to new documents and is exchanged with other computers via the transfer of the information in the infected documents. Macro viruses are easy to propagate and, at least for the known strains, easy to detect.

### Email Viruses

Once upon a time, in a cyberspace long ago, the ability to send messages from one computer system to another was relatively simple and so were the email messages. However, it did not take developers long to migrate the ability to execute macros from major applications into that simple everyday email. Today, in our modern world with our powerful computers, the common email message is anything but a simple text file. To develop and transport these sophisticated packages of glitter and glitz, vendors developed email to magically package any file (text, data, or the most complex program), slap on an email header, and send it off to thousands of users. When the email arrives at its destination, it can be magically executed with the click of a mouse—sometimes by a user that has no idea of the danger that may be lurking just on the other side of the *click*. Nobody recognized the opportunities for a hacker to wreak havoc.

Perhaps the most startling example happened early in the summer of 1999. Almost in concert, email systems around the world developed problems. Mail servers that had operated normally for months and years suddenly started gasping, then died. The cause was a particularly insidious virus that came to be known as *Melissa*. So prevalent had the simple email become ingrained in our high-tech society, that the virus was propagated around the world in less than 24 hours and within 24 more hours systems were shutting down. It took almost four days to develop defenses to bring our trusty email back to normal.

Could it happen again? Will the sun rise in the east tomorrow?

### General Virus Categories

So far we have shown on a few examples of virus technology. Many others exist:

◆ *Boot sector virus*—Designed to infect the master boot record, usually of a floppy disk formatted with the system files on it. This type of virus spreads to the master boot record of the hard drive, and then infects any floppy disk you format on that computer.

◆ *Polymorphic virus*—Changes its makeup every time it moves from one host to another, increasing the difficulty of detection.

◆ *Worm*—Uses the network system to transport itself from one computer to another. With the rapid growth of the Internet, worms have taken on an entire new dimension.

◆ *Bacteria*—A variation of the virus theme. Bacteria reproduce at an exponential rate. The colony grows larger and larger until it overcomes memory and bandwidth and the system locks up. At that point the only option is to reset the computer. That kills it; well almost. The initial germ is still there and the problem is, once the computer has been reset, the bacteria immediately begins reproducing all over again. Isn't that a fun concept?

### Are You Happy Yet? (Our Last Example)

A while back my lab associate asked me to look at something interesting. We went to his office where he fired up his desktop computer, and when the login banner popped up he immediately canceled it. Please note that he was not authenticated to the network. His next step was to load a program that immediately scanned the network and came back with a list of IP addresses. He then selected an address from the list and received a request for a password, which he entered.

At this point his desktop attached itself to the computer at the IP address he entered. By using various combinations of *hot keys*, he examined the files on the remote PC's hard drive, saw what was on its screen, watched what characters the user was typing in, and so on and so on. The really disturbing thing about this is that he was not logged in to the network. All he needed was the TCP/IP protocol stack loaded and bound to a network interface card in the remote PC.

All that was made possible because of a particularly nasty trojan horse firus named *Back Orifice 2000*. We caution you not to mess with this critter, it is particularly dangerous. For more information go to **www.symantec.com** and track it down.

Once infected, the virus modifies the Windows registry, so that the virus is loaded immediately after the TCP/IP protocol stack. It then will advertise the appropriate IP address to the network, and sit back and wait. Oh, one other thing, it also modifies the email program to attach automatically a copy of the virus to every item of email sent out. To activate the virus requires the other part of the program, which is a remote terminal emulator available off the Internet. When the remote terminal is activated, it polls the network for all available devices on a particular port. That's where the list of IP addresses comes from. Once an IP address is selected, the virus receives the hot key commands over the network, and performs the appropriate task.

This is a real nasty virus. Using this virus, it is possible to copy keystrokes as the user types them in from the keyboard, so it can be used to steal passwords before they are encrypted and sent to the server. It also modifies the Windows Registry, which makes it particularly hard to kill. Finally, it attaches itself to every item of email sent by the host computer, which in some cases makes it almost impossible to track.

I told you it was a nasty virus, didn't I? The user will eventually find out about this virus because it attaches itself to every email sent out, and sooner or later someone is going to tell this user that something is not right. However, it is very easy to create a similar virus that imbeds itself in a particular computer and doesn't attach itself to outgoing email. It this case, the user is completely unaware that the virus is there, and someone else is watching every keystroke they make.

How do you locate this type of virus and how do you get rid of it? Even better, how do you prevent this type of infection in the first place? We keep asking these same questions all through this section, and the answer is almost always going to be the same. So in order to keep from repeating ourselves, we are going to put the answer further down in this chapter.

Many viruses are floating around the Net today. We have mentioned a few types here in order that you may get an idea of what types of viruses exist.

## Viruses And Hardware

The question about the ability of a virus to cause problems in hardware is difficult to answer. Most hardware devices on a computer are controlled by software instructions—that is, lines of code executed by the computer system. As such, they can be taken over and controlled by a virus.

As an example, let's take a look at an SVGA video adapter card. The modern SVGA video adapter is capable of outputting video to the monitor in several resolutions, ranging all the way from the original 480 x 350, up to and beyond an astounding 1920 x 1400. The number of reproducible colors also varies depending on the amount of available video RAM. All this versatility is controlled through the use of software instructions.

Not all video monitors are capable of supporting all the available outputs from the video adapters. In many cases the switching capability of multisync monitors is controlled by small relays inside the monitor that sense the signal on a particular conductor and close or open a set of contacts based on that input.

If a programmer developed a virus that infected the video driver portion of the computer system, and systematically and repeatedly changed the horizontal and vertical sweep rates at a high rate of speed, no monitor would successfully operate for an extended period of time. In this case, the answer to the question about viruses and hardware would be *yes*. The virus is capable of destroying the hardware, given enough time.

Has this particular type of virus ever been developed? You bet. However, I have also heard talk of viruses that could reprogram the ROM BIOS and destroy the hard disk drive. All of this falls within the realm of being possible. But so far, I have yet to encounter a virus that could destroy a hard disk drive or reprogram a ROM chip. I have seen boot sector viruses that could cause the data on the hard disk drive to become unusable. But this could always be cured by running FDISK, deleting the partition, and starting over, but isn't that bad enough?

## Virus Defenses

The damage that a virus can do ranges anywhere from being a nuisance all the way to being destructive. If you detect any virus attacking your system, you must counterattack aggressively using every resource at your disposal.

Further down in this chapter we are going to discuss a comprehensive security plan, but for now, here are some steps you can be thinking about. Maybe you'll want to implement some of them before you finish the chapter.

♦ Know that your network will be attacked by a virus. Thinking that it won't is like imitating an ostrich. The best way to protect yourself against any attack is to be prepared to defeat it. As a starting place, convince management to:

　♦ Establish a comprehensive policy detailing how much and what type of files your users are allowed to download from the Internet. Based on the policy, train your support staff on what types of attacks are likely and how to combat them.

　♦ Establish a regular training schedule or good communications scheme with the users to discuss the types of viruses, apparent symptoms, and plan of action on even a suspicion of infection.

　♦ Enforce the management approved policy. Rules are worthless without enforcement. Deliberate, knowing propagation of a virus should result in immediate suspension or termination of an offender. Likewise, policies are worthless if they are squirreled away in a desk drawer or notebook on the top shelf.

♦ Spring for the best virus detector package your budget can afford and subscribe to its updates. Most of the commercial packages available on the market are updated at regular intervals, and these updates are available for download off of the Internet. While you are at it, don't expect a PC virus detector to work on a network system. It just ain't gonna happen. If you have a PC, get a PC virus detector. If you have a network, get a network virus detector.

♦ Use the Internet to keep you and your support staff updated on the latest virus attacks. When a fast-acting virus like Melissa makes the news, notify the users of the danger. Systematically shut down any unnecessary operations that may cause the spread of the virus while you are cranking up your defensive counterattack.

♦ When you learn about a new virus, especially a new macro or email virus, find out as much as you can about how the virus propagates through the network. Check your network system and determine if your network has the vulnerable applications. Concept-A, for example, is exclusive to Microsoft Office applications. If your system relies on Corel Perfect Office, a good chance exists that your system is not susceptible to that particular virus.

♦ Develop a contingency plan for shutting down your system, section by section, to trap and eliminate a virus. You may never need to use that plan, but having it in your notebook is a whole lot better than  answering your boss with a dumb look when she asks, "What are you going to do about it?"

Fortunately, dealing with viruses is more of a nuisance than a tragedy. Most of the time, the top-rated virus detection vendors do an excellent job and the huge majority of viruses are puerile toys. It's when something like Melissa or explorer.zip enters the arena that the delay between initial attack and adequate defense that you are most vulnerable. That's when your planning and the cooperation of your users is most vital. However, a time may come when the viruses start propagating faster than the software vendors can develop the tools to deal with them. When this point is reached, it is hard to predict what the result will be. Okay, okay, I'll stop my impersonation of Mr. George C. Scott impersonating General George S. Patton. Let's move on.

# Denial Of Service

Slipping a virus into your network isn't the only way to spoil your day. Denial of service attacks are not new, but the number and scope of this type of attack seems to be on the rise.

How does a denial of service attack work, anyway? The attack can come about in many ways, and the last thing we wanted to do was to write someone a cookbook. On the other hand, we think you have a need to know what to expect.

So we offer a compromise. Here's a brief description—with one or more critical steps left out—of an earlier method used in a denial of service attack. Thanks to some significant changes on the Internet in the past year or two, this method is very seldom encountered today. It will, however, serve to demonstrate how a hacker can use the available tools and deny Internet service to your network.

### Email Spamming

Email is the most popular service available on the Internet. The number of email messages that cross the Internet every hour is astounding. Most email messages are relatively small, and travel the Internet in less time than it takes for you to phone the recipient and ask them to check their email. For the most part, email works reliably. However, its intrinsic popularity and reliability makes it a favorite tool for a spamming attack.

For a model, we will use a Unix host connected to the Internet. All Unix and Linux computers have a neat little executable *daemon*—that's Unixese for an executable program—called *Sendmail*. The purpose of this program is exactly what the name implies. It *sends* or forwards email from one host machine to another host machine located on the Internet. At one time, almost every Unix machine loaded and executed the Sendmail daemon. In this configuration, almost every Unix machine on the Internet could act as a mail forwarder, forwarding email from one location to another. Internet email is defined by the Simple Mail Transport Protocol, or SMTP for short. Under this protocol, when a mail forwarder transmits a piece of email, it tacks its address into the header, so the recipient could trace the email back to its origin through the headers. Well, this is the way it's supposed to work.

The first thing a good hacker learns to do is to locate a mail forwarder on the Internet. It really doesn't matter where the machine is located; what's important here is that it will forward the email, regardless of where it's coming from. Once that's accomplished, the hacker develops—or downloads from the Internet—an *email spoofing script*, an executable script to strip the header from incoming email before it is forwarded to the next location. Remember that when the mail forwarder sends the email message to the next location, it tacks on the location of the email forwarder into the header. Now, when the mail forwarder sends the message to the final recipient, it looks as if it originated *at* the mail forwarder. The only thing we need now is a script that will create several hundred bogus email messages per second. The content might well be meaningless garbage. We now have all the pieces needed, so let's do it.

The attacker uses a program, maybe FTP, to upload the spoofing script to the file system on the mail forwarder. Then, the attacker uses a remote terminal program, maybe Telnet, to log in to the Unix host and execute the spoofing script. Don't worry about passwords; we used a cracker program for that minor delay. Next, the attacker executes the email creation script on their local machine and sends 5,000,000 email (yes, that's five million) messages to the computer that they want to attack using the mail forwarder to forward the messages. The spoofing script strips the header off its incoming email, so the real attacker is untraceable. The recipient finds their system inundated with 5,000,000 email messages. If each message was 5K, that is 25GB cramming into your system as fast as the bandwidth will allow it.

What would that do to your network? How about the domino effect? First, your system shuts down because: (a) it saturated and didn't have anywhere left to stuff another message, or (b) you, the network administrator, interrupted the service. Next, your ISP is going to love you, because the mail you didn't have room for piled up on his email server until it crashed. Upstream from your ISP...I think by now you get the picture, you can't do much after the fact. In this particular attack, the sender is untraceable.

The scary part is that email is only one of your vulnerable ports. If an attacker slams more data down any of the ports than your network can handle, you'll wish you had put some defenses in place long beforehand.

# System Defenses

We spent most of the first part of this chapter motivating you with a scant few of the different attacks your network system may have to deal with. This is especially true if you have users with sloppy or no protected access to the Internet. Now we're going to try and show you some ways to prevent, or at least lessen, the risks. Call it *safe 'netting*.

## Company Security Posture

At this point in this chapter I want you to stop and think about what has been said so far. In almost every instance where a security breach occurred, one common thread was present. What was it? The correct answer: the unsuspecting user. Make the user secure, and you make your network secure. The problem is, how do you make the users secure?

Read on, and we'll answer that question.

## It All Starts Here

Three tools comprise the tool kit you need if you expect a reasonable degree of success in your security efforts:

♦ A comprehensive, reasonable policy for acceptable network access and use

♦ Training

♦ A good disaster recovery plan

### Policy And Motivation

Because any policy deals with the people that work for the company, a policy on network access and use will naturally deal with the company employees that comprise the troop of network users. In this case, we are not dealing with computers, we are dealing with people.

My opinion is that communication is vital to the health and welfare of not only your network, but the people who use it, as well. That means you must establish a good line of communication, and make every effort to keep that line open.

No normal, reasonably well-adjusted person wants to be made to look foolish. I also believe that normal, well-adjusted people do not willingly want to damage or destroy the means of their livelihood. This means that, for the most part, users will go along with suggestions that certain things they may do can place the network in danger. If you explain to them that violating the acceptable use policies can crash their systems, they will earnestly try and follow the policies.

## How Much Security Is Enough?

I can tell you how to absolutely guarantee that your network will be secure and virus free 100 percent of the time. All you have to do is systematically turn off every item of computer hardware at your facility, and leave it off. Follow that plan and I absolutely guarantee that you will never have a virus or intruder in your system.

While you're at it, don't forget to pick up your pink slip and last paycheck on the way out the door, because the company has no further need for information technologists or network administrators. Needless to say, that's not a real good plan.

A better idea is to adopt a policy that's reasonable, allowing the users the freedom to perform the tasks necessary to accomplish their assignments, without opening the network up to unreasonable risk. I know I'm going to upset a large number of network administrators when I say this, but the policy on network access and use should be set by the users, with information supplied by the network administrators, not the other way around.

As a network administrator it is important that you remember a simple fact. You don't use the network to take care of the company's business, the network *users* do that. It is unreasonable to expect the users to be able to conduct their business burdened with a network access and use policy that hinders every attempt to conduct normal business.

Once the policy has been established, it should be reviewed on a regular basis. A procedure for regular review and implementation of changes should be established. Copies of this procedure should be distributed to all the users of the network. In this way, a user who needs to have a change implemented knows where to start.

## User Passwords—Damned If We Do And Damned If We Don't

My experience with the Internet goes back to when it was considered a private club. At that time access to the Internet was limited, and no commercial activities were allowed. The college where I work had Internet access and everything was fine for a time. Then the

National Science Foundation (NSF) ceased funding for the Internet and commercial enterprise took over. When the big changes occurred, the college remained with the same ISP and kept the same policies about Internet access and use.

One of the restrictions imposed on Internet access by the ISP was the requirement of a password. The network users couldn't change the password themselves; they contacted the ISP and had the password changed to something they wanted. Of course, everyone chose passwords that were easy to remember, the only requirement being a minimum of six characters, at least one of which had to be a number.

You may be wondering what this has to do with network security in general, and passwords in particular. Be patient, I'm getting there.

Within a year of the Internet going prime time, our ISP came under attack. Crackers would break into someone's account, gain access to restricted areas, and trash the files to the point at which the ISP was forced to bring down the system and perform a complete restore from the backup. If it was somewhat of a pain for the users; it was more than that for the ISP.

Within another six months, email spamming and flooding began. At the time, the only passwords needed for email access were the users'. Just like before, crackers would figure out a user's password. Once inside the system, the crackers used the account to send upwards of 50,000 email messages across the Internet. Again, the system was brought to the brink of collapse.

Finally, the ISP had enough. Its management adopted a policy tightening the security. First was the requirement for two passwords—one to log in, the other to access the ISP's services, including email. Another change in the password arena was that users could no longer choose their own passwords. The ISP used a script that generated random passwords. Both the login and the access passwords were at least eight characters long, four letters and four numbers. Each new password was compared to the equivalent of the American Heritage Dictionary of more than 300,000 words. If even a partial match with an existing word was found, the password was discarded, and the process repeated.

The result was that each user was required to have two passwords, each a string of eight characters, half alphabetic and half numeric, no part of which could match any word known in the English language. Not surprisingly, when this policy was put in place, it upset most of the users and many of those dropped this ISP's service. Too bad for them, because as soon as the new policy was implemented, the success rate for the crackers went down to an easily manageable level.

This tells me that the most vulnerable point of attack in a network is the ease with which user passwords can be cracked. The harder it is to crack the passwords, the lower the number of attacks you will experience. Can it really be that simple?

My job requires that I travel and on those occasions I take my laptop along—to check my email in addition to playing bridge and chess. When I'm on the road, I use my AT&T Worldnet account so I can make a local connection wherever I am. One of the first things I noticed when I got my new account was the password. I thought the password at my home base ISP was good, but the one from AT&T is better. My access policy says I'm not allowed to let the browser login panel *remember* my password, and this one is a lonnnnng string of characters. I have a pretty good memory, but I can't remember this one, so I created a special hidden file and saved the password there. When I need the password, I open the file with a text editor and do a cut-and-paste into the dialer's data field. It's a bother, but I don't mind because it keeps my Internet access safe—and that's what I want.

In case you haven't gotten the message yet: The first line of defense in any network system is the user's password. The complexity of the password should be balanced against the degree of threat you perceive to your network and the willingness of the users to buy in to it. If you raise the complexity of the passwords high enough, the majority of crackers—and therefore the majority of the threat—will move to an easier target. Unfortunately, you won't stop the attack, you simply push it off on some easier target.

It would be nice if a way could be found to stop the attacks, but that is unrealistic. In an effort to help you make a decision about what type of password restrictions to implement, I have told you about one ISP and AT&T Worldnet.

I've included an excerpt from the policies at the University of Colorado at Denver to give you one example of getting a password section down in writing in your network access and use policy:

1. Passwords:

    (a)  Access to a multiuser computer system should be governed by passwords with a minimum length (where possible) of eight characters.

    (b)  Ideally, passwords should not be words found in a dictionary and should include one or more numeric characters.

    (c)  Passwords should not be capable of being readily guessed by someone acquainted with the user. For example, they should not be maiden names or names of children, spouses, or pets.

    (d)  Passwords should under no circumstances be written or typed in any document, on a piece of scrap paper, or taped to a computer terminal.

    (e)  Unencrypted passwords should not be included in any electronic mail message, but should be communicated directly between individuals. Telephone transmission of passwords may be a problem, because it may be difficult to verify the other party.

   (f)   Accounts that give access to extraordinary system capabilities (e.g., the ability to read data belonging to others, the ability to modify system software, etc.) should be protected with more than one password and the passwords should be selected with special care.

   (g)   Periodic password change is a good practice.

### Employee Education

Okay, we have established some type of policy. We have a plan for getting the support staff trained. What's next? The hardest part: Train the user.

### Motivation

The first step is to get the user to recognize the need for training. We call this motivation; you may not think in terms quite so nice. However you say it, you need to get the users to recognize that many of them exist, but few of you. When it comes to defending the network against threats and attacks, it takes everyone. How do you do this? We don't know all the answers, but here are some areas you can use to try to get the point across.

### Rewards (And Penalties)

Users are at the front line in a network system. They are the ones that will start to notice a problem first, and they need to be able to recognize the need for blocking the items that are not allowed under the network access and use policy. If you can help the users to see the dangers present, and how they can disrupt their normal operations, chances are pretty good that the majority will be willing to go along with the policy. Keep in mind that this is a two-way street. If you expect the users to listen to you, you have to be willing to listen to the users.

# System Backup

With respect to your network, what qualifies truly as your worst nightmare? Most experienced network administrators will agree that the one thing they fear the most is losing their data. One example should make the point clear. You arrive at work one morning to find the building that housed the center of your computer network system burned to the ground. Totally destroyed, along with everything inside. At one time a few years back it was said that six out of ten businesses over five years old did not survive a complete loss of their computerized records.

So what do you do to prevent a loss of your files? A company can invest large amounts of cash in complex systems for fire control, fire proofing, and other physical means of stopping a catastrophic fire, only to lose everything in a hurricane. You see, prevention is good, but everyone should plan on the worst thing possible happening. My solution is to operate under the assumption that sooner or later, something is going to happen that will cause your network system to lose all the data it contains. If you expect it, you can plan for it (there I go, making another plan). If you plan for it, you will be prepared when it happens. This strategy is called *disaster recovery*. The plan is called a *disaster recovery plan*. The central part of any disaster recovery plan is a well-planned, well-maintained backup procedure.

Back in the BPC era (Before PCs), the operators of the central computer facility had a sign hanging on the window of the equipment room warning that the system would be offline between the hours of such and so. It was usually timed early into the swing-shift; to catch you trying to make up for lost productivity due to system crashes. For an hour or so the mainframe would dump its brains out onto tapes or, if the system had adequate funding, onto multiple-platter hard-disks. Some critical or very large systems would be backed up more than once a day.

Decentralization of the main frame computing scheme transferred the responsibility of backing up the desktop to the user. Responsibility of backing up databases and other shared resources generally stayed in the dominion ruled by the IT manager, along with the servers, router, directories, and myriad other tools required for a smooth running network.

At first, the IT managers and system administrators applauded—until the operating cost of support services began creeping up, and up, and up. A new technology opened up to provide backup facility to the desktop. That spawned an industry developing software and hardware so the desktop users could dump their brains, well—their PC's brains, onto tapes or disks.

No disaster recovery plan is complete without some type of backup strategy. This strategy should be a part of the overall network plan, and should include information about what will be backed up, when it will be backed up, and where it will be backed up. It should also include a statement about what will be done with the backup media after it is completed. This is as much a part of the system security as the firewall, because if everything else falls apart, you can always reach for the backup.

Let's look closer at the backup process, starting with the types of media available.

## Backup Media

Several types of backup media are available off the shelf and one of them might suit your installation. If you can't find a turnkey system that you can just take out of the box and plug in, a host of vendors await the opportunity to devise your custom backup operation. All you have to do is hop into the Internet and ask. Which type you choose will depend mostly on the particular circumstances of your network system.

### *Disks*

*Disks*, more commonly known as *diskettes*, were the first backup media for PCs. They were easy to use, reasonably reliable, and in the very early days actually held an adequate amount of data. Today this is no longer the case. Although diskettes remain easy to use and reliable, the storage capacity of a diskette is nowhere near large enough to even back up most data files today. For this reason diskettes are not commonly used for backup purposes any more.

### CD

Another media that can be used for backup purposes is *writeable* CD, more commonly known as *CDR*. The standard CD recordable disk can store about 640 Meg (give or take some), is robust and not subject to failure, and reasonably priced. With advances in technology, the CD has now become re-writeable, allowing the user to continue recording data until the disk is full.

In addition, a new technology, *Digital Versatile Disk*, or *DVD*, is now making its way into the market. The DVD uses a disk that is very similar in appearance to the CDR disk, except that the storage capacity is much greater, approaching a whopping 10GB. As the cost of the technology and the disks comes down, this will become a good backup media for large storage needs.

Here's a surprise: The one drawback to using CDR and DVD disk for backup is speed. You may be able to retrieve data from them that makes tape look like it is standing still, but they get really pokey when it comes to recording.

Logic will tell you that the more data you have to back up, the longer it requires. Eventually, if the amount of data you have to back up continues to grow, you will reach a point at which it simply is not possible to back up everything overnight.

You need something else, and good old reliable digital storage tape is it.

### Tapes

Only two types of media existed before magnetic tape: punch cards and paper tape. Magnetic tape has been used in all types of computer systems as a means of information storage for many years. And either in spite of or because of new technologies, tape will survive as a storage medium.

Tape is reliable, not easily damaged if proper precautions are taken, and is by far the lowest cost medium on the market. With 4mm and 8mm DAT systems, tape backup systems of up to 20GB per tape are possible. You can have your pick from several different tape backup technologies available on the market today.

## What To Back Up

Most people who are not network administrators would consider the question of what to back up rather foolish. Others of us know better. In a network system the question of what you back up is a key issue.

### Application Software

Of course you should back up the applications, at least once. Many network systems perform a network installation of major software products. Then, when the user needs to have a software product installed, instead of carrying around a large container of software programs, the smart technician simply installs the applications over the network; fast and simple.

At one time it was said that the applications hardly ever change. This is no longer true. Many applications now can be updated over the Internet, and software products are on the market that will automatically perform updates as the newer releases become available. On top of that, different users will set different preferences tailoring an application to their specific needs. I consider it a good practice to back up the applications the first time a new backup system is used, and then do regular periodic backups of the applications to catch changes and updates.

### Data files

Data files must be backed up on a regular schedule. The data change every time a user makes an entry.

### Network Operating System Files

What about the network operating system? Do these files ever change? How often should you back up the operating system? The answer here is a little more complex. The files that make up the operating system itself only change when a new support pack or option is installed. However, other parts of the operating system do change, almost every day.

Take for example Windows NT and, for starters, look at the Windows Registry. This is where the information about the complete makeup of the server, both hardware and configuration, is stored. This changes almost daily. Also, don't forget the Security ID (SID) data file. This changes each time a new user is created, or an existing user changes one of their properties, or changes their profile. This needs to be backed up regularly. The *.ini files and other configuration files should also be backed up regularly.

What about Novell NetWare? If you are using NetWare 5, you may be surprised to learn that NetWare now uses a Registry also. Even if you are not using NetWare 5, you still have the directory tree and/or bindery information that changes. This needs to be backed up.

Do you need to do a complete backup every day? The answer is no, it is not necessary to perform a *complete* backup every day. But you do need to establish a backup system and it will include some files for daily attention.

# A Good Backup System

If you know anything about computer file systems, you should know what an *attribute* is. If you don't, quickly find a good basic text on the subject and read it before continuing. One available attribute is the archive bit that keeps track of when the file was last backed up or copied. When the backup software copies a file—any type of file—it clears the archive attribute. That allows the system to determine if the file has been backed up or not.

By using the right backup software in combination with the archive bit, you can develop a system that is capable of performing three types of backup service:

♦ A *complete backup*—All the files in the system, regardless of type and attribute settings, are copied to the backup. This is the safest type of backup. It is also the type of backup that takes the longest to perform. After the file is copied, the backup software clears the archive bit. The next time a backup is performed, only the files that were changed since the last backup can be identified.

♦ *An incremental backup*—The backup software selects only the files that were modified since the last incremental backup. The backup software selects the files according to the status of the file's archive bit. If the bit is set, the file is backed up. If the bit is clear, the file is skipped. After the file is copied, the backup software clears the archive bit.

♦ *A differential backup*—The backup software backs up the files that have been changed since the last complete backup. The main difference between this and an incremental backup is that the archive bit is *not* cleared during a differential backup. This way, the next time a backup is performed, all the files that have been changed since the last complete backup will be copied.

Why do we have three different types of backup procedures? The answer has to do with the restore process. Let's look at a backup system built around each of the three methods.

### Method One, A Complete Backup Every Night

I'm not reneging on my earlier statement. It is not necessary for you to perform a complete backup every night, but it is by far the safest backup to perform if your system resources allow it.

First, I'm going to presume that your single day's tape capacity exceeds the amount of data you are going to back up. This may require more than one reel or cartridge and in that case when I refer to the *tape* or *tapes*, you will understand that I mean the collection of tapes for one day.

To begin with, you will need a minimum of four tapes. The fourth tape should be new and still in its wrapper. It will be used only if one of the other three goes into retirement or dies of old age.

Perform a complete backup using tape one on Monday. On Tuesday, use tape number two for your backup. The goal there was to *not* use your most recent backup tape, so on Wednesday you are going to leave tape two safely in its cubby and reuse tape one. Leapfrogging this way protects you in case something goes wrong during the backup process. In the worst case, you may have to fall back a few days to the last weekly, but only if your daily tape gets messed up somehow. Remember, tape is cheap compared to the cost of restoring.

Now, on Friday I want you to use the tape for that day—at this point it should be tape number one—for your *weekly* backup. Your backup procedures won't change, just the label for the tape and the fact that you are going to archive it for one week. If you use tape number two on schedule the following Monday and slip number three in on Tuesday, you are beginning a tape rotation that will apply equal time to each tape.

Tape rotation is an important thing to consider. Nominal life-time for tapes is around 100 passes, including both backups and restores. That implies you need to devise some record keeping and order replacement tapes far enough in advance so you can retire the old ones. If you are unlucky enough to have to put tape number four in service, order another one immediately.

The restore process for this system is a snap. If your system crashes completely, get it repaired back to tip-top condition, then perform a complete restore from the most recent backup tape. You might save some time if you determine that only a partial—maybe only one file—restoration is needed.

One downside to complete daily backups is the time required. The larger the system, the more time required. With a large enough system, multiple backup machines may be needed. You can solve this problem in some cases by automatic backups during off-peak hours. Plug in the tape, press a couple of keys, and go away—the backup starts after everyone has left the office for the day and is complete by the time you get to work in the morning.

The one glitch to this plan is for the volume to be backed up to exceed the capacity of one tape. In this case, someone has to be present to change tapes during the backup or you must employ multiple machines and segment the task.

One last consideration: time. Typical backup speed touted by the upper echelon of vendors is around 70MB per minute. If you have a data volume of 12GB, it is going to take most of three hours to do the backup. Build that time into your backup plan.

### Method Two—Complete Backup Once A Week And Incremental Backup Nightly

Keeping track of the tapes used in this scheme is more involved that the simple nightly complete backup. You will do one complete system backup every week and an incremental backup on all the other days. Pay close attention to the number of tapes you need for this *and* the schedule for reusing a tape. I may not have made it canon in the last section, but I made a strong point that you should never use your most recent backup tape. The same is true here, but pause for a moment and consider what is encompassed by *most recent backup*. In this case, the four incremental tapes following each weekly backup are unique. Each incremental tape will contain some data that are not on any of the others.

In order to do a system restore, you must first do a restore from the last weekly complete backup. Then follow that with a restore from each incremental backup—in order—up to and including the last one on the shelf. Yes, it is complicated and hopefully you won't ever have to do a restore. In the meantime, what you have done is saved lots of time by doing the incremental backups. So what if now and then the inconvenience of restoration comes back and takes a bite at you—in the long run you will have saved labor time, a very expensive commodity in any enterprise, large or small. I won't leave you hanging here. By my count, you need no less than nine tapes, including my penchant for one new and unopened.

### Method Three—A Complete Backup Weekly With A Nightly Differential Backup

This method only needs four tapes and the scheduling is a compromise between the two previous methods. First, you perform a full backup to get started, then each day for the rest of the week do a differential backup. Differential, remember, does not clear the archive bit in the file information block. That means each day the volume of data will increase and the backup will take noticeably longer by the end of the cycle.

The payback comes if you must do a restore. Again, this is a compromise between daily and incremental. To perform a complete restore for a crashed system, use the last complete backup first to restore all the files, then use the last differential tape to restore all the files that have changed since the last complete backup. Restoring a single file uses the same procedure. Restore from the last complete backup first, then use the last differential backup.

### Variations On A Theme

As you can see, plenty of versatility exists in backup methods. You can find the backup procedure that works best for your operations. A word of caution is in order here. If you use the incremental or differential method, use one or the other. Never mix the two together.

I once consulted for an accounting firm that did the books for several companies. Now, accounting firms perform operations based on accounting periods, either 12 or 13 periods per year. At the end of each period, the books are closed for that period, and rolled over to the next.

This accounting firm performed differential backup every night, up to the last day of the accounting period. Then, before the period was closed, it performed a complete backup. The tapes were then placed in archival storage for five years in compliance with IRS record-keeping rules. If any question about a particular accounting period came up, the accounting firm was fully prepared to restore the backup for a complete examination of the books. Of course, the accounting firm charged for that service, but they were able to provide it because they developed a backup procedure that allowed them to.

# On-Site Storage Vs. Off-Site Repository

Every company that performs a regular backup has some place to keep the backup tapes on-site. In many cases this is a small fire-proof safe that will protect the backup for a limited period of time. But if the fire or other hazard is not contained in time, the safe will eventually fail.

Most experts agree that the weekly complete backup should be archived in an offsite location. That is a good idea. A safe deposit box at your company's bank is a good choice. By implementing this archive system into your procedure, you will almost always have data available that is no more than 30 days old.

# Hardware

Sooner or later we had to get to the hardware. It is, after all, a necessary part of our overall security posture. In this section we are going to discuss the following:

♦ Firewall server

♦ Proxy server

♦ Caching server

## Firewall Systems

As you made your way through this book, you have occasionally seen different applications for firewalls. Actually, the term *firewall* is almost always misused. We define a firewall as a computer with two network connections. One connection comes from a *protected* network, the other connection goes to an *open* network. In VPN terminology as it is used by Novell, the protected network is known as the *private* network, and the open network is known as the *public* network.

In reality, when most people use the term firewall, they actually mean a system comprising several components, which may or may not include a *proxy server*, a *cache device,* and, of course, a *firewall.* As you will see, the functions of the system are quite complex, requiring combinations of hardware and software designed to work in concert to provide blocking functions for unwanted TCP/IP data packets. In Chapter 5 we showed you some firewall configurations: the screened host, the screened subnet, and the dual-homed gateway. Many different methods and configurations for constructing firewall systems exist. Advantages are present with each different system configuration. If you plan on implementing a firewall system, you should perform a fairly thorough study before jumping in.

We are not going to introduce any new configurations or show any systems that differ substantially from what you have already seen. Instead, we are going to provide you with some theory about firewall design, and some detail in how that design is implemented.

### Architecture

An explanation of firewall architecture requires a basic understanding of TCP/IP. As if we have not talked about TCP/IP enough already, we shall look at it from a different viewpoint—without, I promise, lengthy discussions of IP addresses or subnets. This time we're going to talk about sessions, sockets, and ports. To help us out with this discussion, I am going to call on my old friend, Linux.

The Linux operating system is patterned very closely to that of Unix. Engineers at AT&T Bell Labs developed Unix as a time sharing, multiuser/multitasking operating system that could be implemented on a single processor. Unix operates in a TCP/IP environment for its network interface and serves as a host system. In this environment, Unix can run different applications for different users and do it concurrently. Unix—and its clone, Linux—are indeed very powerful operating systems.

The engineers designed the Linux system architecture so that when a user logs in to the system it creates the equivalent of a separate logical computer. Then Linux assigns that logical computer to the user. Because these logical computers exist within the confines of the real physical computer, any number of them can be created. Each logical computer is switched in to the physical computer for a short period of time—the essence of time-sharing—then switched out while the other logical computers are switched in. This way, the physical computer can serve all the logical computers that it created.

Consider each logical computer as a *session*. Each time a new user logs in, a new session is created. The interesting thing about this is that the users are not always at the physical computer's console. More often they are on the computer's network. The physical computer doesn't care where the user is coming from; all it cares about is creating another session.

Having a physical Linux computer running multiple sessions for multiple users is the concept of *multiuser* capability. As each user operates within the confines of his or her session, they may execute more than one application. Each time a user performs a different function or task, they start a different application. Often, one user may perform several different tasks at the same time during a session. Hence, the term *multitasking*.

Okay, now we have multiple users on separate sessions performing multiple tasks on one physical computer via a network. Good grief—you need to understand how Linux keeps all this stuff straight.

It starts by assigning an identifier to each session. Each application that requires input and output is assigned a logical device commonly called a *port* in Linuxese. NetWare and NT refer to these logical devices as *sockets*. These ports or sockets are logical devices, and each different port is assigned a unique number. In Linux, port numbers are 16 bit numbers, allowing a range of up to 65,536 ports. The operating system reserves the first 255 ports for specific applications used within Linux and TCP/IP for specific application protocols. A list of typical protocols and port numbers is shown in Table 10.1.

In order to keep this stuff straight—and assure that the right session uses the correct port to process a particular datum and send it over the network to the intended user—the port numbers are stuffed into the UDP/TCP header when the packet is formed. The transport and session layers of the OSI network model described back in Chapter 3 take care of this chore for us.

**Table 10.1  TCP/IP port assignments.**

| Port Number | Keyword | Description |
| --- | --- | --- |
| 1 | TCPMUX | TCP Port Service Multiplexer |
| 5 | RJE | Remote Job Entry |
| 7 | ECHO | Echo |
| 11 | USERS | Active Users |
| 13 | DAYTIME | Daytime |
| 17 | QUOTE | Quote of the Day |
| 19 | CHARGEN | Character Generator |
| 20 | FTP-DATA | File Transfer (Default Data) |
| 21 | FTP | File Transfer (Control) |
| 23 | TELNET | TELNET |
| 25 | SMTP | Simple Mail Transfer |
| 37 | TIME | Time |
| 42 | NAMESERVER | Host Name Server |
| 43 | NICNAME | Who Is |
| 53 | DOMAIN | Domain Name Server |
| 67 | BOOTPS | Bootstrap Protocol Server |
| 68 | BOOTPC | Bootstrap protocol Client |
| 69 | TFTP | Trivial File Transfer |
| 79 | FINGER | Finger |
| 80 | HTTP | HyperText Transfer |
| 102 | ISO-TSAP | ISO-TASP |
| 103 | X400 | X.400 |
| 104 | X400-SND | X.400-SND |
| 109 | POP2 | Post Office Protocol—Version 2 |
| 110 | POP3 | Post Office Protocol—Version 3 |
| 137 | NETBIOS-NS | NetBIOS Name Service |
| 138 | NETBIOS-DGM | NetBIOS Datagram Service |
| 139 | NETBIOS-SSN | NetBIOS Session Service |
| 144 | NEWS | News |
| 146 | ISO-TP0 | ISO-TP0 |
| 147 | ISO-IP | ISO-IP |
| 161 | SNMP | SNMP |
| 162 | SNMPTRAP | SNMPTRAP |
| 163 | CMIP-Manage | CMIP/TCP Manager |
| 164 | CMIP-Agent | CMIP/TCP Agent |
| 165 | XNS-Courier | Xerox |
| 201 | AT-RMTP | AppleTalk Routing Maintenance |
| 202 | AT-NBP | AppleTalk Name Binding |
| 203 | AT-3 | AppleTalk Unused |
| 204 | AT-ECHO | AppleTalk Echo |
| 206 | AT-ZIS | AppleTalk Zone Information |
| 246 | DSP3270 | Display Systems Protocol |

Okay, when the packet arrives at the destination, the receiving protocol stack decodes the port number and routes the data to the proper application—and everyone lives happily ever after. Well, almost; some things you need to keep in mind: The assignment of port numbers to applications is not an option; it is a requirement. The first 256 ports are reserved for protocols used and managed by the Internet. The remainder, up to 65,536, are available for general use, and any programmer can use them if they understand the protocol for making the assignments.

Now that I have driven you down this road that seems to lead nowhere, it's my job to explain how a firewall works and what it is good for. Firewalls work by blocking unwanted TCP/IP datagrams and allowing needed TCP/IP datagrams to pass through. Some of those unwanted datagrams may be bogus attempts sent by hackers to attack your system. The firewall does its job simply by determining which port is being used by an application and selectively rejecting all ports that are not allowed. In reality it is a bit more complex than this and you will learn more when we get to the proxy server.

### *Firewall Design Philosophy*

In the world of firewalls, two different camps man the bulwarks. Each has its own philosophy and its own design. As we have done in previous discussions when different approaches were apparent, I will discuss each design as objectively as possible. But sometimes my bias leaks through.

Let me reinforce a point I made earlier. Firewalls are generally placed at the connection between the Internet (public network) and the intranet (private network). The term *firewall* is generally misused to describe a complete system. For the purpose of this section, I am using firewall to define a single computing device with two network connections. This device is generally configured to allow traffic to flow freely from the intranet (private network) to the Internet (public network), and restrict traffic flowing from the Internet to the intranet. In other words, any and all traffic can go out, but only allowed traffic can enter. The process of selecting specific TCP/IP packets to pass through the firewall is generally referred to as *filtering*.

This leads us to the primary difference between the two design philosophies. The differences are as simple as they are a world apart. They revolve around what to allow and what to block, in the *original default configuration*. The difference can be stated like this:

♦ Allow nothing unless it is specifically requested.
♦ Block nothing until you are specifically told to do so.

In the first configuration, filters are put in place to block all TCP/IP packets (although we have not talked about it, the same capability is available for IPX/SPX protocols) at the time the firewall is installed. This, of course, has the effect of immediately shutting off access to the Internet completely. The network administrator then enables only those TCP/IP protocols needed for network operation. This firewall allows the network administrator to keep track of what can and cannot go through. Unfortunately for the users, it causes some problems. When users are accessing information located around the Internet, the originator of the information will use a specific port assignment to pass that information. If the network administrator has blocked that port with a filter, the information will not pass through the firewall.

In the second case a firewall initially has no effect on Internet traffic in either direction. The network administrator must specifically enable the filters to block the required ports. Only those specifically enabled filters will affect Internet access. The idea behind this firewall is to place as few restrictions on the users as possible, while maintaining some degree of control over Internet access. The downside is that it is fairly easy for the administrator to miss a port or two, or possibly a range, and leave windows of opportunity open to attack.

Both systems perform exactly as the manufacturer specifies after they are properly configured. But before they are configured, the two systems are as different as night and day. I don't know enough about your network to tell you which is better for you. You must balance your perception of required protection against the degree of user frustration you are willing to withstand. This is especially true if your business is rather small, and you are depending on an outside vendor to perform configuration changes on your network.

My recommendation is that you take a hard look at what you want in a firewall system. Then look at different products and find the one that matches your needs as closely as possible. I will say this much: After looking at both the Windows NT VPN implementation and the Novell BorderManager VPN implementation, I feel that both adequately serve the needs of their customers without placing undue hardship and configuration problems on the network users. I say this keeping in mind that some basic philosophical differences exist between the Novell approach to networking and the Microsoft approach to networking.

## Proxies

We made the statement earlier that the firewall was only one part of the complete system. Another part of a firewall system is the proxy server. I said it before: I guarantee that as long as your network is not connected to the Internet, you will not have to worry about attacks from that direction. Because that defeats the very concept of VPN, you don't have that option. Instead, let's build a computer with special programming that can be configured to perform the following operations:

♦ Intercept outgoing traffic addressed to the Internet, then replace all information in the TCP/IP packets that identify your specific computer and IP network with information that would point back only to itself.

♦ Forward the reconfigured outgoing packets over the Internet to the destination.

♦ Intercept the incoming packets, strip off its own address, and replace it with your computer's identity on your network.

♦ Forward the reconfigured incoming IP packets to your computer.

What you see is a device that performs the equivalent—in a logical manner—of isolating your computer from the Internet. It acts on your behalf to send and receive data to and from the Internet, while hiding your computer and your network. This device becomes your *proxy* for Internet operations.

That is what a proxy server does. The proxy server uses the information included in the TCP/IP headers to identify the source and destination computers, and the protocol port numbers. It assigns a *request identifier tag* to each request coming from the network headed for the Internet, and removes the information that identifies your computer and your network from the TCP/IP headers. This information is appended to the request identifier tag and set aside within the proxy server.

The proxy server then appends the request identifier tag and information that points to itself to the TCP/IP headers and shoots it off into cyberspace. When information arrives from the Internet, the proxy server looks for the request identifier tag in the TCP/IP header. If a tag is present, the proxy locates the original header information, strips out the proxy server identification and replaces it with yours, and sends you the message.

The operation of a proxy server is complex. It requires a large amount of storage and a high performance platform. In many cases proxy servers are proprietary devices loaded with a combination of hardware and software, specifically designed to perform only proxy server functions. All of that is intended to enhance the proxy server's performance. Novell (in their BorderManager product) and Microsoft manufacture proxy server software products. The performance of these products is reported to be as good as any on the market.

As you would expect, it takes a huge amount of RAM to keep a proxy server happy. This led to a proxy server enhancement known as a *caching server*. A cache is a section of memory—generally RAM, but in some cases hard drive storage can be used—set aside to hold frequently requested information. Passing information over the Internet is much slower than at the local network speed. When multiple users access the same Internet site repeatedly, it makes sense to keep the site information on a local network machine rather than continually receiving the information from the Internet. That's the job of the caching server.

Proxy servers, by necessity, have a large amount of memory on a high performance platform. It makes good sense to combine the features proxy and caching server into one package called a *proxy cache* server—a combination of two products that serves each function well.

### In The Firewall Nutshell

As I pointed out back in Chapter 5, you can configure firewall systems in many different ways. That not only adds to the complexity, but it also makes the decision about which way to go that much more difficult.

In considering a firewall system, I recommend you first take a close look at the type of information present on your existing network and the complexity of your existing network. Talk with your peers in your particular area of business and learn how attractive networks like yours are to outside attack.

If your network doesn't invite outside attack and its information is not all that confidential or critical, then adopt a firewall system that primarily meets the needs of your users. If your network is attractive to attack, and it processes mission-critical operations, then you need to implement a firewall system with a high degree of security. In any case, you must balance the security posture against the effect it has on the users.

In all probability, your firewall system will fall somewhere in the middle—offering moderate security against the most common attacks, and allowing the users a reasonable degree of freedom for their Internet needs.

# Software

Hardware is only a part of your security defenses. Software plays a significant part. We will start our discussion with a short look back at some network protocols, then move into encryption techniques.

## Protocols

The network protocol is the foundation of the system. Like all foundations, if not designed properly, the entire structure is subject to weak spots and the whole thing might crumble with your fingers still poised above the keyboard. In this section we will take a quick look back at some of the protocols, and what security measures have been applied to them.

### PPP

In Chapter 3, we said the Point-to-Point protocol (PPP) is a serial-line protocol used primarily for remote access through PSTN networks. Among its advanced features are the abilities to:

♦ Operate over more multiple protocols than TCP/IP. For example, PPP supports IPX/SPX and Appletalk on the same connection at the same time.

♦ Support DHCP, allowing network administrators to assign IP addresses on an as needed basis.

♦ Support IP header compression to allow for faster data transmission.

The security aspects of the PPP protocol deal primarily with authentication. In this respect PPP works well with two other protocols, both related to establishing secure connections. These are:

♦ Challenge Handshake Authentication Protocol (CHAP)

♦ Password Authentication Protocol (PAP)

In addition, when used with the Microsoft VPN protocol PPTP, PPP supports:

♦ User authentication using clear text, encrypted, or Microsoft-encrypted authentication

♦ The ability to create PPP datagrams that contain encrypted IPX, NetBEUI, or TCP/IP packets

Used with PPTP, PPP encryption is based on the MD4 hash using the shared secret encryption method. The user password, which is known to the user and recorded in the SID on the NT server, is the shared secret. This makes a good policy on passwords an absolute must for access using a PPTP VPN.

When using CHAP, the node on the network receiving the incoming connection initiates a series of data packets called the *challenge sequence*. The caller then modifies the challenge sequence and sends it back. That becomes the *handshake*. If the handshake is satisfactory, the remote user is authenticated by the network.

PAP uses a different procedure to perform the same function. In the PAP a series of ID/Password pairs from the remote user is compared against a list of authorized ID/Password pairs. If a match is found, then the incoming call is validated and the user is allowed access to the network. Both protocols authenticate the remote user before allowing access to the network.

### PPTP

Because the members of the PPTP Forum have such a diverse range of products, it is difficult to target a single implementation architecture. However, they all have some similarities:

♦ *Authentication based on CHAP or enhanced MS-CHAP*—This usually incorporates the shared secret key encryption.

♦ *Authorization*—If necessary, users can be assigned policies to allow different authorization levels. If authorization is implemented, it is usually provided by policies stored in a RADIUS database.

♦ *Data encryption*—Before data is transmitted over the Internet, it should be encrypted to prevent intercepted data from being read by unauthorized clients.

♦ *Key management*—To create and refresh encryption keys for servers and clients.

♦ *Multiprotocol support*—So heterogeneous clients can communicate over the VPN.

PPTP VPN connections are made with initial 40-bit or 128-bit encryption keys, depending on the end unit's country of origin. When used in NT 4, PPTP depends on two proprietary protocols, MS-CHAP and MPPE, to protect user data.

### Note
*With a few notable exceptions like Canada and some privileged concerns, United States government policy restricts distribution of 128-bit technology.*

### L2TP

For a review of layer-2 protocol features, let's look at excerpts from **msdn.microsoft.com/workshop/server/feature/vpnovw.asp**.

♦ *User authentication*—Layer 2 tunneling protocols inherit the user authentication schemes of PPP, including the EAP methods discussed below. Many Layer 3 tunneling schemes assume that the endpoints were well known (and authenticated) before the tunnel was established. An exception to this is IPsec ISAKMP negotiation, which provides mutual authentication of the tunnel endpoints. (Note that most IPsec implementations support machine-based certificates only, rather than user certificates. As a result, any user with access to one of the endpoint machines can use the tunnel. This potential security weakness can be eliminated when IPsec is paired with a Layer 2 protocol such as L2TP.)

♦ *Token card support*—Using the Extensible Authentication Protocol (EAP), Layer 2 tunneling protocols can support a wide variety of authentication methods, including one-time passwords, cryptographic calculators, and smart cards. Layer 3 tunneling protocols can use similar methods; for example, IPsec defines public key certificate authentication in its ISAKMP/Oakley negotiation.

♦ *Dynamic address assignment*—Layer 2 tunneling supports dynamic assignment of client addresses based on the Network Control Protocol (NCP) negotiation mechanism. Generally, Layer 3 tunneling schemes assume that an address has already been assigned prior to initiation of the tunnel. Schemes for assignment of addresses in IPsec tunnel mode are currently under development and are not yet available.

♦ *Data compression*—Layer 2 tunneling protocols support PPP-based compression schemes. For example, the Microsoft implementations of both PPTP and L2TP use Microsoft Point-to-Point Compression (MPPC). The IETF is investigating similar mechanisms (such as IP Compression) for the Layer 3 tunneling protocols.

♦ *Data encryption*—Layer 2 tunneling protocols support PPP-based data encryption mechanisms. Microsoft's implementation of PPTP supports optional use of Microsoft Point-to-Point Encryption (MPPE), based on the RSA/RC4 algorithm. Layer 3 tunneling protocols can use similar methods; for example, IPsec defines several optional data encryption methods that are negotiated during the ISAKMP/Oakley exchange. Microsoft's implementation of the L2TP protocol uses IPsec encryption to protect the data stream from the client to the tunnel server.

♦ *Key management*—MPPE, a Layer 2 protocol, relies on the initial key generated during user authentication, and then refreshes it periodically. IPsec explicitly negotiates a common key during the ISAKMP exchange, and also refreshes it periodically.

♦ *Multiprotocol support*—Layer 2 tunneling supports multiple payload protocols, which makes it easy for tunneling clients to access their corporate networks using IP, IPX, NetBEUI, and so forth. In contrast, Layer 3 tunneling protocols, such as IPsec tunnel mode, typically support only target networks that use the IP protocol.

### IPsec

The IPsec protocol suite encompasses a large number of different protocols that cover a like number of different areas. These areas can be divided into three primary groups:

♦ *Authentication*—Developed in the form of an Authentication Header, or AH.

♦ *Tunneling*—Developed using the IP Encapsulating Security Payload, or ESP.

♦ *Encryption*—Developed using a choice of several different encryption protocols and key management protocols.

We covered IPsec thoroughly in Chapter 4, so all we need here is a quick refresher.

First, for authentication purposes, IPsec provides a protocol known as the *Authentication Header*, or AH. The IP Authentication Header (hereafter called AH) provides the following services:

♦ Connectionless integrity

♦ Data origin authentication

♦ An optional anti-replay service

AH has two modes of implementation, transport or tunnel. When AH is implemented in transport mode it provides protection primarily for upper layer protocols because the IP datagrams are not encrypted. When AH is implemented in tunnel mode the protocols are applied to tunneled IP packets.

In the datagram, the AH is placed between the ESP and the outer IP header and is made up of several fields:

♦ *Next Header*—Indicates what the higher level protocol following the AH is, for example, ESP or TCP.

♦ *Payload Length*—An 8-bit field specifying the size of the AH.

♦ *Reserved*—For future use.

♦ *Security Parameters Index* or *SPI*—A set of security parameters to use for this connection.

♦ *Sequence Number*—Incremented by one for each packet sent with a given SPI.

♦ *Authentication Data*—A digital signature for this packet.

IPsec requires specific algorithms for implementing both ESP and AH. These *minimum requirement* algorithms guarantee minimal interoperability between entities implementing IPsec. All IPsec implementations must support HMAC-MD5 and HMAC-SHA1 for the AH.

Second, the tunneling protocol for IPsec is based on the IP Encapsulating Security Payload, a versatile method of datagram encapsulation. ESP is a process that provides integrity and confidentiality to IP datagrams. ESP can be implemented separate from IPsec, and when used separately, ESP does not require an AH. If authentication is desired, it is implemented as an AH. Because ESP can be implemented either with or without AH, ESP can provide the three basic operations of:

♦ Confidentiality and integrity of IP datagrams only

♦ Authentication only

♦ Both authentication and confidentiality and integrity of IP datagrams

Which one of these three services is implemented is determined by the choice of algorithm and algorithm mode. When ESP is implemented as a part of the IPsec protocol suite, the Authentication Header or AH is always implemented.

ESP provides confidentiality and integrity by encrypting data and placing them in the data—or payload—portion of the IP Encapsulating Security Payload. When the mode selected is tunnel-mode ESP, the original IP datagram is placed in the encrypted portion of the ESP and then the entire ESP frame is placed within a datagram having unencrypted IP headers. This process is slightly different from previous encapsulation protocols in that, when using ESP, the original datagram, including the datagram headers, is encrypted and becomes the Encapsulating Security Payload.

The structure of an ESP datagram is different from other IP datagrams. In the first part of the ESP, the payload is placed in the unencrypted field(s), then comes the encrypted datagram. In addition to the unencrypted IP address information, the unencrypted ESP datagram header contains information that tells the intended receiver how to properly decrypt and process the data. This information is in the form of a special data field known as a *Security Parameters Index*. The SPI negotiates an agreement between the two endpoints relating to what type of security should be implemented and how strong the security should be. This agreement between the two endpoints is the *Security Association*.

### Encryption

When using ESP, you can use a number of different encryption algorithms. You can enable a number of tunnels, each using ESP and each using a different encryption algorithm to encrypt the data. You can also include padding by inserting null characters in the datagram before it is encrypted. That makes all the datagrams the same size after encryption, which further prevents security breaches through an attack called *traffic analysis*.

By default IPsec specifies a 56-bit DES-CBC cipher. This guarantees minimal interoperability between IPsec entities.

### The Security Association(s)

To provide reliable secure transport operation you need a method that assures entities on both ends of an IPsec implementation are properly authenticated and that both understand the proper methods used to encapsulate and decapsulate the datagram. In addition, the datagram must meet all the standards for traditional IP protocols in order to provide reliable transport from the origin to the destination.

A *security association* (SA) established between the origin and destination provides this service. When you consider all the different algorithms and protocols involved in IPsec, you begin to see what we mean when we say the SA is fundamental to the operation of IPsec.

An SA is a simplex virtual connection that provides security services to the data carried by it. Unlike the ESP and AH, in which either one or the other or both can be used, in the SA security services are provided by either AH or ESP, but not both. Because both AH and ESP can be applied to a traffic stream, two SAs must be established when both AH and ESP are implemented. Establishing duplex communications between two security gateways requires you to establish an SA for each direction.

Each SA is uniquely identified by three components:

♦ A Security Parameter Index, or SPI (previously defined in the AH header)

♦ An IP destination address

♦ A security protocol, either AH or ESP

We said two types of SAs are defined: transport and tunnel. A transport mode SA is made between two hosts. A tunnel mode SA is applied to an IP tunnel. If an SA is made between two security gateways, or between a security gateway and a host, then that SA must use tunnel mode. VPNs use the tunnel mode SA.

The datagram in a tunnel mode SA contains two IP headers called the *outer* and *inner headers*. The outer header specifies the IPsec processing destination, such as the security gateway at the destination network, and the inner header specifies the ultimate destination for the packet. As you can see, the outer header may have its contents altered by the routers the datagram passes through on its path through the Internet. The inner IP header will not change and is therefore securely protected by both AH and ESP.

We also said the processes place the AH between the inner and outer headers. That header carries information for the IPsec processing destination entity used in processing the received datagram. As I said, SAs can be combined to provide multiple levels of security, as well as transport or encapsulation capabilities. When SAs are combined, the result is called an *SA Bundle*. A *bundle* is a sequence of SAs through which traffic must be processed. Each SA in the bundle satisfies a requirement of the total security policy. In actual implementation, the security administrator develops the SA bundles in the installation and configuration process. Only in rarest of cases should it be necessary for the administrator to get down to the code or configuration-file level. However, a knowledge of the final outcome helps to make the configuration process more understandable.

The Security Association concept in IPsec is complex. A critical part of the SA concept is the SPI. The SA exists on a virtual level, but the SPI is a real number in every datagram that is forwarded using the IPsec protocol stack. The SA is only one part of the complete protocol. The second part is the encryption and the generation and management of encryption keys.

### Key Management Protocol With Oakley Key Exchange

Passwords work fine for authentication to the network. However, for encryption we need something stronger. The best encryption techniques are derived through algorithms. The numbers produced as a result of the encryption process are technically known as *ciphers*.

The more commonly used term for the sets of numbers used to generate a cipher is *key*, or *keys*. In the world of encryption, you will find two types of keys: *public* and *private*.

A private key is a large group of numbers known by as few people as possible. Without a doubt, a well-maintained private key encryption system is very secure. As the number of people involved in the encryption algorithm increases, the chance of a mishap involving the key increases and increases yet again when the group of people are displaced over a large geographical territory. Private key encryption works best if you only have one or two individuals involved.

Public key encryption is the other method. Today the most dominant form of public key encryption is the *RSA Public Key Cryptosystem*, named after its developers, Rivest, Shamir, and Adleman. RSA is based on the same principal as private key encryption using very large numbers as keys manipulated through a mathematic algorithm. The difference between public key and private key encryption is the existence of *two* keys, public *and* private, generated by the same algorithm. Either key can encrypt the cipher, but only the other key can decrypt it. In other words, if the public key is used to encrypt the data, the private key must be used to decrypt the data and vice versa.

You can use the public key encryption scheme by itself for encrypting and decrypting data sent between two individuals. However, when combined with AH and ESD, the reliability and security are increased dramatically. When a connection is made between two endpoints, the endpoints are authenticated first, then a public key/private key pair is generated. After the endpoints are authenticated, one of the keys is sent to the other end. When both endpoints have a key, then they can encrypt outgoing data and decrypt incoming data.

The chances of someone discovering one of the keys increases over time. It makes good sense then to periodically change the public key/private key pairs that have been issued. You can do this individually, because all the users do not have to be present when you update the keys.

As with public key/private key encryption, a well maintained public key encryption system is reliably secure, but remember, the encryption system must be properly maintained.

### Proving You Are Who You Say You Are—The Certificate Of Authority

A *Certificate of Authority*, or CA, is nothing more than a trusted independent third party, an entity whose identity you can prove and who then can provide proof that others are who they say they are. A good analogy to this is a Notary Public.

The CA is based on public key/private key encryption, only this time, signatures are what are being encrypted—digital signatures. The CA makes a large public key available through several different locations. When you register with a CA, the system requests you to produce a digital signature. The digital signature is a group of characters that uniquely identifies you to the system. The CA then produces a key pair then sends one to you and keeps the other along with your digital signature in its secure database. A business (let's say the business you wish to set up a VPN with) will also register with the CA.

Now, let's step through the process together and see how it works. This seems like a long, drawn-out process, but it will be over before you can think of the next key to press. Here goes:

1. You, as the remote user make a connection to the Internet, contact the business wanting to establish a secure VPN.

2. The business uses IPsec AH to authenticate a connection with you. As a part of establishing the SA, the AH requests your digital signature.

3. Your computer encrypts your digital signature with the CA key pair and sends one to the business.

4. The business forwards the bundle to the CA requesting confirmation that you are who you say you are.

5. The CA looks up your name in its secure database, gets the matching key, and uses it to decrypt your digital signature and compare it to the signature on file.

6. If it is a match, the CA prepares a certificate stating that the signatures match and uses the private key half of the CA's public key/private key pair to encrypt the certificate.

7. The CA sends the encrypted certificate to the business which then uses the public key part of the public key/private key pair to decrypt the bundle.

8. Provided everything still matches, the business will then generate a key pair, and send one to you via the authenticated, but as yet unencrypted, tunnel.

9. Each end uses its respective key to encrypt outgoing traffic and decrypt incoming traffic.

**Note**

*The AH header contains the SDI field. If anyone tampers with the datagram in route the SDI will not match and IPsec will negate the process. When the SA has been established, ISAKMP will manage the SA until the connection is torn down. If necessary, ISAKMP will change keys on a regular basis using the Oakley key exchange system.*

You need more than encryption to establish a reliable and secure communications channel between two entities. First, an authentication process must take place before the first datagram is transported (AH). Second, a method of encryption agreeable to both ends must be applied to the encapsulation security payload (ESP). Third, the encryption process must be *well maintained.*

In the IPsec protocol stack, the ISAKMP provides for regular exchange and update of the keys used to encrypt and decrypt the ciphers. These keys are exchanged over the channel after both ends have been authenticated using the AH.

# Encryption

*Encryption* simply means to make a message unintelligible. In geological terms, encryption is relatively new—having really only been around since the late 1800s. For an example of early cryptography look at **www.bokler.com/eapoe.html**. Over the past century experts have developed several techniques for encrypting information, but it was not until the development of the computer that powerful techniques became possible.

Cryptography and encryption is complex. If you want to pursue the subject in greater detail, take a trip to **home1.gte.net/mcorphan/bookstores.html** and find a bookstore that suits your tastes.

According to Novell's Encyclopedia of Networking, Encryption is "...*a process used to transform text into an unreadable form, known as ciphertext.*" Mathematicians have devised many types of encryption based on one or another type of algorithm. I have mentioned encryption several times so far. Now it is time to add some additional information about how encryption works and perhaps point out some strengths and weaknesses of a few algorithms.

Our investigation will center primarily on three encryption techniques:

♦ *Symmetric block cipher*—as used in the Data Encryption Standard, DES.

♦ *Hash algorithms*—as used in MD5 and other closely related algorithms.

♦ *Public key cryptography*—as used in the RSA algorithm.

We will then look at two other lesser-known encryption algorithms, Blowfish and the emerging IDEA.

## Data Encryption Standard—DES

A good place to start is the Data Encryption Standard (DES), probably the most widely used encryption scheme. DES was adopted in 1977 by the National Bureau of Standards as Federal Information Processing Standard 46 (FIPS PUB 46). In using the DES encryption method, 64-bit blocks of data are encrypted using a 56-bit key.

The original DES was developed to meet an RFP issued by the National Bureau of Standards in 1973. At the time, IBM had completed a research project in computer cryptography led by Horst Feistel. The result of the IBM research project was a cryptography algorithm designated LUCIFER. It is a Feistel block cipher that takes as input data blocks of 64 bits and, using a key size of 128 bits, produces an output block of 64 bits.

Mathematicians modified the algorithm to eliminate weaknesses found by the National Security Agency and the key size was reduced to 56-bit to allow it to be placed on a single chip. The result was accepted by the Bureau of Standards and officially adopted in 1977.

A detailed analysis is not possible here because we are not privy to the classified algorithm. But you can find a neat tutorial at **www.zolatimes.com/V2.28/DES.htm**. All we will give you is the general procedure. Keep in mind that DES requires data input in the form of a block of 64 bits, and a key of 56 bits. Plain text processing takes three phases:

1. The initial 64 bits of plain text is processed through an initial permutation. The output is a 64-bit block with the order of the bits rearranged and called the *permuted input*.

2. Next comes 16 rounds of repeating function involving both permutation and substitution. The 64-bit output is a function of the permuted input and the key. The left and right halves of the output are then swapped, to produce the *preoutput*.

3. The preoutput is subjected to a final permutation, the inverse of the permutation used in the initial step, to generate the final 64 bits of ciphertext.

Since the adoption of DES as an encryption standard, controversy has existed over the level of security provided. The large majority of concerns about DES have been raised in two areas: key size and the algorithm used.

### Cracking DES

All that led to a challenge from RSA Laboratories. They offered $10,000 to anyone who could find a DES key, given a ciphertext for a known plain-text message. The method of attack was a brute-force program distributed over the Internet. As new challengers picked up the gauntlet, they were assigned a section of the 56-bit key to use in their attack. Eventually, more than 70,000 computers and their masters were struggling with the puzzle. It took more than 96 days for someone to finally claim the prize. By then, about one-fourth of the possible keys had been examined.

Keep in mind that the brute force attack worked in part because the attacker knew the plain text that was used to create the ciphertext. That factor seems to be a requirement in any brute-force attack. The project did not accomplish it's goal of drawing attention to the weaknesses of the DES standard, spurring discussion about alternatives for conventional encryption standards.

The other discussion revolves around the nature of the algorithm used in DES. Some ongoing concern exists about the possibility that cryptanalysis is possible just by exploiting the characteristics of the DES algorithm. This concern centers around the eight substitution tables, or S-boxes, used in the iterations. The rumor is that someone knowledgeable about the weaknesses of the S-boxes can do the cryptanalysis. Despite a number of irregularities and unexpected behaviors of the S-boxes, no one has so far bragged in public and proved that they have found the supposed fatal weaknesses.

Amidst all the hubbub, investigation into new cryptography standards has caused mathematicians to develop the following variations of the DES standard:

♦ Double-DES, with two encryption stages, and two 56-bit keys.

♦ Triple-DES with two keys. This one was developed to counter the man-in-the-middle attack that hackers launched against double-DES with its two keys.

# MD5

The *message-digest algorithm (MD5)* was developed by Ron Rivest at MIT. It is what is known as a *hash algorithm*. According to Thawte Consulting in Raleigh, North Carolina, "A **hash** is simply a 'summary', or 'tag', which is generated from a digital document using a mathematical rule or algorithm. It is designed so that a small change in the document would produce a big change in the hash. Hashing algorithms are 'one-way': you can create a hash from a document, but you cannot recreate the document from a hash. A hash is *not* an encryption of the document. Most importantly, it's very difficult to find two documents that have the same hash." You can read more about what they say by visiting their Web site: **www.thawte.com/support/crypto/hash.html**.

The MD5 algorithm has an input message of arbitrary length, and produces from this input a 128-bit message digest. The input is processed in 512-bit blocks in the following manner:

1.  Append padding bits so that its length in bits is congruent to 448 modulo 512.

2.  Append length of the result in step one with a 64-bit representation of the original message length.

3.  Initialize MD buffer—a 128-bit buffer to hold intermediate and final results of the hash function.

4.  Process the message in 512-bit blocks.

5.  Output the result—after all 512-bit blocks have been processed, the output is the 128-bit message digest.

Despite the hash algorithm's complexity, MD5 is considered by a growing population to be vulnerable to a variety of attacks. That is leading a gradual movement for adopting a new hash algorithm. The National Institute of Standards and Technology developed a *secure hash algorithm (SHA)* based on the MD4 algorithm.

MD5 and SHA-1 evolved from MD4 and hence, are similar in design. This results in similarity in their strengths. The primary difference between them is that the SHA-1 digest is 32 bits longer than the MD5. This longer digest increases the difficulty encountered in a brute-force attack.

# RSA

The trio of Ron Rivest, Adi Shamir, and Len Adleman, all from MIT, are responsible for developing the RSA algorithm. The crypto-community recognizes all three as leading cryptanalysts. First published in 1978, RSA has reigned supreme as the leading general-purpose approach to public-key encryption. As with the hash algorithm, the RSA algorithm is relatively complex, and we are not going to eviscerate it here. Try going to **world.std.com/~franl/crypto/rsa-guts.html** to get a closer look.

We have also hashed out (no pun intended) the subject of private and public keys enough so that we are sure you fully understand the concept. We will limit the discussion to a very few words for refresher. Any public key algorithm is dependent on the development of two keys, one public and one private. The private key is kept a secret; however, the public key can be released to the public. If the message is encrypted with the public key, the private key must be used to decrypt it. The opposite is also true: A message encrypted with the use of the private key can only be decrypted with the public key.

In the public key algorithm, key generation and key management are crucial factors. As with the other cryptographic algorithms, the RSA algorithm can be attacked. The most likely attacks to succeed are the following:

♦ *Brute force*—Trying all possible keys until you stumble accidentally across one that works.

♦ *Mathematical attacks*—The equivalent of factoring the product of two primes.

♦ *Timing attacks*—Based on the running time of the decryption algorithm.

So far, the RSA wizards have devised adequate solutions to counter each of these three attacks and allowed the RSA public key algorithm to continue to provide reliable encryption.

# Blowfish

*Blowfish* is a lesser known symmetric block-cipher developed by Bruce Schneier. He designed it to have the following characteristics:

♦ Blowfish encrypts data on 32-bit microprocessors at a rate of 18 clock cycles per byte.

♦ In some applications Blowfish requires less than 5K of memory.

♦ The structure of Blowfish is simple, and easily implemented.

♦ The key length size is variable, and can be as long as 448 bits.

Blowfish encrypts 64-bit blocks of plain text into 64-bit blocks of cipher-text implementing a variable bit key length. It is implemented in a number of products, and has at one time or another undergone considerable investigation. Up to now, no information can be found challenging the security of Blowfish. In his book, *Cryptography and Network Security: Principles & Practice*, William Stallings said "...with regard to brute-force attacks, Blowfish is virtually invulnerable with suitable choice of key length." But then, it hasn't been around as long as DES, either.

# IDEA

The *International Data Encryption Algorithm (IDEA)* is the new kid on the block. This is another symmetric block-cipher developed by Xuejia Lai and James Massey of the Swiss Federal Institute of Technology. IDEA is one of several conventional encryption algorithms vying to replace DES.

IDEA inputs data block sizes of 64-bits with a 128-bit key. From a design standpoint, IDEA's cryptographic strength is based on the following philosophy:

- *Block length*—Should be long enough to deter statistical analysis and at the same time avoid the complexity that grows exponentially with block size. Thus the use of a block size of 64 bits.

- *Key length*—Should be long enough to prevent exhaustive key searches. Thus, the key length of 128 bits.

- *Confusion*—Should depend on the plain text and key in a complicated and involved way. To achieve this goal IDEA uses three different operations, as compared to the XOR operation found in DES.

- *Diffusion*—When every plain-text bit and key bit should influence every cipher-text bit. By spreading out the individual plain-text bits over many cipher-text bits, the statistical nature of the plain text is effectively hidden.

IDEA is designed to allow implementation in either hardware—using very-large-scale-integration chips—or software. When implemented in hardware, high-speed operations are the expected result. IDEA is one of several encryption algorithms presented as a replacement for DES. IDEA is seeing the greatest success of any of the current proposals in the area of adoption, and is included in PGP, which enjoys widespread adoption world over.

# Chapter 11

# *VPN Management And Maintenance*

*Key Topics:*

♦ *Developing a performance baseline*

♦ *Capturing Windows NT4 statistics*

♦ *Capturing BorderManager statistics*

♦ *How to use the VPN statistics*

♦ *Administrative checklists*

♦ *VPN maintenance tasks*

♦ *Troubleshooting the VPN*

Now that you have successfully installed your VPN, the next order of business is to keep it running efficiently. In this chapter we will help you do just that by looking at some traditional administrative and management tasks—with the viewpoint of the VPN in mind. We will show you some tasks that are more related to VPN than to anything else.

We put all the troubleshooting procedures in this chapter for good reasons. Many times the procedure you will use to troubleshoot network-related problems is the same, regardless of what software you are using. Rather than stretch troubleshooting over several chapters, repeating the same procedures each time, we decided it would help you more if we placed all the procedures in one place. The last section of this chapter is devoted entirely to troubleshooting both VPN-specific items and, because it is often difficult to separate the two, a section on troubleshooting common TCP/IP problems.

## Moving From Implementation To Operations

After you have the VPN initially set up and have allowed access to a few users, you will find several places that will require tweaking to improve performance. Most administrators consider this the final part of the installation phase. At some point, this tweaking will move from being part of the implementation phase to being a part of the operation phase. The move from the implementation phase to the operations phase of the VPN installation should take place in an orderly manner. In fact, you probably will not recognize the point at which that happens.

In any given network system, operations are basically the same. The only difference is the type and configuration of the equipment involved. You can divide operations into three individual steps, each of which is equally important:

♦ *Monitoring*—Usually performed by equipment configured to monitor and/or record data traffic related to a specific part of the system.

♦ *Administration*—Usually adding and removing users or groups, assigning passwords, and maintaining good overall security.

♦ *Troubleshooting*—Usually performed after a problem has occurred (reactive troubleshooting).

A significant portion of the operations phase should be devoted to monitoring. If you have the correct equipment, monitoring becomes nothing more than properly configuring specific types of equipment and monitoring them on a regular basis.

## Developing A Performance Baseline—If You Don't Know Where You're Going, Any Road Will Get You There

I teach my troubleshooting classes that to troubleshoot anything, you must know three things:

♦ What does normal operation of the system look like?

♦ What does the operation of the system look like when the problem is present?

♦ What system devices are involved that can affect the system in such a way as to cause the difference?

Numbers two and three are easy to come by. We make the assumption that the system has a problem, because you are working on it. If you connect the proper monitoring equipment to the system—more about this in a bit—you can get a fairly good idea of the operation of the system when the problem is present.

With an accurate network diagram, you can locate the devices involved between the input and output points of the system. You only need a little knowledge to determine which equipment can cause your system's problem.

The most difficult information is what comprises *normal system operations*. The manufacturers will provide you with data sheets for all the individual elements connected to your network, but that won't tell you what the *system* should look like under *normal* operations. The only way to do that is to monitor the system and develop, over a period, a *baseline for normal operations*.

## Gathering The Information For A Baseline

You may already have a performance baseline for your company's LAN. Although this information will be valuable for isolating problems in that LAN, in all likelihood it won't help much in establishing a VPN baseline because:

♦ The percentage of network utilization figure will not be correct because the LAN bandwidth of 10MB or 100MB will determine the figure.

♦ The information on the number of packets transmitted and received is for all packets, and you are concerned with only those packets that apply to the VPN.

♦ You usually will not have a method of tracking lost or retransmitted packets.

You need to develop a performance baseline by monitoring the network interfaces used by the VPN tunneling server. Start by monitoring:

♦ Generic information common to both VPN protocols

♦ Information specific to Microsoft PPTP protocol

♦ Information specific to Novell IPSec protocol

Because the information you need to monitor is the same, regardless of what type of VPN you have installed, let's first look at some items you should monitor, then discuss specifics about how to gather the information.

## Statistics You Should Monitor

Regardless of what type of VPN system you are using, you should monitor certain parameters for the VPN tunnel activities. I offer Table 11.1 as a minimum list, with the caveat that it is by no means everything available. Feel free to add additional items to meet your specific requirements.

By the way, the terminology used here may vary from one vendor to another (and I mean it as a general guide, not to name a specific tag). For example, what Windows NT refers to as *frames*, BorderManager calls *packets*. In either case, the monitored category refers to the same logical group of data bits. One last point: In some cases you may not find corresponding data in both products.

**Table 11.1   Elements to monitor for establishing a VPN baseline.**

| Tunnel Details | Connections | Transfer Operations |
| --- | --- | --- |
| Status (up or down, with times listed) | Active connections (current and maximum) | IP encrypted packets sent |
| Successful client connections (with list of times) | Connection type (client-to-site or site-to-site) | IP encrypted packets received |
| Failed client connections (with list of times) | Duration | Unencrypted packets sent |
| IP packets sent | | Unencrypted packets received |

*(continued)*

**Table 11.1**  **Elements to monitor for establishing a VPN baseline** *(continued)*.

| Tunnel details | Connections | Transfer operations |
| --- | --- | --- |
| IP packets received | | Sent packets discarded |
| IPX packets sent | | Receive packets discarded |
| IPX packets received | | Total packets sent |
| Total packets sent | | Total packets received |
| Total packets received | | Total bytes sent |
| Total bytes sent | | Total bytes received |
| Total bytes received | | |
| Total sent packets discarded | | |
| Total receive packets discarded | | |
| ◆Data should include total and packets or bytes per second | | |

# How To Capture Statistics

Novell's Lanalyzer for Windows and HP's Open View are very good protocol analyzers for monitoring the VPN. Lest you think we are giving short shrift to the rest of the world, consider the number of protocol analyzers and the differences between them far beyond the scope of this book. If you have another brand and are comfortable using it, consult its user guide for the best method to perform the monitoring functions required.

If you do not have a protocol analyzer, the software provided by Microsoft and Novell both will perform some basic needs. The methods for collecting the data will vary between them, but we will take a quick look at each.

### *Microsoft Windows NT 4*

Capturing statistical information about the network is straightforward and relatively painless with Windows NT. The tool you will use most is *Network Monitor Agent*. It is not installed by default; to see if it was installed, use the following procedure:

1. Click on Start | Settings | Control Panel to open the Windows NT control panel, as shown in Figure 11.1.

2. Click the Network icon in the control panel and open the network properties pages. Click on the Services tab to open the network services properties page shown in Figure 11.2.

3. If the panel lists Network Monitor Agent as one of the installed services, you can skip the rest of this procedure. Otherwise, click the Add button and open the Select Network Service dialog box, as shown in Figure 11.3.

**Figure 11.1**
Windows NT control panel.

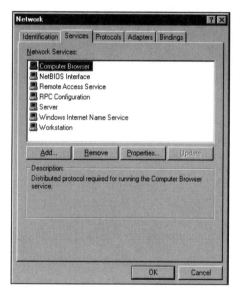

**Figure 11.2**
This panel allows you to select various Network properties for modification.

4. Scroll through the list and select the Network Monitor Agent, as shown. When you have selected the Network Monitor Agent, click on OK.

5. The installation process will probably need to copy some files, either from the CD-ROM or from another location. Mount whatever volumes the program requests. When the installation process is complete, a dialog box prompts you to restart the computer to finish the addition of the Network Monitor Agent.

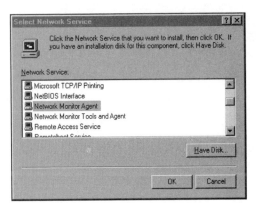

**Figure 11.3**
Network services selection panel.

After you restart the computer, the Network Monitor Agent sends information to the Performance Monitor. This is the part of Windows NT that records statistics about the various components making up the NT server. You must configure the performance monitor to capture and display the information provided by the Network Monitor Agent. Let's do that now:

1. Click on Start | Programs | Administrative Tools | Performance Monitor, as shown in Figure 11.4.

**Figure 11.4**
Typical Performance Monitor panel.

2. To add the network statistics to the Performance Monitor chart, click on Edit to open the drop-down menu. Select Add to Chart, as shown in Figure 11.5, and click to open the Add to Chart dialog box, as shown in Figure 11.6.

3. Click the list arrow next to the Object property to open the object list shown in Figure 11.7. Click on NBT Connection and the dialog box changes to that shown in Figure 11.8, allowing you to select the specific items you wish to monitor.

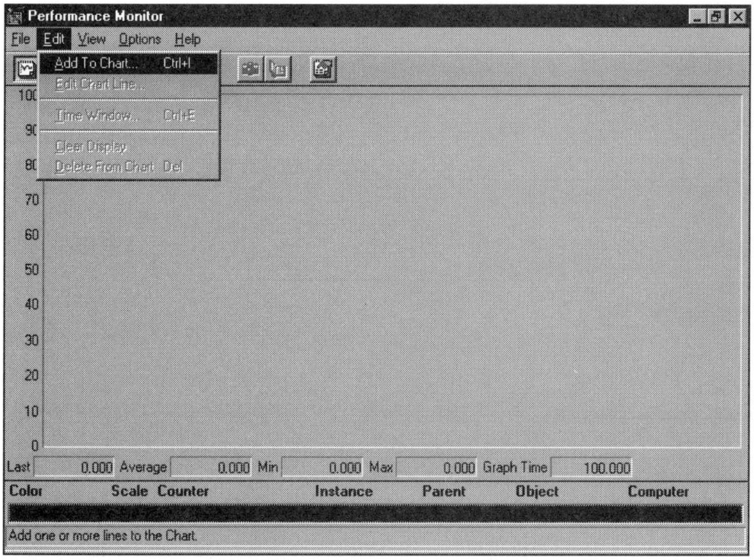

**Figure 11.5**
Drop-down menu for editing the Performance Monitor.

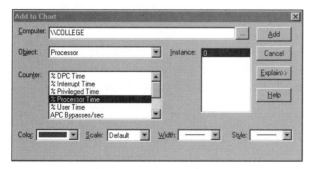

**Figure 11.6**
Add to Chart dialog panel.

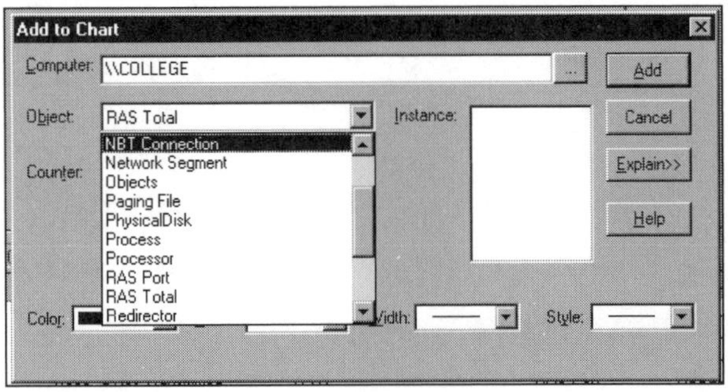

**Figure 11.7**
NBT Connection is selected for adding to the chart.

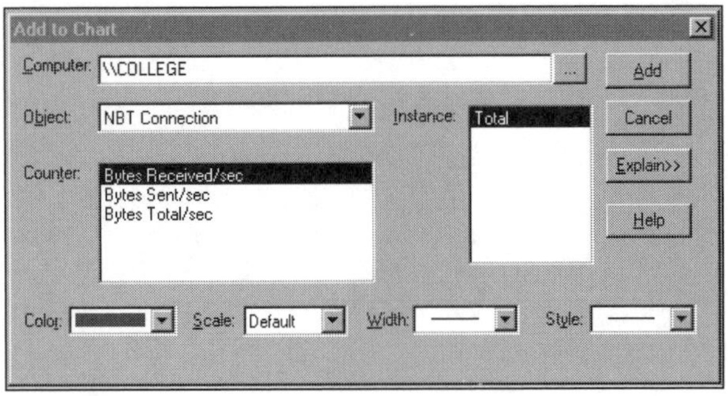

**Figure 11.8**
One item under the NBT connection is selected for display.

4. To add an item to the performance monitor, highlight it in the list box and click Add.

5. When you are finished selecting items, click on Done. That closes the dialog box and returns you to the Windows NT Performance Monitor.

To add to the repertoire, go back through the preceding five steps. This time, select RAS Port instead of NBT Connection to open the Add to Chart dialog box shown in Figure 11.9. Then select RAS Total, which opens the Add to Chart dialog box, shown in Figure 11.10.

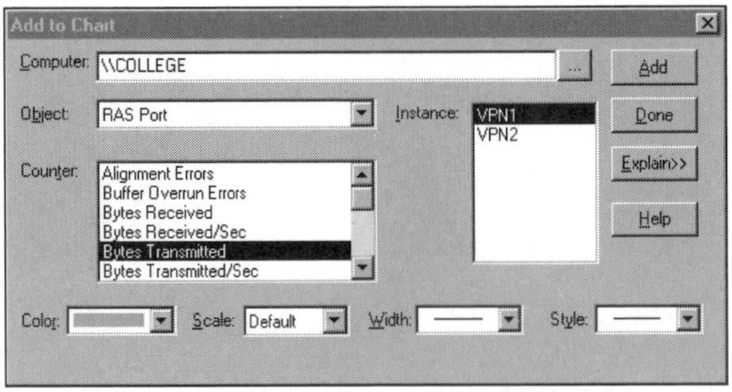

**Figure 11.9**
RAS Total is now selected in the Add to Chart panel.

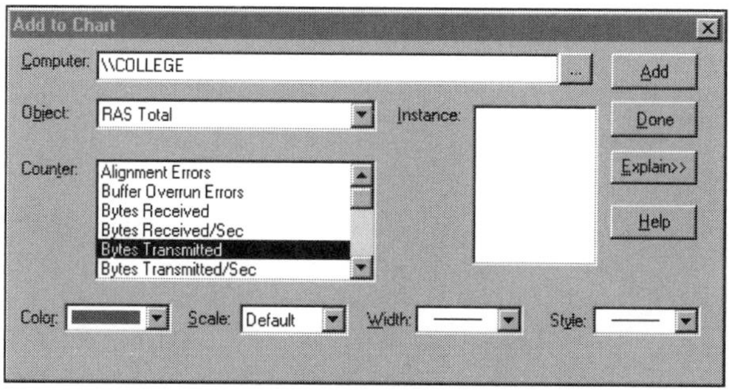

**Figure 11.10**
One item under the RAS Total is selected for display.

If you need to change the configuration of the chart after selecting some items to monitor, click on Edit to open the selection list, then click on Edit Chart Line. (This is not available unless the chart has at least one valid statistic to monitor.) With the Edit Chart Line dialog box open, as shown in Figure 11.11, you can change the chart's configuration to suit your preferences.

The Windows NT performance monitor presents the statistics in a chart form, with each item assigned a different color. The performance monitor continues to monitor the statistics until you close and remove it from the active services. The next time you want to record statistics, you will have to reconfigure the performance monitor.

### Note

*The more items the performance monitor charts at the same time, the greater the resource load. During high load times, the performance monitor may require more resources than the benefit received from using it. If the system bandwidth is adversely impacted by the performance monitor, the next best solution is to use a separate protocol analyzer not on the PPTP Tunneling server.*

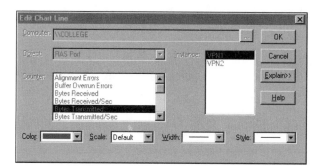

**Figure 11.11**
You can tailor color, scale, width, and style to suit the user.

### BorderManager And NWAdmin

Novell recommends that you have only one NDS Tree containing all the objects, including all the servers, in that single tree. Although Novell says—in fact, recommends—that you can have more than one Admin object, in many networks this is not the case.

That can lead to an interesting problem. When you install NetWare, the process places NWAdmin in a subdirectory on each NetWare server. When you install BorderManager Services on a NetWare server, you must install the Border Manager Snap-In on *all* NetWare servers that you may possibly use to administer the BorderManager server. If you don't, then you may find yourself in a situation when you launch NWAdmin, only to find that the system did not add pages for the BorderManager features to the NetWare server.

### Novell BorderManager Services

You will perform most BorderManager VPN monitoring with the NetWare administrator program, NWAdmin, on the administrator workstation. That can be any computer on the network running Windows 95, 98, or NT. However, before you can use NWAdmin, you must install the BorderManager Snap-In, an addition to the NWAdmin program included in the BorderManager Services package. We covered the installation of the BorderManager Snap-In in Chapter 7. If you have not yet installed the Snap-In, this is a good time to take care of that chore.

## Accessing Statistics For BorderManager

To access the statistics for the BorderManager Services VPN, use the following procedure:

1. From an administrator workstation, log in as a user with admin equivalence to the tree containing the VPN servers you want to monitor.

2. Launch NWAdmin. Navigate through the tree to the container holding the VPN and double-click on that object to open the server object properties page.

3. Click the BorderManager Setup button, and select the VPN tab. That opens the VPN properties page, as shown in Figure 11.12.

4. Double-click the listing for Master Site-to-Site under the Enable Service to open the Master Site-to-Site dialog panel, as shown in Figure 11.13.

5. Click the Status button, which opens the VPN Synchronization Status dialog box, as shown in Figure 11.14. This screen shows the status of the VPN as one of three possibilities:

   ♦ *Up-to-Date*—Indicates that the server is configured with the latest topology and encryption information. Note: This does not indicate the status of the VPN Tunnel, only the synchronization between the master and slave VPN servers.

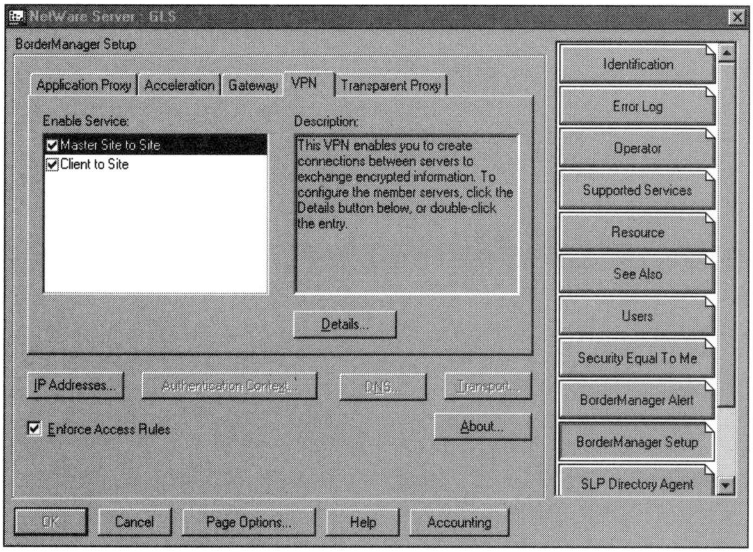

**Figure 11.12**
BorderManager setup panel.

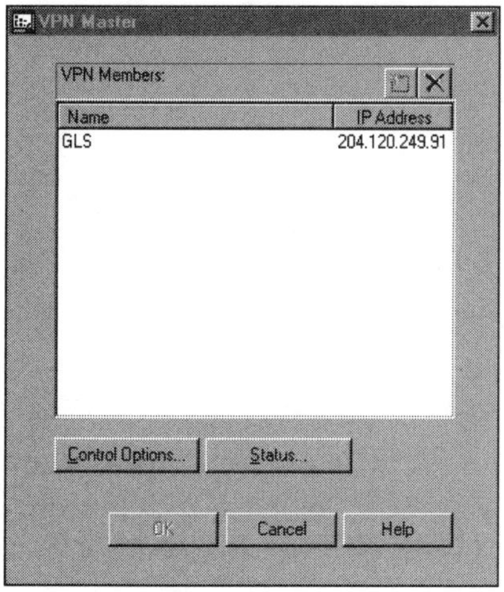

**Figure 11.13**
Master Site-to-Site dialog panel.

- *Being Configured*—Indicates that the server has not received the newest topology and encryption information from the master server.
- *Being Removed*—Indicates that the server is being removed from the VPN.

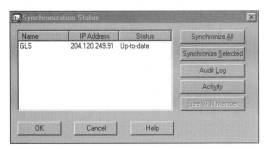

**Figure 11.14**
Synchronization status panel.

---

> **Note**
>
> *Novell says that any server state that remains at Being Configured or Being Removed for a long period of time indicates a failure (or other problem) in the communications link between the Master and Slave VPN servers. If this is a problem, you can remove the VPN server from the list by clicking on Free VPN Member.*

6. To monitor the statistical information for a VPN server, select the appropriate server in the list and click the Activity button. This opens the VPN Activity properties page as shown in Figure 11.15. The following sections give a summary of each group of statistics. For a more detailed description, refer to the online documentation supplied with the BorderManager Services product or online at **support.novell.com**.

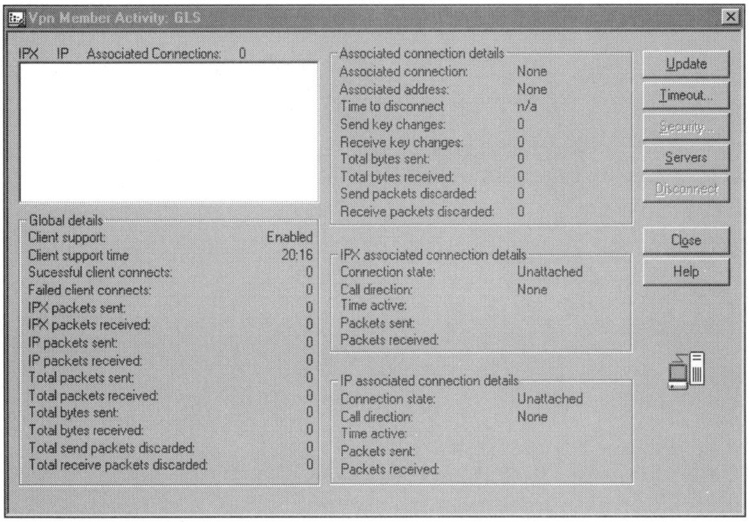

**Figure 11.15**
VPN activity monitoring page for BorderManager.

- *VPN Associated Connections*—The panel in the upper-left quadrant of the screen displays the real-time activity of the currently selected VPN server and associated tunnel connections. A series of colored arrows represents the activity as follows:

  - *Green Up arrow*—Currently active tunnel: packets have been received within the last 35 seconds.

  - *Light Blue Up arrow*—Currently active tunnel; packets have been received from 35 to 70 seconds earlier.

  - *Yellow Up arrow*—Currently Active tunnel; packets have not been received within the last 70 seconds.

  - *Magenta Up arrow*—Previously established tunnel; the connection is currently unattached.

  - *Red Up arrow*—Tunnel is in the process of being established.

  - *Red Down arrow*—Encryption tunnel is currently down; no packets were ever received. (This indicates a problem. For more details, check the Audit Log)

- *VPN Tunnel Global Details*—Items in this group provide global VPN connection information.

- *Associated Connection Details*— Provides statistics about the tunnel between the selected VPN member and the VPN member at the other end of the tunnel.

- *IPX Associated Connection Details*—Provides statistics about the IPX traffic that has passed through the tunnel between the selected VPN member and the VPN member at the other end of the tunnel.

- *IP Associated Connection Details*—Provides statistics about the IP traffic that has passed through the tunnel between the selected VPN member and the VPN member at the other end of the tunnel.

7. To view statistical details relating to the security items, such as encryption and authentication key parameters, click the Security button.

8. If you configured the VPN as a Client-to-Site VPN, you can click the Client button to view the same statistical information about the client connections. Note that this button toggles between Server and Client statistics. Clicking on the Client button changes the display to the client VPN member activity, as shown in Figure 11.16.

Global statistics recorded by the system for the BorderManager VPN are cumulative and the program retains the totals for as long as the VPN server is running. When you release a connection, the system quits monitoring details of that specific connection. You should rely on the global statistics to develop your baseline for normal operations. For troubleshooting purposes, use the associated connection details and the VPN audit log.

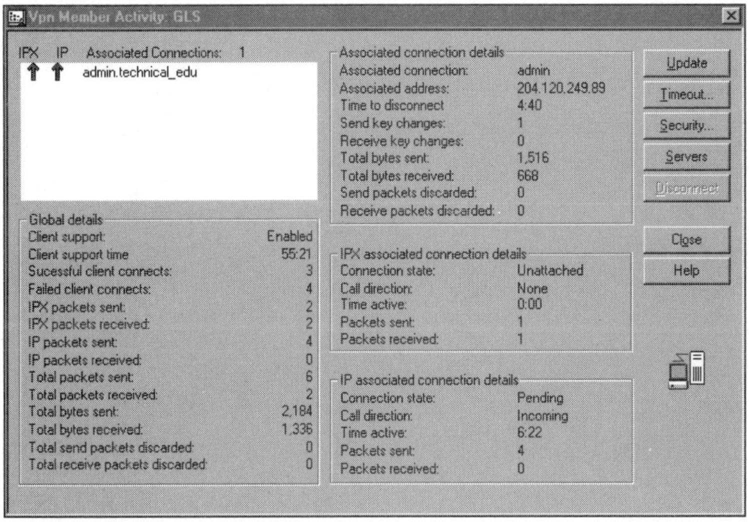

```
Vpn Member Activity: GLS                                              [X]

IPX  IP  Associated Connections:  1      ┌Associated connection details──────┐   [ Update  ]
 ↑   ↑   admin.technical_edu             │ Associated connection:   admin    │
                                         │ Associated address:  204.120.249.89│   [ Timeout... ]
                                         │ Time to disconnect:      4:40     │
                                         │ Send key changes:        1        │   [ Security... ]
                                         │ Receive key changes:     0        │
                                         │ Total bytes sent:        1,516    │   [ Servers  ]
                                         │ Total bytes received:    668      │
                                         │ Send packets discarded:  0        │   [ Disconnect ]
                                         │ Receive packets discarded: 0      │
 ┌Global details──────────────────┐      └───────────────────────────────────┘
 │ Client support:        Enabled │                                             [ Close ]
 │ Client support time:   55:21   │      ┌IPX associated connection details──┐
 │ Sucessful client connects:  3  │      │ Connection state:    Unattached   │   [ Help  ]
 │ Failed client connects:     4  │      │ Call direction:      None         │
 │ IPX packets sent:           2  │      │ Time active:         0:00         │
 │ IPX packets received:       2  │      │ Packets sent:        1            │
 │ IP packets sent:            4  │      │ Packets received:    1            │
 │ IP packets received:        0  │      └───────────────────────────────────┘
 │ Total packets sent:         6  │
 │ Total packets received:     2  │      ┌IP associated connection details───┐
 │ Total bytes sent:       2,184  │      │ Connection state:    Pending      │
 │ Total bytes received:   1,336  │      │ Call direction:      Incoming     │
 │ Total send packets discarded:  0│     │ Time active:         6:22         │
 │ Total receive packets discarded: 0│   │ Packets sent:        4            │
 └────────────────────────────────┘      │ Packets received:    0            │
                                          └───────────────────────────────────┘
```

**Figure 11.16**
Client statistics.

## Maintaining And Using The Baseline

Once you have developed a baseline for so-called normal operations, you may think that you do not have to continue monitoring normal operations. However, you must remember LAN operations, in general, and VPN operations, in particular, change over time. Especially remember that Internet operations, the substance of your VPN, change daily. Don't be shy about changing your baseline to accommodate trends. However, do it only when you know the trend is not a function of an internal breakdown in your system's performance.

Periodic monitoring should continue to be a routine part of your network operations. Study your monitored data for any large scale changes from the baseline. Look for areas that might cause noticeable difference in operations. Use this method to identify trouble spots before they start having a degrading effect on normal operations.

# Administrative Checklists

As a part of normal operations, the network administrator must perform certain administrative tasks that we have conveniently divided into daily, weekly, and monthly intervals. I suggest you distribute the weekly and monthly tasks across the calendar so you don't have to cope with one inordinately long day each week and one impossibly day every month. I suggest that you need not perform the weekly and monthly activities (except for the 24-hour scan of Internet traffic) at the same time each week or each month. This may or may not fit your particular circumstance. With that thought in mind, use the following as suggestions and mix and match to fit your particular needs. One final note: I wrote the items in what *I* consider the order of importance—that is, the first item on the list is the most important. Skip any items that your configuration does not enable.

# Daily

The daily tasks are:

♦ Retrieve the new backup tape and examine the backup and verification logs. If you don't see any errors, archive the backup log.

♦ Prepare the daily backup.

♦ Check the error logs and record errors that occurred in the past 24 hours. Scan the error logs for the previous five to seven days for any developing pattern.

♦ Check the traffic logs. Record the volume of traffic and the time the traffic occurred. Scan the previous traffic logs for developing patterns in the network traffic. Plan for future upgrades in areas where needed.

♦ If you have a major scheduled upgrade or other major network activity planned for this day, do it now.

♦ Check your road warrior list. Remind any who are in the home office to turn in their laptop computers for the latest software updates.

♦ Perform weekly administrative tasks scheduled for this day.

♦ Create and delete users, modify user profiles, and configure software for users as needed.

# Weekly

Simply because this section is titled weekly does not mean the listed tasks must be performed on a particular day of the week. In fact, it will probably work out to everyone's advantage—especially yours—if you distribute the tasks throughout the week. Plan the distribution to cause the minimal perturbations in your daily administrative procedures. The weekly tasks are:

♦ Prepare for the weekly backup.

♦ Download network client updates and application software updates from the Internet as applicable. If your system automatically updates remote users when they log in, make sure the configuration includes the latest updates.

♦ Review all VPN-related network traffic logs from the past week. If the preparation of summary reports and trend analysis is part of your job description, do that now.

♦ Meet with your VPN support team—include all people directly or indirectly involved. Discuss the Internet trend analysis report, the need for any changes, upgrades, or modifications, and upcoming scheduled activities. If necessary, finalize the plans for any event you scheduled for the coming week.

# Monthly

As in the weekly tasks, you don't need a magic day for monthly administrative tasks. Typically, these items affect a large population of the users. When planning them, you must consider causing the minimum disruption to services and facilities when they are accomplished. Part of that is publicizing the event and wherever possible doing it during off-peak hours. The monthly tasks are:

♦ Apply any required Windows Service Packs or Novell Support Packs to the network system. But make sure you test them on a spare machine in the lab before you stuff them into a network machine.

♦ If your network system is Novell NetWare, perform any major changes to the Directory Tree—merging partitions, relocating containers, relocating servers within the tree structure, and so forth.

♦ Install new software applications—such as migrating from MS Office 97 to MS Office 2000. This is especially important with respect to the remote or traveling users when downloading via the VPN is not practical.

♦ Perform a 24-hour Internet traffic scan for baseline analysis.

**Note**

*I recommend that this be performed on the same day of the week, in the same week of the month, on a regular basis. In this way Internet traffic patterns can be baselined and a trend log can be developed and used to track changing conditions on the Internet.*

♦ Conduct monthly training sessions, especially for your remote/traveling users.

# VPN Maintenance Tasks

Now and again, a network newbie will ask, "Exactly what is the Internet?" Because you are reading this book, you probably have an answer and chances are that answer is about as good as any. Occasionally, the newbie turned neophyte will come up with a more interesting question, like *who takes care of the Internet?* That's a good question, especially when you're having a problem and you think the Internet might be part of it.

The answer to the second question is, of course, about as easy—or difficult—to answer as the first question. If the Internet is a large network of individual networks, it stands to reason that Internet maintenance is performed by the individuals responsible for maintaining those individual networks.

If your company has a VPN so its users can access the company network from the Internet, you own a small part of the responsibility for the overall health of the Internet. The problem is finding out who takes care of the rest of it.

## Keeping Up With The Internet

With respect to Internet maintenance, you need to work closely with your ISP. Not only is the Internet a collection of individual—and we left out independent—networks, it is a collection of different software operating systems. At one time, the only Internet operating system was Unix, flawed as it was in the early days. Now, the majority of the operating systems currently in use on the Internet today are still Unix, albeit much improved, but many more operating systems are parked in cyberspace that are every bit as capable of giving satisfactory performance.

To maintain your chunk of the Internet in your part of cyberspace, you only need to know the syntax for your operating system. No one should expect you to know the syntax for every possible Internet operating system. Therefore, if you have a problem, and you trace that problem outside your network, you are going to have to locate the person responsible for maintenance of another network and work with them to get things back in shape.

Thankfully, the majority of the time you only have to make your ISP aware of the problem and pass the responsibility across the chain. Of course, that requires you to work with others—regardless of what you may think of their skill, knowledge, and capabilities compared to your own.

I said it before and I will remind everyone: In networks, the majority of troubleshooting is a social exercise—the problem is not fixed until the user says it's fixed. If the problem is located within the fabric of the Internet, you will find the tables have turned. Then, you are the user and you will rely on someone to provide you with the service you need. You might find yourself in the role of a frustrated user that has to put up with a service technician with an attitude.

Fortunately, very few service technicians I have dealt with have an attitude. Of course, it helps when the individuals at both ends of the line are knowledgeable and understand the terminology involved.

## Tracking Traffic Patterns

Back in Chapter 7, we made a point that the performance of your network, at least the VPN part of it, is now conjoined with the Internet in a symbiotic relationship. In real terms, a problem on your VPN could actually be a problem on the Internet—somewhere. To keep your LAN and VPN at peak health, you must be able to perform statistical monitoring of the Internet.

A good starting place is your VPN interface with the Internet. You can easily collect the following statistical information:

♦ Total number of packets transmitted

♦ Total number of packets received

♦ Number of packet errors

♦ Overall application throughput

♦ Typical route through the Internet for a data packet

---

### *Monitoring WAN Link Usage*

The typical route through the Internet for a data packet may not be as easy to get. One utility you can try is called *TraceRoute*. Under normal circumstances, this program sends a data packet from one location to the another, sending back an ICMP message packet from every router it encounters. This may not work very well with a VPN because it encapsulates the TraceRoute packet. In that case, you may need a protocol analyzer.

I know of two useful programs for gathering this type of information. One is named *Cloud,* from Shunra Software; the other is named *Chariot,* from Ganymede Software. Either will prove useful for gathering information on latency and the number of dropped packets.

---

# Troubleshooting Your VPN

The procedures for troubleshooting a VPN follow the same basic pattern as any technically complex device. If your network is based on TCP/IP, you can use the same tools and procedures you use for troubleshooting any network problem. Keep in mind that you must temporarily reconfigure the filters to use certain types of tools. Having said that, I would now like to point out that in all likelihood, the majority of the procedures that follow are procedures you are already doing. For those of you new to troubleshooting—and those of you old enough to have learned that no one knows everything—I'll make an effort to include all the steps I normally follow in troubleshooting a problem. However, because this chapter deals with troubleshooting VPNs, I'll leave out a lot of the details until we get into the actual VPN troubleshooting procedures.

## On The Network Level

You can divide troubleshooting any technically complex system into a series of smaller steps.

1. Obtain a *problem report*—It is important to get as much detailed information as possible about the nature of the problem. Reports usually originate from a user who is anxious to help so they can get back to work. Sometimes the user will get hooked on a symptom and not the cause of the trouble. Getting a detailed description of the trouble helps isolate the problem. Have the person who reported the trouble demonstrate exactly what the problem is.

2. Isolate the *problem*—Systematically eliminate parts of the system until you have isolated the problem to a single section or part of the network system. Start with your log of previous trouble reports and look for a reoccurrence. If that doesn't help, do a Sherlock Holmes. Analyze the system logically and draw up a list of possible culprits. Don't be shy about laying your system drawings out on a table to get the big picture.

3. Determine the *fault*—Once you have isolated the problem to a section of the network, use your tools to determine what is happening in the system at the point of failure. You can then compare what is happening with what is supposed to happen—and use your knowledge of the system to locate the fault.

4. Correct the *fault*—After you locate the fault, use your skills to correct the problem, and restore normal operation.

5. *Test and document*—When the system has been thoroughly tested and restored to normal operation, it is time to document the repair. As a minimum, your documentation should include the:

   ◆ Problem as it was reported

   ◆ Equipment and/or software involved

   ◆ Test procedures used to isolate the problem and locate the fault

   ◆ Exact nature of the fault

   ◆ Exact nature of the repair

   ◆ Tests you performed to verify normal operation

**Note**

*You should provide as much detail as possible about the nature of the fault and what you did to fix it. This documentation should be copied into the master trouble log—either a paper log or an electronic database.*

## Down To The Desktop

Computers are complex systems of both virtual and real parts. In a desktop PC system with no applications running, we can divide the system into three areas:

◆ *Hardware*—The physical devices that make up the PC system.

◆ *Software*—With no applications running, the only software involved is the operating system.

◆ *Configuration*—This is all the information entered by you, the user, or default settings that tell the software how to interface with the hardware.

With applications running, the scope of the configuration increases to include the application software and the configuration may include both the operating system and the peripherals.

## Spreading Out

A LAN has the same three areas on each desktop, plus the same three areas that comprise the network as a system. Expanding still further to a WAN increases the overall scope, adding still more hardware and configuration items. Finally, expanding to include a VPN expands the possible trouble areas to the Internet itself—which is vastly more complex.

Having painted that picture of gloom and doom, let me add some sunshine and show that it's not all as bad as it looks. To begin with, most application software today is—in spite of popular opinion—reasonable reliable. That means that if you're having a problem with an application, it is most likely caused by configuration problems as opposed to a bug in the code.

Most software and hardware vendors have Web sites on the Internet where you can go and download the latest patches and drivers. Many of these same vendors devote a separate section of their Web site for listing common users' problems, along with fixes for them. This provides a factory direct support capability right at your keyboard for many of the more common problems encountered.

### Getting Help For The VPN

You won't have to solve VPN problems on your own; you will have a virtual army of ISPs to back you up. This is their bread-and-butter, and they want to keep their customers happy.

Back in Chapter 1, we told you how the ARPANET evolved to provide redundant paths between networked computers. Back then, the scheme was that if one path broke down, the data would reach its destination via an alternate path. Well, guess what? That same scheme is alive and well today—only it is more complex than its originators ever imagined. That complexity of the Internet, with its redundancy and alternate pathways, can be very intimidating to the neophytes, but it makes the Internet very reliable.

## What You Need In Your Toolkit

Many enterprises divide their support operations into areas such as PC computers (including the operating system) and peripherals, applications software, and networking. For the purposes of this chapter, we are going to assume that one person does it all. If your organizational divides troubleshooting among different individuals or groups, encourage everyone involved in this to read this chapter, and then divide the tasks up, as you feel necessary.

Quite often, locating faults in complex systems is a process of elimination—making tests and measurements to prove a piece of equipment is *not* the cause of the problem. Suppose a protocol analyzer indicates a larger than normal number of packet errors related to a particular node address. The cause of the errors could be a faulty NIC or a noisy connector on the network cable. If a network cable tester verifies that the cable is okay, the test eliminated a potential culprit by the process of elimination.

You must have adequate tools in order to troubleshoot and repair a problem in a complex system. The larger and more complex the network system, the more important the proper tools become. Of course, the flip side of this is that tools are expensive, and justifying the purchase of specific tools—like a laptop computer—to perform a test may or may not be possible. Notwithstanding, here is what I think you should have to troubleshoot problems in a network with a VPN.

### Documentation

You should have the following documentation:

- First and foremost on the list, you must have good documentation. I cannot over-emphasize the importance of this, especially as your network grows. The larger your network becomes, the more important will be the documentation. (I personally don't think anyone ever has enough documentation about their computer/network system.) This documentation should be in two parts:

  - *Network*—You need network diagrams and wire-maps (complete with wire numbers) for every section of wire in your network system. You also need a complete list of all the hardware—servers, routers, switches, hubs, transceivers, and other miscellaneous items, including any configuration information about that hardware. Finally, you should know about any software used in the fabrication of your network.

  - *Desktops*—You should have a complete list of the hardware and software installed in each PC in your network, complete configuration parameters (especially the network properties), and a copy of the Windows Registry (or the equivalent file if your operating system is not MS Windows).

**Note**

*Keep this information in a database of some type. If that is not possible, keep it in an organized file system so the total information on a particular item in the system will be easy to locate.*

### Hardware And Software Tools

You should have the following hardware and software tools:

- A laptop computer loaded with Windows 98 or NT, a network card compatible with the network you are working on, the latest network client for the version of network system you are working on, a 56K V.90 modem, and at least a 2GB hard disk drive. At one time, a few people considered this a nice thing to have; today it is an absolute necessity for troubleshooting networks. While you're at it, load the troubleshooting database on the laptop so the technician can have that information available.

- A small (4 or 6 port) 10MB or 100MB twisted pair Ethernet hub.

- Three or four twisted-pair patch cables that you know work properly. Use the cable tester and verify these cables to be good before you go out on a trouble call.

- A protocol analyzer to troubleshoot a fully configured VPN implementation. Several third party vendors, like Hewlett Packard and Computer Associates (formerly Network General), have them on the market. Microsoft and Novell offer protocol analyzer software that is quite satisfactory for basic VPN troubleshooting. Microsoft's product is the SMS *Network Monitor*, and Novell calls its product *Lanalyzer for Windows*.

**Note**

*Microsoft includes a modified version of the Network Monitor software as a part of the Windows NT Server package. Unfortunately, it will not operate in promiscuous mode and will not capture packets on the network that are not addressed to the NT server. That means that by the time the packet is addressed to the NT server, it is out of the VPN tunnel. This limits the adequacy of the bundled capability for trouble-shooting.*

♦ A diagnostics software program for a PC computer. You can purchase any one of several different programs for this task. When I run diagnostics on a PC, I personally like to move as far away from the existing operating system on the PC as possible. For that reason, I prefer a diagnostics program on a bootable floppy disk or, even better, a bootable CD. That only works when you can configure the PC to boot from the CD drive and your CD-ROM writer can produce bootable discs.

♦ You need information about software configurations and jumper settings for your hardware devices. Some companies produce libraries of diagrams and configuration information for a wealth of different mainboards, network adapters, hard disk drives, and so on. They supply the information on a CD, and periodically update the data. For more information about this type of product, visit our Web site at **www.sldenterprises.com**.

♦ Your troubleshooting resources should include a library of the latest drivers for the hardware and peripherals in your system. The library must include operating system patches, drivers for video and sound cards, printer drivers, drivers for network adapters, and the latest version of all network clients. Here again, companies provide this information on regularly updated CDs. In addition, with the ready availability of CD-ROM writers, I think the idea of investing some time to download all the newest drivers from the Internet on a regular basis and burn them on a CD is a good idea.

♦ No system toolbox should be caught without a virus checker capable of detecting and eradicating all known viruses. You must update it as soon as new information is available from the manufacturer. Here again, a CD-ROM writer comes in handy.

♦ Keep a few blank diskettes handy; formatted for the type of system you are working on. You just never know when you will need them.

♦ Have a good cable tester handy that will perform the following tests:

    ♦ Wire-map

    ♦ Attenuation

    ♦ Noise

    ♦ Near End Cross Talk (NEXT)

*Note*

*I recommend investing in a cable tester with an auto-test feature that will run a suite of tests and compare them to an internal library of specifications. It will speed up the testing process and cut down on errors.*

♦ If you don't already have one, invest in a PC toolkit with the hand tools to assemble and disassemble PCs in the field. Make sure it includes an anti-static mat and static wrist strap.

*Note*

*I am assuming that you know about the dangers caused by static electricity and the methods used to prevent static damage to components. In your troubleshooting and repair procedures, always follow accepted procedures for preventing static damage to components.*

♦ If your enterprise has a shop in which the technical support staff can perform their work, it should have a POTS line directly to the outside world, circumventing any phone switching equipment the company has for handling incoming calls. You will use this outside line to troubleshoot laptop computers used by remote or traveling users that use the VPN to dial in and access the network.

### Software Tools

You should also arm yourself with software tools. Novell NetWare and Microsoft Windows NT come with an array of software tools specifically designed to aid you in isolating and correcting problems in their associated VPN products. Here are abbreviated lists of available products from each of the two vendors.

*Novell Netware*—Tools for troubleshooting BorderManager VPNs:

♦ NetWare Administrator VPN Audit Log

♦ CALLMGR

♦ Monitor

♦ Ping

♦ TPing

♦ IPXPing

♦ TCPCON

♦ IPXCON

♦ FILTCFG

♦ SLPINFO/D displays the status of the configured directory agents.

♦ NETSTAT -R displays the client's routing table.

♦ TRACERT [ip_address] displays the route that packets take to reach the destination address.

> **Note**
>
> *The last three items are VPN DOS commands for troubleshooting problems from a client workstation.*

*Microsoft Windows NT*—Tools for troubleshooting problems from a Windows VPN client machine. You will find these in the Administrative Tools section of the Program List on the Start toolbar:

♦ *Remote Access Admin*—You can use this to:

  ♦ Monitor the statistics of the RAS.

  ♦ Start, stop, and pause the RAS.

  ♦ Select a domain or server to monitor.

  ♦ Assign users to the RAS.

  ♦ Monitor active user connections.

♦ *Performance Monitor*—Used to monitor statistics about the RAS and VPN servers in chart format.

♦ *Windows NT diagnostics*—Used to perform diagnostics tests on the operation of the NT Server, RAS, and VPN tunneling server.

Also, Ping, TRACERT, Netstat, and Route are available from the DOS prompt. For information about the capabilities and proper syntax for these commands, enter the command name followed by /? at the DOS prompt.

> **Note**
>
> *I know this list of tools is quite long. Some of you probably think the only tool you need is a screwdriver. Well, sometimes that works—if your network is small and you are blessed with eidetic memory. But as the size of the network grows, it will become more and more difficult to keep all the details in your head. I suggest you plan on getting a good start up front.*

## Some Thoughts About Deskside Manners

We covered most all of the tangible tools needed to do a good job of locating and fixing problems. However, we left out the most important one—that tool is you.

I don't know why, but most computer users become very defensive and evasive when circumstances force them to finally call for help with their PC. It might be because they are afraid something they did caused the computer to quit working. In trying to find out what the problem with their computer is, often you find you must be diplomatic in asking them what the problem is. You may also find that asking the same question in a different way yields a different answer. I honestly don't think the person is being evasive. I think they are embarrassed about not knowing all the technical aspects of their computers and networks.

Another problem you are going to encounter is when a person tried to load a new or different program on their computer. In the process, they made a mistake and, of course, it crashed when they tried to restart it. Sometimes, you are going to come up against individuals that will deny they did anything to the computer. "Gosh," they say, "all I did was turn it on and it wouldn't work." Even when shown evidence that someone tried to load a different set of files on the PC, they will deny it was their fault.

You could raise a fuss, but I personally don't think that will accomplish very much. My suggestion is to show them any files you find out of order and ask them if they want to keep them. If the answer is yes, and the company policy allows it, create a directory and move the files there. If policy prohibits keeping the files, explain the reason and remove them.

Starting an argument with a user about copying files or loading a program on the computer is not going to get anyone anywhere, and it certainly is not going to improve their opinion of you as a PC repair technician. It is up to you to keep encounters from escalating into a war. Do your best to reassure the user that it probably wasn't their fault. Maybe the PC decided this was the day to go belly-up. Moreover, after all, on occasion any PC *is* subject to fail. If the battery on the mainboard droops below a marginal voltage, the CMOS RAM can lose the setup. In a large office building, just the machinery it takes to keep the functions of the building operating can create the equivalent of an electrical storm on the wiring inside the building. High voltage spikes can get through the power supply and cause havoc with the digital ICs. Stuff happens, and it's not anyone's fault.

In short, I suggest you adopt a rather good deskside manner. If it isn't his or her fault, reassure the user that they did nothing wrong. Fix the PC and get on with your life. In the long run, getting upset and carrying a grudge against the users doesn't hurt them nearly as much as it hurts you.

Now that I have you pretty well decked out, done up, and brainwashed into making the users think what nice person you are, let's figure out how to do some serious troubleshooting.

# Problem Isolation

In a large complex system with a VPN, the first question is how to get started. It is one thing to say the first step is to isolate the problem to a single section of the network. It is another thing to jump in there and do it—especially without some type of plan.

I'll tell you about the scheme I use most of the time. I won't guarantee that this will work in all cases, but I can vouch for the fact that it works in the large majority of them. Now and again, I may find it necessary to change things to fit specific cases and so will you. I seem to like to use steps a lot in this chapter, so let's break my scheme down into some steps:

1. Use the tools you have and your knowledge of the system to isolate the source of the problem to a specific network location or item of equipment.

2. Once the problem is isolated to a specific location or item of equipment, make an educated guess about the source of the fault. Is it related to hardware, software, or configuration?

3. Again, using the tools you have and your knowledge of the system, determine where the fault is.

4. Using approved procedures, correct the fault and return the system to normal operation.

5. Document the trouble call. *The job's not finished till the paperwork's done.*

# Isolate The Source

You know by now that I am a strong proponent of logical procedures and checklists. That includes keeping notes as I go through a procedure. You should follow my example and write down what you do *when* you do it.

### Step One

Begin by doing the following:

1. Get as accurate a description of the trouble as possible from the person, probably a user that encountered the problem. Things to find out include:

   ◆ A detailed description of the problem.

   ◆ What time did the problem occur?

   ◆ Did the problem clear up later?

> **Note**
>
> *These three items are very important on the VPN. If more than one user had a similar type of problem at about the same time of the day and later the problem cleared up, it could very easily have been a temporary problem with your ISP.*

   ◆ Has the system ever worked satisfactorily, or is this a new implementation of a software product?

   ◆ What specific action the user took when the problem occurred. Did the user make any changes on their computer just before the problem occurred?

   ◆ What specific action the user took after the problem occurred.

   ◆ Any error messages that the user encountered.

   ◆ Any other operations (programs running in the background, print jobs working, and so on) that the user had going on when the problem occurred.

2. Check the error logs and see if other users are reporting the same or similar type problems. It is important to check the VPN *and* non-VPN error reports because you are looking for any patterns that will point you toward the problem. If you find related problems, take time to talk to the other users.

3. Using the PC where the problem occurred, attempt to duplicate the problem using the same procedure, as closely as possible, reported by the user. If possible, have the user there when you do this or perhaps even let them demonstrate the trouble.

*Always to try to repeat the problem. You may discover a simple procedural error that caused the problem, and get the user back online quickly and without any hassle.*

4. Analyze the information you've collected on the error and narrow your efforts to that part of the system (hardware, software, configuration) most likely to contain the problem.

### Step Two

I recommend two reliable methods for isolating problems on wide area networks. Like me, you will wind up using some combination of them. Loosely defined, the two methods are:

♦ From the source end, use TCP/IP tools designed for that purpose. This is a good starting point, especially if you need to extend your reach beyond your local network.

♦ On the local end, use physical network tracing and troubleshooting.

Both have good and bad features. The trick is knowing which one to start with—and when to switch.

## Using TCP/IP Tools—Ping And TraceRoute

*Ping* and *TraceRoute* are two common tools you can use to locate problems in the transmission of TCP/IP packets. Ping is used primarily to determine if a path exists to a particular IP address or if a particular host machine is reachable. TraceRoute (TRACERT) is used to trace the route that IP packets follow in their trip through the Internet. You can use both tools to locate incorrect address configurations and network dead spots.

**Note**
*Both Ping and TRACERT use ICMP echo and information packets to perform their tasks. In order for them to work, all routers and the final destination host must not have any TCP/IP filters set to block ICMP packets. By default, a VPN sets filters to block this type of packet and prevents the use of both Ping and TraceRt. If you want to use either Ping or TraceRt, you must disable the filters and allow the ICMP packets through.*

Both Ping and TRACERT are DOS command line or system prompt commands. Microsoft does not provide the equivalent Windows-based utilities, but several third-party software products do. You can find an abundance of shareware utilities for Windows on the Internet. A good place to start your search is "The Ultimate Collection of Winsock Software," (TUCOWS) (pronounced two-cows), **www.tucows.com**. TUCOWS started off as a collection of Internet utilities designed for Windows and has since grown to include all manners of shareware tools designed for all platforms, including the Apple Mac and Linux systems.

The use of Ping is considered so basic that almost every vendor includes it with its TCP/IP stack. The use of traceroute is almost the same. We will look at Ping first.

### *Ping*

Ping is especially useful for determining if a valid path exists through a network, including the Internet, to a specific IP address. When you execute this simple program from a command line, Ping typically sends out a minimum of three special format packets called *echo packets*. The target system, that is the system that is being *pinged*, will return the echo packets to the originating station—provided a route back can be found. The DOS syntax is straightforward; typing in *PING 204.120.249.65* will return a result similar to that shown in Figure 11.17.

Generally, all devices with a real or virtual IP address will honor the ping request and return the echo packet to the originating source address. For example, consider the WAN shown in Figure 11.18, consisting of two LANs tied together through a T1 link. The support technician at workstation 209.127.58.20 wants to test the network equipment in the circuit between the user's PC and the HOU server. The network diagram gives up the assigned IP addresses for the devices located in the network between the two ends—that is, the user's PC and the HOU server.

To check the operation of the equipment, start with the IP address closest to you. Each time the ping returns successfully, ping the next IP address in the chain. The sequence would go like this:

1. Ping the IP address assigned to the user's PC (209.127.58.20).
2. Ping the IP address assigned to the LAN side of the GLS Inner Security Gateway computer in the Firewall (204.127.58.2).

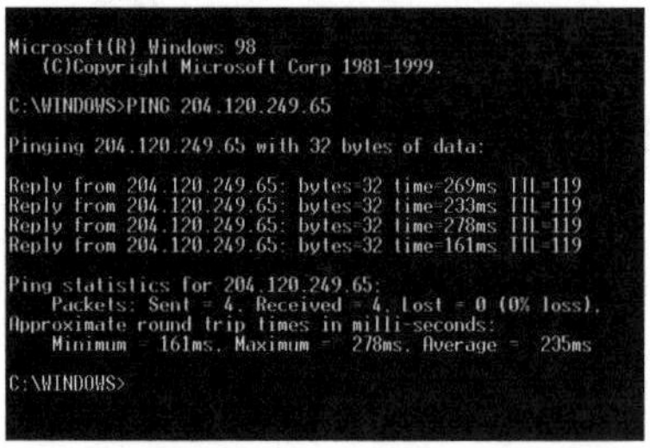

```
Microsoft(R) Windows 98
   (C)Copyright Microsoft Corp 1981-1999.

C:\WINDOWS>PING 204.120.249.65

Pinging 204.120.249.65 with 32 bytes of data:

Reply from 204.120.249.65: bytes=32 time=269ms TTL=119
Reply from 204.120.249.65: bytes=32 time=233ms TTL=119
Reply from 204.120.249.65: bytes=32 time=278ms TTL=119
Reply from 204.120.249.65: bytes=32 time=161ms TTL=119

Ping statistics for 204.120.249.65:
    Packets: Sent = 4, Received = 4, Lost = 0 (0% loss),
Approximate round trip times in milli-seconds:
    Minimum = 161ms, Maximum = 278ms, Average = 235ms

C:\WINDOWS>
```

**Figure 11.17**
Results of a PING command to IP 204.120.249.65.

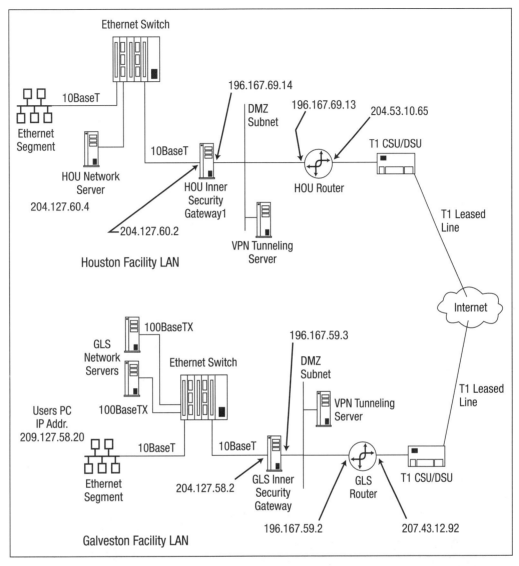

**Figure 11.18**
An example network for using the Ping command.

3. Ping the IP address assigned to the DMZ Subnet side of the GLS Inner Security Gateway computer in the Firewall (196.167.59.3).

4. Ping the IP address for the DMZ Subnet side of the GLS Router (196.167.59.2).

5. Ping the IP address for the WAN side of the GLS Router (207.43.12.92).

6. Ping the IP address for the WAN side of the HOU Router (204.53.10.65).

7. Ping the IP address for the DMZ Subnet side of the HOU Router (196.167.69.13).

8. Ping the IP address of the DMZ Subnet side of the HOU Inner Security Gateway computer in the Firewall (196.167.69.14).

9. Ping the IP address of the LAN side of the HOU Inner Security Gateway computer in the HOU Firewall (204.127.60.2).

10. Ping the IP address of the LAN connection of the HOU Server computer (204.127.60.4).

### TraceRoute (TRACERT)

This TCP/IP utility sends a special type of ping-packet with instructions for each router that it encounters to send its name and IP address to the originator. That shows you each hop the packets took between your machine and the final destination. From the DOS prompt, enter TRACERT [IP Address] for the final destination. For example: TRACERT 204.120.249.65. Your results should look similar to the trace shown in Figure 11.19.

### Other TCP/IP Utilities

Several other TCP/IP utility programs exist as Unix command line utilities that most ISPs find useful. For troubleshooting your specific network problems some may prove helpful, others may not. Among those that I like to keep on my laptop computer are the following:

♦ *Resolver*—Resolves a host name to an IP Address, or vice-versa.

♦ *Whois*—Returns information about a particular host or domain.

In addition to those utilities, the following application programs will prove useful:

♦ *Telnet*—Allows you to log in to a remote host. Usually the remote host has to be a Unix machine. This is the most common program used for retrieving and modifying router tables and DNS tables.

♦ *FTP*—The TCP/IP file transfer program. The DOS and Unix versions have a syntax that might prove a bit sticky, but some slick Windows versions exist.

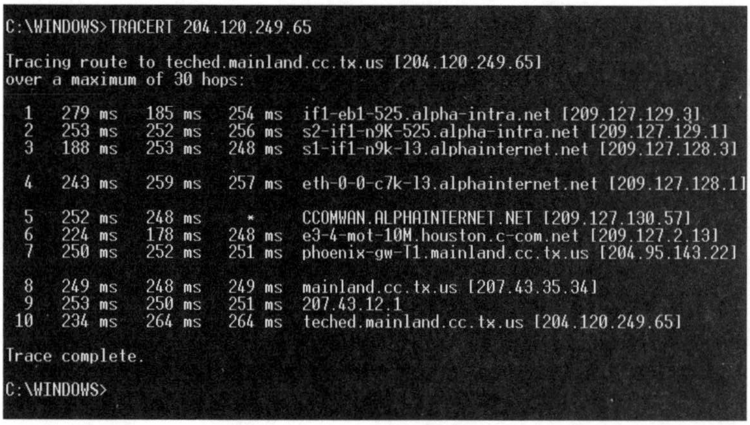

**Figure 11.19**
A typical TraceRoute result. Yours will depend on the route from your machine to the destination.

### A Final Word

Both Ping and TRACERT show you if a path exists between the client workstation and the host or other resource. Both are useful, but both are also limited in scope—neither returns information about software problems, incorrect configurations, routers that will not allow certain packets through, and so on. You are going to have to learn when to stop using this set of tools and start using the others.

## Suspected Hardware Faults

I have some suggestions for isolating faulty segments, should your troubleshooting lead you to suspect the problem relates to hardware items in a large network system. Try this:

- Start at the signal source and work toward the destination. We shall define source and destination as:

    - The remote user's PC, in which case we define the destination as the LAN computer the remote user is attempting to attach to. This would be the case of a client-to-site VPN.

    - A user's PC on the local LAN, in which case the destination will be the computer at the remote site the VPN user is attempting to access. This would be the case of a site-to-site VPN.

- Start at the signal destination and work backward to the source. The same source and destination definitions apply here as well.

- Start in the middle, and divide the system into progressively smaller sections, eliminating sections as you go—more commonly known as *divide and conquer.*

A wide area network with a VPN is huge. Starting at the source or the destination and working towards the other end, you might have to cover most of the network system to locate the problem area. In that case, where everything is spread over a large area, but you can easily gain access to the network from the middle, you should use the divide and conquer plan.

If the errors lead you to suspect that the problem is hardware related, identify the equipment on the network diagram that exists between the source and destination. That includes hubs, switches, routers, DSU/CSUs, modems, and ISDN terminal adapters. Then, locate points where you can gain access to the network with as little change as possible to the current configuration. The best point for that is a network hub.

The next best point would be a port on a switch, but using switches to gain access requires minor changes to network configuration. If you cannot find any existing point of access, you will have to make one. This is where the small twisted-pair hub and the patch cables come in. You select a port off a switch or router, unplug the cable (after you tell the users what is going to happen), and patch the hub into the line to create yourself a point of access without changing the configuration.

After you map out the network access points, load the software necessary to emulate the user's activities with your laptop. Copy the user's configuration as closely as you can into your laptop, and select a point near the middle of the network system. Configure your laptop to gain access at that point and plug it in.

From this vantage point, attempt to access the network resource that generated the original error. If the system works, you can assume the network is good from where you currently are to the downstream resource and the trouble lies in the other direction. If you get the same error as before, then you can assume the problem lies between you and the resource.

So far, you have eliminated about half of the network as the problem source. Now use the network diagram to select another point halfway from where you are up or down the bad half and repeat the process to narrow the focus to a quarter. Keep chopping the remaining segment in half until you isolate the problem to a single network element.

## Suspected Software Faults

Your options are severely limited if the problem is software related. The most common software faults are located at the network client running on the user's PC or a network resource the user is attempting to access, such as a network file server. Other devices, such as routers and switches, have software, but in most cases, it is loaded from ROM or a boot disk. Problems in those devices relate more to configuration than actual software failures.

To troubleshoot a suspected software fault, your best first step is to use a different computer, preferably your laptop, to access the same program or file and see if the error persists. If it does, then chances are the error is on the server. If it does not, then the error is located in the user's PC software. If the problem points to software on a router or switch, use the procedures listed in the preceding section, "Suspected Hardware Faults," to isolate the hardware.

### Configuration Errors

Configuration is where you are most likely to encounter the largest number of problems. Every device that uses software to operate has some user configurable sections; including the:

♦ Network client on the user's PC

♦ Software-defined operations on the network equipment within the network, those routers, switches, and so forth

- ◆ VPN tunneling servers
- ◆ Resource that the user is trying to access—that is, file servers, RAS, and so forth

Fortunately, isolating problems of this nature down to a single section is not any more difficult than any of the others. Consider the following:

- ◆ If the problem exists on a major resource that is accessed by more than one user, it will, in almost all cases, show up as a problem for more than one user.
- ◆ If the problem exists on an item within the network, such as a router, switch, or hub, you can isolate it using the procedure outlined in "Suspected Hardware Faults."
- ◆ If the problem is with the VPN tunneling server, it usually affects more than one user. If the problem is an incorrect configuration that shows up only for the one user, you can isolate it by applying the methods outlined in the "Suspected Hardware Faults" section. Eventually, you will narrow the search down to the VPN tunneling server.
- ◆ An incorrect configuration problem on the user's PC will disappear when you connect a different computer in its place.

## TCP/IP And IPX Packet Filtering Configurations

Selectively blocking specific types of data packets is a normal function of any TCP/IP router. The system assigns a port and user ID to each TCP/IP protocol. When the protocol makes the packet up, this port (or socket) and user ID becomes a part of the UDP or IP header. A router uses each packet's header information to allow selected packets through and block unwanted packets. In addition, firewalls and VPN tunneling servers commonly filter packets. Let's take a quick look at packet filtering configurations, starting with firewalls.

### Firewall Configuration Considerations

The default configuration of most firewall implementations is a two-part process. First, filtering blocks all packets; in other words, nothing gets through the firewall. Then exceptions are made through some type of configuration program to allow specified packet types to pass.

This is important if your VPN tunneling server is installed inside the firewall. In this case, you must make exceptions for VPN packets used by either the PPTP or IPSec. For the Windows NT implementation of the PPTP, you also need to configure the firewall to allow TCP Port 1723 and IP User ID 47.

For the BorderManager implementation of the IPsec protocol, the configuration is a bit more complex. Table 11.2 shows the configuration recommended by Novell.

**Table 11.2   Recommended filters for BorderManager VPN.**

| Description of Filter | Protocol | Source Address | Source Port | Destination Address | Destination Port |
|---|---|---|---|---|---|
| VPN mstr srvr to allow incoming traffic | TCP (ID=6) | Any | Any | VPN public addr | 353 |
| (same) | TCP (ID=6) | Any | 213 | VPN public addr | Any |
| (same) | SKIP (ID=57) | Any | Any | Any | Any |
| (same) | UDP (ID=17) | Any | 2010 | VPN public addr | 2010 |
| (same) | UDP (ID=17) | Any | 353 | Any | 353 |
| VPN mstr srvr to allow outgoing traffic | TCP (ID=6) | Any | 353 | VPN public addr | Any |
| (same) | TCP (ID=6) | Any | Any | VPN public addr | 213 |
| (same) | SKIP (ID=57) | Any | Any | Any | Any |
| (same) | UDP (ID=17) | Any | 2010 | VPN public addr | 2010 |
| (same) | UDP (ID=17) | Any | 353 | Any | 353 |
| VPN slave srvr to allow incoming traffic | TCP (ID=6) | Any | Any | VPN public addr | 353 |
| (same) | TCP (ID=6) | Any | Any | VPN public addr | 213 |
| (same) | SKIP (ID=57) | Any | Any | Any | Any |
| (same) | UDP (ID=17) | Any | 2010 | VPN public addr | 2010 |
| (same) | UDP (ID=17) | Any | 353 | Any | 353 |
| VPN slave srvr to allow outgoing traffic | TCP (ID=6) | Any | 353 | VPN public addr | Any |
| (same) | TCP (ID=6) | Any | 213 | VPN public addr | Any |
| (same) | SKIP (ID=57) | Any | Any | Any | Any |
| (same) | UDP (ID=17) | Any | 2010 | VPN public addr | 2010 |
| (same) | UDP (ID=17) | Any | 353 | Any | 353 |

If you encounter problems using the VPN and your tunneling server is inside the firewall, you should check to see that the installation configured the firewall to allow VPN packets to pass.

### VPN Tunneling Server Filter Configurations

Both Windows NT and BorderManager set default configurations when you install the product. During initial installation of the Windows NT PPTP tunneling server, filtering was enabled through the Protocols tab, located in the network pages of the Control Panel. Only two options exist—to enable PPTP packet filtering or not. When you enable filtering, the server passes only PPTP packets. If you attempt to troubleshoot your network with Ping or TRACERT, be sure to turn off PPTP packet filtering.

In Chapter 4, we made a point that the IPsec protocol is more complex than PPTP. In BorderManager, a need exists for more control over packets forwarded by the VPN tunneling server. After BorderManager installation, the NetWare server controls packet filtering using FILTCFG.NLM. Remember, don't remove any filters that the system automatically installed during BorderManager VPN installation. The VPN installation automatically adds IP filters to:

♦ Block RIP updates of the public IP address form being sent out through the VPN tunnel.

♦ Block RIP updates of the VPN tunnel from being sent out through any interface.

♦ Block RIP from advertising a default route through the VPN tunnel interface.

**Note**
*Caution: Removing any of the above filters will cause a potential security breach through the VPN tunnel.*

## Fault Determination

For this section, we assume that you have:

♦ Isolated the problem area to the VPN.

♦ Tested or proven that the network cabling is adequate for the job.

♦ Tested or proven that the hardware is operating satisfactorily.

In other words, the problem is with the VPN tunnel software or configuration.

Unfortunately, when most network technicians reach this point, they think they have a handle on the solution and fix the problem without ever knowing the actual fault mechanism. You don't think so? Answer this: How many times have you fixed a problem with Windows 95 or 98 by simply rebooting? Sure, the fix worked, but exactly where was the fault?

I can put my finger on two reasons for this: First, isn't it human nature to take the easiest path to fix a problem? Second, everyone is applying lots of pressure to get the problem fixed without *wasting* any more time. Also, many technicians don't like paperwork, and will avoid it if possible.

Those reasons have validity from the technician's point of view. However, those same technicians don't recognize it when the majority of troubleshooting problems are recurring and they could prevent them by analyzing the real cause. By taking time to document the fault, they could remove the cause, have a record of the fault, and not have to troubleshoot the problem again down the road.

### *Some Tips On Configuration Problems*

Here are some tips to solve configuration problems:

♦ List the checks to perform. Prioritize the list in order of most to least likely.

♦ Group the steps into related areas. More than five checks per area makes it difficult to determine which check fixed the problem, and you are back to square one.

♦ Now comes the hard part—testing the VPN after you perform each group of checks. That may not be as difficult as you think; it just requires some thought on your part. You don't want to wear out the system by rebooting it, nor do you want to become a pest to the users. So you have to put some thought into developing an efficient testing plan.

♦ With your plan developed, perform the checks in a related group and mark them off the list as you go. When you finish a group of checks, perform the operational test you developed to see if you have fixed the problem.

♦ When you have fixed the problem, your checklist will provide you with the information you need for your documentation.

# Stick With A System

The key to troubleshooting is to perform a systematic series of steps designed to help you determine the exact nature of the fault. If you follow this procedure, you will be amazed at your ability to determine the actual fault instead of just isolating the problem down to a section of the system. In a complex LAN/WAN/VPN environment, fault determination is important. The larger the scope of the network, the greater the importance of determining the fault's location.

Because the model VPN systems we employed in this book are considerably different in their implementation, we have to apply specific troubleshooting methods based on the software you are using. We will start with BorderManager and finish with Windows NT.

## Novell BorderManager VPN

When troubleshooting problems in a BorderManager VPN tunneling server, check the following configuration items with the appropriate tool. You can check most of these with the NetWare Administrator program, NWAdmin:

♦ A machine can be a member of only one VPN.

♦ If the VPN server is located behind a firewall, make sure the firewall is configured to pass VPN packets destined for TCP and UDP port 353, UDP port 2010, and TCP port 213, with a protocol ID of 57.

♦ Do not use IPTUNNEL or IPRELAY with a VPN.

♦ Each VPN tunnel server, master and slave, must have unique IP addresses.

- All VPN members must be in the same VPN tunnel network or subnet. In other words, the network address portion of the IP address for each VPN member must be the same.

- Travelers on the Internet should never see your VPN outside the tunnel, so you need not register it.

- The VPN tunnel address must not be advertised to the Internet. Although this will not effect the operation of the VPN, it is a serious security breach.

- Your private network must know the VPN tunnel address.

- The dial-up connection must be configured with "Type of Dial-Up Server" set to Novell Virtual Private Network.

- The "Reply To Get Nearest Server" option must be set to ON at the VPN server. (Do this from the server console.)

- If you use the same computer for Novell Client 32 and accessing a VPN, the Client 32 must be version 2.2.0.0 or later.

- Do not delete the filters that were automatically added when a VPN server was configured.

## Microsoft Windows NT

When troubleshooting a Windows NT tunneling server, check the following items for proper configuration. The configuration for the majority of these items can be determined through the Network Properties option in the Windows NT Control Panel. Verify that:

- The VPN devices have been added as RAS capable devices.

- The Receive calls only option in the Port Usage dialog box is selected.

- Only TCP/IP is checked in the Server Settings dialog box in the Network Configuration dialog box.

- Require Microsoft encrypted authentication is selected in the Network Configuration dialog box of the Remote Access Service Properties.

- Require data encryption is selected in the Network Configuration dialog box of the Remote Access Service Properties.

- Enable PPTP Filtering is selected in the TCP/IP Protocol Properties, under the Protocols tab of the Network options in the Control Panel.

- The TCP/IP protocol is configured to enable IP forwarding.

- Default routes have been suppressed by adding a Registry entry in the Windows NT Registry, and that the entry has been made correctly.

- Static routes pointing to the private network have been added to the router table. To verify this, use NETSTAT–R from the DOS command line.

## Problem Correction

This last section deals with correcting the problem after you have determined where the fault is. This is sort of anti-climactic. When you determine the exact nature of the fault, you more than likely correct it at the same time. For example, replace a faulty cable with a good patch cable and the problem will immediately disappear. With configuration errors, this is even more true. If, when going down the configuration checklist you developed, you reset an incorrect packet filter, the system will come up as it's supposed to do.

All manner of problems are possible on a system as complex as a LAN/WAN/VPN. Cables become noisy over time if the fabricator goofed when making it up, ports on hubs and switches develop faults and stop working, and so on. Any item of hardware is subject to failure.

But what about configuration items? How can the configuration on a VPN tunnel server change, seemingly of its own accord? Ask yourself another question: Has anyone changed anything in the configuration from the default? If the answer is yes, what have you or anybody else done to prevent the system from restoring the defaults in the event of an automatic reboot after a power failure or other event that will cause the server to restart? If you can't answer that question, the problem is not fixed—only patched until the next time you re-start the server or it automatically reboots.

It is important that you understand the difference and take every precaution to implement a permanent fix instead of a temporary patch.

## The Job's Not Finished Till The Paperwork's Done

We touched on the subject of documentation here and there throughout this chapter. Now it's time to promote it. Without referring to your logs, what malfunction were you called on to investigate on April 31 of last year? Yeah, okay, it was a trick question, April only has 30 days. I think you get the point—it is important to document what the nature of the fault is, and the steps you took to correct the problem.

One important use of documentation is identifying repeating problems. By building a searchable database, you can easily spot trends even over periods that might not make sense. Of course, that implies you are going to use the data during your troubleshooting.

Another benefit of good documentation is future planning. Often the need for additional resources in a particular part of the system is not readily apparent unless a number of problems can be associated with overloaded conditions. Of course, for either of these to become a reality, you not only have to document the service call, but you periodically have to review the total log.

# Summary

In this chapter, we looked at procedures for managing and maintaining your VPN after it is up and running. We took a short look at some troubleshooting procedures and made some recommendations to you in that area. We want you to keep in mind that your VPN is merely an extension of your existing network, another resource using the Internet to provide a transport medium.

I am sure we passed over a topic or two. You may also have noticed that we didn't deal with specific problems, but concentrated on developing procedures to follow instead. We detailed some configuration items we felt were important and left out some that—in our opinion—were maybe not as important. We might not have covered it all, but we will bet that more than once you said, "...been there, done that."

We have just about reached the end of the road in our cyberspace travels through this book. In the next chapter, we will put it all together. Don't put the book down just yet, I think you might find the next chapter interesting.

## Chapter 12

# *Connecting Your Network To The World*

*Key Topics:*

♦ *Predictions*

♦ *Interoperability issues*

♦ *VPN recommendations*

You are almost finished. Before we bail out completely, how-ever, we would like to bend your ear for just a little while longer. Before we go, we want to polish up the crystal ball and take a quick look at the future. We also promised earlier in the book to make some recommendations. Who knows, one of us might even take off the wraps and let our true colors show.

## What The Future Looks Like

Looking into the future of networking, especially in Internet re-lated areas, is very exciting. The virtual army of manufacturers, developers, engineers, and computer scientists is creating new prod-ucts that will continue to improve the performance of the Internet and fuel its unparalleled growth.

### Interoperablility—Will Wintel Conqure The World?

A casual observer of the PC computer industry might think that Microsoft and Intel have almost succeeded in shoving the com-petition out of the PC market. Some folks scattered around in places like San Jose and Cupertino [California], Provo [Utah], Austin [Texas], and Ontario [Canada], will disagree with that. In fact, companies exist in direct competition with Microsoft and Intel. Not only are they enjoying increased sales; they make prof-its for their stockholders.

463

Although the share of the market governed by Microsoft and Intel has increased a small percentage each year, the market has grown much faster—ballooned by competitor's products. In the meantime, the overall PC industry is setting uniform standards for the competition. For example:

♦ The Universal Serial Bus (USB) is a relatively new interface that allows PCs with different architecture—for example, Apple or Intel—to share an entire range of products, from scanners to Zip drives.

♦ Microsoft and Apple Computer, long time archrivals, are cooperating on some software products like Microsoft's Internet Explorer Web browser. Can it be that the computer industry has finally figured out that enough market exists for everyone?

# Prediction #1

As world demand for a more unified PC environment increases, companies will continue to invest in building interoperability features into their products to allow heterogeneous operation with other companies' products. I predict that this will include the marketplace for VPN technologies. Consider this:

♦ The members of the PPTP forum, including Microsoft, submitted a draft paper to the IETF with the goal of adopting PPTP as the standard Internet protocol. The draft never made it to the RFC stage because it was surpassed by the IPsec protocol.

♦ Although Novell developed its BorderManager VPN solution using the IPsec protocol, it is a known fact that BorderManager is compatible with Microsoft's implementation of PPTP. Novell published a white paper that details how to configure the BorderManager Server for PPTP.

♦ Microsoft announced that support for IPsec will be available in Windows 2000.

♦ Cisco developed their VPN strategy around L2TP to take advantage of the built-in capabilities of identifying ISPs and the capability of supplying *Bandwidth on Demand*. At the same time, Cisco has announced plans to support IPsec for their customers that want it.

♦ Most third party vendors have a line of VPN products that support IPsec or have announced plans to support it in the future.

## Working Together—Defining Interoperability

What we see is a slow movement toward unification to one standard encryption and encapsulation protocol. Enterprises demand this to connect supplier, manufacturer, vendor, and customer networks through secure encrypted VPN tunnels. Their goal is the rapid exchange of information that will reduce the start-stop scheduling and production practices in place today. Interoperability promises to allow better production schedules with fewer delays.

But wait, there's more. We touched briefly in the early part of this book on new technologies in the WAN network area. Among these were:

- *Integrated Service Digital Network*—ISDN is in place in many areas and offers higher bandwidths to home subscribers.
- *Asymmetric Digital Subscriber Line*—ADSL offers even higher bandwidth than ISDN.
- *Cable Modem Technologies*—CMT offers unprecedented speed and capability at a cost affordable by the individual home user.

# Prediction #2

What do all these mean to society as a whole? Quite probably, within a few years we will see startling changes in the workforce in this and other industrialized countries. It is quite possible that the majority of people processing and exchanging information will work from their homes as telecommuters—they won't commute daily back and forth to the office. The result will be reduced traffic jams, pollution, and reduced stress in dealing with the daily hassle of surviving a connected industrialized society.

## Building The Infrastructure

Of course, all this high-speed home access will eventually swamp the Internet with a glut of data packets, right? Interestingly enough, I have been hearing that for about four years now; yet, during that time the number of people using the Internet has increased by more than an order of magnitude and I've noticed a significant increase in speed.

What the doomsayers have not noticed is that along with the improvement in speed for the users at the front end, an even more significant speed improvement has occurred in the infrastructure. AT&T, Sprint, GTE, MCI, and other major carriers are spinning a glass Web throughout the industrialized countries of the world. Equipment manufacturers are developing routers and switches to communicate on this glass Web in the gigahertz, and hundreds-of-gigahertz ranges. Couple this new equipment to protocol developments such as ATM and GigaBit Ethernet, not to mention the already established FDDI and Frame Relay backbones, and the movement of data between computers over the Internet just gets faster and faster.

In underdeveloped countries, the development of a copper wire infrastructure is being bypassed in favor of wireless technology implementing satellite relays instead. By using wireless transmission, these countries are spared the cost of expanding their copper wire infrastructure. This almost puts them one step ahead of the industrialized nations.

Now, when you add emerging VPN technology, with secure encrypted data tunnels, the wireless traffic is made reasonably tamper proof and very hard to eavesdrop on. That itself is a major plus in many cases.

# Prediction #3

Overall, the future looks very bright, especially for the implementation of VPN technology based on the IPsec and PPTP protocols. What will be the result of this? My prediction is that in the new millennium, everyone will be the benefactor.

# Some Closing Words

We set out to write this book about Virtual Private Networks with the goal of telling you what they are, where they came from, how they are configured, and how they are implemented. In the introduction, we said this book is intended for network administrators, and any others that wish to know how to configure a basic Virtual Private Network. With that thought in mind, we made a special effort not to get carried away in detailed explanations about how the basic concepts are implemented, but at the same time to provide you with enough information so that you could acquire a basic understanding of the subject.

Our experience is that the more you understand something, the better you are able to put it to use. So we took you on a journey designed to help build your understanding of VPN technology—an extension of your private network to a remote site that uses the Internet as the transmission medium. With our objectives laid out, we devoted the first part of this book to reviewing networking and the Internet. We presented three technology areas:

♦ LAN and WAN theory

♦ Origin and history of the Internet

♦ Origin and development of concepts that became the Virtual Private Network paradigm

In our efforts to avoid a technical morass, we left out the more juicy stuff—such as specifics on the operation of a layer 3 and layer 4 switch. We kept reminding ourselves that this book is about VPN, not the ins and outs of Internet-related hardware, and hoped you wouldn't mind.

We did, however, make an effort to scratch below the surface to explain the process of developing the Internet through the use of RFCs. That was important, as it is an ongoing process that will never become outdated. RFCs made the Internet the premier means of information data exchange in less than a flicker on the historical perspective scale.

As soon as we had everyone on more or less equal footing in the area of network technologies, we jumped in and demonstrated in three chapters how to incorporate and configure a VPN in a modern network system using the two most popular network systems in the market today, Novell NetWare and Microsoft Windows NT. We could have used other examples, but space didn't permit, so we played the odds that your existing network operating system is produced by one of these two vendors. Although Novell and Microsoft are not the only VPN manufacturers by any means, they are the two major producers. Both have a VPN product for networks that ranges in size and scope from very small to very large. It wasn't always easy to remain neutral and unbiased in our presentation, but we tried.

# Our Recommendations About Your VPN

If you read this far assuming that sooner or later we would recommend one product over the other; you're in luck. We in turn assume that you have read the majority of the book and know something about the protocols used because they affect our judgements.

Pete says, "Before I offer my recommendations, I want to state up front that I like Novell NetWare. I have been installing and using NetWare since it was first introduced in 1983, and it is my considered opinion that no better network operating system is on the market today, bar none. So having said that, can I still make a good recommendation for your VPN implementation? I'll let you be the judge."

Our recommendation depends on three things:

♦ The size of the enterprise

♦ The intended VPN applications

♦ Your level of satisfaction with your existing network system

### The Size Of The Enterprise

If the enterprise is small- to medium-sized and has at least one person on hand that can take care of your network operations, then either the Windows NT or BorderManager VPN will adequately serve the need. If the business is small and does not have a person dedicated to network operations, I think it should consult an ISP about implementing a VPN solution through them before making a decision. Although most VPNs are not subject to failure after the network administrator completes a careful setup and configuration, the long distance implications beg for continuing support.

Pete says: "I personally think the PPTP product available with Windows NT is a bit easier to configure, but the IPsec product offered with BorderManager is a bit more secure." From a realistic standpoint, consider the following items:

♦ In spite of numerous rumors to the contrary, neither Microsoft nor Novell have had any significant security breaches.

♦ Despite the seeming complexity of configuring one system over the other at the server end, you can painlessly configure either system. Both are provided with excellent documentation and both systems are well known enough to have several sources of support available. Support sources for noncritical issues exist for both products for the cost of an Internet connection. And, of course, for a fee both companies provide incident support on critical issues.

If your company is a major corporation, with hundreds or even thousands of traveling/remote users, a third party system from a vendor like Cisco or IndusRiver Software is our recommendation. These VPN companies are geared toward installations for major corporations, and provide quality products with support to back them up.

### Consider The VPN Application You Need

This is more important than the issue of company size. For the most part, if your intended use for the VPN is to allow remote users access to the home network on a regular basis, either product will provide you with an easy to use interface and a reliable level of security. Your company can conduct normal day-to-day operations using either the Windows NT

PPTP or Novell BorderManager IPsec products. From the client's viewpoint, establishing a connection is so similar between the two products that no issue exists.

If your application involves confidential information, transfer of funds, or for any other reason requires the highest possible level of security, then my recommendation is to use the IPsec. You don't have to use Novell's BorderManager, but I don't think you will find a better IPsec implementation. Granted, some IPsec implementations are advertised as operating under the Windows NT network system. If you must have the highest security level, you need IPsec—which is the bottom line.

### Working In An Existing Network System

In the end, it really boils down to this: If you already have a network system you like, why change? If your company already has a network system and you are expanding it to include a VPN, only one reason should make you opt for changing to a different network product— that is, your present network operating system can't perform to your expectations.

As with everything, exceptions to that can be argued. If your network system is Unix- or Linux-based TCP/IP, perhaps you should seriously consider using Cisco Systems L2TP or IPsec implementation.

On the other hand, you may have a fairly large network system with some Novell NetWare here, some Windows NT over there, and maybe a little Unix or Linux hither and thither. In that case, use this book as one part of a more detailed study to make your recommendations for system improvements.

One more case might sadly exist where the residents of mahogany row have made the decision without your consultation. You, the network administrator/support technician/major guru, have been simply told to get it installed and up and running—regardless of what they picked for you. We hope you find this book to be helpful anyway.

# Things We Missed And Mistakes We Made

This book has been a big undertaking. We have covered a lot of ground over a vast and complex topic. Along the way we have undoubtedly left out some things that you think should be here. We have probably even made one or two small errors. We, the authors, welcome your comments, preferably by email, but you can send us letters in care of the publisher too.

We mentioned **www.sldenterprises.com** several times in the text. That's our Web site, and we plan to have a section of the site devoted to this book. A form there will tell us of any mistakes or discrepancies you find. We also plan to have an errata file for corrections.

You needn't find mistakes in order to visit us. You will find other tips, hints, and resources to make a visit worthwhile. Drop by the Web site and sign the guest log, fill out the comment sheet about the book, and feel free to tell us what you like and don't like. Hopefully you'll tell us how useful you found the book. We never get tired of hearing compliments.

### An Involuntary Omission

It was our original intention to include the VPN products offered by Cisco Systems in this book. Cisco is a very large player in the Internet today. Time, scheduling, and the planned size of the book precluded writing in Cisco's products on this go-around. If we get a chance for a second edition, Cisco will top our list.

## Recommended Reading

More than once we mentioned providing you with a list of titles for recommended reading. If you want to find out more about a particular point or peruse some information touched on briefly in this book, go to the list in Appendix E. All of these books are good, and most of them were written at the technical instead of engineering level.

## Coming Events

As we put this project to bed, Microsoft is geared up to release Windows 2000. The folks at Redmond say it will include IPsec protocol support in its VPN capabilities.

Novell recently released BorderManager Version 3.5, with enhancements to its IPsec VPN functions and a new BorderManager VPN Client. The client, by the way, will work with the BorderManager 3 product, and is available for free download from **support.novell.com**.

## Conclusion

Time marches on, and technology changes exponentially, creating new products every day. In five years, the Internet will pervade our planet. It will, in all probability, predominate information exchange, surpassing even television. In all probability you will find it not just desirable but absolutely necessary to have your company represented in this vast network system—connecting your network to the world.

For many people the magnitude of impending change instills fear—perhaps it is a fear of the unknown. Others jump on new technology the instant it becomes available, without giving much thought to the cost and consequences. Next come the people who know that change is inevitable. They accept change as a challenge, and set out to learn how best to implement new products and technology to improve the quality of life in our society. If you are involved in PC technology, you know changes are a daily occurrence and that every one is a new challenge. Many people in this world wouldn't have it any other way and we like to think you're one of them.

If you're a part of this fast moving crowd, then you know what we mean when we use these lines from a rather popular song by the Eagles as a parting comment:

"Life in the fast lane.

Everything!

All the time!"

# *Appendix A*
# *Acronyms*

This list contains almost all of the acronyms used in this book, plus a few more. From our vantage point, these are the most common networking acronyms. If we missed your favorite, we invite you to send it via email to be added to the list found on our Web site at **www.sldenterprises.com**.

**3DES**—Triple Data Encryption Standard

**AAA**—Authentication Authorization and Accounting

**AARP**—AppleTalk Address Resolution Protocol

**ABR**—Available Bit Rate

**ACP**—Access Control Protocol

**ADS**—Active Directory Service

**ADSL**—Asymmetric Digital Subscriber Line

**AH**—Authentication Header

**ANSI**—American National Standards Institute

**API**—Application Program Interface

**ARA**—AppleTalk Remote Access

**ARAP**—AppleTalk Remote Access Protocol

**ARCNet**—Attached Resource Computer Local Network

**ARP**—Address Resolution Protocol

**ARPA**—Advance Research Projects Agency

**ASCII**—American Standard Code for Information Interchange

**AT&T**—American Telephone and Telegraph

**ATM**—Asynchronous Transfer Mode

**BBN**—Bolt, Beranek, and Newman

**BDC**—Backup Domain Controller

**B-ISDN**—Broadband ISDN

**BITNET**—Because It's Time NETwork

**BNC**—Undefined—A MilSpec term for a type of coaxial cable connector; possibly an abbreviation for *bayonet connector*.

**BRI**—Basic Rate Interface

**CAD**—Computer Aided Drafting

**CAP**—Competitive Access Provider

**CCITT**—Committ∂ Consultatif International de Tϑlϑgraphique et Tϑlϑphonique

**CERN**—Undefined, European Laboratory for Particle Physics

**CHAP**—Challenge Authentication Protocol

**CLI**—Command Line Interface

**CO**—Central Office

**CPE**—Customer Premise Equipment

**CPU**—Central Processing Unit

**CSM**—Cisco Service Management System

**CSMA/CD**—Carrier Sense Multiple Access with Collision Detection

**CSNET**—Computers and Science Network

**CSU/DSU**—Channel Service Unit/Data Service Unit

**DARPA**—Defense Advance Research Projects Agency

**DAT**—Dynamic Address Translation

**DCE**—Date Communications Equipment

**DEC**—Digital Equipment Corporation

**DES**—Data Encryption Standard

**DHCP**—Dynamic Host Configuration Protocol

**DLCI**—Data Link Connection Identifier

**DLL**—Date Link Layer

**DMZ**—Demilitarized Zone

**DNIS**—Dialed Number Identification String

**DNS**—Domain Name Service, Server, System

**DoD**—Department of Defense

**DoJ**—Department of Justice

**DOS**—Disk Operating System

**DPT**—Dynamic Packet Transport

**DS0**—Digital Signal 0–64 Kbps

**DS1**—Digital Signal 1–1.544 Mbps

**DSL**—Digital Subscriber Line

**DSP**—Digital Signal Processing

**DTE**—Digital Terminal Equipment

**EAP**—Extensible Authentication Protocol

**EBCDIC**—Extended Binary Coded Decimal Interchange Code

**ECSA**—Exchange Carriers Standards Association

**EIA**—Electronics Industries Association

**EISA**—Enhanced Industry Standard Architecture

**ELAP**—EtherTalk Link Access Protocol

**ENIAC**—Electronic Numerical Integrator And Computer

**ESP**—Encapsulating Security Payload

**FDDI**—Fiber Distributed Data Interface

**FTP**—File Transfer Protocol

**GAN**—Global Area Network

**GRE**—Generic Routing Encapsulation

**GTE**—General Telephone and Electric

**GUI**—Graphical User Interface

**GW**—Gateway

**HHL**—Host-To-Host Layer

**HMAC**—Hashing Method Authentication

**HMAC-MD5**—(a variation)

**HMAC-SHA1**—(a variation)

**IAB**—Internet Activities Board

**IBM**—International Business Machines (nicknamed "Big Blue")

**ICMP**—Internet Control Message Protocol

**I-D**—Internet Draft

**IEEE**—Institute of Electrical and Electronic Engineers

**IETF**—Internet Engineering Task Force

**IGMP**—Internet Group Management Protocol

**IGP**—Interior Gateway Protocol

**IIA**—Internet Industry Almanac

**IMP**—Interface Message Processor

**IP**—Internet Protocol

**IPNG**—IP New Generation

**IPSEC**—Internet Protocol Security

**IPVPN**—IP-Based Virtual Private Network

**IPX**—Internet Packet Exchange

**IRTP**—Indus River Tunneling Protocol

**ISA**—Industry Standard Architecture

**ISAKMP**—ISA Key Management Protocol

**ISDN**—Integrated Services Digital Network

**ISO**—International Organization for Standardization

**ISP**—Internet Service Provider

**IT**—Information Technology

**ITU**—International Telecommunications Union

**JVM**—Java Virtual Machine

**KHz**—Kilohertz; 1,000 cycles per second

**KMP**—Key Management Protocol

**L2F**—Layer 2 Forwarding

**L2TP**—Layer 2 Tunneling Protocol

**LAN**—Local Area Network

**LATA**—Local Access Transport Area

**LCP**—Link Control Protocol

**LDAP**—Lightweight Directory Access Protocol

**LEC**—Local Exchange Carrier

**LEM**—Lunar Excursion Module

**LLC**—Logical Link Control

**LSL**—Link Support Layer; also Local Subscriber Loop

**LSP**—Link State Protocol

**MAC**—Message Authentication Code; also Media Access Control

**MAN**—Metropolitan Area Network

**Mbps**—Mega-Bits-Per-Second

**MCSP**—Microsoft Certified Service Provider

**MD5**—Message Digest 5

**MHz**—Megahertz; 1 million cycles per second

**MILAN**—Microsoft LAN

**MILNET**—Military Network

**MIS**—Management Information Services

**MLID**—Multiple Link Interface Driver

**MPEC**—Microsoft's Encryption Control Protocol

**MPLS**—Multi-Protocol Label Switching

**MPPC**—Microsoft Point-To-Point Compression

**MPU**—Microprocessor Unit

**MSX**—Multi-Service Access Switch

**MTBF**—Mean Time Between Failure

**MTTR**—Mean Time To Repair

**NAS**—Network Access Server

**NAT**—Network Address Translation

**NCP**—Network Control Protocol

**NDIS**—Network Device Interface Specification

**NDS**—Novell Directory Services

**NetBEUI**—NetBIOS Extended User Interface

**NI**—Network Interface

**NIC**—Network Interface Card

**NIL**—Network Interface Layer

**NLAM**—Network Layer Address Management

**NLM**—NetWare Loadable Module

**NLSP**—NetWare Link State Protocol

**NOS**—Network Operating System

**NSF**—National Science Foundation

**NSFNET**—National Sciences Foundation Network

**NT**—New Technology

**OC**—Optical Carrier

**ODI**—Open Datalink Interface

**OEM**—Original Equipment Manufacturer

**OSI**—Open Systems Interconnect

**OSPF**—Open Shortest Path First

**PAP**—Password Authentication Protocol

**PARC**—Palo Alto Research Center

**PC**—Personal Computer

**PCAP/TAP**—Packet Capture and Trace and Performance

**PCI**—Peripheral Component Interconnect

**PDC**—Primary Domain Controller

**PDN**—Public Data Network

**PET**—Personal Electronic Transactor, a Commodore Computer

**PHY**—Physical Layer

**PKIX**—Public Key Infrastructure using X.509 standards

**POP**—Point Of Presence

**POTS**—Plain Old Telephone Service

**PPP**—Point-To-Point Protocol

**PPTP**—Point-To-Point Tunneling Protocol

**PRI**—Primary Rate Interface

**PSTN**—Public Switched Telephone Network

**PVC**—Permanent Virtual Circuit

**QOS**—Quality Of Service

**RADIUS**—Remote Authentication for Dial-In User Services

**RAM**—Random Access Memory

**RAS**—Remote Access Server

**RBOC**—Regional Bell Operating Company

**RDBMS**—Relational Database Management Systems

**RFC**—Request For Comment

**RIP**—Routing Information Protocol

**ROBO**—Remote Office/Branch Office

**ROM**—Read-Only Memory

**RSA**—Rivest-Shamir-Adelman Public-Key Cryptosystem

**RTT**—Round Trip Time

**SA**—Security Authentication

**SAP**—Service Access Point

**SATNET**—Satellite Net

**SCO**—Santa Cruz Operation

**SDH**—Synchronous Data Hierarchy

**SHA-1**—Secure Hash Algorithm

**SKIP**—Simple Key Exchange Internet Protocol

**SLIP**—Serial Line Internet Protocol

**SMTP**—Simple Mail Transfer Protocol

**SNA**—Simple Network Architecture

**SNMP**—Simple Network Management Protocol

**SOHO**—Small Office/Home Office

**SONET**—Synchronous Optical NETwork

**SPI**—Security Parameters Index

**SPX**—Sequenced Packet Exchange

**SRI**—Undefined, formerly a research department at Stanford University, now privatized.

**SRP**—Spatial Reuse Protocol

**ST**—[as applied to optical fiber]

**STP**—Shielded Twisted Pair

**STS**—Synchronous Transport Signal

**SVC**—Switched Virtual Circuit

**TACACS**—Terminal Access Controller Access Control System

**TCP**—Transmission Control Protocol

**TCP/IP**—Transmission Control Protocol/Internet Protocol (actually the Internet protocol suite)

**TCU**—Texas Christian University

**TelNet**—Undefined—RFC 0854: "Its primary goal is to allow a standard method of interfacing terminal devices and terminal-oriented processes to each other."

**TIA**—Telephony Industries Association

**TMA**—Tunnel Management

**TMS**—Tunnel Management Server

**TOS**—Terms Of Service

**TSR**—Terminate and Stay Resident

**UDP**—User Datagram Protocol

**UNI**—User Network Interface

**UNIVAC**—Universal Automatic Computer

**USA**—United States of America

**UTP**—Unshielded Twisted Pair

**UUCP**—Unix-To-Unix Copy Protocol

**VG**—Voice Grade

**VLAN**—Virtual LAN

**VLM**—Virtual Loadable Module

**VoIP**—Voice over Internet Protocol

**VPDN**—Virtual Private Dial-up Network

**VPN**—Virtual Private Network

**VTP**—Virtual Tunneling Protocol

**W2K**—Windows 2000

**WAN**—Wide Area Network

**XNS**—Undefined—An early network system developed by PARC.

**Y2K**—Year 2000

# Appendix B
# *Selected Requests For Comments*

T he *Request for Comments* (RFC) is one of the powerful tools in the arsenal of the Internet developer. The original developers of the ARPANET created the RFC scheme to provide a means for distributing ideas and experimental results.

## Internet-Related Standards Organizations

Far from complete, but good places to start:

**Internet Society (ISOC)**—A nonprofit, nongovernmental, international, professional membership organization. It focuses on standards, education, and policy issues. Its more than 150 organizations and 6,000 individual members world-wide represent a veritable who's who of the Internet community. (**www.isoc.org**)

**Internet Corporation for Assigned Names and Numbers (ICANN)**—The new nonprofit corporation that was formed to take over responsibility for the IP address space allocation, protocol parameter assignment, domain name system management, and root server system management functions now performed under U.S. Government contract by IANA and other entities. (**www.icann.com**)

**Internet Assigned Numbers Authority (IANA)**—The new independent IANA organization will have responsibilities in three interrelated areas: Internet protocol addresses, domain names, and protocol parameters. This includes the root server system and the work carried out currently by the existing IANA. The new IANA's goal is to "preserve the central coordinating functions of the global Internet for the public good." (**www.iana.com**)

**Internet Architecture Board (IAB)**—A technical advisory group of the Internet Society. Its responsibilities include: (**www.iab.org**)

◆ *IESG selection*—The IAB appoints a new IETF chair and all other IESG candidates from a list provided by the IETF nominating committee.

◆ *Architectural oversight*—The IAB provides oversight of the architecture for the protocols and procedures used by the Internet.

◆ *Standards process oversight and appeal*—The IAB provides oversight of the process used to create Internet standards. The IAB serves as an appeal board for complaints of improper execution of the standards process.

◆ *RFC series and IANA*—The IAB is responsible for editorial management and publication of the Request for Comments (RFC) document series, and for administration of the various Internet assigned numbers.

◆ *External liaison*—The IAB acts as a representative of the interests of the Internet Society in liaison relationships with other organizations concerned with standards and other technical and organizational issues relevant to the world-wide Internet.

◆ *Advice to ISOC*—The IAB acts as a source of advice and guidance to the Board of Trustees and Officers of the Internet Society concerning technical, architectural, procedural, and (where appropriate) policy matters pertaining to the Internet and its enabling technologies.

**Internet Engineering Task Force (IETF)**—A large open international community of network designers, operators, vendors, and researchers concerned with the evolution of the Internet architecture and the smooth operation of the Internet. It is open to any interested individual. (**www.ietf.org**)

**Note**

*The actual technical work of the IETF is done in its working groups, which are organized by topic into several areas (for example, routing, transport, security, etc.). Much of the work is handled via mailing lists. The IETF holds meetings three times per year.*

**International Telecommunication Union (ITU)**—Headquartered in Geneva, Switzerland, ITU is an international organization within which governments and the private sector coordinate global telecom networks and services. The ITU is the leading publisher of telecommunication technology, regulatory, and standards information. (**www.itu.int**)

**International Trademark Association (INTA)**—Founded in 1878 as The United States Trademark Association. The Association changed its name in May 1993 to International

Trademark Association to reflect the scope and interests of its members worldwide. The Association is dedicated to promoting trademarks as essential to world commerce. (**www.inta.org**)

**World Intellectual Property Organization (WIPO)**—An intergovernmental organization with headquarters in Geneva, Switzerland. It is one of the 16 specialized agencies of the United Nations system of organizations. WIPO is responsible for the promotion of the protection of intellectual property throughout the world through cooperation among states, and for the administration of various multilateral treaties dealing with the legal and administrative aspects of intellectual property. (**www.wipo.org**)

# Tips On Searching For *The* RFC You Need

Quite often you may find that searching RFCs for the exact detail you are looking for can be challenging. The reasons for this are many, among which are the following:

◆ Not all RFCs have exactly the correct title.

◆ RFCs are numbered by order of submission and acceptance, not by order of subject matter.

◆ RFCs are built on top of each other, often referring to a previous RFC that in turn refers to a previous RFC, and so on.

◆ Every now and then, the entire RFC database is reviewed and updated, and older RFCs are replaced by newer RFCs. This makes the sequence difficult to follow.

## Tips And Techniques

In an effort to make it a little easier to locate what you are looking for, I offer the following suggestions. Feel free to use all or none of them, as you wish.

Several sites exist that archive the RFC list. The next section lists some of them. Although the RFCs at each site are all the same, you may find that each site is a little different. Try a few out, find one you like, learn the nuances of the site you like, and stay with it.

As a bare minimum, an RFC archival site should have a full text search engine that will allow you to search for RFCs by number, title, and, as a last resort, a full text search through the entire RFC. Some sites also make available the publications of various standards organizations, and this may prove helpful too.

No site is worth using if it isn't fast and reliable. The site you choose should be capable of delivering the information you need in a reasonable time frame, without unnecessary disconnection. Usually, but not always, the closer the site is to your location, the more reliable the service. Somehow it just doesn't make sense for a user in Fort Worth, Texas, to want to download RFCs from a site located in Hong Kong, when Rice University in Houston, Texas, has the identical stuff.

Each RFC has an abstract. Reading it will save you a lot of time in deciding if that particular RFC contains information on your subject. If online time is important, download the titles and abstracts for the RFCs pertinent to your subject and peruse them at your leisure while offline.

Likewise, each RFC has a reference section at the end of the RFC crediting previous RFCs used in its development. You should probably download this reference section and, unless you are good at screen switching, print it out.

Most RFCs are referenced by number and not title, so you can spend a lot of time reading RFCs, only to find out that they really don't pertain to your subject. To get around that problem, you can download the entire list of RFC numbers and titles. This is a large file, but if you are digging in deep, you may find the download helpful. It does not take long to build up a long thread of RFCs that contain information you are looking for.

The RFCs' process began long before the proliferation of word processors. The early ones were all written with a text editor, with very few fonts, and no graphics at all. What illustrations are there are developed using the ASCII character set, so don't think you are going to find lots of pretty pictures and fancy fonts. A few sites have the more recent RFC files in both text version and downloadable files in fancy formats.

If you use the Web to access RFC sites, you will find that the RFCs are generated dynamically by a CGI script that simply takes the RFC text file and encapsulates it (now where have I heard that before?) in an HTML document. When you download this, you will have an HTML document, which in reality is not very useful for doing serious searching.

---

### The Author's Scheme

When I search the RFC archives, I start with the newest RFC and go to the reference section to see what other RFCs are referred to. Then, I make an educated guess about which of the RFCs I need, and download the batch of them. Next, I go to the reference section of each of those and follow the same procedure. This is where having the list of RFC numbers and titles will come in handy. Finally, I review the abstracts to decide which complete RFC documents to download.

After I have downloaded what I think are all the RFCs I need, I use my processor to convert the HTML or TXT documents to its native format. Now comes the boring part: reading. When I come to a reference to a previous RFC, I usually open up the referenced RFC title, and perform a search using text from the referring RFC as keywords. By using this method I avoid having to read the entire referenced RFC, unless I find it necessary—or desirable—to do so.

One thing I forgot to mention—while I am reviewing all these RFCs, I also have the document that I am working on open, and can switch back and forth between my document and any of the open RFCs. I find this works pretty well.

Well, that's about it. I hope you find some of these tips to be useful. Have fun and don't forget to come up for air every now and then.

---

## How, And Where, To Find RFCs

My number one resource for chasing down RFCs for this book was **www. faqs.org/rfcs**. If you do a search for RFC archives and search engines you will find lots—more than we are going to include in this appendix. Just for starters you can go to any one of these:

♦ www.nexor.com

♦ www.rfc-editor.org

♦ www.csl. sony.co.jp/rfc

♦ www.pmg.lcs.mit. edu/rfc.html

If you already know the RFC number—RFC 1927, for example—any of the previous sites lets you plug the number in directly. If, on the other hand, you are doing a blind search with only keywords, it is all right to use this method, also. One thing about keywords: The more you have, the more RFCs you will winnow out of the list; just try doing a search with the keyword *security* and see what happens. By the way, you should go to one or another of the previous RFC archive sites and read RFC 1927.

# Selected Requests For Comments

We may have not captured one or more of the RFCs we used to put this book together and for that we apologize. We did our best to collect them all here to save you most of the agony of digging for them on your own.

**1075, Distance Vector Multicast Routing Protocol**—D. Waitzman, C. Partridge, November 1988. This memo describes an experimental routing protocol, named DVMRP, that implements internetwork multicasting. DVMRP combines many of the features of RIP with the Truncated Reverse Path Broadcasting (TRPB) algorithm described by Deering.

**1234, Tunneling IPX Traffic Through IP Networks**—D. Provan, June 1991. This memo describes a method of encapsulating IPX datagrams within UDP packets so that IPX traffic can travel across an IP Internet. This RFC allows an IPX implementation to view an IP Internet as a single IPX network. An implementation of this memo will encapsulate IPX datagrams in UDP packets in the same way any hardware implementation might encapsulate IPX datagrams in that hardware's frames. IPX networks can be connected thusly across Internets that carry only IP traffic.

**1241, Scheme for an Internet Encapsulation Protocol: Version 1**—R. Woodburn, D. Mills, July 1991. For several years researchers in the Internet community have needed a means of "tunneling" between networks. A *tunnel* is essentially a source route that circumvents conventional routing mechanisms. Tunnels provide the means to bypass routing failures, avoid broken gateways and routing domains, or establish deterministic paths for experimentation.

**1264, Internet Routing Protocol Standardization Criteria**—R. Hinden, October 1991. The purpose of this document is to provide more specific guidance for the advancement of routing protocols. All levels of the standardization process are covered. Two types of routing protocol are currently in the Internet. These are Interior Gateway Protocols (IGP), sometimes called Intra-Domain Routing Protocols, and Exterior Gateway Protocols (EGP), sometimes called Inter-Domain Routing Protocols. This document uses the terms IGP and EGP.

**1504, AppleTalk Update-Based Routing Protocol: Enhanced AppleTalk Routing**—A. Oppenheimer, August 1993. This document provides detailed information about the AppleTalk Update-Based Routing Protocol (AURP) and wide area routing. AURP provides wide area routing enhancements to the AppleTalk routing protocols and is fully compatible with AppleTalk Phase 2.

**1825, Security Architecture for The Internet Protocol**—R. Atkinson, August 1995. This memo describes the security mechanisms for IP version 4 (IPv4) and IP version 6 (IPv6) and the services that they provide. Each security mechanism is specified in a separate document. This document also describes key management requirements for systems implementing those security mechanisms. This document is not an overall security architecture for the Internet and is instead focused on IP-layer security.

**1827, Track IP Encapsulating Security Payload (ESP)**—R. Atkinson, August 1995. This document describes the IP Encapsulating Security Payload (ESP). ESP is a mechanism for providing integrity and confidentiality to IP datagrams. In some circumstances it can also provide authentication to IP datagrams. The mechanism works with both IPv4 and IPv6.

**1827, IP Encapsulating Security Payload (ESP)**—R. Atkinson, August 1995. This document describes the IP Encapsulating Security Payload (ESP). ESP is a mechanism for providing integrity and confidentiality to IP datagrams. In some circumstances it can also provide authentication to IP datagrams. The mechanism works with both IPv4 and IPv6.

**1853, IP in IP Tunneling**—W. Simpson, October 1995. Daydreamer Category: Informational Status of this Memo. This memo provides information for the Internet community. It does not specify an Internet standard. Distribution of this memo is unlimited, IESG.

**Note**

*This memo is an individual effort of the author. This document reflects a current informal practice in the Internet. An effort is underway within the IETF Mobile-IP Working Group to provide an appropriate proposed standard to address this issue. Abstract: This document discusses implementation techniques for using IP Protocol/ Payload number 4 Encapsulation for tunneling with IP Security and other protocols.*

**2002, IP Mobility Support**—C. Perkins, October 1996. This document specifies protocol enhancements that allow transparent routing of IP datagrams to mobile nodes in the Internet.

**2003, IP Encapsulation within IP**—C. Perkins, October 1996. This document specifies a method by which an IP datagram can be encapsulated (carried as payload) within an IP datagram. Encapsulation is suggested as a means to alter the normal IP routing for datagrams by delivering them to an intermediate destination that would otherwise not be selected by the (network part of the) IP Destination Address field in the original IP header. Encapsulation can serve a variety of purposes, such as delivery of a datagram to a mobile node using Mobile IP.

**2004, Minimal Encapsulation within IP**—C. Perkins, October 1996. This document specifies a method by which an IP datagram can be encapsulated (carried as payload) within an IP datagram, with less overhead than "conventional" IP encapsulation that adds a second IP header to each encapsulated datagram.

**2005, Applicability Statement for IP Mobility Support**—J. Solomon, October 1996. As required by RFC 1264, this report discusses the applicability of Mobile IP to provide host mobility in the Internet. In particular, this document describes the key features of Mobile IP and shows how the requirements for advancement to Proposed Standard RFC have been satisfied.

**2119, Key Words for Use in RFCs to Indicate Requirement Levels**—S. Bradner, March 1997. In many standards track documents, several words are used to signify the requirements in the specification. These words are often capitalized. This document defines these words as they should be interpreted in IETF documents.

**2194, Review of Roaming Implementations**—B. Aboba, J. Lu, J. Alsop, J. Ding, W. Wang, September 1997. This document reviews the design and functionality of existing roaming implementations. *Roaming capability* can be loosely defined as the ability to use any one of multiple Internet service providers (ISPs), while maintaining a formal, customer-vendor relationship with only one. Examples of cases where roaming capability might be required include ISP "confederations" and ISP-provided corporate network access support.

**2341, Cisco Layer Two Forwarding (Protocol) L2F**—R. Atkinson, August 1995. This document describes the IP Encapsulating Security Payload (ESP). ESP is a mechanism for providing integrity and confidentiality to IP datagrams. In some circumstances it can also provide authentication to IP datagrams. The mechanism works with both IPv4 and IPv6.

**2344, Reverse Tunneling for Mobile IP**—G. Montenegro, May 1998. Mobile IP uses tunneling from the home agent to the mobile node's care-of address, but rarely in the reverse direction. Usually, a mobile node sends its packets through a router on the foreign network, and assumes that routing is independent of source address. When this assumption is not true, it is convenient to establish a topologically correct reverse tunnel from the care-of address to the home agent.

**2356, Sun's Skip Firewall Traversal for Mobile IP**—G. Montenegro, V. Gupta, June 1998. The Mobile IP specification establishes the mechanisms that enable a mobile host to maintain and use the same IP address as it changes its point of attachment to the network. Mobility implies higher security risks than static operation, because the traffic may at times take unforeseen network paths with unknown or unpredictable security characteristics. The Mobile IP specification makes no provisions for securing data traffic. The mechanisms described in this document allow a mobile node out on a public sector of the Internet to negotiate access past a SKIP firewall, and construct a secure channel into its home network.

**2401, Security Architecture for the Internet Protocol**—S. Kent, R. Atkinson, November 1998. This memo specifies the base architecture for IPsec compliant systems. The goal of the architecture is to provide various security services for traffic at the IP layer in both the IPv4 and IPv6 environments. This document describes the goals of such systems, their components, and how they fit together with each other and into the IP environment. It also describes the security services offered by the IPsec protocols, and how these services can be employed in the IP environment.

**2402, IP Authentication Header (AH)**—S. Kent, R. Atkinson, November 1998. The IP Authentication Header (AH) is used to provide connectionless integrity and data origin authentication for IP datagrams (hereafter referred to as just *authentication*), and to provide protection against replays. The receiver can select this latter, optional service when a Security Association is established. (Although the default calls for the sender to increment the Sequence Number used for anti-replay, the service is effective only if the receiver checks the Sequence Number.) AH provides authentication for as much of the IP header as possible, as well as for upper level protocol data.

**2411, IP Security Document Roadmap**—R. Thayer, N. Doraswamy, R. Glenn, November 1998. The IPsec protocol suite is used to provide privacy and authentication services at the IP layer. Several documents are used to describe this protocol suite. This discusses the interrelationship and organization of the various documents covering the IPsec protocol. It also provides an explanation of what to find in which document, and what to include in new encryption algorithm and authentication algorithm documents.

**2412, The OAKLEY Key Determination Protocol**—H. Orman, November 1998. This document describes a protocol named OAKLEY, by which two authenticated parties can agree on secure and secret keying material. The basic mechanism is the Diffie-Hellman key exchange algorithm. The OAKLEY protocol supports Perfect Forward Secrecy, compatibility with the ISAKMP protocol for managing security associations, user-defined abstract group structures for use with the Diffie-Hellman algorithm, key updates, and incorporation of keys distributed via out-of-band mechanisms.

**2459, Public Key Infrastructure Certificate and CRL Profile**—R. Housley, W. Ford, W. Polk, D. Solo, January 1999. This memo profiles the X. 509 v3 certificate and X. 509 v2 CRL for use in the Internet. An overview of the approach and model are provided as an introduction. It describes the X. 509 v3 certificate format in detail, with additional information regarding the format and semantics of Internet name forms (for example, IP addresses).

It also describes standard certificate extensions and defines one new Internet-specific extension. It specifies a required set of certificate extensions. It describes the X. 509 v2 CRL format and also defines a required extension set. It describes an algorithm for X. 509 certificate path validation. It provides supplemental information describing the format of public keys and digital signatures in X. 509 certificates for common Internet public key encryption algorithms (that is, RSA, DSA, and Diffie-Hellman). ASN.1 modules and examples are provided in the appendices.

**2473, Generic Packet Tunneling in IPv6 Specification**—A. Conta, S. Deering, December 1998. This document defines the model and generic mechanisms for IPv6 encapsulation of Internet packets, such as IPv6 and IPv4. The model and mechanisms can be applied to other protocol packets as well, such as AppleTalk, IPX, CLNP, or others.

**2574, User-Based Security Model (USM) for Version 3 of the Simple Network Management Protocol (SNMPv3)**—U. Blumenthal, B. Wijnen, April 1999. This document describes the User-Based Security Model (USM) for SNMP version 3 for use in the SNMP architecture [RFC 2571]. It defines the Elements of Procedure for providing SNMP message level security. This document also includes a MIB for remotely monitoring/managing the configuration parameters for this Security Model.

# Appendix C
# *VPN Vendors*

We did our best to round up as many VPN product vendors as we could. They are listed in alphabetical order and inclusion or omission of any vendors is not to be construed in any way.

Some of the names will jump out at you, and some won't be nearly as familiar. Some of the companies specialize in hardware, while others are in the software business. Visit their Web sites to become more familiar with their wares. As we collect more names, we'll post them on **www.sldenterprises.com**. Drop in there for a visit from time to time.

**Ascend Communications, Inc.**
1701 Harbor Bay Parkway
Alameda, CA 94502-3002
Tel: 510-769-6001
Fax: 510-747-2300
**www.ascend.com**

**Ashley Laurent, Inc.**
707 West Avenue, Suite 201
Austin, TX 78701
Tel: 512-322-0676
Fax: 512-322-0680
**www.osgroup.com**

**Assured Digital Inc.**
P.O. Box 248
Littleton, MA 01460
Tel: 978-486-0555
Fax: 978-486-3772
**www.assured-digital.com**

**Aventail Corporation**
808 Howell St., Second Floor
Seattle, WA 98101
Tel: 206-215-1111
Fax: 206-215-1120
**www.aventail.com**

**Cisco Systems, Inc.**
170 West Tasman Drive
San Jose, CA 95134
Tel: 408-526-4000
**www.cisco.com**

**Citadel Data Security**
P.O. Box 1272
Sea Point, South Africa 8060
Tel: +27 21 423-6065
Fax: +27 21 424-3656
**www.oms.co.za**

**Cylink Corporate Headquarters**
P.O. Box 3759
Sunnyvale, CA 94088-3759
Tel: 800-533-3958
**www.cylink.com**

**Data Fellows Inc.**
675 N. First Street, 8th Floor
San Jose, CA 95112
Tel: 408-938 6700
Fax: 408-938 6701
**www.datafellows.com**

**Digital Link**
217 Humboldt Court
Sunnyvale, CA 94089-1300
Tel: 408-745-6200
Fax: 408-745-6250
**www.digitallink.com**

**Fortress Technologies**
2701 N. Rocky Point Drive, Suite 650
Tampa, FL 33607
Tel: 813-288-7388
Fax: 813-288-7389
**www.fortresstech.com**

**Indus River Networks, Inc.**
31 Nagog Park
Acton, MA 01720
Tel: 978-266-8100
Fax: 978-266-8111
**www.indusriver.com**

**InfoExpress, Inc.**
425 First Street, Suite E
Los Altos, CA 94022
Tel: 650-947-7880
Fax: 650-947-7888
**www.vtcp.infoexpress.com**

**Information Resource Engineering, Inc.**
8029 Corporate Drive
Baltimore, MD 21236
Tel: 410-931-7500
Fax: 410-931-7524
**www.ire.com**

**Internet Devices, Inc.**
1287 Anvilwood Avenue
Sunnyvale, CA 94089
Tel: 408-541-1400
Fax: 408-541-1406
**www.internetdevices.com**

**Network Associates, Inc.**
3965 Freedom Circle
Santa Clara, CA 95054
Tel: 408-988-3832
Fax: 408-970-9727
**www.nai.com**

**Nortel Networks**
One Brunswick Square
Atrium, Suite 100
Saint John, NB
Canada E2L 4V1
Tel: 800-4Nortel
**www.nortelnetworks.com**

**PSINet, Inc.**
510 Huntmar Park Drive
Herndon, VA 20170
Tel: 703-904-4100
Fax: 703-904-4200
**www.psi.com**

**RADGUARD**
575 Corporate Drive
Mahwah, NJ 07430
Tel: 201-828 9611
Fax: 201-828 9613
**www.radguard.com**

**RedCreek Communications**
3900 Newpark Mall Road
Newark, CA 94560
Tel: 510-745-3900
**www.redcreek.com**

**Shiva**
28 Crosby Drive
Bedford, MA 01730-1437
Tel: 781-687-1000
Fax: 781-687-1001
**www.shiva.com**

**Signal 9 Solutions, Inc.**
580 Terry Fox Drive, Suite 406
Kanata, Ontario
Canada K2L 4B9
Tel: 613-599-9010
Fax: 613-599-7010
**www.signal9.com**

**TimeStep Incorporated**
593 Herndon Parkway
Herndon, VA 20170
Tel: 800-383-8211 ext. 4500
Fax: 703-736-6260
**www.timestep.com**

**V-One Corporation**
20250 Century Blvd., Suite 300
Germantown, MD 20874
Tel: 301-515-5200
Fax: 301-515-5280
**www.v-one.com**

**VPNet Technologies, Inc.**
1530 Meridian Avenue
San Jose, CA 95125
Tel: 408-445-6600
Fax: 408-445-6611
**www.vpn.com**

# Appendix D

# *Installation And Administration Checklists*

You have permission to photocopy the checklists for your personal use so you can mark them up as you proceed through a VPN installation or configuration. The lists are organized by chapter, as shown in the four tables that follow:

**Table D.1** Checklists from Chapter 7 for installing and configuring a VPN using Novell NetWare BorderManager.

| Checklist # | Subject | Found On Page |
| --- | --- | --- |
| 1 | Equipment Required | 499 |
| 2 | Support Needs | 499 |
| 3 | Pre-Implementation | 500 |
| 4a | Using the Internet Configuration Program | 502 |
| 4b | Install BorderManager Software on the NetWare Servers | 502 |
| 4c | Install BorderManager Snap-In for the NetWare Administrator Utility | 504 |
| 4d | Configure the Master Server | 505 |
| 4e | Configure the Slave Server | 507 |
| 4f | Add the Slave Server to the VPN | 509 |
| 5 | Post-Implementation | 511 |
| 6 | Managing Your VPN | 512 |
| 7 | Future Planning | 512 |

**Table D.2  Checklists from Chapter 8 for installing and configuring a VPN using Windows NT.**

| Checklist # | Subject | Found On Page |
|---|---|---|
| 1 | Equipment Required | 513 |
| 2 | Support Needs | 513 |
| 3 | Pre-Implementation | 514 |
| 4a | Install PPTP and Select the Number of VPN Devices | 515 |
| 4b | Add the VPN Devices as RAS Ports, Configure Encryption and Authentication Options, and Configure the RAS Server | 515 |
| 4c | Make an Entry in the Registry to Prevent the Server from Building a Default Route | 517 |
| 4d | Add Static Routes in the Routing Table | 518 |
| 4e | Configure IP Packet Forwarding | 518 |
| 4f | Enable PPTP Packet Filtering | 519 |
| 4g | Verify that the VPN Networking Routines have been Installed with Windows 98 | 519 |
| 4h | Install the Microsoft Virtual Private Network Adapter | 520 |
| 4i | Create a Dial-Up Networking Object | 521 |
| 4j | Configure the Dial-Up Networking Object | 521 |
| 4k | Make a Connection with the PPTP VPN | 522 |
| 5 | Post-Implementation | 522 |
| 6 | Managing Your VPN | 523 |
| 7 | Future Planning | 523 |

**Table D.3  Checklists from Chapter 9 for expanding an existing VPN to accommodate remote users. When not generic, the checklists are identified as BorderManager (BM4 series) or Windows NT (NT4-series).**

| Checklist # | Subject | Found On Page |
|---|---|---|
| 1 | Equipment Required | 524 |
| 2 | Support Needs | 525 |
| 3 | Pre-Implementation | 525 |
| BM4a | Configure a BorderManager VPN Server for User Access Via the Internet | 526 |
| BM4b | Install the Novell VPN Client | 529 |
| BM4c | Create a Dial-Up Networking Icon | 529 |
| BM4d | Configure Dial-Up Networking | 530 |
| BM4e | Make the Connection | 531 |
| NT4f | Verify that the VPN Networking Routines have been Installed from the Windows 98 CD | 533 |
| NT4g | Install Microsoft VPN Adapter | 534 |
| NT4h | Create a Dial-Up Networking Icon | 534 |

*(continued)*

**Table D.3**   **Checklists from Chapter 9 for expanding an existing VPN to accommodate remote users. When not generic, the checklists are identified as BorderManager (BM4 series) or Windows NT (NT4-series).** *(continued)*.

| Checklist # | Subject | Found On Page |
|---|---|---|
| NT4i | Configure the VPN Dial-Up Connection Icon | 535 |
| NT4j | Establish a Connection to the ISP | 536 |
| NT4k | Establish Communications with the PPTP VPN Server and Make a Secure Connection to the NT Network. | 536 |
| 5 | Post-Implementation | 536 |
| 6 | Managing Your VPN | 537 |
| 7 | Future Planning | 537 |

**Table D.4**   **Checklists are from Chapter 11 on managing the VPN.**

| Checklist # | Subject | Found On Page |
|---|---|---|
| 1 | Daily Administrative Tasks | 538 |
| 2 | Weekly Administrative Tasks | 538 |
| 3 | Monthly Administrative Tasks | 539 |

# Chapter 7: Basic NetWare VPN Model

### *BorderManager VPN, Checklist 1: Equipment Required*

The following checklist is for equipment required:

❑ An exact plan of the network changes you are going to implement.

❑ Detailed drawings that include all IP addresses.

❑ A list of items you will require to complete the project.

❑ Configuration forms for each item of new equipment required.

### *BorderManager VPN, Checklist 2: Support Needs*

The following checklist is for support needs:

**Note**

*These are suggestions of whom you may need to contact for help resolving problems with your installation and configuration.*

❑ NetWare software vendor, especially if they are a Certified Novell Service Center.

Name: _____

Company: _____

Phone: (____)_____

❑ Hardware vendor:

Name: _____

Company: _____

Phone: (____)_____
❑ Internet Service Provider:

Name: _____

Company: _____

Phone: (____)_____
❑ PSTN or PDN provider:

Name: _____

Company: _____

Phone: (____)_____
❑ Other support options:

Name: _____

Company: _____

Phone: (____)_____

## BorderManager VPN, Checklist 3: Pre-Implementation

The following is a pre-implementation checklist:

❑ Create a contingency plan; preferably with a time line and point-of-no-return established.

❑ Notify users, especially those directly involved with the VPN, that you are working on the network and service may be interrupted from time to time.

❑ Verify that the PSTN/PDN carrier has signed off connectivity.

❑ Verify that add-on (new) hardware is functional, and, if necessary, upgraded to meet specifications required:

    ❑ Hard drive space

    ❑ Network interface cards

    ❑ RAM

    ❑ Transport media (cables—UTP and fiber-optic)

    ❑ Other

❏ Verify that all rollover (existing) hardware is functional, and, if necessary, upgraded to meet specifications required:

    ❏ Hard drive space

    ❏ Network interface cards

    ❏ RAM

    ❏ Transport media (cables—UTP and fiber-optic)

    ❏ Other

❏ Perform diagnostics test on all UPS devices.

❏ Verify that you have enough registered IP addresses available for new added Internet connections.

❏ Check your detailed drawing and make sure that you have assigned an IP address to the network connection on each new item of equipment.

❏ Physically locate any new hardware equipment and install any and all new cables.

❏ Power up the new equipment and assure yourself that it is all functioning correctly.

❏ Perform the following five steps before you take down your existing WAN link between the two sites. This is necessary in order for the directory tree to synchronize between the two sites with the new equipment located in the tree.

    ❏ If necessary, install the Novell NetWare 5 operating system on the computer desig-nated for the BorderManager server. Run VREPAIR on the NetWare SYS: volume to assure that no volume errors have cropped up.

    ❏ Determine that all equipment involved in the implementation has the proper proto-cols assigned, proper addresses assigned, and that routing has been established between subnets.

    ❏ If you haven't already done so, upgrade the version of DS.NLM on all servers to the latest recommended by Novell. The latest version of DS.NLM is available by down-load from **support.novell.com**.

    ❏ When you install the NetWare 5 system on the servers, you should also install them at their appropriate locations in the NDS directory tree. If your tree is relatively small, my recommendation is that you place the BorderManager servers in the same container. However, this may not always be possible.

    ❏ Make sure that the directory is fully synchronized and no directory-related problems exist. Run DSREPAIR on all servers that have a replica of the partition that will contain the BorderManager VPN servers.

❏ Install and configure the TCP/IP protocol and set up initial routing functions.

### *BorderManager VPN, Checklist 4a: Using The Internet Configuration Program*

The following checklist is for using the Internet configuration program:

Run INETCFG.NLM on the NetWare/BorderManager servers.

❏ At the server console, shown in Figure 7.10, type "INETCFG" and press Enter. This will load the Internet configuration program, and, if this is the first time this utility has been run, open an information box, as seen in Figure 7.11.

❏ The information dialog box will inform you that all load and bind commands will be copied to the configuration files maintained by INETCFG, and that all future configurations must be done using INETCFG. Select Yes and press Enter to copy the necessary configuration information and change the dialog box to look like Figure 7.12, asking if you want to restart the computer.

❏ Select No and press Enter. The dialog box will change, as shown in Figure 7.13, asking if you wish to use the Multiprotocol Router Fast Setup method.

❏ Select No, use the standard method, and press Enter to go to the INETCFG opening screen shown in Figure 7.14.

❏ Press Esc and an information box will display, as shown in Figure 7.15, confirming that you want to exit the INETCFG utility.

❏ Select Yes and press Enter to exit INETCFG and return to the server console.

### *BorderManager VPN Checklist 4b, Install BorderManager Software On The Netware Servers*

The following is a checklist for software on the Netware servers:

❏ Insert the BorderManager CD in the CD-ROM drive and mount the CD as a NetWare volume by typing CDROM at the server console and pressing Enter. A slight delay will occur while the server locates the CD-ROM index. At that point, the CD will be mounted as a NetWare volume, as shown in Figure 7.16.

❏ If the GUI interface is not loaded, type "STARTX" at the server console and press Enter. You should end up with the screen in Figure 7.17.

❏ Click the Novell logo in the lower-left corner of the screen for a pop-up menu, as shown in Figure 7.18.

❏ Click on Install. A window will display, as shown in Figure 7.19, listing the currently installed products.

❏ Click on New Product and the Source Path dialog box, shown in Figure 7.20, will open.

❏ Replace the default path A:\ with the path to the CD-ROM drive. Alternatively, you can click on the Browse icon to open the screen shown in Figure 7.21 and browse to locate the CD-ROM drive. When you have the correct path entered, click on OK to open the BorderManager Services Installation program, as shown in Figure 7.22.

❏ Click on Next to begin the installation. This will open the window shown in Figure 7.23 presenting the license agreement.

❏ After you have read the license agreement, click on I Accept.

❏ Insert the license diskette. Enter the path to the disk drive if the default path is incorrect. Click Next. If more than one license is available on the disk, an information dialog box will display, as shown in Figure 7.25, informing you that a browser will open allowing you to select the license you wish to install.

❏ Click on OK. The Select License to Install browser will open, as shown in Figure 7.26, displaying the available licenses, and allowing you to choose the license you wish to install.

❏ Select the license you wish to install and click on OK. The Select License to Install browser will close, and the BorderManager Services Installation dialog box will open, as shown in Figure 7.27, displaying information on the licenses to be installed.

❏ Review the license display. You can click Back to go back and make changes. When you are satisfied with the license(s) to be installed, click Next. At this time, a warning dialog box may open, as shown in Figure 7.28, informing you that the current version of Novell Internet Access Server will be overwritten, but the configuration will be retained.

❏ When you are satisfied with the license selection, click Next. That will open the login screen shown in Figure 7.29, prompting you to login to NDS.

❏ Enter your fully distinguished username. Press the Tab key—or click on the password entry line—and enter your password. Press the Enter key—or click on OK—to close the login screen and open a window displaying the NICs installed and configured in this computer. See Figure 7.30.

**Note**

*You must log in as a user with administrator rights at the [ROOT] of the tree for administrator rights at the container level in which the server object is located. Administrative rights are required to extend the NDS schema and configure the NICs.*

❏ Review the list of NICs and their IP bindings. Each interface must be specified as public (the Internet), or private (your LAN). One selection is required for each network interface. If your BorderManager Server is located inside the firewall, and has only one network interface, I recommend that you specify that interface as connected to the private network.

❏ Specifying, a private interface activates the HTTP proxy for the All Private Interfaces option. The next checkbox enables access control restrictions for Web browsers. I recommend you leave it *un*checked. (For more information about the HTTP proxy, see the Novell Documentation.)

❏ Click Next, and the BorderManager Services Installation window, shown in Figure 7.31, will open, prompting you to enter a unique DNS domain name for your network.

❏ Click Next. The BorderManager Services Installation window will change, as shown in Figure 7.32, and you will be prompted to enter the IP addresses for up to three DNS servers.

❏ Click Add to open a dialog box allowing you to enter the IP address of at least one, and up to three, servers. The search order will be the order you list the DNS servers. You can change the listed order moving them with the Up and Down arrows. When the search order is as you want it, click Next. The BorderManager Services installation screen will change, as shown in Figure 7.33, to display a list of product options for you to install.

❏ Select the products for your installation, verify that they are correct, then click Finish. That will open the information window shown in Figure 7.34 and display the installation progress.

❏ Click Reboot, and restart the server.

**Note**
*You have now completed the installation of the BorderManager services. Don't forget that you have to complete this process on the servers on both networks.*

### BorderManager VPN Checklist 4c, Install BorderManager Snap-In For The Netware Administrator Utility

The following checklist is used with the snap-in for the Netware Administrator utility:

❏ Log in to the directory tree as a user with admin rights at the root of the tree or container level where the master VPN server will be located.

❏ Click on Start, then point to Run and click again. The Run Programs dialog box will open, as shown in Figure 7.36, prompting you to enter the name of the program to run.

❏ Type in the path to the SYS:\PUBLIC\BRDRMGR\SNAPINS\SETUP.EXE file, and click Next. (You could click on Browse, and use the browser to locate the program.) The setup program will load, and the Installing BorderManager screen will open, as shown in Figure 7.37, with the appropriate information.

❏ Click Next. The setup program will search for the directory that contains the NWAdmin.exe program. When it has located this program, the Choose Destination Location dialog box will open, as shown in Figure 7.38, prompting you to choose the destination for the installed files.

❏ Click Next to stick with the default, or follow the instructions on the setup screen as appropriate for your specific configuration. The setup program will proceed with the chore of copying and configuring the necessary files. When the setup is complete, an information dialog box will open, as shown in Figure 7.39, asking if you wish to view the README file at this time.

❏ If you wish to view the README file, click Yes; otherwise click No. If you click No, the information dialog box will close, and another information dialog box will open, as shown in Figure 7.40, informing you that the BorderManager files have been installed, and asking if you want to launch the NW Admin utility now.

❏ If you wish to launch the NW Admin utility, click Yes. If you do not wish to launch the NW Admin utility at this time, click No. If you click No, the setup screen will close and the Windows Desktop will become the active screen.

### BorderManager VPN, Checklist 4d, Configure The Master Server (NIASCFG.NLM)

The following checklist is used to configure the master server (NIASCFG.NLM):

**Note**

*This configuration procedure is performed at the server console—on the server that will be the master VPN server.*

❏ At the server console type "LOAD NIASCFG" and press Enter. This will load the NIASCFG configuration utility, and the server screen will look like Figure 7.41. If this is the first time you have run NIASCFG, you will see an information box informing you that all load and bind commands will be moved to the NETINFO.CFG file.

❏ Press Enter to continue. The NIASCFG utility will verify that the appropriate commands have been relocated to the correct file. A new information box will open, shown in Figure 7.42, informing you that you must restart the server before any new changes will take place.

❏ Press Enter to continue. The NIASCFG utility opening screen will appear, shown in Figure 7.43.

❏ Select Configure NIAS, and press Enter. The Select Component to Configure box will open, shown in Figure 7.44.

❏ Select Virtual Private Network, and press Enter. If this is the first VPN Server (either master or slave) you are installing in the tree, the directory schema will have to be extended. In this case, the VPN Configuration dialog box will open, as shown in Figure 7.45, and the following substeps will be performed, one time only:

  ❏ You will be prompted to login to the NDS tree as a user with administrative rights at the root of the tree—usually this is the ADMIN user. Enter the fully distinguished name of the user and press Enter, enter the password, and press Enter again to log in to the directory. After NDS has authenticated the username and password, the directory schema will be extended to include the new VPN objects. An information dialog box will open, shown in Figure 7.46, informing you that the extension has been done.

❑ Press Enter. The information dialog box will close, and the VPN Configuration screen, Figure 7.47, will display.

❑ Select Master Server Configuration, and press Enter. An information dialog box will open, shown in Figure 7.48, informing you that each VPN can have only one master VPN server, and asking you to confirm that this is the only master VPN server for this VPN.

❑ Select Continue and press Enter. The Master Server Configuration menu box will open in the VPN server configuration screen, shown in Figure 7.49.

❑ Select Configure IP Addresses, and press Enter. The Configure IP Addresses dialog box, shown in Figure 7.50, will open.

❑ Enter the public IP address for the VPN master server. This will most likely be an address in the range of addresses assigned by your ISP. After you have entered the public IP address, press Enter, then enter the IP net mask for the master VPN server public IP address. When you have entered the mask, press Enter.

❑ Enter the VPN tunnel IP address. This address should be unregistered, as it will never be seen outside your private network. (Remember that all VPN servers in the same VPN must be in the same IP subnet.) Press Enter, and then enter the IP net mask for the master VPN tunnel IP address. A dialog box similar to Figure 7.51 will appear.

❑ When the IP address information is correct, press Esc. A confirmation dialog box will open, as shown in Figure 7.52, asking you to confirm that you want to save the new IP addresses.

❑ Select Yes, and press Enter. An information dialog box will open, as shown in Figure 7.53, informing you that the VPN packet filters were successfully added.

❑ Press Enter. The information dialog box will close, and you will be returned to the Master Server Configuration menu box shown in Figure 7.49.

❑ Select Generate Encryption Information and press Enter. The Enter Random Seed dialog box will open, shown in Figure 7.54, prompting you to enter a seed for the encryption algorithm.

## Note

*The value you type in as the random seed serves only to provide a more random selection value to start the process of generating the encryption public key. You will not need it again, so don't worry about remembering the random seed number you invent.*

❑ Type in any combination of up to 255 characters and press Enter. An information dialog box will open, shown in Figure 7.55, informing you that the encryption information has been generated successfully.

❑ Press Enter to continue. A new information dialog box, shown in Figure 7.56, will inform you that the VPN attributes have been successfully updated.

❏ Press Enter to continue and you will return to the Master Server Configuration menu box shown in Figure 7.49.

**Note**

*At this time the VPN public key resides in the master encryption information file, named MINFO.VPN. You will need to send this file to the slave VPN server site where it will be required for configuring the encryption algorithm there. It is advisable to copy this file to a floppy diskette. This is the next step in the configuration process.*

❏ Select Copy Encryption Information, and press Enter. A dialog box will open, as shown in Figure 7.57, prompting you to enter the path to the disk drive where you will copy the encryption information. (The destination can be a floppy diskette or the hard disk.)

❏ Enter the path information, and press Enter. When the process is complete, an information dialog box will open, as shown in Figure 7.58, telling you the action was successful.

❏ Press Enter to continue. A different dialog box will open, shown in Figure 7.59, informing you that the VPMASTER.NLM—this is the master VPN server core program—has successfully loaded.

❏ Press Enter to continue and you will be returned to the Master Server Configuration menu box, shown in Figure 7.49.

❏ Press Esc repeatedly until a confirmation dialog box opens, as shown in Figure 7.60, asking you to confirm that you want to exit from this NLM.

❏ Select Yes, and press Enter. The NIAS configuration utility will close, and you will be returned to the server console.

**Note**

*This completes the configuration of the master VPN server. Label the floppy disk with the encryption information and store it in a protected location. You will need it to configure the slave VPN server.*

### BorderManager VPN, Checklist 4e: Configure The Slave Server (NIASCFG.NLM)

The following checklist is used to configure the slave server (NIASCFG.NLM):

❏ At the server console type "LOAD NIASCFG" and press Enter to load the NIASCFG configuration utility. The server screen will look like Figure 7.61. If this is the first NIASCFG run, an information box will tell you that all load and bind commands will be moved to the NETINFO.CFG file.

❏ Press Enter to continue. The NIASCFG utility will verify that the appropriate commands have been relocated to the correct file and a new information box will open, as shown in Figure 7.62, telling you to restart the server before any changes will take place.

❏ Press Enter to continue. The NIAS options dialog box will open, as shown in Figure 7.63.

❏ Select Configure NIAS and press Enter. The Select Component to Configure box will open, as shown in Figure 7.64.

❏ Select Virtual Private Network and press Enter. This will open the VPN Server Configuration menu, as shown in Figure 7.47.

❏ Select Slave Server Configuration and press Enter to open the menu box, shown in Figure 7.67.

❏ Select Configure IP Addresses and press Enter; the Configure IP Addresses dialog box will open as shown in Figure 7.68.

❏ Enter the public IP address for the VPN slave server, press Enter, type in the IP net mask for the slave, and press Enter.

❏ Enter the VPN tunnel IP address; this address should be unregistered, as it will never be seen outside your private network. Remember that all VPN servers within the one VPN must be in the same IP subnet. Next, press Enter and type in the IP net mask. After you enter the net mask, the dialog box should appear similar to the one in Figure 7.69.

❏ After verifying that the IP address information is correct, press Esc to open a confirmation dialog box, as shown in Figure 7.70. Select Yes and press Enter. The information dialog box in Figure 7.71 will open to tell you that the VPN packet filters were successfully added.

❏ Press Enter to close the information dialog box and return to the Slave Server Configuration menu box, shown in Figure 7.72.

❏ Select Generate Encryption Information and press Enter for the Enter Pathname dialog box shown in Figure 7.73, prompting you to enter a path to the encryption information file, MINFO.VPN.

❏ If you have not already done so, insert the disk containing the MINFO file in the floppy disk drive, confirm that the path listed is correct, and press Enter. An information dialog box will open, shown in Figure 7.74, displaying the message digest value.

❏ At this point you need to verify that the message digest value generated at the slave VPN server matches the message digest value generated at the master VPN server. If the message digest values match, select Yes and press Enter. The Enter Random Seed dialog box will open, as shown in Figure 7.75.

❏ Type in any combination of up to 255 characters and press Enter. The information dialog box shown in Figure 7.76 will open to inform you that the encryption information has been generated.

❏ Press Enter to continue and a new information dialog box will open, shown in Figure 7.77, to inform you that the VPN attributes have been successfully updated.

❏ Press Enter to return to the Slave Server Configuration menu box, shown in Figure 7.78.

❑ Select Copy Encryption Information and press Enter to open a dialog box like the one in Figure 7.79, prompting you to enter the path to the disk drive where the encryption information will be saved. You can copy the information to a floppy diskette, or to a specific location on the hard disk drive. In this case, you should choose the floppy so you can send the information back to the master location.

❑ If the default value shown in the dialog box is not correct, type in the appropriate path information and press Enter. After the encryption information has been copied, an information dialog box like the one depicted in Figure 7.80 will inform you that the encryption information has been successfully copied.

❑ Press Enter to close this information dialog box and return to the Slave Server Configuration menu box, shown in Figure 7.81.

❑ Press Esc to close this menu and an information dialog box will open, shown in Figure 7.82, informing you that VPSLAVE.NLM—the slave VPN server core program—has loaded successfully.

❑ Press Enter to continue. The information dialog box will close, and you will be returned to the VPN Server Configuration menu box, as shown in Figure 7.47.

❑ Press Esc repeatedly until the confirmation dialog box shown in Figure 7.83 appears and asks if you really want to exit from this NLM.

❑ Select Yes, and press Enter. The NIAS configuration utility will close, and you will be returned to the server console.

### BorderManager VPN, Checklist 4f: Add The Slave Server To The VPN (NWADMIN)

The following is used to add the slave server to the VPN (NWADMIN):

❑ Log on to the directory tree as a user with Admin rights at the root of the directory tree or the container level where the master VPN server will be located.

❑ Click on Start, point to Run, and click again. The Run Programs dialog box will open, as shown in Figure 7.84, prompting you to enter the name of the program to run.

❑ Type in the path to the SYS:\PUBLIC\WIN32\NWADMIN32.EXE file, and click Next or Browse, then use the browser to locate the program. The NWADMIN program will load, and the directory tree will open, as shown in Figure 7.85.

**Note**

*What your actual screen looks like depends on where your last context was, and what the configuration of your tree is like.*

❑ Navigate to the container that has the object representing the master VPN server, point to the server object, and double-click. The details dialog box for the server object will open, as shown in Figure 7.86.

❏ Click on the BorderManager Setup Page button. The BorderManager setup page will open, as shown in Figure 7.87.

❏ Click the VPN tab to open the VPN dialog page, as shown in Figure 7.88.

❏ Under the Enable Service window, double-click the Master Site-to-Site listing. This will open the dialog box shown in Figure 7.89.

❏ Click the Add icon; the left one of the two in the upper-right-hand corner of the list box shown in Figure 7.90. This will open the File Open dialog box, as shown in Figure 7.91, prompting you to enter the location of the encryption information file (SINFO.VPN) for the slave server you wish to add.

❏ If you have not already done so, insert the disk with the encryption information file in the disk drive on the computer at which you are running the NWADMIN program. Type in the path to locate the encryption information file for the server you want to add or, if the file is stored on the master VPN server, enter the path to the location of the file. Click Open to open and read the file, and the master VPN server will use this information to calculate a message digest value. An information dialog box will open displaying this value, as shown in Figure 7.92.

❏ Contact the slave server administrator and compare the value of your message digest with the one generated at the slave server console. If the two are equal, click Yes; otherwise, click No. When you click Yes, an information dialog box will open, as shown in Figure 7.93, informing you that the slave server has been added to the VPN. This same dialog box will prompt you if you want to add to the list of protected networks and hosts on this VPN accessible through the slave server.

❏ Click Yes. The protected IP Networks and Hosts dialog box will open, as shown in Figure 7.94.

❏ Click on the Add icon. The Add Protected Network input box will open.

❏ Enter the IP address and network mask for the network or host connected to the slave VPN server. When you have the information correct, click on OK. The Add Protected Network input box will close, and the new network or host will be listed in the Protected Networks and Hosts list box.

❏ Click on OK. The Protected Networks and Hosts list box will close, and the Master Site-to-Site dialog box will become active. The newly added slave VPN server will now appear in the list, as shown in Figure 7.96.

❏ Click the Status button. The Synchronization Status dialog box will open, as shown in Figure 7.97.

❏ Click Synchronize All. The status of the VPN servers will change to Configuring. After a short time they should show a status of Up-to-Date. At this time the slave and master servers will synchronize, and a virtual tunnel will be created between them.

❏ If the two servers lost communications when the master VPN server was configured, a new communications channel will be established through the VPN tunnel, and within a short time communications between the two servers should be established.

**Note**

*Now, we only covered the configuration of one slave VPN server in this chapter; if you have configured more than one slave VPN server, you will have to perform this process for each of the slave servers you want to be a part of the VPN.*

❏ Click on OK until you exit from the BorderManager Setup page.

❏ Close and exit from the NWADMIN Utility.

### BorderManager VPN, Checklist 5: Post-Implementation

The following checklist is for post-implementation:

❏ Check all the replicas of the NDS tree, and make sure that they are all synchronized, and that no NDS errors are flagged. For that you can use DSREPAIR.NLM, or your favorite Directory Service diagnostics program. How fast the directory is synchronized depends on how many replicas you have, their locations, and the size of your directory tree. In extreme cases, it may take as long as 24 hours for the directory to sync up.

❏ Make sure all the servers are communicating with each other and that the time is fully synchronized across the complete WAN.

❏ When you are satisfied that the directory is in good shape and all the servers are communicating with each other, take down the existing (old) WAN link. This will force the two networks to start using the VPN; they should already be using the VPN (more about that later). At this time, you should see no difference in the operation of the network, the directory, or communications between existing servers on either network.

❏ If you have a protocol analyzer, you can capture some packets destined for the network on the other side of the VPN and decode them. The data in the packets should be encrypted, and you should not be able to recognize any information.

❏ Notify all the users that they are now operating on the VPN and ask them to report any problems they may encounter. Start a trouble log and log all problems reported.

❏ Remove any temporary restrictions or other implementations you may have put in place on a temporary basis.

**Note**

*In configuring the NetWare Server to support BorderManager, Novell assumed the server would be used as a firewall and that users would not log onto the server. For the most part this is correct, however, an exception can happen when using the newly released BorderManager VPN Client for a secure connection from the BorderManager server to your remote user's computer. In this case, change the set parameter on both the master and slave VPN servers to: SET REPLY TO GET NEAREST SERVER = ON, and login to the BorderManager VPN server using the VPN Client.*

### BorderManager VPN, Checklist 6: Managing Your VPN

The following checklist is to be used for managing your VPN:

**Note**

*You can perform most of the administration tasks related to the VPN from a Windows NT/9x computer using the NetWare Administrator, NWADMIN.*

❑ Selecting the VPN server response time.

❑ Tuning master-slave server synchronization.

❑ Synchronizing VPN servers.

❑ Check and monitor statistics relating to the VPN. Among the statistics you should watch are the following:

    ❑ VPN server activities

    ❑ VPN server audit logs

    ❑ VPN realtime monitoring

    ❑ VPN client connection status

    ❑ Latency

    ❑ Number of dropped packets

    ❑ Overall application throughput

    ❑ Typical route through the Internet for a data packet

### BorderManager VPN, Checklist 7: Future Planning

The following checklist should be used for future planning:

**Note**

*You should be watching for change, usually in the form of an increase in demand, in the following areas:*

❑ Network expansion:

    ❑ User population

    ❑ Connect time

    ❑ Bandwidth utilization

❑ VPN capacity:

    ❑ Tunnel server capacity

    ❑ Supporting systems capacity

    ❑ Bandwidth use

❏ Longer-term network growth:

  ❏ Remote users

  ❏ Accessibility to client sites (extranet)

  ❏ Accessibility to vendor sites (extranet)

❏ Future interoperability issues

# Chapter 8: Basic VPN Using Microsoft Solutions

### *Windows NT VPN, Checklist 1: Equipment Required*
The following checklist will help you determine the equipment required:

❏ Develop an exact plan for the network changes you will implement.

❏ Develop detailed drawings for the network, include all IP address changes.

❏ Construct configuration forms for the new equipment.

❏ List all items required to complete the project.

### *Windows NT VPN, Checklist 2: Support Needs*
The following checklist will help you determine your support needs:

❏ Software vendor for Windows NT 4, especially if it is a Microsoft Certified Solutions Provider (MCSP):

Name:_____

Company:_____

Phone: (____)_____
❏ Hardware vendor:

Name:_____

Company:_____

Phone: (____)_____
❏ Internet Service Provider:

Name:_____

Company:_____

Phone: (____)_____
❏ PSTN or PDN provider:

Name:_____

Company:_____

Phone: (____)_____

❑ Other support options:

Name:_____

Company:_____

Phone: (____)_____

### *Windows NT VPN, Checklist 3: Pre-Implementation*

The following is a pre-implementation checklist:

> **Note**
>
> *If at all possible, go through the implementation process on a test network before applying it to your main system.*

❑ Create a contingency plan; preferably with a time-line and established point-of-no-return.

❑ Notify users, especially those directly involved with the VPN, that you are working on the network and that service may be interrupted from time to time.

❑ Verify PSTN/PDN carrier has signed off on all connectivity issues.

❑ Verify that add-on and all rollover (existing) hardware (especially if used) is functional and upgraded, if necessary, to meet required specifications. The important factors are the following:

  ❑ Hard drive space

  ❑ Network interface cards

  ❑ RAM

  ❑ Transport media (cables—UTP and fiber-optic)

  ❑ Other

❑ Perform diagnostics tests on Uninterruptible Power Supply (UPS).

❑ Verify that you have enough registered IP addresses available for Internet connections.

❑ Assign an IP address to the network connection on each new item of equipment.

❑ Verify installation of NT 4 Server operating system on the RAS.

**Note**

*Most of the preceding steps apply to the servers at both ends of the VPN. It is better to install both servers at the same time.*

### Windows NT VPN, Checklist 4a: Install PPTP And Select The Number Of VPN Devices

The following checklist will help in installing PPTP and selecting the number of VPN devices:

❏ Open the Windows NT Control Panel by clicking on Start | Settings | Control Panel.

❏ Double-click on the Network icon; see Figure 8.3.

❏ Click on the Protocols tab; see Figure 8.4.

❏ Click on Add; see Figure 8.5.

❏ Select Point-To-Point Tunneling Protocol, as shown in Figure 8.6.

❏ If the default location listed in Figure 8.7 is not correct, type in the location of the NT Server Version 4 Installation Files and click on Continue. (If the files are being copied from the CD, don't forget to insert the CD at this time.) At this point the software will copy PPTP files and load them into the server.

❏ When the file copy procedure is complete, the PPTP Configuration dialog box will open, as shown in Figure 8.8.

❏ Enter the number of VPNs you want this server to support by clicking on the drop-down arrow for the Number of Virtual Private Networks. Click the increase or decrease arrows until the correct number is indicated. You can also highlight the figure in the box and type in a number.

❏ Select the correct number and click on OK.

❏ Click on OK.

**Note**

*At this point you have completed the process of installing the PPTP protocol on a Windows NT server; however, the changes will not take effect until the server is shut down and restarted.*

### Windows NT VPN, Checklist 4b: Add The VPN Devices As RAS Ports, Configure Encryption And Authentication Options, And Configure The RAS Server

The following checklist should be used when adding VPN devices as RAS Ports, configuring encryption and authentication options, and configuring the RAS server:

❏ Open the Windows NT Server Control Panel, shown in Figure 8.3, by clicking on Start | Settings | Control Panel.

❏ Double-click on the Network Icon.

❏ Open the Remote Access Setup Properties dialog box by performing the following sub-steps:

> ❏ Click the Services tab to open the Services Page, then click Add to open the Select Network Service dialog box, shown in Figure 8.11.

> ❏ Select Remote Access Service and click on OK. At this point the Windows NT Setup dialog box opens, prompting you for the location of the Windows NT Installation Files.

> ❏ If the default location listed is not correct, type in the location of the files (if you chose to restart the server after the installation of the PPTP Protocol steps, you will have to insert the CD at this time). Click the Continue button. The Remote Access Server files are copied, then the Remote Access Service dialog box opens, followed immediately by the Add RAS Device dialog box.

❏ Add the VPN devices as RAS ports by performing the following steps for each VPN device:

> ❏ The Add RAS Device dialog box shown in Figure 8.10 should already be open. Point to the RAS Capable Devices list arrow and click to display the VPN devices that must be added.

> ❏ Select a VPN device and click on OK. That device is added to the RAS, the Add RAS Device dialog box closes, and the Remote Access Setup panel shown in Figure 8.12 opens.

> ❏ If you have more VPN Devices to add, click on the Add box to reopen the Add RAS Device dialog box.

> ❏ Go back and continue, repeating each step until you have added all the VPN devices to the RAS server.

❏ Verify that all the added VPN devices are configured for Receive Calls Only by performing the following sub-steps for each new VPN device.

> ❏ Select a VPN port and click on Configure.

> ❏ The Configure Port Usage dialog box for that device will open, as shown in Figure 8.14.

> ❏ Verify that the Receive Calls Only Radio Button in the Port Usage dialog box is selected.

> ❏ Click on OK to return to the Remote Access Setup Properties dialog box.

> ❏ Repeat this operation for each of the VPN devices you have created.

❏ Configure the network for the VPN Device by selecting the encryption and authentication options. To do this, click on the Network button (located in the Remote Access Setup Properties dialog box) to open the Network Configuration dialog box, shown in Figure 8.15.

❏ Verify that only TCP/IP is checked in the Server Settings.

❏ Verify that the Require Microsoft Encrypted Authentication radio button is selected.

❏ Check the Require Data Encryption checkbox.

❏ Click on OK. This opens the RAS Server TCP/IP Configuration dialog box, shown in Figure 8.16.

❏ Verify that the Allow Remote TCP/IP clients to Access the Entire Network Radio Button is checked.

❏ Check the Use Static Address Pool radio button.

❏ Type in the beginning IP address you have selected.

❏ Type in the ending IP address. All addresses must be in the same subnet, they must be contiguous, and you must add at least one more than the total number of RAS ports you have configured.

❏ When all the information is correct, click on OK. The RAS Server TCP/IP Configuration dialog box closes, and the Remote Access Setup Properties dialog box opens.

❏ Click Continue to install the RAS. When this operation is complete, a Setup Message information box opens to inform you that the Remote Access Server has been successfully installed.

❏ Click on OK to return to the Network window.

❏ Click Close to close the Network window. This opens a Network Settings Change information box, informing you that you must shut down and restart your computer before the new settings will take effect.

❏ If you copied the installation files from the CD, remove it now.

❏ Click Yes to restart your computer.

### Windows NT VPN, Checklist 4c: Make An Entry In The Registry To Prevent The Server From Building A Default Route

The following checklist should be used when making an entry in the Registry to prevent the server from building a default route:

❏ Click on Start and point to Run, then click. This opens the Run dialog box, shown in Figure 8.17.

❏ Type in "regedit," and click on OK. This opens the Registry Editor shown in Figure 8.18.

❏ Click the plus (+) sign next to the following folders as they appear:

    ❏ HKEY_LOCALMACHINE

    ❏ SYSTEM

    ❏ CurrentControlSet

    ❏ Services

❑ Scroll down through the *service* entries until you find a NIC to change or investigate. Click on its plus sign, then click on Parameters and TCP/IP. The Registry information for this NIC appears in the right-hand window of the Registry Editor dialog box, shown in Figure 8.20.

❑ Click on Edit to open the drop-down menu, then select New‡DWORD Value, and click to create a space for a new entry in the *Properties* window on the right side, as shown in Figure 8.21.

❑ Type in the following name for the new entry: "DontAddDefaultGateway," and press Enter. This adds the DontAddDefaultGateway entry, with an initial value of 0x00, into the properties for the NIC card entry, as shown in Figure 8.22.

❑ Now change the value of this entry to 0x01. To do this click on Edit to open the edit drop down menu, then click on Modify. This opens the Edit DWORD Value dialog box, shown in Figure 8.23.

❑ Verify that the value name is DontAddDefaultGateway and the hexadecimal radio button in the base section is selected, then type "01" in the value data section. If all this is correct, click on OK. The Edit D_WORD Value dialog box closes, and the Registry Editor becomes active again. The entry for the DontAddDefaultGateway property now has a value of 0x00000001 (1), as shown in Figure 8.24.

❑ Finally, click on the Close button in the upper-right-hand corner of the Registry editor. After making the change in the Windows NT Registry, restart the computer to have the change take effect.

### Windows NT VPN, Checklist 4d: Add Static Routes In The Routing Table

The following checklist should be used when adding static routes in the routing table:

❑ Click Start | Programs | Command Prompt. This opens a virtual MS-DOS session window, shown in Figure 8.25.

❑ At the DOS prompt, type the following: "route -p add dest.ip.addr interface.ip.addr" (without the quotation marks) and press Enter. This makes a static entry in the router table identifying the interface for routing data packets to the computer with IP address dest.ip.addr.

### Windows NT VPN, Checklist 4e: Configure IP Packet Forwarding

The following checklist should be used for configuring IP packet forwarding:

❑ Click Start | Settings | Control Panel to open the NT Control Panel.

❑ Double-click the Network Icon to open the Network Control Panel.

❑ Click the Protocols tab to open the Protocols panel, select TCP/IP, and click on the Properties button to open the TCP/IP Properties dialog box.

❑ Click the Routing tab to open the Routing page, as shown in Figure 8.26.

❏ Check the Enable IP Forwarding checkbox, then click on OK. This closes the TCP/IP Properties Routing Page, and the Network Control Panel becomes active.

❏ Click on OK to close the Network Control Panel. This opens a Network Settings Change Information box, informing you that changes made will not take effect until the computer is restarted.

❏ Click Yes to restart the computer. The Windows NT server shuts down and the computer restarts.

### *Windows NT VPN, Checklist 4f: Enable PPTP Packet Filtering*

The following checklist should be used for enabling PPTP packet filtering:

❏ Click Start | Settings | Control Panel.

❏ Double-click the Network icon to open the Network Control Panel.

❏ Click the Protocols tab to open the Protocols panel, select TCP/IP, and click on the Properties button to open the TCP/IP Properties dialog box.

❏ Click the IP Address tab to open the IP Address dialog box, then click Advanced to open the Advanced IP Addressing dialog box, as shown in Figure 8.27.

❏ Click the Network Adapter drop-down arrow and select the adapter connected to your ISP. Click the Enable PPTP Filtering checkbox.

❏ Click on OK to close the Advanced IP Addressing dialog box and drop back to the TCP/IP Properties dialog box.

❏ Click on OK to close the TCP/IP properties dialog box and the Network Control Panel displays. Click Close to get a Network Settings Change information box, informing you that changes will not take effect until the computer is restarted. Click Yes to restart the computer. NT server shuts down and the computer restarts.

### Note
*Do the previous procedure only on the NIC that connects to the Internet.*

### *Windows NT VPN, Checklist 4g: Verify That The VPN Networking Routines Have Been Installed With Windows 98*

The following checklist should be used for verifying that the VPN networking routines have been installed with Windows 98:

❏ Click Start | Settings | Control Panel. The panel in Figure 8.28 displays. How you have the preferences set determines whether the HTML format displays on the left side of the screen, as shown in the Figure 8.28; however, that's not critical. The main stuff is the icons on the right.

❏ Double-click on the Add Remove Programs icon and your screen will look like Figure 8.29.

❏ Click on the Windows Setup tab to open the Properties page, as shown in Figure 8.30.

❏ Use the scrollbar to move through the available components window, and select Communications. Then click on the Details Button to open the Communications components dialog box shown in Figure 8.31.

❏ Using the scrollbar, look through the available components until you locate Virtual Private Networking. If it is not there, check the checkbox for Virtual Private Networking. Click on OK to close the details window and return to the Add/Remove Program Properties Control Panel, as shown in Figure 8.30. Click on OK to close it.

❏ Click on OK and open a Copying Files dialog box like the one in Figure 8.33. If the default path shown for the location of the Windows 98 installation files is not correct, type in the correct path. If you are copying the files from the Windows 98 CD, insert the CD in the CD-ROM drive at this time and click on OK. The file copy procedure will start.

❏ Click on OK and the remaining files will be copied. After the file copy procedure has completed, the Add/Remove Programs Properties window closes and the Control Panel becomes active. Remove any diskettes and/or CDs and restart the computer.

### Windows NT VPN, Checklist 4h: Install The Microsoft Virtual Private Network Adapter

The following checklist should be used for installing the Microsoft Virtual Private Network adapter:

❏ Click Start | Settings | Control Panel. Double-click on the Network icon, as shown in Figure 8.28 to open the Network Control Panel shown in Figure 8.35.

❏ Click the Add button to open the Select Network Component Type dialog box, shown in Figure 8.36.

❏ Select Adapter, then click Add. This opens the Select Network adapters dialog box, as seen in Figure 8.37.

❏ Using the scroll arrows for the left-hand window, scroll through the list of manufacturers until you find Microsoft; then click on it. This opens the list of Microsoft Network Adapters in the right-hand window, as shown in Figure 8.38.

❏ Select Microsoft Virtual Private Networking Adapter in the right-hand window, then click on OK to return to the Network Control Panel. Click on OK to close the Network Control Panel. This opens a System Settings Change information box, as shown in Figure 8.39, informing you that the settings will not take place until the computer is restarted. Click on Yes to restart the computer.

**Note**

*This completes the installation of a Microsoft Virtual Private Networking Adapter for Windows 98.*

### Windows NT VPN, Checklist 4i: Create A Dial-Up Networking Object

The following checklist should be used for creating a Dial-Up Networking object:

❑ Click on Start | Programs | Accessories | Communications | Dial-Up Networking. This opens the Dial-Up Networking group, as shown in Figure 8.40.

❑ If you have no dial-up connections at this time, the Make New Connection dialog box automatically opens, as shown in Figure 8.41. If you already have one or more dial-up connections configured, then double-click on the Make New Connection icon to open the new connection dialog box.

❑ Type in any name you want to use to describe the connection. After you've entered the name, press the Tab key to move the cursor to the Select A Device data area. Click the drop-down arrow to the right of the data area, then point to Microsoft VPN Adapter, and click again. The Microsoft VPN adapter should be selected in the data area, as shown in Figure 8.42.

❑ Click on the Next button to open the Host Name or IP Address data entry area as shown in Figure 8.43.

❑ Type in the IP address of the computer you are making a connection to on the other end of the VPN tunnel. If you have made a DNS entry for the *host name* for that computer, you can enter that. When you have the IP address or host name entered correctly, click on Next. This opens the Make New Connection information screen, shown in Figure 8.44, telling you that a new dial-up networking connection with the name you assigned has been created.

❑ Click on Finish to close the Make New Connection dialog box, and open the Dial-Up Networking group window in Figure 8.45, showing the new connection.

### Windows NT VPN, Checklist 4j: Configure The Dial-Up Networking Object

The following checklist should be used for configuring the Dial-Up Networking object:

❑ Point to the VPN Dial-Up Connection you created, and right-click. Click Properties to open the dialog box for the connection you have created, as shown in Figure 8.46.

❑ Click on the Server Types tab to open the server types dialog box, as shown in Figure 8.47.

❑ In the Advanced Properties Area, make sure the Require Encrypted Password and Require Data Encryption checkboxes are checked; the rest are optional.

❑ In the Allowed Network Protocols area, make sure that the TCP/IP checkbox is checked. The other checkboxes in the allowed Network Protocols area are optional, but TCP/IP is required for PPTP. Click on the TCP/IP Settings button to open the dialog box shown in Figure 8.48.

❑ If you want the PPTP Server to assign an IP address, then verify that the Server Assigned IP Address radio button is selected. If you want to assign an IP address, select the Specify an IP Address radio button and enter a valid address. (Remember that if you specify an IP address, the address must match the range of addresses you entered when you configured the TCP/IP protocol settings on the PPTP server.)

❑ If you want the PPTP server to assign an address for the name server, then verify that the Server Assigned Name Server Address radio button is selected. If you want to use a specific name server address, select the Specify Name Server Address radio button and enter the IP address of at least one DNS or WINS server that will be accessible to this computer.

❑ If your system can support IP Header compression and you want to use the default gateway on the remote system, leave the appropriate checkboxes selected. When the TCP/IP configuration is correct, click on OK to return to the server types dialog box and click on OK to return to the Dial-Up Networking Group window.

**Note**

*At this point you have created and configured a dial-up interface to connect to the PPTP server.*

### Windows NT VPN, Checklist 4k: Make A Connection With The PPTP VPN

The following checklist should be used when making a connection with the PPTP VPN:

❑ If the Dial-Up Networking window is not open, click on Start | Programs | Accessories | Communications, and click on Dial-Up Networking to open the panel in Figure 8.40.

❑ Double-click the icon for the VPN connection you created in the Dial-Up Networking window. This opens a Connect To dialog box, shown in Figure 8.49.

❑ Enter your username and password, make sure the IP Address or Host Name is correct, and click on Connect. An information window saying Connect To VPN Device will appear.

❑ After a short period the Microsoft Client Logon Screen opens, prompting you to enter the network password. Type in the correct password and click on OK. The Microsoft Client logon screen closes, and you will be connected to the NT server.

**Note**

*At this point you should be able to perform any tasks appropriate for the type of user you are logged on as.*

### Windows NT VPN, Checklist 5: Post-Implementation

The following checklist should be used in post-implementation:

❑ Make sure all the servers can communicate with each other, and that no apparent incorrect configurations exist, especially in establishing static routes.

❏ When you are satisfied that everything is in good shape, all the servers are configured correctly, and the necessary client workstations have been configured with the dial-up VPN adapter, take down the existing (old) WAN link. From this point on your users will have to start using the VPN via the dial-up adapter. At first this additional step may be a bit awkward, but given time to adapt to the new interface, the users should see no difference in the operation of the network.

❏ If you have a protocol analyzer available you can capture some packets destined for the network on the other side of the VPN and decode them. The data in the packets should be encrypted, and you should not be able to recognize any information.

❏ Notify all the users to be sure and report any problems they may encounter. Start a trouble log and log all problems reported.

❏ Remove any temporary restrictions, or other implementations you may have put in place on a temporary basis.

### Windows NT VPN, Checklist 6: Managing Your VPN

The following checklist should be used for managing your VPN:

❏ Select network protocols used by the VPN. The PPTP VPN can be configured to use both TCP/IP and IPX/SPX protocols. If you have any need to support IPX/SPX protocols, you can do this quite easily.

❏ Add static routes to the router table. In this case, using Windows NT, you need to open a virtual DOS session and use the ROUTE ADD command.

❏ Configure data encryption and data authentication methods.

❏ Select links.

❏ Tune for optimum performance.

❏ Monitor statistics and bandwidth usage on the NICs.

On a more local scene, your particular interface could monitor the following statistics:

❏ Latency

❏ Number of dropped packets

❏ Overall application throughput

❏ Typical route through the Internet for a data packet

### Windows NT VPN, Checklist 7: Future Planning

The following checklist should be used for future planning:

❏ Network expansion

  ❏ User population

  ❏ Connect time

  ❏ Bandwidth utilization

❑ VPN capacity

  ❑ Tunnel server capacity

  ❑ Supporting systems capacity

  ❑ Bandwidth use

❑ Longer-term network growth

  ❑ Remote users

  ❑ Accessibility to client sites (extranet)

  ❑ Accessibility to vendor sites (extranet)

❑ Future interoperability issues

# Chapter 9: Expanding The VPN

### Expanding The VPN, Checklist 1: Equipment Required

The following checklist should be used in determining the equipment required:

❑ Develop a configuration plan that includes the following items.

  ❑ Determine to which of the VPN tunneling servers this client will attach if you have configured a site-to-site VPN connecting two LANs.

  ❑ List the IP addresses for the tunneling server.

  ❑ List the protocols to be sent over the VPN tunnel (TCP/IP, IPX/SPX etc.).

  ❑ Determine what applications are needed, such as email, word processing, spreadsheet, and so forth.

  ❑ If your VPN is Novell NetWare-based, you should record the location of the user in the tree.

❑ Fill out a configuration form for the client equipment. I advise you to use a separate form for each new client, include at least the information shown in Table 9.1.

❑ List the items you require on the workstation to complete the installation and configuration of the VPN software. This should include the following:

  ❑ A computer capable of running Microsoft Windows 98 or your favorite client operating system reliably. Make sure that this computer has a sufficient amount of RAM (64MB recommended), and a Pentium processor (166 MHz or better recommended).

  ❑ Microsoft Windows 98, or your favorite client operating system, installed. If you did not install Windows 98 yourself, verify the installation of dial-up-networking. This is the default, but it never hurts to check.

❑ A high-speed modem (56K V.90 recommended). The modem can be either internal or external, depending on the preferences and capabilities of the user and the computer. The modem should be installed, tested, and working reliably.

❑ The computer should have a CD-ROM drive installed and tested.

### Expanding The VPN, Checklist 2: Support Needs

The following checklist should be used in determining support needs:

❑ Software vendor for Windows NT 4, especially if it is a Microsoft Certified Solutions Provider (MCSP):

Name:_____

Company:_____

Phone: (____)_____

❑ Hardware vendor:

Name:_____

Company:_____

Phone: (____)_____

❑ Internet Service Provider:

Name:_____

Company:_____

Phone: (____)_____

❑ PSTN or PDN provider:

Name:_____

Company:_____

Phone: (____)_____

❑ Other support options:

Name:_____

Company:_____

Phone: (____)_____

### Expanding The VPN, Checklist 3: Pre-Implementation

The following checklist should be used in performing pre-implementation:

❑ Create a contingency plan, preferably with a time-line and point-of-no-return established and share it with the user. This is especially important if you are configuring the user's computer, and the user is doing without in the meantime.

❑ Notify users, especially those on the VPN of interest, that you are working on the network and that service may be interrupted from time to time. Even though you are only installing a client, Murphy may toss a glitch into the system requiring you to reboot the server. Telling people ahead of time may reduce the infernal jangling of the telephone when you have both hands full of troubleshooting charts.

❑ Verify that all hardware, new or rollover (existing), on the client computer is functional and, if necessary, upgraded to meet specifications required.

❑ Check your detailed drawing and make sure that you have assigned an IP address to the network connection on each new item of equipment.

❑ Determine that all equipment involved in the implementation has the proper protocols and addresses assigned.

❑ Make sure that all software to be used, especially Novell NetWare, Microsoft Windows NT, and Novell BorderManager, have all had the latest support packs installed as per recommendations by either Novell or Microsoft. For the newest list of recommended upgrades, check each vendor's Web site.

❑ If you haven't already done so, upgrade the version of the network clients to the latest recommended by the software vendor. Check for the latest clients at the Web sites for either Microsoft or Novell (or any other vendor whose product you are installing).

### Note
*The next step is very important because BorderManager makes full use of Novell Directory Services.*

❑ If you are installing the NetWare BorderManager VPN, make sure that the directory is synchronized fully and no directory-related problems exist. Run DSREPAIR on all servers that have a replica of the partition that will contain the BorderManager VPN Servers. A Directory Tree that has problems can cause client problems.

❑ Install and configure the TCP/IP protocol and set up initial routing functions.

❑ Power up the equipment, and run some diagnostics tests to assure yourself that it is all functioning correctly. The goal here is to eliminate as many potential problem sources as possible. The more variables you eliminate, the less tools Murphy has to work with.

### Expanding The VPN, Checklist BM4a: Configure A BorderManager VPN Server For User Access Via The Internet

The following checklist is used for configuring a BorderManager VPN server for user access via the Internet:

*In this series of checklists we have combined the BorderManager and Windows NT portions into separate checklists. Those lists that deal primarily with the BorderManager product are identified as BM4x. Those lists that deal primarily with the Windows NT product are identified as NT4x. You should use the checklist that is appropriate for your implementation.*

❑ Log on as a user with Admin rights in the container where the VPN server you want to configure is located.

❑ Click on Start | Run. This opens the Run dialog box, as shown in Figure 9.5.

❑ Type in the path shown in Figure 9.5; or as an option, you can click Browse and navigate your way through the path to the Nwadmin32.exe file.

❑ Click on OK. The NetWare Administrator program will start, as shown in Figure 9.6.

❑ Double-click on the server object representing the VPN server. The server property page will open, as shown in Figure 9.7.

❑ Click on BorderManager Setup; this will open the BorderManager Setup properties page, as shown in Figure 9.8.

❑ Click on the VPN Tab. This opens the VPN property page, as shown in Figure 9.9.

❑ Place a checkmark in the Client to Site checkbox, and click on Details. This opens the VPN Client details page, as shown in Figure 9.10.

❑ To enable the encryption of IPX data, you must enter a valid IPX network address in the WAN Client IPX Network Address data entry box.

*Note*

*If you enter an address here, it must be a valid, unique IPX address. It cannot be the same IPX address that is already bound to another adapter in the computer. This is the IPX address that will be assigned to the user upon connection to the VPN tunnel. When IPX support is enabled for a VPN client, the client's IPX LAN connection will be disabled when the dial-in VPN IPX connection is established. This is a normal function of the software and also occurs when the dial-up client is not using the VPN.*

❑ If you do not want the client and server to negotiate the data encryption and data authentication methods, you can put a checkmark in the Restrict Clients To Use Server Preferred Security checkbox.

❑ If you want to specify a limited number of networks that the client will be able to access using data encryption, select the Encrypt Only Networks Listed Below radio button. If you select this radio button, you must add the specified networks by clicking the Add icon and entering the specified networks.

**Note**

*By default, IP encryption is enabled for all networks.*

❏ If you wish, you can select the amount of time allowed before the VPN expires. To do this select the appropriate time in the Inactivity Timeout selection boxes.

❏ If you wish, you can enable the VPN server to send "keep alive" packets periodically. To do this, place a checkmark in the Keep Alive Automatically checkbox.

❏ To view the Information Digest code that is sent to the client, click on the Digest button. You should record this information, as you will need to provide it to the clients for their initial login to this server from a new workstation.

**Note**

*If you are not sure about what configuration to use with any item, I suggest you take the default for now. For the most part, the default settings will work correctly for the largest percentage of users.*

❏ When you have configured the VPN client information, click on OK. You will be returned to the VPN properties page, as shown in Figure 9.9.

❏ Click on the BorderManager Access Rules button. This will open the BorderManager Access Rules properties page, as shown in Figure 9.11.

❏ You must now add the users that are authorized to gain access to the network through the VPN. To do this, click on the Add icon to open the Access Rule Definition properties page, as shown in Figure 9.12.

❏ Under Action, select the Allow radio button.

❏ Under Access Type, select VPN Client from the selection drop-down menu.

❏ In the Source section, select the Specified radio button.

❏ Click on the Browse icon to open the VPN User Specification properties page, as shown in Figure 9.13.

❏ Click on the Add icon to open the Select Object dialog box, as shown in Figure 9.14.

❏ Use the Browse context list to navigate your way through the tree until the object you wish to add is shown in the Available objects window. Select the object you want to add in the Available objects window and click on OK. This returns you to the VPN User Specification properties page, with the object you selected now listed.

❏ If you need to add more objects, repeat the previous two steps until you have all the objects you wish to add. When you have finished adding objects, click on OK. This returns you to the Access Rule Definition property page, with the specified objects listed in the Source dialog box.

❏ When you have completed the Access Rule Definition configuration procedure, click on OK. This returns you to the BorderManager Access Rules properties page, as shown in Figure 9.11, with the new Access Rule listed in the Rules list.

❏ When you have completed configuring all the BorderManager Access Rules, click on OK. This activates the new rules at the VPN server, and the screen will return to the NetWare Administrator opening page, as shown in Figure 9.6.

❏ Click the Exit icon to close the NetWare Administrator.

Make sure to supply the clients with the following information:

❏ The NDS username and password assigned to each user.

❏ The actual IP address of the VPN server.

    ❏ If necessary, the Digest of the VPN server security authorization information.

### *Expanding The VPN, Checklist BM4b: Install The Novell VPN Client*

The following checklist is used when installing the Novell VPN client:

❏ Mount the Novell BorderManager CD in the CD-ROM drive.

❏ Click Start | Run to open the Run dialog box, as shown in Figure 9.15.

❏ Type in the path, as shown in Figure 9.15. As an option you can click Browse, and navigate your way through the path to the setup.exe file. Click on OK. This starts the setup program. The Novell Virtual Private Network Client Installation screen will open, as shown in Figure 9.16.

❏ Click on Next. The dialog box will change to an information box, as shown in Figure 9.17. Verify that the conditions listed are correct.

❏ Click on Next. The information in the dialog box will change to that shown in Figure 9.18, informing you that you need to install the Novell VPN adapter, and that you may need the Windows 98 CD.

❏ Click on Next. The setup program will perform a file copy operation. After a short time an Insert Disk dialog box will open, as shown in Figure 9.19, prompting you to insert the Windows 98 CD-ROM.

❏ Click on OK. The Copying Files dialog box will open, as shown in Figure 9.20, prompting you for the path to the Windows 98 files.

❏ Enter the path to the Windows 98 files, and click on OK. The dialog box will close, and a new box will open, shown in Figure 9.21, telling you that the VPN client has been installed and you will need to make a new connection in the Dial-Up Networking group.

❏ When you are ready to continue, click Next. The information dialog box will close, and the Dial-Up Networking group will be opened on the Desktop.

### *Expanding The VPN, Checklist BM4c: Create A Dial-Up Networking Icon*

The following checklist should be used to create a Dial-Up Networking icon:

❏ To create an icon in the Dial-Up Networking group, click on Start | Programs | Accessories | Communications | Dial-Up Networking. This will open the Dial-Up Networking group, as shown in Figure 9.22.

❏ Double-click on the Make New Connection icon to open the new connection dialog.

❏ Type in a name to describe the connection.

❏ After you've entered the name, press the Tab key once to move the cursor to the Select a device drop-down menu. Open the menu and select the modem you want to use for this dial-up connection. The menu will close and your modem will be listed in the Select a device data area, as shown in Figure 9.24.

❏ Click on the Next button to open the Make New Connection dialog box, as shown in Figure 9.25, prompting you for the phone number of the computer you want to call.

❏ Consult your ISP information sheet, and fill in the appropriate information. Click on Next. A new dialog box will open, shown in Figure 9.26, informing you that a new dial-up networking connection with the name you assigned has been created.

❏ Click on Finish to close the Make New Connection dialog box and return to the Dial-Up Networking group window, as shown in Figure 9.27, and notice that your new connection is now available.

### Expanding The VPN, Checklist BM4d: Configure Dial-Up Networking

The following checklist should be used for configuring Dial-Up Networking:

❏ Point to the dial-up connection you just created, and right-click to open the selection drop-down menu, then left-click on Properties. That opens the Dial-Up Connection properties pages, shown in Figure 9.28, for the new connection.

❏ Click on the Server Types tab to open the Server Types properties page, as shown in Figure 9.29.

❏ For a dial-up connection to a BorderManager VPN, the server type must be Novell Virtual Private Network. When you select this server type, all the Advanced Options and Allowed Network Protocols will be grayed out, except for the TCP/IP protocol.

❏ Click on the TCP/IP Settings button to open the TCP/IP properties page, as shown in Figure 9.30.

❏ Consult your ISP configuration sheet and verify if the called server will assign an IP address. Otherwise, click the Specify name server addresses radio button, and fill in the appropriate information for the primary and secondary DNS servers. Verify that the checkboxes for Use IP header compression and Use default gateway on the remote network are checked as appropriate. When the TCP/IP properties are filled in correctly, click on OK. This returns you to the Server Types properties page, shown previously in Figure 9.29.

❏ Click on OK. The property pages will close and you will be returned to the Dial-Up Networking group, shown in Figure 9.27.

❏ Click on the close box ("X" in the upper-right corner of the dial-up networking panel) to close the window and return to the Novell Virtual Private Network Client Installation screen, as shown in Figure 9.31.

❏ When you are ready to continue, click Next. The Install Novell BorderManager VPN Client dialog box will change, as shown in Figure 9.32, prompting you to enter the type of dial-up connection for the VPN server.

❏ Click the Indirect through an ISP radio button to make an Internet connection through an ISP. If you will always be connecting to the same VPN server, consult your configuration sheet and type in the actual IP address for the public interface. On the other hand, if you are going to be using this same configuration to connect to different VPN servers, or you don't have the IP address of the VPN server, you can leave this entry blank, and the software will request an address each time you initiate a connection.

❏ When you are ready to continue, click Next. The information in the Install Novell BorderManager VPN Client dialog box will change, as shown in Figure 9.33, and gives you the options to View the Readme file and Create a shortcut on the Desktop for the VPN login. Both options are selected in the default settings.

❏ When you are finished, click Next to continue and close the box. The Reboot dialog box, as shown in Figure 9.34, displays next, prompting you to restart your computer.

❏ To restart your computer, remove any diskettes and/or CD-ROMs from the appropriate drive(s) and click Finish. The setup program will close.

**Note**

*We recommend that you restart before continuing the installation process.*

### Expanding The VPN, Checklist BM4e: Make The Connection

The following checklists should be used for making the connection:

❏ Start the Novell VPN Client one of the following three ways:

    ❏ If you choose to create a VPN Login icon for the Windows Desktop, double-click that icon.

    ❏ Click Start | Programs | Novell | VPN client | VPN Login.

    ❏ Double-click the VPN Dial-Up Network entry. When the specified connection is established, the Novell VPN Login program is launched.

❏ We will assume that you double-clicked the VPN Login icon on the Desktop. That action started the VPN Login program and opened the Novell BorderManager VPN Client, as shown in Figure 9.35.

❏ Use the information sheet provided from the BorderManager Client Configuration and fill in the following information in the appropriate fields:

    ❏ NDS username

    ❏ NDS password

> **Note**
> *This username and password may be different from the ISP Internet password.*

❑ NDS context

❑ VPN server's actual IP address

❑ Select the Dial-Up tab and change to the VPN Login Dial-Up property page, as shown in Figure 9.36.

❑ Use the configuration information sheet for the ISP and put the following information in the appropriate areas:

❑ Name you used when you created a dial-up networking icon.

❑ Username assigned by the ISP for the dial-up user.

❑ The password assigned by the ISP for the dial-up user. This entry is optional and if used will replace any entry made in a similar area in the Dial-Up Networking entry.

❑ One or more phone numbers for accessing the ISP. This entry is optional, and if used, will replace any entry made in a similar area in the Dial-Up Network entry.

❑ If you are using RADIUS to authenticate users, you can automatically use the NetWare username/context and password used in the RADIUS account by placing a mark in the Use NetWare username and password checkbox.

❑ When the dial-up property information is correct, click on the NetWare Options tab to open the next page, as shown in Figure 9.37.

❑ Here you select from the available options to meet your specific needs. The installation selects all by default. Except for the Enable ipx checkbox, the options are self-explanatory; enable ipx enables IPX encryption over the VPN. If you don't select this option, you can't use IPX for this VPN session. If you enabled IPX encryption on the VPN server when you went through the configuration process, you should leave this option enabled here.

❑ To launch an application after the VPN tunnel is established, you can click on the Launcher tab and go to the Launcher property page shown in Figure 9.38. You can then click the Browse button and navigate through the path and select an application to launch.

❑ When you have all the information entered correctly, click on OK.

❑ If this is the first time that you have connected to this VPN from this workstation, you will be presented with a dialog box containing the digest information from the VPN server. This is the same digest information presented during the VPN server configuration. Hopefully, you recorded the information when you were configuring the server for client access. Verify that it is correct and click on OK.

❑ During the initial connection and login process, the Novell VPN Login dialog box will change to the VPN Status tab so you can monitor the progress of the login from this page.

❏ After the connection is established and you have logged in to the Tree, the default login script will execute and the VPN Login dialog box will close. The software will create an icon representing the VPN connection and place it in the Taskbar. Double-click on that icon to monitor the VPN statistics.

### Expanding The VPN, Checklist NT4f: Verify That The VPN Networking Routines Have Been Installed From The Windows 98 CD

The following checklist should be used for verifying that the VPN Networking routines have been installed from the Windows 98 CD:

❏ Click Start | Settings | Control Panel. The panel in Figure 9.39 will open. How you have the preferences set will determine whether you have the HTML format displayed on the left side of the screen as shown in the figure; however, that's not critical. The main stuff is the icon field on the right.

❏ Double-click on the Add Remove Programs icon and your screen will look like Figure 9.40.

❏ Click on the Windows Setup tab to open the Properties page, as shown in Figure 9.41.

❏ Use the scrollbar to move through the Components window and select Communications, then click on the Details button. This opens the Communications components dialog box, shown in Figure 9.42.

❏ Using the scrollbar, look through the available components until you locate Virtual Private Networking. If not already checked, check the box for Virtual Private Networking. Click on OK to close the Details window and return to the Add/Remove Program properties Control Panel, shown in Figure 9.41. Click on OK to close it.

❏ If you checked Virtual Private Networking, an Insert Disk dialog box will open, as shown in Figure 9.43, informing you that you need to insert the Windows 98 CD.

❏ Click on OK and open a Copying Files dialog box like the one in Figure 9.44. If the default path shown for the location of the Windows 98 Installation Files is not correct, type in the correct path. If you are copying the files from the Windows 98 CD, insert the CD in the CD-ROM drive at this time and click on OK. The file copy procedure will start.

❏ After the first of the files have been copied, a Dial-Up Networking Setup information box will open, as shown in Figure 9.45, informing you that after the Add/Remove Programs has completed you will need to restart your computer before proceeding with the Dial-Up Networking configuration.

❏ Click on OK and the remaining files will be copied. After the file copy procedure has completed, the Add/Remove Programs properties window will close, and the Control Panel will become active. Remove any diskettes and/or CDs and restart the computer.

### *Expanding The VPN, Checklist NT4g: Install Microsoft VPN Adapter*

The following checklist should be used for installing the Microsoft VPN Adapter:

❏ Click Start | Settings | Control Panel. Double-click on the Network icon (Figure 9.39) to open the Network Control Panel, shown in Figure 9.46.

❏ Scroll through the list for Microsoft Virtual Private Networking Adapter. If it is already installed, you can skip the rest of this section. Otherwise, click the Add button to open the Select Network Component Type dialog box shown in Figure 9.47.

❏ Select Adapter, then click Add to open the Select Network adapters dialog box shown in Figure 9.48.

❏ In the left-hand window, scroll through the list of manufacturers, then click on Microsoft. This opens the list of Microsoft Network Adapters in the right-hand window, as shown in Figure 9.49.

❏ Select Microsoft Virtual Private Networking Adapter in the right-hand window, then click on OK to return to the Network Control Panel. Click on OK to close the Network Control Panel. This opens a System Settings Change information box, as shown in Figure 9.50, informing you that the settings will not take place until the computer is restarted. Click Yes to restart the computer.

### Note

*That completes the installation of a Microsoft Virtual Private Networking adapter for Windows 98.*

### *Expanding The VPN, Checklist NT4h: Create A Dial-Up Networking Icon*

The following checklist should be used to create a Dial-Up Networking icon:

❏ Click Start | Programs | Accessories | Communications | Dial-Up Networking to open the Dial-Up Networking group, as shown in Figure 9.51.

❏ If you have no dial-up connections at this time, the Make New Connection dialog box will automatically open, as shown in Figure 9.52. If you already have one or more dial-up connections configured, double-click on the Make New Connection icon to open the new connection dialog.

❏ Type in any name you want to use to describe the connection. After you've entered the name, press the Tab key once and the cursor will move to the Select a device data area. Open the drop-down menu to the right of the data area and click on Microsoft VPN Adapter. The Microsoft VPN adapter should be selected in the data area, as shown in Figure 9.53.

❏ Click on the Next button to open the Host name or IP address data entry area, as shown in Figure 9.54.

❏ Type in the IP address of the computer you are making a connection to on the other end of the VPN tunnel. If you have made a DNS entry for the *host name* for that computer, you can enter that, then click on Next. This opens the Make New Connection information screen, shown in Figure 9.55, telling you that a new Dial-Up Networking connection with the name you assigned has been created.

❏ Click on Finish to close the Make New Connection dialog box will close and open the Dial-Up Networking group window in Figure 9.56, showing the new connection.

**Note**

*You are not restricted to the number of dial-up connections you create.*

### Expanding The VPN, Checklist NT4i: Configure The VPN Dial-Up Connection Icon

The following checklist should be used for configuring the VPN Dial-Up Connection icon:

❏ Right-click on the VPN Dial-Up Connection you created. Click on Properties; this opens the dialog box for the connection you have created, as shown in Figure 9.57.

❏ Click on the Server Types tab to open the Server Types dialog box, as shown in Figure 9.58.

❏ In the Advanced option area, make sure the Require Encrypted Password and Require Data Encryption checkboxes are checked; the rest are optional and can be checked as desired.

❏ In the Allowed network protocols area, make sure that the TCP/IP checkbox is checked (it is required).

❏ Click on the TCP/IP Settings button to open the dialog box shown in Figure 9.59.

❏ If you want the ISP to assign an IP address, verify that the Server assigned IP address radio button is selected. If you want to assign a specific IP address, then the Specify an IP address radio button, and enter a valid IP address.

❏ If you want the ISP to assign an address for the name server, verify that the Server assigned name server address radio button is selected. If you want to use a specific name server address, select the Specify name server address radio button, and enter the IP address of at least one DNS or WINS server that will be accessible to this computer.

❏ If your ISP can support IP header compression and you want to use the default gateway on the remote system (these are the defaults), then leave the appropriate checkboxes checked.

❏ When the TCP/IP configuration is correct, click on OK twice.

**Note**

*You have created and configured a dial-up interface to connect to the PPTP server. You can, for your convenience, create a shortcut to this interface on your Windows Desktop.*

### Expanding The VPN, Checklist NT4j: Establish A Connection To The ISP

The following checklist should be used to establish a connection to the ISP:

❏ Double-click on the appropriate connection icon in the Dial-Up Network group (or on the Desktop if you have a shortcut) for the ISP you wish to use to initiate the client end of the VPN. This opens the Connect To dialog box, as shown in Figure 9.60.

❏ Fill in the appropriate password, and change the other information as necessary, then click on Connect. This initiates the connection and starts the modem dial sequence. An information dialog box will open, as shown in Figure 9.61, informing you of the progress of the connection.

❏ When a connection has been established, the information dialog box will close and the Connection Monitor icon will appear in the Taskbar.

### Expanding The VPN, Checklist NT4k: Establish Communications With The PPTP VPN Server And Make A Secure Connection To The NT Network

The following checklist should be used to establish communications with the PPTP VPN server and to make a secure connection to the NT Network:

❏ Double-click on the appropriate connection icon in the Dial-Up Network group (or on the Desktop if you have a shortcut) for the PPTP VPN tunnel connection. This opens the Connect To dialog box for the PPTP VPN connection, shown in Figure 9.62.

❏ Verify that the information is correct, then click on Connect to initiate the connection and start the VPN tunnel development sequence. An information dialog box will open, as shown in Figure 9.63, displaying the progress of the connection.

❏ With the connection established, the screen will display the profile the administrator has established for you on the Windows NT server. A second connection monitor icon will appear in the Taskbar; the first is for the dial-up connection to the ISP, and the second is for the PPTP VPN connection.

❏ To disconnect, click on Disconnect.

### Checklist Number Five: Post-Implementation

The following checklist should be used for post-implementation:

❏ If your operating system is BorderManager running on NetWare, perform a check of the Directory Tree and make sure no problems exist there.

❏ If you have a BorderManager Site-to-Site VPN, as well as a Client-to-Site VPN, run NWAdmin from a workstation and verify that the master server and all slave servers are synchronized correctly.

❏ If you are using Windows NT 4, and you have added any new features on the NT server, go back and reinstall the Windows NT Service Pack 4. This must be reinstalled each time new features are added to the NT server.

❏ If you are using BorderManager and have not done so yet, install the latest Support Pack. Read the technical document for each support pack, and upgrade any other necessary items, including VPN clients and snap-ins for NWAdmin on all the NetWare servers.

❏ Remove any temporary cable patches, temporary hubs, switches, and routers you may have needed for the installation.

❏ In configuring the NetWare Server to support BorderManager, Novell assumed the server would be used as a firewall and that users would not log onto the server. For the most part this is correct; however, an exception can happen when using the newly released BorderManager VPN Client for a secure connection from the BorderManager server to your remote user's computer. In this case change the Set parameter on both the master and slave VPN servers to: SET REPLY TO GET NEAREST SERVER = ON, and login to the BorderManager VPN server using the VPN client.

### Checklist Number Six: Managing Your VPN
The following checklist should be used for managing your VPN:

This list is items that you should be aware of in regard to remote user administration.

❏ Software updates

❏ Data backups

❏ Maintaining a list of ISPs

❏ Building and maintaining an ISP database

❏ Developing a script that will auto-download the database update

### Checklist Number Seven: Future Planning
The following checklist should be used for future planning:

Monitor your VPN on a regular basis, watching for change in the following areas.

❏ Network expansion

　❏ User population

　❏ Connect time

　❏ Bandwidth utilization

❏ VPN capacity

　❏ Tunnel server capacity

　❏ Supporting systems capacity

　❏ Bandwidth use

❏ Longer-term network growth

　❏ Remote users

　❏ Accessibility to client sites (extranet)

　❏ Accessibility to vendor sites (extranet)

# Chapter 11: VPN Management And Maintenance

## VPN Management Checklist 1: Daily Administrative Tasks

The following checklist should be used to perform daily administrative tasks:

❏ If you perform your backup overnight, retrieve the new backup tape and examine the backup and verification logs. If no errors exist, archive the backup log. While this is not a VPN-specific function, it is still a part of daily administration and should not be overlooked.

❏ Depending on your shift schedule and your backup schedule, you may have to set up the daily backup.

❏ Check any error logs you have enabled, and record any errors that occurred in the past 24 hours. Take a few minutes and scan the error logs for the previous five to seven days, looking for any pattern developing in the errors. This is a major key in making your troubleshooting proactive instead of reactive.

❏ Check any traffic logs, record the volume of traffic, and the time the traffic occurred. If you have a protocol analyzer, or if you use the Network Monitor feature in Windows NT Server, this is very easy to do. Just as you did with the error logs, take a few minutes and scan through the traffic logs looking for developing patterns in the network traffic. This will help you spot developing trends, and possibly allow you to plan for future upgrades in areas where needed.

❏ If you have a major scheduled upgrade or other major network activity planned for this day, perform that activity at this time.

❏ Check your list of remote/traveling users and see who is going to be in their office today. Contact those that are in, and verify that they have turned in their laptop computers to have the latest software updates applied. This is especially true with the remote/traveling users, as they do not normally get their software updated automatically when they login to the network over the VPN.

❏ Perform weekly administrative tasks as necessary. (See the first paragraph of the next section for an explanation of this item.)

❏ Perform daily administrative tasks such as creating and deleting users, modifying user profiles, and configuring software for users as needed.

## VPN Management Checklist 2: Weekly Administrative Tasks

The following checklist is used to perform weekly administrative tasks:

❏ Depending on your shift schedule and your backup schedule, you may have to set up the weekly backup.

❏ Check your software update schedule, and download software updates from the Internet as applicable. Of particular interest should be network client updates and application software updates. If you use software on your network that automatically updates the user's network client and software applications each time they log in to the network, perform the necessary configuration to enable the latest updates to be downloaded.

❑ Review all the logs from all VPN-related network traffic for the past week. If the preparation of summary reports and trend analysis falls within your job description, summarize the logs and produce a one page report with trend analysis.

❑ Have a team meeting with all the individuals directly or indirectly involved in supporting the VPN. Discuss the Internet trend analysis report, and the need for any changes, upgrades, or modifications. Discuss upcoming scheduled activities, and, if necessary, finalize a plan for a monthly scheduled event to take place within the week.

### *VPN Management Checklist 3: Monthly Administrative Tasks*

The following checklist should be used to perform monthly administrative tasks:

**Note**

*Monthly administrative tasks are items that generally affect a fairly large segement of the network, and should be scheduled. They should be scheduled and users notified of possible network use disruptions.*

❑ Apply any network system Service Packs (Windows NT) or Support Packs (Novell NetWare) as needed.

❑ If your network system is Novell NetWare, perform any major changes to the Directory Tree (merging partitions, relocating containers, relocating servers within the tree structure, etc.) that will affect more than a few users.

❑ Install any new software applications (not just patches and fixes for the same version) or major version upgrades (that is, moving from MS Office 97 to MS Office 2000). This is especially important with respect to the remote/traveling users that access the network through the VPN, as they usually need the software loaded on their computer, not accessible over the network.

❑ Perform a 24-hour scan of traffic on the Internet in order to build a baseline of Internet traffic patterns. I recommend that this be performed on the same day of the week, in the same week of the month, on a regular basis. In this way Internet traffic patterns can be baselined and a trend log can be developed and used to track changing conditions on the Internet.

❑ Schedule regular ongoing training sessions monthly, especially with your remote/traveling users. Use this training time to demonstrate new features of the network clients, new features of the VPN software they may be interested in, and so forth.

# Appendix E
# *Recommended Reading*

Between the two of us, we have several yards of reference books. We have sorted through the dozens of titles and offer the following list for your perusal with our recommendations. Over the coming months, as new titles hit the shelves, we will include reviews of some of them on our Web site **www.sldenterprises.com**.

## Networking And Internet

*Troubleshooting TCP—IP: Analyzing the Protocols of the Internet*
Author: Miller, Mark A.
Publishing Date: 9/1995
Publisher: IDG Books Worldwide
Binding: Paperback
ISBN: 1-55851-268-3
List Price: U.S. $44.95

*Novell's Internet Plumbing Handbook*
Author: Rybaczyk, Peter
Publishing Date: 2/1998
Publisher: IDG Books Worldwide
Binding: Paperback
ISBN: 0-76454-537-X
List Price: U.S. $34.99

*Novell's Encyclopedia of Networking*
Author: Shafer, Kevin
Publishing Date: 12/1997
Publisher: IDG Books Worldwide
Binding: Hardcover
ISBN: 0-76454-511-6
List Price: U.S. $69.99

*An Introduction to Ethernet Switching*
Authors: Hein, Mathias, and David Griffiths
Publishing Date: 1/1997
Publisher: International Thomson Computer Press
Binding: Mass Market
ISBN: 1-85032-166-3
List Price: U.S. $44.95

## Protocols

*Internetworking with TCP/IP, Vol. 1*
Author: Comer, Douglas E.
Publishing Date: 3/1995
Publisher: Prentice Hall
Binding: Cloth Text
ISBN: 0-13216-987-8
List Price: U.S. $65.00

*IP Fundamentals: Addressing, Routing, and Troubleshooting*
Author: Maufler, Thomas A.
Publishing Date: 3/1999
Publisher: Prentice Hall
Binding: Paper Text
ISBN: 0-13975-483-0
List Price: U.S. $49.99

*Gigabit Ethernet*
Authors: Kadambi, Jayant, Ian Crayford, and Mohan Kalkunte
Publishing Date: 4/1998
Publisher: Prentice Hall
Binding: Cloth Text
ISBN: 0-13913-286-4
List Price: U.S. $48.00

*Cryptography and Network Security: Principles and Practice*
Author: Stallings, William
Publishing Date: 6/1998
Publisher: Prentice Hall
Binding: Cloth Text
ISBN: 0-13869-017-0
List Price: U.S. $67.00

## Microsoft Windows 98 And Windows NT 4

*Microsoft Windows 98 Resource Kit*
Author: Microsoft Corporation Staff
Publishing Date: 6/1998
Publisher: Microsoft Press
Binding: CD-ROM, General Hardcover
ISBN: 1-57231-644-6
List Price: U.S. $9.99

*Microsoft NT Server Resource Kit*
Author: Microsoft Corporation Staff
Publishing Date: 9/1996
Publisher: Microsoft Press
Binding: Boxed, Slipcased, and/or Casebound CD-ROM, General Paper Text
ISBN: 1-57231-344-7
List Price: U.S. $149.95

*Windows NT 4.0 Connectivity Guide*
Author: Grace, Richard
Publishing Date: 1/1998
Publisher: IDG Books Worldwide
Binding: Paperback
ISBN: 0-76453-160-3
List Price: U.S. $39.99

*Windows NT 4.0 Server Security Guidebook and CD-ROM*
Author: Gonsalves, Marcus
Publishing Date: 4/1998
Publisher: Prentice Hall
Binding: CD-ROM, General Paperback
ISBN: 0-13679-903-5
List Price: U.S. $44.95

## Novell NetWare And BorderManager Services

*Novell's Guide to NetWare 5 Networks*
Author: Hughes, Jeffrey F., and Blair W. Thomas
Publishing Date: 2/1999
Publisher: IDG Books Worldwide
Binding: CD-ROM, General, Hardcover
ISBN: 0-76454-544-2
List Price: U.S. $74.99

*IntranetWare BorderManager*
Author: Gaskin, James
Publishing Date: 9/1997
Publisher: Sybex, Incorporated
Binding: Hardcover
ISBN: 0-78212-138-1
List Price: U.S. $49.99

## Internet Resources

If you work with Novell NetWare or other Novell products, the authors recommend that you subscribe to the Novell Research AppNotes. For more information about AppNotes go to: **developer.novell.com/dev_resources/faq/researchfaq.htm**.

In addition to the previous titles, an abundance of vendor-specific technical articles await your inspection at these and other sites on the Internet:

- **support.novell.com**
- **support.microsoft.com**
- **www.cisco.com**
- **www.indusriver.com**
- **www.fortresstech.com**

# Index

1Gbps Ethernet, 31, 33
10base2 Ethernet, 33, 51
10base5 Ethernet, 33
10baseF Ethernet, 33
10baseFL Ethernet, 33
10baseT Ethernet, 33
10Mbps Ethernet, 31
100baseFL Ethernet, 31
100baseTX Ethernet, 31
100baseVG Ethernet, 31
100Mbps Fast Ethernet, 31
1000baseT Ethernet, 31
3Com, PPTP Forum, 154
3-way handshakes, 129

## A

ABR connections, 83
Access charges, ISPs, 371
ACS, 166
Address Resolution Protocol. *See* ARP.
Administrative checklists, 436–438
Advanced Research Projects Agency. *See* ARPA.
Advanced Research Projects Agency Network.
  *See* ARPANET.
AHs, 137, 138–139, 141
Airports
  computer theft, 370
  security scanners, 369–370
American National Standards Institute. *See* ANSI.
**AND** function, masking, 89
ANSI, 16
AnyLAN, 31
Apple Macintosh. *See* Macs.
AppleTalk protocol suite, 6, 40
Application layer, OSI model, 22
Application software, backing up, 399–400
Architecture
  Cisco Systems' approach, 164–166
  current, VPN design, 185–189
  FDDI, 81–82
  firewalls, 404–407

ISA, 16
LANs, 16–18, 185
Micro Channel, 18, 60
NetWare, 56, 160–161
NetWare VPN model, 200–201
PPTP Forum, 155
WANs, 66–67, 186, 188
ARCNet systems, 51
ARP, 90
ARPA, 3–4
ARPANET, 7, 33–34
  dismantling, 34
  security, 135–136
Ascend Communications, PPTP Forum, 154–155
ASDLs, 78, 465
Asymmetric Digital Subscriber Lines. *See* ASDLs.
Asynchronous technology, 73
Asynchronous transfer mode. *See* ATM.
ATM, 82–85
  data packets, 83
  DPT, 83–85
  older protocols, 82
  packet length solution, 83
ATM Forum, 82
AT&T WorldNet, 370–371
Authentication, 155
  Indus River Software, 170
  PPP, 129
Authentication, Authorization, and Accounting (AAA),
  L2F, 132, 133
Authentication Headers. *See* AHs.
Authorization, 155
Available bit rate. *See* ABR connections.

## B

Backbone, collapsed, 54
Backbone cable, 46
Backbone routers, 53
Backdoor users, viruses, 385
Back Office 2000 virus, 388
Backup. *See* System backup.

Backup domain controllers. *See* BDCs.
Bacteria, 388
Bandwidth, 29–32
   Ethernet, 31–32
Basic rate interface. *See* BRI.
BDCs, 63, 276
Because It's Time NETwork. *See* BITNET.
B-ISDN, 76–77
BITNET, 6
Blowfish, 421–422
BNC Tee, 51
Boot sector viruses, 388
Bootstrap (boot) programs, 42
BorderManager, 211–215
   accessing statistics, 432–436
   adding Snap-In utility, 234–237
   client-to-site VPN implementation, 353
   configuring master VPN server, 237–247
   encryption, 215
   firewalls, 212, 221
   installation, 224–234
   NWAdmin, 432
   theory of operation, '213–215
   troubleshooting, 458–459
Boundary routers, 150
Break-out cable, 48
BRI, 76
Bridges
   LANs, Ethernet, 53–54
   WANs, 85–87
Broadband ISDN. *See* B-ISDN.
Broadcasting, 50
Brouters, 101–102
Bulletin boards, 6
Bus expansion unit (bus slot), 42

# C

Cable Modem Technologies. *See* CMT.
Cables
   backbone, 46
   break-out, 48
   coaxial, 45–46, 47
   fiber-optic, 47–49
   twisted-pair, 44–45
Cache devices, 404
Caching servers, 409
Carrier Sense Multiple Access with Collision Detection.
   *See* CSMA/CD.
CAs, 417–418
Catastrophic failure, 114

CDRs, backing up, 399
CDs, backing up, 399
Cerf, Vinton, 5
CERNET, 5
CERN European Laboratory for Particle Physics, 5
Certificates of Authority. *See* CAs.
Challenge Handshake, Authentication Protocol. *See* CHAP.
CHAP, 113–114, 129
Chariot, 271, 440
Chat rooms, 6
Cheaper net, 51
Checklists, implementation approach, 209–210
Ciphers, 142–143, 416
CiscoSecure Access Control Server (ACS), 166
Cisco Service Management System. *See* CSM.
Cisco Systems, 164–167, 469
   approach to network architecture, 164–165
   collaborations, 167
   DPT, 83–85
   history, 164
   L2F, 132–134, 153–154
   management systems, 167
   partnership approach, 165
   VPN implementation architecture, 165–166
   VPN protocols, 166
Classes, IP addresses, 88
Client installation procedure, 328–333
   checklist approach, 328–329
   equipment checklist, 329–330
   implementation procedure checklist, 333
   pre-implementation checklist, 332–333
   support checklist, 331
Clients, NetWare, 56–58
Client-to-site VPN, 319–378
   client installation procedure. *See* Client installation
     procedure.
   ISP interface, 323–324
   NetWare. *See* NetWare client-to-site VPN implementation.
   PPTP. *See* PPTP client-to-site VPN implementation.
   product comparisons, 326–328
   remote user administration. *See* Remote user administration.
   server interfaces, 324–325
   site-to-site VPN versus, 320–323
   troubleshooting. *See* Remote user troubleshooting.
Cloud, 271, 440
CMT, 465
Coaxial cable, 45–46, 47
Code division multiplexing, 75
Cold boot loader, NetWare, 56
Collapsed backbone, 54

Collisions, Ethernet protocol, 29
Commodore, 5
Compatibility, VPN implementation, 189–192
Complete backups, 400–402
Compulsory tunneling, 273
Computers
    building in help, 374–375
    connecting into LANs, 43–51
    historical background of, 2–3, 5
    LANs, 41–43
    laptop, remote, 368–370
    theft, 370
Computers and Science Network. *See* CSNET.
Concentrators, 51
    Ethernet, 51, 52
Concept-A virus, 387, 391
Configuration errors, 454–455
Connection-oriented services, 69
Connectivity, ISO standards, 19
Console One, 59
Copper cable, 44–47
    coaxial, 45–46, 47
    twisted-pair, 44–45
Costs, VPN implementation, 192–193
Counter rotating rings, FDDI, 81
CPE, 166
CPUs, 42
Crackers, 383. *See also* Security.
CSM, 167
CSMA/CD, 26, 28–29
CSNET, 6, 34
Customer premises equipment. *See* CPE.

**D**

Daemons, 392
Daily administrative checklist, 437
Daisy chains, 52
DARPA, 4–5, 33–34
DASs, 81–82
Data, telephony services, 73
Data backups, laptop computers, 368–369
Databases, ISPs, 371–372
Data cabinets, 46
Data encryption, 155
Data Encryption Standard. *See* DES.
Data files, backing up, 400
Datagrams, 123
    OSI model, 21
    source route, 124
    TCP/IP, 35

Data link layer. *See* DLL, OSI model.
Data Service Unit/Channel Service Unit. *See* DSU/CSU.
*De facto* standards, 17–18
Default gateways, 90
Defense Advanced Research Projects Agency. *See* DARPA.
Demilitarized zone. *See* DMZ.
Demodulation, 72
Demultiplexing, 74
Denial of service attacks, 381, 391–393
DES, 166, 419–420
DHCP, 109
Diagnostics software programs, 444
Dial-in, security concerns, 113–114
Dial-up connections, problems, 324
Dial-up networking icons
    configuring, 309–312, 346–350, 363–364
    creating, 307–309, 343–346, 360–362
Differential backups, 401, 403
Digital data, 73
Digital subscriber lines. *See* DSLs.
Digital Versatile Disks. *See* DVDs, backing up.
Digital voice circuits, 73
Diplomacy, troubleshooting, 446–447
Directory services, WANs, 105–106
Directory tree, NetWare, 55
Disaster recovery, 398
Disks, backing up, 398
Distance vector routing protocols, 97–98
DLL, OSI model, 21, 23
DMZ, 150, 186, 188
DNS, 37–38
Documentation
    for troubleshooting, 443
    of troubleshooting, 460
Domain names, 37–38
Domain Name System. *See* DNS.
Domains, Windows NT, 62–63
The DOS Requestor, 57
Dotted decimal notation, 88
DPT, 83–85
Dropped packets, 194
DSLs, 78
DSU/CSU, 74
Dual attachment stations. *See* DASs.
Dual-homed proxy hosts, 150–151
DVDs, backing up, 399
Dynamic Host Configuration Protocol. *See* DHCP.
Dynamic Packet Transport. *See* DPT.

# E

Eavesdropping, wireless communications, 50
ECI Telecom, PPTP Forum, 154
Eckert, J. P, 3
ECSA, 75
EIA/TIA 568 standard, 44, 46
EISA, 16
ELAP, 40
Electronic Numerical Integrator and Computer. *See* ENIAC.
Email, 6
   creation, 4–5
Email flooding, 381, 392–393
Email spoofing scripts, 392
Email viruses, 387–388
Encapsulating Security Payload. *See* ESP.
Encapsulation, 123. *See also* Tunneling.
   GRE, 130
Encryption, 142, 414–415, 418–422
   Blowfish, 421–422
   BorderManager, 215
   ciphers and keys, 142–143
   definition, 418
   DES, 419–420
   IDEA, 422
   Indus River Software, 171
   MD5, 420–421
   NetWare client-to-site VPN implementations, 337
   public key, 416
   RSA, 421
Encryption algorithm, 121
End users, training, 195
Enhanced ISA. *See* EISA.
ENIAC, 2–3
Enterprise Network, 65
E-series leased lines, 74
ESP, 136–139, 166
   confidentiality and integrity, 137–138
Ethernet, 6, 28–29
   bandwidths, 29–32
   bridges, 53–54
   concentrators and hubs, 51, 52–53
   connections, 51
   switches, 54
EtherTalk, 28, 40
Ether Talk Link Access. *See* ELAP.
Exchange Carriers Standards Association. *See* ECSA.
Executive overloads, 4
Expansion, VPN implementation, 191–192
Extranet VPN, 188, 192

# F

Fabrication, network attacks, 384
Failures
   catastrophic, 114
   personnel training in management, 183
Fast Ethernet, 31
Fast packet switching, 79–80
Fault determination, 457–458
FDDI, 80–82
   architecture, 81–82
Fiber Distributed Data Interconnect. *See* FDDI.
Fiber-optic cable, 47–49
Fido Net, 6
Filtering, 407–408
Firewalls, 114, 148–151, 186, 188, 404–408, 410
   architecture, 404–407
   BorderManager, 212, 221
   configuration, 455–456
   design philosophy, 407–408
   dual-homed proxy host, 150–151
   screened host gateway, 149–150
   screened subnet, 150
Frame relay, 79–80
Frames, 79, 425
Frequency division multiplexing, 75
FTP, 452

# G

GANs, 65, 66
Gateways
   default, 90
   Novell BorderManager, 161
   screened host, 149–150
   security, 144
   WAN routing, 95–98
Gel-filled fiber-optic cable, 49
Generic Routing Encapsulation Protocol. *See* GRE.
Global Area Networks. *See* GANs.
Graphical User Interfaces. *See* GUIs.
GRE, 130
GTE Net, 370–371
GUIs, 59

# H

Hackers, 381. *See also* Security.
Hardware. *See also specific hardware*.
   expanding capabilities, 42
   suspected faults, 453–454
   viruses, 389–390
   VPN implementation, 193

Hardware routers, 106
Hashes, 420
Hashing Message Authentication. *See* HMAC.
HDLC protocol, 73
Hello packets, 98
Help desk, 184
    software packages, 368
Help systems, 374
HHL, TCP/IP, 35
High-level data link control. *See* HDLC protocol.
HMAC, 139–140
Hollerith, Herman, 2
Hop count, 96
Host names, 37
    WANs, 88
Hosts, TCP/IP, 34
Host-to-host layer. *See* HHL, TCP/IP.
Hot keys, viruses, 388
Hubs, 51
    Ethernet, 51, 52–53
    manageable (smart), 52–53
    switching, 54

# I

IAB, 136
IBM
    Micro Channel architecture, 18, 60
    SNA, 19
IBM PC, 5
IBM PC DOS, 60
IBM XT, 5
ICMP, 35, 92
IDEA, 422
I-Ds, 117
IEEE, 16
IEEE 802 model, 23–24
IEEE standards, ISO model compared, 24–26
IESG, 117
IETF, 136
IGP, 97
Imagery, 6
Impedance, cables, 44–45
IMPs, 34
Incremental backups, 401, 402–403
Indus River Software, 168–171
    approach to networks, 168–169
    client-to-site VPNs, 326
    ISP database service, 371–372
    VPN protocols, 169–171
Industry Standard Architecture. *See* ISA.

INETCFG.NLM program, 221–224
Infrastructure, 465
Inside attacks, 381–383
    crackers, 383
    impersonation, 382
    unattended logged-in computers, 382
    unauthorized access, 381–382
Installing
    BorderManager software, 224–234
    Microsoft VPN adapter, 357–360
    NetWare client software, 340
    Novell VPN Client for Windows 98, 340–343
    PPTP on Windows NT server, 283–287
    PPTP VPN client, 354–357
    Windows NT as member server, 276
Institute of Electrical and Electronics Engineers.
    *See* IEEE entries.
Integrated Services Digital Network. *See* ISDN.
Intel, interoperability, 463–464
Interception, network attacks, 384
Interface message processors. *See* IMPs.
Interior Gateway Protocol. *See* IGP.
International Data Encryption Algorithm. *See* IDEA.
International Organization for Standardization. *See* ISO.
International Telecommunications Union. *See* ITU.
Internet
    configuring Novell server for user access via, 333–350
    growth, 11–12
    keeping up with, 438–439
    monitoring with NetWare VPN implementation, 270–271
    monitoring with PPTP VPN implementation, 315–316
    NetWare development, 55–56
    site-to-site versus client-to-site VPNs, 321
    WANs, 71–72
Internet Activities Board. *See* IAB.
Internet Control Message Protocol. *See* ICMP.
Internet Drafts. *See* I-Ds.
Internet Engineering Steering Group. *See* IESG.
Internet Engineering Task Force. *See* IETF.
Internet layer, TCP/IP, 35
Internet performance monitoring, 194
Internet Protocol Suite. *See* TCP/IP.
Internet Registry, 37
Internet Service Providers. *See* ISPs.
Internet VPN, 188, 191
Internetwork Packet Exchange/Sequenced Packet
    Exchange. *See* IPX/SPX.
Interoperability, 463–465
Interruption, network attacks, 384
Intranets, VPN applications, 9
Intranet VPN, 188, 191–192

Intra-NetWare, 56
Inverse multiplexing, 74–75
IP addresses, 34, 36–37
   assignment, 37
   classes, 36, 88
   limited supply, 37
   parts, 36
   static assignment in BorderManager, 220
   WAN routing, 88
IP headers, 140–141
IPNG, 136
IP New Generation. *See* IPNG.
IP packet forwarding, configuring, 298–299
IPsec, 134–141, 154
   encapsulation, 136–141
   need for security, 135–136
   security, 413–414
IPX addresses, NetWare client-to-site
   VPN implementations, 337
IPX internal network numbers, 58
IPX packet filtering configurations, 455–457
IPX/SPX, 28, 38–39
   NetWare, 58–59
ISA, 16
ISA bus architecture, 42
ISDN, 465
   add-ons, 77–78
   deregulated charges, 77
   ISDN interfaces, 76–77
   local subscriber loops and ISDN, 75–76
ISO, 16
ISO model, IEEE model compared, 24–26
ISPs, 8, 319
   access charges, 371
   assistance available from, 189
   client-to-site VPN interface, 323–324
   databases, 371–372
   independent, 371
   maintaining list for remote users, 370–372
   mobile users, 127
   training personnel to find in remote places, 182–183
   turnkey services, 127
ITU, 69

## J

Java Virtual Machine, NetWare, 59
Jobs, Steve, 5

## K

Kahn, Bob, 5
Key management, 155
Key Management Protocol, *See* KMP.
Keys, 142–143, 416–417
KMP, 141–143

## L

Lanalyzer for Windows, 426, 443
LAN Manager, 62, 152
LAN protocols
   AppleTalk, 40
   EtherTalk, 40
   IPX/SPX, 38–39
   NetBEUI, 39–40
   TCP/IP. *See* TCP/IP.
LAN routers, 34
   backbone, 53
LANs, 15–64
   architecture, 16–18, 185
   bandwidth, 29–31
   cables, 43–49
   computers, 41–43
   concentrators, hubs, and switches, 51–52
   Ethernet, 28–29, 31–32
   Ethernet switches, 53–54
   IEEE and ISO models, 24–26
   Internet protocol suite. *See* TCP/IP.
   managed network devices, 52–53
   network operating systems. *See* NOSs.
   OSI model, 18–24
   overview, 15–16
   physical addressing, 32
   security, 64
   virtual, layer-4 switching, 104
   wireless communications, 49–51
LAN server interface, client-to-site VPNs, 325
Laptop computers, remote, 368–370
Lasers, safety, 50
Latency, 194
Layer Two Forwarding (L2F) protocol, 132–134, 153–154, 166
Layer Two Tunneling Protocol. *See* L2TP.
LDAP, 163
Lightweight Directory Access Protocol. *See* LDAP.
Limited broadcasts, 92
Linear bus, 52
Link State Protocol functions, 98

Linux
    firewalls, 405
    WAN implementation, 112
Local area networks. *See* LANs.
Local subscriber loop. *See* LSL.
Logical link control layer, IEEE 802 model, 25
Logical objects, NetWare, 55
LSL, 76
L2F, 132–134, 153–154, 166
L2TP, 134, 154, 156–157, 166
    security, 412–413
LUCIFER, 419

# M

MAC addresses, 32, 36
    resolvers, 95
Macintosh computers. *See* Macs.
MAC layer, 61
    IEEE 802 model, 25
MAC layer devices, 85
Macro viruses, 387
Macs, 5
    AppleTalk protocol suite, 6, 40
    EtherTalk, 40
    TCP/IP, 40
Maintenance, 438–440
    keeping up with Internet, 438–439
    tracking traffic patterns, 439–440
Maintenance operations, 266–268
Malicious programs, 385
Manageable hubs, 52–53
Man in the middle attacks, 138
MANs, 65, 66
Masking, WAN routing, 89–90
Master/slave configuration. *See also* Slave servers.
    Novell BorderManager, 161, 214, 220
    synchronization, 220
Mauchly, J. W., 3
MD5, 420–421
Media access control. *See* MAC addresses; MAC layer.
Media types, LANs, 32–40
Melissa virus, 388
Member servers, installing Windows NT as, 276
Message-digest algorithm. *See* MD5.
Message digest value, 215
Messages, OSI model, 22
Metropolitan Area Networks. *See* MANs.
Micro Channel architecture, 18, 60
Microprocessing unit. *See* MPU.

Microsoft
    interoperability, 157, 463–464
    PPTP Forum. *See* PPTP Forum.
Microsoft Windows. *See* Windows *entries.*
Military Network. *See* MILNET.
MILNET, 6
Mission critical, 66
MLIDs, 57
Mobile users, tunneling, 127
Modem banks, 107
Modems, 72
Modification, network attacks, 384
Modulation, 72
Monitoring Internet
    NetWare VPN implementation, 270–271
    PPTP VPN implementation, 315–316
Monitoring statistics, 424–436
    accessing statistics for BorderManager, 432–436
    capturing statistics, 426–432
    maintaining and using baseline, 436
    NetWare VPN implementation, 269–270
    parameters, 425–426
    performance baseline, 424–426
    PPTP VPN implementation, 315
Monitoring WAN link usage, 440
Monthly administrative checklist, 437–438
MPU, 42
MS-NET, 152
Multimode data transmission, fiber-optic cable, 48
Multiple Link Interface Drivers. *See* MLIDs.
Multiplexing, 74–75
Multiprotocol support, 155
Multitasking, 405
Multiuser capability, 405

# N

NASs, 154
NAT, 37
National Science Foundation, release of Internet restrictions, 6
NCP, 4
NDIS, 61
NDS, 55, 159
    Novell BorderManager, 163
    version 8, 106, 111–112
    WAN implementation, 111–112
NetBEUI, 28, 39–40, 60, 61
    Windows NT, 63
NetBIOS, 60
NetBIOS Extended User Interface. *See* NetBEUI.

NetWare, 55–60, 158–164
    adaptability, 58
    architecture, 56
    client operating systems, 56–58
    client-to-site VPNs, 326–328
    evolution, 55
    history, 158–159
    installing client software, 340
    Internet's impact, 55–56
    IPX/SPX, 38–39, 58–59
    Novell's approach to networks, 159–160
    security, 159–160
    troubleshooting tools, 445–446
    version 5, 59–60
    VPN architecture, 160–161
    VPN protocols implemented with BorderManager, 162–163
    WAN implementation, 110–112
    Windows NT with, 63–64
NetWare Client 32, 57–58
NetWare client-to-site VPN implementation, 333–353
    accessing server via Novell VPN client, 350–353
    BorderManager, 353
    configuring servers for user access via Internet, 333–350
    dial-up networking icons, 343–350
    installing NetWare client software, 340
    installing Novell VPN Client for Windows 98, 340–343
NetWare Link Suite Protocol. See NLSP.
NetWare Loadable Modules. See NLMs.
NetWare management software, 53
NetWare shell, 57
NetWare site-to-site VPN implementation, 199–272
    adding slave server to VPN, 258–265
    architecture, 200–201
    BorderManager. See BorderManager.
    equipment checklist, 215–217
    future planning, 203–207, 271
    implementation checklist, 220–221
    INETCFG.NLM program, 221–224
    installation and configuration items, 207–210
    maintenance, 266–268
    management, 266, 268
    monitoring Internet, 270–271
    monitoring statistics, 269–270
    network access and use policy, 203
    NIASCFG.NLM program, 247–258
    post-implementation steps, 265–266
    pre-implementation checklist, 218–220
    support checklist, 217–218
    traffic patterns, 202
  Network Access Servers. See NASs.

Network Address Translation. See NAT.
Network attacks, 384
Network Basic Input/Output System. See NetBIOS.
Network Control Protocol. See NCP.
Network Device Interface Specification. See NDIS.
Network interface cards. See NICs.
Network interface layer. See NIL, TCP/IP.
Network layer, OSI model, 21, 23
Network masks, 89–90
Network media, TCP/IP, 34
Network Monitor Agent, 426–432
Network numbers, 58
Network operating systems. See NOSs.
Network Solutions, 37
Network terminators. See NT1s.
NetX, 57
Newsgroups, 5
NIASCFG.NLM program, 237–258
    configuring slave servers, 247–258
NICs, 21, 43
    collision detection, 29
    Registry entry names, 293–297
NIL, TCP/IP, 35
NLMs, 56
NLSP, 112
Node IDs, 32, 36
Noise, retransmission by Ethernet devices, 52
NOSs, 54–64
    backing up, 400
    IBM PC DOS, 60
    NetWare. See NetWare entries.
    OS2, 60
    Windows. See Windows entries.
Novell BorderManager, 160–163
Novell Directory Services. See NDS.
Novell NetWare. See NetWare entries.
NSFNET, 34
NT1s, 77
NuBus architecture, 42
NWAdmin, BorderManager, 432
NWADMIN program, monitoring statistics, 269–270

# O

Oakley Key Exchange. See OKE, security.
OCs, 75
Octets, 36, 88, 123
ODI, 57
OKE, security, 416–417
Open Datalink Interface. See ODI.
Open networks, 404

Open Shortest Path First. *See* OSPF protocol.
Open standards, 17
Open Systems Interconnection (OSI) standard. *See* OSI model.
Open View, 426
Operating systems, 42–43. *See also* NetWare; NOSs;
   Windows *entries; specific operating systems.*
Operational cycle, 267
Optical carriers. *See* OCs.
**OR** operator, masking, 89
OSI model, 18–24
   layers, 20–24
   transmission process, 22–23
OSI standard. *See* OSI model.
OSPF protocol, 98
OS2, 60

# P

Packet filtering, PPTP, enabling, 299–301
Packets, 425
   ATM. *See* ATM.
   dropped, 194
   OSI model, 21
   TCP/IP, 34
Packet switching, 4, 34
   fast, 79–80
PAP, 113–114, 129
Password Authentication Protocol. *See* PAP.
Passwords, 394–397
   viruses, 385
Payload padding, 141
PC, historical background of, 5
PDCs, 63, 276
PDN, 69
   V-series standards, 73
PDNs, 66
Peer-to-peer network systems, 40
Performance baseline, 424–426
Performance metrics, 194
Permanent virtual circuits, 79–80
Permission to transmit, 80
Personal Electronic Transactor. *See* PET.
PET, 5
Physical addressing, 32
Physical layer
   IEEE 802 model, 24
   OSI model, 20–21
Ping, 449–452, 453
Plain Old Telephone Service. *See* POTS.
Points of Presence. *See* POPs.

Point-to-point leased lines, 73–78
   definitions, 74–75
   ISDN. *See* ISDN
   standards, 74
   trunks and trunk lines, 75
Point-to-point mode, 50
Point to point protocol. *See* PPP.
Point-to-Point Tunneling Protocol. *See* PPTP *entries.*
Policies, 174–179
   current use, 174–176
   items to detail, 177–179
   network access and use, 203
   reasons to implement, 176–177
   security, 393–394
Polymorphic viruses, 388
POPs, 84
Port numbers, 35
Ports, 405–407
POTS, 68
   cable, 44
   leased lines. *See* ISDN; Point-to-point leased lines.
PPP, 109, 128–129
   authentication, 129
   negotiation spoofing, 156
   security, 410–411
PPTP, 40, 119–120, 128–129
   definition, 130–131
   installing on Windows NT server, 283–287
   PPP, 128–129
   security, 129, 411–412
   VPN protocols, 155–157
PPTP client-to-site VPN implementation, 353–367
   accessing VPN server via VPN client, 365–366
   dial-up networking icon, 360–364
   installing Microsoft VPN adapter, 357–360
   installing PPTP VPN client, 354–357
   post-implementation checklist, 367
PPTP Forum, 152–158
   approach to networks, 154–155
   history, 152–154
   RedCreek, 157
   VPN implementation architecture, 155
   VPN protocols, 155–157
   Windows 2000, 158
PPTP site-to-site VPN implementation, 273–317
   adding VPN devices as RAS ports, 288–291
   configuring RAS server for IP packet routing, 292–301
   domain controllers, 276
   equipment checklist, 278–280
   future planning, 316–317

implementation procedure checklist, 283
installing PPTP on Windows NT server, 283–287
maintenance, 314–315
management, 315
management checklist, 313–314
monitoring Internet, 315–316
monitoring VPN statistics, 315
post-implementation checklist, 313
pre-implementation checklist, 281–283
scheme, 274–278
support checklist, 280–281
testing, 312–313
Windows 98, 301–312
Presentation layer, OSI model, 22
PRI, 76
Primary domain controllers. *See* PDCs.
Primary rate interface. *See* PRI.
Private keys, 143
Private networks, 404
Problem isolation, 447–458
fault determination, 457–458
isolating source, 448–449
suspected hardware faults, 453–454
suspected software faults, 454–455
TCP/IP and IPX packet filtering configurations, 455–457
TCP/IP tools, 449–453
Process/application layer, TCP/IP, 36
Protocol analyzers, 193–194
Protocols. *See also specific protocols.*
conversion by bridges, 86
older, ATM, 82
routing, 97–98
security, 410–418
standards versus, 119–120
Proxy servers, 114, 404, 408–409
Novell BorderManager, 161
PRTNs, 68–69
PSTNs, 66
Public data networks. *See* PDNs.
Public key encryption, 416
Public keys, 143
Public networks, 404
Public switched telephone networks. *See* PRTNs.
Public switched telephone networks. *See* PSTNs.
Punch-down blocks, 46
Punch-down tools, 46

# Q

Quality of service. *See* QOS.
QOS, 83
layer-4 switching, 104–105

# R

Radio frequencies, wireless communication, 51
RADIUS, 131–132
AA, 132, 133
Microsoft modifications, 132
RAM, 42
Random access memory. *See* RAM.
RAS, 129, 152, 325
RAS ports, adding VPN devices as, 288–291
RAS servers, configuring for IP packet routing, 292–301
RedCreek Communications, PPTP Forum, 157
Registry entries, 293–297
Remote access, WANs, 107–109
Remote Access Server. *See* RAS.
Remote Authentication Dial In User Service. *See* RADIUS.
Remote server interface, client-to-site VPNs, 325
Remote user administration, 367–372
laptop computers, 368–370
maintaining ISP list, 370–372
Remote user troubleshooting, 372–378
accessing remote computer from support site, 377
areas involved, 373
back-up plan for, 377–378
building help into computer, 374–375
help systems on computers, 374
user's checklist, 375–376
Requests for Comments. *See* RFCs.
Resolver program, 452
Resolvers, 38, 90–91
MAC addresses, 95
RFCs, 34, 116–118
1075, 123–124
1171, 128
1172, 128–129
1241, 125–126
1700, 121
1701, 121
1702, 130
1827, 136–137
1853, 121
1994, 129
2058, 131–132
2401, 134
authorship, 117
comment cycle, 117–118
genesis, 117
system administrators, 123
tunneling, 122
RIP, 97–98
RiverMaster Management Application, 169
RiverPilot Universal Access Manager, 169

RiverWay Subscription Service, 169
RiverWorks Management Server, 169
RiverWorks Tunnel Server, 169
RJ-45 connectors, 46
Routers. *See also* LAN routers; WAN routers; WAN routing
   boundary, 150
   Windows NT-PPTP servers as, 276
Router tables, 95–96
Routing
   configuring RAS servers for IP packet routing, 292–301
   WANs. *See* WAN routing.
Routing Information Protocol. *See* RIP.
Routing tables, 292–293
   static entries, 297–298
RSA Public Key Cryptosystem, 143, 416, 421

# S

SA Bundles, 416
Safety, lasers, 50
SAs, 138, 139–140, 415–416
SASs, 81
SATNET, 5
SatelliteNet. *See* SATNET.
SDH, 75
Secure hash algorithms. *See* SHAs.
Security, 379–422
   amount, 394
   attacks from within, 381–383
   company security posture, 393–394
   definition, 380–381
   encryption. *See* Encryption.
   firewalls. *See* Firewalls.
   IPsec. *See* Ipsec.
   LANs, 64
   NetWare, 159–160
   passwords. *See* Passwords.
   PPP, 129
   PPTP VPN implementation, 282
   protocols, 410–418
   proxies, 408–409
   system backup. *See* System backup.
   viruses. *See* Viruses.
   VPN implementation, 179–180
   WANs, 68, 113–114
   wireless communications, 50
Security associations. *See* SAs.
Security gateways, 144
Security scanners, 369–370
Sendmail program, 392
Serial Line Internet protocol. *See* SLIP.
Server-centric model, NetWare, 56

Server interfaces, client-to-site VPNs, 324–325
Service layer, TCP/IP, 35
Services
   NetWare, 56
   TCP and UDP protocols, 35
Session layer, OSI model, 22, 23
Sessions, 405
SHAs, 421
Shielded twisted-pair. *See* STP cable.
Simple Network Management Protocol. *See* SNMP.
Simple servers, 63
Single attachment stations. *See* SASs.
Single-mode data transmission, fiber-optic cable, 48
Site-to-site VPNs, 319
   client-to-site VPN versus, 320–323
   NetWare. *See* NetWare site-to-site VPN implementation.
   PPTP. *See* PPTP site-to-site VPN implementation.
Slave servers
   adding to VPN, 258–265
   configuring, 247–258
SLIP, 109
Smart hubs, 52–53
SMS Network Monitor, 443
SNA, 19
Sneaker net, 4
Sniffers, 138
SNMP, 52–53
Software
   application, backing up, 399–400
   for help desk, 368
   security, 410–418
   suspected faults, 454–455
   VPN implementation, 193–194
Software routers, 106
Software updates, laptop computers, 368
SONETs, 75
Source route IP datagrams, 124
Spatial Reuse Protocol. *See* SRP.
Spamming, 381, 392–393
SRP, 84–85
Stackable hubs, 52
Standard Ethernet, 31
Standards. *See also specific standards.*
   *de facto*, 17–18
   pen, 17
Static routes, 94
Statistics
   monitoring with NetWare VPN implementation, 269–270
   monitoring with PPTP VPN implementation, 315
Stealth users, viruses, 385
Store and forward method, 79

STP cable, 44
STS, 75
Subnets, screened, 150
Subnetworks, 98
    OSI model, 21
Support, 195–197. *See also* Remote user troubleshooting.
    end-user operations, 196–197
    technical operations, 196
Support staff, training needs, 184
Switches
    Ethernet, 54
    layer-3, 102–103
    layer-4, 103–105
    WANs, 102–105
Switching hubs, 54
Synchronization, master and slave, 220
Synchronous digital hierarchy. *See* SDH.
Synchronous optical networks. *See* SONETs.
Synchronous technology, 73
Synchronous transport signal. *See* STS.
System administrator, RFCs, 123
System backup, 397–404
    backup media, 398–399
    on-site versus off-site repository, 403–404
    types of backup, 400–403
    what to back up, 399–400
Systems Network Architecture. *See* SNA.

# T

Tabulating machine, 2
TACACS, 133
Talk and Listen method, Ethernet protocol, 28–29
Tapes, backing up, 399
TCP, 5
TCP/IP, 5, 17, 26–27, 33–38
    development, 33–35
    domain name system, 37–38
    IP addresses, 36–37
    layers, 35
    Macs, 40
    packet filtering configurations, 455–457
    port assignments, 406
    troubleshooting tools, 449–453
    VPN standards, 115–116
    WAN implementation, 112
    Windows NT, 63
Telecommunication Standardization Sector, ITU, 69
Telecommuting, 9, 12–13
Telephone services, 69
Telephony, 6
    voice and data signals, 73

Teleprinters (teletypes; teletypewriters), 2
Telnet, 452
Terminal Access Controller Access System. *See* TACACS.
Terminate and stay resident programs. *See* TSR programs.
ThickNet, 46
Time bombs, 385
Time division multiplexing, 75
Token rings, 80
Tokens, 80
TollSaver Connection Manager, 169
Tomlinson, Ray, 4–5
Top level domain, 37
Topology, 23
TraceRoute utility, 440, 449–450, 452–453
Traffic analysis, 414
Traffic patterns, tracking, 439–440
Training, 181–185, 194–195
    amount, 184–185
    for end users, 195
    failures, 183
    finding ISPs in remote areas, 182–183
    help desk, 184
    for support staff, 184, 194–195
    workstations, 181–182
Transatlantic cable, first, 1–2
Transceivers, Ethernet protocol, 29
Transmission Control Protocol. *See* TCP.
Transmission Control Protocol/Internet Protocol. *See* TCP/IP.
Transport layer, OSI model, 21–22, 23
Transport mode SAs, 140
Traps, 53
Trojan horses, 385, 388
Troubleshooting, 440–461
    BorderManager VPNs, 458–459
    correcting problems, 460
    desktop level, 441
    diplomacy toward users, 446–447
    documentation, 460
    isolating problems. *See* Problem isolation.
    network level, 440–441
    remote users. *See* Remote user troubleshooting.
    tools, 442–446
    Windows NT VPNs, 459
T-series leased lines, 74, 75
TSR programs, 57
Tunneling, 59, 120–128. *See also* Encapsulation.
    compulsory, 273
    Indus River Software, 170
    ISP enterprise, 128
    mobile users, 127
    process, 126–127

RFC 1075, 123–124
RFC 1241, 125–126
server filter configurations, 456–457
site-to-site versus client-to-site VPNs, 322
transmission problem, 124–125
Tunnel mode SAs, 140
Turnkey approach, 10, 208
Twisted-pair cable, 44–45

# U

UDP, 35, 123
USB, 464
U.S. Navy, virus attack, 386
UNIVAC, 3
Universal Automatic Computer. *See* UNIVAC.
Universal Serial Bus. *See* USB.
Unix
    crackers, 383
    email spamming, 392
    virus attack, 386
    WAN implementation, 112
Unix-to-Unix Copy Protocol. *See* UUCP.
Unshielded twisted-pair. *See* UTP cable.
USB, 464
Usenet, 5
User Datagram Protocol. *See* UDP.
User datagrams, 123
User problems, site-to-site versus client-to-site VPNs, 323
US Robotics, PPTP Forum, 154
UTP cable, 44
UUCP, 5

# V

Vendors. *See also* specific vendors
    implementation independent from, 208–209.
Video adapter cards, viruses, 389–390
Virtual channels, 83
Virtual LANs, layer-4 switching, 104
Virtual Loadable Modules. *See* VLMs.
Virtual Private Dialup Networks. *See* VPDNs.
Virtual Private Networking. *See* VPN.
Viruses, 384–391
    defenses, 390–391
    detection, 387
    email, 386–388
    general categories, 388
    hardware, 389–390
    macro, 387
    nonreplicating, 385

    self-replicating, 386
    spread, 386
VLMs, 57
Voice, telephony services, 73
Voicenet, 13
Voice-Over Internet Protocol. *See* VoIP.
VoIP, 13
VPB, origin, 121
VPDNs, 154
VPN
    advantages and disadvantages, 7–10
    applications, 9
    definition, 118–119
    future, 10–14
    hardware and software decisions, 9–10
    historical background of, 1–7
    implementation levels, 8–9
    infrastructure, 465
    recommendations, 466–468
    turnkey approach, 10, 208
VPNet Technology, Inc., 10
VPN implementation, 173–197
    benefits and considerations, 204–205
    checklist approach, 209–210
    compatibility, 189–192
    current architecture, 185–189
    developing procedure, 207–208
    hardware, 193
    hidden costs, 192–193
    planned phased approach, 205–207
    policy planning, 174–179
    security, 179–180
    software, 193–194
    support, 195–197
    training, 181–185, 194–195
    vendor independent plan, 208–209
VPN maintenance, 266–268
    PPTP VPN implementation, 314–315
VPN management, 266, 268
    PPTP VPN implementation, 313–314, 315
VPN protocols
    Cisco Systems, 166
    Indus River Software, 169–171
    Novell BorderManager, 162–163
    PPTP, 155–157
VPN standard implementation, 147–171
    Cisco Systems, 164–167
    firewalls, 148–151
    Indus River Software, 168–171
    Novell, 158–164
    PPTP Forum. *See* PPTP Forum.

VPN standards, 115–145
  IPsec. *See* Ipsec.
  KMP, 141–143
  L2F, 132–134
  PPTP. *See* PPTP.
  protocols versus, 119–120
  RADIUS, 131–132
  RFCs. *See* RFCs.
  TCP/IP, 115–116
  tunneling. *See* Tunneling.
VPN types, 188
V-series standards, 69, 70–71, 72

# W

WAN emulation and testing software, 194
WAN protocols, 78–85
  ATM, 82–85
  FDDI, 80–82
  frame relay, 79–80
  implementation by software vendors, 109–112
  X.25, 79
WAN routers, 66, 87–88
  hardware, 106
  IP addressing, 88
  software, 106
WAN routing, 89–107
  ARP, 90
  brouters, 101–102
  to different network, 93–94
  directory services, 105–106
  gateways, 90, 95–98
  masking, 89–90, 91–92
  paradigm, 99–100
  problems, 100–101
  resolver functions, 90–91
  switches, 102–105
WANs, 65–114
  architecture, 66–67, 186, 188
  bridges, 85–87
  gateways, 95–98
  implementing, 66–67
  Internet's impact, 71–72
  monitoring link usage, 440
  PDN, 69, 73

point-to-point leased lines, 73–78
  PSTN, 68–69
  remote access for users, 107–109
  routing. *See* WAN routers; WAN routing.
  security, 68, 113–114
  standards, 69–71
Weekly administrative checklist, 437
Whois, 452
Wide area networks. *See* WANs.
Windows, NetBEUI, 39–40
Windows 3x, 61, 175
  NetWare interface, 57
Windows 9x, 61, 176
  NetWare interface, 57
Windows 98
  client-to-site VPNs, 326
  installing and configuring PPTP, 301–302
  installing Novell VPN Client for Windows 98, 340–343
Windows 2000, 158
  WAN implementation, 110
Windows for Workgroups, 61
Windows NT, 62–63, 152, 175
  capturing statistics, 426–432
  client-to-site VPNs, 326, 327
  domains, 62–63
  NetWare with, 63–64
  troubleshooting, 459
  troubleshooting tools, 446
  VPN implementation. *See* PPTP client-to-site VPN implementation; PPTP site-to-site VPN implementation.
  WAN implementation, 110
Windows NT Advanced Server, 152
WinSock, 40, 61, 323
Wire closets, 46
Wireless communications, 49–51
Workstations. *See also* Clients.
  training personnel in use, 181–182
World Wide Web, 6–7
Worms, 388
Writeable CDs (CDRs), backing up, 399

# X

X.25 protocol, 79
X-series standards, 69, 70, 71–72